Medieval Legal and Political Thought

Medieval Legal and Political Thought:

From Isidore and the Quran to Maimonides and the Incas

By

Larry May

Cambridge Scholars Publishing

Medieval Legal and Political Thought:
From Isidore and the Quran to Maimonides and the Incas

By Larry May

This book first published 2022

Cambridge Scholars Publishing

Lady Stephenson Library, Newcastle upon Tyne, NE6 2PA, UK

British Library Cataloguing in Publication Data
A catalogue record for this book is available from the British Library

ISBN (10): 1-5275-7582-9
ISBN (13): 978-1-5275-7582-0

TABLE OF CONTENTS

Section IV. War and Peace

Part B: Islamic and Canon Law

Section V. Divine and Natural Law

Section VI. Legal Status

Section VII. Crime and Punishment

Part D: Neo-Aristotelian Jurisprudence

Section XIII. Natural Law, Equity, and Procedural Law

Section XIV. Status and Criminality

GENERAL INTRODUCTION

Medieval legal and political thought encompasses the period from approximately 500 CE to 1500 CE. The term "Medieval" signifies a period in the middle–and for us it refers to the legal and political thought from the time of the late Roman Empire to that of the Renaissance. The legal and political thought of the Middle Ages is overwhelmingly characterized by the increasing role that religion played in influencing politics and law. By the high Middle Ages, we find the great theorists, Averroes, Maimonides, and Aquinas linking law to their respective religions of Islam, Judaism, and Christianity.

In my previous book on ancient legal and political thought, "Ancient Legal Thought," I argued that from some of the earliest of times, notably Hammurabi's code from 1750 BCE, ancient legal and political thinking was not primitive either conceptually or normatively. Indeed, a concern for justice and especially for equity was the hallmark of the prefaces that accompanied many legal codes. In addition, I argued that it is a mistake to think that legal and political thought became more humane over time, with the thought of the Greeks and Romans at the pinnacle of that thought. Instead, especially if we looked to China and India in ancient times the story that must be told was not one that fit a developmental picture.

In "Medieval Legal and Political Thought," I argue that the so-called Dark Ages has very significant ideas about the law, especially how violence is to be contained, that makes this early Medieval period anything but "Dark." I also argue that the Christianization and Islamicisation of legal and political thought created almost as many problems as solutions to the increasingly diverse times that arose in the middle of the Middle Ages. And I also argue that the late Middle Ages already held many of the most important legal and political ideas of the Renaissance–showing that there was no clear break from the Medieval to the Modern periods of legal and political thought. Of central importance is the way that the development of the idea of conscience made the natural law theories of the Medieval times a robust set of ideas that is still felt quite strongly today.

My method is largely comparative in two senses. First, ideas from one society are compared to ideas from the same society of a somewhat later time. Second, ideas of one society at a certain time are compared to ideas on a similar topic from another society at about the same time. Often the comparison is not just between two "Western" societies but between Western and Eastern societies. In this sense this work is meant to be multi-cultural and hence we find significant treatment of Islamic legal and political thought as well as that of Indigenous legal and political thought in the Americas and Africa at the end of the Medieval period.

"Medieval Legal and Political Thought" is not a comprehensive history but rather a set of snap-shots–meant to be representative of the history of Medieval legal and political thought to be sure. The category of "legal and political thought" applies quite broadly here to encompass not only the writings of legal and political theorists and lawmakers, but also the understanding of laws and actual institutions as well as their justifications in the way laws and policies were discussed, discarded, and changed. I will be especially interested in laws concerning criminality, the role of women, and slavery.

I am very grateful to editing, formatting, and indexing help that I received from my daughter, Elizabeth May, as well as for many discussions of nearly all of the topics in this book with my wife, Marilyn Friedman.

PART A:

GERMANIC LAW AND BYZANTIUM

INTRODUCTION TO PART A

The first of the Medieval periods is often called the Dark Ages. As we will see, this is a mischaracterization in that there were exciting legal and political ideas of this period, hardly the wasteland that the image of a dark age calls forth. In addition, the Germanic law codes are often known as "barbaric" codes. Today, if not in earlier eras as well, there is such a strongly negative connotation to the idea of anything barbaric that I will not use that term but talk more straight-forwardly of Germanic law. And finally, the rise of Christianity especially in the early medieval period is often contrasted with what is called "pagan" religion. Once again, because of the strongly negative connotations of the term "pagan" I will not use that term either but refer to the various Germanic views of religion.

"Germanic" will refer to the peoples often said to have a similar heritage who lived north of the Rhine River and eventually "invaded" or simply migrated south into various parts of the Roman Empire, principally the Visigoths, Franks, Burgundians, Lombards, and Anglo-Saxons, as well as to a lesser extent the Bavarians and Alamans. There will be much to contrast between the German laws that were promulgated in the Western Roman Empire and the laws promulgated in the Eastern Roman Empire. Here the term "Byzantine" is used, and despite this term having some negative connotations as well, I will employ this term.

One quite fascinating feature of the early medieval period is that the Germanic people who moved across the Rhine River into the Western Roman Empire did not have a fully developed legal system; indeed they often did not have even a written code of law until they encountered the Romans. The Germanic peoples came to develop written legal codes starting from their unwritten customs, as was also true for various ancient peoples. So, there was a clash between peoples who were just developing written codes of law out of the ancient customs of their people with a Roman society that had one of the most highly intricate legal codes of any era and was already many centuries old. The way the Germanic codes of law were developed in reaction to the law of the Roman Empire will be seen to be utterly fascinating. This is significantly different from the earlier clash of legal ideas between those of the Roman Empire and the Rabbinic tradition, for instance, since the Rabbinic tradition was actually older than the Roman when they confronted each other.

> In a set of additional enactments to the Burgundian Code we find that when there is no law that governs a certain set of facts, the assembly is to be consulted along with the group of counts, the regional political rulers. Since cases of this kind arise within our realm for which no provision has yet been made by law, we decree by the present enactment what ought to be observed among our people following a discussion held with our counts (*comites*).[4]

In addition, we find that provisions are made that bind both Burgundian and Roman political leaders.

> We command this especially, that all counts (*comites*), Burgundian as well as Roman, shall maintain justice in all their decisions; let them avenge and punish severely those who have committed violence, assault, or any crime, so that no one may be presumed to commit such acts within our realm. Let them judge all cases according to the laws so that the judge may be bound by the ordinances of justice as the laws of our ancestors sets forth.[5]

Even though the Burgundians generally allowed Romans to be judged by Roman law, when there was a gap in the laws it was the customary laws of the Burgundians that should be used to judge both Burgundians and Romans alike. In the Burgundian Code justice was the key consideration and justice was defined as deciding cases "according to the laws." When the laws, even the customary laws, are not followed, "the people are debased."[6]

The idea that Romans are to be generally judged by Roman law is repeated throughout the Burgundian Code, for example in the following Edict concerning foundlings:

> Since we have learned at the worthy and laudable suggestion of that venerable man Bishop Gimellus that exposed children whom compassion would cause to be taken in are neglected because those who would shelter the foundlings fear that they would be taken from them by legal charges, and so because of lagging compassion the souls of these children perish wretchedly; whereas, having been moved by the just suggestion which has been raised in this case by our father of

[4] Ibid., p. 93.
[5] Ibid., p. 95.
[6] Ibid., p. 95.

> when they render decisions so that no one is excused on grounds of ignorance.[2]

Romans were to be judged by Roman law and Burgundians by Burgundian law even though these two peoples were living side by side in Burgundy.

In this chapter we will first consider how the Burgundian Code differed from other Germanic codes in the fifth and sixth centuries CE concerning conceptions of justice. Then in the second section we will compare the Burgundian and other Germanic codes to the Roman codes existing at that time, principally the Theodosian Code from the fifth century CE as well as the Laws of the Isaurian era dating from the eighth century CE in Byzantium. In the third section we turn specifically to ideas concerning equity in Germanic codes and the codes of Byzantium. In the fourth section we will examine some of the theoretical writing about justice and equity in this period, from the Visigoth, Isidore of Seville, and also the Roman jurists. Finally, we will turn to the writings of Augustine of Hippo who attempts to provide a distinctly Christian take on justice and equity in this early Medieval period.

I. The Early Germanic Codes

The Preface to the Burgundian Code shows that justice and equity were prime considerations for those who drafted the Code:

> For the love of justice, through which God is pleased and the power of earthly kingdoms acquired, we have obtained the consent of our counts (*comites*) and leaders (*proceres*), and have desired to establish such laws that the integrity and equity of those judging may exclude all rewards and corruptions from themselves.[3]

Notice that in addition to the respect shown to justice, integrity, and equity, there is also a testament to the consent of the counts, the main regional leaders of the Burgundians. It therefore seems that whoever drafted the Burgundian code submitted it first to an assembly (of counts) for approval–this was not a code that was imposed on the Burgundian people from on high.

---

[2] Ibid., p. 20.

[3] Ibid., p. 18.

> In a set of additional enactments to the Burgundian Code we find that when there is no law that governs a certain set of facts, the assembly is to be consulted along with the group of counts, the regional political rulers. Since cases of this kind arise within our realm for which no provision has yet been made by law, we decree by the present enactment what ought to be observed among our people following a discussion held with our counts (*comites*).[4]

In addition, we find that provisions are made that bind both Burgundian and Roman political leaders.

> We command this especially, that all counts (*comites*), Burgundian as well as Roman, shall maintain justice in all their decisions; let them avenge and punish severely those who have committed violence, assault, or any crime, so that no one may be presumed to commit such acts within our realm. Let them judge all cases according to the laws so that the judge may be bound by the ordinances of justice as the laws of our ancestors sets forth.[5]

Even though the Burgundians generally allowed Romans to be judged by Roman law, when there was a gap in the laws it was the customary laws of the Burgundians that should be used to judge both Burgundians and Romans alike. In the Burgundian Code justice was the key consideration and justice was defined as deciding cases "according to the laws." When the laws, even the customary laws, are not followed, "the people are debased."[6]

The idea that Romans are to be generally judged by Roman law is repeated throughout the Burgundian Code, for example in the following Edict concerning foundlings:

> Since we have learned at the worthy and laudable suggestion of that venerable man Bishop Gimellus that exposed children whom compassion would cause to be taken in are neglected because those who would shelter the foundlings fear that they would be taken from them by legal charges, and so because of lagging compassion the souls of these children perish wretchedly; whereas, having been moved by the just suggestion which has been raised in this case by our father of

[4] Ibid., p. 93.
[5] Ibid., p. 95.
[6] Ibid., p. 95.

CHAPTER 1

JUSTICE AND EQUITY IN GERMANIC LAW AND BYZANTIUM

Let us begin our first chapter by discussing the Burgundians, a Germanic people who seem to have peaceably settled in Roman Gaul (now principally France) starting in the fifth century CE. The Burgundians were recognized by the Roman Empire as "foederati"–a sovereign nation but existing as part of the Empire. Here is Katherine Drew's account:

> the Burgundians had entered the valley of the Rhone peacefully, and perhaps even at the invitation of the Roman provincials who sought to enlist their military aid, so there was not much incentive for either people to enforce their laws or customs on the other. Since the Burgundians were foederati of the Empire and as such entitled to a part of the lands before held entirely by the Romans, there was naturally much need for a code of law to govern commercial and social relations between the two peoples. The Burgundians were evidently willing to live up to the trust which the Gallo-Romans had put in them when they were practically invited to become their rulers, and we find that the Burgundians did not forcibly subject the Roman population of their kingdom to the Burgundian customary law, but rather they attempted to establish codes of law that would be fair to both Burgundians and Romans.[1]

Thus, we find this provision in the Preface of the Burgundian Code, probably compiled between 483 and 517 CE:

> we command that Romans be judged by the Roman laws just as has been established by our predecessors, let them know that they must follow the form and statement of the written law

[1] *The Burgundian Code*, translated with an introduction by Katherine Fischer Drew, Philadelphia, PA: University of Pennsylvania Press, 1949, 1976, p. 5.

SECTION I.

JUSTICE AND JURISDICTION

> when they render decisions so that no one is excused on grounds of ignorance.[2]

Romans were to be judged by Roman law and Burgundians by Burgundian law even though these two peoples were living side by side in Burgundy.

In this chapter we will first consider how the Burgundian Code differed from other Germanic codes in the fifth and sixth centuries CE concerning conceptions of justice. Then in the second section we will compare the Burgundian and other Germanic codes to the Roman codes existing at that time, principally the Theodosian Code from the fifth century CE as well as the Laws of the Isaurian era dating from the eighth century CE in Byzantium. In the third section we turn specifically to ideas concerning equity in Germanic codes and the codes of Byzantium. In the fourth section we will examine some of the theoretical writing about justice and equity in this period, from the Visigoth, Isidore of Seville, and also the Roman jurists. Finally, we will turn to the writings of Augustine of Hippo who attempts to provide a distinctly Christian take on justice and equity in this early Medieval period.

I. The Early Germanic Codes

The Preface to the Burgundian Code shows that justice and equity were prime considerations for those who drafted the Code:

> For the love of justice, through which God is pleased and the power of earthly kingdoms acquired, we have obtained the consent of our counts (*comites*) and leaders (*proceres*), and have desired to establish such laws that the integrity and equity of those judging may exclude all rewards and corruptions from themselves.[3]

Notice that in addition to the respect shown to justice, integrity, and equity, there is also a testament to the consent of the counts, the main regional leaders of the Burgundians. It therefore seems that whoever drafted the Burgundian code submitted it first to an assembly (of counts) for approval–this was not a code that was imposed on the Burgundian people from on high.

---

[2] Ibid., p. 20.

[3] Ibid., p. 18.

CHAPTER 1

JUSTICE AND EQUITY IN GERMANIC LAW AND BYZANTIUM

Let us begin our first chapter by discussing the Burgundians, a Germanic people who seem to have peaceably settled in Roman Gaul (now principally France) starting in the fifth century CE. The Burgundians were recognized by the Roman Empire as "foederati"–a sovereign nation but existing as part of the Empire. Here is Katherine Drew's account:

> the Burgundians had entered the valley of the Rhone peacefully, and perhaps even at the invitation of the Roman provincials who sought to enlist their military aid, so there was not much incentive for either people to enforce their laws or customs on the other. Since the Burgundians were foederati of the Empire and as such entitled to a part of the lands before held entirely by the Romans, there was naturally much need for a code of law to govern commercial and social relations between the two peoples. The Burgundians were evidently willing to live up to the trust which the Gallo-Romans had put in them when they were practically invited to become their rulers, and we find that the Burgundians did not forcibly subject the Roman population of their kingdom to the Burgundian customary law, but rather they attempted to establish codes of law that would be fair to both Burgundians and Romans.[1]

Thus, we find this provision in the Preface of the Burgundian Code, probably compiled between 483 and 517 CE:

> we command that Romans be judged by the Roman laws just as has been established by our predecessors, let them know that they must follow the form and statement of the written law

[1] *The Burgundian Code*, translated with an introduction by Katherine Fischer Drew, Philadelphia, PA: University of Pennsylvania Press, 1949, 1976, p. 5.

> In a set of additional enactments to the Burgundian Code we find that when there is no law that governs a certain set of facts, the assembly is to be consulted along with the group of counts, the regional political rulers. Since cases of this kind arise within our realm for which no provision has yet been made by law, we decree by the present enactment what ought to be observed among our people following a discussion held with our counts (*comites*).[4]

In addition, we find that provisions are made that bind both Burgundian and Roman political leaders.

> We command this especially, that all counts (*comites*), Burgundian as well as Roman, shall maintain justice in all their decisions; let them avenge and punish severely those who have committed violence, assault, or any crime, so that no one may be presumed to commit such acts within our realm. Let them judge all cases according to the laws so that the judge may be bound by the ordinances of justice as the laws of our ancestors sets forth.[5]

Even though the Burgundians generally allowed Romans to be judged by Roman law, when there was a gap in the laws it was the customary laws of the Burgundians that should be used to judge both Burgundians and Romans alike. In the Burgundian Code justice was the key consideration and justice was defined as deciding cases "according to the laws." When the laws, even the customary laws, are not followed, "the people are debased."[6]

The idea that Romans are to be generally judged by Roman law is repeated throughout the Burgundian Code, for example in the following Edict concerning foundlings:

> Since we have learned at the worthy and laudable suggestion of that venerable man Bishop Gimellus that exposed children whom compassion would cause to be taken in are neglected because those who would shelter the foundlings fear that they would be taken from them by legal charges, and so because of lagging compassion the souls of these children perish wretchedly; whereas, having been moved by the just suggestion which has been raised in this case by our father of

[4] Ibid., p. 93.
[5] Ibid., p. 95.
[6] Ibid., p. 95.

> holy memory, we declare by this proclamation and the provisions of the present edict and we state in this declaration of our law that in this matter the rules of the Roman law be observed among Romans and let such litigation as has arisen between Burgundians and Romans be concluded as has been established by us…[7]

To avoid conflicts of law, Romans are to be bound by Roman law and when Burgundians and Romans are in a legal dispute Burgundian law prevails.

Some of the most significant provisions of the Burgundian Code concern the penalties for judges who abuse the system to the disadvantage of litigants:

> our zeal for equity repudiates from ourselves those things which we forbid to all judges under our rule, let our treasury accept nothing more than has been established by the laws concerning payment of fines. Therefore let all nobles, counselors, bailiffs, mayors of our palace, chancellors, counts of the cities or villages, Burgundian as well as Roman, and all appointed judges and military judges know that nothing can be accepted in connection with those suits which have been acted upon or decided, and that nothing can be sought in the name of promise or reward from those litigating; nor can the parties (to the suit) be compelled by the judge to make a payment in order that they receive anything (from their suit). But if any of those mentioned, corrupted against our laws, or even judging justly, has been convicted of receiving rewards from suits or decisions, and the crime has been proved, let him be punished capitally as an example to all.[8]

The use of the death penalty applied to corrupt judges and other officials extended to all Burgundians as well as to Romans. And it is the concept of equity, of basic fairness in how officials treat litigants, which is the key– indeed it is a "zeal" for equity that is said to motivate the Burgundian Code.

This code, compiled in the late 5th and early 6th centuries, displays such sensitivity to the ideas of justice and equity that it would be a misnomer to call it "barbaric" as this term is used in even some of the most recent translations, albeit perhaps for lack of a better term. Some of the other Germanic codes from this period displayed more or less contact

---

[7] Ibid., p. 92.
[8] Ibid., p. 18.

with Roman law. The Visigothic code shows perhaps the most contact and the codes of Anglo-Saxons the least. The most original of the Germanic codes is that compiled by the Lombards, which governed most of the Western Roman Empire long after the Franks defeated the Lombards.

Here is part of the Preface to the Edict of Rothair, who was a king of the Lombards:

> The most noble Rothair, king of the Lombards, together with his principal judges, issues this lawbook in the name of the Lord...The collection which follows makes evident how great was and is our care and solicitude for the welfare of our subjects; for we recognize that it is not only the numerous demands of the wealthy which should carry weight, but also the burdensome trials of the poor are important... We desire that these laws be brought together in one volume so that everyone may lead a secure life in accordance with law and justice...[9]

This code of laws was issued in 643 by Rothair and it, along with other Lombard laws, remained in effect until the 10th century. Unlike the Burgundian Code, the Lombard laws remained in effect even after the Lombards were conquered by the Franks in 775.[10]

We can see from the preface of Rothair's Edict that justice was to be even-handed, with the interests of the wealthy as well as the poor considered important. Yet it seems that the Burgundian Code considered the interests of the poor, especially foundlings, to be given strong weight that required judges to show compassion to them but not to those who could help and chose not to do so. It is not completely clear that this is the case since the Burgundian Code has little to say about the wealthy. What is clearer is that the Lombard laws were more comprehensive than the Burgundian Code. As we next see, the Visigothic Code was even more comprehensive than these other two, making it a competitor of the Theodosian Code which governed the affairs of the Romans at this period.

Like the other Germanic codes of law of the early medieval period, the Visigothic Code begins by discussing the role of justice in law-making and law-interpreting.

> In all legislation the law should be fully and explicitly set forth, that perfection and not partiality, may be secured....The

[9] King Rothair, "Rothair's Edict," in *The Lombard Laws*, translated by Katherine Fischer Drew, Philadelphia, PA: University of Pennsylvania Press, 1973, p. 39.

[10] See ibid., p. 21.

SECTION I.

JUSTICE AND JURISDICTION

> law is the rival of divinity; the oracle of religion; the source of instruction; the artificer of right; the guardian and promoter of good morals; the rudder of the state; the messenger of justice; the mistress of life; the soul of the body politic...The law should be plain, and not lead any citizen to commit error or fraud. It should be suitable to the place and time, according to the character and custom of the state; prescribing justice and equity... For men are better armed with equity than with weapons; and the prince should rather employ justice against an enemy than the soldier his javelin; and the success of the prince will be more conspicuous when a reputation for justice accompanies him...[11]

Here justice is conceived as a moral value that law must aspire toward. In this respect we see already the influence of Roman Stoicism as well as early Christianity that makes early medieval legal and political thought different from the legal and political thought of the late ancient period even though it is still the Roman Empire that plays a crucial role.

We can cite one more of the Germanic codes at the beginning of our study to show the growing influence of theological considerations in the formation of law codes, in this case the law of the Salian Franks, which begins as follows:

> With the aid of God, it was decided and agreed among the Franks and their notables in order that peace be established among themselves, that all increase in litigation be curtailed so that just as the Franks stand out from other peoples living around them by the strength of their arms so also they shall excel them in the authority of their laws. Thus they [the Franks] will provide an end to criminal actions according to the nature of the cause. Therefore from among many men four were chosen...These men, meeting together in three different courts and discussing the causes of all disputes, gave judgment in each case in the following fashion.[12]

Here, we have really two grounds for the authority of law–"the aid of God" and also the agreement or consent of the Franks to be governed by the laws that the chosen four had promulgated.

---

[11] *The Visigothic Code*, Title II, sections 1-6, translated by S. P. Scott, Boston: The Boston Book Company, 1910, pp. 5-6.

[12] *The Laws of the Salian Franks*, translated by Katherine Fischer Drew, Philadelphia: University of Pennsylvania Press, 1991, p. 59.

II. The Theodosian Code and Laws of the Isaurian Era

The Theodosian Code compiled in the Eastern Roman Empire can be profitably contrasted with the Germanic codes of the West. This code was promulgated at about the same time as the Burgundian Code, and we can cite a few provisions to see some contrasts with the Germanic codes. While justice had an important place in the legal thought of the Roman Empire, the Theodosian Code makes it clear that it is the emperor, not the judges, who shall have the last word in what counts as the just interpretation and application of the law.

> There must be no dispute concerning an imperial judgment, for it is a kind of sacrilege to doubt whether the person whom the Emperor has selected is worthy. If, therefore, any judge should be found who supposed that his own arrogance should be preferred to the imperial judgment, his office staff shall be compelled to pay five pounds of gold...[13]

And here we see one of the clear differences between at least some of the Germanic codes of law and that of the Roman Empire–it is not an assembly of the people that is the source of law's authority, but the emperor.

As with the Code and Digest of Justinian (promulgated a century later but at the time never recognized as superior to the Theodosian Code), the writings of five Roman Jurists are considered sources of law:

> We confirm all of the writings of Papinian, Paulus, Gaius, Ulpian, and Modestinus, so that the same authority shall attend Gaius as Paulus, Ulpian and the others, and passages from the whole body of his writings may be cited... Moreover when conflicting opinions are cited, the greater number of the authors shall prevail, or if the number should be equal, the authority of that group shall take precedence in which the man of superior genius, Papinian, shall tower above the rest...[14]

As we will see, it will later be Christian authors who are given this status as sources of law, but in the early medieval period Roman jurists before the Christianization of the Empire are those jurists most highly regarded.

---

[13] Emperor Theodosius II, *The Theodosian Code*, I.6.9, translated by Clyde Pharr, Princeton, NJ: Princeton University Press, 1952, p. 19.
[14] Ibid., Book I.4.3, p. 15.

Justice and equity are crucial concepts for any legal system, and this is certainly true of the Byzantine legal system of the Eastern Roman Empire. By the time of *The Ecloga*, promulgated in 741, we find that the severity of the Theodosian Code as well as that of Justinian, has been softened. *The Ecloga* begins as follows:

> A selection of the laws compiled in a concise form by Leo and Constantine, the wise and piety loving emperors, from the Institutes, Digest, Code, and Novels of Justinian the Great, and corrected to be more humane… Let those who have been appointed by our piety to judge cases and entrusted with the just weighing of our pious laws consider and understand these things, and conduct themselves accordingly…and by these we hope to restore in us the ancient standard of justice of the state.[15]

Notice here the explicit reference to the correction of the previous codes of the Roman Empire so as to make them more humane. Also note that the authors of *The Ecloga* think that justice has been besmirched and that there is a need to return to "the ancient standard of justice."

The Ecloga was largely a compilation of laws from earlier codes including that of Theodosian and Justinian. But the task of the drafters of the Ecloga and later codes was to make those corrections and changes that brought the law codes into better harmony with the distinctly Christian understandings of mercy, especially for those who were oppressed.

It is thus somewhat surprising that the Ecloga speaks of returning to more ancient conceptions of justice. One possible interpretation here is that certain ancient understandings of law, especially concerning the ancient Athenians, but also some of the much earlier views of the Babylonians and Israelites, tasked the lawgiver with the role of protecting widows, orphans, the poor, and aliens. As I have argued at great length elsewhere, ancient legal codes also stressed that they were authoritative insofar as they were espousing humane treatment especially of those who were weak or oppressed.[16]

---

[15] *The Ecloga*, in *The Laws of the Isaurian Era*, translated by Mike Humphreys, Liverpool: Liverpool University Press, 2017, pp. 34-37.

[16] Larry May, *Ancient Legal Thought*, Cambridge: Cambridge University Press, 2019.

III. Equity in the Early Medieval Codes

In the Burgundian Code, as we have seen, a "zeal for equity" is claimed to govern all judges. In addition, integrity is linked with equity as inspiring judges to "exclude all rewards and corruptions."[17] And in the Visigothic Code, we are told that "men are better armed with equity than with weapons."[18] And it is equity again that is appealed to when judges are corrupted:

> If any judge should render judgment for the sake of gain, and direct that anyone should be treated with injustice, he who has been benefitted by the decision of the said judge shall make restitution. And the judge himself, who has thus acted contrary to the precepts of equity, shall surrender to the losing party the same amount of his own property, as he has ordered him to be deprived.[19]

As in the Roman law codes, equity is given pride of place, along with justice, in the Germanic codes.

Yet, equity seems to be given a somewhat broader definition in the Germanic codes than in Roman legal thought. In the Burgundian and Visigothic codes we have just quoted, equity seems to be a matter of fair decision-making, where it is corruption rather than the overly strict justice that is the main concern. Theorists like Isidore of Seville, as we will see, have a conception of equity more closely connected to the Roman ideas.

In the legal code of Alfred the Great, promulgated in the late 9th century, we find that the Anglo-Saxon idea of mercy is given prominence. Here are some provisions:

> Injure ye not the widows and the step-children, nor hurt them anywhere: for if ye do otherwise, they will cry unto me, and I will hear them, and I will then slay you with my sword; and I will so do that your wives shall be widows, and your children shall be step children. If thou give money in loan to thy fellow who willeth to dwell with thee, urge him not as a 'niedling,' and oppress him not with the increase. If a man have only a single garment wherewith to cover himself, or to wear, and he

---

[17] *The Burgundian Code*, translated with an introduction by Katherine Fischer Drew, Philadelphia, PA: University of Pennsylvania Press, 1949, 1976, p, 18.

[18] *The Visigothic Code*, Title II, sections 1-6, translated by S. P. Scott, Boston: The Boston Book Company, 1910, p. 6.

[19] Ibid., p. 28.

> give it [to thee] in pledge; let it be returned before sunset. If thou dost not so, then shall he call unto me.[20]

Here these Anglo-Saxon laws display mercy and humaneness even if not specifically identified as forms of equity.

We can also look at the most important of the Roman codes of this period, The Theodosian Code, to see how equity was treated in Byzantium. Here is a provision of Book I of that code:

> When We are persuaded by entreaty to temper or to mitigate the rigor of the law in a special case, the regulation shall be observed that rescripts that are interpreted before the posting of the edict shall have their own validity, and a prior rescript shall not be derogated by a later one… it is necessary that We alone shall investigate an interpretation that has been interposed between equity and the law.[21]

Here equity is connected with the idea of mitigating the rigor of the law. But just a bit later, equity is linked with the proper understanding of justice and the law:

> With reference to those persons that demand that a decision rendered by a governor or by any other judge be invalidated, the examination of the case by Your Sublimity shall proceed under the limitation that if, when the fundamental features of the case have been examined in every detail, it should be clearly evident that the decision departed from law and justice, that decision shall be completely abolished, and the controversy shall come to an end in accordance with equity.[22]

And here equity can allow for the overriding of a statute law if equity is consistent with a broader understanding of justice and the law. Indeed, in a slightly earlier law, equity is linked with the eternal law for its source[23]–hence eternal law in effect overrides statute law if there is a conflict.

---

[20] King Alfred, "The Laws of King Alfred," in *Ancient Laws and Institutes of England,* vol. I, edited by Benjamin Thorpe, Cambridge: Cambridge University Press, 1840, p. 53.

[21] *The Theodosian Code*, I.2.3, translated by Clyde Pharr, Princeton, NJ: Princeton University Press, 1952, p. 13.

[22] Ibid., Book I.5.3, p. 16.

[23] See *The Sirmondian Constitutions*, Title 15, in *The Theodosian Code*, I.2.3, translated by Clyde Pharr, Princeton, NJ: Princeton University Press, 1952, p. 485.

IV. Isidore on Equity

In his work, the *Sententiae*, Isidore of Seville has much to say about the nature of equity. In this early 7th century work, Isidore says this about judges:

> There are four ways in which human judgment is perverted: by fear, greed, hatred, and love. By fear when we are afraid to speak the truth out of fear of someone's power; by greed when we are corrupted by the reward of some bribe; by hatred when we are stirred up to be an adversary of someone; by love when we strive to prefer a friend or family member. In these four ways equity is often violated and innocence is often harmed.[24]

Here equity is a feature of good or fair judgment. And Isidore also tells us that impartiality, which is a synonym for equity, is a balancing of justice on one side and mercy on the other.[25]

Isidore is especially concerned with what he calls the "oppressors of the poor." These oppressors "should know that they are deserving of more serious sentences."[26] It seems that the more severe sentences than would otherwise be deserved according to strict justice are also justified on grounds of equity–the intermediate between justice and mercy. While the text is not completely clear in this respect, Isidore seems to capture what other ancient legal theorists had called equity when he seeks that virtue of judges who consider the special circumstances of those people such as the poor. Isidore is also concerned with what he calls "wicked judges" who have the capacity to "maim poor people more gravely than the cruelest of enemies."[27]

In one of Isidore's other major works to survive, the *Etymologies*, he gives the following account:

> People are for the most part unaware of the origin of certain terms. Consequently we have included a number in this work for their informational value… Fair (*aequus*), meaning "naturally just," from 'equity' (*aequitas*), that is after the idea of what is

[24] Isidore of Seville, *The Sententiae*, book III.54.7, translated by Thomas Knoebel, NY: The Newman Press, 2018, p. 207.
[25] Ibid., Book III.52.4, p. 201.
[26] Ibid., Book III.57.1, p. 208.
[27] Ibid., Book III.52.7, p. 204

> equal (*aequus*)–whence likewise 'equity' is so-called after a certain equalness (*aequalitate*).[28]

Isidore elaborates on the conceptual idea of equity in an earlier part of the *Etymologies*:

> Law (*lex*) is the ordinance (*constitutio*) of the people, which the nobility have solemnly ratified with the common people. What a king or emperor proclaims (*edicere*), is called an ordinance (*constitutio*) or edict (*edictum*). The basis of fairness (*aequitas*) is twofold, sometimes in laws, sometimes in customs (*mores*). Between law and custom there is this difference, law is written, while custom is usage (*consuetudo*) tested and found good by its antiquity, or unwritten law.[29]

Here equity is equated with legal or customary fairness. Aristotle and Cicero had similar accounts as they presented it hundreds of years earlier, but as we will see, Isidore characteristically adds a dimension of religion not often mentioned in ancient writings on equity.

Isidore goes on to explain the difference between what is legal and what is customary:

> Indeed, law (*lex*) is so named from 'reading' (*legere*), because it is written. Custom (*mos*) is longstanding usage, taken likewise from 'moral habits' (*mores*, the plural of *mos*). 'Customary law' (*consuetudo*) moreover is a certain system of justice (*ius*), established by moral habits, which is received as law when law is lacking; nor does it matter whether it exists in writing or in reason, seeing that reason commends a law. Indeed, if law amounts to reason (*ratio*), the law will consist of everything that already agrees with reason, provided that it accords with religion, befits orderly conduct, and profits welfare. Customary law is so-called because it is in 'common use' (*communis usus*).[30]

In this detailed account of how equity is related to law, custom, and reason, we find many of the most important elements of medieval legal and political thought, or for nearly any form of legal and political

---

[28] Isidore of Seville, *The Etymologies*, Book X, translated by Stephen A. Barney, W. J. Lewis, J. A. Beach, and Oliver Berghof, Cambridge: Cambridge University Press, 2006, p. 213.

[29] Ibid., Book II, p. 73.

[30] Ibid.

thought for that matter. Let us note here that equity is important both in written law and also in customary, unwritten law. In this respect, Isidore suggests that there might be different senses of equity in these different usages, perhaps explaining how equity can be seen as a narrow concept concerning written law but a much wider concept concerning custom. It seems that both conceptions of equity are modified or limited by considerations of religion, once again speaking to one of the characteristic differences between ancient and medieval legal thought.

There was an emerging notion that equity was a concept of fairness that was linked to divine law as understood in these early Christian days. Both justice and equity were given a distinctly religious character as we will see in the final section of this chapter. As Augustine, for example, conceives it, judgment on earth should mirror the judgment of the final days when people will be judged by divine law. True justice only comes when God rules.[31]

V. Early Christianity and Justice

To get a sense of how justice and equity were conceptualized in the early medieval period, we should not ignore the outsized role that early Christianity played in both the Germanic codes and the codes promulgated in Byzantium. Consider in this respect the *Novels of Irene* promulgated in 797 as supplements to, and as corrections of, *The Ecloga*.

> But at the end of days, He himself, the son of God and our God, shall come to save our race. Bringing in this way the Old Law given through Moses to completion and illuminating all peoples with the knowledge of His truth, He gave to us, we who are to be perfected, knowledge of His perfect law from His grace… concerning which, the present edict has been toiled upon by us…[32]

Like *The Ecloga*, these Byzantine laws are couched in references to the Bible and to the role of God in inspiring the laws.

The emerging tradition in Europe of seeing the civil law as an interpretation of God's divine law can be traced to Augustine the Bishop

[31] Augustine, *The City of God*, Book XIX, Ch. 24, translated by Henry Bettenson, NY: Penguin Books, 1984, pp. 890-891.

[32] Emperor Irene, *The Novels of Irene*, in *The Laws of the Isaurian Era*, translated by Mike Humphreys, Liverpool: Liverpool University Press, 2017, pp. 164-165.

of Hippo who wrote the masterpiece, *The City of God*. Augustine begins the Preface to his work as follows:

> Here, my dear Marcellinus, is the fulfillment of my promise, a book in which I have taken upon myself the task of defending the glorious City of God against those who prefer their own gods to the Founder of that City. I treat of it both as it exists in this world of time, a stranger among the ungodly, living by faith, and as it stands in the security of its everlasting seat. The security it now awaits is steadfast patience, until "justice returns to judgment;" but it is to attain it hereafter in virtue of its ascendency over its enemies, when the final victory is won and peace is established. The task is long and arduous; but God is our helper.[33]

Augustine looks to divine law in order to understand the way that civil law should be established and how justice should be instituted.

While there had been other Christian thinkers before Augustine, in the domain of political and legal thought Augustine is surely the first of the great medieval theorists. His writings of the early 5th century were referred to at his time and for the next thousand years of the Middle Ages–indeed his work is still highly influential today on such topics as the justification of war. In importance, we then come to the writings of Isidore who is one of the "barbarians" that Augustine worried so much about–yet Isidore had converted to Christianity just as Augustine had. The fact that Augustine was originally a Roman "pagan" and Isidore was originally a "barbarian pagan" hardly seemed to mark much of a difference by the time assessments were made of this work by later medieval legal and political thinkers.

Some commentators attribute to Eusebius the important medieval idea that the emperor established civil law and ruled the earthly kingdom just as God ruled the heavenly kingdom. Augustine surely held this view and defended it throughout *The City of God*. But because Eusebius was a close confidant of Emperor Constantine, D. M. Nicol tells us that Eusebius was one of the first to have expressed the idea:

> that the empire of Constantine is the earthly reflection (*mimesis*) of the Kingdom of Heaven. As there is but one God so there is but one emperor (*basileus*). Thus in imitation of the divine monarchy, Constantine has established himself as sole ruler.

[33] Augustine, *The City of God*, translated by Henry Bettenson, NY: Penguin Books, 1984, p. 5.

> The pagan Roman emperor had been *dominus et deus*. The Christian emperor was lord but not God. Nevertheless it is from God that all imperial power derives; and Eusebius declared that Constantine had a special relationship with God through the Divine Word, the Logos... In Hellenistic theory the king had been guided by the Logos of philosophy and the reason of the law. In Eusebian theory the Christian emperor was guided by the Logos of God... Monarchy was the best form of government; and since there was only one God, one Supreme Being, there could only be one emperor.[34]

The Christian idea that there was just one God was used as a basis for the claim that there should be only one ruler, the emperor.

In Greek political and legal thought, reason was the ruler of all people, both individually and collectively. When the Christian thinkers connected reason to God the authority of law became grounded in a religious conception of reason. Justice and equity were then also reconceived in light of theological doctrines as well. In the early medieval period, we find that justice and equity were understood in similar ways to the late ancient period, but with the overlay of Christian religious doctrine. As this part of the text continues we will have many occasions to see how specific ideas, such as concerning the legal status of women and slaves, change, and how they do not, as Christianity seizes more attention of the lawmakers.

---

[34] D. M. Nicol, "Byzantine Political Thought," in *The Cambridge History of Political Thought: c. 350 – c. 1450*, edited by J. H. Burns, Cambridge: Cambridge University Press, 1988, pp. 51-82, pp. 52-53.

CHAPTER 2

JURISDICTION AND CONFLICT OF LAWS

Within the Roman Empire there was sometimes a conflict of law, for example where Jews were governed both by the Roman law and by the Rabbinic law of the Mishnah and Talmud.[35] But at just about the same time, and for several hundred years later, there was also a similar kind of conflict, as Carl Von Savigny says:

> The Moderns always assume that the law, to which the individual owes obedience, is that of the country where he lives; and that the property and contracts of every resident, are regulated by the law of his domicile. In this theory, the distinction between native and foreigner is overlooked, and national descent is entirely disregarded. Not so, however, in the middle ages; where in the same country, and often in the same city, the Lombard lived under the Lombardic, and the Roman under the Roman law. The same distinction of laws was also applicable to the different races of Germans. The Frank, Burgundian, and Goth resided in the same place, each under his own law, as is forcibly stated by the Bishop Agobardus, in an Epistle to Louis le Debonnaire. "It often happens," says he, "that five men, each under a different law, may be found walking or sitting together."[36]

As we examine the legal thought of the so-called Dark Ages, the beginnings of the medieval period, we will compare the various Germanic laws with the Roman law and the legal thought that sought to make sense of the overlapping systems of law that governed the peoples of the Western Roman Empire as well as the law of the Eastern Roman Empire, which comes to be called the law of Byzantium.

---

[35] I addressed this issue in the final part of my book *Ancient Legal Thought*, Cambridge: Cambridge University Press, 2019.

[36] Carl Von Savigny, *The History of the Roman Law during the Middle Ages*, translated by E. Cathcart, Edinburgh: Adam Black, 1829, pp. 99-100.

In this chapter, we will contrast the ideas about jurisdiction in the Roman Empire with that of the various Germanic legal codes. The Roman Empire is generally credited with successfully designing institutions that were aimed at treating all equally before the law. Yet, as the empire expanded to cover large portions of the globe, the task of providing a single political and legal institution for the whole empire became increasingly difficult leading to a splitting of the empire into parts, with the Theodosian code largely governing the Western Roman Empire and the Justinian code governing the Eastern (Byzantine) Roman Empire. The Roman Empire's political and legal institutions were strained even more by successive invasions or migrations of Germanic peoples who were different from the Romans and who by and large wanted to be treated differently as well.

In the first section of this chapter, we will set out the ideas of jurisdiction in the Roman Empire at the time of the Germanic migrations, as well as the significantly different ideas of jurisdiction in the Burgundian Code. We will then devote a section to various ways that the Romans and Germans were treated differently in the Germanic nations that had conquered parts of the Western Roman Empire. In the third section we will see examples of how Romans and Germans were sometimes treated the same by the Germanic codes. In the fourth section we then examine the idea of conflict of law when there were overlapping codes of law. And in the final section we will examine the idea of jurisdiction in the legal thought of the early Medieval period. In these chapters we will examine how it was that these codes dealt with matters of jurisdiction and conflict of laws. Most commentators treat these codes as having the same general idea: that the Germanic code was for the Germanic peoples and the Romans continued to be treated according to Roman codes of law. Throughout, I will challenge this generalization showing that there were important differences among these Germanic codes.

I. Equality Before the Law and the Burgundian Codes

The Theodosian Code is quite explicit in saying in several prominent places that the code applies to all those in the Empire. Here is how Book II of this code begins:

> It is Our will that the judges of the provinces shall assume the power of due authority, so that the same discipline which governs the provincials shall govern the overseers and all other persons of Our imperial estates. Prisons shall hold the scoundrels when they are convicted, torturers shall tear them in

> pieces, the avenging sword shall destroy them. For in this way the license of the inveterate lawlessness of desperadoes is restrained, if they understand that they must live with one and the same aspiration as do all others.[37]

In Roman law, jurisdiction is established territorially–by the province where the act was committed that is the object of the suit. Anyone in a given province will have the same judge regardless of who that person is.

We see the strongest contrast between Roman and Germanic treatment of jurisdiction when we examine the early parts of the Burgundian Code, one of the earliest of the Germanic codes. At the beginning of this code we have what appears to be a very clear jurisdictional statement: the laws concern "the welfare" of the Burgundians. And then we find these statements creating personal not territorial jurisdiction:

> we command that Romans be judged by the Roman laws just as has been established by our predecessors...If indeed anything is not covered by the statement of our laws, we order those judging to refer the matters to us... Let no Roman or Burgundian count, in the absence of the other judge, presume to decide any case however often they may desire it, so that consulting frequently they may not be in doubt concerning the provisions of the laws.[38]

There were to be different laws and even different judges for Burgundians and for Romans.

We find that procedurally, Romans could not employ Burgundian attorneys, as is clear in this provision:

> Whatever Roman hands over a case which he has with another Roman to be transacted by a Burgundian as advocate, let him lose the case, and let him who receives it pay a fine in the amount of twelve solidi.[39]

And we also find that Burgundians were not allowed even to involve themselves at all in Roman legal affairs:

---

[37] *The Theodosian Code*, Book I, title I.1, translated by Clyde Pharr, Princeton: Princeton University Press, 1952, p. 37.

[38] *The Burgundian Code*, translated by Katherine Fischer Drew, Philadelphia: University of Pennsylvania Press, 1949, 1976, pp. 17-21.

[39] Ibid., p. 39.

> Inasmuch as it has been established under certain penalty that no barbarian [Burgundian or other German] should dare to involve himself in a suit which a Roman has brought against another Roman, we advocate a stricter handling of these cases, and command that the law remain just as we have ordered it in earlier times.[40]

There was a strict separation of the legal affairs of the Romans and of the Burgundians. This gives rise to the idea put forward forcefully by the early twentieth century legal theorist Paul Vinogradoff that the Germanic peoples held to a view of personal jurisdiction.

> Whole nations, such as the Burgundians, the Visigoths, the Ostrogoths, the Franks, were admitted as allies (*federati*) within the limits of the Empire, and quartered in the provinces in a way that made them practically masters of a third, sometimes even of two-thirds, of the land. This influx of alien immigrants in the provinces of the West was bound to make itself felt in the legal domain. The Empire was forced to recognize to some extent the legal customs of the various tribes, and the idea of wiping out these customs in favor of the civilized law of Rome was never entertained... barbarians in general were left to follow their own legal customs with regard to transactions among themselves. This raises a question which came to be of vital importance somewhat later, namely, how were members of different tribes to transact business when they met? The supreme authority of the Imperial Courts and of Roman Law did not allow these divergences to assume a sharp and uncompromising aspect but as alien customs were allowed within the boundaries, the principle that a man must be made answerable primarily to his own personal law existed already in germ in the closing centuries of the Western Empire.[41]

This Germanic idea of personal jurisdiction, where the ethnicity of the person determined the jurisdiction, stood in sharp contrast to the Roman idea that jurisdiction was to be determined by where an act occurred, or perhaps where the actor resided. But as we will see, the principle of personal jurisdiction was not uniformly supported across Germanic codes of law and in any event began to fade away over time in favor of the principle of territorial jurisdiction that the Roman Empire had employed and continues to be employed today.

---

[40] Ibid., p. 63.

[41] Paul Vinogradoff, *Roman Law in Medieval Europe*, London: Harper and Brothers, 1909, pp. 6-7.

II. Differential Treatment for Romans and Germans

In the introduction to her translation of the laws of the Salian Franks, Katherine Fischer Drew comments:

> Before the Germanic barbarians entered the Roman Empire they had no written codes of law… It is conjectural how this early customary Germanic law was applied in practice; the law was almost certainly not royal law… Before the evolution of "royal power," obtaining justice resided largely in the hands of the families or kin groups; and there may have been more or less popular courts attended by the more important members of the community if not by all freemen. Since enforcement of law resided in the family and kin rather than the state, there could hardly be such a thing as territorial law. So for the Germans law was essentially personal (i.e. a man was judged by the law of his ancestors, not by the law of the place he happened to be)… By A.D. 500, the Western Roman Empire had given way to a number of Germanic kingdoms, but how "Germanic" these kingdoms were has always been a matter of dispute. Certainly the Germans constituted a minority of the population so that the new kings found themselves ruling essentially in two guises: as kings to their own German people and as magistrates toward their Roman population.[42]

The Salian Franks seem to have recognized the different jurisdictional standing of Romans and Germans quite clearly.

For some Germanic tribes, different codes of law were produced for Germanic people and for Romans. This is true of the Visigoths and the Burgundians–where the Roman codes governing Romans living under Germanic rule were based in a compilation of laws from the Theodosian and Justinian Codes, along with passages from Roman jurists such as Paulus and Gaius. The differential legal treatment of Germans and Romans was thus clearly marked by having separate codes for each people.

Louis Halphen comments on how the principle of personal jurisdiction was understood in certain Germanic codes at the beginning of the sixth century.

> A fusion had not yet been accomplished between the old population and the conquerors: Roman and German lived side

[42] *The Laws of the Salian Franks*, translated and with an introduction by Katherine Fischer Drew, Philadelphia: University of Pennsylvania Press, 1991, pp. 20-21.

> by side, each group endowed with its own laws, and at least in the territory of the Visigoths, mixed marriages were formally prohibited. Frankish legislation went so far as to distinguish between "barbarians" and "Romans" in providing that the penalty usually be doubled when the victim of an aggression or a simple criminal act was barbarian rather than Roman… The barbarians thus arrived at the idea of "personality of law" according to which every person carried with him, wherever he went to dwell and whoever was the sovereign under whom he established himself, the juridical status of the nation of his origin.[43]

Halphen goes on to summarize this arrangement as follows: "Subjects of the same king, residing in the same place, the Burgundians and Romans continued to live side by side almost as strangers."[44]

Yet, the differential treatment was not always due to different codes but often due to differential treatment in the same code. We can see this clearly in the *Pactus Legis Salicae*, a code of the Salian Franks:

> He who ties up a freeman without cause shall be liable to pay twelve hundred denarii (i.e. thirty solidi)…
> If a Roman ties up a Frank without cause, he shall be liable to pay twelve hundred denarii (i.e., thirty solidi).
> If a Frank ties up a Roman without cause, he shall be liable to pay six hundred denarii (i.e. fifteen solidi).[45]

Notice that the same fine is assessed in cases where a Frank is tied up regardless of who does it, another Frank or a Roman; but there is only half of this fine if it is a Roman who is tied up by a Frank. What governs the penalty is who the person is not where the assault took place.

There are also differential penalties assigned for homicide later in the *Pactus Legis Salicae*.

> He who kills a free Frank or other barbarian who lives by Salic law, and it is proved against him, shall be liable to pay eight thousand denarii (i.e., two hundred solidi).

---

[43] Louis Halphen, "Germanic Society in the Early Sixth Century," in *The Barbarian Invasions: Catalyst of a New Order*, edited by Katherine Fischer Drew, Huntington, NY: Robert E. Krieger Publishing Company, 1977, pp. 31-32.
[44] Ibid., p. 33.
[45] *The Laws of the Salian Franks*, translated and with an introduction by Katherine Fischer Drew, Philadelphia: University of Pennsylvania Press, 1991, p. 93.

> He who kills a Roman who is a table companion of the king and it is proved against him shall be liable to pay twelve thousand denarii (i.e., three hundred solidi).
> If a Roman landholder who is not a table companion of the king is killed, he who is proved to have killed him shall be liable to pay four thousand denarii (i.e., one hundred solidi).[46]

So, killing a Roman landholder is assigned only half the penalty as for killing a free Frank, but if the Roman is a friend of the king then the penalty is higher than for a free Frank. The determining factor is the status of the Frank who is killed or who is the friend of the one who is killed, with the Roman victim not being as important as the Frank.

We find similar differential treatment in other Germanic codes, especially the Lombards, as we see in this law from King Liutprand:

> If a Roman man marries a Lombard woman, and acquires her mundium, and if after his death the widow marries another man without the consent of the heirs of her first husband, feud and the penalty for illegal intercourse shall not be required; for after she married a Roman man and he acquired her mundium, she became a Roman and the children born of such a marriage shall be Roman and shall live according to the law of their Roman father. Therefore the man who marries her after the death of her first husband ought not to pay composition for illegal intercourse just as he would not pay it for another Roman woman.[47]

It is highly interesting here that a woman who marries a Roman man is thereafter treated according to Roman law, and this is also true of the children of such a marriage even if the woman later marries a Lombard. As we will see in later chapters, cases like this make us aware that sometimes Germanic law treated women as property. There is a sense that a woman's personal status in terms of legal jurisdiction is determined by the man who controls her mundium (guardianship). We have much more to say about the legal status of women in the early Medieval period in Chapter 5.

---

[46] Ibid., pp. 104-5.

[47] King Liutprand, "Laws of King Liutprand," in *The Lombard Laws*, translated by Katherine Fischer Drew, Philadelphia: University of Pennsylvania Press, 1973, pp. 199-200.

III. Territoriality Seems to Dominate in Germanic Law

Despite the generally perceived idea that Germanic law was one of personal jurisdiction rather than one of territorial jurisdiction, we can find examples where this idea does not seem to hold. Here is an example from the Lombard code of King Rothair:

> All foreigners who come from outside our frontiers into the boundaries of our kingdom and yield to the jurisdiction of our power ought to live according to the Lombard laws, unless through our grace they have merited another law. If they have legitimate children, these heirs shall live just as do the children of the Lombards.[48]

In this early law of Rothair we seem to have a conflict with the somewhat later law of Liutprand we just examined. Drew thinks that the Lombards are an exception to the general idea that Germanic law followed the principle of personal jurisdiction. But if so then the law of Liutprand is anomalous. Perhaps a better explanation is that Romans who were already residing in the territory taken over by the Lombards were treated differently than the other foreigners who came into the already established territory of the Lombards.

There are other examples of where Germanic law seems to follow territoriality rather than personality. Here is a law from the Visigothic Code:

> If any freeman or slave has a cause of action against anyone residing outside the province in which he lives, and within the jurisdiction of another judge, the judge of the district to which the plaintiff belongs shall send a letter under his signature and seal, to the other judge, and direct him to hear the cause of the complainant, without delay; and if he should neglect or deny this request, then the judge in whose district the plaintiff resides, shall seize as much of the property belonging to the judge to whom he sent the letter, as the sum amounts to, concerning which the plaintiff brought the suit.[49]

---

[48] King Rothair, "Rothair's Edict," in *The Lombard Laws*, p. 124.

[49] *The Visigothic Code*, translated by S. P. Scott, Boston: The Boston Book Company, 1910, pp. 42-43.

While this Visgothic law is a bit difficult to comprehend, what seems clear is that the law to be followed is the law of the judge in the jurisdiction where the plaintiff resides.

The various laws of the Lombards display the most sophistication of any of the Germanic codes. We can see this in the way the lawmakers chose often to give rationales for laws, especially if the new law was a change from an older law.

> If men who reside in a district under the same judge but under two different schultheis [local officials] are involved in a suit, then that one who is the complainant should go with a representative or letter from his own schultheis to that one under whose jurisdiction the person lives against whom he is bringing suit. If he [the latter schultheis] does not render justice within four days, that schultheis who neglects to take action shall pay six solidi as composition to him who brings the suit, and he shall also pay six solidi to the judge.[50]

Here the plaintiff is compensated when the officials in his own jurisdiction delay justice because seemingly of a dispute among officials.

The Lombards also were sensitive enough to the difficulties of jurisdiction when there is a dispute over which judge should handle a given case.

> If anyone has a case [with a man who lives] in another judicial district, he shall go with a letter from his own judge to that judge who presides in the other place. If that judge delays to do justice for him and has not settled the suit within eight days, he shall pay twenty solidi as composition to him who brought the suit and another twenty solidi to the king.[51]

In these two laws of King Liutprand, the Lombards recognized that employing territorial jurisdiction could result in problems, especially of delayed justice.

The Lombard codes addressed the difficulties that could result from disputes about jurisdiction in terms of how the parties felt–indeed the basis for appeal seems to be simply that one party felt that he had not achieved justice.

---

[50] *The Lombard Laws*, p. 156.

[51] *The Lombard Laws*, pp. 156-157.

> In those cases which have been settled by a decision and he [against whom the case was brought] does not believe that it was judged according to law and therefore he appeals to the king, he shall not be liable to blame. And if the judge had judged contrary to law, he shall pay forty solidi in composition… If the judge heard the case and made his decision and his judgment did not appear to be right, he shall not be guilty if he can offer an oath to the king that he did not judge that case with evil intent nor had he been corrupted by a bribe, but as the law appeared to him; and he shall be cleared.[52]

Here we see quite a subtle set of considerations. Judges are generally held personally liable for wrongful decisions that neglect the law that is relevant to the case. But if the judge can show that he was innocent but merely negligent, the judge will not be penalized for a wrongful decision. These are especially important considerations when there are the kinds of conflicts of laws which we will next consider.

IV. Conflict of Laws

Some commentators seem to believe that the personal jurisdiction of the German codes creates conflicts of laws that are nearly irreconcilable. At the beginning of this chapter I quoted Bishop Agobardus, in an Epistle to Louis le Debonnaire who said "It often happens that five men, each under a different law, may be found walking or sitting together." [53] The picture presented is that when these five men engage in a crime the judge will have to try each according to very different laws, making the trial impossible even to imagine.

Let us try to imagine the situation anyway, hypothetically pursuing these five people interacting with each other who each come from different Germanic tribes. Let's assume that three of them conspire to assault a fourth and the fifth learns about the assault but does nothing to stop it from occurring. The victim's legal status may be determinative but so might any of the three assailants and the fifth person may or may not be culpable since the various codes at the time treat accomplice liability differently from each other.

The question here is one of how to choose which body of law for the judge to consider. If one of the five people is Roman should this fact

---

[52] *The Lombard Laws*, p. 157.

[53] Quoted in Carl Von Savigny, *The History of the Roman Law during the Middle Ages*, translated by E. Cathcart, Edinburgh: Adam Black, 1829, pp. 100.

determine which law to use concerning his liability? Or should Roman law, regardless of why it might be appealed to, always take a subsidiary position to Germanic law? We have already seen that in some jurisdictions, Romans are treated not as well as Germans who do the very same act with the same consequences.

Today, especially in international law, jurisdiction based on the nationality of the victim sometimes is employed and sometimes it is jurisdiction based on the nationality of the perpetrator. In some cases, jurisdiction is determined based on where the act in question took place. In still other cases, jurisdiction is regarded as universal if the crime is of such seriousness that it offends all people–and in that case any judge can assert jurisdiction over the perpetrator, assuming he or she can be brought before the judge. In these four types of jurisdiction we see how complex jurisdiction can be. When we add that the nationalities of the parties calls for different jurisdictions the example of the five people all from different national groups gets incredibly complex.

Again let us hypothetically assume that the perpetrator and victim are of different national groups–one a Roman and one a Visigoth for example. There then seems to be a conflict of laws–two system of law overlap and perhaps call for different results based on whether we decide jurisdiction in favor of the perpetrator or victim. Now let us say we can decide the matter according to the principle that it is the perpetrator whose status should have sway. What next? If the perpetrator is Roman but the judge in whose jurisdiction the perpetrator is found is a Visigoth, the judge would seemingly have to apply a Roman code to the facts of the case. Yet, judges were not routinely trained in multiple systems of law–indeed they were barely trained in their own systems. One possibility is to have multiple judges in each case just so that one of them might know the law that will need to be employed. This seems to be the practice in the Visigothic system of law, where there was much interaction between Roman jurists and Visigothic jurists. But in other domains, especially in Anglo-Saxon domains there was no such Roman interaction and hence the problem of overlapping jurisdictions for judges remains.

In the Burgundian Code, sometimes Romans and Germans are treated the same, as for example in the following law:

> If anyone solicits another's bondservant, or anyone, either native Burgundian or Roman, presumes to take in theft a horse, mare, ox, or cow, let him be killed: and let him who lost the bondservants and animals mentioned above, if he is not able to

> find them in the possession of the solicitor or thief, receive compensation in fee simple...[54]

But as we have enumerated so far there are also examples from the Burgundian Code and from other Germanic law codes that Romans are to be treated less well than native Germans who have done the same act or who have suffered the same misfortune.

So now we have yet another complicating factor. In some domains Romans are treated according to their own system of laws with their own penalties and procedures. In other domains, Romans, for example, are treated according to the same code as Germans, but the Romans are treated less well. Here there are serious questions of fairness–people are treated differently for having committed the very same act. This would be especially problematic today–but in these early Medieval times people of different status within the same national group (slaves or women versus freemen, for instance) are treated differently at law also for having committed the same act. So, perhaps fairness was regarded differently then as opposed to now–yet our investigation in the first chapter of this study did not reveal any stark contrast in how equity as fairness was understood.

Conflict of laws is one of the most difficult and fraught areas of law today and this was seemingly true in Medieval times as well. As we will next explore, the idea of jurisdiction, and especially possibly conflicting jurisdiction, was not resolved in these early Medieval times. The idea that a person should be held to account for violations of his or her own national laws has certain advantages but probably at least as many conceptual and practical problems as other systems for deciding jurisdiction, such as asking instead where the act in question took place.

V. Jurisdiction in Early Medieval Legal Thought

Today, questions of jurisdiction are often complicated matters, and I assume that the same would be true in previous times. As I have said, it is sometimes held that it is the victim's domain that should dominate, and sometimes it is held that it is the perpetrator's domain. In addition, there are questions, especially in a federated legal system like that in the United States, whether it is local, state, or federal law that should be applied. In the early Medieval period there is the added problem that there are different laws that could apply based on the nationality of one or both of the parties. The key conceptual idea is that in applying law

[54] *The Burgundian Code*, p. 21.

to a particular case, a judge must determine whose law is to be used–a task made even more difficult if some of the possible laws in question are customary and not available in written form.

These conflict of law and jurisdictional issues are especially significant if judges are not trained in the multiple systems of law that could apply to the cases before them. In some respects what is important for the stability of the society is that a judge chooses some law to apply and does so in a way that is not arbitrary. But there are other issues at stake–such as providing notice of possible illegality, to the people who might come before a certain judge, that an action these people are contemplating is likely to be seen as legal or illegal.

If all judges working in Germanic kingdoms in what had been the Western Roman Empire did treat all people as having a right to the law of their personal heritage things would still be difficult but perhaps more manageable. But what we have seen is that some Germanic legal systems employed territorial jurisdiction rather than personal jurisdiction. Indeed, the task for the judge is very difficult in light of the differences concerning which principle of jurisdiction is supposed to be employed. Indeed, the question of whether a given judge is even the appropriate judge to adjudicate the case at issue is itself a jurisdictional question that cannot be solved until it is determined which law is supposed to apply to that case. It should be no surprise that today the first question often asked by a judge is why he or she as a jurisdictional matter is thought to be the correct judge to be handling the case at issue.

What I have just called a jurisdictional issue is actually today sometimes understood as a philosophical issue–which theory of jurisdiction should guide the judge in determining which body of law to apply to the facts of the case? And do we wish to give to the defendant the choice of law since it is he (or she) whose position is most precarious? Or should it be the victim who chooses given that he (or she) had no choice over being the victim in this case? Even of greater political significance, shouldn't it be the political leader whose domain it was where the assault occurred who should decide? After all, the kingdoms in question were supposed to have a certain amount of sovereignty and that sovereignty would be undermined if some other political kingdom got to decide which law was to apply to assaults perpetrated in the first kingdom's domain. Kingship sovereignty was not what it is today, but even at the beginning of the Medieval period, deference was paid to the king in whose domain various actions occurred.

Embedded in the questions I have just asked is the issue of the authority of the law. If a person is in a certain political domain, but carries his own law around with him as a shield, does this assault the rule of law in that domain? Law attains authority in several different ways but most clearly when law is found to be deserving of respect by the populace. But this idea of authority is generally premised on the idea that all people in a certain territory are treated equally before the law. What we have seen is that people in the same territory were often treated very differently in terms of the Germanic and Roman codes at the time of the early Medieval period.

In addition, if it was hard for a judge to figure out what law to apply to a given person, it must have been even harder for the average citizen or subject to see that the law was being applied properly. And there is a strong likelihood of abuse that follows when law is so unclear that judges have nearly unfettered discretion. Jurisdiction is supposed to be the idea that judges cannot justifiably rule unless it is clear that the judges do indeed have a legitimate legal basis for ruling concerning a certain person in a certain domain. When jurisdiction is muddled or allows for multiple interpretations then the likelihood of abuse arises and people lose respect for the authority of the law–the ability of the law to speak in the name of the people and to tell those people what they must do.

We should note that in ancient times, jurisdiction was handled often in the simplest possible way–if you were in a certain territory you were governed by the laws of that territory. The rise of the Roman Empire brought to the fore jurisdictional issues not previously recognized. When the Romans conquered one nation after another, stretching very far from Rome, it was difficult to keep a single jurisdiction over such a vast territory. And in addition, many of the conquered people had a strong respect for their own legal systems and resented any attempt by Rome to ignore their laws in favor of Roman laws.

When various Germanic peoples invaded or merged with parts of the Roman Empire, even more difficult issues arose than when Rome was the conqueror. Most of the Germanic tribes did not have written law codes, but they were nonetheless deeply committed to their customary laws. In confrontation with Roman written codes the Germanic peoples set about, often with Roman help, to craft a written code from their customary laws as well as out of those Roman laws the Germans found to be worthy of including in their own codes. And because Germanic people sometimes moved from place to place, establishing jurisdiction on the basis of location or territory did not seem to make sense for some of these Germans. As Carl Von Savigny concisely put it: "The true and general principle, on this subject, is - that birth determined the law… voluntary departure from that law was utterly impossible."[55] Yet, we have seen that there was variation in the way that jurisdictional problems were solved.

The idea that people carry their own law with them wherever they travel is a deceptively simple solution to the jurisdictional problems of large domains. But the simplistic formulation is not simple at all in execution. Indeed, the societies that initiated personal jurisdiction seem to have abandoned this practice after a few years and moved to a system of territorial jurisdiction. As we have seen, especially in early Medieval times, where judges were not well trained in their own law let alone the laws of other national groups, territorial jurisdiction was actually simpler to execute than personal jurisdiction.

[55] Carl Von Savigny, *The History of the Roman Law during the Middle Ages*, translated by E. Cathcart, Edinburgh: Adam Black, 1829, p. 135.

SECTION II:

LEGAL PERSONHOOD AND STATUS

CHAPTER 3

VALUING LIVES: THE FREE, THE HALF-FREE, AND THE WERGELD

We begin our section on legal status in the early Medieval period by discussing how people, especially men, were understood and valued in the Germanic codes and Eastern Roman Empire laws. This attention to the valuing of human life is a major difference between ancient and early Medieval legal thought. In ancient times there clearly were social hierarchies where one person's life was of greater value than that of another. But the obsessive attention to differential valuing, especially in monetary terms, seems to separate Medieval from ancient legal and political thought.

There were at least two ways that the value of a life could have been assigned. In the early Medieval Germanic codes, lives were valued differentially, not equally, in terms of the social hierarchy. Today, it is often claimed that lives are valued as roughly the same, certainly this is true in criminal law. It is worth mentioning at this early point in our discussion that in tort law in the US, for example, lives are not valued equally today. How much you are expected to have made in income matters, as does your place in a family structure, such as whether people were depending on your support. In valuing a life in terms of wrongful death cases, a calculation is made that has been compared to how life insurance companies decide what a person, or that person's family, is owed in actuarial terms. So, even today lives are valued differently–and the Medieval texts signal a significant shift in this direction.

In this chapter we will first look at the idea of the wergeld–the Germanic idea of the value of human life in monetary terms. In the second section we will look at the social hierarchies in Germanic as well as Eastern Roman terms. In the third section, we look specifically at how male free citizens were treated in law. And in the fourth section we contrast the free person with the person who was only half-free, the *aldii*. And in the final section we discuss the differences of group or collective thinking versus individualistic thinking. Throughout I argue that while the wergeld was instrumental in solving a vexing problem about the blood feud there were significant problems that further entrenched social hierarchies in ways that made the overall worth of the wergeld system not ultimately positive.

I. The Wergeld and the Valuing of Life

The wergeld is the Germanic term for the value (calculated largely in monetary terms) of a life. The idea behind the wergeld was that there was a need to stop the blood feud that would result when a member of one group killed or harmed a member of another group. Early medieval law codes imposed a strong penalty on anyone who continues the blood feud. And the idea was that some kind of substitute had to be found that would satisfy the members of the group whose member had been harmed. Here is where the valuing of a life comes in: instead of revenge following from harm there is a compensation that is owed. According to the underlying idea behind the wergeld, the receiving of the compensation for the loss of a member of one's group was often all that a group was entitled to. And since especially when egregious harms also disrupted the peace, there was also a compensatory penalty owed to the society at large.

The wergeld is referred to in several Germanic codes. In this section we will be especially focused on the Lombard laws and the Anglo-Saxon codes where we will see a detailed sense of how the idea of the wergeld was understood in legal codes that were not strongly influenced by Roman legal concepts. Here is how one historian summarized the beginning idea of the wergeld:

> The classic view of the social structure of early English society, drawn from a reading of those laws, has been that its bedrock was the thriving free peasant, the *ceorl*, who worked land sufficient to support his household and some dependants and owed only modest service to his lord, if he had one. His primary support system was his kindred, who were entitled to compensation for offenses against his person and his household, and who might enforce such compensation, if all else failed, by the feud. But, although they take the freeborn man as the basic element of society, the laws also assume a high degree of social differentiation and allude to complex hierarchies of rank. The great variation in wergeld, the compensation due to a

> family for the killing of one of its members, suggests that there were very considerable inequalities in early English society.[56]

The wergeld varies according to a person's status and is meant to stop the blood feud.

While different terms are sometimes employed, the wergeld or *bote*, refers to the compensation owed for the wrong done: "If the king calls his [people] to him, and any one there do them evil, [let him compensate with] a two-fold *bote* and [an amount of] shillings to the king."[57] There is also an additional fine, referred to in Anglo-Saxon law as the *wite*, which is due to the crown for the social disruption due to the offense.[58]

It is clear that the penalties were meant to stop the revenge-seeking of the blood feud. Here is a law from the Lombard King Rothair:

> Concerning the man who seeks revenge after accepting composition. If a freeman or slave is killed and composition paid for the homicide and oaths offered to avert the feud, and afterwards he who received the composition tries to avenge himself by killing a man belonging to the associates from whom he received the payment, we order that he repay the composition twofold to the relatives of the freeman or the slave's lord. In like manner concerning him who tries to avenge himself after accepting compensation for blows or injuries, he shall restore that which he accepted in double amount. In addition, he shall pay compensation, as provided above, if he has killed the man.[59]

From this law we learn rather clearly that once the compensation (called composition) of the wergeld had been paid revenge taking was legally forbidden under penalty of very steep fines for the one who seeks revenge.

---

[56] Alan Thacker, "England in the Seventh Century," in *The New Cambridge Medieval History, Vol. I: c. 500-c.700*, edited by Paul Fouracre, Cambridge: Cambridge University Press, 2005, p. 490.

[57] King Aethelbirht, "The Laws of King Aethelbirht," 2, in *Ancient Laws and Institutes of England*, vol. I, edited by Benjamin Thorpe, 1840, Cambridge: Cambridge University Press, p. 3.

[58] See the notes accompanying the first and second laws of King Aethelbirht, in *Ancient Laws and Institutes of England*, vol. I, edited by Benjamin Thorpe, 1840, Cambridge: Cambridge University Press, p. 3.

[59] King Rothair, "Rothair's Edict," 143, in *The Lombard Laws*, translated by Katherine Fischer Drew, Philadelphia: University of Pennsylvania Press, 1973, pp. 74-75.

The wergeld was due if one killed a freeman, but it was also due in some cases if one killed a freewoman as well. Indeed, in a law of the Lombard King Grimwald we find that the wergeld could be owed to a woman who had been falsely accused of adultery.

> If anyone maliciously and without legal cause, accuses his wife of having committed adultery or having conspired against the life of her husband, that woman may clear herself by the oath of her relatives or by combat… he shall pay the wergeld of that woman in composition, such an amount as if he had killed her brother, half to the king and half to the relatives of the woman.[60]

Here the value of the woman is determined by the value of her brother since women are generally not given their own status in Germanic societies, as we will see in Chapter 5.

In the Anglo-Saxon laws we also get a good sense of the differential wergeld based on standing in the social hierarchy. Thacker tells us that

> Below the noble rank lay the thriving ceorl, traditionally regarded as the mainstay of the early English society. His status is quite difficult to define. 'Peasant' carries the wrong connotations, in many ways his property and his privileges before the law placed him closer to the noble than the poor and economically dependant tenants and laborers. The ceorl, assigned by [King] Ine a wergeld of 200 shillings (one sixth of that of the landed royal companion), held sufficient land to support a single household, himself, his family, his servants, unfree tenants, and slaves.[61]

In the next section we will see added layers to the social hierarchy and begin to get a sense of how to distinguish the value of the members of these various strata.

---

[60] King Grimwald, "Laws of King Grimwald," 7, in *The Lombard Laws*, translated by Katherine Fischer Drew, Philadelphia: University of Pennsylvania Press, 1973, p. 134.

[61] Alan Thacker, "England in the Seventh Century," in *The New Cambridge Medieval History, Vol. I: c. 500-c.700*, edited by Paul Fouracre, Cambridge: Cambridge University Press, 2005, p. 491.

II. Social and Legal Hierarchies

Here is how one historian describes the different legal classes that we find in Germanic legal codes:

> The distinction of different legal classes is so widespread and frequently documented throughout the West that it must be judged as one of the most important (perhaps the most important) social phenomenon of this period… The graduated wergeld and the attempts to retain one's liberty, prove, however, such a portent.[62]

In this section we will survey the various social and legal classes that existed among the Germanic peoples living in the early Medieval period in Western Europe.

In her edition of the Burgundian Code, Katherine Fischer Drew provides a fascinating account of the various classes among the Burgundian as well as the wergeld for each:

The Unfree:
- An ordinary slave–30 solidi
- A trained house servant or messenger–60 solidi
- A private person's agent–100 solidi
- A royal agent (steward)–150 solidi

The Freemen:
- Lower class (*minores personae*)–150 solidi
- Middle class (*mediocres*)–200 solidi
- Nobility (*optimates*)–300 solidi[63]

This is a highly graduated hierarchy, where a freeman who was a noble was valued at 10 times the ordinary slave. Or to put the value of the slave in greater relief (in addition to the much fuller treatment of the legal status of slaves in Chapter 4) we could note that the composition in case of theft of an ordinary horse was 5 solidi, and so an ordinary slave was six times more valuable than an ordinary horse.

Concerning the Lombards, we have a similar social stratification as we learn from the translator of *The Lombard Laws*:

---

[62] Hans-Werner Goetz, "Social and Military Institutions," in *The New Cambridge Medieval History II: c. 700-c.900*, edited by Rosamond McKitterick, Cambridge: Cambridge University Press, 1995, p. 417.

[63] See *The Burgundian Code*, translated by Katherine Fischer Drew, Philadelphia: University of Pennsylvania Press, 1949, note 4, pp. 192.

> Composition was the sum paid by the guilty party for offenses other than homicide... A considerable portion of *Rothair's Edict* (Titles 41 to 125) is taken up with a schedule of fines to be paid in each of a long number of injuries. Ordinarily, the composition to be paid varied with the quality of the person injured: an injury to a freeman involved a larger payment than a corresponding injury to an *aldius* (half-freeman) or to a personal or household slave (*servus ministerialis*), and such an injury to an *aldius* or household slave likewise involved a larger payment than a corresponding injury to an agrarian slave (*servus rusticus*).[64]

It is also true that the beneficiary of the composition was only paid to someone who had "his own legal power" based also on legal status: "In case of an injury to a woman, the composition was paid to her husband or legal guardian (*mundwald*); in the case of a minor, to his guardian; in the case of an *aldius* or freedman, to his patron (*patronus*); and in the case of a slave, to his lord."[65]

III. The Freeman

In the law of the Roman Empire, there were clear divisions of social class. The slave and freeman were distinguished and treated quite differently across a wide realm of laws. In addition, there were higher and lower class freemen recognized in such texts as the Theodosian Code that was the ruling code in the Roman Empire at the beginning of the Middle Ages.

> When slaves are proved by the testimony of witnesses or by their own confession to have committed violence, if they committed this crime without the knowledge of their masters. We decree that they shall be surrendered and shall atone for their deeds by the supreme penalty. But if they committed the violence because of fear or the exhortation of their masters, it is clear according to the Julian Law, that the master shall be pronounced infamous and that he cannot use as a defense the dignity of his station or of his birth; but slaves who are proved to have obeyed the madness of their masters shall be sentenced to the mines. Low and infamous persons, moreover, and those who are convicted of having committed violence twice or more

---

[64] *The Lombard Laws*, translated by Katherine Fischer Drew, Philadelphia: University of Pennsylvania Press, 1973, pp. 27-28.
[65] Ibid., p. 28.

> frequently shall be held liable to the penalty prescribed by the divine imperial constitutions.[66]

We see here that there were low class persons as well as people who were noble by birth, and both are classed as Roman citizens. And while Roman citizens were generally treated equally before the law in Rome, there are exceptions. The free citizen was at the peak of the social and legal hierarchy in the Roman Empire, although priests and senators were sometimes treated with more respect.

The freeman was also at the peak of the social and legal hierarchy in Germanic societies at the beginning of the Medieval period. But within this category of freemen there was a hierarchy as we have seen, where quite different values were placed on freemen based on whether or not they were nobles; and among those who were not nobles there was a significant difference between whether these freemen were middle or lower class.

There is a sense that the middle class freeman was the center of concern in the Germanic legal codes, as was also true although not to the same extent in the Roman Empire's legal codes. Here is how Katherine Fischer Drew described this situation:

> The social and economic organization of the Lombard kingdom must be inferred from references in some of the laws. At the top of the social scale were the Lombard freemen whose status was reflected in the amount of their wergeld. Two classes of such freemen were clearly distinguishable, their status being determined, it would seem, by whether or not they possessed land. The landholders (who belonged to the "first" class) had a wergeld of 300 solidi; the landless freemen (the lesser men, *minores homines*) had a wergeld of 150 solidi… All Lombard freemen above the age of eighteen were legally competent. In addition to his own independence, the Lombard freeman might enjoy the right of legal protection (*mundium*) over a number of other persons: his wife and unmarried daughters, minor sons, *aldii*, and slaves. The Lombard freeman to whose household these legal incompetents belonged represented these persons in all matters: he appeared for them in court and paid out and received composition in their stead.[67]

---

[66] *The Theodosian Code*, 9.10.4, translated by Clyde Pharr, Princeton: Princeton University Press, 1952, p. 234.

[67] *The Lombard Laws*, translated by Katherine Fischer Drew, Philadelphia: University of Pennsylvania Press, 1973, pp. 28-29.

In law, the freeman was the center of attention and was called upon to represent the interests of his family members and others in his extended household.

IV. The *Aldius*: the Half Free

We can get a sense of how the *aldius*–the half-free man–was treated in Lombard law by looking to two laws of Rothair's Edict:

> 76. Concerning the *aldius*. It is not lawful for an *aldius* or anyone who has not been made legally independent (*amundius*) to sell either land or bondsmen without the consent of his patron, nor may he set any free.[68]
> 205. On the rape of *aldiae*. He who rapes another man's *aldia*, that is, one who was born of a free mother, shall pay forty solidi as composition.[69]

These laws are seemingly straightforward but betray the complex legal status of the *aldius*.

There are several important things about the *aldius* in these two short laws. First, we learn that the *aldius* is in the class of those who are not legally independent; in other words the *aldius* is legally dependent. And, second, we learn that the person to whom the *aldius* is dependent is his patron. Third, in order to exercise certain legally basic liberties, such as selling land or bondsmen, or setting bondsmen free, the *aldius* must have the consent of his patron. Fourth, female *aldia* are characterized as having a free mother (and presumably an unfree father). If one rapes a female slave the composition is only 20 solidi, seemingly setting the value of a female *aldia* as twice that of a slave.[70] In between the law on raping an *aldia* and raping a slave woman there is a law of Rothair's Edict that says that the rape of a freedwoman requires a composition of twenty solidi, the same as the rape of a slave.[71] Why is the rape of an *aldia* worth more than the rape of a freedwoman? Drew speculates that perhaps "this is an indication of the fact that an *aldia* is still classed as a man's property."[72]

---

[68] King Rothair, Rothair's Edict, in *The Lombard Laws*, translated by Katherine Fischer Drew, Philadelphia: University of Pennsylvania Press, 1973, p. 65.
[69] "Rothair's Edict," in ibid., p. 92.
[70] "Rothair's Edict," 207, in ibid., p. 92.
[71] "Rothair's Edict," 206, ibid., p. 92.
[72] *The Lombard Laws*, translated by Katherine Fischer Drew, Philadelphia: University of Pennsylvania Press, 1973, note 57, p. 247.

In several significant ways the *aldius* and slave are treated as having the same legal status but their differential compositions or wergeld make these quite different statuses.

> 124, VIII. He who strikes an *aldius*, or *aldia*, or a male or female slave, and they are crippled as a result of the blow shall pay to their lord or patron as composition half the price (*pretium*) which he would have paid had he killed them. If he causes wounds or injuries he shall pay composition as is provided in an earlier edict.[73]

But it seems that the *aldius* is nonetheless similar to that of the household slave.

> 76. Concerning the half-free (*aldii*) and the household slave (*servi ministerius*). We call those "household slaves" who have been taught, nourished, and trained in the home.
> 77. He who strikes another's *aldius* or household slave so that the wound or bruise is apparent shall pay one solidus as compensation for one blow. He who strikes two blows shall pay two solidi. He who strikes three, three solidi. He who strikes four shall pay four solidi, If, however, more blows than this were endured, they shall not be counted.[74]

One possible interpretation is that the *aldius* has equivalent legal status to the household slave, but not the ordinary slave who is untrained. An indication that this may be the correct interpretation of the Lombard Laws is that the Burgundian Code sets the value of the household slave as twice that of the ordinary slave.

Yet, there are other Lombard Laws that take a different approach to differentiating the *aldius* from the household slave, such as the following laws from *Rothair's Edict*:

> 129. On killing *aldii*. He who kills an *aldius* shall pay sixty solidi as composition.
> 130. On killing household slaves. He who kills another's household slave–one who has been trained or taught as above–shall pay fifty solidi as composition.

---

[73] "Laws of King Liutprand," in *The Lombard Laws*, translated by Katherine Fischer Drew, Philadelphia: University of Pennsylvania Press, 1973, p. 199.
[74] "Rothair's Edict," in *The Lombard Laws*, translated by Katherine Fischer Drew, Philadelphia: University of Pennsylvania Press, 1973, p. 65.

> 131. In the case of another household slave who is found to be subordinate to him… but is nevertheless called a *ministerialis*: whoever kills such a one shall pay twenty-five solidi as composition.[75]

Here the *aldius* is valued at ten more solidi than is the household slave. In addition the *aldius* is valued at 35 more solidi than is true of the ordinary slave.

It is hard to know how to make sense of these precise differences, but the idea is clear that the *aldius* is valued more highly than the ordinary slave, but more like that of the slave who has training and education, implying that the *aldius* also probably has specialized training, and that this accounts for his higher value not necessarily his half-free status. The half-free status denotes a lack of independence, which the *aldius* shares with all of the classes of slaves. Yet, there is perhaps a difference marked when the Germanic laws speak of the "patron" of the *aldius* but the "lord or master" of the slave.

The *aldius'* patron seems to be different from the lord of the slave but also different from the guardian of a female or child. In some respects the patron seems to be an employer, but that would not explain why the *aldius* is said to be half-free. Perhaps it is worth exploring at this stage the status of the serf who will later in the Middle Ages play a large role in feudal society. The serf was still referred to as a *servi* which was also the term for slaves. But the idea developed that the serf had a different relationship to the person he was dependent on than had the slave.

> In the Carolingian age a growing number of clients had paid clevage, though on condition of keeping or receiving the status of free men. For the slave had a master who could take everything from him; not a defender to whom payment was due for the protection given. Gradually, nevertheless, this obligation of clevage, once considered perfectly honorable, came to be associated with baseness, and eventually to be counted by the courts among the characteristic features of serfdom.[76]

---

[75] "Rothair's Edict," in *The Lombard Laws*, translated by Katherine Fischer Drew, Philadelphia: University of Pennsylvania Press, 1973, p. 72.

[76] Marc Bloch, *Feudal Society, Volume I: The Growth of Ties of Dependence*, translated by L.A. Manyon, Philadelphia: University of Pennsylvania Press, 1973, p. 261.

We will later spend time tying to understand the conditions of feudal society. At the moment I just wish to suggest that the *aldius* may be thought of as on the road to serfdom. The aldius was tied to his patron for protection, and the patron treated the *aldius* not like a common slave but rather like an employee, yet one who definitely had his liberty restricted in several legally significant ways. As Marc Bloch has argued, slaves virtually disappeared in Frankish and other Germanic societies in Western Europe, eventually partially replaced by serfs who were tied to their patrons by the land on which they lived and worked.

In our legal sources from the early Medieval period, there emerges a status category that is somewhere between the freeman and the slave, half-way between being fully free and being fully unfree. In one source we find that the *aldius* is in this half-way status because only one of his parents was free at the time of his birth. In earlier times, there were laws governing such situations that depending on circumstances made such a person either free or slave but rarely was there an intermediate legal status. One exception is the status of the *muskenum* in ancient Babylonia. Here is an account of this person's status by a legal scholar: "Clearly, then, the *muskenum* is inferior in rank and circumstances to the ordinary free man but superior to the free man's slave."[77] The *muskenum* was under the protection of the crown, even perhaps "a servant of the palace" but was able to make a marriage of the ordinary type and even to own slaves.[78] This category of legal status is relatively unique in ancient societies.

One significant difference between the ancient legal status of the *muskenum* and the *aldius* in early Medieval legal texts is that the life of the *aldius*, along with all the other Medieval legal statuses, is given a precise value in monetary terms. In the next section of this chapter, I will explore the idea of legal status drawn in monetary terms by considering how such valuation seems to move us from collective ideas of legal status to individualistic ones. As the Germanic societies moved away from the blood feud by legally defining the wergeld for each person, so the Germanic legal codes began establishing legal rights in individualistic terms. We certainly can see the roots of such a movement in both ancient Greek and Roman legal thought, but the valuation in precise monetary terms added a significant element that we need to confront directly.

---

[77] G. R. Driver and John C. Miles, *The Babylonian Laws*, Oxford: Oxford University Press, 1952, vol. I, p. 92.

[78] Ibid., p. 93.

V. The Group and the Individual Begin to Separate

Louis Halphen provides us with a good beginning to this section when he discusses the Visigothic Code's treatment of responsibility:

> With the concept of marriage… we see the legislator here making an effort to substitute the principle of a strictly personal responsibility for the collective responsibility of all members of the family. "The father," says one provision of the old articles of the [Visigothic] code, "must not be disturbed on account of the son, nor the son for the father, nor the wife for the husband, nor the brother for the brother. He alone will be accused who has actually committed a blameworthy act, with the author of the act, the accusation will die."… The Burgundian legislator likewise provided that in a case of homicide only the murderer was to be pursued.[79]

There was "a struggle taking place among the Visigoths against the principle of family solidarity" but as we will see there is much evidence to think that individualistic conceptions were mostly winning out over collective conceptions.

So, we can see at least two sources of an individualistic turn in Germanic law in the early Medieval period. First, the idea of responsibility was devolving on the discrete individual, not the family unit. This was seen in the way that criminal responsibility was treated. Second, and related, the way that the penalties of the law were arranged showed that the idea of individual worth or value was the key consideration, and quite a bit more important than the collective unit that the individual was a part of.

The attempt to give precise monetary values to individuals based not on their group or even family status but due to the role in the society these individuals played is highly significant. This is also true of the attempt to provide exact amounts of money that given injuries would call for as penalties. This is perhaps exemplified best in Rothair's Edict in the Lombard Laws, of which these are just a few instances:

> 46. He who hits another man on the head so that the skin which the hair covers is broken shall pay six solidi as composition…

---

[79] Louis Halphen, "Germanic Society in the Early Sixth Century," in *The Barbarian Invasions: Catalyst of a New Order*, edited by Katherine Fischer Drew, Huntington, NY: Robert E. Krieger Publishing Company, 1977, p. 36.

> 47. He who hits another man on the head so that the bones are broken shall pay twelve solidi as composition….
> 48…. In the case where someone gouges out another man's eye, composition shall be computed as if for death, that is, according to the rank of the person…
> 49. … He who cuts off another man's nose shall pay half of that one's wergeld as composition…
> 63… He who cuts off the thumb of another man's hand shall pay that one as composition a sixth part of the wergeld at which he would have been valued if he had been killed.
> 64… He who cuts off the index finger from another man's hand shall pay sixteen solidi as composition.
> 65… He who cuts off the middle finger from another man's hand shall pay five solidi as composition.[80]

Penalties like these could easily be used today for assigning compensation in workmen's compensation cases in the US.

The idea behind these elaborate penalties is to ascertain what functional part of a human's life is lost due to injury, and to attempt to compensate as closely as possible for that loss. We find something similar in other Germanic codes as well. Here is just a bit of the Salic Frank's code:

> He who maims another with his hand or foot or gouges out or strikes out his eye or cuts off his ear or nose and it is proved against him shall be liable to pay…one hundred solidi.
> If he has cut the hand and the hand remains hanging there he shall be liable to pay…sixty-two and a half solidi…
> He who cuts off another man's thumb or big toe and it is proved against him shall be liable to pay…fifty solidi…[81]

These Salic laws, like the Lombard laws, aim to set penalties quite precisely based on the functioning that was lost. Again, such laws are highly individualized.

In these Germanic codes there are some laws that treat of collective rather than individual responsibility, which we will examine in much more detail in Chapter 6. But even these laws try to ferret out the individual responsibility of the members of a collective rather than to

---

[80] "Rothair's Edict," in *The Lombard Laws*, translated by Katherine Fischer Drew, Philadelphia: University of Pennsylvania Press, 1973, pp. 61-64.

[81] King Clovis, *Pactus Legis Salicae*, *The Laws of the Salian Franks*, translated by Katherine Fischer Drew, Philadelphia: University of Pennsylvania Press, 1991, pp. 92-93.

blame the whole collective as can be seen in this example from *Rothair's Edict*:

> 11. On plots involving death. If freemen without the king's consent plot another man's death, but that one does not die as a result of the agreement, then each shall pay twenty solidi as composition, as stated above. But if that one [conspired against] dies as a result of the plot, then the doer of the deed shall pay the victim's wergeld, according as he is valued, as composition.[82]

Even in these collective acts of wrongdoing, it is the individuals who are penalized.

It is worth wondering whether and to what extent the monetary valuing of different classes affects other valuing. In some ancient societies we can see something similar, but compared to earlier Germanic societies, the use of monetary values seems to constitute an abrupt change. It is clearly the case that the monetary fees set for homicide as well as for various injuries was aimed at stopping the blood feud.

The first issue then is how it was thought that the setting of monetary fines would in fact overcome the feud. Paul Vinogradoff provides this account:

> The blood feud generally resolves into a system of composition, or material compensation for the injury inflicted. It is easy to understand that in primitive societies, when a wrong done to a single individual might lead to retribution by a whole group of kindred, there was a constant danger of private war, which would be exceedingly injurious to society at large, unless checked by arbitration. The incipient state did all it could to render conciliation acceptable to the individual disputants and it did not always have an easy task. The desire for personal vengeance was very strong…[83]

This is the normal story of why Germanic codes had penalties that were meant to provide very precise penalties for injuries or death–it was to stop the blood feud.

---

[82] "Rothair's Edict," in *The Lombard Laws*, translated by Katherine Fischer Drew, Philadelphia: University of Pennsylvania Press, 1973, p. 54.

[83] Paul Vinogradoff, *Outlines of Historical Jurisprudence*, Oxford: Oxford University Press, 1920, vol. I, p. 310.

But there is a second issue that is related to the first and at least as important conceptually: why did the law favor the individual over the collective? Law generally operates better in terms of justice and also compliance when it focuses on the individual perpetrator and the individual victim. Getting a clear picture of who did what to whom requires an attention to the individuals, and can be obscured when looking at the group or collective.

The turn from collective guilt to individual guilt is in stark contrast to the often told story that the early Middle Ages devolved *into tribalism* and away from the rule of law. If we look at the Germanic codes we see something quite different in legal and political thought. The Germanic peoples were moving *away from tribalism* toward a personalized sense of the authority of law. The attempt to set precise values on individual lives, and even individual body parts, is a way to counter the idea that the individual's value can only be seen in its relation to the person's group.

When other ancient societies moved from collective to individualized legal and political thought there was not the attention to precise numerical valuing that we have seen in the Germanic codes. As we will see in later chapters, such precise numerical valuing played a very large role in the way that criminal law was conceived in Germanic legal thought as well. Not only was the blood feud countered but the idea of the rule of law for each individual arose in these Germanic codes. Law became something that individuals feared but also something that these individuals valued, especially when the individuals were not likely to be helped by their tribes. The idea of the law seen as a protector of the weakest members of the society was crucially premised on the idea of individual rather than collective identity and responsibility. We next turn to the way that slaves and women were conceptualized in these individualized ways before turning to the important advances in criminal law that can be found in the supposedly dark ages of the early Medieval period.

CHAPTER 4

SLAVERY AND MANUMISSION

Enslavement came in many forms in the early Medieval period, and probably set the stage for the idea of serfdom that was the cornerstone of the feudal societies of the later Middle Ages. One of the crucial differences from ancient ideas of slavery is that in the early Middle Ages slavery was increasingly seen as a penalty or punishment for having violated the law in a serious way. Here we find strong influences of the Catholic Church, as with many things in the Middle Ages. During the early Medieval period there were also new ideas of how to understand the release from enslavement. In this chapter I will argue that enslavement varied significantly in the early Medieval period and that some forms of enslavement did in fact have characteristics similar to the later idea of serfdom. In addition, I will argue that we can see in this period the ideas that will shape later conceptions of imprisonment, as a kind of legally mandated enslavement.

In the first section, we will discuss the Byzantine ideas of enslavement. In the second section we will explore the various ways that a person became enslaved in the Germanic codes of the early Medieval period. In the third section we will look in more detail at the idea of penal enslavement. In the fourth section we will analyze the various forms of manumission that are discussed in the Germanic codes. And in the final section we will compare the ideas of enslavement of the early Medieval period with the ideas of serfdom in the later Medieval period. Throughout we will try to understand why enslavement remained so common even as it had seemed to be dying out in the late Roman Empire.

I. Byzantine Ideas of Enslavement

The law of the Roman Republic drew a firm distinction between free men and slaves as we see from this famous passage from the great second century Roman jurist, Gaius:

> The whole of the law observed by us relates either to persons or to things or to actions. Let us first consider persons.
> The primary distinction in the law of persons is this, that all men are either free or slaves. Next free men are either *ingenui* (freeborn) or *libertini* (freedmen). *Ingenui* are those born free, *libertini* those manumitted from lawful slavery. Next, of freedmen there are three classes: they are either Roman citizens or Latins or in the category of *dediticii*.[84]

In the law of the Roman Republic, there was a clear distinction between slaves and those who were free; and a very clear difference between those who were free from birth and those who attained freedom by being manumitted as slaves. Freedmen, freed slaves, were treated differently from free men.

The Theodosian Code that was in force in the Medieval Roman Empire has this rather clear law concerning the manumission of slaves that also tells us something about the status of slaves:

> If any person with pious intention should grant deserved freedom to his favorite slaves in the bosom of the Church, he shall appear to give it with the same legal force as that with which Roman citizenship was customarily bestowed under observance of the usual formalities. But it is Our pleasure that such right to manumit in the churches shall be allowed only to those persons who give freedom under the eyes of the bishops.[85]

Manumitted slaves who are freed by seeking sanctuary in churches are granted full citizenship rights in Roman law. We see here that the status of being a freedman is no longer treated as a distinctly different category to that of a freeman.

By the time of Justinian's Code, a century or so after the Theodosian Code, the distinction between freedman and freeman was abolished, regardless of where the manumission of the slave took place: "all rights of patronage are abolished… We prefer that [Our Empire] be inhabited rather by freeborn persons than those who have been

[84] Gaius, *Institutes*, translated by Francis De Zulueta, Oxford: Oxford University Press, 1946, vol. I, p. 5.

[85] *The Theodosian Code*, 4.7.1, translated by Clyde Pharr, Princeton: Princeton University Press, 1952, p. 87.

emancipated from slavery."[86] Alice Rio comments: "In the sixth century, Justinian eventually abolished the distinction between freedman and free citizen..."[87] During the height of the Roman Empire, slavery became less common and less important in the law.

We also find a similar Roman law in Justinian's Novels, where manumission is said to entail elevation to full citizenship:

> 78.1. Therefore we order that if anyone, when manumitting a male or female slave, should declare him or her to be a Roman citizen (and, indeed, he is not allowed to do otherwise), he is hereby notified that, in accordance with the terms of this law, the person who received freedom shall at once, and ever afterwards, have the right to wear a gold ring, and be classed as originally freeborn; that he shall not be required to petition the Emperor for this purpose, or to observe any other formality, but all these things will result from his grant of freedom...[88]

Again we see here that manumission resulted in free citizenship not the status of being merely a freedman by the time of this late act of Justinian.

There were some sources of enslavement that were connected to violating the criminal law, but most slaves were simply born to slave parents or had been forced into slavery by debt or capture. The category of being "a slave of punishment" is recognized in the Theodosian Code,[89] and there were some laws that had slavery as the punishment in the earlier Roman codes. The best known case of enslavement as a punishment concerned a free woman who "lived with the slave of another person after notice (*denuntiatio*) by the owner that he forbade it" resulting in the woman being enslaved.[90] Yet, by the time of Justinian in the sixth century, penal enslavement had ceased in the Roman Empire.

> We manifest Our indulgence in an instance in which the severity of the law was formerly exhibited... We now annul

---

[86] Emperor Justinian, *Justinian's Code,* Book VI, Title 4.3, in *The Civil Law*, translated by S.P. Scott, Cincinnati: The Central Trust Co., 1932, vol. 13, p. 302.

[87] Alice Rio, *Slavery After Rome: 500-1100*, Oxford: Oxford University Press, 2017, p. 78.

[88] Emperor Justinian, *Constitutions of Justinian – Sixth Collection, Seventy-Eighth New Constitution*, Chapter 1, in *The Civil Law*, translated by S.P. Scott, Cincinnati: The Central Trust Co., 1932, vol. 16, p. 291.

[89] See *The Theodosian Code*, 10.10.30, translated by Clyde Pharr, p. 278.

[90] W. W. Buckland, *The Roman Law of Slavery*, Cambridge: Cambridge University Press, 1908, p. 412.

> this provision and do not permit any person who was well born in the beginning to become a slave as part of his punishment; for We by no means desire anyone who is free to be reduced to a servile condition, as we have long since embraced every opportunity to promote the manumission of slaves.[91]

Here we see that Justinian supported the eventual elimination of slavery, and that in the mean time he abolished penal slavery. Byzantine law, as well as that of the Roman Empire in the West seemed to be moving away from slavery just as the Germanic codes were being written to give a large role for slavery. The codes differed on how much slavery was countenanced as we will see.

II. Forms of Non-Penal Enslavement

As in previous times, in the early Middle Ages a person could become a slave primarily in the following ways:

a) by being born to slave parents
b) by being captured on the battlefield
c) by contracting into slavery in lieu of payment of a debt
d) by being captured in a "slave raid"
e) by being convicted for certain crimes.

In this section we will examine the first three of these forms of enslavement and consider the fifth form of enslavement in the following section.

Alice Rio provides a good summary of the primary ways in which a person became a slave.

> Capture and sale constituted the most disruptive imaginable form of enslavement, but there were many other ways of entering an unfree condition. These involved the recruitment of insiders: people who, prior to their enslavement, had been integrated in the same community in which they continued to reside as unfree persons... Sometimes it was clearly coercive and disruptive of people's lives to an extent comparable to violent capture, and their victims had just as little say. In other cases, however, the attribution of unfree status could involve

[91] *Constitutions of Justinian – Sixth Collection, Twenty-Second New Constitution*, Chapter 8, in *The Civil Law*, translated by S.P. Scott, Cincinnati: The Central Trust Co., 1932, vol. 16, p. 114.

> negotiation between enslaver and enslaved to a surprising extent. Self-sale or self-gift, when people either sold themselves for a price or simply gave themselves to more powerful people, happened in the evident expectation of a trade-off...[92]

People could literally sell themselves for a price, although this was generally condemned, or they could give themselves to someone who they expected to be able to provide food and shelter for their family that could not be provided otherwise.

I will attempt to reconstruct how slavery was viewed from the plentiful legal texts primarily of the Germanic codes. I should note that this method is limited to be sure, and so I will occasionally also discuss some social and political records. It is unclear to what extent the legal codes did represent legal thought in this period, although it is also not clear what is a better source for us to consider.

To begin, let us consider how the Germanic codes treat debt enslavement, a form of enslavement that we can trace back at least to ancient Babylonia of about 1800 BCE. Here is a law from the Visigothic Code, a code that is closest to the codes of the Roman Empire:

> Any freeman who permits himself to be sold, and shares the price with the vendor, and afterwards, desiring to cheat the purchaser, publishes the fact for the sake of reclaiming his liberty, shall not be heard, but shall remain in slavery; for it is dishonorable that a freeman should voluntarily subject himself to servitude. But if he who sold himself, or permitted himself to be sold, shall have sufficient property to redeem himself... the person who is the object of the sale shall regain his freedom.[93]

Here we see that the selling of oneself into slavery is recognized as a valid sale in Visigothic law.

There were important restrictions to the idea of being sold into slavery for debt, as we see in this section of the Visigothic Code:

> It shall not be lawful for parents to sell, give away, or pledge their children. And no one who purchases or receives a child under such circumstances, shall have any legal right to it

---

[92] Alice Rio, *Slavery After Rome: 500-1100*, Oxford: Oxford University Press, 2017, p. 42.

[93] *Visigothic Code*, Book V, Title IV.10, pp. 162-163.

> whatsoever, but on the other hand, he shall lose the price or the amount advanced as a loan, which he paid to the parents of said children.[94]

The Visigoths seem to accept someone selling himself into slavery, but, unlike many societies before them, they reject the idea that a child can be sold into slavery by his or her parents.

The Frankish formularies of Angers give us an idea of how self-sale came to be seen as a way into slavery:

> No. 19. To A forever my lord B. Both because of the necessity of these times and of life, and also because I am oppressed by the combined weight of hunger and poverty, I am unable to act in any other way than to transfer my entire [free] status into your service. It is therefore established that I, compelled by no one, but with my fullest will… and I received from you in exchange for my aforementioned [free] status the price which pleased me, worth n. solidi in gold, so that from this day you may have the power in every way, with God's favor, to do whatever you want with me, as with the other unfree servants in your service…[95]

The self-sale contract is seen in these Frankish formularies as a way into permanent slavery.

In the Lombard laws we find an especially good contrast with the formularies of the Frankish kings where we have an account of how enslavement was not viewed as a permanent form of self-gift as contrasted with enslavement as punishment:

> If a man out of his own goodness enters the service of a judge or of some other man and serves him or his sons or his nephews and if it is manifestly true that his own relatives are all free, if afterward he [whose service the man entered] wishes to keep him in servitude claiming that he has served him or his relatives for as much as thirty years, he cannot keep him by this kind of possession, for it is unreasonable and contrary to the commands of God that, while all his relatives are free, he alone who served voluntarily should be retained in servitude for possession alone. But if a man has been handed over to someone to serve on account of theft or by any other offense,

---

[94] *Visigothic Code*, Book V, Title IV.12, pp. 163-164.

[95] *The Formulary of Angers*, No. 19, in *The Formularies of Angers and Marculf*, translated by Alice Rio, Liverpool: Liverpool University Press, 2008, p. 64.

> and this is proved, then he shall continue to serve, as the law provides.[96]

Here we have a rejection of the idea that self-sale could constitute permanent servitude and a good transition to the idea of penal servitude, accepted by the Lombard King Aistulf.

III. Penal Enslavement

A form of enslavement in the early Middle Ages that was only rarely seen in ancient times was penal enslavement–enslavement as a state ordered penalty or punishment for having committed certain crimes. In some respects this form of enslavement was employed because, by and large, there were not public prisons to which a person could be sentenced in this period. As we will see in this section there were many Germanic laws that had as their penalty that the convicted person be enslaved. And in many of these cases the person was sold into slavery to a private person who was able to control the slave as part of his household or farm employees.

The Visigoths clearly recognized that various severe crimes could warrant the punishment of enslavement:

> If any freeman should carry off a virgin or widow by violence, and she should be rescued before she has lost her chastity, he who carried her off shall lose half of his property, which shall be given to her. But should such not be the case, and the crime should have been fully committed, under no circumstances shall a marriage contract be entered into with him; but he shall be surrendered, with all his possessions, to the injured party; and shall, in addition, receive two hundred lashes in public; and, after having been deprived of his liberty, he shall be delivered up to the parents of her whom he violated, or to the virgin or widow herself, to forever serve as a slave.[97]

The crime here involves kidnap and rape of a woman who had not yet lost her virginity and the penalty is one of the most severe short of death. The implication is that enslavement could occur as punishment for such very serious crimes.

---

[96] King Aistulf, "Laws of King Aistulf," 22. XIII., in *The Lombard Laws*, translated by Katherine Fischer Drew, Philadelphia: University of Pennsylvania Press, 1973, p. 237.

[97] *Visigothic Code*, Book III, Title III.1, pp. 88-89.

Here is another Visigothic law that also concerns rape with the punishment of enslavement:

> If any one should carry off a woman betrothed to another we hereby decree that half of the property of the ravisher shall be given to the girl, and the other half to the betrothed. But if he shall have little or no property, he shall be given up, with all his possessions, to those above mentioned; so that the ravisher having been sold as a slave, they may have an equal share of the price for him.[98]

This law seems to treat the crime of kidnap and rape of a betrothed woman, as contrasted with an unbetrothed virgin, as a crime that could be punished only with the transfer of half of the property of the ravisher. Only when the ravisher cannot pay as much is he then subject to enslavement. So, this is a mixed case of enslavement for punishment and enslavement for inability to pay a monetary penalty.

Adultery is also a crime that can carry the punishment of enslavement, and for both parties:

> If a marriage contract has been entered into… and afterwards the girl or the woman is convicted of having committed adultery, or of having betrothed herself to another man, or of having married; she along with her unlawful husband, or adulterer, or betrothed to whom she has given herself contrary to her solemn agreement, shall be delivered up as slaves, with all their property, to the person to whom she was first betrothed…[99]

We find similar treatment of prostitution to that of adultery:

> If any freeborn girl or woman should publicly practice fornication, be known as a harlot, and be shamelessly given to soliciting men; after having been arrested by the governor of the city, she shall receive in public two hundred lashes, and shall be sent away, under the condition that she shall not, afterwards, be guilty of similar conduct, or ever again enter the city. And if she should ever return, she shall be sentenced by the governor to receive three hundred lashes more, and shall be

[98] *Visigothic Code*, Book III, Title III. 5, pp. 90-91.
[99] *Visigothic Code*, Book III, Title IV. 2, p. 95.

> given as a slave to some pauper, and never be permitted to go freely about the city again.[100]

Being placed in servitude to a pauper was seen as especially harsh punishment.

The Visigoths in addition punished the woman who obtains an abortion similar to the woman who performs these other sexual crimes.

> If anyone should administer a potion to a pregnant woman to produce abortion, and the child should die in consequence, the woman who took such a potion, if she is a slave, shall receive two hundred lashes, and if she is freeborn, she shall lose her rank, and shall be given as a slave to whomever we may select.[101]

There were other Visigothic laws that called for the punishment of enslavement but the paradigm case seemed to be these violations of sexual norms.

When a person is adjudged guilty and is penalized a certain amount of money, the failure to pay the monetary penalty can then result in enslavement as we see in this Visigothic law:

> Where an individual has been guilty of offenses against many persons, or owes debts to different creditors, he who first establishes a claim either in writing or by oral testimony… shall have the preference; and said person shall be required to satisfy the claim, regardless of its priority in time, or shall be sentenced by the judge for the offense he has committed against the law. Where several parties to whom he is indebted, should proceed against him at one and the same time, he shall satisfy his obligations to such persons according to the value of the claims; or, if he should prove insolvent, he shall serve all of them as a slave.[102]

So, either for failure to pay criminal penalties or for failure to pay debts enslavement is the punishment.

And there is a similar law but this one concerns the person who accuses another person of such crimes as witchcraft, poisoning, or theft:

> When anyone is accused of crime, that is to say, of poisoning, witchcraft, theft, or any other unlawful act, his accuser must go

---

[100] *Visigothic Code*, Book III, Title IV. 17, p. 103.

[101] *Visigothic Code*, Book VI, Title III. 1, p. 206.

[102] *The Visigothic Code*, Book V, Title 6.5, p. 179.

> before the governor of the city, or the judge who has jurisdiction in the district, in order that the case may be investigated according to law; and as soon as the commission of the crime has been established, the governor or the judge shall cause the culprit to be arrested; and if he should not be convicted of a capital offense, the accuser shall be compelled to give him pecuniary satisfaction; and where the latter has not the means to do so, he shall be delivered up to him as a slave.[103]

Enslavement here is used as a punishment for the crime of accusing an innocent person of a crime, which was considered one of the most serious offenses.

IV. Manumission

Freeing a slave could be accomplished in several ways as illustrated in the Germanic codes, for instance, by paying off the debt that had caused a person to be sold into slavery. There are other forms of manumission found in the Germanic codes, and several are relatively unique. Consider this law from Rothair's Edict:

> 222. On marrying one's own woman slave. If any man wishes to marry his own woman slave, he may do so. Nevertheless, he ought to free her, that is, make her worthy born (*vurdibora*), and he ought to do it legally by the proper formal procedure (*gairethinx*). She shall then be known as a free and legal wife and her children may become the legal heirs of their father.[104]

This relatively humane law concerning manumission follows another law that is not humane at all: "The slave who dares to marry a free woman or girl shall lose his life."[105]

There were various formal procedures by which a master could free his slave, either during the master's life or as part of his stipulated will concerning how to proceed after his death. Here is a rather clear law on manumission in Rothair's Edict:

> 224. On manumission. He who wishes to free his own man or woman slave shall have that right if it pleases him. He who

---

[103] *The Visigothic Code*, Book VII, Title 1.5, p. 235.
[104] "Rothair's Edict," 222, in *The Lombard Laws*, translated by Katherine Fischer Drew, Philadelphia: University of Pennsylvania Press, 1973, p. 95.
[105] "Rothair's Edict," 221, in ibid., p. 95.

> wishes to make his slave folk free and a stranger to himself, that is, legally independent (*haamund*), ought to do it thus. The lord shall first hand the servant over to the hand of another freeman and confirm it by formal action (*gairethinx*). And the second man shall hand the servant over to a third in the same manner, and the third shall hand him over to a fourth. And this fourth man shall lead him to a place where four roads meet and give him arrow and whip, and say: "From these four roads you are free to choose where you wish to go." If the act is done thus, the former slave will then be legally independent and completely free. Afterwards his patron will not have the right to require any liability of him or of his children.[106]

This procedure of giving the slave the choice of four roads is repeated in other Germanic codes and the symbolism is quite striking.

A master or patron may choose instead to make his slave only half-free (an *aldius*) but that requires a different procedure: "He who wishes to raise his slave to the status of an *aldius* should not give him the choice of the four roads."[107] It was also possible to be given the choice of the four roads but not in addition to be a stranger, that is, to be fully legally independent. In that case, "he shall live with his patron as with a brother or other related free Lombard."[108] And it is also possible for a slave to be freed by the king's command and here the slave is given the choice of the four roads and is not dependent on anyone henceforth.[109]

Another means of manumission is set out in the laws of the Lombard King Liutprand:

> 9.III. On freedmen. If anyone hands over his man or woman slave to the king and the prince himself sets him or her free by handing him or her over to the hands of a priest in front of the holy altar, he or she shall remain free just as those who become folkfree. He who obtains the mundium of such a woman freed by the prince shall have it as for a woman who is folk free; and there shall be no further [servile] condition either for her or for her children.[110]

Unlike for the Romans, in some of the Germanic codes there does not appear to be an intermediate class of people who are freedmen and who

---

[106] "Rothair's Edict," 224, in ibid., p. 96..

[107] Ibid.

[108] Ibid.

[109] Ibid.

[110] "Laws of King Liutprand," 9.III, in *The Lombard Laws*, ibid., p. 148.

are different from freemen. The freed slave did not become a member of an intermediate class but became fully free by this procedure, unless the prince or other person freeing the slave withheld the mundium, that is, the power or right of guardianship.

Yet, there are other Germanic codes that do distinguish freemen, freedmen, and slaves. The Bavarian Laws, for example, draw this distinction in the differential way that penalties are assessed for the same injuries. Here are three laws to compare:

> IV. 1. If anyone strikes a freeman in anger, which they call *pulislac*, let him give one solidus…
> V. 1. If anyone strikes him [a freedman], which they call *pulislac*, let him compensate with one-half solidus…
> VI. 1. If anyone strikes another's slave in anger, let him compensate with one tremissis.[111]

So, the penalty for striking a freeman is twice the penalty of striking a freedman and three times that of striking a slave (a tremissis is worth one-third of a solidus).

In these Bavarian laws, the penalty for striking a slave (one-third of a solidus) is only slightly less than the penalty for striking a freedman (one-half of a solidus). The worth of a slave is closer to the worth of a freedman than the worth of the freedman is to the worth of a freeman. And so, there is a significant difference between being free and being freed for the Bavarians just as was true for the Romans at various times. Slaves are treated differently in the various Germanic codes, perhaps reflecting how strongly these codes were derivative of the Roman codes at the time.

Because of the differential in how freed slaves were treated, the institution of manumission is likewise seen somewhat differently by different Germanic codes as well. And it mattered whether the slave was freed completely or only partially. Such considerations mattered quite a bit in terms of rights of marriage and inheritance, not just the different penalties that attached to injuries of the slaves and freemen. Manumission could be of enormous value, especially if the freed slave became a full citizen. But manumission could be considerably less significant if the freed slave still did the same jobs and for the same compensation as when he or she was a slave.

---

[111] *The Bavarian Laws*, in *Laws of the Alamans and Bavarians*, translated by Theodore John Rivers, Philadelphia: University of Pennsylvania Press, 1977, pp. 130-135.

V. On the Road to Serfdom?

Here is how the historian Alice Rio characterizes some of the differences between slavery and serfdom:

> I would characterize the difference in the following way: while both slavery and serfdom are designed to place a certain category of people at a fundamental disadvantage in terms of rights, slavery primarily concentrates on denying rights altogether, whereas serfdom is, instead, fundamentally geared towards charging for access to them instead. Central medieval lords allowed access to all sorts of fundamental rights–such as marriage, family life, and inheritance–in exchange for a range of traditional payments, which, taken together, constituted excellent tools for obtaining and consolidating the serfs' recognition of their own dependent status. The granting of rights to family and property, far from reflecting an easing of the lords' hold over their dependents, amounted to a reassertion of their domination–at least in the areas that they were interested in. Serfdom was not, as it is sometimes described, a straightforward improvement in the situation of the unfree dependants; it was more a displacement in the aims to which the category was put, accompanied by an adjustment in methods.[112]

One of the main questions of this section is whether or not it is fair to characterize some of the enslavement practices of the early Middle Ages as on the road to serfdom, even if it is nonetheless true that slavery and serfdom were very different from each other in certain respects.

The first issue to take up is that there was a legal status recognized in the Germanic codes, *colonus*, which is sometimes translated as serf. The reason that this category, which was also recognized by the Romans, is likened to being a serf is that the person was bonded to the land rather than to a person.[113] Here is the assessment of P. D. King:

> it is clear that many slaves–especially, no doubt, the erstwhile *coloni*–did work the land free from the direct control of their lords: those laws which allude to the payment by slaves themselves are significant in this respect, while one law refers

---

[112] Alice Rio, *Slavery After Rome, 500-1100*, Oxford: Oxford University Press, 2017, p. 14.

[113] See P.D. King, *Law and Society in the Visgothic Kingdom*, Cambridge: Cambridge University Press, 1972, p. 161.

> specifically to a slave's acquisition of immovables on the estate of someone other than his owner. The property which such a slave possessed, his *peculium*, might consist of lands, a house, animals, even other slaves–as well as the bits and pieces he had gathered around him, and might be added to by inheritance or payment from outsiders. But such property was not his to dispose of at will. For, the slave was a chattel, to be used as his master might lawfully desire...[114]

Here we see that the slave in question seemed to have some of the rights that serfs were said to have, but not to have unrestricted rights. Indeed the slave's master still had control over how the slave exercised the limited rights in such cases. The slave as *colonus* was free from direct control but never really free from the master's ultimate control.

The *colonus* is seemingly in between a slave and a serf in that the *colonus* was not mainly defined by the rights he was denied but by the attachment to land and the proto-rights he had vis-à-vis the land. And it is attachment to the land, rather than attachment to a person, that was to characterize the serf. The *colonus* had that attachment to land, but also had attachment to the master. How precisely this arrangement worked is a matter of some considerable debate among historians. But it does appear to me that the form of slavery of the *colonus* can be seen as at least on the way to serfdom.

The Burgundian Code can also be consulted about the category of the *originarii*, a term which is sometimes translated as serf.

> This procedure will be observed among Burgundians and Romans: if a crime is charged to anyone which cannot be proved at the present, we order that it be observed that whether it be a slave (*servus*) of Burgundian or Roman who is accused of the crime, let his master not be compelled to take oath either for slave (*servus*) or serf (*originarius*); but when a crime has been charged either let the value of the slave (*servus*) or serf (*colonus*) be established according to his condition, which value the master to whom the slave (*servus*) or serf (*colonus*) belongs shall receive from the accuser in person, or let him (the master) receive a slave (*mancipium*) of like value...[115]

---

[114] Ibid., p. 170.

[115] *The Burgundian Code*, translated by Katherine Fischer Drew, Philadelphia: University of Pennsylvania Press, 1949, p. 28.

This fairly confusing law does not seem to distinguish between slave and serf, and what is translated as serf is both *originarius* and *colonus*. So we seem to have the idea of slave and serf being mixed together in various parts of the Burgundian Code.

There is a contradiction in seeing a slave as a chattel (like a beast of burden who has no rights) but also as someone who can own land or even other slaves. Strictly speaking chattel cannot own anything. We are thus already in a mixing of ideas that perhaps constitute the beginning of the road to serfdom. Yet, we find similar conceptual problems concerning slaves in much earlier ancient legal thought as well–in ancient Mesopotamia slaves could be bought and sold, but were also entitled to own businesses as well as own other slaves.

Especially in the case of penal enslavement we can easily see the beginnings of the ideas of penal imprisonment that had already begun to emerge in the Roman Empire. Insofar as enslavement could be conditioned on who was to be the master in penal enslavement, we also see the idea of enslavement that was not necessarily perpetual or that called for the same rights restrictions across all cases. For the Germanic codes that stuck closest to the codes of the Roman Empire, specifically the Visigothic and Burgundian Codes, we find the continuation of the change in the status of slaves to be more open to different arrangements between slave and master. Especially in the agricultural domain, slaves who were identified as the *coloni* were identified in Rome, as being tied increasingly more to the land rather than to a person who is the master or lord. We will see related ideas of how crime was understood on the new Christian model of sin that also changed the relations among different classes. To see this we will in the next part of the book dive more deeply into the ideas of criminality. Before doing this though we will examine the changing status of women in Byzantine and Germanic legal thought.

CHAPTER 5

WOMEN AND THE FAMILY

In the early Medieval period, especially among the Germanic legal codes, there was a wide variety of laws stipulating the roles that women were assigned in family life and in the public sphere. At least some commentators have argued that the introduction of Christianity improved the status of women, and we will see this to be partially true. But we will also see that in certain important domains women were treated differently and arguably better in Germanic societies before the rise of Christianity, or so I will argue in this chapter.

In the first section of this chapter I will discuss the value of a woman in Germanic codes in terms of the price of compensation, the wergeld. In the second section I will contrast the views of divorce that we find in the codes of the Roman Empire and the Germanic codes. I will start here because in divorce we have the most graphic illustration of the wide differences but also arguably the better treatment of women by the Germanic "barbarians" than by the Christianized Romans. In the third section we will examine the laws concerning rape and kidnap, where it appears that the Germanic laws were much less humane than the Roman codes. In the fourth section we will tackle the issue of marriage, considering especially the gifts that were required to make betrothal binding. And finally, I will attempt to draw some conclusions about the legal status of women at the beginning of the Middle Ages and the rise of Christianity, a status that was independent of their price as brides.

I. The Value of a Woman

In an earlier chapter we have seen that the value of various persons was established as their wergeld, the price of compensation if the person was killed. We begin by noting that in many Germanic codes the value of a woman was set at twice that of a man. This curious fact does not necessarily indicate that women's place in Germanic society was exalted or superior to that of men; in fact it appears that it was quite the opposite. As one scholar has noted:

> The high value placed on the life of women by the Germanic codes has been interpreted as evidence of the significant appreciation of women during the early Middle Ages. But it would appear that women's ability to bear children, rather than their worth as helpmates or prophetesses, was prized.[116]

We will see that while these matters are fairly complicated this conclusion can be strongly supported in various ways.

The Burgundian Code has some of the most elaborate gradations of wergeld compensation.

> If anyone shall steal a girl, let him be compelled to pay the price set for such a girl ninefold, and let him pay a fine to the amount of twelve solidi.
> If a girl who has been seized returns uncorrupted to her parents, let the abductor compound six times the wergeld of the girl; moreover, let the fine be set at twelve solidi.[117]

Let us delve into the implications of this law for how women and girls were valued.

Here we see that the wergeld compensation of a girl is increased dramatically if someone corrupts her, or in other words her value is much greater if she is still a virgin. So, if she is captured but returned still a virgin the compensation is also much less than if she is returned now no longer a virgin. This Burgundian law also tells us that the increased value of a girl is not merely that she has the ability to bear children but that the children she bears are clearly those of a man to whom she is married. Perhaps more cynically it may be that the value of a girl is increased if she has not yet had sexual relations–so that the first to have sex with her will have the most enjoyment and must compensate accordingly.

The Alamannic laws are even more extreme in setting the wergeld price of an unbetrothed, and presumably virgin, girl.

> If anyone takes another's unbetrothed daughter for himself as a wife, let him return her and compensate for her with forty solidi, if her father demands her back.

---

[116] Suzanne Fonay Wemple, *Women in Frankish Society: Marriage and Cloister 500 to 900*, Philadelphia: University of Pennsylvania Press, 1981, p. 29.

[117] *The Burgundian Code*, XII, translated by Katherine Fischer Drew, Philadelphia: University of Pennsylvania Press, 1949, 1976, p. 31.

> If however, this woman dies under his [custody], before he acquired her guardianship [*mundium*] from her father, let him pay 400 solidi for her to her father.[118]

The value of a girl or woman is dramatically increased here, by a factor of ten–from 40 to 400 solidi–if she dies. Why might this be?

If it is a matter of the woman's worth being measured in terms of the children she can bear, then it might be that the compensation for her increases as her ability to bear children is forcibly diminished. But why would the compensation to her father increase so dramatically if she is killed? It appears to me that the increase cannot be explained simply in terms of child bearing but must include the value of the woman or girl in other terms. Yet, the wergeld price for a murdered woman is set as similar to that of a man: "If anyone murders a man or a woman who is [free], let a lawful wergeld be paid ninefold."[119]

The Bavarian Code is perhaps a bit easier to make sense of in terms of the value of women and girls, which sets the compensations for injuries to women at twice that for men:

> If any of these acts happens to the women of those freemen, let all be compensated for twofold. Since a woman cannot defend herself with weapons, let her obtain a double compensation. If, however, she wishes to fight through boldness of heart, just as a man does, her compensation will not be twofold.[120]

The rationale for the greater price, or wergeld compensation value, of a woman compared to that of a man has to do not with childbearing potential but with the supposed weakness of women to be able to defend themselves against attacks. It is of interest that the value of women in the Bavarian Code is much more a valuing of who they are than is true of the Alamannic Code that sets the value of women in terms of utilitarian interests of her father or husband.

---

[118] *The Alamannic Laws*, LIII, in *The Laws of the Alamans and Bavarians*, translated by Theodore John Rivers, Philadelphia: University of Pennsylvania Press, 1977, p. 84.

[119] *The Alamannic Laws*, LXIX, in ibid., p. 93.

[120] *The Bavarian Laws*, VI.29, in ibid., p. 134.

II. Varieties of Divorce

In the pre-Christian Roman Empire, divorce was relatively easy to obtain; yet under Christianity divorce became increasingly difficult for women to obtain. We can also see a similar pattern existing between customary law in Germanic societies concerning divorce, which were rather loose, and the increasingly difficult task for women to obtain divorce in the Christianized Germanic codes, especially of the Franks.

We begin with the *Theodosian Code* of the Romans, which seems to have had an impact on the Burgundian laws.

> It is our pleasure that no woman, on account of her own depraved desires, shall be permitted to send a notice of divorce to her husband on trumped up grounds, as for instance, that he is a drunkard or a gambler or a philanderer, nor indeed shall a husband be permitted to divorce his wife on every sort of pretext.[121]

We then find this more general law concerning the right of the wife or husband to divorce for cause:

> It remains to say that if a woman who withdraws, shall prove serious grounds and conscience involved in great crimes, she shall obtain possession of her dowry and shall also retain the betrothal bounty, and she shall regain the right to marry after a period of five years from the day of the divorce.... if the husband should be the first to give notice of divorce , and if he should charge his wife with great crimes... he shall acquire the unrestricted right to marry another woman immediately.[122]

It appears that for Roman law in the early Medieval period, divorce could be secured either for cause or by mutual consent, although the terms of divorce certainly favored the divorcing husband over the divorcing wife.

The Visigothic Code speaks more clearly than nearly any other source in the following prohibition on divorce:

> If the violation of the wife of another is a crime, how much more is she to be condemned who voluntarily commits this sin. For the reason that there are many reckless men who either

[121] *The Theodosian Code*, 3.16.1, translated by Clyde Pharr, Princeton: Princeton University Press, 1952, p. 76.

[122] *The Theodosian Code*, 3.16.2, ibid., p. 77.

> through ambition or desire, or induced by some fraud, and despising their own wives, seek those of others, we therefore decree by this law, which is to be perpetually observed, that no man, except for the manifest charge of fornication, shall at any time leave his wife, nor shall he divorce himself from her.[123]

Here we see the strong condemnation of the husband who divorces his wife without good reasons grounded in her own infidelity.

We also find that a similar portion of this Visigothic law dealt with a wife who divorces her husband:

> And, for the reason that women are accustomed very frequently to cause scandal by leaving their husbands, on account of attachment to kings and judges; therefore we decree that if any woman either by the aid of the king, or through inducements held out to her by anyone else, should separate from her husband, or consent to marry another man; she shall be surrendered, with all her property, into the hands of her lawful husband, and shall be liable to the same penalty imposed on the husband under similar circumstances, as hereinafter stated, and her property shall be disposed of in a similar manner.[124]

So, the Visigoths did not countenance divorce initiated by either the husband or the wife over the objections of the other spouse.

And while it remains unclear from the above Visigothic laws whether or not mutual consent to divorce was also prohibited, most commentators believe that divorce by mutual consent was approved, at least until the strong effects of later Christianity.[125] Indeed, for many Germanic societies, the loose rules for obtaining a divorce by mutual consent were hard for the Catholic Church to overturn.

The Burgundian Code treats the divorcing wife or husband quite severely (although much more severely for the wife) but countenances divorce when a husband simply abandons his wife.

> XXXIV. Of Divorces. 1. If any woman leaves (puts aside) her husband to whom she is legally married, let her be smothered in mire.

---

[123] *The Visigothic Code*, Book III, Title VI.2, translated by S. P. Scott, Boston: The Boston Book Company, 1910, p. 114.

[124] *The Visigothic Code*, Book III, Title VI.2, in ibid., p. 115.

[125] See P. D. King, *Law and Society in the Visigothic Kingdom*, Cambridge: Cambridge University Press, 1972, p. 235.

> 2. If anyone wishes to put away his wife without cause, let him give her another payment such as he gave for her marriage price, and let the amount of the fine be twelve solidi.
> 3. If by chance a man wishes to put away his wife, and is able to prove one of these three crimes against her, that is, adultery, witchcraft, or violation of graves, let him have full right to put her away: and let the judge pronounce the sentence of the law against her, just as should be done against criminals.
> 4. But if she admits none of these crimes, let no man be permitted to put away his wife for any other crime. But if he chooses he may go away from the home, leaving all household property behind, and his wife with their children may possess the property of her husband.[126]

The situation of divorce here for the Burgundians seems uncomplicated, much as was true for the Visigoths. But such was not true for the Lombards and Franks.

There is no mention of divorce in the codes of the Lombards or Franks, but there is some evidence that the Franks might have accepted divorce by mutual consent. Katherine Fischer Drew argues:

> There are no provisions for divorce in the Frankish laws but, considering the strong legal position of the woman, dissolution with mutual consent may have been in effect. Although no law can be cited to support this contention, there is a story related by Gregory of Tours that suggests dissolution even without the consent of one of the spouses… After Chlotard killed her brother, Radegund left her husband (over his protests), took the veil, and founded a monastery (the Holy Cross) at Poitiers. Radegund's life is interesting because her husband was unable to prevent her from deserting the marriage and, since she was thereafter able to found and endow a monastery, she undoubtedly was able to take her property with her.[127]

It is fascinating to think that a Frankish wife had the legal right to divorce her husband, even over his objections, and take her property with her as she left.

Suzanne Fonay Wemple provides us a good comparative assessment of how Germanic and Roman codes approached divorce:

---

[126] *The Burgundian Code*, XXXIV, translated by Katherine Fischer Drew, Philadelphia: University of Pennsylvania Press, 1949, pp. 45-46.

[127] *The Laws of the Salian Franks*, translated with an introduction by Katherine Fischer Drew, Philadelphia: University of Pennsylvania Press, 1991, p. 230-231.

> Divorce laws also enshrined double standards. It was not more difficult, at least for a man than to break his engagement. Divorce was a simple affair in the Frankish kingdom. In addition to the dissolution of a marriage by mutual consent, allowed by both Roman and Germanic law, the Germanic laws made it easy for a husband to repudiate his wife. Under Roman law a husband could escape from an unwanted union only if his wife gave her consent to the dissolution of the marriage, or if she had committed adultery, sorcery, or acted as a procuress. If he divorced her for any other reason, she had the right to reclaim her dowry and nuptial gift, and her husband could not remarry. Should he remarry, she could claim his whole property. Under Germanic law, a man could repudiate a woman for her inability to bear children, as well as for any serious crime. If she were beyond reproach, he could unilaterally divorce her as long as he was willing to relinquish control over her property and to pay her a compensation equal to her bridegift.... A wife, however, did not have these options. She had to remain faithful and obedient.[128]

In this analysis, the Roman laws concerning divorce were more liberal than those of the Germanic codes.

We have seen though that such a comparison must be more nuanced since the Germanic codes differed sometimes quite substantially among themselves. The situation of women also changed quite significantly as we move later into the Medieval period and find women's roles more closely monitored and circumscribed by the Catholic Church, although there is reason to think that how women were treated in the cloister differed from how they were treated in the family unit. We explore some of that evidence in the final section of this chapter.

III. Rape, Kidnapping, and Fornication

As we saw in a previous section, according to the Burgundian Code, those who kidnapped a girl had a very high wergeld price to pay. Here is more of that Burgundian law:

> But if the abductor does not have the means to make the above-mentioned payment, let him be given over to the parents

[128] Suzanne Fonay Wemple, *Women in Frankish Society: Marriage and Cloister 500 to 900*, Philadelphia: University of Pennsylvania Press, 1981, p. 42.

> of the girl that they may have the power of doing to him whatever they choose.
> If indeed, the girl seeks the man of her own will and comes to his house, and he has intercourse with her, let him pay her marriage price threefold; if however she returns uncorrupted to her home, let her return with all blame removed from him.
> If indeed a Roman girl, without the consent or knowledge of her parents, unites in marriage with a Burgundian, let her know she will have none of the property of her parents.[129]

We can learn several important things from this Burgundian law.

It is the abductor (and probably rapist) who is most severely penalized. But then things change if it turns out that the girl had consented to be abducted, or at least if this was not against her will. In such a case it is treated as if there was a marriage except that the abductor has to pay three times the normal marriage price. We also learn that the key is the lack of consent of the parents, at least in the intermarriage of a Burgundian and a Roman.

We also learn that, as was hypothesized in an earlier section, it is the having of intercourse, or not, that seems to matter significantly in terms of the penalties. If the idea was that a girl or woman's worth was based on her ability to have children, then it is hard to see how having intercourse outside of marriage would matter. And it is even harder to see why rape and kidnap are condemned. Of course, if it is the lack of the girl or woman's consent then it is easier to understand why rape would be penalized heavily. The lack of consent on the parents' part is still a curious matter to hang the penalties for rape and kidnap on unless the girl is considered in some sense the property of the parents.

Let us look at another set of laws, those of the Lombardian king Rothair, to try to get a better idea of why kidnap and rape were seen as wrongs.

> 186. On violence. If a man violently seizes a woman and takes her unwillingly as a wife, he shall pay 900 solidi, half to the king and half to the woman's relatives. And if she does not have relatives, then the entire 900 solidi shall be paid to the king's fisc. The woman then gets to choose who shall have in his power her mundium…
> 187. On the forceful seizure of free women. If anyone takes a wife by force he may pay composition, as above, and then

[129] *The Burgundian Code*, XII, translated by Katherine Fischer Drew, Philadelphia: University of Pennsylvania Press, 1949, p. 31

> acquire her mundium. But if by chance it happens that, before he has acquired the right to her guardianship, she dies, then her property shall return to relatives and the man who took her to wife by force must pay composition for her death.[130]

It is laws like these that have given rise to claims that Germanic law did not value women for their own sake.

Indeed, in law 189 of Rothair's Edict we learn that a man who has illegal intercourse with a free girl or woman gets to decide whether or not to take her as a wife.

> 189. On fornication. If a free girl or woman voluntarily has intercourse with a freeman, her relatives have the right to take vengeance on her. If it is agreed between both parties that he who fornicated with her take her to wife, he shall pay twenty solidi as composition for his offense, that is, for the illegal intercourse. If it is not agreeable that he have her to wife, then he must pay 100 solidi as composition, half to the king and half to whom her mundium belongs.[131]

There are several things to say about this law.

First, initially it does appear that the man who engages in illegal intercourse gets to decide whether or not to take her as a wife. But it also appears that the decision of whether or not she is taken as a wife involves mutual consent. This must be qualified since it also seems that the two parties who must agree are the man and the girl or woman's relatives, not merely herself. While marriage by mutual consent is recognized, if there is illegal contact between the man and woman (or girl) things seem to change. And in any event, there must be a bridegift paid to the relatives as we will see in the next section.

It is also of note that the price for his offense is twenty solidi if he takes her as his wife but five times this amount (100 solidi) if he chooses not to marry her. This takes us back to the question of the worth or value of a girl or woman. If the girl or woman consents to marry her fornicator, her value is much less than if she is not chosen as his wife. It is hard to understand such a calculus, but perhaps after a more careful discussion of marriage and the bridegift things will get somewhat clearer. The relatives of a free girl or woman still play a significant role in decisions of

---

[130] "Rothair's Edict," in *The Lombard Laws*, translated by Katherine Fischer Drew, Philadelphia: University of Pennsylvania Press, 1973, pp. 86-87.

[131] "Rothair's Edict," in *The Lombard Laws*, translated by Katherine Fischer Drew, Philadelphia: University of Pennsylvania Press, 1973, p. 87.

marriage. And another of Rothair's laws make it clear that this is to "avert the feud" that could break out between the woman or girl's clan and that of the man.[132] (We will discuss the idea of the blood feud in much more detail in the next chapter, chapter 6).

Let us end this section by looking at the law of the Salian Franks about rape and abduction. Here is a set of laws established by Clovis:

> XIII. Concerning the Abduction of Freemen or Freewomen.
> 1. If three men take a girl from her house or workroom, the three shall be liable to pay twelve hundred denarii (i.e., thirty solidi)...
> 4. The abductor shall be liable to pay twenty-five hundred denarii (i.e., sixty-two and one-half solidi)...
> 14. He who attacks on the road a betrothed girl with her bridal party being led by her husband and forcibly has intercourse with her shall be liable to pay eight thousand denarii (i.e., two hundred solidi).[133]

Taking a girl from her house is valued at much less than taking a girl when she is just about to be married–thirty solidi as compared to two hundred solidi.

As with the other laws we have examined, the reason for this difference in valuing of girls is not fully clear. But we may surmise that a marriageable girl is more valuable than one for whom it is not clear that she is marriageable. It is also possible that the girl who has already been paid for, or for whom her mundium has been sold, is more valuable than a girl for whom it is not clear what her mundium will be valued at. In order to make more sense of the differences in these laws it is useful next to consider directly the valuing of girls and women in marriage.

IV. The Bridegift and Inheritance

When marriages are dissolved in the early Medieval period one of the main questions concerns the disposition of money and property brought into the marriage by the wife. Considerations such as these give us a window into how women are valued in and out of marriage. Let us consider several of the Lombard laws of Rothair on this subject.

---

[132] "Rothair's Edict," 188, in *The Lombard Laws*, translated by Katherine Fischer Drew, Philadelphia: University of Pennsylvania Press, 1973, p. 87.

[133] *Pactus Legis Salicae*, in *The Laws of the Salian Franks*, translated by Katherine Fischer Drew, Philadelphia: University of Pennsylvania Press, 1991, pp. 77-78.

> 184. On nuptial gifts. If when a father hands over his daughter to another as wife or a brother hands over his sister, one of his friends gives something to the woman and the gift is accepted, then that gift will be under the control of the man who has acquired her mundium since the husband must make the return gift (*launigild*) himself if one is required.[134]

So, the exchange of gifts concerns the girl or woman but is undertaken by the man in the marriage. In fact, there is an obligation to provide a return gift to anyone who gives a gift, but things are more interesting when marriage is the subject of the gifts.

In other laws of Rothair, we find that there is an amount of money that is required to be paid by the prospective husband and by the family of the prospective wife.

> 181. On marriage. If a father gives his daughter to a husband or a brother gives his legitimate sister, the bridegroom must be content with that amount of the father's or mother's property which the father or brother gave him on the day of the carrying out (*traditio*) of the nuptials. He should not seek more.[135]

Here the father or brother of the wife must give something to the husband on the morning after the night of the wedding.

In one of Rothair's laws we find that marriage is referred to as the act of selling the mundium of a female to a male. The mundium is the right of control over a girl or woman. Initially the mundium is owned by the father, and marriage is then characterized as the purchase of the mundium from a female's father (or other male relative): "If anyone purchases the mundium of a free woman or girl and she is handed over to him as wife"[136] is the phrasing that is crucial to determining how property should be distributed after the marriage is dissolved

We find out a significant amount about the value of girls or women in the law governing the disposition of property when the woman becomes widowed.

---

[134] "Rothair's Edict," in *The Lombard Laws*, translated by Katherine Fischer Drew, Philadelphia: University of Pennsylvania Press, 1973, p. 86.

[135] "Rothair's Edict," in *The Lombard Laws*, translated by Katherine Fischer Drew, Philadelphia: University of Pennsylvania Press, 1973, p. 85.

[136] "Rothair's Edict," 183, in *The Lombard Laws*, translated by Katherine Fischer Drew, Philadelphia: University of Pennsylvania Press, 1973, pp. 85-86.

> 182. On the rights of the widow. If anyone has given his daughter or other relative in marriage and it happens by chance that her husband dies, then the widow shall have the right, if she wishes, to go to another husband, provided he is free. Moreover, the second husband who wishes to marry her should give, from his own property, for her marriage portion to him who is the nearest heir to the first husband half of the amount which was offered when the first husband betrothed her. If the heir does not wish to accept this amount, then the woman shall give it together with [her first husband's] morning gift (*morgengab*) and that which she brought with her from her own relatives, that is, her father's gift (*faderfio*). Her relatives then have the right to give her to another husband where both they and she desire it, and the relatives of the first husband shall not have her mundium because they refused her consent: therefore her mundium shall return to the near relatives who first gave her to a husband. And if there are no legitimate relatives, then her mundium shall belong to the king's fisc.[137]

The first thing to note is that the mundium, the right to control the life of the woman, is never given to her–there must be a male who has it, even as a last resort going to the king. The Lombard laws did not consider women capable of deciding how to lead their lives even after marriage and widowhood.

Yet, there are some interesting wrinkles to the Lombard law concerning widows that seemingly recognize that the wife has some rights nonetheless. Notice that the decision about who the woman can remarry is a joint decision of her and her relatives–"where both they and she desire it" - presumably this means that she can block a remarriage. Even more significantly the widow does get to keep her morning gift along with the gift that her dead husband's heirs are willing to provide for her remarriage and the gift that her father gave that had been given to her husband.

So, while the widow never gets her mundium after becoming a widow she seems to be able to realize quite a large amount that she can take out of the marriage and hold as her own. We do find that the value of the woman diminishes after her first marriage has been dissolved–"half of that amount which was offered when the first husband betrothed her"–but the widow still has value and some say over how her life will be led as a widow. We also find in Rothair's laws that when a betrothal is broken by the man due to abandonment or refusal to marry her, "the marriage portion

[137] "Rothair's Edict," in *The Lombard Laws*, translated by Katherine Fischer Drew, Philadelphia: University of Pennsylvania Press, 1973, p. 85.

which had been [demanded and] paid shall be in the control of the girl or woman because the betrothed man neglected to take her to wife."[138]

V. Women Outside of Marriage

We end this chapter by considering some of the Germanic laws that govern women who never marry in order to get a better sense of how women were valued independently of marriage. We began this chapter by looking at unmarried women and inheritance, and considered several important changes that occurred in the later Lombard laws. Another way to discuss the value of women outside of marriage is to look at how women were valued when they entered a monastic order and pledged not to marry. We will end this final section by attempting to glean some insight from this status of women.

There were significant changes in the way women, especially unmarried women came to be seen in terms of inheritance. Here is a 735 CE law of the Lombard King Liutprand:

> 145.III. We call to mind that provision has already been made concerning the man who dies and leaves one or more daughters as well as one or more unmarried sisters, that both the sisters and daughters ought to succeed him in similar fashion and equally; if one of the sisters dies unmarried, her surviving sister(s) shall equally succeed her. But now a controversy has arisen between brothers and sisters over a niece who died unmarried, the question being who should succeed her: we decree that the paternal uncles who held the mundium ought to succeed to her share. The sisters of the dead girl's father shall receive none of her portion, but they should have such a share as they would have had if their niece had continued to live.[139]

We see here that unmarried girls and women were recognized as able to succeed in inheritance, even those who were unmarried and had married sisters. This is highly significant because it shows that over time the Lombard laws changed to recognize girls and women as having rights of inheritance independent of their rights assigned them when they married.

---

[138] "Rothair's Edict," 178, in *The Lombard Laws*, translated by Katherine Fischer Drew, Philadelphia: University of Pennsylvania Press, 1973, p. 84.

[139] "Laws of King Liutprand," in *The Lombard Laws*, translated by Katherine Fischer Drew, Philadelphia: University of Pennsylvania Press, 1973, p. 211.

There are also late Lombard laws that treat girls and women the same, whether married or not, in terms of respect that should be shown to all these females. Here is a curious law of Liutprand that speaks to the status of girls and women.

> 135.VI. It has been made known to us that a certain perverse man took all of a woman's clothes while she was bathing in the river; as a result the woman was naked and everyone who walked or passed through that place considered her condition to be the result of her sinful nature. She could not, moreover, remain forever in the river and, blushing with shame, returned naked to her home. Therefore we decree that the man who presumes to do such an illicit act shall pay his wergeld as composition to that woman to whom he did that shameful thing. We say this because if the father or husband or near relatives of the woman found him, they would have entered into a violent fray (*scandalum*) with him and he who was the stronger would have killed the other man. Therefore it is better that the culprit, living, should pay his wergeld as composition than that a feud develop over a death and produce such deeds that the eventual composition be greater still.[140]

The man who shows such disrespect for a woman, regardless of whether she was married or not, must pay a very high penalty showing that women's value was here also beginning to be separated from her value in terms of being married for a price.

We finally turn briefly to the way women were treated if they entered religious communities either as virgins or widows. Here is how Suzanne Fonay Wemple characterized the place of women in Christianized Frankish law:

> Religion in the Frankish Kingdom, as in the late Roman Empire, offered women an opportunity to transcend biological and sexual roles and to seek spiritual fulfillment. Women were involved in a broader range of religious functions under Christianity than paganism. Except for a few vestal virgins, women in the pagan Roman Empire were only passive participants in the state religion or the mystery cults. Whereas some of the mystery cults excluded women altogether from membership, Christianity welcomed both men and women to its worship and ritual. Although women were barred from the

[140] "Laws of King Liutprand," in *The Lombard Laws*, translated by Katherine Fischer Drew, Philadelphia: University of Pennsylvania Press, 1973, pp. 204-205.

> Christian priesthood, they could share in pastoral care as priests' wives, deaconesses, or virgins and widows dedicated to the service of God. They could also pursue the contemplative life, devoting themselves to prayer and meditation as professed virgins and widows, members of a religious community, or recluses.[141]

In this respect the women who entered religious life were treated at least as well as were unmarried daughters and sisters.

The value of women was initially understood as closely tied to the price they could garner as brides. But as the Germanic laws changed over time they came to reflect what the law of the Roman Empire also recognized: women had value over and above their price as brides. Christianity had something to do with this change, but there are examples that we have highlighted where the law changed seemingly independently of the Christianization of the Germanic laws.

[141] Suzanne Fonay Wemple, *Women in Frankish Society: Marriage and Cloister 500 to 900*, Philadelphia: University of Pennsylvania Press, 1981, p. 127.

SECTION III.

CRIMINALITY: INDIVIDUAL AND COLLECTIVE

CHAPTER 6

COLLECTIVE GUILT AND THE BLOOD FEUD

The Germanic tribes held to the idea of some kind of collective guilt before they were amalgamated with the Western Roman Empire. We can see this best in the way that crimes were treated–where the tribe of a person injured or killed then exacted revenge on the tribe of the perpetrator. The perpetrator's tribe then sought to exact revenge for what the victim's tribe had done to them, and so on. In the early Germanic codes we find the remnants of collective responsibility in several laws that treated groups of perpetrators often more severely than individual perpetrators. We also can see how the emerging Germanic criminal law tried to stop the blood feuds by assigning quite specific values or prices to the assaults and deaths, as we began to see in Chapter 3, that when paid were meant to stop any further repercussions of the assault. There is also a story to be told about how the Christianization of the later Germanic laws may have reintroduced collective guilt ideas. Throughout we will explore the fascinating ideas of collective guilt and responsibility in early Medieval Germanic legal and political thought. I will argue that, contrary to what many might think, some of these ideas are highly defensible.

In the first section we will reexamine the general idea of the blood feud in Germanic legal thought. Then in the second section we will examine how the legal codes of the Germanic tribes tried explicitly to circumvent the feuds. In the third section we will see how certain ideas of collective responsibility remained in these Germanic codes. In the fourth section we will also see how concepts of group responsibility and even bystander liability became part of Germanic legal thought. Then in the final section I will argue that contrary to many accounts of these developments, some of these ideas of collective responsibility and even collective guilt can be defended as plausible.

I. The Blood Feud

The blood feud was a collectivist rather than an individualist legal and political conception. But contrary to some commentators, the blood feud was not completely replaced by an individualist conception. The idea behind the blood feud in Germanic political thought was that extended families and clans were the basic unit of society. The idea behind the *pater familias* of Roman legal thought was also about the family and how the members of the family owed primary allegiance to the male head of that family. It is sometimes said that Christianity changed these ideas by focusing on the individual whose soul was the most important unit of society. But as Walter Ullmann has argued, especially in the early Christian writings of St. Paul, the Church was a corporate body in which each person was a part and where baptism made a person a member of the body of Christ.

> It was Paul who used the human body as a model in order to demonstrate the various functions within the *unum corpus christi*. This organological or anthropomorphic thesis meant that each part of the human body functioned for the sake of the whole, not for its own sake. If we translate this into terms of the corporate public body, we are presented with the theory that the individual did not exist for his own sake, but for the sake of the whole society.[142]

Ideas of corporate life, especially of corporate responsibility were still at the core of Medieval legal and political thought even as it moved away from the blood feud and toward a limited individualism.

Katherine Fischer Drew also tells us that the idea of collective responsibility was employed to force the family or clan to pay the composition that came to replace the revenge taking of the blood feud.

> The kin group was important because the individual alone, or even with his immediate family, was in a precarious position in Frankish society. One needed the support of a wider kin to help bring offenders against his peace before the courts, and one needed kin to help provide the oathhelpers that a man might be required to present in order to make his case or establish his own innocence before the court. These roles of the kin are familiar to all the Germans. But the Frankish kin group had further responsibilities and privileges…The right of the kin group to share in the receipt of composition involved also the

[142] Walter Ullmann, *The Individual and Society in the Middle Ages*, Baltimore, MD: The Johns Hopkins University Press, 1966, p. 42.

> responsibility for helping members of the group to pay composition.[143]

So the blood feud gave rise to the idea that a civil law of collective responsibility was needed to stop revenge taking but also to allow the composition that replaced revenge taking to be spread among one's kin group.

According to Louis Halphen, there were various strategies aimed at eliminating the blood feud:

> In order to avoid quarrels and to limit the feud, the lawgiver fixed in advance with a meticulous and almost puerile care the tariff of fiscal compensations to be rendered in each case to the injured party, compensation that would serve as a redemption from the vengeance, on behalf of his victim, to which the guilty one exposed himself. Everything, even human life was assessed a tariff….These different amounts were called "compositions," that is they represented the price of transaction to which the two parties in a suit were held to have agreed in advance. The payment of the sum did not take the place of public punishment… but it cut short all later claims from the parties involved and stopped the exercise of private vengeance.[144]

And as J. M. Wallace Hadrill has written: the "vendetta (the normal Germanic way of settling differences arising from bloodshed) was not the law of the jungle but a duty regulated by custom that one owed to the community for maintenance of order. It was sometimes bloodthirsty and even rather wasteful, but it was all the Germanic tribesmen had."[145]

As we have seen the establishment of a wergeld, a price or value of a life, was an attempt to shift from the idea of revenge to one of retribution. Yet "in cases in which the wergeld was paid, it was neither paid nor received by the individual, but by his kindred, by his *Sippe*."[146]

---

[143] *The Laws of the Salian Franks*, introduction and translation by Katherine Fischer, Philadelphia, PA: University of Pennsylvania Press, 1991, p. 40.
[144] Louis Halphen, "Germanic Society in the Early Sixth Century," excerpted in *The Barbarian Invasions: Catalyst of a New Order*, edited by Katherine Fischer Drew, Huntington, NY: Robert E. Krieger Publishing Company, 1977, pp. 34-35.
[145] J. M Wallace-Hadrill, "Roman Survivals in Frankish Gaul," excerpted in *The Barbarian Invasions: Catalyst of a New Order*, edited by Katherine Fischer Drew, Huntington, NY: Robert E. Krieger Publishing Company, 1977, p. 44.
[146] Walter Ullmann, *The Individual and Society in the Middle Ages*, p. 41.

Consider one of the Laws of King Ine at the beginning of the eighth century in England:

> If a man demand the 'wer' of the slain, he must declare that he slew him for a thief; not the associates of the slain, nor his lord: but if he conceal it, and after a time it becomes known, then makes he room for an oath on behalf of the dead man, that his kindred may exculpate him.[147]

The wergeld is demanded and paid by the kindred.

Here is a provision of the Laws of King Alfred in late ninth century England concerning feuds that goes to the same point as that of the laws of King Ine:

> We also command: that the man who knows his foe to be home-sitting, fight not before he demand justice of him. If he have such power that he can beset his foe, and besiege him within, let him keep him within for vii. days, and attack him not, if he will remain within. And then, after vii. days, if he will surrender, and deliver up his weapons, let him be kept safe, and let notice of him be given to his kinsmen and his friends.[148]

Notice that this law that attempts to stop the blood feud was still aimed at the kinsmen of the perpetrator in order to obtain justice.

II. Confronting the Blood Feud

The wergeld was paid by the perpetrator's kinsmen in order to redeem him and avoid the ensuing life for life feud. We find that various laws are aimed explicitly at ending the blood feud. Here is one of Rothair's laws for the Lombards:

> 74. In the case of wounds and injuries mentioned above, involving freemen as they do, we have set a higher composition than did our predecessors in order that the *faida*, that is the

[147] "The Laws of King Ine," 21, in *Ancient Laws and Institutes of England*, Vol. I, edited by Benjamin Thorpe, Cambridge: Cambridge University Press, 1840, 2012, p. 117.

[148] "The Laws of King Alfred," 42, in *Ancient Laws and Institutes of England*, Vol. I, edited by Benjamin Thorpe, Cambridge: Cambridge University Press, 1840, 2012, p. 91.

> blood feud, may be averted after receipt of the above mentioned composition, and in order that more shall not be demanded and a grudge shall not be held. So, let the case be concluded and friendship remain between the parties.[149]

In this law, we see that the payment of the wergeld was meant to stop the blood feud by disallowing any other revenge taking.

We also find in a law of Rothair that stiff penalties would be assigned if revenge is still sought after receiving composition.

> 143. Concerning the man who seeks revenge after accepting composition. If a freeman or slave is killed and composition paid for the homicide and oaths offered to avert the feud, and afterwards he who received the composition tries to avenge himself by killing a man belonging to the associates from whom he received the payment, we order that he repay the composition twofold to the relatives of the freeman or to the slave's lord. In like manner concerning him who tries to avenge himself after accepting composition for blows or injuries, he shall restore that which he accepted in double amount. In addition, he shall pay composition, as provided above, if he has killed the man.[150]

These very stiff penalties are aimed at dissuading victims from continuing a feud on the understanding that the society ruled by law was different than the older society that had been ruled by customs and that had allowed for groups to continue to exact revenge.

We can also understand how collective responsibility is treated in Germanic law by considering how the law dealt with groups of people committing violence as revenge.

> 19. He who falls upon another with armed hand in order to vindicate some injury, or who leads an armed band containing up to four men into a village, shall die for his unlawful presumption or shall at least pay 900 solidi as composition, half to the king and half to him who was wronged. Each of those with him, if freemen, shall pay eighty solidi as composition, half to the king and half to him who was wronged. And in addition, if they have burned houses in that

---

[149] "Rothair's Edict," 74, in *The Lombard Laws*, translated by Katherine Fischer, Philadelphia, PA: University of Pennsylvania Press, 1973, pp. 64-65.
[150] "Rothair's Edict," 143, in *The Lombard Laws*, translated by Katherine Fischer, Philadelphia, PA: University of Pennsylvania Press, 1973, pp. 74-75.

> village or killed any man there, then they shall pay composition, according as the damage is assessed, to him whose houses were burned or whose relative or slave was killed.[151]

Here we have a clear illustration of the way law was used to stop the blood feud. In this case the law intervenes to stop the use of violence to "vindicate some injury." And the case of leading "an armed band"–presumably a group of one's kinsmen bent on revenge–is also treated severely, even if they did not do injury, Just being in a "band" that sought revenge calls forth stiff penalties as a way to stop the blood feud. We also learn in law #45 that the penalties are aimed toward making it the case that "the blood feud (*faida*) shall cease.[152]

In the Formularies of Marculf we find a document that is aimed at preventing future revenge-taking after compensation has been paid.

> To my lord brother A,B. Since at the instigation of the devil, you were seen to kill my brother C, which you should not have done, you could have been in danger of [losing your] life because of this; but through the intervention of the priests and great men, whose names are added below, we were seen to restore the harmony of peace in this matter, so that you were to give me *n. solidi* in compensation for this, which you were seen to deliver by your pledge, and we were seen to relinquish this claim against you by the rod. Therefore, according to what was agreed, it pleased us to write this document of security for you, so that you should not fear any further claim or accusation or penalty regarding this death of our brother, whether from me or from my heirs or his, or from a judiciary power, or from anybody, but you will be seen as free and absolved in every way. And if perhaps, I myself or one of my heirs or anyone else wants to trouble you regarding this, and is not prevented by me, we will pay to you, the fisc compelling [us], twice what you gave us. And let him be unable to assert his claim, but let the present document of security made by me remain firm.[153]

---

[151] "Rothair's Edict," 19, in *The Lombard Laws*, translated by Katherine Fischer, Philadelphia, PA: University of Pennsylvania Press, 1973, p. 56.
[152] "Rothair's Edict," 45, in *The Lombard Laws*, translated by Katherine Fischer, Philadelphia, PA: University of Pennsylvania Press, 1973, p. 61.
[153] *The Formulary of Marculf*, II, 18, in T*he Formularies of the Angers and Marculf: Two Merovingian Legal Handbooks*, translated by Alice Rio, Liverpool: Liverpool University Press, 2008, p. 204.

According to this formulary, the person who would otherwise have a claim of revenge relinquishes such a claim in recognition of the fact that an adequate compensation has been paid by those responsible for the death of this person's kin. Such documents gave further protection to those who paid compensation to protect them from further revenge-taking, thereby further deterring the blood feud.

III. Collective Responsibility in the Germanic Codes

Let us next consider several Germanic laws that provide evidence that the idea of collective guilt or responsibility survived from more ancient customs. Here are three laws of the Lombard King Rothair:

> 10. If any freeman plots against another man's life and that one does not die as a result, then the plotter shall pay twenty solidi as composition
> 11. On plots involving death. If freemen without the king's consent plot another man's death, but that one does not die as a result of the agreement, then each of them shall pay twenty solidi as composition, as stated above [Rothair 10]. But if that one [conspired against] dies as a result of the plot, then the doer of the deed shall pay the victim's wergeld, according as he is valued, as composition.
> 12. If two or three or more kinsmen commit a homicide together, and wish to associate themselves so that as one they may pay composition for that one [the man killed] according as he is valued, such an agreement is permitted to them. If one of them separates himself from the others and is not able to clear himself as the law provides, namely [he is not able to prove] that he inflicted none of the blows against that man who was killed, then he is as guilty as the others who paid the composition, If he does clear himself, however, he shall be free of blame in connection with the homicide. If [he is accused of being] in the counsel [of the conspirators], he shall pay twenty solidi as composition, as stated above [Rothair 10] unless he can clear himself of involvement in the conspiracy.[154]

Here violence was penalized unless it was committed with the king's consent. In addition, groups are allowed to band together to pay composition. But merely being in the company of conspirators is here penalized unless he can prove that he committed no violence personally. In

---

[154] "Rothair's Edict," 10-12, in *The Lombard Laws*, translated by Katherine Fischer, Philadelphia, PA: University of Pennsylvania Press, 1973, pp. 54-55.

effect, the burden of proof is shifted in collective responsibility cases forcing the individual member to prove that he was not an active member of the group.

In the laws of the Lombard King Liutprand we have a clear recognition of the idea of conspiracy and of how to parcel out guilt among the members.

> 107.IIII. If a number of men enter into an agreement confirmed by a charter, providing therein a penalty [for breach of the agreement], and if afterwards one or more of the men wish to withdraw from this agreement and break the contract, each of them shall individually pay the full composition as established in the pact; for all consented unanimously and no one forced them to make such an agreement. Therefore let each man who breaks the agreement pay composition just as each voluntarily consented.[155]

The idea that the members of a conspiracy are each liable for full damages of what the group does is a radical notion but one that has also been embraced today in certain circumstances.

We can get an even better sense of how conspiracies were treated by examining one other Lombard law of King Liutprand.

> 134.V. If men living in the same village are involved in a controversy over their fields or vineyards, meadow or forest, or some other property and one party of them collect themselves together for the purpose of driving their opponent forth by force from that place, and if they go on and commit violence (*scandalum*) there or inflict wounds or injuries or kill the man, we decree that they shall pay composition for the wounds or injuries or for killing the man in accordance with our earlier edict which our glorious King Rothair established and which we [have supplemented] ourselves [Rothair 43-73]. Moreover, for their illegal presumption in collecting themselves together thus, they shall pay twenty solidi as composition to the party who labored in the field or vineyard or meadow or forest.[156]

---

[155] "Laws of King Liutprand," 107.IIII, in *The Lombard Laws*, translated by Katherine Fischer, Philadelphia, PA: University of Pennsylvania Press, 1973, pp. 190-191.

[156] "The Laws of King Liutprand," 1913.V, in *The Lombard Laws*, translated by Katherine Fischer, Philadelphia, PA: University of Pennsylvania Press, 1973, p. 204.

Here again is a law that tries to stop people from taking matters into their own hands. Rather this case is regarded "as the same as giving evil counsel, or plotting a death." Indeed, it is explicitly aimed at making sure "that no one may presume to incite or perform such evil deeds."[157]

Even though there is generally not as much attention to collective liability in the Visigothic Code as in the Lombard Laws or the Laws of the Salian Franks, there is a concern about incitement as we see in this Visigothic law:

> Whoever collects a mob for the purpose of committing bloodshed, and makes an attack upon another, whereby he sustain bodily injury; or incites or orders others to commit such acts; as soon as the judge shall be informed of the same, he shall, at once, cause the guilty party to be arrested. And in order that he may be rendered publicly infamous, he shall receive fifty lashes in the presence of the judge, and shall be compelled to name all who were with him, or participated in his offense; and if his said associates should not be under his patronage, every freeman shall receive fifty lashes. If, however, slaves are participants in the crime, and belong to another master, they shall each receive two hundred lashes publicly, and in the presence of the judge, as a warning to others.[158]

Here incitement and collecting others together into a mob are penalized quite harshly.

Incitement is seen as a key to the survival of the blood feud and something that needs especially to be severely punished. It is interesting that collective responsibility and punishment is employed to stop the collective action of the clan in a blood feud and one of the main ancillary things to stop is the act of incitement that spurred members of a clan or family to use violence to take revenge for past wrongs. The Germanic codes tried to ferret out and stop all aspects of the blood feud so as to bring stability and order to their societies. But we see that some forms of collective responsibility were also countenanced.

The Laws of the Salian Franks also employs ideas of collective responsibility as we see in this law of the Lex Salica Karolina:

---

[157] Ibid. p. 204.

[158] *Visigothic Code*, Book VIII, Title III, translated by S. P. Scott, Boston: The Boston Book Company, 1910, pp. 264-265.

> 1. If anyone, having gathered together his band of men, attacks a freeman in his home and kills him there, he shall be liable to pay twenty-four thousand denarii (i.e., six hundred solidi).
> 2. But if the man who was killed was an antrusian of the king's (*in truste dominica*), he [who killed him] shall be liable to pay seventy-two thousand denarii (i.e., eighteen hundred solidi).
> 3. But if the corpse of the man killed has three or more wounds, the three who are charged and, because they are in that group of men, are convicted, will be compelled individually to pay the above amount in full.
> And three others from that band of men shall each be liable to pay thirty-six hundred denarii (i.e., ninety solidi). And in the third place, three more from that same band of men will each be liable to pay eighteen hundred denarii (i.e., forty-five solidi),
> 4, If indeed a Roman or a half-free man (*lidus*) has been killed by such a band of men, half the above amounts shall be paid as composition.[159]

Like the Lombard laws, the laws of the Franks had very severe penalties for collective actions that caused harm. And the reason for these penalties was an attempt to deter the blood feud and other group criminal action that was thought to be inconsistent with the maintenance of public peace.

IV. Collective Action and Bystanders

An earlier law, the *Pactus Legis Salicae*, also had various laws for the Franks concerning collective action:

> 1. If at a banquet where there are four or five men present one of these is killed, those who remain must give up one of their number to be convicted or all will pay for the death of that man. This rule should be observed where there are up to seven men at a banquet.
> 2. If indeed there are more than seven men at the banquet, not all of them shall be held liable to punishment; but those against whom the crime is proved must pay according to this rule.
> 3. If a man has been killed by a band of men (*contubernio*) while he is outside of his house or making a journey or standing in a field, if he has suffered three or more wounds,

[159] Emperor Charlemagne, *Lex Salica Karolina*, XII (XLIV), in *The Laws of the Salian Franks*, translated by Katherine Fischer Drew, Philadelphia, PA: University of Pennsylvania Press, 1991, pp. 181-182.

> then three members of that band against whom it is proved shall each pay composition for the death of that one. And if there are more members of that band against whom it was not proved, three of them shall each pay twelve hundred denarii (i.e., thirty solidi) and three more of the band shall be liable to pay six hundred denarii (i.e., fifteen solidi).[160]

Here we see that it was of special concern what happened at banquets where families or clans were likely to congregate and because of the heavy consumption of alcohol quite likely to cause harm that then would be subject to a blood feud. The law of the Franks set out a complicated penalty scheme aimed at thwarting this type of feud.

Let us consider one other law of the Franks concerning collective responsibility or liability.

> If anyone from a band of followers (*contubernio*) presumes to attack a free woman or a girl on the road or in some other place, both one or more who have proved to have committed this crime shall be liable to pay two hundred solidi. And from that band of followers, if some still remain who did not commit the crime but were known to have been there, if they were more or fewer than three in number, they shall be liable to pay forty-five solidi.[161]

Notice that the passive bystanders are penalized quite heavily in this law of the Franks.

Collective action problems are especially difficult because some members of a group do not appear to have done anything and hence seemingly are not liable to punishment or to pay compensation. But if there is a sense in which there is a group, and a given person is a member of that group, then when the group acts there is a sense that the member acts as well. Those who are merely bystanders pose an especially difficult problem even if one accepts the legitimacy of collective responsibility ascriptions. For bystanders to be caught up in the collective responsibility net, there must be a sense that they could have (and also should have) intervened to stop the group from acting wrongly.

The Frankish law, *Pactus Legis Salicae* LXIII cited above, speaks of someone who is a member of a group but is merely present when

---

[160] *Pactus Legis Salicae*, LXIII, in *The Laws of the Salian Franks*, translated by Katherine Fischer Drew, Philadelphia, PA: University of Pennsylvania Press, 1991, pp. 107-108.

[161] Ibid., p. 131.

harmful action is taken by the group to which one belongs. The persons identified as those "known to be there" where the crime was committed, are said to be liable to pay compensation. The idea seems to be that by being a member of a group that does wrong, and being present where the group does this harm, the passive members incur liability for what they did not do, namely trying to stop their fellow group members from doing harm.

Collective action problems are especially nettlesome because of how responsibility is attributed to the members, passing through the group that is said to have acted. In part, the Germanic codes speak of collective liability because the family or clan was customarily the main social unit. As the family or clan recedes as an important legal site of liability, there seem to be uses of collective responsibility that remain. In the last section of this chapter I will attempt to defend some uses of collective responsibility even as I recognize that some other uses are fraught with peril.

V. The Uses of Collective Liability

The blood feud is problematic for a number of reasons. It is a form of guilt by association–a person is penalized merely for being a member of a group regardless of what that person has done or not done. The blood feud was also a form of vigilante justice in so far as members of clans and families sought revenge outside of the framework of formal law. Of course, when the blood feud was an acceptable part of the customary Germanic law it was not mere vigilante justice but had the force of customary law ultimately behind it.

We should recognize that one of the ways that the Germanic codes tried to restrict or end the blood feud was by employing another collective responsibility scheme. When a person was convicted and told to pay composition, that person could then appeal to his family or clan members to aid him or her in making payment. Indeed, the laws required members of one's family or clan to come to the aid of those who could not pay composition. In this section I will discuss possible justifications for such a practice as well as other uses of collective responsibility schemes that were employed in the Germanic codes.

In order to confront the blood feud, which was incredibly destabilizing of the society as a whole, a payment scheme had to be designed that members of a family or clan would find an acceptable alternative instead of seeking vengeance. The payment schedule that was developed, based on the social status of each type of person in the society, had to include payments that were indeed likely to be acceptable substitutes for vengeance. Yet the problem was that individuals often did not have the resources to pay the composition and thus there was a risk that the members of the victim's family or clan might still seek vengeance.

So, there emerged a revised kind of collective responsibility–the family or clan was not responsible for exacting vengeance in the name of the victim against the family or clan of the perpetrator, but the family or clan of the perpetrator was responsible for making sure the perpetrator paid the composition so as to stop the blood feud. The family or clan of the perpetrator was the object of both forms of collective responsibility, but the enforcer was significantly different. In the older customary law case, the enforcer was the victim's family or clan, but in the newer version it was the society or state that acted to make sure that justice was done and the perpetrator, along with his or her family or clan, was penalized.

The other collective responsibility scheme of note is to hold liable members of groups who had only a passive role, if even that role, in the perpetration of harm caused by the group. In a sense this appears to be a throwback to the ancient customary practices of the Germanic societies since the focus is the group rather than the individual. But the use of collective responsibility in this sense is actually not significantly different from what we can see today in the legal systems of many societies. The law of conspiracy is employed to achieve the result of holding all members of a group liable even if some particular members did not do much, if anything, which was otherwise illegal.

In many of the Germanic Codes there is much attention paid to gangs, mobs, and other groups that do harm. As a normative matter, I think there is nothing wrong with this focus of the criminal law, especially given the customary law that was premised on the idea of the group as the main social entity. Focusing on how groups came together and how they were able to act, such as the way some members allowed other members to act for the group, makes sense if the legal authorities are trying to wrest control from families and clans. When it is clear that there has been a collectivity formed that perpetrates harm, the emerging Germanic states needed to deter other collectivities from retaliating. But the idea that a group could be help responsible is itself defensible if it was truly engaged in a group effort.

The difficulty is that at the same time that the law codes were attempting to deter collective retaliation, they seemed to be also acknowledging the efficacy of collective action. This apparent conflict dissolves when it is recognized that the legal and political thought of the early Medieval period never fully moved away from the focus on the group. In claiming for the state the right to settle disputes and assign penalties as well as punishments, we have in a sense the substitution for one group, the family or clan, with another group, the society or the state.

Indeed, the Medieval period followed certain developments in Roman law in seeing institutions, such as churches and states, responsible with the ensuing idea that the members of institutions could be held liable through their membership in these corporate or group entities. But it was the institutional collectivity that remained the focus. We do not see a genuinely full turn toward the legal subject as a discrete individual until, arguably, the beginning of the modern period with such theorists as Thomas Hobbes and John Locke. There was still somewhat of an organic unity of subjects (surely not citizens) that was the focus of the law during the Medieval period.

As we saw at the beginning of this chapter, Walter Ullmann argued that Medieval legal and political thought remained focused on the group even after the blood feud was significantly deterred. Indeed, Ullmann recognized that there were differences as we move from the beginning to the middle of the Medieval period, especially those that were brought on by the rise of Christianity. But the focus remained on the group–in the case of the Christianization of the Germanic societies, the group was the church, understood as a collective body of which the individual was primarily seen as a mere member of the church as the body of Christ. The texts of the Germanic legal codes do not show a full turn toward the individual as the subject of responsibility and liability, but in some respects the replacement of one group by another.

Collective liability and responsibility are understood in the early Medieval Germanic codes as a special focus because of the influence of three sources:

1) the customary Germanic law's emphasis on self-help by clans in seeking settlement of disputes by collective revenge;
2) the Roman law's emphasis on the family and its pater familias for settling many contentious matters within the family;
3) and the growing influence of the Catholic Church with its idea of the importance of religious institutions in nearly all aspects of civil life.

One could add, perhaps, the economic idea that few people could survive outside of one group or another.

In discussing the early Medieval emphasis on collectivities, we should not forget that the idea of the state was also discussed in terms of collective concepts. In ancient Greek ideas, the people were formed from individuals and the ruler of the state was in various ways responsible to the people. By the time of Charlemagne, just as was true for the earlier Roman emperors, there was a break between the people and the king. The king was to take care of the people but was not answerable to the people. Indeed, we find increasingly in the Germanic codes the Christian idea that it was God to whom the king was answerable. Here is one example from the early eighth century:

> We acted for the salvation of our people and to alleviate the vexations of the poor when we gathered together new laws to add to the body of this lawbook in five previous issues: for this we believe that the mercy of God will reward us for such good works because we have done it for the fear and the love of God alone so that all controversies may be ended with reason and justice, that error may cease and that His justice will become clear; whence the name of the Lord will be blessed without end.[162]

Here the Lombard King Liutprand speaks of a collectivity, the people, as benefiting but it is "God alone" to whom the king is answerable.

[162] "The Laws of Liutprand," from the twelfth year, in *The Lombard Laws*, translated by Katherine Fischer Drew, Philadelphia, PA: University of Pennsylvania Press, 1973, p. 166.

CHAPTER 7

COMPENSATION TO THE STATE FOR CRIME

As we have seen Germanic codes tried in various ways to deter and eliminate the blood feud, a form of private revenge-taking. The alternative system seen in several of the Germanic codes was to provide an exact monetary payment for each crime that was to be paid to the victim or his or her family. As Louis Halphen says:

> These different amounts were called "compositions," that is they represented the price of a transaction to which the two parties in a suit were held to have agreed in advance. The payment of this sum did not take the place of public punishment, which in most cases was exacted in the form of fines… but it cut short all later claims from the parties involved and stopped the exercise of private vengeance.[163]

In this seventh chapter we will discuss the "compositions" in more detail and also begin to explain the system of public fines and punishments that the state exerted for the violation to the public peace that the offenders had caused.

I will argue that the "compositions" and the public fines as punishments were a unique contribution to the conceptualization of crime in the history of legal and political thought. In the first section we will encounter some examples from the Germanic codes of compositions plus public fines for certain crimes. In the second section we will look more deeply at the idea of "composition" especially in Frankish society of the sixth century. In the third section we closely examine the idea of the public fine which was added to the "compositions." And in the fourth section we examine the idea of public punishment sometimes employed instead of the public fine. Then in the final section we will assess the Germanic codes' confrontation with crime and spell out the way in which it was a unique

---

[163] Louis Halphen, "Germanic Society in the Early Sixth Century," excerpted in *The Barbarian Invasions: Catalyst of a New Order*, edited by Katherine Fischer Drew, Huntington, NY: Robert E. Krieger Publishing Company, 1977, p. 35.

contribution to the legal and political thought of the history of criminal justice.

I. Penalties for Criminal Acts

Let us start by considering a Lombard law of King Rothair who provided one of the most complete codes of law during the early Medieval period.

> 280. On seditious acts committed by field slaves. If, for any reason, rustics (*homines rusticani*) associate together for plotting or committing seditious acts such as, when a lord is trying to take a bondsman or animal from his slave's house, blocking the way or taking the bondsman or animal, then he who was at the head of these rustics shall either be killed or redeem his life by the payment of a composition equal to that amount at which it is valued. And each of those who participated in this evil sedition shall pay twelve solidi as composition, half to the king and half to him who bore the injury or before whom he presumed to place himself.[164]

Notice first of all that the ringleader is either to be capitally punished or he can redeem his life by paying a composition based on the wergeld. Then also note that the members of the gang must pay six solidi to the injured person and an equal amount to the king. The latter amount is the added fee that is for the maintenance of peace and should be understood to be a public penalty in recognition of the public nature of the harms in question.

As a point of contrast, consider how criminal action was dealt with in the Theodosian Code that governed Byzantium:

> Our glorious father had ordered that vengeance be taken very harshly against ravishers. We however have established only capital punishment, in order, of course, that any delay in punishing the crime may not arise under the pretext of a too severe decision. But the full measure of the laws must be employed against the audacity of slaves with a different kind of punishment, that is, that they shall be subjected to burning by fire, unless they are restrained from such great crime at least by the severity of the penalties.[165]

[164] "Rothair's Edict," 280, in *The Lombard Laws*, translated by Katherine Fischer Drew, Philadelphia, PA: University of Pennsylvania Press, 1973, p. 109.

[165] *The Theodosian Code*, 9.24.2, translated by Clyde Pharr, Princeton, NJ: Princeton University Press, 1952, p. 245.

We do not find here the splitting of the penalty between private compensation and public punishment. And, contrary to what might be otherwise assumed, the punishment for the slave who rapes is much more barbarous than the punishments for the same act in the Germanic codes.

The mark of a criminal punishment for Byzantine law was that it was very severe. For the Germanic codes, the victim had to be compensated and then on top of this was added a kind of compensation for the king or the state. Since the victim received nothing as compensation in the Byzantine law it was clear that the convicted rapist needed to repay the society. In the Germanic codes there was also this kind of public punishment or penalty, yet the victim also received compensation. Because there were two penalties, it was in my view clearer in the Germanic codes that there was here a difference from normal civil penalties.

II. A Closer Look at Composition

For the Lombards, the fee paid to the king or the fisc is here equal to the amount to be paid to the injured victim or his or her family. We can think of the second part as the compensation–a kind of private law settlement between the two parties. But the first part paid to the king is clearly a public penalty as is the death sentence meted out to the ringleader since killing the ringleader does not compensate the victim in any meaningful sense.

The Burgundian code also calls for two payments as we see in the following laws concerning fighting.

> XV. Of Starting a Fight.
> 1. If any freeborn Burgundian enters another's house to fight, let him pay six solidi to him to whom the house belongs; and let the fine be twelve solidi. Furthermore we wish this to be observed equally among Burgundians and Romans.
> 2. Indeed if a slave enters another's house by force or violence, let him receive a hundred blows for punishment, and let the master of the slave suffer no loss on this account.[166]

Notice that for the Burgundians the public penalty was in this case twice what was owed to the victim. Also note that for slaves, who it was presumed had no resources from which to draw to pay the victim, the

[166] *Book of Constitutions*, XV, in *The Burgundian Code*, translated by Katherine Fischer Drew, Philadelphia, PA: University of Pennsylvania Press, 1949, p. 33.

public penalty was the only penalty and in this case it was very severe corporal punishment. And Romans and Lombards are to be treated the same.

In contrast to both of the Lombardian code and the Burgundian code, we can look briefly at an example of laws from the code of the Salian Franks.

> XXXII. Of the Tying-Up of Freemen
> 1. He who ties up a freeman without cause shall be liable to pay twelve hundred denarii (i.e., thirty solidi).
> 2. He who ties up someone else and takes him bound to another place shall be liable to pay eighteen hundred denarii (i.e., forty-five solidi).
> 3. If a Roman ties up a Frank without cause, he shall be liable to pay twelve hundred denarii (i.e., thirty solidi).
> 4. If a Frank ties up a Roman without cause, he shall be liable to pay six hundred denarii (i.e., fifteen solidi).
> 5. He who through arrogance or force takes a bound man away from the count must pay composition for his life.[167]

The Franks did not divide the composition between the private settlement and the public penalty, at least in these laws. Notice that the penalties are different if the victim is a Frank or a Roman, with the Roman getting only half of what the Frank is to get for the same criminal act.

Finally, to these three Germanic codes we can add some more from the Anglo-Saxon King Alfred.

> Of Kinless Men
> 27. If a man, kinless of paternal relatives, fight, and slay a man, and then if he have maternal relatives, let him pay a third of the 'wer'; his guild-brethren a third part; for a third let him flee. If he have no maternal relatives, let his guild brethren pay half, for half let him flee.
> Of Slaying a Man Thus Circumstanced
> 28. If a man kill a man thus circumstanced, if he have no relatives, let half be paid to the king; half to his guild brethren.[168]

---

[167] *Pactus Legis Salicae*, XXXII, in *The Laws of the Salian Franks*, translated by Katherine Fischer Drew, Philadelphia, PA: University of Pennsylvania Press, 1991, p. 95.

[168] "The Laws of King Alfred," 27 and 28, in *Ancient Laws and Institutes of England*, Volume I, edited by Benjamin Thorpe, Cambridge: Cambridge University Press, 1840, pp. 79-81.

While difficult to understand completely, these laws seem to call for a division of the composition into thirds–one part to the relatives of the victim, one part to the members of the victim's clan, and a final third is a public penalty for letting the perpetrator escape with his life. And in the case of a victim having no relatives then the division is half to the victim's guild and half to the king.

III. Public Fines

Louis Halphen lucidly summarizes the Frankish idea of the public fine when he comments as follows:

> whatever atrocity he committed, the code provided no penalty other than a fine. This fine, which was added to the so-called composition, was designed to wipe out the right of revenge sought by the victim or his family; it was payable to a representative of the royal authority in repayment for keeping the order and the public peace. It was only if he was unable to acquit himself from his own resources or those of his family...that the guilty party was liable to pay for his crime with his blood or, to use the language of the time, to "make composition with his life."[169]

The fine was collected for the royal treasury and was a form of public settling with the society for the crime.

The Burgundian, somewhat similar to the Frank, could extricate himself by paying a simple fine the amount of which was fixed in advance (usually 3, 6, or 12 solidi) and added to the composition."[170] The Visigoths seem to have had a more severe form of public fining. "On almost every page of the Visigothic code freemen of modest rank, and sometimes even of the highest rank, were threatened with forty, fifty, one hundred, or two hundred lashes in addition to the payment of fines and composition."[171] And it is not clear how many people could survive two hundred lashes.

---

[169] Louis Halphen, "Germanic Society in the Early Sixth Century," excerpted in *The Barbarian Invasions: Catalyst of a New Order*, edited by Katherine Fischer Drew, Huntington, NY: Robert E. Krieger Publishing Company, 1977, p. 39.
[170] Louis Halphen, "Germanic Society in the Early Sixth Century," ibid., p. 38.
[171] Louis Halphen, "Germanic Society in the Early Sixth Century," ibid., p. 37.

IV. Public Punishment

Capital and corporal punishment was employed in some of the Germanic codes. In this section we examine examples of such laws as one of the ways that the state intervened into what had been a private dispute mechanism of Germanic customary law before the Germanic tribes' legal system intermingled with that of the Romans. Slaves and people of limited financial means were those who were most often subject to physical punishment if they could not pay the public fines dictated by the law of composition. At least in part, the use of corporal and capital punishment seems to be meant to satisfy the victim or his or her family, and hence to stop the blood feud. But I will suggest that it seems also that the public punishments were aimed at making sure that the state got something for restoring the public peace.

We can begin with the Visigothic Code which has many references to flogging and other forms of corporal punishment, not restricted to the lowest classes. Here is one representative law:

> VIII. Where a Slave Carries Off a Freewoman by Force.
> It is the province of equity to make laws concerning the future, where doubt exists in the present. Where slaves with the knowledge of, or under the order of their master, carry off any woman by force, the master shall be required by the judge to give satisfaction required by law. And if slaves should perpetrate such crimes against the will of their master, they shall be arrested by the judge, and after having been scalped, shall receive three hundred lashes with the scourge. Any slave who has violated a free born woman shall undergo the extreme penalty of the law.[172]

In the next law we learn that the master is to pay a hundred solidi on behalf of his slave in such circumstances.[173] The punishment of 300 lashes is virtually equivalent to the death sentence.

Here is another Visigothic law that features corporal punishment but is not restricted to slaves.

> XII. Concerning Freemen and Slaves Who are Proved to Have Been Implicated in the Crime of Rape.

---

[172] *The Visigothic Code*, Book III, Title III.VII, translated by S. P. Scott, Boston: The Boston Book Company, 1910, p. 92.
[173] *The Visigothic Code*, Book III, Title III.IX, translated by S. P. Scott, Boston: The Boston Book Company, 1910, p. 92.

> Any one who is known to have assisted, or to have been present, at the carrying off of any woman by force, if he is a freeman, shall pay a fine of six ounces of gold, and shall publicly receive fifty lashes with the scourge. If he is a slave, and acted without the consent of this master, he shall receive a hundred lashes. But if he should commit this crime with the consent of his master, the latter must make such satisfaction in his stead as has already been stated.[174]

Here the freeman who commits rape is subject to a monetary penalty as composition and then in addition there is a corporal punishment meted out by the state.

One more set of laws, on homicide, display the use of corporal and capital punishment by the Visigoths.

> V. Where One is Killed While Intervening in a Quarrel.
> If any freeman should interfere in a quarrel for the purpose of making peace, and should be killed as a consequence, and he who struck him shall be able to prove, either by his own oath, or by the testimony of respectable witnesses, that the act was not committed intentionally, because the party who struck the fatal blow did not wish to commit the assault or homicide upon the person who was killed, shall pay a pound of gold to the relatives of the person who lost his life; and in like manner, if any wound was inflicted under similar circumstances, the person who inflicted it shall pay a third part of the aforesaid sum, for the reason that the death of him who interfered for the purpose of making peace should not go unavenged.
> XI. Where One Man Intentionally Kills Another.
> Every man who kills another intentionally, and not by accident, is liable to punishment for homicide.
> XII. … Where one Freeman Kills Another.
> …if after an investigation, it is evident that the crime has been committed, the culprit shall receive… the punishment of death, which he deserves.[175]

Here it is clear that the standard punishment for intentional homicide is the death penalty. For killing that is not intentional the purpose of imposing penalties is that the state, and not the victim's family, avenges the death.

---

[174] *The Visigothic Code*, Book III, Title III.XII, translated by S. P. Scott, Boston: The Boston Book Company, 1910, p. 93.

[175] *The Visigothic Code*, Book III, Title III.XII, translated by S. P. Scott, Boston: The Boston Book Company, 1910, p. 222.

We can also turn to some of the other Germanic codes that employed public corporal and capital punishment to satisfy the need to have an avenging of the death of a person whose family would otherwise seek private vengeance. Such public punishments were not aimed at compensating the family or clan of the victim but to deter them from a blood feud. Consider the Burgundian laws on murder:

> Of Murders.
> 1. If anyone presumes with boldness or rashness bent on injury to kill a native freeman of our people of any nation or a servant of the king, in any case a man of barbarian tribe, let him make restitution for the committed crime not otherwise than the shedding of his own blood.
> 2. We decree that this rule be added to the law by a reasonable provision, that if violence shall have been done by anyone to any person, so that he is injured by blows of lashes or wounds, and if he pursues his persecutor and overcome by grief or indignation kills him, proof of the deed shall be afforded by the act itself or by suitable witnesses who can be believed. Then the guilty party shall be compelled to pay to the relatives of the person killed half his wergeld according to the status of the person: that is, if he shall have killed a noble of the highest class, we decree that the payment be set at one hundred fifty solidi, i.e., half his wergeld; if a person of middle class, one hundred solidi; if a person of the lowest class, seventy-five solidi.
> 3. If a slave unknown to his master presumes to kill a native freeman, let the slave be handed over to death, and let the master not be liable for damages.
> 4. If the master knows of the deed, let both be handed over to death.[176]

This very rich legal text helps us understand both the means and the point of the criminal punishments and penalties that were issued by the Burgundians. Restitution is called for, but often so is punishment that is aimed at the state not at the victim's family. Notice that there is a graded scale for restitution payments based on the social class of the victim. Notice also that slaves and freemen were subject to the death penalty as the penalty the state exacted. There is perhaps a reference to a *lex talionis* principle when the first of these laws calls for the shedding of blood as punishment for the perpetrator having himself shed the blood of the victim.

---

[176] *Book of Constitutions*, XV, in *The Burgundian Code*, translated by Katherine Fischer Drew, Philadelphia, PA: University of Pennsylvania Press, 1949, p. 23.

One last code to examine is that of the Lombard King Rothair's edict to which we have often referred already.

> 13. He who kills his lord (*dominus*), shall be killed himself. The man who tries to defend this murderer who killed his lord shall pay 900 solidi in composition, half to the king and half to the relatives of the dead man. And he who refuses to aid in avenging the man's death, if his aid is sought, shall pay fifty solidi as composition, half to the king and half to the man to whom he refused aid.[177]

Here we have a mixture of capital punishment for killing and then composition for those who defend or fail to aid in the capture of the killer. As in many of the Lombard laws, the wergeld is split evenly between the victim's family and the king. The payment to the king, as we saw in Section III, is for maintenance of the people's peace by above all else stopping the blood feud.

It is not always clear what precisely the corporal or capital punishment is for. It can be a kind of restitution if understood as replacing the compensation that the victim's family would seek under the customary law standards. But there is also a clear sense that the state is demanding especially capital punishment for itself not for the victim's family. And we have also seen, what the king demands is sometimes such a payment and sometimes not really a penalty so much as a comparable punishment to what the private revenge might have sought. In the final section of this chapter we will explore this point in more detail.

V. Criminal Law and the Germanic Peoples

Unlike other societies, the Germanic peoples start to conceptualize what we now would call criminal law as a way to override the blood feud by which private vengeance had been the main remedy for criminal acts. What is relatively unique to the Germanic codes in the history of legal and political thought is the way it was made clear that in addition to compensation or composition paid to the victim or the victim's family, the state in the form of the king required an additional public payment or punishment. And it is this clear division of penalties that marks out the case of criminal liability from that of mere "civil" liability.

---

[177] "Rothair's Edict," 280, in *The Lombard Laws*, translated by Katherine Fischer Drew, Philadelphia, PA: University of Pennsylvania Press, 1973, p. 55.

Yet, it is significant that the Germanic codes look to satisfying the victims so that they do not pursue private vengeance. The idea seems to be that merely punishing the perpetrator with corporal or capital punishment does not assuage the victim's demand for something that recognizes his or her pain and suffering. So, on my construal, criminal sanctions are linked to a kind of civil sanction, a payment to the victim or his or her family in addition to the penalty or punishment that the state extracts in its own behalf.

The Germanic codes provide a response to the oft-heard complaint today that criminal law does not address the victim. Prosecutors and police often say that they are motivated by trying to do something for the victim. But putting the perpetrator in prison, or even executing him or her, does not really provide the victim anything direct. There is a kind of vicarious vengeance, I suppose, in that the victim or his or her family see the perpetrator suffer for what he or she has done. But vengeance carried out by the victim is nonetheless significantly different from vicarious vengeance carried out by the state. And vengeance is not really the right way to think of the public punishment in any event.

Public penalties and punishments are best seen as directed at what the society has been made to suffer at the hands of a perpetrator. In US criminal law today the victim is not even named in the title of the complaint–it is instead the state or the ruler that is the complainant. And this nomenclature belies the way the proceedings are organized–often the victim or the family plays no role at all. This is at least one of the reasons that victims and their families often feel disconnected and ultimately unsatisfied by criminal trials and the public punishments that follow upon conviction of the perpetrator. We will return to the advantages of the Germanic codes in dealing with criminal acts, but let me sketch some of the problems first.

One way to understand the underlying motivation of the way the Germanic codes dealt with criminal matters is to see how slaves were treated if they killed someone. Here is a fascinating statement about the Visigothic Code and its difficulties by P. D. King:

> The law took the view that responsibility for an offense committed by a slave at the orders or with the knowledge of his master lay entirely at the latter's door, except on very rare occasions when the slave was also held punishable. The slave-owner suffered the consequences of his slave's act as if he himself had been the actor.[178]

[178] P. D. King, *Law and Society in the Visgothic Kingdom*, Cambridge: Cambridge University Press, 1972, p. 174.

This was true unless it was clear that the slave truly did act on his or her own. In this latter case another problem arose.

> The practical difficulty lay in the manner of punishment, for the imposition of composition and fines to the crown upon a criminous slave directly penalized the master. Very frequently therefore, punishment took a corporal form when the same offense committed by a freeman involved payment of some sort.[179]

Here we can see how the need to provide some composition to the victim meant that slaves had to be treated quite differently and much more harshly than freemen. As we saw, composition depended on the perpetrator having monetary resources in the first place, and slaves normally did not.

In addition, the slave's master often wanted to solve the problem privately since the master was legally recognized as having complete control over the slave. But allowing this kind of private punishment was even further removed from the desire for vengeance that was felt by the victim or his or her family. Once again, vicarious vengeance did not seem to work when it became too attenuated.

One last problem to consider is that the various Germanic codes handled criminal matters very differently, so differently that when combined with the idea of personal jurisdiction we discussed in chapter 2, made for a disjointed and chaotic system that was not clearly delivering justice and equity in a reasonable manner. The victim was left without a clear idea of how or even when justice would be meted out.

To get a clearer idea of the patchwork nature of the criminal law under the various Germanic codes let us look at the differences that existed among these codes. We can start with the Roman code of Theodosian that was the law of the land in the Empire at the time of the Germanic migrations into the Roman Empire. As we have seen, there was one penalty or punishment that attached to the convicted perpetrator of an assault. Rape was punished in most cases by the death penalty, except for slaves who were burned alive.

The code of the Salian Franks in many respects follows the Roman code more closely than any of the other Germanic codes. We saw that the Franks had but one penalty or punishment and that was a public one administered to the convicted perpetrator of an assault. The Burgundian code makes it clear that the composition is to go to the family

[179] Ibid.

of the victim. This was still a publicly executed penalty, so as to stop the private vengeance-taking. Here composition was the main thing that the law sought to provide.

The Visigothic code is often said to be closest to the Roman code, but in most cases there were two public penalties or punishments for the convicted perpetrator of assault. There is composition and public corporal punishment but it is not clear that the composition is earmarked for the victim's family, as we saw in the case of rape where there was both a monetary penalty and a corporal punishment. So, while there is often a two part penalty, it seems that both parts were public and owed to the state rather than compensation to the victim's family, although this is not as clear as one would like. The two part penalty was, though, of prime importance in other Germanic codes that advanced criminal law in important ways.

The codes of the Anglo-Saxons, and especially the codes of the Lombards, mark the distinctive form of criminal sanctions that were imaginative and ingenious. As we have seen the Anglo-Saxons sometimes divide the composition penalty into three parts, one-third to the state and the other two thirds divided between the victim and his or her family or guild. This bears little resemblance to the Roman codes and it is generally thought that the Anglo-Saxons took from Roman law the least amount of any of the Germanic peoples. The early Anglo-Saxon laws are unfortunately not as easy to understand because the terminology employed is so different from anything else in the Germanic codes as to be sometimes nearly indecipherable.

The Lombards are an especially interesting case since they are generally seen as being most concerned by jurisprudential matters and their codes had the greatest effects on other Germanic peoples even as the Lombards as a people were conquered by the Franks and did not have a lasting political influence on the later Middle Ages. Let us examine an especially clear example of how the Lombard laws dealt with wrongful acts in an early Lombard law, from Rothair's Edict, which deals with seizure of a woman.

> 214. He who takes to wife a free girl without the advice and consent of her relatives shall pay twenty solidi as composition for the seizure, as above and another twenty solidi to avert the feud. Concerning her mundium, moreover [let it be arranged] just as it is agreed and the law allows provided nevertheless both man and girl are free.[180]

---

[180] "Rothair's Edict," 214, in *The Lombard Laws*, translated by Katherine Fischer Drew, Philadelphia, PA: University of Pennsylvania Press, 1973, pp. 93-94.

We see here that there are two penalties one paid to the relatives of the seized girl and the other earmarked for the state to stop whatever feud might be contemplated by these relatives.

Another example comes from the Lombard Laws of King Grimwald on a similar matter.

> On Abandoned Wives.
> 6. If anyone puts aside his wife without legal cause, and receives over her another woman into his house, he shall pay 500 solidi as composition, half to the king and half to the relatives of the wife; and moreover, he shall lose the mundium of the woman whom he put aside. If the wife does not wish to return to her husband, she may return to her relatives together with her property and her mundium.[181]

We see here again there are two penalties, one half of the total which goes to compensate the woman's relatives and the other half goes to the state. In addition, we see an especially humane law where the woman who has been abandoned is given the choice of either returning to her husband or leaving him with her property and mundium, that is, regaining the power of control over herself.

Looking at these two Lombard laws, one from King Rothair and one from King Grimwald, we can see that the portion of the composition that goes to the state is variously described as for the king but also "to avert the feud." The other half of the composition is really for compensation for the victim or his or her family or clan. But the part for the king or for the state is what today looks like a fairly straight-forward criminal penalty or punishment aimed at deterrence. And in these centuries when there was no established idea of a public police or prison one can see the fees collected as the public half of the composition perhaps going to shore up the emerging police powers of the state. So, in this sense the Lombard laws set the stage nicely for the modern idea of criminal justice, as do some of the other Germanic codes in the early Medieval period.

What is different from the modern ideas of criminal justice is that in Lombard criminal law there is a clear attempt to pay compensation to the victim, placing the victim squarely in the criminal proceedings at least conceptually. Criminal justice was a matter of both compensating the victim and also deterring private vengeance. We don't see this kind of

---

[181] "Laws of King Grimwald," 6, in *The Lombard Laws*, translated by Katherine Fischer Drew, Philadelphia, PA: University of Pennsylvania Press, 1973, p. 134.

approach taken much in our own contemporary times, although it is also clear that there would be support for such an idea today.

To look at things in a somewhat different way, the Lombard criminal laws combine the Roman idea of criminal law being primarily about the state acting as if it were to defend itself from the perpetrator of assault, and the even older set of ideas that "criminal" law was not terribly different from "civil" law in that it was mainly about compensation for the victim or his or her family or clan. In this respect one could see the Lombard laws as an intermediary stage of criminal justice between the quite old idea of compensating victims and aiding the deterrence goals of the state. But I want to suggest that that is not the only or even the best way to understand the Lombard criminal laws.

Seeing criminal law as being either about compensating victims or about shoring up the deterrence goals of the state is to fail to see that these aims are both important and can be combined together. And it is my view that such an idea needs serious consideration today as victims and especially victims' advocacy groups try to make the criminal law more responsive to the victims of assault and other criminal acts. Let me end this chapter with a few more reflections, positive and negative, about remaking criminal law so it is responsive to both of the goals.

The main thing to say against something like the Lombard model is that it diminishes the place of the perpetrator's guilt in the criminal trial. When the interests of the victim are discounted it allows criminal justice institutions to focus only on the guilt or innocence of the alleged perpetrator. In this respect we find the idea of fairness to the perpetrator to be of paramount concern. I have supported such an idea in several of my previous books, especially in international criminal law where there is a strong tendency to allow institutional interests to predominate. But there are reasons to be leery of this approach to the entirety of criminal law.

As I have said, there is a strong movement today to let the voices and interests of victims gain a greater role in criminal law proceedings. It is often said: if not for the victim being wronged there would be no point to a criminal having trials. Victims need to have "their day in court" and focusing the criminal proceedings to be about, at least in part, reasonable compensation for the victim makes perfect sense. The Lombard laws can thus be seen as not an intermediary stage in the full development of criminal justice but as a new and highly reasonable idea of how to view criminal justice.

CHAPTER 8

CRIME AND SIN

At the same time that Medieval Germanic codes of law were refining ideas of criminality there were also ideas of sin that clerics were propounding as well. In it simplest form, we can say that crime is a violation of the King's law, whereas sin is a violation of God's law, especially with the rise of Christianity. The ideas of crime and sin were not as easy to separate though if the authority of the King itself came from God. In addition, by the time of Charlemagne the kings were regularly inserting themselves into religious affairs and in some cases enforcing religious laws. In this chapter we take up the myriad of ways that crime and sin were interlinked in early Medieval times.

In the first section of this chapter I will set out the background of understanding violations of God's law. Here we will see how the Hebrew Bible dealt with this issue and what the salient differences are between that bible and the Christian Gospels. In addition we will encounter the controversy about providing sanctuary to criminals. In the second section we will discuss the emerging doctrine that the king ruled on the basis of divine authority. In the third section we will look at civil legal texts that set out general conditions for crime. In the fourth section we will look at early ecclesiastical laws that set out the conditions and remedies for sin. And in the final section we will discuss how crime and sin interrelated. I will argue in this chapter that crime and sin were often characterized in quite similar ways. And indeed, there were laws that seemed to conflate the ideas of crime and sin. This dispute mirrors the larger dispute abut how secular and ecclesiastical regimes were separated and yet often overlapping.

I. Sin and Sanctuary

The ancient idea of sanctuary was that criminals could go to a church or other religious place to escape sentencing. Sanctuary was discussed in the Hebrew Bible and in ancient Greek times as an amalgam of two different types of law: God's law and the law of particular kings.

Here is how one scholar has described the problem of sanctuary in the early Medieval period:

> Anglo-Saxon legislation provides us with rich material for understanding the interplay between sanctuary, royal law, and feuding practices. Anglo-Saxon sources, like Carolingian, provide evidence that kings were trying to bring sanctuary to heel through written legislation in the ninth century and thereafter. In the Anglo-Saxon case, royal authority tried to discipline sanctuary by integrating it within the laws and norms that governed the blood feud. The results were mixed. Sanctuary laws were not fully assimilated into processes of royal penal law, and sanctuary practices remained governed by an amalgamation of ecclesiastical sensibilities, feuding norms, and royal authority.[182]

The Carolingian kings tried to rein in sanctuary because it wrecked havoc with criminal law generally and with the attempt to stop or at least curtail the blood feud.

We can also learn from the Burgundian code which addressed sanctuary in several key laws:

> if a freeman has been slain by a freeman, and the homicide has fled to a church, he himself who admits to the homicide, shall with half of his goods be placed in servitude to the heirs of the slain; the remaining half of the homicide's possessions shall be relinquished to the heirs of the slain. If indeed anyone's slave has been killed by a freeman, and the homicide runs to the church, it is considered that the price paid to the slave's lord in recompense will be according to the quality of the slave…[183]

Here the Burgundians are attempting to offset the blood feud by establishing a price to be paid by the person who commits homicide independently of whether sanctuary is initially declared by the perpetrator.

As we have seen, the way to stop the blood feud was to make it clear that a killer or other perpetrator would be punished by the king. If a killer could seek amnesty from punishment by entering a religious sanctuary, then the need for revenge would not be satisfied and the relatives of the victim would still seek their own vigilante justice. And in addition, if how sanctuaries operated was put in the hands of the clergy

---

[182] Karl Shoemaker, *Sanctuary and Crime in the Middle Ages, 400-1500*, NY: Fordham University Press, 2011, p. 78.
[183] Quoted in ibid., p. 79.

then this was a disruption of the king's justice. This is why sanctuary had to be disciplined and incorporated into civil law and taken out of the domain of ecclesiastical law in the early Medieval period.

The New Testament injunction to give to Caesar the things that are Caesar's and to give to God the things that are God's was the articulation of a principle for keeping either the King's law or God's law from encroaching on each other. But as I said, the King was increasingly seen as deriving his authority from God–indeed, in some cases the King was thought to rule by divine right. This idea was hard to reconcile with the idea that civil matters and religious matters should be kept separate. And as the Middle Ages went on some Kings claimed the right to prosecute and punish those who had violated God's laws. So, crime and sin began to merge in some Medieval societies.

We can also see that in some cases there was literally a confusion of crime and sin–so that what is at one point called a crime is also called a sin, sometimes in the very same law. As an example, consider two ecclesiastical laws concerning confession enacted under the Anglo-Saxon King Edgar:

> 10. For all I pray my Lord's forgiveness, that the devil may never steal upon me, so that I am without confession and amendment of my sins; as I today confess all my crimes before the Lord Savior Christ, who ruleth the heavens and the earth…
> 11. And thou, Savior Christ, be merciful and forgiving to my soul, and blot out my sins and my crimes, that late or early I have perpetrated; and lead me to thy realm on high… that I may atone for my sins and crimes, and eschew others such, so that the Lord may sustain me, who liveth and reigneth over without end, to eternity.[184]

Here crimes and sins are seemingly mixed together and God is asked to forgive both and to issue penances as punishment of violations of both God's law and the King's law. And in a later ecclesiastical law we learn that "If a priest be criminal, and he celebrates mass against the archdeacon's command, let him pay xii. ores."[185] We seem to find here that the crimes of priests are being punished by their spiritual supervisors.

---

[184] *Canons Enacted Under K. Edgar*, *De Confessione*, 10-11, in *Ancient Laws and Institutes of England*, translated by Benjamin Thorpe, Vol. II, London: The Commissioners of the Public Records of the Kingdom, 1840, p. 265.

[185] *Law of the Northumbrian Priests* 7, in *Ancient Laws and Institutes of England*, translated by Benjamin Thorpe, Vol. II, London: The Commissioners of the Public Records of the Kingdom, 1840, p. 291.

In ancient times, we find that there were strong injunctions on committing sin. The Hebrew Bible is the best known source of such injunctions, but we also find other ancient religious texts decrying sin and calling for it to be punished in a god's name. There is also a strong concept of natural law that can be found in the early Medieval period. In a sense, natural law was said to be the grounding for both all civil laws and also all of God's laws. If one takes this view seriously then again it is hard to reconcile it with the idea that civil law and ecclesiastical law are to be kept separate insofar as breaches of certain civil laws constituted a crime but violations of ecclesiastical law was a sin. In some writing on these topics, the separation was drawn in terms of punishments–where the punishment for a violation of the King's law was death, corporal punishment, or imprisonment whereas violations of ecclesiastical law would largely be punished in the next life.

II. The King and Divine Rule

Roman emperors proclaimed themselves to be gods, or at least representatives of a god. In early Christianized Germanic codes the king was not seen as a god or God, but there was an attempt to characterize the king's authority as in some sense divinely constituted. Here is how A. J. Carlyle puts it:

> The ruler is not only the minister of God's remedy for sin, but the instrument of his punishment… St. Optatus of Milevis, in his treatise on the Donatist schism in North Africa, expresses the conception that the ruler is the representative of God… replies by urging that St. Paul's commands to Christian men, that they should offer up prayers for kings and those in authority, and asserts that the Empire is not in the Church, but the Church in the Empire, and that there is no one over the Emperor but God only, who made him Emperor.[186]

Various ways are employed by Medieval writers to characterize the divine authority of the king. "The title of "Vicar of God" is important as summing up the conception that the authority of the ruler is derived from God Himself."[187]

---

[186] A. J. Carlyle, *A History of Medieval Political Theory in the West*, Vol. I, London: William Blackwood and Sons LTD., 1970, p. 148.

[187] Ibid., p. 149.

The idea that the king ruled by divine authority poses conceptual as well as practical problems for the separation of civil and ecclesiastical law as well as the separation of sin as an offense against God and crime as an offense against the king. It is perhaps surprising that it is Christian prelates who affirmed the idea that the king ruled by divine authority. The Augustinian idea that there is a distinction between the city of God and the city of man is strained if the ruler of the city of man is himself divinely authorized to be an enforcer of God's laws.

It is also somewhat surprising that the idea of divine authority for the king was also used to claim that the people should obey their rulers even if those rulers appear to be harming the people over whom they rule. As Carlyle writes:

> We have then a theory that the ruler is the representative of God, and whatever his conduct may be, he does not cease in some sense to have this character. St. Augustine expresses the same conception with a certain added emphasis. He mentions Nero as an example of the worst type of ruler, but adds that even such rulers receive their power through the providence of God… The character of the ruler is adapted to the character of the people: if they are good God will give them a good ruler; if they are evil God will set an evil ruler over them.[188]

Evil rulers are not to be disobeyed since they are, even as being evil, God's representative on earth.

Here is how the Lombard King Rothair talks about himself and his connection to God: "In the name of the Lord, I, the most noble Rothair, seventeenth king of the Lombards [issue this lawbook] with the aid of God."[189] We then find more explicit connections between the king and God in the codes of later Lombard kings. Here is part of the prologue of the laws of King Liutprand:

> This Catholic Christian prince has been influenced to promulgate these laws and to judge wisely not by his own foresight but through the wisdom and inspiration of God: he has conceived [these laws] in his heart, studied them in his mind, and happily fulfilled them in his word. For the heart of the king is in the hand of God… believing ourselves inspired by divine providence, we shall delete and add things in like

---

[188] Ibid., p. 151.

[189] "Rothair's Edict," Prologue, in *The Lombard Laws*, translated by Katherine Fischer Drew, Philadelphia: University of Pennsylvania Press, 1973, p. 39.

> manner which seem fitting to us according to the law of God, and such we have ordered to be written on the present page.[190]

We see a much closer connection between the king and God in this prologue, and in addition we see the connection between the law of God and the civil laws of the Lombards.

Four years after the prologue of King Liutprand's laws we find an addendum being offered by Liutprand with even a more explicit connection to God:

> In the name of God Almighty, I, Liutprand, most excellent king of the most happy and Catholic, favored by God, nation of the Lombards, take occasion to remember that those laws issued earlier by us can now be found in the lawbook of the Lombards… we with foresight add these provisions which we believe to be pleasing to God…[191]

Here we have the king saying he is favored by God and that he has issued laws that he believes to be pleasing to God. And in later addenda, Liutprand also says that he is "God favoring"[192] and that he is king "of the divinely chosen Catholic nation of the Lombards."[193] This last reference comes close to calling himself divinely ruling.

And one of the most explicit references to this idea is found in the addition to the lawbooks by Liutprand in his Fifteenth Year of reign: "in defense of our Christian and Catholic law we make provision that no one may presume to wander from the faith of Christ, that we may have God as a defender and helper firmly and permanently in all things."[194] Here the civil law is said to be justified by the fact that "no one may presume to wander from the faith of Christ." We have then a quite explicit connection between the king and God and also an explicit connection between obeying the civil law and having faith in God. And in the Lombard laws of King Ratchis we find obedience to law linked to "salvation of our own

---

190 "Laws of King Liutprand," From the First Year of his Reign, Prologue, in *The Lombard Laws*, translated by Katherine Fischer Drew, Philadelphia: University of Pennsylvania Press, 1973, pp. 144-145.

191 "Laws of King Liutprand," From the Fifth Year, Prologue, in *The Lombard Laws*, translated by Katherine Fischer Drew, Philadelphia: University of Pennsylvania Press, 1973, pp. 146-147.

192 "Laws of King Liutprand," From the Eighth Year, in ibid., p. 150.

193 "Laws of King Liutprand," From the Ninth Year, in ibid., p. 153.

194 "Laws of King Liutprand," From the Fifteenth Year, in ibid., p. 180.

souls and the souls of all of our people."[195] Such mixing of the King's law and God's law of salvation is now firmly and expressly put forward by the middle of the 8th Century during the reign of the Lombard King Ratchis.

III. Punishing Crime

In earlier chapters we have already seen that the criminal laws of the Germanic peoples were focused on ending or limiting the blood feud by articulating a fee schedule for the taking of a life, where there was the promise that the state would take over from the victim's family the seeking of retribution against perpetrators of violence. Penalties and punishments meted out by the state were crucial above all else at ending the system of private vengeance so as to promote the overall stability of the society. We can turn to the laws of Rothair for an important statement of this principle.

> 74. In the case of all wounds and injuries mentioned above, involving freemen as they do, we have set a higher composition than did our predecessors in order that the *faida*, that is the blood feud, may be averted after receipt of the abovementioned composition, and in order that more shall not be demanded and a grudge shall not be held.[196]

The criminal penalties are here quite explicitly said to be justified to stop the blood feud.

We can also turn to another law of the Lombard king Rothair about additional measures aimed at curtailing the blood feud.

> 143. Concerning the man who seeks revenge after accepting composition. If a slave is killed and composition paid for the homicide and oaths offered to avert the feud, and afterwards he who received the composition tries to avenge himself by killing a man belonging to the associates from whom he received the payment, we order that he repay the composition twofold to the relatives of the freeman or to the slave's lord. In like manner concerning him who tries to avenge himself after accepting composition for blows or injuries, he shall restore that which he had accepted in double amount. In addition, he

---

[195] "Laws of King Ratchis," in ibid., p. 215.

[196] "Rothair's Edict," 74, in *The Lombard Laws*, translated by Katherine Fischer Drew, Philadelphia: University of Pennsylvania Press, 1973, pp. 64-65.

> shall pay composition, as provided above, if he has killed the man.[197]

This law seeks to punish severely anyone who accepts the wergeld or the composition that is offered by the state and yet still seeks private revenge as well.

Here is a Burgundian law about murder that shows the central place of matching the punishment to the crime:

> II. Of Murders
> 1. If anyone presumes with boldness or rashness bent on injury to kill a native freeman of our people of any nation or servant of the king, in any case a man of barbarian tribe, let him make restitution for the committed crime not otherwise than by the shedding of his own blood…
> 7. In such cases let all know this must be observed carefully, that the relatives of the man killed must recognize that no one can be pursued except the killer; because just as we have ordered the criminals to be destroyed, so we will suffer the innocent to sustain no injury.[198]

There are several important principles affirmed here. First, the punishment must be proportionate to the crime; and second, only the perpetrator should be punished, not a member of the perpetrator's family or tribe.

The Visigothic Code also administers criminal law in a proportionate although nonetheless very severe manner as we see in this law concerning punishments:

> If several freeborn persons by common agreement, should plan the perpetration of a homicide, he who struck the blow, or actually committed the deed, shall be put to death. The others, however, who are convicted of having plotted the crime, although they did not take an active part in its perpetration, shall nonetheless, on account of their wicked counsel, each receive two hundred lashes in public, and undergo the ignominy of being scalped. And, in addition, each shall be compelled to pay fifty solidi to the nearest relatives of the deceased, and should any of them not be possessed of such a

---

[197] "Rothair's Edict," 143, in *The Lombard Laws*, translated by Katherine Fischer Drew, Philadelphia: University of Pennsylvania Press, 1973, pp. 74-75.

[198] *Book of Constitutions*, II, in *The Burgundian Code*, translated by Katherine Fischer Drew, Philadelphia: University of Pennsylvania Press, 1949, pp. 23-24.

> sum, he shall be delivered over to them to be their slave forever.[199]

Punishing crime was a major task of the King and other civil rulers. The administration of a criminal justice system was seen as one of the most important tasks of civil rulers. But as we will next see, civil rulers sometimes also saw themselves as tasked with administering a system of religious laws and punishing those who had sinned.

IV. Punishing Sin

We can begin to understand the changes brought about by the rise of Christianity as it affected the tasks of the civil state by looking at the laws of Byzantium in the 8th Century. Here is one such law from the Ecloga:

> Since, therefore, He [God] has entrusted us the rule of the empire, as it pleased Him, which made plain our love for Him in reverential fear, and since, according to Peter, the supreme head of the Apostles, He ordered us 'to be shepherds' of his most faithful 'flock', we can think of nothing in return which ranks higher with Him or is more important than steering 'in judgment and righteousness' those entrusted to us by Him, so that thereby 'the bonds of all injustice are loosed, and the knots of violent dealings dissolved and the assaults of sinners beaten back… and the empire is made peaceful for us and the state steadfast.[200]

Notice that the role of the civil rulers is closely connected to dealing with sinners.

In another law from the same period we see the civil role in the eradication of sin quite clearly, concerning marriage:

> 2,9,1, The wisdom of God the Maker and creator of all things teaches that marriage is an indissoluble union of those living together in the Lord. For He who brought mankind from nothingness into being did not form man and woman in the same fashion, although able to, but created her from the man in

---

[199] *The Visigothic Code*, Book VI, Title 5.12, translated by S. P. Scott, Boston: The Boston Book Company, 1910, p.224.

[200] *The Ecloga*, Prologue, in *The Laws of the Isaurian Era*, translated by Mike Humphreys, Liverpool: Liverpool University Press, 2017, p. 35.

> order that He might wisely ordain the indissolubility of marriage, uniting in 'one flesh' two persons. He did not separate them... but punished the sin and did not break the union. Moreover this active law was confirmed anew by the Creator... And we who follow and obey shall not ordain anything more beyond this.[201]

In this law we see that marriage is regulated in the way that the Bible commanded with the civil rulers essentially enforcing God's law concerning how to treat sinners. In this respect, sin became something that Byzantine law sanctioned, just as crime was sanctioned as well.

Indeed, it is quite clear that the Byzantine rulers incorporated large sections of the Biblical law into the civil law, often taking the Biblical injunctions verbatim, as we see in these laws:

> Title 5. From Deuteronomy, Chapter 87.
> Fathers shall not be put to death for their children, and sons shall not be put to death for their fathers; each shall die for their own sins....
> Title 7. From Deuteronomy, Chapter 86.
> Do not rob the wages of the poor and needy of your brothers, or from the strangers in your cities. Pay him his wages on the same day; the sun shall not go down upon it, for he is poor and anxious for it. Otherwise he may cry to the Lord against you, and you shall be guilty of sin.[202]

Here we find that the civil rulers and judges are to take into account the Mosaic law and enforce its provisions against sin.

The Christianization of the Roman Empire proceeded, including both Byzantium in the east and the Germanic peoples intermixing with the Romans in the West. In some respects including punishing of sin by the civil rulers followed the increasing intermingling of Christian ecclesiastical law and civil law. Indeed, we have already seen examples of how this idea played out in the West, and can see it also in the following law of the Burgundians:

> CII Of Jews Who Presume to Raise Their Hands against a Christian

---

[201] *The Ecloga*, 2.9.1,, in *The Laws of the Isaurian Era*, translated by Mike Humphreys, Liverpool: Liverpool University Press, 2017, pp. 50-51.

[202] *A Selection from the Mosaic Law*, Titles 5 and 7, in *The Laws of the Isaurian Era*, translated by Mike Humphreys, Liverpool: Liverpool University Press, 2017, pp. 145-146.

> 1. If any Jew presumes to raise a hand against a Christian with fist, shoe, club, whip, or stone, or has seized his hair, let him be condemned to the loss of a hand.
> 2. But if he wishes to redeem his hand, we order him to redeem it with seventy-five solidi, and let the fine be twelve solidi.
> 3. Besides this, we order that if he has presumed to raise a hand against a priest, let him be handed over to death, and let his property be given into our treasury.[203]

This multi-part law essentially provides that the criminal law will be used to punish those who violate Christians and their priests.

Another law that criminalizes the religious practices of the Jews can be seen in the Visigothic Code:

> I hereby renounce all the rites and observances of the Jewish sect, and without reserve, express my utter abhorrence of all their ceremonies and solemnities which I have practiced and kept in former times, until now; and I pledge myself that I will, hereafter, observe none of said rites or ceremonies, nor will I adhere to any of my former errors; that is to say that I will not retain them in my mind, or in any way carry them into effect. Henceforth renouncing all things which are condemned and prohibited by the doctrines of Christianity: -I believe in one God, the Omnipotent Father, Maker of Heaven and Earth, the Creator of all things visible and invisible, and in our Lord Jesus Christ, the only Son of God, begotten by the Father before all the centuries…[204]

This Visigothic law is fascinating in that it outlaws any doctrine or practice of the Jews and any other non-Christian religion. In addition it makes the belief in the religious canons of the Catholic Church matters that should be sworn to by all those in the Visigothic kingdom. In effect, this law authorizes the central tenets of the Catholic faith to be enforced by the civil law, fully absorbing Christian law into Visigothic civil law.

And Visigothic law also makes the practice of Jewish religion subject to very severe criminal penalties:

> If any Jew should presume to offer an insult to the Christian religion, or, by arguments, should induce anyone to abandon

---

[203] *Book of Constitutions*, CII, in *The Burgundian Code*, translated by Katherine Fischer Drew, Philadelphia: University of Pennsylvania Press, 1949, p. 86.

[204] *The Visigothic Code*, Book XII, Title 3.14, translated by S. P. Scott, Boston: The Boston Book Company, 1910, pp. 395-396.

> the Christian faith, or should defend the weakness of his own sect, or while fleeing from the doctrines of the Christian religion, should conceal himself in any part of our kingdom, or should escape to foreign countries, for the purpose of concealment, or if anyone should offer a hiding place to a transgressor of this law, knowing he is a fugitive, any of said parties guilty of any of the above-named offenses shall be punished with a hundred lashes, have his head shaved and, after his property has been confiscated for the benefit of the king, shall be subjected to the miseries of slavery.[205]

The criminal law is here employed in the service of Christian religious law and, so it seems, sin is punished as crime had also been punished by the use of severe civil penalties and punishments.

Jews were subject to discriminatory treatment in the laws of the Roman Empire that preceded Christianity, but these laws were not aimed at advancing the agenda of a different religion, although some religious practices were protected in civil law. When Emperor Constantine embraced Christianity and required that his subjects convert, it became a goal of the civil law to aid in this effort of Christianizing the Empire. Treating sins as if they were crimes was a large part of that effort. We next look at conceptual as well as practical similaritics to the way that crimes and sins were treated in the Christianized Roman and Germanic laws.

V. Medieval Treatment of Crime and Sin

Carlyle makes a fascinating comparison to the way that slavery and coercive government were viewed among early Christian writers:

> Slavery was contrary to the natural law of the primitive condition of human innocence, but is proper and even useful under the actual conditions of human nature. It is the same with the institution of government. Coercive government has been made necessary through sin and is a divinely appointed remedy for sin. It is interesting to find this conception developed by Christian writers from a very early date. We have already considered St. Paul's treatment of the institution of government and the sanctity which belongs to it. He affirms

[205] *The Visigothic Code*, Book XII, Title 3.9, translated by S. P. Scott, Boston: The Boston Book Company, 1910, pp. 389-390.

> its sanctity and explains this as arising from the fact that its purpose is to repress evil and reward good.[206]

Just as government and its laws were doing good by protecting slaves even as they set harsh penalties for them, so government and its laws were protecting all people by repressing sin.

As medieval governments became Christianized they saw law as the vehicle for confronting sin in similar ways to the confrontation of crime, which remained also a goal of law. Indeed, in some legal texts sin and crime were seen as nearly synonymous. And Carlyle goes on to suggest that these early Christian thinkers were inspired by the Hebrew Bible where the King of Israel drew authority from God and saw his task as punishing both sin and crime.[207]

There were monumental disputes between religious and political leaders about who was the most important judge of sin: was the bishop supposed to keep the King in line or was the King to keep the bishops in line to make sure that sin was properly confronted? These disputes reached a crescendo in the later Middle Ages as the Church used its power to confront and even attempt to remove kings. But in the early Middle Ages, these powers were still somewhat aligned over the importance that legal punishments be used to repress sin.

Walter Ullmann provides another important idea from Medieval sources that explains why political rulers concerned themselves with both sin and crime.

> The law, as the soul ruled the corporate entity, ruled the body, be it the Church or a kingdom, or an empire. When we read in the Visigothic Laws of the seventh century that *Lex est anima totius corporis popularis* [the law is the soul of the body politic[208]], we have pretty clear proof of how strongly entrenched was the idea of law as the regulating and animating force of society, even at that early time.[209]

---

[206] A. J. Carlyle, *A History of Medieval Political Theory in the West*, Vol. I, London: William Blackwood and Sons LTD., 1970, p. 128.
[207] Ibid., p. 159.
[208] See *The Visigothic Code*, Book I, Title 2.2, translated by S. P. Scott, Boston: The Boston Book Company, 1910, p. 5.
[209] Walter Ullmann, *The Individual and Society in the Middle Ages*, Baltimore, MD: The Johns Hopkins Press, 1966, p. 47.

The law was seen as what inspired the society and kept it together. And in this respect, the protection of the soul of the society required laws that enforced both civil law and religious law.

In the Anglo-Saxon Confessional laws, the priest is supposed to punish sin by requiring prayer and good works as penance. So, the question is why punishing egregious sin was considered not just the role of the priest but also the civil authorities. One possible explanation is that especially egregious sin was seen as a threat to the body politic not merely a threat to the soul of the penitent.

The punishment for sins has a strikingly similar form to that for crimes, as we can begin to see in this Canon concerning penitents of King Edgar:

> Where it be needful, various punishments are proper for sins: bonds, or blows, or "pollupas," or prison-darkness, or earthworms, or swine; and sometimes mutilation of limbs, and sometimes loss of life…
> Roughly he fares who constantly criminates himself; and yet is he happy, if he never relax, till he make full "bot"; no man in the world is so very criminal, that he may not make atonement to God, let him undertake it fervently.[210]

We see here that the full panoply of punishments employed for crimes is applied to those who have sinned. And in addition, we see once again a conflation of sinful behavior with criminal behavior.

Since Church officials lacked the means to carry out these punishments for sin, it was left to the civil authorities to do so. Thus, the state and its means of punishment came to be used to confront sin as well as crime. And we also see that the punishments for sin are referred to as "bot" the term used to describe the compensation or amends that is the term used in criminal law of the Anglo-Saxons. It is clear that the king is expected to step in and punish sinners as we see in the Institutes of Polity of the Anglo-Saxons:

> It is the duty of a Christian king, in a Christian nation, to be, as it is right, the people's comfort, and a righteous shepherd over a Christian flock. And it is his duty, with all his power, to upraise Christianity, and everywhere further and protect God's

[210] *Canons Enacted Under K. Edgar, Of Penitents*, in *Ancient Laws and Institutes of England*, translated by Benjamin Thorpe, Vol. II, London: The Commissioners of the Public Records of the Kingdom, 1840, pp. 279-283.

> church...He shall evil-doing men vigorously chastise with secular punishments...[211]

Notice once again that the king is supposed to confront evil and sin by the use of secular punishments.

One further point of similarity between sin and crime is worth considering. The person who is said to be criminal or sinner can redeem himself from certain punishments by accepting alternative sanctions of various kinds.

> Herein is declared, how a sick man may redeem his fast–A man may redeem one day's fast with one penny; a man may also redeem one day's fast with ccxx. psalms; a man may also redeem a fast of twelve months with xxx. shillings; or let a man be freed who is worth that money... and with xxx. masses a man may lighten a xii. months' fast; if he will, with true love of God, supplicate for himself, and confess his sins to his confessor, and so atone for them as he shall direct him, and carefully ever abstain.[212]

As we have seen in this and other chapters, the convicted criminal can similarly sometimes redeem himself from harsh penalties and punishments by paying a certain amount of money instead.

In this chapter I have argued that the treatment of crime and sin in early Medieval legal and ecclesiastical codes is quite similar. And we have also seen that there is a very practical reason for this similarity, namely that the ecclesiastical leaders often did not have the means or power to punish sin in an effective way. But what this means then is that criminal law and punishment is used for both sin and crime in a way that creates conceptual confusion even if it could be practically justified.

---

[211] *The Institutes of Polity*, II, in *Ancient Laws and Institutes of England*, translated by Benjamin Thorpe, Vol. II, London: The Commissioners of the Public Records of the Kingdom, 1840, p. 305.

[212] *Canons Enacted Under K. Edgar*, *Of Penitents*, in *Ancient Laws and Institutes of England*, translated by Benjamin Thorpe, Vol. II, London: The Commissioners of the Public Records of the Kingdom, 1840, pp. 385-387.

SECTION IV.

WAR AND PEACE

CHAPTER 9

WAR, VIOLENCE, AND CHRISTIANITY

It is commonly thought that the so-called "Dark Ages" that we have been investigating had no use for the laws of war that the Roman jurists had developed. One prominent commentator has said:

> In the Dark Ages, between 476 and 800 AD, international law reached its nadir in the West. The war-practice of the Teutons stamps them as barbarians devoid of all conception of international right. The Goths, Vandals, and Turingians, like the Vikings of the North in later days, burned, pillaged and slew without mercy. They ravaged fields, uprooted vines, cut down olive trees, and burned without distinction all buildings, sacred and profane, leaving their track behind them in smoldering ruins... They slew in attack alike priest and layman, man and woman, and put to death their prisoners in the most cruel fashion... Even after the formal adoption of Christianity, the war-practice of the Barbarian Conquerors was more than brutal. The history of the wars of Clovis, the hero of that orthodox clergy, is the tale of savage murder and the most hateful treachery. A peculiar faithlessness distinguished the Frank even among his treacherous Teutonic kinsmen.[213]

I will challenge this uncompromising assessment, although I will mainly address the legal and philosophical tracts rather than the war practices themselves.

In the first section of this chapter I will look for evidence in support of Walker's claims in the law codes and commentaries of the period. In the second section, I will assess contrary evidence from the law codes that seems to speak of a humane approach to violence and war. In the third section I will pursue this issue by examining writings of religious and political leaders of the early Middle Ages. In the fourth section I will consider the seeming disparity between practice and theory in the legal

---

[213] Thomas A. Walker, *A History of the Law of Nations*, Vol. I, Cambridge: Cambridge University Press, 1899, pp. 64-65.

and political thinking of the early Medieval period. And in the final section I will consider the claim that Christianity did not restrain but actually emboldened aggressive war.

I. "Barbarians" at War

The Roman historian, Tacitus, is responsible for first setting out a picture of the time just before the main Germanic invaders of the Roman Empire. And he is often unsparing in his assessment of the atrocities in the first century CE.

> I am entering on the history of a period rich in disasters, frightful in its wars, torn by civil strife, and even in peace full of horrors. Four emperors perished by the sword. There were three civil wars; there were foreign enemies; there were often wars that had both characters at once. There was success in the East, and disaster in the West.... Italy was prostrated by disasters either entirely novel, or that recurred after a long succession of ages, cities in Campania's richest planes were swallowed up and overwhelmed; Rome was wasted by conflagrations, its oldest temples consumed, and the Capitol itself fired by the hands of citizens; Sacred rites were profaned; there was profligacy in the highest ranks; the sea was crowded with exiles, and its rocks polluted with bloody deeds.[214]

If this was the condition of the Roman Empire before the main Germanic invasions, it is clear that barbarous behavior was not restricted to the Germans that we have examined but already consumed Romans, at least in the West.

Yet, there have been historians who have tried to make the case for thinking that the Germanic invaders were much worse than their Roman hosts. Here is a selection from Prosper Boissonade's work describing the fifth century CE effects on Rome of the Germanic invaders:

> All the guarantees with which the expiring civilization of the ancient world had surrounded the life and possessions of the individual disappeared in the anarchy let loose by the barbarians. Even among the Visigoths, Ostrogoths, and Franks, who were already half Romanized by a long sojourn within the

[214] Tacitus, *The Histories*, Book I, Preface, translated by Alfred John Church and William Jackson Brodribb, Encyclopedia Britannica, 1952, reprinted by Franklin Mint Corporation, Franklin Center, PA: The Franklin Library, 1979, pp. 347-348.

> empire, the sudden awakening of ancestral ferocity transformed these "guests" into unchained murderers. Alaric and his followers in Boeotia, Attica, Thessaly, and Macedonia slew the inhabitants and carried off the women and cattle. "For us," says Salvian, Archbishop of Marseilles, himself the apologist of the barbarians, "there is neither peace nor security." Another contemporary, Prosper of Aquitaine, cries, towards 416: "It is ten years since we fell beneath the sword of the Vandals and Goths, the people has perished, even children and young maids they slew… The war bands which took part in the great invasion of 406 in Italy and Gaul, spread terror far and wide by their atrocious exploits: they transformed the town of Treier into a charnel-house, in which the naked bodies of men and women were devoured by dogs and birds of prey. In Aquitaine and in Spain the faithful and the clergy were beaten, thrown into chains, and burned alive. Everywhere, at the sack of cities and towns, women suffered the supreme outrage.[215]

This account, while challenged by many historians today, is nonetheless representative of the accounts of the war crimes committed by the Germanic invaders.

It is clear that even the use of the term barbarian was meant to signify that the Germanic peoples did not adhere to laws that Romans had adhered to, both the civil law and the law of nature. Yet, as we will see the Germanic codes were not a reversal of Roman law so much as an attempt to adapt that law to the new circumstances that were faced by the declining influence of the Roman Empire in the West.

II. Violence and War in the Germanic Codes

As we have seen, the Germanic codes are generally focused on diminishing the blood feud and replacing it with a system of monetary compensation. And while there is quite a lot of state-imposed violence for the most egregious crimes, there are procedures in place to minimize the possible arbitrary or unfair administration of that state violence. In what follows in this section we will see similar concerns and procedural constraints on those times when peace does not prevail.

Let us first examine some of the laws in Rothair's Edict. Several of the first seven of these laws (out of 388) concern matters of war and peace. Here are these laws:

---

[215] Prosper Boissonade, *Life and Work in Medieval Europe,* translated by Eileen Power, London: Routledge & Kegan Paul Ltd., 1927, pp. 22-23.

> 1. That man who conspires or gives counsel against the life of the king shall be killed and his property confiscated…
> 4. He who invites or introduces enemies into our land shall be killed and his property confiscated.
> 5. He who hides a spy (*scamaras*) within the land or gives him provisions shall either be killed or shall pay 900 solidi as composition to the king.
> 6. That one while on campaign raises a revolt against his duke or against him appointed by the king to command the army, or that one who raises a revolt in any part of the army, shall be killed.
> 7. He who during a battle with the enemy abandons his comrade or makes him *astalin*, that is, betrays him and does not remain with him, shall be killed.

It is of note that these are among the first laws of Rothair's Edict, and that they call for the death sentence to those who conspire with the enemy or insight rebellion among the army.

Those who hide spies are here also subject to the death penalty, but in other Germanic codes certain spies are encouraged insofar as they help enforce the law against those who would violate it. Rothair is clear though that, despite the harshness of how he treats those who conspire against the king, he aims for a merciful treatment of his citizens:

> The collection which follows makes evident how great was and is our care and solicitude for the welfare of our subjects; for we recognize that it is not only the numerous demands of the wealthy which should carry weight, but also the burdensome trials of the poor are important. Therefore, trusting in the mercy of Almighty God, we have perceived it necessary to improve and to reaffirm the present law… We desire that these laws be brought together in one volume so that everyone may lead a secure life in accordance with law and justice, and in confidence thereof will willingly set himself against his enemies and defend himself and his homeland.[216]

Peace and stability are the goals of Rothair's Edict and of other Germanic codes.

Later Lombard kings refined and corrected Rothair's Edict in ways that altered somewhat how violence was viewed. Here is a revision of how killing is understood according to King Liutprand:

---

[216] "Rothair's Edict," in *The Lombard Laws*, translated by Katherine Fischer Drew, Philadelphia: University of Pennsylvania Press, 1973, p. 39.

> 20.II. On homicide. If any freeman in self-defense kills another freeman and it is proved that he killed that man while defending himself, he shall pay composition for him [the man killed] just as is provided in an earlier law established by King Rothair of glorious memory. But whoever falls upon another man and kills him for any other reason shall lose all his property. [217]

Self-defensive killing is here treated very differently than killing for all other reasons. We can extrapolate that a consistent application of the principle behind this law would also affect how killing in war was regarded, and indeed we do see such extrapolation, but not for several centuries.

In a yet later law of King Liutprand, there are further refinements and corrections to the law concerning self-defense.

> 62.VIIII. I am mindful of the manner in which we have already established that anyone who [deliberately] kills a freeman shall lose his entire property and that he who kills a man while defending himself shall pay composition according to the quality of the person. Now we set forth the means whereby that quality should be determined. For it is the custom that a lesser person (*minima persona*) who is a freeman (*exercitalis*) shall have a wergeld of 150 solidii and he who is of the first class (*primus*) shall have a wergeld of 300 solidii.[218]

Self-defensive killing was not excused, and here in this refinement of the self-defense law we see that there are quite serious penalties assigned for killing even in self-defense.

The Christianized Lombard laws of violence mirrored to a certain extent the Christian ideas of war that saw no complete excuse for the use of violence–violence should be a last resort and even so it still created a liability on the one who used the violence. Isidore's account of what makes war just has as one of the legal bases of such war that an enemy is driven off, as we will next see. But self-defensive wars, while just, are still not to be pursued unless there is conformity with the natural law.

---

[217] "The Laws of King Liutprand," 20.II, in ibid., p. 155.

[218] "The Laws of King Liutprand," 62.VIIII, in ibid., p. 170.

III. Religious and Political Leaders on Violence

The early Church Fathers were often pacifists, and also likely to speak out against slaughter and violence during war. Here is the apologist Justin writing in the early Christian period:

> We who were filled with war and mutual slaughter and every wickedness have each through the whole world changed our warlike weapons–our swords into ploughshares and our spears into implements of tillage–and we cultivate piety, righteousness, philanthropy, faith, and hope.[219]

Louis J. Swift comments on this passage that:

> Despite Justin's words cited above about Christians turning "swords into ploughshares," the apologist insists on their strong loyalty in paying taxes and acknowledging the emperor's authority. In about 177, the Greek apologist Athenagoras assures Marcus Aurelius that Christians pray for the empire's increase "with all men becoming subject to your sway" while at the same time he condemns the slaughter and destruction which often attends the pursuit of that end.[220]

Even those Christians who were not pacifists nonetheless condemned the slaughter and destruction that is employed in war.

Political Leaders like the Lombard kings in addition to striving to undermine the blood feud called for foreigners to be treated well and not treated as if they are enemies. Rothair sets the following law:

> 367. On Foreigners (*waregang*). All foreigners who come from outside our frontiers into the boundaries of our kingdom and yield to the jurisdiction of our power ought to live according to the Lombard laws, unless through our grace they have merited another law. If they have legitimate children, these heirs shall live just as do the children of Lombards. If they do not have legitimate children, it shall not be in their power to give away

---

[219] Justin, *Dialogue with Trypho* 110.3, translated by A. Robinson and J. Donaldson, quoted in Louis J. Swift, "Early Christian Views on Violence, War, and Peace, in *War and Peace in the Ancient World*, edited by Kurt A. Raaflaub, Oxford: Blackwell Publishing Ltd., 2007, p. 281.

[220] Louis J. Swift, cited in ibid., pp. 280-281.

> any of their property or to alienate it by any means without the king's consent.[221]

It here seems that the Lombard King Rothair takes special interest in protecting foreigners and their offspring, as long as these foreigners act peaceably.

We can also gain insight by consulting one of the most famous of the Lombard religious leaders, Isidore of Seville. Isidore divides war into four categories:

> Now there are four kinds of war: just, unjust, civil, and more than civil. A just war is that which is waged in accordance with a formal declaration, and is waged for the sake of recovering property seized or driving off the enemy. An unjust war is one that is begun out of rage, and not for lawful reasons.... Civil war occurs when factions rise among fellow citizens and hostilities are stirred up...A "more than civil war" is where not only fellow-citizens, but also kinfolk fight... brother struggled against brother, and father bore arms against son.[222]

Isidore follows Cicero in thinking that there can be just wars, but that not all wars are just. Indeed, Isidore speaks of "lawful reasons" for going to war as the determining factor to whether war is just.

In an earlier chapter of his *Etymologies*, Isidore says that "repulsion of violence by force... is never unjust, but is held to be natural and fair."[223] In this respect he says that he is referring to natural law which exists everywhere. It seems that for Isidore wars are just if they conform to natural law (and are also begun with a formal declaration). War fought in self-defense or defense of others is the paradigmatic just war insofar as such wars involve repulsing violence by force.

The writings of prominent political and religious leaders in the "Dark Ages" suggest that there was sometimes an enlightened view of war and violence. The idea that some wars can be just in the sense that they are started for good reasons and waged with restraint is an idea that is somewhat derived from Cicero but now also having Biblical support as well. One of the problems is how to reconcile war with the saying of Jesus

---

[221] "Rothair's Edict," 367, in *The Lombard Laws*, translated by Katherine Fischer Drew, Philadelphia: University of Pennsylvania Press, 1973, p. 124.

[222] Isidore of Seville, *The Etymologies*, Book XVIII.i, translated by Stephen Barney, W. J. Lewis, J.A. Beach, and Oliver Berghof, Cambridge: Cambridge University Press, 2006, p. 359.

[223] Ibid., Book XVII.iv., p. 359.

that one should turn the other cheek–an idea that the early Church fathers relied on to support their pacifist positions.

Augustine had developed the idea that war was horrible but that it could be justly employed in order to counter that which was even more horrible. In fact, Augustine spoke of "the laws of war" in his work, *The City of God*:

> the first just men were set up as shepherds of flocks, rather than as kings of men, so that in this way God might convey the message of what was required by the order of nature… The origin of the Latin word for slave, *servus*, is believed to be derived from the fact that those who by the laws of war could rightly be put to death by the conquerors, became servi, slaves, when they were preserved, receiving this name from their preservation.[224]

In Augustine's doctrine, the laws of war not only specified when wars were initiated justly but also how wars were to be waged justly–in this instance sparing the lives of those who are captured on the battlefield, even as one then is entitled to enslave these prisoners.

In his *City of God*, Augustine sets the main rationale for a doctrine of the Just War:

> Those wars are now past history; and yet the misery of these evils is not yet ended…If I were to try to describe, with an eloquence worthy of the subject, the many and multifarious disasters, the dour and dire necessities, I could not possibly be adequate to the theme, and there would be no end to this protracted discussion. But the wise man, they say, will wage just wars. Surely, if he remembers that he is a human being he will rather lament the fact that he is faced with the necessity of waging just wars; for if they were not just, he would not have to engage in them, and consequently there would be no wars for a wise man. For it is the injustice of the opposite side that lays on the wise man the duty of waging wars; and this injustice is assuredly to be deplored by a human being since it is the injustice of human beings, even though no necessity for war should arise from it.[225]

---

224 Augustine, *The City of God*, Book 19, chapter 15, translated by Henry Bettenson, London: Penguin Books, 1984, p. 874.

225 Augustine, *City of God*, Book 19, Chapter 7, translated by Henry Bettenson, London: Penguin Books, 1972, pp. 861-862.

So some wars should be fought to confront injustice, and those wars are just.

One of the most important components of Augustine's doctrine of the Just War is that war is to be pursued only so that a just peace can be achieved.

> To begin with, therefore, a man has a responsibility to his own household... This is where domestic peace starts, the ordered harmony about giving and obeying orders among those who live in the same house. For the orders are given by those who are concerned for the interests of others... they do not give orders because of a lust for domination, but from a dutiful concern for the interests of others, not with pride in taking precedence over others, but with compassion in taking care of others.[226]

It is through compassion not from lust or vengeance that a just war is to be pursued.

Yet, it is also part of the Augustinian doctrine that there can be cases where peace is achieved but it is not a just peace. We are all imperfect sinners and we do not always pursue what is just rather than what is convenient. And in addition, unless God rules over the city or the state "that city is devoid of true justice."[227] The later Catholic doctrine following Augustine held that the lack of true justice can be seen, among many other ways, in the methods used in war. All forms of violence and coercion, which are the hallmarks of war, are seen as not truly just. But it is possible to achieve some kind of justice and peace nonetheless, however imperfect it will be.

IV. Theory and Practice in the Early Middle Ages

Throughout my work in the history of legal and political thought a problem has seemed to arise when the practice of kings is not in line with the legal and political theory that seems to undergird the laws of a kingdom. And war is often the example that is used to illustrate the disparity between theory and practice. Wars were common in the "Dark Ages" and yet the laws and the commentary on the laws were full of restraint. Wars waged for gain or out of rage were condemned but nonetheless still pursued and even feted. And the period we are examining

---

[226] Ibid., Book 19, Chapter 14, pp. 873-874.
[227] Ibid., Book 19, Chapter 24, p. 891.

was at the threshold of the idea of a "holy war" waged by Christian soldiers who sought to retake the holy lands from the "infidels." The idea was emerging that war could be justified by religious reasons, despite the sanctioning of violence in the codes of law at the time.

It is not surprising that there is a disconnect between theory and practice. In particular it has been common for kings to portray themselves, or get others to praise them, as peacemakers and those who use violence only as a last resort. Kings are far more likely to mandate that others restrain themselves than that kings should do so. This is one of the reasons that the rule of law has been successfully presented as a progressive advance in the history of legal and political thought.

We have seen in our previous chapters on early Medieval legal and political thought that it is crucial that law apply not only to those who are less powerful but also to those who are more powerful in a given society. Indeed, the idea that even the king is subject to obey the law has been an important development over the centuries and millennia. If even the king is subject to obey the law then it is fair to demand that ordinary citizens do so as well.

It remains true though that all states exercise violence and claim that they have the exclusive right to use violence. In this respect, there is surely a disconnect between the theory that all people including the king should be subject to law and that the king stands somehow above the law. And it was thought that if the king did not have the right to use violence it would be nearly impossible to secure the obedience of the people to obey the law. And so we are faced with a disconnect here between the theory that all are subject to the law and the "necessary" practice that some members of the society are above the law.

One way for there not to be such a strong disconnect between theory and practice is for even the king and his agents to be *restrained* in their use of violence. And here there are two domains where problems are posed. In the domestic setting, restraining the violence of the state may mean that potential law-breakers are not sufficiently deterred. But it needs to be pointed out that there is not good data on how deterrence works and how violence is most effectively administered in any event.

The more dangerous domain in which violence might be restrained is internationally. Restraining the king's war-making powers and other uses of violence employed to protect the people from enemies may mean an ineffective defense. Restraint on the battlefield (to say nothing of pacifism on the battlefield) would often lead to disastrous results. If war is necessary to protect the people or the homeland, then it seemingly makes little sense to restrain the use of violence by the state to show that the state leaders are subject to the law in the same way ordinary citizens are. So, in one respect it is almost inevitable that there will be a gap between theory and practice concerning the use of violence.

It is also true that codes of law set a kind of ideal for the society but where adherence to the law is not always recognized by the elites especially by the most powerful political elites. In this respect the law codes are not designed or aimed at the rulers but at the ruled. Of course such a view is at odds with the emerging doctrine of the rule of law, as I've been suggesting. But the rule of law is only one value in law and society. What seems important is that there are laws the rulers must obey even if they are not the very same as the rules for the normal citizens. We will next turn to ask what effect the rise of Christianity seemed to have on laws concerning violence and war.

V. Did Christianity Adversely Impact the Laws of War?

In the early days of Christianity many of the church leaders were pacifists–until the time of Augustine. In part the pacifism was a response to the war crimes of the Romans. But once the Roman Empire was Christianized at the time of Constantine, more and more church leaders supported the view that some wars could be justified, especially wars that furthered the spread of Christianity. It is perhaps too simplistic to suggest that the Catholic Church's position on war changed once there were Christian kings rather than "pagan" kings who were waging war. Indeed, the evidence is quite mixed. In this final section I will attempt to assess such evidence.

Christian apologists and theologians had to reconcile the strong emphasis on love in the New Testament with the duties that all citizens had to obey commands and generally defend the king. John von Heyking writes of Ambrose as having tried to resolve such conflict:

> Ambrose attempted to reconcile Christian love with the duties of political power and was nearly successful in achieving a synthesis of Christian and Ciceronian ethics. Specifically, he articulated rules for war-making and incorporated a Ciceronian understanding of military glory into Christianity. He surpassed the disastrous efforts of Eusebius and his own earlier efforts of glorifying leaders like Constantine… Ambrose attempted to persuade them of the superiority of peaceful statesmanship formed by the love of and service to God and neighbor… [he

> argued for] the higher pursuits of statesmanship, philosophy, and faith.[228]

In this view, when peaceful statesmanship has failed then and only then can resort to war be justified. But even in such a case, the motivation to go to war must be some sense of love, most especially love of those who are being attacked unjustly.

Another attempt to reconcile the demands of Christian love and loyalty to the King can be seen in Paul's letter to the Romans:

> Recompense to no man evil for evil. Provide things honest in the sight of all men.
> If it be possible, as much as lieth in you, live peaceably with all men.
> Dearly beloved, avenge not yourselves, but rather give place unto wrath: for it is written, Vengeance is mine; I will repay, saith the Lord.
> Therefore if thine enemy hunger, feed him; if he thirst, give him drink: for in so doing you shalt heap coals on his head.
> Be not overcome by evil, but overcome evil with good.[229]

These famous passages extol the virtue of living peaceably and not seeking vengeance even against one's enemies. But Paul also says that Christians have a duty to obey and support the civil authorities where they reside. And the beginnings of a Just War doctrine can be seen in the injunction "to overcome evil with good." This doctrine has often been cited as a cornerstone of the Just War idea that war can be a good if it is aimed at countering evil.

Various problems arose in the history of this idea as it was justified in employing the instruments of war as long as one had a good intent in doing so. Some of these problems included various problems where the line was to be drawn where the good intention was not enough to justify violent tactics. In its later incarnations, the idea of the Just War separated the justification of initiating war from the justification of the use of specific tactics and weapons of war. In the early Christian articulation of the Just War, it is the justification of the initiation of war that is stressed. And one of the problems is that it appears that any weapons and

---

[228] John von Heyking, "Taming Warriors in Classical and Early Medieval Political Theory," in *Ethics, Nationalism, and Just War*, edited by Henrik Syse and Gregory M. Reichberg, Washington, DC: Catholic University of America Press, 2007, p. 52.

[229] Romans,12.17-21.

tactics can be justified as long as they are intended to be used to confront evil.

There is another worry with the formulations in the quotation from Paul we just observed. Paul says that we "should not be overcome by evil." There is at least one way to interpret this formulation that is problematic because it seems to countenance anything done in war as long as it is in league with not allowing ourselves to be overcome by evil. There is more than a hint of the doctrine that the ends justify the means, and even more of the doctrine that it is worse to let one self be harmed than to do harm, which is the reverse of the ancient Socratic doctrine that it is better to suffer than to do evil.

In another context I have examined the doctrine popularized by the Jesuits that morality is a form of casuistry where we need to think carefully about the details of any given situation before we can be in a position to tell what is the right thing to do in that situation. In this doctrine, even very small changes in circumstance could be the difference in determining what the morally correct action is called for.

The question to take up at the end of the current chapter is whether or not the various contributions to the doctrine of the Just War in the early Middle Ages, especially in the early Christian writers, advanced a humane agenda. Of course, in one sense the beginnings of the doctrine of the Just War were a humane advance over the ideas in support of an unrestrained war doctrine. But in another sense, the Just War doctrine seems not to have been an advance over the doctrine of pacifism of the earliest of Church Fathers, such as Tertullian. Let us take up these issues in reverse order.

If humane treatment is advanced more by pacifism than any other doctrine then the doctrine of the Just War was not a humane advance. Prohibiting most forms of state violence is a hallmark of the doctrine of pacifism. But it is also true, as some Christian authors argued, that it is more of a necessity that those who are made to suffer should be aided and that those who created that suffering be confronted. The slaughter of the innocent is such an overwhelming evil that stopping that slaughter even by the use of violence is itself humane.

Yet, if the alternatives are unrestrained war or the Just War doctrine then the latter is surely the more humane alternative. And even if pacifism is an alternative there could certainly be situations where defending the weak or even defending oneself is necessary and where turning the other cheek is likely to produce a slap on that other cheek as well. Augustine believed that war was only very rarely justified, but when it was justified it was as a necessity that war be employed to stop evil. Yet,

Augustine also seems to have been led to this position because of respect for his secular Roman rulers.

One of the problems is that once war is morally countenanced it is hard to stop its most extreme forms. And in these early versions of the Just War doctrine there was not a clear necessity requirement. The early Christian doctrine of the Just War was an outgrowth of the doctrine that obedience is owed to Caesar–where this meant that morally challenging the king is not necessarily virtuous. On the other hand, once violence is morally ruled out then the case where utter destruction is risked is harder to confront than it would be when a less extreme view of violence is accepted.

It is clear that Augustine and other prominent early Christians saw a need to moderate the emerging doctrine of the laws of war. One prominent criticism is that the early Christians were pacifists while they did not hold any significant political roles but that once kings like Constantine embraced Christianity, Christian apologists abandoned pacifism to allow these kings to continue to wage war as they had before being converted to Christianity. As far as I can see there is no explicit evidence of such a view, although we will end this chapter with examining a few more remarks by Augustine on this topic.

In *The City of God* and other works, Augustine argued that Christians needed to fight against evil in its various forms, including those infidels who refused to hear and embrace the word of the true God.

> justice is found where God, the one supreme God, rules an obedient City according to his grace, forbidding sacrifice to any being save himself alone; and where in consequence the soul rules the body in all who belong to this City and obey God, and the reason faithfully rules the vices in a lawful system of subordination; so that just as the righteous man lives on the basis of faith, which is active in love, so the association, or people, of righteous men lives on the same basis of faith, active in love, the love which a man loves God as God ought to be loved, and loves his neighbor as himself. But where this justice does not exist, there is certainly no "association of men united by a common interest of right and by a community of interest"… And because God does not rule there the general characteristic of that city is that it is devoid of true justice.[230]

---

[230] Augustine, *City of God*, Book 19, Chapter 24, translated by Henry Bettenson, London: Penguin Books, 1972, pp. 890-891.

Notice that here Augustine says that justice does not occur without the people manifesting obedience to both religious and secular authorities.

Yet, there is another important point made by Augustine in the above quotation: Christian love means love of neighbor as well as love of God. Any doctrine of violence or war must be consistent with the idea of love of neighbor. And this explains why the laws of war must be grounded in the idea that we should all be ready to go to the aid of our neighbors. Christianity adds this important idea to what the Greeks and Romans had seen as the possibility of a just war.

A just war for Augustine is grounded in love for one's neighbor as well as for God. When applied to one's neighbor, we get the highly plausible idea that sometimes violence must be used to aid an otherwise defenseless neighbor, whether this is a fellow member of our society, or a people outside our society. But there are possible problems when love of God is said to lead to justified war-making. Here as we will see in later chapters, the very problematic idea of the Crusades was grounded, a highly fraught type of war that saw one's enemies in terms of those who held other religious beliefs than the Christian ones.

Part B:

Islamic and Canon Law

Introduction to Part B

In this part of the text, we examine the two most prominent systems of religious law in the Middle Ages, the Islamic law grounded in the Quran, the Ahadith, and the Sunnah as well as other religious texts, and Canon law grounded in the Gospels and the writing of the Church fathers as well as the various edicts of popes. The central idea is that God's divine law binds believers in certain crucial ways: both concerning rituals, such as daily prayer, but also in terms of certain offenses that are not to be engaged in–with clear otherworldly as well as this-worldly penalties and punishments for the offenders. Sexual and family matters are especially regulated. But in addition, there are special laws for those who have roles within the religion, such as priests or imams or those who dedicate their lives to religious worship.

Certain criminal matters are often covered by these religious laws, and here again we have a mixing of the ideas of sin and crime in ways that will cause us to investigate in more detail how religious law was to be enforced by civil authorities. As is true virtually throughout the Middle Ages, heresy and apostasy were some of the most severely punished crimes. And ideas of penance and confession are also very important to determining how offenders are to be regarded.

In addition, we have a thoroughly world-wide phenomenon of the Christian Crusades and the corresponding jihads waged to counter the crusaders, each of these supported by the religious legal systems of Islam and Catholicism. These wars, which covered several centuries, were occasions for examining and reexamining the laws of war that had been first discussed in ancient Greek and Roman times. In the context of both Islamic and Canon law, the obligation to wage God's war drove masses to join crusades and jihads.

SECTION V:

DIVINE AND NATURAL LAW

CHAPTER 10

DIVINE LAW AND JUSTICE

Islamic law is the law that derives from the Quran and the sayings of Muhammad. Canon law, or ecclesiastical law, is the law of the Catholic Church that derives from the Hebrew Bible, the Gospels, and the edicts of church leaders. Canon law and Islamic law can be at least partially classified as divine laws, that is, laws that derive their authority from God. Islamic and Canon law rose to prominence in approximately the same time–the 7th through 10th centuries CE. As in the case of Talmudic law, Islamic and Canon law govern both matters of religious practice and also matters of family and sexuality as well as other matters of the daily life of members of the Catholic and Islamic religions. As we will see especially in the last chapter of this part of the book, Islamic and Canon law also played a prominent role in how to view non-believers, both as a matter of conversion but also as a matter of lethal confrontation. The material we will survey somewhat overlaps with the legal materials of Germanic and Byzantine law, although we will focus now on the explicitly religious laws or laws which derive from religious sources.

In the first section of this chapter I will set out the way divine law is characterized in Islamic and Canon law. In the second section I will explain the ways that divine law is connected to the ideas of justice and equity in these early medieval centuries. In the third section we will examine some of the specific sources that are referred to by Islamic and Canon lawyers and religious leaders. In the fourth section we will tackle the often fraught ways that religious and civil law intersected and sometimes clashed. And in the final section we will discuss several significant differences between Islamic and Canon law in the early Medieval period.

I. Ideas of Divine Law

In the Quran's second book we find this account of what is to be contained in the Quran:

> This is the Book in which there is no doubt, a guidance for the reverent, who believe in the Unseen and perform the prayer and spend from that which We have provided them, and who believe in what was sent down to thee, and what was sent down before thee, and who are certain of the Hereafter. It is they who act upon guidance from their Lord, and it is they who shall prosper.[231]

And then in the third book we find that the Quran is placed on the same level of revealed authority as the Bible.

> He sent down the Book upon thee in truth, confirming what was before it, and He sent down the Torah and the Gospel aforetime, as a guidance to mankind… He it is Who has sent down the Book upon thee; therein are signs determined… And none know its interpretation save God and those firmly rooted in knowledge. They say, "We believe in it; all is from the Lord."[232]

The Quran is said to be the revealed word of God, just as is said to be true of the Torah and the Gospels of the New Testament.

The Quran is said to be delivered by God through his angel and memorized by Muhammad. An Islamic scholar of the early 9th century, Al-Shafi'i, summarized the main doctrine of the divine impetus for Islamic legal and political thought. Not only is the Quran divinely revealed but so are the sayings of Muhammad (the Ahadith) as well as his practices (the Sunnah). Laws which emanate from the Quran or from the sayings and practices of Mohammad, are themselves grounded in divine revelation, anchoring Islamic law firmly in divine law.

It is perhaps not surprising that the Canon, or ecclesiastical, law developed especially in the sixth through ninth centuries would also be said to be grounded in divine law. Canon law is defined and explained by Constant Van de Wielin in his *History of Canon Law*, as follows:

> Canon law is a normative system that includes *canones, decreta, decretalia, constitutiones, praecepta, responsiones, rescripta, epistolae*, and legal customs…"Canon" comes from the Greek word *kanon* and means, in its proper sense, the stem of a reed… a rule by which straight lines are drawn…With the rise of Christianity, *kanon* received a new meaning:

---

231 *The Study Quran*, 2:2-2:5, translated and edited by Seyyed Hossein Nasr, NY: HarperCollins, 2015, pp. 13-14.

232 *The Study Quran*, 3.3-3.7, pp. 128-129.

> "commandments of God," or in Latin *regulae fidei* (truth of faith), and *regulae morum* (behavioral rules). *Kanon* also indicates the definitive list of the sacred books containing the truths of faith, the moral and liturgical rules, and especially the unchangeable prayer of the consecration and regulations for priests and monks... Although civil laws are also behavioral rules, the word "canon" was, from the outset, used exclusively for Church laws. The Council of Nicea (325), the first of the Eastern councils (325-869), used this term for the first time.[233]

Canon law was composed of the Bible and pronouncements by church officials who were said to be authoritatively interpreting God's laws. In addition to God's direct pronouncements, either through Moses or Jesus' disciples, Constant Van d Wiel says: "the bishops, as successors to the Apostles, derive their collegial legislative power directly from divine law."[234]

In his book *On the Liturgy*, Amalar of Metz writing in the early 9th century, says of his motivation for his study:

> I, your servant, although the least of all, was once moved by a desire to know the purpose behind the order of our Mass, which we celebrate in accordance with established custom. I was struck even more by the diversity of our celebrations–how sometimes one epistle is read, sometimes two, and other matters that also relate to the other offices. This past summer I found myself as if in a crypt, when a ray of light concerning the matter that I desired shone through the window as far as my small person. Eager with long-lasting hunger, I did not allow fear of my teacher to rein me in, but immediately offered mental thanks to God and wrote what I felt.[235]

The translator of Amalar Metz's work, Eric Knibbs, comments:

> This particular moment of inspiration, must have occurred in the early 820s at the latest but these sentiments were not new or especially exceptional for Amalar... Abbot Peter of Nonantola wrote to ask Amalar for a copy of an earlier Mass commentary. The work has been completed, as Peter puts it,

---

233 Constant Van de Wiel, *History of Canon Law*, Louvain: Peeters Press, 1991, p. 11.

234 History of Canon Law, ibid., p. 16.

235 Amalar of Metz, *On the Liturgy*, Preface 2, edited and translated by Eric Knibbs, Cambridge, MA: Harvard University Press, 2014, vol. I. p. 19.

> "through the dictation of the Holy Spirit." And a decade and a half later, Florus of Lyon reports that, when Amalar was pressed during his trial about the source of his ideas, he responded that he had read them "in his spirit."[236]

Amalar thus seemed to believe that his writings were conveyed to him, as dictation, from God just as Muhammad and his immediate followers characterized their inspiration as well.

In both Islamic and Canon law, there were tribunals that interpreted and applied divine law to particular cases here on earth. Insofar as the judges in these tribunals were religious officials who derived their adjudicatory authority from divine sources the decisions of these tribunals were also seen as at least grounded in divine law even if they were not thought to be themselves instances of divine law.

II. Justice, Equity, and Divine Law

In the Quran we have this simple statement of doctrine: "God bears witness that there is no god but He, as do the angels and the possessors of knowledge, upholding justice."[237] In most cases, justice is identified with upholding God's law in both Islamic and Canon law. Justice is identified with following God's law. Casuistry in Islamic law concerns ferreting out the divine law when the sources of divine law are not clearly applicable to a particular case. Passages in the Quran as well as in the Ahadith are studied carefully to see what is revealed. This is somewhat similar to the way that Canon lawyers studied the Bible as well as the teachings of the Church fathers, especially Augustine, Paul, and Jerome. But when it is unclear what the primary sources of divine law can teach about how to decide a particular case, then justice is served by careful reasoning from analogy, as is true in many systems of law.

According to Seyyed Hossein Nasr, who edited *The Study Quran*, the legislative parts of the Quran, especially the part on women, show a strong concern for justice.

> Establishing and upholding justice in society is a key concern of the Quran. God establishes justice by setting *the Balance* within creation itself (15:19; 55:7; 57:25) by commanding justice among human beings through revelation (7:29; 16:90; 42:17; 57:25) and by weighing deeds in a set balance on the

---

[236] Ibid., p. xx.
[237] *The Study Quran*, 3:18, p. 134.

> Day of Judgment (21:47). In 3:18, God is described as *upholding justice*.[238]

The question then arises about how strictly the sources of divine law must be interpreted. Does a judge or lawyer have discretion to decide cases on the basis of his sense of fairness or is the jurist restricted significantly and not allowed to consider matters from his own intuitions about what is most fair. Put in other words, is there room for considerations of equity in systems of rules that are governed by divine law? And can considerations of equity outweigh sources of divine law when it seems that following divine law will produce counter-intuitive results.

We find that the age-old conflict between justice and equity is also represented in Islamic law. Here is how Abdur Rahim puts it:

> It sometimes happens that a rule of law deduced by the application of analogy to text is in conflict with what has been expressly laid down by some other text, or by the unanimous opinion of the learned. All the four Sunni Schools of Law agree that in such cases the former must give way to the latter. It may happen that the law analogically deduced fails to commend itself to the jurist, owing to its narrowness and in adaptability to the habits and usages of the people and being likely to cause hardships and inconveniences. In that event also according to the Hanafis, a jurist is at liberty to refuse to adopt the law to which analogy points, and to accept instead a rule which in his opinion would better advance the welfare of men and the interest of justice.[239]

The doctrine that allows for such discretion and flexibility is named *istihsan*, and is normally translated as juristic equity.

It should be noted though that the Quran can be cited for the centrality of justice, both civil and religious, that rules out a subjective consideration of equity:

> O you who believe! Be steadfast maintainers of justice, witnesses for God, though it be against yourselves, or your parents and kinsfolk, and whether it be someone rich or poor, for God is nearer unto both. So follow not your caprice, that

[238] Ibid., p. 253.

[239] Abdur Rahim, *The Principles of Muhammadan Jurisprudence*, pp. 163-165.

> you may act justly. If you distort or turn away, truly God is aware of whatsoever you do.[240]

Equity is important but should not overrule justice when the sources of justice are clear. As Nasr puts it commenting on the above passage: "It is not the people's prerogative to bend the laws to achieve what they may consider ultimately just: that would be *following* their *caprice*."[241]

A very similar treatment of the conflict between justice and equity can be found in the Canon law as espoused by Gratian in his *Treatise on Laws*.

> Law [*ius*]–so called because it is just [*iustum*], as no one is said to be a judge [*iudex*] unless he is just. But sometimes something is lawful that is not equitable or just. For example, one whose wife is adulterous may not be promoted, which I understand to mean that he may not if he has relations with her afterwards, for he should not be punished without a fault of his own. Again, it is equitable and just that no one become richer through another's loss. Nevertheless, usucaption and prescription have been instituted contrary to this equity. Again, it is iniquitous that one be punished in place of another, for punishment should not go further than putting right the wrong. But many laws speak against this equity. But you may say that in all these cases a rigor contrary to natural equity has been instituted for a purpose and for the sake of peace or society. But sometimes a rigor contrary to equity has been instituted without a purpose, and then the only reason for it is that the law was written that way.[242]

Gratian here provides an account of the relationship between law and justice as well as between equity and justice that seems to hearken back to Aristotle and Cicero's writings on these topics and seems similar to the Quranic verses as well.

Law, along with strict justice defined as faithfully following the law, comes into conflict with equity, often seen as a moral as well as a legal concept. Equity can call for something less than rigorously maintaining justice. But there is also a wider notion of justice hinted at in these texts, which would encompass equity. In Islamic law, the early

---

[240] *The Study Quran*, 4:135, pp. 252-254.

[241] Ibid., p. 253.

[242] Gratian, *The Treatise on Laws* (Decretum DD 1-20), Distinction One, cc. 2-4, translated by Augustine Thompson, Washington DC: The Catholic University of America Press, 1993, p. 4.

jurists, like Al-Shafi'i have established rules for when one must stick closely to the main sources of divine law and when divergence is allowable. Here are several passages from his *Epistle on Legal Theory*:

> The sum total of legislative statements that God has provided for His creation in His book–concerning those obligations to which He has subjected them, according to what He has foreordained–are several: One type includes what God has stated in the form of an explicit text, like His general obligations to wit… He has provided explicit texts concerning unlawful sexual intercourse, wine-drinking, and the eating of carrion, blood, and swine flesh… Another type of legislative statement includes those matters the obligation of which He has affirmed in His book and then how they are to be performed through the words of His Prophet, like the number of prayers, alms and the times they fall due… Another type of statement includes those things for which God's Emissary has established a practice in respect to which God has provided no explicit text of a rule. In His Book, God has imposed the obligation to obey His Emissary and to abide by his rulings.[243]

In each case, examining the source of divine law can help a jurist decide how much latitude is available for reaching a decision that may favor equitable considerations over strict justice.

Canon law seems to have followed Roman law in how to resolve the conflict between equity and strict justice. Here is how Lord Kames has summarized the Roman idea of equity:

> the judge ought not to interpose, unless he can found his decree upon some rule that is equally applicable to all cases of the kind. If he is under no limitation, his decrees will appear arbitrary, though substantially just–and what is worse, will often be arbitrary and substantially unjust.[244]

Canon lawyers were especially interested in the doctrine of equity, as Cicero understood it.

The Ciceronian idea about equity is that it countenances an exception to the normal bindingness of the law, specifically an "excuse"

[243] Muhammad ibn Idris Al-Shafi'i, *The Epistle on Legal Theory*, edited and translated by Joseph Lowry, NY: New York University Press, 2013, p. 15.

[244] Lord Kames, Henry Home, *Principles of Equity*, London: Alex, Lawrie, and Co., 1765, p. 13.

for not following the law. Here is a concise statement by Cicero of his position on the honorableness of appeals to equity:

> He will point out that there is no law which requires the performance of any inexpedient or unjust act; that all penalties provided by law were established to punish wickedness or vice… After all, he will ask his opponents: "Suppose that I had so and so; suppose that so and so had happened–mentioning any of those acts for which there is a most honorable excuse or a certain plea of necessity–would you still accuse me?" But the law makes no exception. Therefore all cases are not covered by exceptions, expressed in writing, but some that are self-evident are covered by exceptions understood but not expressed.[245]

The law makes no explicit exceptions and should in that sense be interpreted strictly, and yet it is counter-intuitive to ignore self-evident exceptions that must be allowed for the law to be considered itself to be just, now understood in the broad sense that encompasses equity.

III. Sources of Law

Here are how Islamic sources of law are characterized by one scholar, Abdur Rahim:

> The primary source of laws in the Muhammadan system is revelation. Revelation has been of two kinds–manifest and internal. Manifest revelation consisted in communications which were made by the angel Gabriel, under the direction of God, to Muhammad either (1) in the very words of God, or (2) by hints, and (3) of such knowledge as occurred in the mind of the Prophet through the inspiration of God. Internal revelation consisted in the opinions of the Prophet embodied in the form of ratiocination and delivered from time to time on questions that happened to be raised before him. The Quran is composed of such manifest revelations as were made in the very words of God. Matters which formed the subject of manifest revelation by hints from Gabriel, or by inspiration, or of internal revelation are known as Ahadith (plural of hadith) i.e., precepts or traditions.[246]

---

[245] Cicero, *De Inventione*, II.XLVII, in *Cicero II*, translated by H. M. Hubbell, Cambridge, MA: Harvard University Press, 1949, pp. 307-309.
[246] Abdur Rahim, *The Principles of Muhammadan Jurisprudence*, London: Luzak & Co., 1911, p. 69.

The Quran and the Ahadith are the foundational sources of the Islamic law.

The Ahadith are understood as filling gaps that existed in the legal provisions of the Quran. In this respect the Ahadith are fully equivalent to the Quran as sources of law. Other sources of Islamic law are not granted this status, and this includes the sayings of the most famous of the disciples of Muhammad and later experts in Islamic jurisprudence. This is true even though these other sources have some claim to be divinely inspired as well. Of the immediate successors of Muhammad, Al-Shafi'i is considered one of the most important sources of law. Al-Shafi'i is the founder of one of the four early medieval schools of Islamic jurisprudence. The other three schools of jurisprudence are those founded by Hanafi, Maliki, and Hanbali, respectively. Al-Shafi'i is considered to have been the most moderate in terms of how strict a believer must adhere to the word of the Quran.

Much of Islamic legal reasoning involves analogies drawn from past cases where a rule has been successfully applied. There is much discussion in the early Islamic legal texts about how to resolve differences among the various sources of Islamic law. As Al-Shafi'i tells us, it matters if there are conflicting rules or if the sources are silent about what is the law for a particular case. Here is how Joseph Schacht puts it in his *An Introduction to Islamic Law*:

> Although Islamic law is 'sacred law,' it is by no means essentially irrational; it was created not by an irrational process of continuous revelation but by a rational method of interpretation, and the religious standards and moral rules which were introduced into the legal subject-matter provided the framework for its structural order… One of the most striking features of traditional Islamic law is the casuistical method which is closely connected with the structure of its legal concepts, and both are the outcome of an analogical, as opposed to an analytical, way of thinking which pervades the whole of it. Islamic law represents an extreme case of 'jurists' law'; it was created and developed by private specialists; legal science and not the state plays the part of a legislator, and scholarly handbooks have the force of law.[247]

Islamic law is both divinely inspired law and also law that proceeds by analogy from previous cases. We will have occasion to explore these

[247] Joseph Schacht, *An Introduction to Islamic Law*, Oxford: Oxford University Press, 1982, pp. 4-5.

features of Islamic law later but at the moment we should note that the analogical reasoning allowed for the non-rigid application of divinely inspired texts to new cases.

In the tradition of Canon law, we find a host of sources that like the Islamic sources had to be reconciled with each other and for which controversies arose about how to handle new cases not directly covered by the Canonical sources. Here is a passage from the English Abbot Aelfric's *Pastoral Epistle* that partially resembles the Islamic views we have just summarized:

> Three periods are reckoned in this world. One period was before God's law, in the time of the Patriarchs, who were of yore. The second, under God's law in the time of Moses and the prophets. The third under Christ's own grace, in the Christian time, after Christ's advent… the Almighty God, in the time of Moses, the great leader, established, as a guide to mankind, the five books in which is God's law; and Moses wrote them, and commanded mankind… Then at last, verily, the righteous Christ himself, the Son of Almighty God, who created all things, came into this world with real humanity… himself giving example.[248]

Here is a statement of sources of Canon law from the tenth century that traces back to God's law delivered to Moses and contained in the five books of the Hebrew Bible, and also includes the teaching and example of Jesus, as recorded in the Gospels.

In the Canon law tradition there were the old and new testaments of the Bible along with the various accounts of the sayings and example of Jesus. In addition, there were increasing numbers of Papal pronouncements and writings by Church fathers who, like Islamic legal scholars, also laid claim to be sources of divinely-inspired law. And controversy similarly arose when these texts, even though they were divinely inspired, seemed to conflict when applied to particular cases.

IV. Religious and Civil Law

Islamic law is a mixture of religious and civil law as even a cursory reading of the Quran will demonstrate. It is much less clear that

---

[248] Abbott Aelfric, "Aelfric's Pastoral Epistle," in *Ancient Laws and Institutes of England*, edited by Benjamin Thorpe, Cambridge: Cambridge University Press, 1840, vol. II, p. 367.

Canon law is also a mixture of religious and civil law. Yet this is indeed the case, as we will see in this section. In this respect we can once again see a parallel between Rabbinic law on the one hand and Islamic and Canon law on the other. In all three systems of law, the main area of law where religious and civil laws overlap concerns family and sexuality matters. But it is also true that some criminal matters are addressed in all three systems of law as well. Indeed, as with earlier medieval law, the ideas of sin and crime are often mixed in ways that make distinguishing them very difficult.

Parts of the Quran are legislative in nature such as concern "women and their rights along with various conditions of marriage, marital relations, and the law of inheritance" and also concerning rights and obligations as involving war and peace. Indeed, the fourth book of the Quran concerns all of these matters and Nasr says that this book is considered "among the most important and fundamental for Islamic jurisprudence."[249]

One of the nine volumes of the Ahadith prepared by Al-Bukhari, who edited the Ahadith during the 9th century, is largely taken up with criminal matters. We will devote much time to this work in later chapters, but it is useful to see some of the ways that early Islamic law dealt with criminal matters such as killing. Here are some selections from Book 87 in volume 9 of Al-Bukhari's edition of the Ahadith:

> O you who believe! *Al-Qisas* (the Law of Equality in Punishment) is prescribed for you in case of murder: The free for the free; the slave for the slave; the female for the female. But if the killer is forgiven by the brother (or the relatives) of the killed against blood-money, then adhering to it with fairness and payment of the blood-money should be made to the heir in fairness. This is an alleviation and mercy from our Lord. So after this, whoever transgresses the limits (i.e. kills the killer after taking the blood-money) he shall have a painful torment
>
> To question the killer till he confesses; and confession in cases where Divinely prescribed punishments are imperative.[250]

The determination of what to do with a killer and how to assess his or her guilt was one of the main matters of Islamic law.

---

[249] *The Study Quran*, translated and edited by S. H. Nasr et al, p. 188.

[250] *Ahadith: The Translation of the Meaning of Sahih Al-Bukhari*, hadith 6875, translated by Muhammad Muhsin Khan, Riyadh, Saudi Arabia: Maktaba Dar us Salam, 2015, vol. 9, pp. 18-19.

In 802, Charlemagne issued a Capitulary that attempted to set the boundaries between religious and civil law proclaiming that the clergy should follow Canon law, even as it also proclaimed that the emperor could adjudicate matters of religious as well as civil law. Here are some brief selections from the *Capitulary of Charlemagne*:

> let no one, through his cleverness or astuteness–as many are accustomed to do–dare to oppose the written law, or the sentence passed upon him, or to prevail against the churches of God… The monastic clergy should altogether observe in their actions a canonical mode of living, far removed from turpid gains; nuns should keep diligent guard over their lives; laymen and secular clergy should make proper use of their privileges without malicious fraud; all should live together in mutual charity…[251]

Here we see that Charlemagne sets the law for clergy and laymen alike, even as he recognizes that the clergy will be bound by canon law and the laymen by civil law. Charlemagne continues the argument in his Capitulary:

> every man in his whole kingdom–ecclesiastic or layman, each according to his vow and calling–who had previously promised fealty to him as king should now make this promise to him as emperor…[252]

Here we see that clergy and laymen all owe fealty to the emperor.

And then in Charlemagne's Capitulary we see how ideas of sin and crime are intermingled:

> the guilty man shall make no delay in paying the wergeld. When, moreover, through the influence of sin, this shall have happened, that any one shall have slain his brothers or his relative, he shall straightaway submit himself to the penance imposed, according as his bishop decides and without any circumvention.[253]

---

[251] Emperor Charlemagne, "Capitulary of the Emperor Charlemagne," in *A Reader of Medieval Laws, Edicts, and Orders*, translated by E. F. Henderson, Washington, DC: Madison and Monroe Press, 2013, p. 148-149.
[252] Ibid., p. 149.
[253] Ibid., pp. 155-156.

Bishops are to issue punishments for killings. Indeed, we find the curious pronouncement that "bishops, abbots, and abbesses, shall have bailiffs and sheriffs and judges skilled in the law" where they are "on no account … to depart from the model of the canons or the rule."[254] So, there will be Canon law judges and even sheriffs under the direction of the bishops, but ultimately subject to Charlemagne, just as is true of lay sheriffs and judges.

A battle was to rage between the emperors and bishops over who was responsible to whom. But there is no dispute that bishops had the authority to adjudicate such criminal matters as that concerning killing, as well as matters of family affairs, sexuality, and inheritance, and to do so according to principles of Canon law at the time of Charlemagne in the early 9th century.

V. The Divine Origin of Islamic and Canon Law

The Quran incorporates many of the ideas of the Torah into its text, but does not recognize the Christian idea that Jesus was the son of God, and so the ideas of the New Testament do not feature prominently in the Quran. Jesus is said to be one of the Prophets, a group that is said to end with Muhammad, the last Prophet. So, it can be said that the Quran and at least the so-called Old Testament share in common the idea that these books are the revealed word of a monotheist God–the divine law of Islam and Canon law is said to derive from the same source: God's revealed word. Canon law also recognizes the revealed word of the so-called New Testament but Islamic lawyers did not accept the New Testament teachings as anything other than the word of a good person and his followers. Canon lawyers did not recognize the teaching of the Quran as revealed authority either. So, there certainly are differences between Islamic and Canon law in terms of how the sources of divine law were understood. The question addressed in the final section of this chapter is whether such differences and others made a major difference in the accepted law of the Canonists and Islamists.

One possibility, sometimes articulated by scholars, is that the reason Islamic law is more Draconian than Canon or Ecclesiastical law was that the humane foundation of the New Testament, i.e., "love thy neighbor as thyself," is not recognized in Islamic law. But while many clerics and emperors espoused the New Testament doctrine of love, it is not clear at all that in practice their laws were more humane than those of

---

254 Ibid., p. 151.

Islam. In this respect it might be useful to compare in a preliminary way the laws concerning adultery in Canon and Islamic law, a topic I will explore in greater detail in a later Chapter 13.

Initially, it appears that the punishment of death by stoning for a woman who is convicted of adultery can be found in both Canon and Islamic law leading to the conclusion that these systems of divinely inspired law are not that different in terms of humaneness. While there is some support for the idea of stoning to death as a punishment for adultery, there are other passages in the Quran that are more measured. Here we can cite verse 24:2–"As for the adulterer and the adulteress, flog them each one hundred lashes, and let not pity for them overcome you concerning God's Judgment."[255]

A long footnote in the Study Quran that accompanies verse 24:2 takes up the evidence from the Ahadith that adulterers are to be stoned. As the commentary says, the major problems are twofold. First, when there is a passage as clear as verse 24:2, a hadith would not normally be thought to overrule the Quran.

> The central legal problem pertaining to stoning to death for adultery is that 24:2 lays out a clear and detailed punishment for adultery, describing how and by whom the punishment is to be carried out, while making no mention of stoning or distinguishing between married and unmarried persons. In Islamic jurisprudence, abrogating or partly overturning an unambiguous text of the Quran requires a high standard for evidence–and it is only possible if one accepts that a hadith can abrogate a part of the Quran, a view rejected by most religious authorities.[256]

The authority of the Ahadith mainly concerns the filling of gaps left unaddressed in the Quran, not overturning something that is straightforwardly addressed as in the case of verse 24:2, which calls for flogging rather than stoning as punishment for adultery.

The second problem is that the non-Quranic texts are not consistent in saying that stoning is the punishment for adultery.

> With respect to the relevant Ahadith, the various versions of individual stoning accounts–such as that of Malik–often contradict each other on important details and contain errors and inconsistencies, such as misquotations from the Torah…

[255] *The Study Quran*, 24:2, p. 865.

[256] *The Study Quran*, note on 24:2, p. 866.

> There are moreover, substantial incongruities… some speculate that those incidents of stoning [by Muhammad], even if taken as historical events, took place before the revelation of 24:2 and thus 24:2 is the final and abrogating punishment for adultery…[257]

So, while there is difference of opinion it can at very least be said that the Islamic law does not unambiguously call for stoning of adulterers.

In Canon law, there is often not as detailed a treatment of a topic as in Islamic legal scholarship. Often, the first place to start is with the Torah. And here we can clearly see the difference between Islamic law and Canon law. Leviticus verse 20:10-14 says:

> If a man commits adultery with the wife of his neighbor, both the adulterer and adulteress shall be put to death… If a man takes a wife and her mother also, it is a depravity, they shall be burned to death, both he and they, that there may be no depravity among you.[258]

Here the Torah punishment of death for adultery is clearly less humane than the sentence of one hundred lashes for adultery in the Quran.

The Gospel according to Luke says simply, "Anyone who divorces his wife and marries another commits adultery and whoever marries a woman divorced from her husband commits adultery."[259] The latter punishment for such crimes is excommunication, clearly more humane yet than the Torah or the Quran, but there is evidence that civil authorities were much harsher. As the following chapters unfold, we will have greater occasion to see what differences there are between the religious texts that also have many pieces of legislation in them.

---

[257] *The Study Quran*, note on 24:2; p. 867.

[258] *The Study Bible* (New Revised Standard Edition), edited by Wayne A. Meeks, NY: Harper Collins, 1989, p. 181.

[259] *The Study Bible*, p. 1796.

CHAPTER 11

REASON AND NATURE

In Islamic and Canon law, as we have seen, divine law was the most authoritative source of human law. And texts that displayed the direct word of God, such as the Quran or the Bible, were considered to be the direct word of God. Legislation contained in these texts was the highest and most authoritative source of law. But these texts did not contain a comprehensive set of legislative acts covering all cases of human behavior that may come before a court for adjudication. If Islamic or Canon law was restricted to legislation contained in the Quran or the Bible most acts would not be covered by law. Seeing the need for additional sources of law, other than the direct word of God, Islamic and Canon lawyers argued that judges should be able to extrapolate from the divine law to cover cases that were not strictly speaking covered by that law. In both traditions, reason and nature were appealed to as additional sources of law for cases not covered by the direct word of God. We will explore these sources and the arguments about them in this chapter. I will once again argue that there are more commonalities than divergences between Islamic and Canon law on these issues.

Medieval legal and political thought, especially Catholic legal thought, developed new ways to understand the ancient idea of natural law as a source of law that filled in when divine law was silent. And natural law was closely linked with human reason as a source of law–this was true of early Islamic legal thought even more so than early ecclesiastical or Canon law. It is well accepted that divine law was linked to natural law in Medieval Catholic legal thought. It is controversial at best even to talk of natural law in the context of Medieval Islamic legal thought. But the crucial link is in the way that both traditions discuss the role of reason as a source of law.

I will begin this chapter by discussing the role of reason in Islamic legal thought, especially in the work of Al-Shafi‘i. Then in the second section I discuss the role of reason in Canon law, especially in the work of Gratian. In the third section I discuss the idea of nature as a source of law in Canon law. In the fourth section I discuss the controversial idea that Islamic law also in a sense can be seen as supporting an idea of natural law, or at least the idea that nature can provide reason for sources of law. In the final section I discuss some differences between Islamic and Canon law on the topic of reason and nature as sources of law.

I. The Idea of Reason as a Source of Islamic Law

In the 9th century Islamic text, *The Epistle on Legal Theory*, Al-Shafi'i discusses an example that commentators have seen to be especially apt in understanding how gaps in the divine law are to be filled. The example is how Muslims are to conform to the Quranic injunction that they should face toward the Kasbah in Mecca when praying. When Muslims lived in Mecca and could see the Kasbah it was easy to understand how to conform to the Quranic injunction about where to face when praying. But for those Muslims who could not see the Kasbah, and especially those Muslims who lived quite far from Mecca, it was a problem because the Quran did not explain how a Muslim could figure out where he or she should face when praying.

Here are some passages from Al-Shafi'i's *The Epistle of Legal Theory* for us to consider at the beginning of our discussion of what to do when divine law needed to be supplemented.

> Thus, He indicated to them (sublime His praise) that if they were distant from the Sacred Mosque itself, a correct result would be arrived at through interpretation, an obligation which He imposed on them in conjunction with the intellects He placed in them, which can distinguish between things and their opposites, and those signs that He set up for them apart from the Sacred Mosque itself, toward which he commanded them to face. So He said: "He placed the stars for you, for you to be guided by them in the darkness of land and sea" and "And signs. And men can guide themselves by the stars." These signs consisted of mountains, night, and day; winds of well-known names even though their directions might differ; and the rising of the sun, the moon, and stars, risings whose locations within the heavens were well known. God obligated them to use interpretation in order to face toward the Sacred Mosque, indicating its direction for them as I have described. And so long as they engaged in such interpretation, they did not abandon God's command (sublime His praise).He did not

> allow them to pray in whatever direction they wished when the Sacred Mosque itself lay distant from them.[260]

The idea of interpretation is here seen as a type of intellect "which can distinguish between things." We also see that the intellect is something God has "placed in them" and which can be a source of law as ultimately derived from God. We should also note something that will be of crucial importance later in our chapter that the intellect or reason is to operate on natural objects such as moon and stars in order to fill in the command to face Mecca's Sacred Mosque when praying.

In addition, Al-Shafi'i discussed the role of inference and analogical reasoning in his *Epistle* as sources of law for Muslims as supplements to the Quran. Here is another passage from Al-Shafi'i's *Epistle*:

> Thus did He inform them of His decree: "Does man think he will be left without guidance?" "Without guidance means to be neither commanded to do something nor prohibited from doing something. This all indicates that no one other than God's Emissary may pronounce on the law except by means of inference, as I have just described, or on what makes someone just such that they may be appointed a witness, or on the legal equivalent of game wrongly killed. Neither may anyone express opinions based on subjective interpretation, since to do so is to pronounce according to mere preference, something that is simply invented and not based on a prior example. Included in the foregoing category are rulings in regard to which God (blessed and exalted) indicated for His creatures the way to determine a correct result based on appearances only.[261]

This is an important passage for several reasons. We find Al-Shafi'i distinguishing between subjective and objective interpretation. Judges are not left unguided to use their own preferences when deciding cases that do not fall squarely within the legislation of the Quran. Interpretation is understood in terms of inference and analogical reasoning that proceeds from God's divine commands. Interpretation is not untethered from the divine word of God for Al-Shafi'i.

---

[260] Muhammad ibn Idris Al-Shafi'i, *Epistle on Legal Theory*, edited and translated by Joseph E. Lowry, New York: New York University Press, 2013, p. 17.

[261] Al-Shafi'i, *The Epistle on Legal Theory*, ibid., p. 19.

Legal interpretation is not based on the mere opinions of the judge, even when there is no clear legislation in the Quran that is on point. For Al-Shafi‘i, God has given an indirect way to arrive at correct judgments that remains centered in divine law even if it is only indirectly connected rather than directly connected as is the Quran or the Ahadith. Yet, there is also another way that reason can lead a judge to a proper disposition of a particular case, what Al-Shafi‘i calls consensus.

It is a tenet of Islamic legal thought that God would not allow for a situation where Islamic legal scholars are in agreement about how a certain case should be treated or about a guiding legal principle, and yet treatment of the case or principle is somehow wrong. From what we have already seen, one possible explanation for the acceptance of consensus as a source of Islamic law is that God has imprinted in each person the means for ascertaining, through reason, what is the objective as opposed to the subjective interpretation of the legal obligations of Muslims.

Muhammad Baqir as-Sadr has written lucidly about the principles of Islamic Jurisprudence that can be found throughout Islamic legal thought. Here is a passage from his discussion of the primary procedural principle:

> We intend now to study the commonly shared elements in another situation that arises in derivation, that in which the jurist failed to attain a substantiating argument which indicates a divine-law ruling, the ruling [proper] remaining unascertainable. In this situation, investigation turns toward an attempt to determine a practical position vis-à-vis that unascertainable ruling as a substitute for the discovery of the ruling itself…We must see whether this starting point imposes on us precaution in the situation of doubt and lack of an argument for the prohibition [of smoking] or not. In order to recur to the starting point which obedience to the Master, praised be He, imposes on us, we must determine that starting point. What is the starting point that obedience to the Lawgiver imposes on us and that is mandatory for us to consult concerning our position? The answer is that this starting point is reason, because a human being understands through reason that God, praised be He, has a rightful claim to the obedience of his servants… If reason is what imposes obedience to the Lawgiver on the basis of His rightful claim to obedience, then it is mandatory to have recourse to reason in determining the answer to the question posed… The correct view in our opinion is that the source of law in the case of every injunction that is possible [but not definitely known] is precaution, as a result of the inclusion of possible injunctions in the rightful

> claim of obedience. For reason understands that the Master has a rightful claim of obedience from human beings not in known injunctions alone, but in possible injunctions as well…[262]

When divine law does not provide a principle that is clearly binding in a given situation, such as whether smoking is prohibited by Islamic law, Muslims should proceed with caution and employ reason to ascertain the best possible injunction that could be supported by the Quran and other divine sources. Given that there are many things that are not explicitly prohibited by the Quran or by the Ahadith, in this way reason must be employed and plays a significant role in Islamic law.

There is a wrinkle that is added by the analysis of Muhammad Baqir as-Sadr that we must finally consider. Some divine texts urge that caution need not be shown.

> The primary [procedural] principle, then, is the priority of precaution. [But] the basic procedural principle has been inverted by a ruling of the Lawgiver into a secondary procedural principle, the priority of exemption which advocates the non-mandatoriness of precaution. The cause of this inversion is that we know by way of a clear divine-law proclamation that the Lawgiver is not concerned with possible injunctions to the degree that precaution is required of the legal agent. Rather, He is satisfied with the abandonment of precaution. The argument for the inversion is to be found in numerous divine-law prooftexts. One of the most famous of these is the prophetic prooftext [a hadith from Muhammad] "My religious community is relieved of that which they do not know." [The priority of exemption] can even be inferred from some verses of the Quran, as when God Most High says "We do not punish until [after] We send a Messenger" (XVII: 15). "Messenger" is understood to imply a clear statement and a [substantiating] argument. The verse shows that there is no punishment without an argument. In this way the [effective] procedural principle becomes that precaution is not mandatory, taking the point of departure to be exemption based on divine law rather than engagement [i.e., precaution] based on reason.[263]

We learn here that reason is a source of Islamic law but only in those cases where Quranic verses and Ahadith are absent.

---

[262] Muhammad Baqir as-Sadr, *Lessons in Islamic Jurisprudence*, translated by Yoy Parviz Mottahedeh, Oxford: One World Publishers, 2003, pp. 119-121.
[263] Ibid., pp. 123-124.

II. Reason as a Source of the Canon Law

In Distinction Eight of Gratian's *Treatise on Laws* (the first part of his *Decretum*) we find the following statements:

> The Lord said in the Gospel of [John 14:6], "I am the Truth." He did not say, "I am custom." And so, when truth has become manifest, let custom yield to truth…
> Also, in On Baptism against the Donatists, IV, III:
> Custom opposes reason in vain.
> "In vain," he says, "do these defeated by reason advance custom against us, as if custom were greater than truth, and as if something that the Holy Spirit has revealed to be better in spiritual affairs should not be done." It is clearly true that reason and truth are to be preferred to custom. But when truth supports custom, nothing should be embraced more firmly.[264]

When reason is employed properly it leads us to the truth, and the truth is a firmer guide to right conduct and also a source of law, even than customs of longstanding duration. The idea is that right reason leads to "manifest truth." As we will later see, right reason is firmly linked to natural law for Gratian and for Catholic legal and political theorists generally in the Medieval period.

In Distinction Eleven of Gratian's *Treatise on Laws* we find these additional statements about the importance of reason:

> Custom yields to ordinances according to Isidore in *Synonyms*, II.
> Evil practice is overturned by reason and ordinance.
> Let practice yield to authority; let ordinance and reason vanquish bad practice…
> The authority of longstanding custom and practice is not insignificant; but the power is certainly not of such moment as to prevail over either reason or ordinance.[265]

There is here a kind of battle envisioned where reason is able to prevail over custom when the two are in conflict.

Notice that reason rightly employed is a source of law stronger than even the strong custom of longstanding duration. At least in part this

---

[264] Gratian, *The Treatise on Laws* (Decretum DD. 1-20), DD 8, translated by Augustine Thompson, Washington, DC: Catholic University of America Press, 1993, pp. 27.

[265] Gratian, *The Treatise on Laws* (Decretum DD. 1-20), DD 11, pp. 37-38.

is because God has given us the power to ferret out which customs and practices are evil. In this sense, reason operates by the grace of God, and is God's way of leading to the truth even when the direct word of God is either unclear or is silent on a given matter. Later Medieval theorists, such as Thomas Aquinas, will link right reason even more strongly to natural law than what we have here from Gratian, writing more than a century before Aquinas.

We can then turn briefly to the letters of Pope Gregory IX for elucidation of the status of reason. Gregory, as an author of the Decretals, tells us that custom must conform to reason if it is to count as law: "the theory of the Decretals is clear–namely, that custom, if it is "*rationabilis et legitime prescripta*," that is, if it is not contrary to "reason" and it has continued for a legally defined period of time, overrides even written positive law."[266] What is unclear is whether "contrary to reason" is to be understood as unreasonable or as more strictly failing in its logic or reasoning. One hypothesis is that legal scholars tended to talk in terms of logic and reason whereas Popes and other Church leaders tended to talk in terms of a looser notion of reasonableness.

Let me just say a bit more about the difference between reason as logic and reason as reasonableness. Reasonableness is what a person of a certain character would decide in a given case. This is the standard today as lawyers in the Anglo-American legal tradition appeal to the intuitions of the jurors. Jurors are not supposed to be experts in reasoning such as logicians are. Rather jurors are supposed simply to employ their common sense and think about how an unbiased member of their society would reach a decision. This idea of reasonableness seems to be of later vintage than the texts we are considering in the Medieval period. But some of the statements of Popes seem to look for the "jury" sense of reasonableness rather than the "logician" sense of reason.

III. Nature in Early Islamic Thought

One way to understand natural law is that it blends together morality and law–both are part of God's law governing human behavior. The Quran, as was true of the Torah and the Gospels, does not often distinguish between what is morally wrong and what is illegal. Both morality and legality are part of the natural order. In Islamic as well as Canonist legal thought not following God's law is sometimes referred to

---

[266] A. J. Carlyle, *A History of Medieval Political Theory in the West*, Vol. II, London: William Blackwood & Sons LTD, 1909, pp. 194-195,

as sin and other times as crime. Rules governing family life and sexuality are especially important in Islam and in Canon law–indeed, the rules governing these domains are often talked about as mandating that a traditional or natural way is the right way.

Early Islamic legal theorists grappled with how to understand the relationship between ideas of legality and morality. Here is how Abdur Rahim puts it:

> When a juristic act is the subject of a prohibitive command, it is affected according to Al-Shafi'i in the same way as a prohibited act. But according to the Hanafis, prohibition of a juristic act prima facie means that it is not bad *per se*, but by reason of something else, unless it appears to be otherwise. When an act is found to be prohibited as being bad per se, it is legally void according to all. If it is prohibited by reason of something which is a quality of the act itself, or because of some concomitant circumstance, the act is regarded as legally correct in its essence, and the prohibition is taken to apply to that quality or circumstance. When the prohibition refers to a quality of the act, the act is vitiated as faulty and if to a concomitant circumstance it is abominable.[267]

Here the religious obligation and the legal obligation are mixed in ways it is difficult, although surely not impossible, to disentangle.

Certain acts in Islamic law are simply abominable–what Canon law would call unnatural–and those acts are per se wrong and illegal as well. But many other acts can have different responses from a religious as opposed to a legal point of view. "Whatever the force of the objection from a strictly religious point of view, the principle of law in its secular aspect necessitates, in such cases, the distinction between legal operativeness of a transaction and the religious responsibility of the person entering into it."[268]

As we saw in Section I, Al-Shafi'i discussed how reason was to operate to fill in gaps in the direct word of God found in the Quran. In trying to ascertain which direction was Mecca's Sacred Mosque, the Kasbah, Muslims were to use their reason in reference to the positioning of the stars and the moon, as well as the rising and setting sun. Here is how Wael B. Hallaq describes Al-Shafi'i's views:

---

[267] Abdur Rahim, *The Principles of Muhammadan Jurisprudence*, London: Luzak & Co., 1911, p. 108.

[268] Ibid., p. 109.

> Al- Shafi'i argues that in their prayer Muslims are commanded to face the Kasbah even when beyond the range of their sight. They are under the obligation to attempt to discover the direction of the Holy Site by seeking, through the exercise of their mental faculties, indications and signs which might lead them to know that direction. For after all, he maintains, God has stated that he has created stars, mountains, rivers, light, darkness, etc. and that Muslims may be guided by them.[269]

Muslims are under an obligation to use reason in conjunction with nature to discover how to satisfy their religious obligations.

One scholar, Anver M. Emon, offers the controversial thesis that some early Islamic legal theories should be classed as natural law theories.

> Their theoretical approaches show how nature as a bounty to humanity is fixed and not vulnerable to divine "change of mind" ...Generally under Hard Natural Law, fact and value are fused in nature, thereby rendering nature a normative foundation for reasoned deliberation about the good and the bad and, by implication, for Shari'a obligations and prohibitions. Hard Natural Law jurists presumed that nature is deliberately created by a just God who creates the world to benefit humanity. They justified their presumption by referring to the Quranic verse that states: "[God] created for you [mankind] all that is in the earth. Hard Naturalist jurists denied that God would create the world with no purpose...[270]

Emon goes further than theorists like Hallaq in claiming that reasoning about nature was not only a way to fill in gaps in Islamic law, but also in providing independent normative authority for Muslims.

One of the problems in discussing Islamic legal theory in terms of natural law is that there is no term used in Islamic writings that could be identified with natural law. In addition, natural law theory is well entrenched in Western legal thought, starting with the Roman philosopher Cicero but really beginning already among the ancient Greeks. The term and underlying concept of natural law is key to understanding Catholic writers throughout the Medieval period as well. Nonetheless, scholars such as Emon have made an interesting case for thinking of Islamic legal

---

[269] Wael B. Hallaq, *A History of Islamic Legal Theories*, Cambridge: Cambridge University Press, 1997, p. 23.

[270] Anver M. Emon, *Islamic Natural Law Theories*, Oxford: Oxford University Press, 2010, pp. 40-41.

thought in terms of natural law, even though it is clear that this is a minority view within Islamic legal scholarship.

IV. Gratian and the Natural Law

In Distinction One of his Decretum, Gratian begins, as we have seen, by discussing the relationship between natural law and divine commands of God.

> The human race is ruled by two things, namely, natural law and usages. Natural law is what is contained in the Law of the Gospel. By it each person is commanded to do to others what he wants done to himself and prohibited from inflicting on others what he does not want done to himself. So, Christ said in the Gospel: "Whatsoever you want men to do to you, do so to them. This is indeed the Law of the Prophets.
> Thus Isidore says in Etymologies, V. II:
> Divine ordinances are established by nature, human ordinances by usages.
> All ordinances are either divine or human. Divine ordinances are determined by nature, human ordinances by usages; and thus the latter vary, since different things please different people.
> Morality is divine ordinance. Law is human ordinance.[271]

Here it seems that Gratian virtually equates divine law with natural law. He seems to follow Isidore rather than Cicero or Gaius. Natural law is divine in origin but creates moral prohibitions not ones that are "legal" he says.

Isidore, in his *Etymologies*, draws a close connection between divine and natural law.

> All laws are either divine or human. Divine laws are based on nature, human laws on customs. For this reason human laws may differ, because different laws suit different peoples. *Fas* is divine law; jurisprudence (*ius*) is human law. To cross a stranger's property is allowed by divine law; it is not allowed by human law… Furthermore, if law is based on reason, then law will be everything that is consistent with reason–provided that it agrees with religion, accords with orderly conduct, and is conductive to well-being… Natural law (*ius naturale*) is

[271] Gratian, *The Treatise on Laws* (Decretum DD. 1-20), DD 1, pp. 3-4.

> common to all nations, and because it exists everywhere by the instinct of nature, it is not upheld by any regulation.[272]

Here divine law and natural law are virtually the same, but natural law is also said to be what is common to all nations. Natural law is not written since it is common to all nations, but then one wonders what kind of law it is–is it merely moral law as Gratian says?

It seems that for both Isidore and Gratian to say that natural law is mere morality misses something important. People are obligated to obey natural law because it comes from a divine source and, in any event, is found to be common to all nations. In this sense it is binding on each person who is in a nation and that presumably means everyone. Yet, even though the natural law is imprinted into the hearts of each person, some people still fail to follow that law and are in need of other rules in order to do as God has commanded.[273] Natural law is real law, even more so than human made legislation, but it is motivated as all of morality is motivated–from within the conscience of each person. There is not the external force that is found in secular law.

Canon lawyers like Gratian see natural law as the embodiment of God's law and as superior to human law found in custom. Here is how A. J. Carlyle puts it:

> It is evident to any student that the principles of the canonists as to the nature of law are derived from Roman law; but–and this is a fact of importance–it is derived from Roman law through St. Isidore of Seville... Law must be agreeable to nature, just, devised for the common good, must represent the custom of the country in which it is to be in force. That is, to express this in broader terms, law is not an arbitrary command imposed by a superior, but rather represents the adaptation of the permanent and immutable principles of "nature" and justice to the needs of a community, under the terms of the circumstances and traditions of that community.[274]

Carlyle makes the point even clearer when he says:

---

[272] Isidore of Seville, *The Etymologies*, translated by Stephen A. Barney, et al, Cambridge: Cambridge University Press, 2006, p. 117.

[273] See A. J. Carlyle, *A History of Medieval Political Theory in the West*, Vol. I, London: William Blackwood & Sons LTD, 1909, p. 105.

[274] A. J. Carlyle, *A History of Medieval Political Theory in the West*, Vol. II, London: William Blackwood & Sons LTD, 1909, pp. 96-97.

> To the medieval canonists then, as to the Fathers, the *jus naturale* is identical with the law of God, it is embodied in the "law and the Gospel," for it represents the general moral principles which God has implanted in human nature, and it is, in its essential character, immutable... The *jus naturale* is to the canonists the norm by which any law of institutions must be tried.[275]

The reference to "nature" in natural law is to "human nature"–where God has written his law, and where humans could look to gain knowledge of the unchanging divine law to which all other laws must conform.

Canon or ecclesiastical law is a form of human law that is promulgated largely by religious leaders of the Church–but they like their civil law cousins must conform to natural law. Here is Gratian's account of canon law:

> As an enactment is either civil or ecclesiastical, and that of the civil forum or civil law is a civil enactment, let us examine what an ecclesiastical enactment is. An ecclesiastical enactment is called a canon... some canons are decrees of pontiffs, others are statues of councils. Some councils are universal, others provincial. Some provincial councils are held by the authority of the Roman pontiff, that is to say, with a legate of the holy Roman Church present...[276]

Just as civil law provides rules for humans to direct them toward what God expects of them as subjects or citizens, so Canon law also provides rules for religious life.

The idea of religious life is meant to cover the religious lives of ordinary people as well as the lives of those who were religious clerics, such as priests and nuns. Indeed, some of the most influential writings of the Medieval period in Canon law concern the rules for religious orders of monks, such as the Rules of St. Benedict. These rules were clearly not aimed at the general public–monks and other religious clerics had to conform to different rules or laws than was true for the general public. While there were religious leaders in Islam it does not appear that their conduct was regulated by different rules than the rules for everyone else.

---

[275] Ibid., p. 113.

[276] Gratian, *The Treatise on Laws*, Distinction Three, pp. 10-11.

V. Reasoning about Nature in Islamic and Canon Law

In a sense, Canon lawyers tended to equate divine and natural law; whereas Islamic lawyers tended to treat nature as ancillary to divine law. Canon law, like civil law, is distinguished from both natural law and divine law. Canon law guides people toward satisfying the demands of God's law–what people could know in their hearts but need help in understanding it. Natural law is divine law written into human nature, and once so inscribed people could be guided by understanding what is within them, but sin and selfishness delude people so that they need rules of various sorts to follow when they cannot see in their nature what the true path of justice and equity is.

Nature plays a role in leading people to the truth in Islam as well. Various civil laws aid people to see how to carry out God's law. But nature does not have a law that is the same as what is divine law and there is no discussion of natural law proper. Yet, there are various ideas present in early medieval Islamic legal thought that correspond to the ideas in early medieval Canon law as well.

One way to see a possible similarity between Islamic and Canon law is in the way that reason and nature are meant to interact to lead people toward God's divine law. As we have seen, nature is important in filling in gaps in the Quran, such as aiding reason in determining where the Sacred Mosque is in relation to where a person praying is. It is also true that reason aided by nature can tell people what are the various customs and traditions that are common to all or most societies. The idea that such customs could be what all people should do follows from the natural fact that the customs were being followed by all or most people. While somewhat controversial some scholars such as Anver Emon have made a good case for seeing some Islamic lawyers as supporting natural law in some form or other.[277]

Canon law then can be understood as similar to Islamic law since in equating natural and divine law, nature is inscribed in the hearts of people and then the use of reason could be employed to ascertain what God is demanding of His people. Nature is in us or is part of us as something of our nature so that when reason is employed introspectively, we are able to get to an understanding of God's divine law. Nature is reasoned about in both Islamic and Canon law as a means to get to an understanding of divine law.

---

[277] See Anver M. Emon, *Islamic Natural Law Theories*, Oxford: Oxford University Press, 2010.

But one of the biggest theoretical differences between Canon and Islamic law can be seen in the way that reason and nature interact to point to the way God expects people to behave. The simplest way to see this, and perhaps the most misleading, is that nature is an aid to reasoning about our obligations in Islamic law whereas nature is itself infused with God's law–hence the near equivalence of natural and divine law–in Canon law. Yet, there is a way for these views to be seen as coming closer together when we think in terms of God's law imprinted in the hearts or minds of humans. In both traditions, God's law is so imprinted. And insofar as what is in humans can be seen as a part of human "nature" there is a way for nature to be interlinked with God's law for Islamic and Canon law traditions.

In other terms, most traditions of religious law put the individual's conscience in a prominent place. But this does not mean that the person can decide matters of law and morality as utterly up to him or her. Indeed, Al-Shafi'i explicitly addressed the issue of whether God's law allows for discretion, in a quotation we partially saw earlier.

> Thus did He inform them of His decree: "Does Man think he will be left without guidance?" "Without guidance" means to be neither commanded to do something nor prohibited from doing something. This all indicates that no one other than God's Emissary may pronounce of the law except by means of inference, as I have described, or on what makes someone just such that they may be appointed a witness, or on the legal equivalent of game wrongly killed. Neither may anyone express opinions based on subjective interpretation, since to do so is to pronounce according to mere preference, something that is simply invented and not based on prior example.... A just person is one who practices obedience to God. They had ways to know when a person was just or not.[278]

There are objective truths that an individual can come to know by such use of reasoning with natural objects as aids, as is the case when "men can guide themselves by the stars" to find the direction of the Sacred Mosque.[279]

Another apparent difference is that Islamic legal thought stresses the use of reason to proceed by means of analogy whereas this method does not seem to have been stressed in Canon law. We will discuss the procedural elements of these two legal systems in the next chapter, but we

---

[278] Al-Shafi'i, *The Epistle on Legal Theory*, p. 19.

[279] Ibid., p. 359.

can say initially here that Canon law reasoning up to the time of Gratian was reasoning from authority (or authorities). The early Church Fathers including Isidore of Seville are given pride of place and it is their doctrinal statements rather than their reasoning that is prized. Early Islamic legal scholarship, starting at least with the early ninth century work of Al-Shafi'i was known and prized for its logic and analogical reasoning not merely because these scholars were thought to have embodied doctrinal wisdom.

One last point of comparison concerns reasoning by experts in these two religious views. Canonists stressed the hierarchical nature of the Church, where the Pope and then his bishops are given special epistemic status in terms of their reasoning. Islam is not organized hierarchically, but there are definitely some people, especially certain legal scholars, who are given special epistemic status. Sometimes legal scholars attained specialist status by tracing back various principles and sayings to the Quran or Ahadith. Other scholars achieve special standing because of their superior reasoning in interpreting the Quran and Ahadith.[280]

[280] See Abdur Rahim, *The Principles of Muhammadan Jurisprudence*, p. 74.

CHAPTER 12

TRIALS AND PROOF

As we have seen, Islamic and Canon law declare that the law they are applying is divine law. In this chapter we discuss the question of how it is that divine law is indeed applied–specifically what kind of trial was envisioned and what constituted proof of the various claims and counterclaims made by litigants? I will argue that the kind of trials and proofs are remarkably similar to those for non-religious courts in the Medieval period and that certain of the religious courts are not significantly less humane or more dependent on "superstitions" than non-religious courts.

The judges of religious courts in both of these traditions must be knowledgeable about religious texts upon which the divine law was based. In most cases this meant that the judge was himself a religious official. The main method of proof in both traditions was the oath, although also in both traditions there were critical questions raised about the effectiveness of oaths. Indeed, religious courts seemed to be more skeptical about the reliability of oaths, which called on God to affirm the truth of the oath taker's words, than did non-religious courts that also had relied on oaths since some of the earliest of ancient times.

In the first and second sections I will set out the general ideas of how trials were to be conducted and who the judges should be, first in Islamic and then in Canon law. In the third and fourth sections I will investigate how oaths were understood in these two traditions. And in the final section I will draw some conclusions about how to assess the use of divine law, as opposed to non-religious law, in terms of court procedures.

I. Islamic Judges

Volume 9 of the Ahadith collected by Sahih Al-Bukhari, sets out various qualities that a good judge in Islamic trials must manifest.

> Abu Bakra wrote to his son who was in Sijistan: Do not judge between two persons when you are angry, for I heard the

> Prophet saying, "A judge should not judge between two persons while he is in an angry mood"…
> Muzahim bin Zufar said, "Umar bin 'Abdul- 'Aziz said to us, 'There are five qualities (which a judge should possess), and if he does not have one of them then he has one defect; and those qualities are: He must be an intelligent, patient, honest, stern, and a learned religious scholar and knowledge seeking.'"[281]

So, in addition to having the qualities of intelligence, patience, honesty, and sternness, the Islamic judge needs to be a learned religious scholar. At least in this hadith it is not required that the Islamic judge be an imam although this is at least implied in other Islamic texts.

In another hadith, we learn some very interesting things about how judges should not be swayed by oratory.

> Allah's Messenger said, "I am only a human being, and you people (opponents) come to me with your cases; and it may be that one of you can present his case eloquently in a more convincing way than the other, and I give my verdict according to what I hear. So if ever I judge (by error) and give the right of a brother to his other (brother) then he (the latter) should not take it, for I am giving him only a piece of (Hell) fire."[282]

We see a concern that judges deal fairly with the litigants and not be swayed by rhetoric. And in a similar hadith the right of appeal seems to be recognized in cases where a judge has been overly influenced by the rhetoric of one of the parties to a suit.[283]

Here is an especially important statement of how early Islamic law viewed judges in Joseph Schacht's well regarded book, *An Introduction to Islamic Law*:

> We must now return to the middle of the first Islamic century, when the rule of the caliphs of Medina was supplanted by that of the Umayyads (661-750)… [they] took the important step of appointing Islamic judges or *kadis*. The office of *kadi* was created in and for the new Islamic society which came into being… The jurisdiction of the *kadi* extended to Muslims only; the non Muslim subject populations retained their own

---

[281] *Ahadith: The Translation of the Meaning of Sahih Al-Bukhari*, 7158, 7162, translated by Muhammad Muhsin Khan, Riyadh: Darussalam Publishers, 1997, 2015, vol. 9, p. 174.

[282] Hadith 7169, ibid., vol. 9, p. 177.

[283] Hadith 2458, ibid., vol. 3, p. 368.

> traditional legal institutions, including the ecclesiastical (and rabbinical) tribunals which, in the last few centuries before the Muslim conquest had to a great extent duplicated the judicial organization of the Byzantine state.[284]

The Islamic judges were seen as a new form of judge that was to be unique to the new Islamic state.

Schacht also goes on to give us a good description of how the *kadis* conceptualized their role in Islamic law.

> The earliest Islamic *kadis* gave judgment according to their own discretion, or "sound opinion" as it was called, basing themselves on customary practice which in the nature of things incorporated administrative regulations, and taking the letter and the spirit of the Quranic regulations and other recognized Islamic religious norms into account as they saw fit.... The work of the *kadis* became inevitably more and more specialized, and we may take it for granted that from the turn of the century onwards (c. 715-20) appointments as a rule went to "specialists"... They impregnated the sphere of law with religious and ethical ideas, subjected to Islamic norms, and incorporated it into the body of duties incumbent on every Muslim.[285]

These Islamic judges are thought to have transformed Islamic law into the mixture of religious and customary law that it then epitomized for many centuries thereafter.

II. Judges in Canon Law

In Canon law it was most often the case that the judge was a bishop, although in the battle between secular and religious law in the later Medieval period it was sometimes a count or other secular political leader who was given the job of presiding even over strictly ecclesiastical matters. The need for judges who were trained in the law, both Canon and secular, spurred the rise of the first law schools, the most important of which was in Bologna.

According to James Brundage, experts or specialists were drafted into the profession of judges from the twelfth century.

---

[284] Joseph Schacht, *An Introduction to Islamic Law*, Oxford: Oxford University Press, 1982, pp. 23-25.

[285] Joseph Schacht, *An Introduction to Islamic Law*, ibid., pp. 25-27.

> By the closing years of the twelfth century, and increasingly thereafter, bishops in many parts of Christendom began to delegate most of their judicial duties to legal specialists, usually men who had formal training in law. These trained and often full-time judges functioned as the bishop's alter ego for most legal matters. The bishop's judicial delegate was often described as the bishop's official... By the latter part of the thirteenth century the officials-principal in many diocese presided over a judicial bureaucracy with a staff of clerks who produced and copied documents, a registrar who directed the work-flow and managed the judicial calendar, and one or more apparitors or bailiffs who notified parties when and where they must appear before the judge.[286]

We can here note that the publication of textbook-like works such as Gratian's *Decretal* made it possible to train lawyers in Canon law much easier than it had been true before the twelfth century. The rise of the judge as specialist in Canon law is clearly similar to the rise of the judge as specialist in Islamic law at about the same time.

We should note one last point before concluding this section: the pope was the head of the hierarchical order in which the bishops stood. Given that the bishops were the main judges in the system of Canon law, it was the pope that was the ultimate decider and also the one to whom appeals would be made. Here is Walter Ullmann on this point and on several related points:

> The essential point therefore in considering the nature of the papal office was its exclusively legal character. Indeed, the papacy was nothing but a *nomen jurisdictionis* and, since in the Middle Ages jurisdiction was considered the exercise of governmental authority, the designation of the papacy as a governmental institution would seem to correspond to its own premises.[287]

The Catholic Church was an institution that was legal and political, not merely religious, in the way in which various documents recognized the bishops and ultimately the pope as judges.

As Medieval Canon law heard more and more cases that might otherwise have been heard by secular courts, the bishops became very

---

[286] James A. Brundage, *Medieval Canon Law*, London: Longman, 1995, pp. 121-122.

[287] Walter Ullmann, *Principles of Government and Politics in the Middle Ages*, NY: Routledge, 1961, p. 51.

busy indeed, spending a significant amount of their time travelling to various locales to sit as judges. And the pope, as the highest appellate judge became so busy with legal matters that it was seen as interfering with the other duties that this religious leader should be performing. Here is an excerpt from a letter from St. Bernard of Clairvaux to Pope Eugene III in the middle of the twelfth century:

> I ask you what is the point of wrangling and listening to litigants from morning to night? And would that the evil of the day were sufficient for it, but the nights are not even free!... One day passes on litigation to the next, one night reveals malice to the next; so much so that you have no time to breathe, no time for rest, and no time for leisure.[288]

We see here that the pope was consumed with his role as the ultimate appellate judge in ways that virtually consumed all of his time.

The mixing of religious and legal matters as the proper domain of the religious leaders of the Catholic Church was characteristic of the Middle Ages, including Islamic leaders as legal as well as religious leaders. Some have argued that in both of these domains, Canon law and Islamic law, there was effectively a theocracy. Whether or not this is generally true, the system of judges certainly mixed religion and law in ways that could seem to support this conclusion.[289]

III. Oaths and Evidence in Islamic Law

In various Ahadith, proof by oath-taking is addressed directly as are some of the problems with this means of proof.

> The Prophet said Al-Kabra'ir, "the biggest sins are: To join others (as partners) in worship with Allah, to be undutiful to one's parents" or said, "to take a false oath…"
> …the Prophet kept on questioning him till he confessed…
> Then the Prophet said to them, "Bring your proof against the killer." They said, "We have no proof." The Prophet said,

[288] Quoted in James A Brundage, *Medieval Canon Law*, London: Longman, 1995, p. 124.

[289] See Dominique Bauer, "From Ivo of Chartres to the *Decretum Gratiani*: The Legal Nature of a Political Theology Revolution," in *Law Before Gratian*, edited by Per Andersen, Mia Munster-Swendsen, and Hell Vogt, Copenhagen: DJOF Publishing, 2007, pp. 123-139.

> "Then they (the defendants) will take an oath." They said, "We do not accept the oaths of the Jews."[290]

We see that oaths are treated as a firm basis of proof, as is a confession. But we also see that the oaths of some people, especially the Jews, were regarded suspiciously and not accepted by certain Muslims.

It is perhaps surprising that the testimony of Jews, under oath, was regarded so skeptically since the Quran talked of Jews as People of the Book, who along with Christians were to be treated differently than other non-Muslims. Yet, it should also be remembered that Jews are often criticized in the Quran, for instance for not properly observing the Sabbath (in verses 2:65; 4:47; and 7:163-66).[291]

In another Hadith there is an important qualification concerning which oath-takers were to be accepted by the judge.

> He let me appear before the people and I said, "O Chief of the believers! You have the chiefs of the army staff and the nobles of the Arabs. If fifty of them testified that a married man had committed illegal sexual intercourse in Damascus but they had not seen him (doing so), would you stone him?" He said "No."[292]

To be believable, the oath-taker must have personally witnessed a crime or sin–and this is true regardless of how many oath-takers there are before the court.

Abdur Rahim tells us that early Islamic law, like Canon law in the Christian world, developed an appreciation for documentary evidence to supplement the rise of importance of circumstantial evidence as well.

> Besides human testimony facts and circumstances may also be relied on as proof. But circumstantial evidence will only be acted upon if it is of a conclusive nature. For instance, if a person is seen coming out from an unoccupied house in fear and anxiety with a knife covered with blood in his hand and in the house a dead body is found with its throat cut, these facts will be regarded as a proof that the person who was seen coming out murdered him.[293]

---

[290] Ahadith, 6870, 6876, and 6898, ibid., vol. 9, pp. 16, 19, 30-31.
[291] See Quran, 16:124, and the commentary of this verse in *The Study Quran*, pp. 690-691.
[292] Hadith 6899, ibid., p. 31.
[293] Abdur Rahim. *The Principles of Muhammadan Jurisprudence*, London: Luzak and Company, 1911, pp. 381-382.

So, while oaths were given pride of place as evidence, early Islamic law recognized other forms of evidence as well.

Rahim also explains what forms of evidence are accepted and how they are regarded vis-à-vis oaths.

> Sometimes documents are accepted as a substitute for oral testimony. But the Court is not to act on a sealed deed or any other document unless it is free from the suspicion of being forged and is such as is customary for people to enter their transactions therein.... The Court generally accepts an admission without regard to requiring any further proof from the claimant. An admission must, however, be unconditional, and it must be voluntary, so that if obtained by coercion it is not binding nor if made in jest.[294]

We see again the concern for testimony, whether based on oaths or not, to be beyond suspicion. The concern about the truthfulness of testimony is a problem that runs through the history of legal thought and seems to be no less a problem for systems of law built upon divine sources than systems of law that are fully secular.

Finally, in this section, let us return to the earlier idea of being suspicious about eloquent litigants and their defenders, expressed in a passage from the Sunna:

> What matters is not speech and its eloquence; rather, regard should only be given to what it contains in knowledge and proof. It is possible that a little educative speech would be much more beneficial than much speech of eloquence that you cannot derive except a little benefit from. And this is the reality of our time; as the speech (usually delivered) is much and little knowledge (is derived from it). Reciters are becoming many while scholars are becoming few.[295]

This text from the ninth century reminds us again of the worries of suspicious speech, especially speech that presents itself as the truth because the speaker is able to present testimony eloquently.

---

[294] Ibid., p. 382.

[295] Imam al-Barbahari, *Sharh as-Sunnah*, translated by Abdus-Sami' Abdus-Salam, Birmingham: Dar Makkah International, 2014, vol. 1, p. 88.

IV. Oaths and Evidence in Canon Law

Leonard Levy gives us a good place to start to understand Canon law's early ideas of proof.

> the Canon law, influenced by the Roman law of the later empire, developed a highly sophisticated system of evidence, later known as the theory of legal proofs, which supposedly would help the accused by preventing the conviction of the innocent… Innocent III, for example, cautioned inquisitors against convicting on merely "violent presumptions" in a matter as heinous as heresy. What the Canon law required was perfect or complete proof that in a later day was specified with considerable complexity and quasi-scientific exactness. Complete proof was a proof clearer than the sun at midday. It consisted, ideally, in the testimony of two eyewitnesses, neither impeached nor impeachable, to the same fact; they must have seen the prisoner commit the crime.[296]

We see here the concern that witnesses had to personally see the commission of the crime, as was true of Islamic law at the same time.

In attempting to distinguish the ordeal from the oath, Robert Bartlett says that the oath was actually conceived as a kind of ordeal.

> The oath, the corner-stone of Medieval judicial procedure, was, in some sense, an ordeal, but one which relied upon God's eventual rather than his immediate judgment… recourse to oath might be inappropriate in two situations: when the individual's own oath was no longer credible, or when the necessary number of compurgators could not be mustered.[297]

When these conditions obtained, then recourse was made to physical ordeals as we will next see.

In 895 the Council of Tribur called for the hot iron ordeal if the oath was inappropriate. And the cases where this would occur were when the accused: "has been caught in theft, perjury, or false witness." In those cases "let him not be admitted to an oath."[298] Canon law followed Roman law in that both oaths and physical ordeals were meant to test the accused

---

[296] Leonard W. Levy, *The Palladium of Justice: Origins of Trial by Jury*, Chicago: Ivan R. Dee, Publishers, 1999, pp. 32-34.

[297] Robert Bartlett, *Trial by Fire and Water: The Medieval Judicial Ordeal*, Brattleboro, VT: Echo Point Books and Media, 1986, 2014, p. 30.

[298] See ibid., p. 31.

or accuser to see whether God would intervene to show a sign of the truth of the claims made by these parties.

The main types of physical ordeal in the early history of Canon law concerned either fire or water. These ordeals were in common usage from the ninth to the thirteenth century. Here is an example from the poems of Edda, concerning Atli's queen, Gudrun, accused of adultery by her servant Herkja:

> She put her hand into the water
> and gathered up the glittering gems:
> "My lords, you have seen the sacred trial
> prove me guiltless–and still the water boils."
> Atli's heart laughed in his breast
> because Gudrun's hand had not been harmed:
> "Now let Herkja go to the kettle,
> she who hoped to hurt my wife."
> No man has seen a pitiful sight
> who has not looked at Herkja's scalded hands;
> then they forced her into a foul swamp –
> Gudrun's grievance was well avenged.[299]

Putting the hand into boiling water or grasping a red hot poker were types of ordeal used to show, for those who were unscathed, the truthfulness of a witness or the innocence of a party to a suit.

Here is an account of how the "glowing iron" ordeal was administered in the 9th century:

> After the accused has been lawfully made, and three days have passed in fasting and prayer, the priest, clad in his sacred vestments, with the exception of his outside garment, shall take with a tongs the iron placed before the altar… he shall bear it to the fire… After this, the iron shall be placed in the fire and shall be sprinkled with holy water… And straightaway the accused shall carry the iron to a distance of nine feet. Finally, his hand shall be covered under seal for three days, and if festering blood be found in the track of the iron, he shall be judged guilty.[300]

---

[299] "The Third Lay of Gudrun," in *Poems of the Vikings: The Elder Edda*, translated by Patricia Terry, Indianapolis: Hackett Publishing, 1969, p. 204, quoted in Robert Bartlett, *Trial by Fire and Water*, p. 18.

[300] *Formulae Liturgicae in use at Ordeals (Ninth Century)*, reprinted in *A Reader of Medieval Laws Edicts, and Orders*, translated by E. F. Henderson, Washington, DC: Madison and Monroe Press, 2013, p. 243

This very common form of the ordeal is discussed in several documents from the ninth century onwards until the ordeal was outlawed in later Canon law.

As in the earliest recorded laws, it was also common to use a water ordeal–throwing a person into a body of water to see whether that person sank or floated. Unlike in earlier times, in Medieval Canon law, the innocent or truthful party was supposed to sink not float–this caused a problem if the sinking party was not quickly pulled from the water before this innocent person drowned.

As Bartlett tells us, the ordeal was used when there were reasons to doubt the accuracy or efficacy of the oath.

> The most significant limitation on the use of the ordeal was that it was only employed when other ways of discovering the truth were not available… It was used only if there were no "certain proof." Such an attitude was occasionally elevated to a general principle. As it was stated in the twelfth-century England, "the ordeal of the hot iron is not permitted except where the naked truth cannot otherwise be explored."[301]

It is unclear exactly why the ordeal came to be outlawed, but some have argued that the ordeal was seen to be at odds with the rising ideas in support of rationalism.[302]

The ordeal was officially banned by the Fourth Lateran Council in 1215. In some cases the oath was used, now seemingly more trustworthy than the physical ordeal. Perhaps this was due to the fact that the oath relied on the person's fear of punishment by God in the afterlife, and hence was not easily disproved, whereas the ordeal called upon God to intervene directly in affairs of this life rather than the afterlife. In addition, it should be noted that the ordeal, and even the oath, was being replaced by the testimony of "legitimate witnesses" or by the confession of the accused. Here is a statement by the French jurist Stephen of Tornai in 1165:

> The defendant shall be summoned before his own judge and be legitimately called by three edicts or one peremptory edict. He must be permitted to have legitimate delays. The accusation must be formally presented in writing. Legitimate witnesses must be produced. A decision must be rendered only after

[301] Quoted in Robert Bartlett, *Trial by Fire and Water*, p. 26.

[302] See Robert Bartlett, *Trial by Fire and Water*, pp. 54-55.

> someone has been convicted or confessed. The decision must be in writing.[303]

Here we can see a return in some sense to the Roman model of Justinian. As we know today, though, the oath did not die out as more rationalistic proof methods were being developed; and proof by oath is still used in trials.

V. Procedure and Divine Law

There is an obvious link between the use of oaths as well as the ordeal in systems of law that derive from God's direct word. The law is based on divine intervention to describe the law that is to be followed. And similarly, the forms of proof that draw on the idea that God will intervene directly and at the moment, in the case of ordeals, and the idea that God will punish those who make an untruthful oath, are also based on divine intervention.

Judging can also be seen to follow the idea of the divine origin of law in that it was expected in both early Islamic law and early Canon law that the judge should be well versed in the various religious texts that were thought to contain the direct word of God, or were somehow derived from that source. As we will see in this section, problems arose when judges became more secular–especially when secular rulers claimed to be able to understand and interpret God's law better than the religious scholars and authorities.

In many respects the investiture controversy is as much procedural as it is a matter of substantive belief or orthodoxy. The issue concerned who had the right to appoint bishops, or to put it differently, what procedure must be followed for properly appointing those who were the primary judges of Canon law. We can see this clearly in the Canons of Melfi by Pope Urban II:

> [8] …we forbid that anyone constituted in the clerical order or any monk should dare to receive investiture of a bishopric or abbey, or any ecclesiastical dignity whatsoever from the hand of a layman. Whoever presumes to do so should be punished by deposition...
> [9] …although in the canons it is established that no cleric without permission of his bishop, no bishop without permission

---

[303] Quoted in *Medieval Justice*, edited by Hunt Janin, London: McFarland and Company, Publishers, 2004, p. 33.

> of the metropolitan, should go to a court, commanding we command and prohibiting we prohibit that no one henceforth should retain someone of this sort…
> [11] Lest the holy church should suffer any injury, we wish and we decree that the laity have no jurisdiction over clerics.[304]

We can see here that Urban II in 1089 was so concerned about the investiture problem that he devoted three of his canons, out of only 16, to trying to settle this problem. Yet, it was not for 30 more years until a new pope was able finally to get the emperors to accept that only clergy could appoint bishops and other clerics.

The investiture controversy ended with the Concordat of Worms on September 23, 1122, when Callixtus II regained the right to invest bishops, but also allowed that the investitures were to take place in the presence of the emperor. Here are some of the terms of the Concordat of Worms:

> That the Roman Church was founded by God alone.
> That the Roman pontiff alone can with right be called universal.
> That he alone can depose or reinstate bishops….
> That for him alone is it lawful, according to the needs of the time, to make new laws…
> That it may be permitted to him to depose emperors…
> That he himself may be judged by no one.
> That no one shall dare to condemn one who appeals to the apostolic chair.
> That to the latter should be referred the more important cases of every church.[305]

The investiture controversy ended in what was perhaps the most important reassertion of the right of the pope to be head of the system of Canon law. Here is an account of what led up to the Concordat of Worms described by E.F. Henderson: "The forbiddal of lay investiture was especially directed against Henry IV, who had recently, disregarding the papal candidate, taken into his own hands the election of an archbishop of Milan. It was one of the boldest moves imaginable."[306]

---

304 *The Canons of Melfi*, in Robert Somerville, *Pope Urban II*, Oxford: Oxford University Press, 1996, p. 261.

305 Pope Calixtus II, "The Dictate of the Pope," reprinted in *A Reader of Medieval Laws, Edicts, and Orders*, translated by E. F. Henderson, Washington, DC: Madison and Monroe Press, 2013, pp. 315-316.

306 E. F. Henderson, ibid., p. 272.

The increasing reliance on specialists trained in either Canon law or Islamic law made it easier to see how the judge was indeed working from the divine texts, but there was also the problem of how to see judge-made law as also sufficiently connected to the divine law. And here is where having clerics as judges, in both Canon and Islamic law, facilitated the recognition of the right to make new law by these people who were seen as directly connected to the divine source of law.

In the early Islamic law tradition, it was highly controversial whether or not judges could make new law. Initially, the authority to make new law was reserved to the Prophet and his closest followers–the caliphs as secular leaders had no such right. Here is how Joseph Schacht puts the doctrine into the mouth of the religious authorities:

> "No one has the right to personal opinion on points settled in the Quran; the personal opinion of the caliphs concerns those points on which there is no revelation in the Quran and no valid Sunna from the Prophet; no one has the right to personal opinion on points settled in a Sunna enacted by the Prophet." And: "There is no Prophet after ours, and no holy book after ours; what Allah has allowed or forbidden through our Prophet remains so for ever; I am not one who decides but only one who carries out, not an innovator but a follower." According to this doctrine, which was consciously adopted very early under the 'Abbasids, the caliph, though otherwise the absolute chief of the community of Muslims, had not the right to legislate but only to make administrative regulations within the limits laid down by sacred Law.[307]

Law was generally not a matter of what had been properly legislated, but a matter of what was divinely ordained, and the only exceptions concerned where the divine law was silent. There was also an exception for those religious leaders who could claim to be in the line of the followers of the Prophet Muhammad, but even here they could not make law that contradicted the Quran and the Ahadith.

Similar issues arose in terms of Canon law, which initially traced its laws back to the Gospels and the Bible, as well as the pronouncements of the popes as standing in the direct line of religious authorities from St. Peter forward. The pronouncements of the popes about Canon law were not as greatly restricted as was true of Islamic law, but popes and bishops

---

[307] Joseph Schacht, *An Introduction to Islamic Law*, Oxford: Oxford University Press, 1982, p. 53.

could not make law that was in direct opposition to the Bible and the Gospels.

Another controversy concerning the role of judges in systems of divine law was whether or not religious judges could overrule secular political authorities, and even whether or not religious judges could declare a secular leader to be acting contrary to divine law and as having dethroned himself by his acts. Here is how Fritz Kern described the controversy in Europe during the Middle Ages:

> the principle [was] that the bad king deprives himself of the capacity to rule, and that by his own misdeeds or ineptitude he *ipso facto* forfeits his royal rights. The unjust king ceases to be king in the eyes of God; for king and right are inseparable ideas. The ruler dethrones himself by his own misdeed; he becomes *tyrannus*, usurper, a man using force without authority… In the Church… there was an established judicial authority, which was competent to recognize the ruler's guilt and so formal judicial process against the king was possible. For the ruler, like every other Christian, was subject to the penal and disciplinary powers of the Church.[308]

When the law was divinely ordained, then those who were the designated interpreters of that law were seen as somehow above the secular political leaders.

Procedurally, systems of divine law, such as Canon and Islamic law of the Middle Ages, pose difficulties for settling controversies about what the law is, as well as how to apply the law to difficult cases. Al-Shafi'i devoted quite a lot of his famous *Epistle on Legal Theory* to trying to resolve such problems. Al-Shafi'i developed an elaborate theory of how properly to use analogy to proceed from known divine sources of law to cover cases that on first viewing did not seem to fit under the known divine laws. Here is a selection from that text, which we partially cited above, on the method of analogy:

> Then he said, "I have heard your opinion concerning consensus and analogy after your opinion about rulings of the Book of God and the Practice of His Emissary. What do you think about the opinions of the Companions of God's Emissary when they disagree with each other?" In that case, I said, we adopt the opinion that agrees with the Book, Prophetic

[308] Fritz Kern, *Kingship and Law in the Middle Ages*, translated by S. B. Chrimes, NY: Frederick A. Praeger Publishers, 1956, pp. 101-102.

> Practice, consensus, or what makes for the most valid analogy. "What do you think," he continued, "about the case in which one of them utters an opinion and no one else is remembered to have agreed or disagreed with it? Can you cite any authority for following it–whether from a scriptural passage, a Prophetic practice, or something people have agreed on–that could serve as a justification of a kind that you could adduce as a report?" We have not found, I replied, any scriptural prooftext or confirmed account of a Prophetic practice pertaining to that. We have found scholars adopting the opinion of one Companion sometimes and not adopting it at other times, and also disagreeing over some of the Companions' opinions that they adopt. "Which of those do you do?" he asked... We rule on the basis of consensus and analogies, which is weaker, but they are a matter of necessity, because it is not allowed to analogize if there is an extant report...[309]

This is how Al-Shafi'i describes the constraints imposed by divine law that must be satisfied before he feels entitled to rule on the basis of analogy.

A system of divine law seemingly resolves problems of sources and interpretation easily by reference to the word of God not the ambiguities of the words of mere mortal legislators. And yet as we have seen there are very many problems concerning sources and interpretation in the divine law systems of Canon and Islamic law. These two systems of divine law had very similar problems and tried to solve the problems also in seemingly similar ways. But the problems often remained since the divine source of the law was not always easy to read or understand, just as was sometimes true of secular sources of law.

[309] Al- Shafi'i, *Epistle on Legal Theory*, edited and translated by Joseph Lowry, NY: New York University Press, 2013, pp. 431-433.

SECTION VI:

LEGAL STATUS

CHAPTER 13

THE STATUS OF WOMEN

In Islamic and Canon law the status of women is improved somewhat from the periods immediately preceding them. But women were not treated as humanely, and not nearly as well, as was true in many ancient societies. In this chapter I will argue that the law that was inspired by divine pronouncements is very different for men than for women. There are a few exceptions to this claim, most notably the requirement of consent to marriage in Islamic law and women who did not marry were given high status in Canon law. But these exceptions also were not so clearly beneficial to women due to the overriding subjugation of women in these systems of religious law. In many respects religiously inspired legal systems are quite conservative and strongly resistant to change even as the circumstances of the world change. Yet, I will argue that it is also remarkable how ideas we would normally think of as modern, such as the treatment of rape, are supported by the religious-legal texts.

In the first section of this chapter I will discuss how women are treated, as contrasted with men, in the Quran and other early Islamic legal texts, especially in the Ahadith. In the second section I will discuss how women are treated in important legal texts in early Canon law, especially in the works of Isidore, Amalar, and Ivo. In the third section I will specifically examine how marriage is understood in Canon and Islamic law. In the fourth section I will look at how rape and other sex crimes are dealt with by Islamic and Canon Law. And I will end this chapter by arguing that the religious foundations of Islamic and Canon law sometimes hinder these legal systems from treating women humanely.

I. Women in the Quran and Early Islamic Law

One of the most widely quoted verses in the Quran equates men with two women when there is a question that calls for testimony by witnesses. Yet elsewhere we see that marriage requires consent on the part of both parties, where a sort of equality seems to be contemplated. In another context, divorce, we also see the Islamic concern for consent and the prohibition of coercion.

> 'Uthman said: A divorce given by a drunk or given under compulsion is not valid.
> And Ibn 'Abbas said: A divorce given by a drunk or given under compulsion is not valid....
> And a divorce is [only] valid when expressed in the language of the nation which the person belongs to.[310]

Ahadith can be cited to show that women are not to be forced into marriage just as they are not to be coerced out of marriage.

In the section of Quran on women (al-Nisa) we find this clear articulation of why men are given the right to control and direct women.

> Men are the upholders and maintainers of women by virtue of that in which God has favored some of them above others and by virtue of their spending from their wealth. Therefore the righteous women are devoutly obedient, guarding in [their husbands'] absence what God has guarded. As for those from whom you fear discord and animosity, admonish them, then leave them in their beds, then strike them. Then if they obey you, seek not a way against them. Truly God is Exalted, Great.[311]

Here we find an expression of one of the pillars of traditional patriarchal views on how men rule over women and women must obey men or suffer sometimes severely painful consequences.

But we also find verses that make one doubt that the Quran can be easily characterized as having a negative attitude toward women's place in society.

> Whosoever does evil shall be requited for it, and he shall find no protector or helper for himself apart from God. And whosoever performs righteous deeds, whether male or female, such shall enter the Garden, and they shall not be wronged as much as the speck on a date stone. And who is better in religion than the one who submits his face to God...[312]

---

[310] Hadith 5269, vol. 7, p. 129.

[311] *The Study Quran*, 4:34, pp. 206-208.

[312] *The Study Quran*, 4:123-125, pp. 247-248.

Seemingly enlightened verses such as these are not uncommon, and yet they sit often within the same section of the Quran as the verses that support male dominance over women.

We also find in Islamic texts a clear reference to men as having to fend off sexual desires that women would expose the men to.

> So Allah's Messenger said, "O young people! Whoever among you is able to marry should marry because it helps him lower his gaze and guard his modesty (i.e. his private parts from committing illegal sexual intercourse, etc.) and whoever is not able to marry should fast, as fasting will diminish his sexual power."[313]

We see that in this translation it seems that it is the private parts of men that commit illegal sexual intercourse, rather than the men themselves. But in any event men are to guard against being led by women into sexual relations that are illegal by getting married as soon as they can. We have no reference here to why women should get married, unless it is so as to be ruled by the men who are superior to them in various ways as the Quranic passage shows above.

In another Hadith, we do find that the wife has certain rights over the husband: "Your body has a right over you, your eyes have a right over you, and your wife has a right over you."[314] We also find this summary of the rights in marriage presented by one Islamic scholar, Khaled Abou El Fadl:

> There is very little room to negotiate the power of husbands. However, in several versions, we find an interesting variation… we find the Prophet supporting a woman's decision. In this version, a father brings his daughter to the Prophet complaining that she refuses to marry anyone. To this the daughter responds, "No, not until you tell me what rights a husband has over his wife." The Prophet reportedly… declares that women cannot be married without their full consent.[315]

We will return to the role of consent in marriage, but we should also note that despite the fact that this idea of consent is one of the most progressive

---

313 Hadith 5066, vol. 7, p. 67.

314 Hadith 5199, vol. 7, p. 93.

315 Khaled Abou El Fadl, *Speaking in God's Name: Islamic Law, Authority, and Women*, London: One World Publications, 2001, pp. 231-232.

ideas in the Middle Ages, nonetheless, there are also very many Quranic verses on the status of women that would not be described as progressive.

II. The Status of Women in Early Canon Law

Many of the authors of early Canon law would also not be considered progressives today, but as we will see in this chapter early Canon law did have elements that were favorable toward women, as we saw also to be true of early Islamic law. Let us start with the early 9th century writings of Amalar of Metz:

> We gathered at church, the men and the women stand separately. We received this practice from ancient custom… we can keep in mind another point of consideration–that the flesh of men and women may be inflamed with lust, each by the other, if they come too close… Ambrose on the letter to the Corinthians: "A woman should cover her head," he says, "because she is not an image of God; rather, so that she may appear subordinated and because transgression arose through her, she should maintain this symbol, so that in church she may not have an uncovered head, but rather one covered with a veil, out of reverence to the priest… Men stand in the southern part of the church and women in the northern, to show through the stronger sex that the stronger saints are always stationed amid the greater temptations of the fire of this world, and through the weaker sex that the weaker have a more fitting place…[316]

Here we find the articulation of women's place as subordinated to that of men, and especially subordinated to the male priest. Women are portrayed as "the weaker sex" despite the fact that they are seen as those who are the ones who transgress the law. We should also note that women, unlike men, are not made in the image of God, and hence must be treated differently than men–even assigning them to a different part of the church, an inferior place, when they come to pray. This last idea is also commonly articulated in Islamic law as well.

We can find similar treatment of women among early Canonists as in the writing of Isidore of Seville in the seventh century, and Ivo of Chartres in the twelfth century. Here is Isidore:

---

[316] Amalar of Metz, *On the Liturgy*, Book III, translated by Eric Knibbs, Cambridge, MA: Harvard University Press, 2014, vol. II, pp. 15-17.

> Indeed, the Lord said to the woman: "your desire shall be for your husband and he shall rule over you" [Genesis 3:16]. Therefore the precepts of Sacred Scripture are to be obeyed, and the man is to be served by a free servitude and a full affection. For the man was not created for the woman but the woman for the man; and since "the head of the woman is her husband," but "Christ is the head of every man" [Corinthians 1:3], whichever wife is not subject to her husband, that is to her head, does a crime of the same sort as that of her husband if he is not subject to Christ, his head. The word of the Lord is blasphemed both when the first teaching of God is held in disrepute and it is accounted as nothing, and the Gospel of Christ is dishonored when, contrary to the law of nature and the faith, she who is Christian and subject to the law of God desires to be superior to man. Even pagan women serve their husbands by the common law of nature...[317]

It is of note that the woman who does not subject herself to her husband commits a "crime" of the same order as when a man does not subject himself to God. And the kind of serving that is required is "a free servitude," that is, where no compensation is asked for.

Despite the fact that Canon law treated men as superior to, and even the masters over, women as servants, we can see some of the beginnings of a more progressive treatment, in the importance given to consent in marriage, as we also saw in Islamic law. Here is how Christof Rolker describes the Canonist Ivo of Chartres's view:

> For Ivo... marriage was first of all a sacrament. However, though being a divine institution, marriage is contracted by individual people. A valid marriage could be contracted wherever there were no marriage impediments, providing there was mutual consent, Ivo wrote, following Roman law. Indeed, for Ivo, consent was the single most important condition for a valid marriage; it required not the agreement of the families involved but the individual consent of the bride and groom. Children under the age of reason could therefore not marry; marriage arrangements on their behalf were legitimate but null and void without the later consent of the couple. Consummation, however, was not necessary to validate a marriage.[318]

---

[317] Isidore of Seville, *De Ecclesiasticis Officiis*, Book II, translated by Thomas Knoebel, NY: The Newman Press, 2008, p. 102.

[318] Christof Rolker, *Canon Law and the Letters of Ivo of Chartres*, Cambridge: Cambridge University Press, 2010, p. 213.

We will have much more to say about marriage in the next section. But here note that Ivo's strong emphasis on consent treats the marriage partners as equals–both man and woman can say no to marriage regardless of what their families say. While a bit of an outlier, Ivo points us toward a progressive element in the Canon law's treatment of women. Once a marriage contract is validly entered into, the wife becomes subject to her husband, but in effect she consents to this arrangement. We find the idea of Roman law's strong emphasis on contracts now being employed to provide a humane element in the way women and men are to be treated in marriage.

III. Marriage in Islamic and Canon Law

As we have just seen, Canon law sometimes characterized marriage as a contract where both parties must freely consent in order for a valid marriage to be formed. The various Canonists differed among themselves on how important consent was for a valid marriage. It seems that consent was an element in a valid marriage, but the disagreement was over how important this element was in establishing the validity of the marriage. Ivo seems to have thought that consent was even more important than consummation, but this was a minority view.

Isidore of Seville's Seventh Century writings on the Ecclesiastical law of marriage are perhaps more representative of early Canon law than Ivo's writings. Here is Isidore:

> The law of nature concerning married people is of the world. For God made Adam and gave him Eve as a helper with the subsequent intention of procreation… After the departure from his blessed home he knew his wife… Therefore the married couple proceeded to the assigned work and enduring "thorns and thistles" [Genesis 3:18], went about fulfilling the task God had first assigned… Whence the apostle predicted, saying: "those who marry will experience distress in life" [1 Corinthians 7:28]. Nevertheless, the beds of the married are not dishonorable [Hebrews 13:4], nor is the marriage bed that is without fruit immaculate.[319]

[319] Isidore of Seville, *De Ecclesiasticis Officiis*, Book II, translated by Thomas Knoebel, NY: The Newman Press, 2008, p. 97-98.

Marriage is here characterized as male dominated yet the hard work of doing God's will is shared between husband and wife according to Isidore.

In another passage from Isidore, we get more of a sense of how marriage is viewed in early Canon Law:

> marriages are good in themselves. They become bad through those things that are done around them… "because of cases of sexual immorality, each man should have his own wife." [1 Corinthians 7:2]. However, this first union having been made in a divine manner, serves as a model that not one man and many women, but one man and one woman are to be married… Adam and his wife Eve engaged in one marital union between themselves… so also there is only one man and one wife…[320]

The union of husband and wife is seen as a kind of exclusive partnership, which could be a progressive idea, even as that same marriage is seen as dominated by the husband as its head.

We also find a continuing differential standard in how ideal husbands and wives are understood:

> In choosing husbands, among the ancients these four things were looked at: virtue, family, attractiveness, and habit of prayer; in women, three things: if she was generous, if she was well-mannered, if she was beautiful. Now, however neither the family nor the customs, but rather riches are pleasing among women. Nor is the woman asked if she is chaste, but rather how shapely, which both feeds the libido of concupiscence and draws the deep breaths of all after it.[321]

Isidore goes on to say that wives should be chaste and faithful according to divine law, whereas the husband should mainly display the example of "continence" that will help by his example to teach his wife how to behave properly as a wife.

As we have seen, Islamic law considers mutual consent to be an essential component in a valid marriage. And this is a major move toward a more humane view of marriage than was often present in ancient societies. Here is how Khaled Abou El Fadl describes one version of the position we have already seen in part, taken in the Ahadith:

> The Prophet tells the daughter to obey her father. To this the daughter responds, "No, not until you tell me what rights a

---

[320] Ibid., p. 98.

[321] Ibid., p. 100.

> husband has over his wife." The Prophet reportedly gives her answers… and she declares, "By the God who has sent you the Truth, I will never get married as long as I live." The Prophet then declares that women cannot be married without their full consent.

The inference to be drawn, says Khaled Abou El Fadl, is that "the symbolism of these reports conveys a compelling message: if need be, women will just have to do without men."[322]

But there are other reports that paint a rather darker picture of how women were regarded by the Prophet Muhammad.

> Abu Hurayrah reported that the Prophet passed a group of women when he addressed them. The Prophet proclaimed, "O women! Increase your prayers, and then give alms for I have seen that women are the majority of the inhabitants of Hell." A wise woman asked, "Why are [women] the majority of inhabitants of Hell, O Prophet of God?" The Prophet responded, "Because you frequently slander and curse, and you are ungrateful to your companions. I have not seen anyone more deficient in intellect and religion, who is able to prevail (mislead) the wise, than you." So they (the women) asked, "And what is [our] deficiency in intellect and religion?" The Prophet said, "[Your] deficiency in intellect is in the fact that the testimony of a man is worth [the testimony] of two women, and the deficiency in religion is that you spend days without fasting or praying (because of the menstrual cycle)."[323]

It should not escape our notice that the "fact" that it takes two women testifying to equal one man is only a fact because Islamic law made it so–it was surely not a natural fact. And it is again Islamic law, not nature, which prevents women from fasting and praying during menstruation.

Islamic law also places a premium on men marrying virgins, and the discussion of this point sometimes displays a lack of concern for the girl or woman as we see in this Hadith:

> When I got married, Allah's Messenger said to me, "What type of lady have you married?" I replied, "I have married a matron." He said, "Why don't you have a liking for the virgins and for fondling them?" Jabir also said: "Allah's Messenger

---

322 Khaled Abou El Fadl, *Speaking in God's Name: Islamic Law, Authority, and Women*, London: One World Publications, 2001, pp. 231-232.

323 Quoted in ibid., p. 225.

> said, "Why don't you marry a young girl so that you might play with her and she with you?"[324]

And while mutual sexual play is contemplated here, we should notice that the Hadith is focused on the man choosing someone to fondle, and the implication is that sexual play is not as satisfying if the man marries a matron.

There is also in the Ahadith a reference to temporary marriages, which seem to be accepted in early Islamic law but later condemned. The idea of temporary marriages is found in a Hadith like the following:

> Narrated 'Abdullah: We used to participate in the holy battles led by Allah's Messenger and we had nothing (no wives) with us. So we said, "Shall we get ourselves castrated?" He forbade us that and then allowed us to marry temporarily by giving her even a garment…

Such a Hadith seems to legalize a form of prostitution, where the giving of something to a woman counts as a proper way to engage in sexual intercourse, which would otherwise be outlawed, because a kind of marriage has occurred. Yet, the temporary marriage can be easily ended without following the normal laws concerning divorce.

IV. Adultery and Sexual Assault

Gratian is quite clear on the wrongness of rape and sexual assault, when he quotes from the works of Labeo:

> In the Title on Extraordinary Crimes: "The seducer of married persons and likewise the spoilers of marriage, even if they are not able to avail in the carrying out of their crime, are punished by an extraordinary process on account of their will for pernicious desire… He who persuades a boy (either an abducted or corrupted companion) to commit debauchery… receives capital punishment for his disgraceful act if it is completed and is deported to an island if it has not been fully carried out.[325]

---

324 Hadith 5080, vol. 7, p. 27.

325 Gratian, *Tractatus de Penitentia*, Distinction I, translated by Atria A. Larson, Washington, DC: The Catholic University of America Press, 2016, p. 7.

The punishments here are quite severe, as is recognized by Gratian, marking the fact that sexual assault is regarded in the Canon law as an especially terrible crime.

Canon law and Islamic law have very severe penalties indeed for sexual assault and rape. It is not always clear though that the concern is one of honor or of more serious concern for the well-being of the woman assaulted. And it is also not clear that men and women should be treated the same in terms of punishment for sexual assault. As Khaled Abou El Fadl tells us, Islamic legal texts rely on "the dubious logic that women should pay the price for the impious failures of men."[326] We can also find references in Canon law to the idea that women are the tempters of men and must bear a large part of the blame if they are sexually assaulted.

James Brundage discusses how sexual assault was treated by ecclesiastical and Canon law courts as follows:

> In addition to their civil jurisdiction, ecclesiastical courts also exercised jurisdiction over a wide variety of criminal matters… Church courts sometimes dealt with marriage problems as criminal matters and exercised, as we have seen, a broad jurisdiction over sex crimes. Perhaps not surprisingly, fornication, adultery, and other common sex offenses usually counted for the largest part of criminal business that came before local ecclesiastical tribunals.[327]

We will next discuss the types of punishments and who was considered the one most responsible but already here we can see that the ecclesiastical courts first took on crimes concerning marriage, since it was considered primarily a sacrament, and then also took up cases that involved sex outside of marriage.

In the ecclesiastical law of Aelfric, we learn that Canon law does not punish clerics very severely when they engage in fornication:

> Beloved: the canons teach us how we should regulate our lives. Canons the right rules are called which direct us, and they ordain, that he who of the lay order takes a widow to wife, or a repudiated wife, be never afterwards deacon or mass-priest;

[326] Khaled Abou El Fadl, *Speaking in God's Name: Islamic Law, Authority, and Women*, London: One World Publications, 2001, p. 235.
[327] James A. Brundage, *Medieval Canon Law*, London: Longman, 1995, pp. 90-91.

> and they direct, that the man in orders, who commits foul fornication, forfeit his order.[328]

Expulsion from holy orders is a serious penalty but not as severe as the physical punishments, and death, that we find frequently assigned to the women who were the fornicators.

A twelfth century canonist, Alger of Liege, addresses severity of punishment even as he often calls for mercy:

> This is to be considered most carefully, that one neither neglects the true severity of true discipline in preserving unity, nor destroys the bonds of Christian society by the excesses of correction.[329]

Indeed, as the Medieval period proceeds, the Canon law punishments, especially of the inquisitions, are notoriously harsh for women who participate in sex crimes or are believed to instigate them.

Islamic law is also especially harsh in treating adultery, whether by the man or woman. Verse 24:2 of the Quran says:

> As for the adulterer and the adulteress, flog them each one hundred lashes, and let not pity for them overcome you concerning God's Judgment, if you believe in God and the Last Day. And let the punishment be witnessed by a group of the believers.[330]

The Study Quran commentary on this passage goes on for several pages. Of interest for us is that other Islamic texts are cited to show that stoning to death was also considered a proper punishment for adultery, although this is somewhat controversial, since the Quran is so specific here–seemingly by its specificity abrogating any other punishment for adultery.

And the commentary on Quran verse 24:2 cites a case where the female in question is punished more severely than the male.

---

[328] Abbott Aelfric, "Aelfric's Pastoral Epistle," 42, in *Ancient Laws and Institutes of England*, Volume II, edited and translated by Benjamin Thorpe, 1840, p. 383.

[329] Alger of Liege, *De Misericordia*, ii. cited and translated in Martin Brett, "Finding the Law: The Sources of Canonical Authority Before Gratian," in *Law Before Gratian*, edited by Per Andersen, Mia Munster-Swendsen, and Helle Vogt, Copenhagen: DJOF Publishing, 2007, p. 66.

[330] *The Study Quran*, pp. 865-868.

> In yet another account, a man attempted to give a kind of compensation for his virgin son's crime of adultery with his employer's wife through a large payment of livestock. The Prophet ordered the virgin's father to take back the goods. He then had the son lashed and exiled, and told the people to go to the woman and ask if she would confess; if she did, they were to stone her. She confessed, and they stoned her to death.[331]

The punishment of being stoned to death for the adulteress is seemingly much more severe than the lashing and exiling of the male adulterer. One might wonder if it is the youth of the adulterer that is taken into account, although there does not appear to be any textual support for this way of explaining the severer punishment for the female than the male.

Here is another account of a law that concerns adultery that results in stoning of the woman in question.

> In another account, a pregnant woman, sometimes as identified as from the tribe of Juhaynah (or its subtribe Ghamid), came and confessed her adultery, and even wondered if the Prophet would try to turn her away as he did with Ma'iz. The Prophet ordered her to go away until she gave birth; when she came back after the baby had been weaned, the Prophet ordered her stoned.[332]

Yet it seems that the Quran itself does not talk of stoning for the crime of adultery.

Consider one commentator's attempt to explain Islamic law's punishment for adultery:

> many commentators and jurists do make the claim that the penalty of stoning to death is *mutawatir*, or "widely transmitted," a technical term that refers to something so widely transmitted that it would be inconceivable for it to have been falsified. Beyond such ambiguities, some basic logical questions arise which are mentioned by al-Razi as objections on the part of the Kharijites. The Quran describes many kinds of transgressions including theft and murder, but does not go into the same level of detail for them as it does for adultery, and thus it is implausible that, in the midst of this detail, stoning, which is a more grievous punishment than all the others mentioned in the Quran, would go unmentioned. It is

---

[331] *The Study Quran*, commentary on verse 24:2, p. 866.

[332] *The Study Quran*, commentary on verse 24:2, p. 866.

> also argued that no solitary hadith could overturn the plain sense of the Quran much less on a question as momentous as imposing the severest of punishments.[333]

So, while there is evidence to think that women are treated more harshly than men who engage in adultery, and evidence that 100 lashes is often the penalty, it is not clear that stoning to death was indeed the approved penalty for adultery by women in Islamic law.

V. Humane Treatment and Religious Law

It is perhaps surprising that the Quran gives more space to the crime of adultery than any other crime including murder. As with Christianity, Islam calls for sex to be restricted to married couples. In order to enforce this religious dogma, severe penalties seem to be called for. But murder is also condemned in no uncertain terms in the Bible and the Quran. It is tempting to say that it is the way that women are seen to be somehow responsible for adultery in ways they are not thought to be responsible for murder that calls for severe punishment. But why would women-centered crimes pose more of a challenge for religious law than other seemingly more serious crimes like murder?

Religious law generally concerns itself with private matters rather than public ones–indeed, secular law is the venue for public matters. In part, it appears that religions are concerned with private matters, especially family relations, because it is in the family that children are socialized into the practices of a given religion. And here we find one primary source of concern in religion for the role of women. For, it is most often women who educate the children into the ways of their religion. And so this line of thinking would go, religion must pay special attention to women to make sure the religious values, rules, and practices are properly conveyed to subsequent generations.

But the attention paid to women in Islamic and Canon law, indeed some would say the obsessive attention paid to women in these systems of law, does not seem to result in an especially humane way that women are to be treated. Women are subjected to various forms of control, such as control by their husbands, which is sanctioned by law. Indeed, here is where religious law becomes harsher toward women than toward men. And it should not go unnoticed that the religious legal authorities are all men in both Canon and Islamic law.

---

[333] *The Study Quran*, commentary on verse 24:2, p. 867.

Islamic and Canon law justify the control of wives by their husbands by claiming that women are weak in body and mind. As we will see in the next chapter, slavery is also justified in terms of the supposedly weak minds of those who are enslaved. Women need to be controlled and subject to the men in their lives so as to help them–and it could be that this claim rests on a kind of humanistic spirit. But the control over women is also clearly set out in a spirit of furthering the superior social position of men.

Women are not treated the same as men in terms of inheritance and also, perhaps most perversely, even in terms of their status as witnesses. Religious law is invoked to subjugate women in the home, but why also in the public arena of court proceedings? Perhaps it is the supposed weakness of the mind of women that justifies the adverse treatment of women in court. It is interesting though that in Islamic law it is the fact that two female witnesses are equivalent to just one male witness that is used to provide evidence for the inferior position of women in the non-public domain. In Canon law we find that women are also subject to differential and unequal treatment as compared to men, again in the household.

In addition, though, as we have seen, Islamic and Canon law stress that consent is necessary for a valid marriage. This provision is especially beneficial to women since they have been historically subject to coercion to marry the person their families want them to. And in the writings about this legal requirement it becomes clear that it is respect for the woman that undergirds the consent requirement. In this respect there is a significant advance in the humane treatment of women in both of these legal systems of the Medieval period.

The insertion of a cornerstone of Roman law, the contract, into religious law of the Medieval period is especially interesting since it is not clear that the Romans had a similar application of contract law to marriage. And perhaps even more interesting is that authorities of Islamic and Canon law would employ the very secular idea of a contract in order to deal with marriage considered to be a sacred arrangement. Perhaps most fascinating of all is that the idea of a contract between equals in marriage, a clearly just and equitable way to treat the marriage couple, was supposedly derived from divine sources.

We have both Islamic and Canon law drawing on the Biblical story of God creating Eve out of the rib of Adam in order to give Adam a helpmate. It would seem that this divine source of law would lead religious authorities to treat women in subordinate ways to men. And this is indeed partially true as we have seen in this chapter. But it is also from divine sources that the idea of a free and equal contract was said to epitomize the marriage relationship. We will see similarly incongruous ideas at play in the way Islamic and Canon law treated slaves as well, in our next chapter.

CHAPTER 14

SLAVERY UNDER RELIGIOUS LAW

In an ideal world, one would hope that morally noxious institutions like slavery would be outlawed in societies that were governed by religious law: such as Islamic and Canon law. At least for those who are believers, Medieval religious law called for equal treatment or at least equal respect for all. And so, we find that various religious doctrines did call for people not to subjugate or oppress. But these doctrines ran up against the reality that slavery was deeply entrenched in most aspects of Medieval life. Slaves were owned even by those who were themselves the leading religious authorities who were supposed to be moral exemplars in those societies. In this case, theory was driven by practice and religious rationales were constructed to justify slavery, even as there were many attempts to protect the slaves from the worst of the abuses perpetrated by their owners.

As we have seen, religious law tends to blur borders between the moral and the strictly legal. This is perhaps most apparent in family situations where religious texts set out not only moral doctrines but legal rules concerning marriage, divorce, inheritance, and sexual practices. Since many slaves are kept in the household one can understand why religious texts sought to regulate slavery practices. Yet, it is also true that many slaves were kept in very large estates which were hardly much like the intimate small-scale family setting that religious law claimed as its purview.

In the first section of this chapter, we will examine the way that slaves are regulated in Medieval Islamic law. In the second section, we then sketch the status of the slave in Medieval Canon law. In the third section, we discuss manumission in Islamic law and in Canon law. In the fourth section we discuss the penalties for those who free slaves or aid in their escape. In the final section we critically assess the disconnect between the often strong humane ideas espoused by religious law and the not very humane ideas about the treatment of slaves.

I. Islamic Law and Slavery

Islamic legal thought casts all believers as equal brothers and sisters but this does not mean that God can not favor some over others in the provisions that God provides. Here are verses 16:70-71 of the Quran:

> God created you; then He takes you [unto Himself]. And among you are those who are brought back to the weakest of ages, such that they know nothing after having had knowledge. Truly God is Knowing, Powerful. And God has favored some of you above others in provision. Those who have been favored do not hand over their provisions to those whom their right hands possess [slaves], such that they would be equal in this regard. Would they thus reject the blessings of God?[334]

And in the notes on this passage in the Study Quran we learn:

> Commentators point out that those *favored…in provision* and those who are servants or slaves (*those whom their right hands possess*) are equal in their humanity; indeed, Muslims are enjoined to think of them as brothers and sisters, and many Ahadith instruct Muslims to feed and clothe them with the same food and clothing they enjoy themselves… v. 71 should not be read to mean that slaves are somehow inferior to free persons spiritually or with regard to their humanity, but only in their physical and social capacities or autonomy in external matters.[335]

It here seems that slaves are in need of the help of non-slaves because they are weak in the ability to govern themselves, even as they are equal to their masters in terms of their spiritual being and humanity. There is no sense that slaves have sinned, as we will find in the Catholic Canonic texts, but there is a characteristic of slaves that makes it imperative that they not be treated as equal except in their humanity.

Yet there is the sense that slaves are indeed somehow inferior to their masters, at least in the same sense that the people of Islam are inferior to their God.

> Unto Him belongs whosoever is in the heavens and on the earth; all are devoutly obedient to Him. He it is Who originates creation, then brings it back, and that is most easy for Him.

---

[334] *The Study Quran*, 16:70-71, p. 676.

[335] *The Study Quran*, pp. 676-677.

> Unto Him belongs the loftiest description in the heavens and on the earth, and He is the Mighty, the Wise. He sets forth for you a parable from yourselves: have you, among those whom your right hands possess [slaves], partners in what We have provided for you, such that you are equal with respect to it, with you fearing them as you fear each other? Thus do We expound the signs for a people to understand.[336]

And then there is this comment in one of the notes accompanying these verses:

> The parable established here compares the relationship between God and those whom the idolaters ascribe as partners to God to the relationship between human beings and their own slaves or servants. The rhetorical questions indicate that no one would envision a slave or a servant having an equal share in the master's wealth or fear that the slave would have an equal right to it, just as God the Absolute Sovereign, would not fear anything else sharing in His Power. The argument is that if one cannot envision this state of affairs for one's own limited sphere of sovereignty, how can one attribute it to the universal sovereignty of God?[337]

So, we have a parallel proposed between God's sovereignty over his people, and the master's sovereignty over his slaves or servants.

Regardless of which recognition comes first, the idea seems to be that God has sovereignty over his people because in some respects they are incapable of governing themselves, and so also masters have sovereignty over their slaves because the slaves are incapable of governing themselves in some respects. At least to this extent the argument here is not unlike that of the Ancient Greeks like Aristotle or the Romans like Cicero, who recognize the equal humanity of slaves and masters but see slavery as a necessary evil in that it helps slaves to keep to the right path.

II. Canon Law and Slavery

One of the differences between Islamic law's treatment of slavery and Canon Law's treatment is that the slave in Canon law is thought to have sinned and stands in need of some way to redeem himself or herself. As we will see, these two religious systems of law are similar in that

---

[336] *The Study Quran*, 30:26-28, p. 990.

[337] *The Study Quran*, p. 990.

slaves are recognized as equal to their masters in their humanity but slaves need something from their masters in order to overcome their positions. For the Canonists, the condition that separated slave from freeman was that of sin.

Here is how A. J. Carlyle describes the dominant idea of the Canonists about slavery:

> The canonists inherited from the later philosophers of the ancient world, from the *corpus juris civilis*, and from the Fathers, the principle that by nature all men are free and equal, that slavery is an institution not of nature or of natural law, but of the *jus gentium* or the civil law… It is sin not nature that has made some men free and some slaves; the origin of slavery is to be found not in some inherent and natural distinction in human nature, but in the fact that sin, as it has depraved men's nature, so it has disordered all relations of human society, and man now needs a discipline which in his original condition would have been unnecessary as it would have been unnatural. Burchard of Worms cites that very important saying of St. Isidore's, which describes slavery as a consequence of the sin of the first man–a punishment, but also a remedy by which the evil dispositions of men may be restrained.[338]

Humans are all free and equal by nature, but some humans have sinned. These are the slaves and we need to search hard for a coherent doctrine of how slaves can be sinners, even from birth, if all humans are equal by nature.

Some of the Canonists seem to take a page from the earliest of the ancient legal theorists to consider slavery–namely, that slaves had been conquered on the battlefield and since their lives were spared despite the fact that they had tried to kill their conquerors, their lives were spared as long as they were taken as slaves instead of being killed. As in ancient times, at least one Canon lawyer, Hrabanus Maurus, traces slavery to the idea of "the slave, servus, as that of one who might be slain, but was spared (servatus)."[339] Hrabanus also links slavery to iniquity–presumably something that has existed since the birth of the slave.

One can understand why slavery would have to be traced to something about the birth of the slave since many household slaves were

---

[338] A. J. Carlyle, *A History of Medieval Political Theory in the West*, London: William Blackwood and Sons Ltd., 1909, vol. II, pp. 117-119.

[339] Quoted in A. J. Carlyle, *A History of Medieval Political Theory in the West*, London: William Blackwood and Sons Ltd., 1909, vol. I, p. 203.

born in their master's house. The question though is what it is about the slave's birth, different from the birth of the free man, that was sinful and in need of punishment as a type of redemption? It cannot be original sin, since all humans are said to have original sin as a result of the sins of Adam and Eve in the Garden of Eden. And original sin was from before birth, not a condition that exists from birth. We can turn to Rufinus for the beginning of an answer, but one that is still problematic:

> Rufinus discusses the question of the apparent contradiction between the law of nature and the civil law with regard to slavery... Natural law shows that freedom is a good condition, and slavery would at first sight seem to be contrary to this, but its real purpose is to correct men's evil desires and criminal passions, and to produce those qualities of humility and innocence in which the natural law is fulfilled. Freedom is, indeed, that condition which is agreeable to natural law, but men are not yet fit for that condition.[340]

In this account, slavery "is adapted not to the ideal of human life, but to the actual imperfections of men's nature."[341] But then why are only some people enslaved?

III. Manumission in Islamic and Canon Law

In the Ahadith, the manumission of slaves is discussed in some detail. Indeed, Book 49 is called "The Book of Manumission." This book begins by quoting from the Quran's verse 90:

> It is the freeing of the slave, or giving food in time of famine to an orphan near of kin, or an indigent clinging to the dust, while being one of those who believe and exhort one another to patience, and exhort another to compassion. These are the companions of the right.[342]

Then Ahadith 2517 and 2518 set the stage for the lengthy discussion of manumission that follows:

---

340 R. W. Carlyle and A. J. Carlyle, *A History of Medieval Political Theory in the West*, London: Blackwood and Sons Ltd., 1909, vol. II, pp. 119-120.
341 Ibid., vol. II, p. 120.
342 *The Study Quran*, 90:13-18, pp. 1516-1517.

> The Prophet said, "Whoever frees a Muslim slave, Allah will save all the parts of his body from the (Hell) of Fire as he has manumitted the body-parts of the slave... I asked the Prophet, "What is the best deed?" He replied: "To believe in Allah and to fight for His Cause." I then asked, "What is the best kind of manumission (of slaves)?" He replied, "The manumission of the most expensive slave and the most beloved by his master."[343]

Freeing one's slave, especially if it costs a person quite a bit to do so, is considered one of the highest of virtues in Islamic legal thought. And the idea behind this rule is that "Slaves are your brothers."[344]

We also find that Islamic legal and political thought supports the idea that slaves who have not or cannot be manumitted should not be abused. Hadith 2559, which ends the chapter on manumission, has this rule: "If somebody beats a slave, he should avoid the face."[345] Of course, it would generally be much more humane not to beat the slave at all, at least as we would understand things today. But the beating of slaves had been a custom of many ancient and medieval societies, and so the restraint of this Hadith can be seen as at least somewhat humane.

There is also another Hadith that speaks of more humane treatment of slaves than 2559:

> Narrated by Al-Mar'ur bin Suwaid: I saw Abu Dhar Al-Ghifari wearing a cloak, and his slave too was wearing a cloak. We asked him about that (i.e., how both were wearing similar cloaks). He replied, "Once I abused a man and he complained of me to the Prophet. The Prophet asked me, 'Did you abuse him by slighting his mother?' He added, 'Your slaves are your brethren upon whom Allah has given you authority. So, if one has one's brethren under one's control, one should feed them with the like of what one eats and clothe them with the like of what one wears. You should not overburden them with what they cannot bear, and if you do so, help them (in their hard job).'"[346]

---

[343] *Ahadith: The Translation of the Meaning of Sahih Al-Bukhari*, 2517-2518, translated by Muhammad Muhsin Khan, Riyadh: Darussalam Publishers, 1997, 2015, vol. 3, p. 402.
[344] Hadith 2544, vol. 3, p. 415.
[345] Hadith 2559, vol. 3, p. 421.
[346] Hadith 2545, vol. 3, pp. 415-416.

This verse reflects better the idea that Islamic law calls for slaves to be humanely treated.

In early Canon legal and political thought, we find the struggle that many ancient and medieval systems of law had also struggled with: slaves were to be treated as free and equal to every other of God's children. But the institutional fact of slavery, where even religious leaders were not immune from owning slaves, and perhaps because of this fact, slavery was not forthrightly condemned. And even the topic of manumitting the slaves owned by the Church or the leaders of the Church presented a tricky problem.

Here is how Carlyle describes the predicament that the canonists found themselves in:

> Freedom is, indeed, that condition which is agreeable to natural law, but men are not yet fit for that condition. The canonists, then, like the Fathers and the jurists, recognize that slavery is contrary to natural law–that is, it is a condition adapted not to the ideal of human life, but to the actual imperfections of men's nature. But the canonists, like the Fathers, while they hold that slavery is not a natural institution, not only tolerate it but justify it; they not only acquiesce in the institution, but hold that it serve a useful purpose. The strongest illustration of this attitude of canon law to slavery is that the Church was itself a slave-owner…[347]

The conflict between ideal morality and institutional need was not easy to adjudicate.

Carlyle then begins his discussion of manumission of slaves in Canon law with this comment:

> Regino includes in his collection some sentences from a canon of a Council of Toledo, which strictly forbid a bishop to emancipate slaves who belong to the Church unless he gives of his own property to the Church; if any bishop should emancipate Church slaves except under these conditions, his successor is to reclaim them.[348]

Church slaves presented an especially difficult topic for canonists.

---

[347] A. J. Carlyle, *A History of Medieval Political Theory in the West*, London: William Blackwood and Sons Ltd., 1909, vol. I, p. 120

[348] Ibid.

There are at least two reasons in favor of not freeing slaves provided by these Canonists. First, some people have sinned and need a way to redeem themselves and being a slave who shows obedience to a master is a very clear way to do this that should not be denied to the slave. And second, slaves are still seen under the dual Roman law categories as persons but also as objects. As objects they are property, and it is improper for property to be taken from its owner without due compensation. And this second rationale against freeing slaves is buttressed by the fact that some slaves are the property of the Church and Church property was especially to be protected.

And there is a very vexed topic for canon lawyers, namely, how to treat slaves who had been ordained into one or another religious order of the Church. These slaves were unfree and yet all members of religious orders must be free. But even slaves who had been ordained were not by that act of ordination freed since there is a canon stating that "no abbot or monk can emancipate a slave" without paying the slave's master the slave's price.[349]

IV. Penalties for Aiding Slaves

Those who free slaves or who aid slaves to escape their masters face serious penalties in both early Medieval Islamic and Canon law. Despite the talk of seeing slaves as brothers or seeing the manumission of slaves as a virtue, the actual freeing of slaves by extra-legal means was very strongly condemned in the religious texts of this period of the early Middle Ages.

Here is how Carlyle characterizes the consensus among Canon law scholars on how to deal with slaves who fled from their masters:

> the canon law accepted and sanctioned the institution of slavery, for they assume that the Church itself was a slave-owner. But the medieval canon law goes further than this, and repeats from earlier Church authorities the very severe condemnation of those who encouraged slaves to fly from their masters, and of fugitive slaves. Burchard of Worms cites the canon of Gangrae… in which the anathema of the Church is pronounced against those who teach slaves to despise their masters and to fly from them, and also part of the letter of Hrabanus Maurus which comments on this and discusses the question whether it was lawful to say mass for a slave who

---

[349] See ibid., pp. 120-121.

> died while in flight. Burchard also cites a canon of the Council of Altheim which professes to repeat a saying of Gregory the Great, that a cleric flying from his church, or a slave flying from his master, is to be excluded from communion until he return. Ivo of Chartres repeats these two canons in his "Decretum," while Gratian cites the canon of Gangrae. The canonists clearly look upon the institution of slavery as in such a sense authorized and sanctioned by God that any revolt against it is sinful.[350]

Notice that excommunication, and rendering someone anathema, two of the strongest punishments of Canon law, are the penalties for aiding the fleeing slave.

As we have seen, there is an entire book of the Ahadith devoted largely to praising the proper manumission of slaves. There is no virtue in freeing slaves against the wishes of the slave's master or without paying the slaves manumission price. Here is a set of verses from a book of volume 3 of the Ahadith as reported by Sahih Al-Bukhari.

> I asked the Prophet… "What is the best kind of manumission (of slaves)?" He replied, "The manumission of the most expensive slave and the most beloved slave." I said, "if I cannot afford to do that?" He said, "Help the weak or do good for a person who cannot work for himself." I said, "If I cannot do that?" He said, "Refrain from harming others for this will be regarded as a charitable deed of your own good."[351]

Freeing slaves can be an act of charity, according to this Hadith, but only if it is done properly by paying the accepted price. Otherwise freeing a slave is a kind of theft.

Yet, there are oddities in the Ahadith, one of which we will cite here before attempting to draw some conclusions:

> Narrated by Jabir bin 'Abdullah: A man amongst us declared that his slave would be manumitted after his death. The Prophet called for that slave and sold him. The slave died the same year.

This Hadith has left some puzzled about the commitment of Islamic law to freeing slaves.

---

350 A. J. Carlyle, ibid., p. 122.

351 Hadith 2518, book 3, pp. 402-403.

We have here an instance of the Prophet Muhammad selling a slave when the slave could have been freed instead. This would seemingly be an odd result given the verses where the Prophet praises those who properly manumit slaves. One translator of this Hadith says: "The liberator was needy, so the Prophet sold the slave for him, permitting him to cancel his promise of manumitting the slave after his death."[352]

We are still left with the oddity that in Islamic law selling a slave, rather than freeing the slave, is preferred in some cases if the master was in need of money. While Islamic legal texts are ambiguous on whether slaves should be freed and whether freeing slaves is condemned, Islamic law nonetheless seems to be better positioned humanely than does Canon law. In any event religious law in the early Medieval period does not give us a fully humane doctrine concerning slavery.

V. Religious Law and Slavery

It is a fact that slavery persisted throughout the Medieval period, and that religious law does not forthrightly condemn slavery. It is not irrelevant that religious leaders, even the most important of religious leaders such as the Muslim Prophet and the Bishops of the Catholic Church owned slaves and did not seem to see themselves as having engaged in immoral or illegal behavior by doing so. Divine and natural law, with their emphasis on equality and dignity for all members of a given religion, are not the sources of condemning slavery in a way we might have expected from our own contemporary perspectives.

The religious law of the canonists is meant to be a more humane law than that of the so-called barbarians of the Germanic peoples; and the religious law of Islam was meant to be a more humane law than the traditional law of the Arabs. But in the matter of owning slaves, the supposed humaneness of these religious legal systems is not apparent. In this final section I will assess the similarities and differences of the Islamic and Canon law in the treatment of slaves.

It should be noted that slaves are clearly some of the worst-off members of societies where slavery is allowed. Traditionally, widows, orphans, aliens, and the poor are recognized as the worst-off members of society. It is rare that slaves were put into that list in ancient legal and political thought. Medieval legal and political thought, especially that of Islamic scholars and the canonists, does recognize the precarious status of slaves–where Islamic law does a better job than Canon law in this

[352] Ibid., p. 410, note 1.

domain–although as we have seen both types of religious law can be seen as urging some humane treatment of slaves.

One possible reason that both Islamic law and Canon law failed to see the freeing of slaves as a moral obligation is that both of these systems of law remained deeply indebted to Roman legal thought, especially to the legal theory of Gaius, as well as the philosophical views of Cicero and even Seneca. The slave was legal property and as such it was simply theft for the slave to be taken from his or her master. The Romans also saw that there was a conflict in that slaves were not only property but also persons. But the slave's status of being a person was a kind of ideal–in Roman law this status was one of the laws of nature but not of the civil law or the law of peoples.

In some respects one can say that ideally slaves should be treated as persons with full rights as were given to other persons, but as a non-ideal matter, given the way the world worked, slaves were most importantly seen as property, basically with no rights or very few. In considering the treatment of slaves, there is more humaneness in the Islamic law than in the Canon law, in that the specific injunctions especially in the Quran are fairly strong whereas the various Canonists often merely speak in a nonspecific way of alleviating the exploitation of slaves.

If it is correct to see the Canon law as well as Islamic law as deeply indebted to Roman law for the treatment of slaves, then it appears that the religious nature of these systems of law is not terribly meaningful. The pagan Romans and Arabs seemingly held the same views of slavery as did the religious Muslims and Catholics. And this poses the question of what the value is of having legal systems grounded in religious creeds and texts.

Divine law, as well as natural law, give to legal systems a kind of moral veneer that is largely lacking in systems of law that arise wholly from the ideas of human legislators. As I have in earlier sections of my work on ancient and medieval legal thought, I use examples like slavery as test cases to determine what changes when one adopts one source of law as opposed to another source. When a fleeing slave approaches a member of a religion that speaks loudly of the virtue of charity toward all, what happens provides a kind of test of how important moral values are in legal arrangements.

In the work of the Canonists, we find that the concept of sanctuary is strongly voiced, especially when considering those who have been unjustly accused of a crime. Indeed, the idea of sanctuary as understood in the Medieval Catholic Church has very recently been seen as a model of how religiously-oriented people should respond to those who are in need of help. But already in the writing of the Canonists we can see that "the Church offers a certain protection to the slave through the right of sanctuary, but the Church must not finally detain the slave or allow the slave to escape from his master by seeking its protection."[353] In a sense, Christian charity does not trump property rights. And this is also true of the idea of sanctuary in Greek and Roman legal thought, which were not grounded in religious ideals. Islamic legal thought is perhaps similarly plagued by the problem that while all people are supposed to act charitably toward each other, the rights of property holders also seem to predominate.

[353] R. W. Carlyle and A. J. Carlyle, *A History of Medieval Political Theory in the West*, London: Blackwood and Sons Ltd., 1909, vol. II, p.133.

CHAPTER 15

RULES FOR RELIGIOUS LIFE

We now come to a domain where the Islamic and Canon law seem to be most distinctly different: the rules for how to practice religion on a daily basis. As we will see, these differences seem most pronounced in the lives led by Jesus and Muhammad that were supposed to operate as exemplars for the followers of these religious leaders. The legal regimes that were set up to sanction the moral rules of correct religious practice on a daily basis also seem to be at the most divergent here.

Yet, as we will see there are many similarities even in the domain of the rules for daily religious life between Islamic and Canon law. In the early Medieval versions of Islamic and Canon law, prayer was highly regulated and required several times a day. Humility was the cardinal virtue, and obedience to God and to God's representatives on earth was paramount. Sexual relations were also highly regulated. Male head of households were afforded near sovereignty over the members of their families. In these respects, and many others, the similarities between Islamic and Canon law were greater than were the differences.

In the first section of this chapter, we will begin with a comparison between the moral exemplars of Jesus and Muhammad. In the second section we will then look to the way the leaders of these religious communities were regulated. And in the third section we will examine the regulation of daily prayer. This will be followed by the regulation of sexual practices. And we will end with a section discussing the way law made a difference in these religious regulations. Throughout I will argue that the similarities are, perhaps surprisingly, greater than the differences.

I. The Moral Exemplars: Jesus and Muhammad

The founders of two of the largest religious organizations were, on first sight, about as different as they could be. According to the traditional account, Jesus never married, whereas Muhammad had nine wives. Jesus preached a version of pacifism, whereas Muhammad led his followers into battle.

Concerning Jesus as an exemplar, we have the following from Amalar of Metz quoting Augustine of Hippo:

> Augustine, in his preface to this Psalm [Ps. 90:1], shows through this psalm how we should appropriately imitate Christ's passion. "In what respect," he writes, "are we to imitate Christ's paths? Surely not in that magnificence through which he was God in the flesh? Or does he exhort or demand of us that we perform miracles like those he performed?"... And a little later: "'Learn of me because I am meek and humble of heart.' What was done on your account is what you should attend to in him, that you might imitate him."... If, therefore, you too suffer the vexations that the devil has prepared in this world, whether openly through men or secretly, as in the case of Job, may you be strong and enduring. You will live "in the aid of the most high," as this Psalm says.[354]

The exemplar of Jesus' life teaches meekness and humility but also strength in the face of evil and wrongdoing. We also find many references to Jesus as the model of how the religious life is best lived as a celibate life.

Concerning Muhammad as an exemplar we find these words from Hadith 3708 concerning appearance and character:

> The Prophet said (to him), "You resemble me both in appearance and character.
> Narrated Abu Hurairah: The People used to say, "Abu Hurairah narrates too many narrations." In fact, I used to keep close to Allah's Messenger and was satisfied with what filled my stomach. I ate no leavened bread and dressed in no decorated striped clothes, and never did a man or woman serve me, and I often used to press my belly against gravel because of hunger, and I used to ask a man to recite a Quranic Verse to me although I knew it, so that he would take me to his home and feed me. And the most generous of all the people to the poor was Ja'far bin Abi Talib. He used to take us to his home and offer us what was available therein.[355]

---

[354] Amalar of Metz, *On the Liturgy*, translated by Eric Knibbs, Cambridge, MA: Harvard University Press, 2014, vol. I, pp. 157-159.

[355] Hadith 3708, vol. 5, pp. 51-52.

According to this Hadith, Muhammad was an exemplar who stressed that one should aid those in poverty and hunger and act modestly as well as not engage in overeating or even eating food that was more tasty.

And we also find in Ahadith 5066 and 5067 that there is no virtue in being celibate, as was true of Muhammad's own life:

> So Allah's Messenger said, "O young people! Whoever among you is able to marry, should marry, because it helps him lower his gaze and guard his modesty (i.e. his private parts from committing illegal sexual intercourse etc.), and whoever is not able to marry should fast, as fasting will diminish his sexual power.
> Narrated by 'Ata: We attended along with Ibn 'Abbas the funeral procession of Maimuna at a place called Sarif. Ibn 'Abbas said: "This is the wife of the Prophet, so when you lift her bier, do not jerk it or shake it much, but walk smoothly because the prophet had nine wives and he used to observe the night turns with eight of them, and for one of them there was no night turn."[356]

The exemplar of Muhammad here instructs all men to marry for the sake of modesty–where this means following Muhammad in having multiple wives, as long as he has sexual power sufficient to give most of his wives a turn.

II. Clerics, Monastics, and Imams

Canon law sets out very strict rules for religious leaders, whereas Islamic law does not distinguish between the rules for religious leaders and those for everyone else. There is a recognized religious leader called the imam, who is mentioned in the Quran as follows:

> We have indeed honored the Children of Adam and We carry them over land with good things, and We favored them above many we have created. On the Day We shall call every people by their imam, whosoever is given his book in his right hand, it is they who shall read their book, and they shall not be wronged as much as the thread of a date stone.[357]

---

[356] Ahadith 5066 and 5067, vol. 7, p. 21.
[357] *The Study Quran*, 17:70-71, pp. 714-715.

The commentary on these verses in the Study Quran is:

> An *imam* is a person or sometimes a source of religious instruction taken as a guide, or model to be imitated. The term derives from a root meaning to be or to stand in front of something; imam can thus refer to one who, standing in front, leads the Muslim congregation in prayer. In the Islamic tradition, *imam* is also a title given to a religious scholar who has acquired great knowledge and influence...Lexically, however, *imam* is a value neutral term, and the Quran mentions, as *imams*, both righteous individuals, such as Abraham, Isaac, and Jacob (2:124; 21:73) and iniquitous ones, such as Pharaoh and his hosts, who are described as *imams calling unto the Fire* (28:41). That people will be called by their leader may mean that they will be called according to the prophet (see 45:28) or the religion that they followed in this life.... the *imams* by which people are called may refer to spiritual leaders, religious scholars, or indirectly the religious schools of thought that they followed in this life.[358]

Imams are religious leaders or scholars in Islamic law. In Canon law there are several different religious leaders and scholars as we will next see–each differentiated in terms of their rules. The undifferentiated imams do not have their rules clearly spelled out, leaving us to assume that they were to follow the same rules as every other Muslim.

According to Canon and ecclesiastical law, there are religious who are monks, priests, nuns, abbots, abbesses, bishops, and popes. The Rule of St. Benedict was the most influential of the monastic rules in the Middle Ages. In the first and third chapters of Benedict's Rule, the regulations for monks are preliminarily set out as follows:

> There are clearly four types of monks. First, there are the cenobites, that is to say, those who belong to a monastery, where they serve under a rule and an abbot. Second are the anchorites or hermits, who come through the test of living in a monastery for a long time, and have passed beyond the first fervor of monastic life.... in every instance, all are to follow the teaching of the rule, and no one shall rashly deviate from it. In the monastery no one is to follow his own heart's desire, nor shall anyone contend with his abbot defiantly, or outside the monastery. Should anyone presume to do so, let him be

---

[358] *The Study Quran*, p. 715.

> subjected to the discipline of the rule. Moreover the abbot must fear God and keep the rule in everything he does.[359]

Obedience and discipline are key components of the monastic rule: Monks should obey their abbots, and the abbots must obey God; both monks and abbots are subject to the monastic rule.

The qualities of the abbot, or the ruler of the monastery, are set out in the second chapter of Benedict's Rule:

> To be worthy of the task of governing a monastery, the abbot must always remember what his title signifies, and act as a superior should. He is believed to hold the place of Christ in the monastery...anyone who receives the name of abbot is to lead his disciples by a twofold teaching: he must point out to them all that is good and holy more by example than by words, proposing the commandments of the Lord... Again, if he teaches his disciples that something is not to be done, then neither must he do it... The abbot should avoid all favoritism in the monastery. He is not to love one more than another unless he finds someone better in good actions and obedience. A man born free is not to be given higher rank than a slave who becomes a monk, except for some other good reason.[360]

Abbots are under the disciplinary rule as leaders of the monastery. They are to be impartial in administering the rule to the monks and lead them by example to do what is good and avoid what is evil.

Along with obedience, humility is to be greatly prized by monks. Chapter seven of Benedict's Rule sets out twelve steps in the path toward the humility that monks should display. Here are a few of those steps:

> The first step of humility, then is that a man keep the *fear of God* always *before his eyes* (Ps. 35[36]:2) and never forgets it....
>
> The fourth step of humility is that in this obedience under difficult, unfavorable, or even unjust conditions, his heart quietly embraces suffering and endures it without weakening or seeking escape....
>
> The sixth step of humility is that a monk is content with the lowest and most menial treatment, and regards himself as a poor and worthless workman in whatever task he is given....

---

359 *The Rule of St. Benedict in English*, chapter 1 and 3,edited by Timothy Fry, Collegeville, MN: The Liturgical Press, 1982, pp. 20 and 26.

360 *The Rule of St. Benedict*, chapter 2, pp. 21-23.

> The ninth step of humility is that a monk controls his tongue and remains silent, not speaking unless asked a question.... The twelfth step of humility is that...Whether he sits, walks or stands, his head must be bowed and his eyes cast down.[361]

Humility here means suffering even unjust conditions, remaining silent in most matters, accepting menial tasks, and keeping his head bowed. Imams as well as Muslims generally are also taught that humility is an important virtue–where keeping one's gaze downcast is one characteristic.

Monks are also restricted in their ownership of property and in the consumption of food and drink. Here are the relevant chapters of Benedict's Rule:

> Above all, this evil practice [private ownership] must be uprooted and removed from the monastery. We mean that without an order from the abbot, no one may presume to give, receive, or retain anything of his own, nothing at all–not a book, writing tablets, or stylus–in short, not a single item, especially since monks may not have free disposal even of their own bodies and wills.[362]

It is a sign of the extreme poverty of the monk's life that Benedict's Rule dictates that monks are not even to possess their own bodies or wills.

And yet there is some leeway in Benedict's Rule, especially concerning the consumption of wine:

> we believe a half bottle of wine a day is sufficient. The superior will determine when local conditions, work or the summer heat indicates the need for a greater amount. He must, in any case, take great care lest excess or drunkenness creep in. We read that monks should not drink wine at all, but since the monks of our day cannot be convinced of this, let us at least agree to drink moderately, and not to the point of excess.[363]

Consuming more than a half bottle of wine a day might perhaps make up for the fact that the monks cannot own even their bodies or wills.

In the Quran, the consumption of wine and spirits is initially allowed but later in the text it is outlawed. There is, as in the Rule of Benedict, a difficulty concerning wine and spirits. It is thought that

---

361 *The Rule of St. Benedict*, chapter 7, pp. 32-37.
362 *The Rule of St. Benedict*, chapter 33, p. 56.
363 *The Rule of St. Benedict*, chapter 40, p. 62.

moderation is best in both of the traditions we are examining. But moderate drinking often leads to excessive drinking. The Quran deals with this problem ultimately by forbidding drinking alcohol, whereas the monastic rules allow for moderate drinking and seek to enforce it stringently, even though allowing for local variations. As we will next see there are other similarities between Canon and Islamic law as well, especially concerning the regulation of how often prayer must be offered in a religious life.

III. Regulating Prayer and Liturgy

Canon law stipulates that monks and some other religious leaders are to pray seven times a day, similar to what we find in the Rule of Benedict of the 6th century:

> The Prophet says: Seven times a day have I praised you (Ps 118[119]: 164). We will fulfill this sacred number of seven if we satisfy our obligations of service at Lauds, Prime, Terce, Sext, None, Vespers, and Compline, for it was of these hours during the day that he said: Seven times a day have I praised you (Ps 118[119]: 164).

So, we have a mandate that clerics pray seven times a day, even being required to get up in the middle of the night to pray.

This requirement also obtained when monks were traveling outside the monastery, if they were given permission to do so. Here again is the Rule of Benedict:

> Brothers who work so far away that they cannot return for the oratory at the proper time–and the abbot determines that this is the case–are to perform the work of God where they are, and kneel out of reverence for God. So, too those who have been sent on a journey are not to omit the prescribed hours but to observe them as best they can, not neglecting their measure of service.[364]

The monastic requirement of praying seven times a day was scrupulously disciplined so that the monk's life of prayer became a habit.

In addition, the various monastic rules, which were part of the larger Canon law documents at the time, also specified which prayers were to be said and when. Here is just a sample of some of the rules:

---

[364] *The Rule of St. Benedict*, chapter 50, p. 72.

> Three psalms are to be said at Prime, each followed by "Glory be the Father." The hymn for this hour is sung after the opening versicle, God, come to my assistance (Ps 69[70]:2), before the psalmody begins... At Vespers, the number of psalms should be limited to four, with refrain after these psalms there follow: a reading and responsory, an Ambrosian hymn, a versicle, the Gospel, Canticle, the litany, and, immediately before the dismissal, the Lord's Prayer.... Each of the day hours begins with the verse, God come to my assistance: Lord, make haste to help me (Ps. 69[70]:2). Then on Sunday at Prime, four sections of Psalm 118 are said.[365]

The meticulous and repeated attention to every detail marked the life of the monk.

Islamic law stipulates that every Muslim is to pray five times a day, as we see in the following passage from the Quran:

> So be steadfast as thou hast been commanded–and those who turn in repentance along with you-and not be rebellious. Truly He sees whatever you do. And incline not toward the wrongdoers, lest the Fire shall touch you–and you have no protector apart from God. Thereafter you will not be helped. And perform the prayer at the two ends of the day and in the early hours of the night. Truly good deeds remove those that are evil. This is a reminder for those who remember.[366]

A commentary on these verses says:

> The prayers here are usually understood to refer to the five daily canonical prayers (*salah*) in Islam. The prayers at *the two ends of the day* are interpreted to be the prayers performed at dawn (*subh/fajr*) and sunset (*maghrib*) or at dawn and the late afternoon (*'asr*), or at midday (*zuhr*) and in the late afternoon; *the early hours of the night* can collectively refer to prayers performed at sunset and during the night (*'isha'*), or to the latter only. A similar range of opinion regarding the five prayers can be seen in identifying the *middlemost prayer* in 2:238.[367]

---

365 *The Rule of St. Benedict*, chapters 17 and 18, pp. 44-45.
366 *The Study Quran*, 11:112-114, p. 586.
367 *The Study Quran*, pp. 586-587.

The Quran does not settle when exactly prayers are to be said, or even how many times a day, but in the Ahadith already we see references to the canonical five prayers a day that Muslims are supposed to practice: *subh/fajr, maghrib, asr, zuhr,* and *isha*. There is no additional number of prayers that the imam is supposed to practice.

Catholic monks, and non-clerics in certain cases, are to kneel when praying; Muslims are to prostrate themselves when saying certain prayers. Both kneeling (as well as genuflecting) and prostrating oneself are meant to show respect and obeisance to God. In Catholicism, Church hierarchy was to be recognized by kneeling as well. Some form of obeisance can also be found in Judaism and other religious traditions such as Hinduism. In all of these cases, prayer is linked to a display of profound subservience to God. We can once again turn to Benedict's Rule to illustrate this point:

> Whether he sits, walks, or stands, his head must be bowed and his eyes cast down. Judging himself always guilty on account of his sins, he should consider that he is already at the fearful judgment, and constantly say what the publican in the Gospel said with downcast eyes: *Lord, I am a sinner, and not worthy to look up to heaven* (Luke 18:13). And with the Prophet: *I am bowed down and humbled in every way* (Ps 37[38]:7-9; Ps 118[119]:107).... the monk will quickly arrive at the *perfect love* of God which *casts out fear* (John 4:18). Through this love, all that he once performed with dread, he will now begin to observe without effort, as though naturally from habit, no longer out of fear of hell, but out of love for Christ, good habit and delight in virtue.[368]

By praying multiple times a day, in a prescribed way and in a subservient manner, religious rules are supposed to become habits of virtuous behavior.

IV. Monogamy, Polygamy, and Celibacy

At least as early as Isidore of Seville's *Ecclesiasticis* we find that the life of clerics is supposed to be "a private life, not only chaste but sober."[369] How "chaste" is understood undergoes considerable change over the centuries. Here is how Isidore puts it:

---

[368] *The Rule of St. Benedict*, Chapter 7, pp. 37-38.
[369] Isidore, *Ecclesiasticis*, p. 69.

> They should avoid overly frequent visits to widows or virgins, they should in no way seek the companionship of unrelated women. They should strive to preserve chastity perpetually inviolate of body, or at least they should be bound by the bond of one marriage.[370]

Here it is being chaste rather than celibate that is mandated.

Yet we also have a somewhat different requirement for bishops also listed by Isidore in his *Ecclesiasticis*:

> That those who are chosen for the order of bishop should be married to only one woman is commanded even in the old Law, and the Apostle wrote it more clearly: "[A bishop must be] married only once" [9Tim. 3:2]. The church seeks a priest for holy orders either from monogamy or from virginity. Priesthood is taken away from one who is married twice.[371]

Chastity is here required of priests and bishops–where this means they can be in a marriage as long as it is their only marriage.

Celibacy for religious leaders enters the Canon law later, with priests and monks allowed to have been in one marriage before the change to celibacy. There is no corresponding rule about celibacy in Islamic law–indeed, everyone is encouraged to marry and to raise a large family. While non-clerics are similarly urged to marry and have large families in Catholicism, chastity is prized among clerics–both women and men. Here is one of the provisions of the monastic rule for Franciscans:

> This is the rule and way of living of the minorite brothers: namely, to observe the holy Gospel of our Lord Jesus Christ, living in obedience, without personal possessions, and in chastity…the ministers shall diligently examine them in the matter of the catholic faith and the ecclesiastical sacraments. And if they believe all these, and are willing to faithfully confess them and observe them steadfastly to the end; and if they have no wives, or if they have them and the wives have already entered a monastery, or if they have given them permission to do so–they themselves having already taken a vow of continence by the authority of the bishop of the

[370] Ibid., p. 69.
[371] Ibid., p. 74.

> diocese, and their wives being of such age that no suspicion can arise in connection with them…[372]

At this point, in the 13th century, it is still possible for those previously married to enter monastic life, but the conditions make it clear that this is already an exception to the rule.

There is no comparable law about celibacy in Islamic law, indeed in some ways the imams are supposed to act the same way as the average Muslims–to have as many children as possible, and with several wives if they can support them. Here is a verse from the Quran:

> O mankind! Reverence your Lord, Who created you from a single soul and from it created a mate, and from the two has spread abroad a multitude of men and women. Reverence God, through Whom you demand your rights of one another, and family relations. Truly God is a Watcher over you. Give orphans their property, and exchange not the bad for the good, nor consume their property with your own. Truly that would be a great sin. If you fear that you will not deal fairly with the orphans, then marry such women as seem good to you, two, three, or four; but if you fear that you will not deal justly, then only one, or those whom your right hand possesses [slaves]. Thus it is more likely that you will not commit injustice.[373]

Here we see that in Islamic law monogamy is not the rule, except in special circumstances. The Study Quran Commentary says: "If a man is unable to adequately provide for multiple wives or treat them equitably, he is advised to take only one."[374] It seems that providing for a wife was mainly a matter of monetary support but also could include providing sexual relations for more than one spouse. And while normal Christians are also supposed to have as many children as they can, there is no provision for multiple wives–indeed, monogamy is the rule.

Augustine writing in the beginning of the fifth century CE first spelled out the Christian conception of marriage, which required sexual fidelity to just one spouse.[375] As we have seen in an earlier chapter, Canon

---

[372] *The Rule of St. Francis of Assisi* (1223 CE), in *A Reader of Medieval Laws, Edicts, and Orders*, translated by E. F. Henderson, Washington DC: Madison and Monroe Press, 2013, p. 266.

[373] *The Study Quran*, 4:1-3, pp. 189-191.

[374] *The Study Quran*, p. 190.

[375] See Augustine, *On the Good of Marriage*, translated by C. L. Cornish, NY: CreateSpace Independent Publishing Co., 2015.

law, especially in the writings of Gratian, required mutual consent for a valid marriage. But the lives of clerics had different rules–largely involving celibacy, at least after joining a religious order.

V. Religious Rules and Codes of Law

It is not surprising that codes of law that arise from a divinely inspired religion would set rules for religious ritual and practice. These rules took on the character of legal requirements in both Christianity and Islam, most evidently in the Medieval period. Codes of Canon law and of Islamic law brought the religious rules of practice under the jurisdiction of civil judges. In this final section I will critically reflect on the problems of having religious practice ultimately governed by civil law codes.

Religious rules governing the family seem to be the most common connection between religion and law. The family, insofar as it is largely a domain outside of the public sphere, seems to be the easiest to carve off from the larger domain of civil law and set rules by religious authorities rather than civil authorities. By association, sexual practices also seem to be a natural fit for regulation by religion rather than civil legislators and judges. But already here, if not already with the family, there is no clear-cut private domain that does not overlap with public matters. Indeed, feminists and other critics of patriarchy have long argued that grave harm can be done to people in families and sexual relationships that are left to religious leaders to police, and this critique extends to the dichotomy between public and private as well.

Religious rules for members of various religions, or for clergy, perhaps make more sense than religious rules governing family and sexual practices. Such rules are like the rules of clubs or fraternal associations–if someone is a member of a group then that person should abide by the rules of the group. The written rules of the group help define the values and taboos of the group and make things clearer than if such matters are left to be transmitted from word of mouth. Canon law could have been circulated only to those members of the clerics who were governed by monastic rules, but in fact this was not what happened since bishops and princes fought for control of more and more of the lives of the people under their jurisdictions.

It is also important to note that for both Canon law and Islamic law, the societies in question were often majority Christians or Muslims respectively. Placing religious rules under civil law where the majority of members of a society are believers in the religious rules is not as bad as having the majority subjected to religious rules that the majority does not believe in. But there is still a problem when the minority of the society is subjected to religious rules it does not believe in. We have an interesting contemporary example in the State of Israel where the majority is Jewish, but not orthodox and yet the religious rules of Orthodox Judaism (such as concerning the Sabbath or marriage) are enforced on those who do not believe in them.

One of the most significant issues we find in the Canon and Islamic law codes is that there is a serious mixing of religious and civil law that can taint both religious and civil law with the connection to the other. Those who do not believe in the religious rules are not the only ones who could be offended by being subjected to civil penalties for not following the religious rules. Resentments toward those religious rules, as well as to the civil laws that enforce them, can lead people not to respect the legal system or to see that legal system as unredeemably biased. Fidelity to religious rules as well as to civil law can then suffer.

Next consider the special case we have taken up in this chapter of the monastic rules for those monks and abbots who are cloistered in monasteries. Here, unlike family life, there really is a cutting off of the group's life from the public world that surrounds it. One could say something similar about family life in Islam, but the codification of Islamic religious practice has made those practices open to examination and criticism in ways that have not always been welcome.

In some respects, the monastic rules are secured from public criticism since they are only enforced internally, not by public sanction. As we will see in later chapters civil punishment was employed for many aspects of Canon law, but the monasteries did remain relatively free from oversight and criticism because the religious rules were only enforced against those who chose to join the monastic communities.

Problems did arise though if a person who had taken final vows nonetheless later decided to leave the monastic community or no longer to follow its rules. Bishops sometimes sought sanctions from civil authorities in such cases, but the sanction of excommunication was the more common response–which in some cases achieved the desired result for the monk who wanted no longer to be bound by monastic rules. These cases were apparently relatively rare and so we will not dwell on them.

It might make sense to compare the ancient Jewish law, especially as codified through the Talmud, with Islamic and Canon law. Because Jews were not by and large in control of their own communities in ancient times, Jewish law did govern religious practices, but it was not enforced by civil authorities. Nonetheless, the laws of kosher, for example, were enforced in Jewish communities for millennia. So, if nothing else this shows that it is not necessary to link religious rules of practice with codes of civil law for those religious rules to be effective.

One obvious question to ask then is why religious rules in the Middle Ages were written into civil law codes. In some respects the answer in the cases of Islamic and Canon law are the same: the civil law was written so as to indicate the religious character of the society governed by that civil law. The idea that a nation was a Muslim state or a Christian state was the expressed reason for codifying religious rules in civil law. Charlemagne, for example, often referred to himself as a Christian emperor as in this document from 802 CE:

> Concerning the embassy sent out by the lord emperor.–The most serene and most Christian emperor Charles did choose from among his nobles the most prudent and wise men–archbishops as well as other bishops and venerable abbots, and pious laymen–and did send them over his whole kingdom; and did grant through them, by means of all the following provisions, that all men live according to law and right... all should live together according to the precept of God... bishops and priests should live according to the canons and should teach others likewise.[376]

Charlemagne here asserts that he is a Christian emperor who will use his civil law to enforce Canon law for the betterment of the Christian nation.

A nation of Muslims is similarly the model for a people governed by Shari'a–where the word Muslim simply means those who submit to God's law. Joseph Schacht clearly expresses this point when he says: "Canon and Islamic law... are dominated by a dualism of religion and state, where the state is not an alien power, but the political expression of the same religion."[377]

In this chapter we have seen that Islamic law and Canon law share much more in common than one might have suspected in terms of the regulation of religious practice of those who are believers. While some of the religious rules differ, many more are similar. For example, there are of course different prayers that people are required to say, and there are differences in how often prayers are to be said. There are also differences in terms of marriage and chastity requirements. But as substantive rules

---

[376] Emperor Charlemagne, "Capitulary of the Emperor Charlemagne," 802 CE, in *A Reader of Medieval Laws, Edicts, and Orders*, translated by E. F. Henderson, Washington, DC: Madison and Monroe Press, 2013, pp. 148-151.

[377] Joseph Schacht, *An Introduction to Islamic Law*, Oxford: Oxford University Press, 1982, p. 2.

go, there is much similarity, especially for instance in terms of the strong requirements concerning the manifestation of humility.

The most striking commonality is the way that religious rules and civil law intersect in Islamic and Canon law, at least in part this is because of the strong identification of their societies' rulers with particular religious views. Intermingling religious rules with civil codes of law is a near hallmark of both Islamic and Canon law societies. There is also a more cynical view of the closeness of religious rules and civil law, especially when the virtue of humility is stressed: it makes it easier for rulers to obtain obedience and dispel rebellion if the religious virtue of humility is elevated to a civic virtue as well. Even the word Muslim is taken from a root having to do with subservience. We also found monks as well as regular lay practitioners of Christianity becoming habituated to kneel in abeyance. And in Islam, believers were to prostrate themselves also as a sign of submission. Religious rules are not by definition so dependent on acts of humility and submission. But we found that in the contemporaneously developing Islamic and Canon law, there was a strong overlap of religious rules and civil law, with subservience as a key component.

SECTION VII:

CRIME AND PUNISHMENT

CHAPTER 16

CRIMINAL INTENT

The idea that there are crimes that are different from civil offenses has been with us since ancient times, since at least the Greek lawgiver, Draco. And the idea that intent matters to such determinations has also been with us, again at least since Roman times and probably earlier. But the conceptual focus on intention is something that appears to be characteristic of Medieval legal and political thought–perhaps starting with Augustine, whose work on the freedom of the will focused on the inner life of the individual, and who seems to have made important advances on the Greek idea of *prohairesis*. Some have even suggested that Augustine discovered the will. But it is the idea of intention that was crucial for criminal law, and we can find this idea especially well developed in Islamic and Canon legal and political thought. I will argue that especially in Medieval Islamic thought the idea of intent was a major concept that set the stage for the development of the idea of criminal intent, and that similar ideas can also be found in Medieval Canon law.

I will explore the general idea of intent in Islamic thought in the first section. And then in the second section I will explore the general idea of intent in Canon law. In the third section I discuss the idea of *criminal* intent in Islamic legal thought. And then in the fourth section I discuss the similar ideas to be found in Canon law. In the final section I draw out some conclusions about how law is developing and whether or not to call such development humane and progressive.

I. Intent in Islamic Legal Thought

Here is how Joseph Schacht begins the chapter on general Islamic concepts of intent in his *Introduction to Islamic Law*:

> A fundamental concept of the whole of Islamic religious law, be it concerned with worship or with law in the narrow sense, is the *niyya* (intent). It applied originally to acts of worship; the religious obligation is discharged not by outward performance as such but only if it is done with a pious intent. But Islamic

> orthodoxy insisted on the performance, and *niyya* from being a state of mind, became an act of will directed towards performing a religious duty; it must, as with a rule, be explicitly formulated, at least mentally. An act of worship without *niyya* is invalid, and so is the *niyya* without the act. The *niyya* thus comes near to the concept of *animus* aimed at producing legal effects and expressed in a declaration of intention.[378]

So, *niyya* (intent) is an inward act but also involves an outward performance. In this sense we are reminded of the Aristotelian idea of *prohairesis*, the forerunner of the will, which was the last act of deliberation before the person decided how to behave. As we will see in Part D of my study, later Islamic thinkers, such as Averroes, were quite outspoken in how their ideas had been influenced by Aristotle.

Already in the early interpretations of the Quran we can find an explicit concern for intention, as is exemplified in a commentary on the following Quranic verse:

> O you who believe! When you rise to perform the prayer, wash your faces, and your hands up to the elbows, and wipe your heads and your feet up to the ankles. If you are in a state of ritual impurity, then purify yourselves, but if you are ill, or on a journey, or one of you has come from satisfying a call of nature, or you have touched women, and you find no water, then resort to clean earth, and wipe therewith your faces and hands. God desires not to place a burden on you, but he desires to purify you and to complete His Blessing on you, that happily you may give thanks.[379]

S. H. Nasr comments on this verse as follows:

> All schools of law consider the *wudu'* [manner of ablution] obligatory before the five daily canonical prayers… In addition to the specific acts mentioned in the verse, The Maliki, Shafi'i, Hanbali, and Twelve Shiite (Jafari) schools of law also require that the *wudu* be preceded by a statement of intention (*niyya*) and that washing of the various bodily parts be done in immediate succession.[380]

---

[378] Joseph Schacht, *An Introduction to Islamic Law*, Oxford: Oxford University Press, 1982, p. 116.
[379] *The Study Quran*, 5:6, pp. 280-282.
[380] *The Study Quran*, commentary, p. 279.

The declaration of intention is thus considered part of the religious law of purification–it is not enough that a person perform the purification acts without the declared intent.

The idea of a declaration of intention is a mixed concept–part internal and part external. And this is why such a concept seems to be very close to the idea of the will–which stands between deliberation and action. And it is, as Schacht tells us also similar to the idea of a certain kind of *animus*: the wrongful intent needed to prove criminality in later systems of legal thought. Declaring specifically what one is trying to do is not definitive for one's state of will or intent, but it is nonetheless important evidence for such a will or intent. As Schacht puts it: "By means of a complicated network of casuistry all possible forms of declaration are tested as to whether they are valid on their own… The investigation often amounts to determining whether a given declaration is compatible with the existence of a certain *niyya* claimed afterwards by the person who made it."[381]

We will later explore some of the problems in determining intent but at this point we can note that the external part of the intent is discussed in terms of a declaration. And yet in a legal proceeding it would surely not be enough that the person's declaration of intent would be sufficient to determine what that intent really was since the person could fail to tell the truth or to know what his or her own intentions were.

The verses of the Quran cited above are discussing the idea of sin and the intention that is needed to establish whether or not a person had the intention to commit an act of sin. In the case of a crime, as we will see, matters are more complicated indeed. The judge can inquire of the defendant what his or her intention was, but more evidence will be needed than a declaration to establish the intention of the defendant.

We can already now see the difficulties of moving from a standard of intention in religious matters to such a standard in legal matters. Schacht explores several of these problems in addition to those we will discuss later in regards to criminal intent:

> Among the defects of declarations, error is taken into limited account in their casuistic interpretation. Error in a confession plays a somewhat more important part in criminal law. As regards to fraud, there is little inclination to protect the victim; it manifests only in the case of "grave deception"…The doctrine of duress is more developed… The effect in civil law

[381] Joseph Schacht, *An Introduction to Islamic Law*, pp. 116-117.

> is that the threat of death, severe beating, and long imprisonment makes the declaration voidable.[382]

Lying or coerced declarations are problematic in many ways and seem to require confirmation by a witness.

II. Intention in Canon Law

Gratian's great work on Canon law contains a long treatise on the concept of penance which gives us a good sense of how intention was understood. At the beginning of this treatise, Gratian quotes Augustine as saying that in confessing "the will is taken to be the work."[383] Gratian then goes on to give his interpretation of Augustine's claim:

> if, as the authoritative text testifies, the will is rewarded, not the work, but the will consists of contrition of the heart, but the work of confession of the mouth, then it must clearly be established that sins are forgiven by contrition of the heart, not by oral confession… and with tears flowing out of true compunction of the heart, they will extinguish the flames of the eternal fire.[384]

Contrition or compunction of the heart is the inner state of intention–in this case the intention not to do the sinful act again and to pray for forgiveness for the past sin.

There is a distinction between secret sins and external sins. The secret sin is the sin of the heart–the intention to do something wrong, or the endeavor to will something that is evil. Even though thoughts alone cannot trigger sin, it is clear that for Gratian there can be sin without external behavior. This is because Canon law is concerned as much with the purity of the heart or soul as it is with the correct behavior of a person. And one's intentions are the key component of the inner or secret states of the person. There is a distinction between confessing orally and confessing in the heart where the latter includes the intention to be good in the future.

We can also consult a sermon by Ivo of Chartres, another great Canon law scholar:

---

382 Ibid., pp. 117-118.

383 Gratian, *Tractatus de Penitentia*, p. 3.

384 Gratian, ibid., p. 17.

> It would not have been fitting for the sinner who sinned of his own will to be forced to do penance; for then he would be as unthankful for his reformation as he was for his original state. Therefore, a medicine has been provided adapted to the need of the patient. By confession clear your consciousness from impurity. This was why the physician came in the fullness of time, saying: "Do penance" and… [you] will be saved."[385]

Christof Rolker adds this interpretation: "Ivo's concept of penance strongly emphasized individual contrition and inner conversion… The principal problem, however, remained. God, but not the Church could see "the secrets of the heart."[386] This problem also existed, as we will see, in law proceedings–the judge could not see the intentions of the accused. In both the religious and legal cases, one had to look at external behavior to get a sense of the inner workings of the mind–unless one is God.

For Ivo and other Canon law scholars, "inner contrition" was necessary for the forgiveness of sins. And the sinner could not be forced to do the penance that would demonstrate such contrition. To be saved, the sinner not only had to change his or her behavior, but the sinner also had to change his heart with the intention to do good. Merely doing good was not sufficient, one also had to have the intention to do good and avoid evil. Indeed, the Canon lawyers insisted that the inner states are more important than the external manifestations.

Ivo, as was also true of Islamic legal thought, found marriage to be an especially important legal consideration concerning intention. Here is how Christof Rolker puts it:

> For Ivo… marriage was first of all a sacrament. However, though being a divine institution, marriage is contracted by individual people. A valid marriage could be contracted where there were no marriage impediments provided there was mutual consent, Ivo wrote, following Roman law. Indeed for Ivo, consent was the single most important condition for a valid marriage… Consummation, however, was not necessary to validate marriage.[387]

---

[385] Ivo of Chartres, *Sermo* VI (PL 162, 565) as quoted in *Canon Law and the Letters of Ivo of Chartres*, translated by Christof Rolker, Cambridge: Cambridge University Press, 2010, p. 191.

[386] Ibid., p. 191.

[387] Ibid., p. 213.

And consent was closely linked to intention–verbal consent was evidence of the intention to make a marriage contract.

But what if there was no verbal consent–what other signs of the intention of the woman or girl could be considered? And how did Ivo stand on one of the issues we will next consider–whether silence could be a sign of consent? The difficulty is that consent is deeply intertwined with the inner state of mind called intention. And it is difficult often to determine a person's state of mind. Perhaps this is why other Canon law scholars did not follow Ivo in fixating on consent instead of what was easier to get evidence of, such as consummation.

III. Criminal Intent in Islamic Law

Abdur Rahim provides us with a good summary of how mental acts are understood in Islamic criminal law:

> According to the accepted Hanafi view, which is substantially the same as that of other Sunni Schools on this point, a man's action is partly within his own power and partly the result of God's interference. It is so far within his power that he is left free to choose between the doing and not doing an act. This power to choose is called *ikhtiar*, that is, will or volition. Having chosen one of two alternatives, namely doing the act, he is said to intend it (*qasd*, *iradat*). If this intention is followed by the act intended, ordinarily it is only so when the act is such, as we are led to expect from the surrounding conditions... Intention with reference to an act is, therefore, according to Muhammadan jurists, that condition of the mind which directly and immediately sets the nerves in motion resulting in the act.[388]

Criminal responsibility requires an act and an intention.

Crime is itself defined in terms of the violation of public rights as Abdur Rahim makes clear:

> When certain primary public rights are violated the wrong is called *maa'si'at*, that is, crime or offence; and it gives rise to certain substitutory public rights in the form of *uq'bat* or punishments. Criminal offences relate mostly to property,

[388] Abdur Rahim, *The Principles of Muhammadan Jurisprudence*, London: Luzak and Company, 1911, p. 220.

> human body, reputation, religion, the state, public peace and tranquility, decency or morals.[389]

And the violation of public rights is only a crime if it is done in an intentional way.

In a Hadith we find the following often cited remark from Muhammad: “The Prophet said, “One’s deeds are to be considered according to one’s intentions.”[390] Muhammad Baqir As-Sadr gives the following comment: “A humane aspect of almost all Islamic law is that it takes into consideration the subjective state of the legal agent when assessing accountability. This consideration includes questions of both capacity and intention.”[391]

It is generally recognized that having an intent requirement for criminal liability is humane in that it rules out people who are coerced or forced to engage in certain conduct. And indeed, as we saw earlier, marriage “acceptance” for instance is not recognized if one of the parties has been coerced. Similarly, if a person has been coerced to participate in a robbery his guilt is minimized if not eliminated altogether. So, even though intent is hard to establish because it is “inside” rather than outside the body, to recognize the agency of the person in terms of what reasons a person had for acting are key considerations in establishing a humane system of criminal justice. In Islamic law, criminal justice as we know it today developed slowly from the idea of *lex talionis*, but intent was crucial from the time of Muhammad in establishing any type of responsibility. Systems of divine law, especially those that can be seen to be in the natural law tradition, strive for treating persons with respect, and one of the most important considerations is that the person’s subjective states be recognized.

It is a humane development in Islamic law that coercion is rendered suspicious in many contexts–primarily because it seems to override the intentions of the person who is coerced. Coercion is often juxtaposed to consent in theoretical discussions today as well. But it is striking how important it was for coercion to be juxtaposed to intention in early Islamic legal thought. We can already see here the idea of the importance of the agency of the person.

In the context of marriage, Islamic legal thinkers were clearly reacting against the non-Islamic Arab culture that countenanced kidnap to

---

389 Ibid., p. 361.

390 Hadith 6940, vol. 9, p. 59.

391 Muhammad Baqir As-Sadr, *Lessons in Islamic Jurisprudence*, translated by Roy Parviz Mottahedeh, Oxford: One World, 2003, p. 25.

secure a marriage partner. The rejection of this practice, and on grounds of the agency of the female marriage partner, is highly significant. The Quran says: "And compel not your female slaves into prostitution if they desire to be chaste… And whoever compels them, then truly God, after their having been compelled, will be forgiving."[392] After this verse is cited, we find the following Hadith:

> Narrated by Khansa' bint Khidam Al-Ansariya that her father gave her in marriage when she was a matron and she disliked that marriage. So she came and complained to the Prophet, and he declared that marriage invalid.
> Narrated Aisha: I asked the Prophet, "O Allah's Messenger! Should the woman be asked for her consent to their marriage?" He said, "Yes." I said, "A virgin, if asked, feels shy and keeps quiet." He said, "Her silence means her consent."[393]

So, while "silence means consent" is problematic, we do seem to find here a testament to the importance of the inner states of the person as agent.

It is interesting to consider that there seems to be a distinction between the consent of the "matron" and that of the "virgin" to the marriage. Perhaps the difference is that the matron is considered to be better informed about what marriage entails. Perhaps there is a simple assumption that the matron is older and wiser than the young virgin. Yet, it is worrisome that the virgin's silence is sufficient to establish her consent–as opposed to her silence being an indication of her lack of consent. Nonetheless, we do see an important movement toward respect for the agent. And in this respect, Islamic legal and political thought clearly is more humane than the earlier Arabic practices.

IV. Criminal Intent in Canon Law

Canon law did not encompass all areas of law–and criminal law was generally left under the purview of civil law authorities, but not always. We can see how extending ideas about sin and penance could be employed to cover the idea of criminality. Here is how James Brundage describes it:

> Medieval canon lawyers also introduced a new and revolutionary approach to criminal law, one that lies at the root of most

[392] *The Study Quran*, 24:33, p. 877.
[393] Ahadith 6945 and 6946, vol. 9, pp. 61-62.

> modern theories of criminal justice. This was the canonical theory of culpability, which taught that the intention of the offender must be an essential element in determining guilt or innocence. Earlier approaches to criminal law had centered on determining what harm the offender had caused and the appropriate compensation that the victim and the community ought to receive. Canonical teachers and writers in the late twelfth and early thirteenth centuries, however, based their ideas about criminal law upon the church's penitential tradition, in which the degree of guilt was primarily a function of the mental and moral intent of the sinner, while the harm that his sinful actions caused became a secondary consideration. Under this theory, what the sinner actually did might be morally neutral, but his reasons for doing it could readily convert a morally indifferent act into a grievous offense[394].

One of the most important canon law scholars, Gratian, took just this route as we will next see.

In Gratian's penitential writings, as we saw above, what is in the sinner's heart is crucial for determining the degree of guilt and the appropriate penance. In a series of comments on quotations from Augustine, Jerome, Cyprian, and other Church fathers, Gratian explains that one can even be guilty of murder if in one's mind one desired the death of another person.

> In wicked deeds, the will is taken to be the work.
> "All iniquity and oppression and injustice is the judgment of blood: and, although you do not kill with the sword, you nonetheless kill with your will."
> "Cain had not already slain his brother when he offered his gift to the Lord, had he? And yet the provident God had already condemned the fratricide conceived in his mind…"
> "He who is moved to do harm kills.
> "The murder forbidden by the law used to be thought to be nothing other than the killing of the body. The Lord thus explained that every wicked inclination to do harm to a brother is considered to be in the genus of homicide."[395]

Gratian gives many examples where the intent to cause harm should be punished as much if not more than the act of harming itself.

---

[394] James A. Brundage, *Medieval Canon Law*, London: Longman, 1995, p. 171.
[395] Gratian, *Tractatus de Penitentia*, edited and translated by Atria A. Larson, Washington, DC: Catholic University of America Press, 2016, p. 15.

Gratian moves from his analysis of sin and penance to his analysis of crime and punishment. In both cases the intent is the key element of the sin or crime. Gratian does not explain though how it is to be determined what the intent is when the act does not occur. In the case of sin, it is clear that God who knows all is able to know what is in the person's heart. But in criminal law, the judge is not all-knowing, and so there is an evidentiary problem that Gratian skirts but does not address directly as a practical matter for a criminal trial.

The judgment that a person has sinned is largely a judgment that is made by the priest substituting for God, according to Canon law. But the judgment that a person has committed a crime is made by a judge or jury and even in a system of divinely-inspired law the judge does not stand in for an all-knowing God. Rather the judge stands in for the king or other worldly political officials of the kingdom. Yet, in both cases of sin and crime the emphasis on intention calls for looking into the heart or mind of the person accused of the sin or crime. In fact, it is often the sinner who is supposed to look at his or her own intentions to determine what an appropriate penance should be.

When Gratian says, "he who is moved to do harm kills," we are then in the position of asking about the will of the accused, where being moved to do harm may not result in any outward manifestations of such a will. It is commendable that Gratian saw that what is wrong is not the final act but the decision to undertake the act. What is not terribly clear is what motivates Gratian to take this stance. In some respects it looks like he simply takes a position that is quite reasonable about the nature of sin and transposes it on to the idea of crime. But the consequences of committing a sin are potentially very different than the consequences of committing a crime. And as we will see in the final section of this chapter, there are also significant evidentiary problems in the determination of criminal intention than in the determination of sinful intention.

Indeed, the realm of sin, as Gratian's arguments display, can be conducted wholly within the heart or mind of the sinner–no one else needs to guess what the intention is for the sinner whereas this must be determined for the criminal. And one can sin merely by having certain kinds of thoughts, such as that a given person should be killed as one plans to execute that thought. In this respect, it is not such an easy task to construct a legal standard of crime by analogizing from a religious standard of sin.

V. Why Intention Matters

Intention is important for criminal liability and responsibility because of the recognition of the defendant as a person making choices rather than a pawn to be manipulated. Making intention one of the elements of a crime puts the subjective life of the defendant front and center in determining whether and to what extent to blame or punish that person for a wrongful act. Indeed, when intention is made an element of a crime, what looks like a wrongful act–because one person has harmed another person–may turn out not even to be wrongful. The crime becomes something like "the intentional harming" not merely "the harming." Unintentional or accidental harming may or may not still be punished, but it won't be punished as severely without the intentional element.

We can see how such an idea could have developed from the idea of inner or secret sins. In this respect it is interesting to note that Gratian makes a distinction between punishing mere thoughts and punishing thoughts that result, or would result, in harm.

> A thought does not deserve punishment by civil law when it is deemed insignificant on its own terms. Nevertheless, such thoughts that lack an effect as far as the law is concerned are distinguished from crimes. For nothing but the mind's judgment is considered in thoughts without legal consequences.[396]

Inner sins which have no connection to outward acts can still be subject to blame, but legally thoughts are subject to punishment only when they have this connection, even as a subjunctive matter.

Intention is a kind of thought but not a mere thought. An intention to do an act already involves some planning toward that act and its consequences. As we have seen, intention in the Medieval period is very similar to will, and will is the mental faculty that Augustine had identified as the source of freedom for each person. The freedom of the will involves the idea that people express their freedom by what they have a will to do, not necessarily by what they actually do.

One of the most significant problems with having intention as an element of crime is evidentiary–how is wrongful intention to be determined? And here is where the focus on intention can lead to regress rather than progress in whether law is humane or not. Consider the case that Gratian takes up after the quotation above–a case from Justinian's Digest:

---

[396] Ibid., p. 11.

> There is no divorce except a valid one, which occurs with a mind fixed on perpetual separation. Thus whatever occurs or is said in the heat of anger is not deemed to be something else until it should persistently appear that such was the judgment of the mind. Therefore, if a wife is returned after a short time after she was sent away, it seems to be a repudiation through the heat of anger and not to have been a true divorce.[397]

Gratian then adds this comment: "here also in the Canons: If anyone should reproach someone for a crime while in a state of anger," etc.[398]

Anger is a state of the mind, but unlike the will anger does not proceed from a deliberation. Because anger is not under the control of one's deliberations it is not thought to be evidence of the intentions of the person in question. Both anger and intention are, in some sense, thoughts. Only intention is a sign of the subjective judgment of the person and hence something for which the person can be held accountable. In the divorce case one sign of the will is that this state of mind tends to last, whereas anger tends to be fleeting.

But as an evidentiary matter, what distinguishes deliberative willing from a different mental state like anger? Gratian, following Justinian, indicates that intention unlike anger is longstanding not fleeting. In general it is hard to distinguish intentions from character traits–both of which are long-lasting. Yet, in examining a person's character it is very easy to be biased in terms of the person's past behavior instead of focusing on what should concern us, namely what the person intended to do at the time in question.

The above evidentiary problems are exacerbated due to the fact that Medieval jurists believed in the existence of miracles as well as devils, sorcerers, and witches. If a person was thought to be associated with, or to be, a witch, for instance, it was thought that all or most of his intentions were evil. Here is a Carolingian capitulary:

> Since we have heard that sorcerers and witches are rising up in many parts of our kingdom, whose magic has killed and injured many men, and since, as the holy men of God have written, it is the king's duty to rid the land of the impious and not to permit witches and sorcerers to live, we command that the counts should take great pains in their counties to search out and seize such people… if the suspects cannot be proved

[397] Ibid., p. 11.

[398] Ibid., p. 13.

> guilty by trustworthy witnesses, let them be tried by the ordeal, and thus by the ordeal either freed or condemned.[399]

It is clear from this capitulary that someone suspected of being a witch was deemed guilty until proven innocent, based solely on the suspected character of the accused.

We can see the evidentiary difficulties in determining intention in a case from 1338 in England. The question was whether a girl of thirteen could form the requisite wrongful intent since it was generally thought that a person had to know right from wrong in order to form such an intent before reaching the age of discretion. Here is how the girl was described in the Year Books of Edward III:

> Also a girl of thirteen years of age was burnt because while she was a servant to a woman she killed her mistress: and it was found to be so and adjudged treason. And it was said that by the old law no one under age was hanged or suffered judgment of life or limb. But Spigurnel found that an infant of ten years of age killed his companion and concealed him: and caused him to be hanged, because of the concealment he showed that he knew how to distinguish evil from good. And so malice makes up for age. [400]

Anthony Musson's comments are directly relevant to our concerns with intention:

> The killing of a mistress by her servant amounted to petty treason. Under the common law, a girl of thirteen had not yet reached the age of discretion and so could not suffer death or mutilation since it was felt that she was too young to realize that what she was doing was wrong. This "old law" is contrasted, however, with more recently decided case law attributed to Henry Spigurnel (d. 1328), which suggests that if the child acts deliberately or there is evidence to show that she acted with premeditation (the law uses "malice" to denote intention) then the child should not be protected by the

---

[399] Quoted in Robert Bartlett, *Trial by Fire and Water*, Brattleboro, VT: Echo Point Books & Media, 1986, p. 24.

[400] Quoted in *Crime, Law, and Society in the Later Middle Ages*, translated and edited by Anthony Musson, Manchester: Manchester University Press, 2009, pp. 95-96.

> presumption that they did not know the difference between rights and wrong.[401]

Premeditation is here thought to show malicious intent. And premeditation is inferred from actions that either show planning to commit the crime or planning after the crime in order to hide its effects.

Yet the evidentiary difficulty is that sometimes people have bad intentions even though they and their past behavior do not indicate that they harbor such intentions. The case of children is especially apt there. And it is a mistake to equate malicious thoughts with intentions in any event. Malice calls up thoughts of devils or witches, and yet what we are trying to gain insight into is the actual state of mind of the offender at the time that he or she acted or was trying to act.

So, what perhaps starts out as an attempt to do something humane by treating people as free choosers rather than merely looking at their external behavior can give rise to significant problems that can be inhumane. In the case of the girl who killed her mistress, there is a reasonable attempt to look inside the girl's head to determine her deliberation. But in other cases, the fact that one is suspected of being a witch then misleads those who attempt to get inside her head.

It is nearly unchallenged today that adding an element of intent to crimes is a good thing in that it forces judges or jurors to look behind the actions of the defendant to the likely deliberations that led him or her to act wrongfully. Yet what we have seen in this chapter is that in the beginning stages of the development of the intention element in crimes, there were serious problems of bias or mistake that were difficult to guard against, especially when the moral rightness or wrongness of states of mind is substituted for criminal intention.

---

[401] Ibid., p. 95.

CHAPTER 17

HERESY AND APOSTASY

In systems of law that are divinely inspired, people who reject the dominant religion are often singled out for especially harsh treatment as criminals. In this chapter we will examine how Islamic and Canon law dealt with two forms of religious dissent or denial: heresy and apostasy. Heresy involves a person espousing religious views different from the dominant religious views, or denying a major tenet of the dominant religious view. Apostasy is similar to heresy in that a person denounces what he or she had previously believed of the dominant religion. In this chapter we will often treat these crimes in similar ways. The thesis of the chapter is that these crimes display one of the most important problems for a divinely inspired legal system because they display a lack of tolerance.

In the first section we will examine how the Quran and other Islamic religious and legal texts treat apostasy. In the second section we will focus on the crime of heresy in Canon law. In the third section, we look to the idea of religious orthodoxy and deterrence in these systems of law. In the fourth section we ask whether the lack of religious tolerance should make people more or less likely to subscribe to the dominant religion, despite what the religious and legal authorities hope for. And finally, we will turn to the question of what would render criminal laws against heresy and apostasy more humane in a legal system. Throughout we will be especially interested in why these crimes are some of the first that religiously based legal systems deal with.

I. Islamic Law and Apostasy

Islamic law is often characterized as intolerant to other religious views despite the fact that Jews and Christians are treated as fellow "people of the Book." We will have occasion to challenge this view but let us start with what we learn from the Quran:

> Is it the judgment of the Age of Ignorance that they seek? And who is fairer in judgment than God, for a people who are

> certain. O you who believe! Take not Jews or Christians as protectors. They are the protectors of one another. And whosoever takes them as protectors, surely he is of them. Truly God guides not wrongdoing people. Yet thou seest those in whose hearts is a disease hastening to them, saying, "We fear lest a change of fortune should befall us." It may be that God will grant victory, or a command from Him. And they shall be remorseful for that which they secretly harbored in their souls. And those who believe will say, "Are these the ones who swore by God with their most solemn oaths that they were with you?" Their deeds have come to naught, and they have become losers. O you who believe! Whosoever among you should renounce his religion, God will bring a people whom He loves and who love Him, humble toward the believers, stern toward the disbelievers, striving in the way of God, and fearing not the blame of any blamer. This is the Bounty of God, which He gives to whomever He will. And God is All Encompassing, Knowing.... "Whomsoever God has cursed and upon whom is His Wrath, among whom He has made some to be apes and swine, and who worship false deities, such are in worse situation, and further astray from the right way."[402]

These verses give us a good sense of the mixed reaction of Islam to different religious views.

First, there is a kind of religious tribalism espoused in these verses–Jews protect each other, Christians protect each other, and Muslims should not look to these other religions to protect them but must look only to Islam. Such a view does not yet condemn those who would believe in the tenets of Judaism or Christianity. But second, we are told that one will go astray by worshipping "false deities." But what makes them false? Is it merely that they are not the deity of Islam? And how should people regard Judaism and Christianity which seem to worship the same God as Islam? And then, third, we are also told that if someone renounces Islam he or she will incur God's wrath. This third point then leads to the condemnation of apostasy.

What is unclear is whether renouncing Islam will incur God's wrath because one turns away from one's religious tribe or because one comes to accept wrong beliefs. There is also the curious phrase "have become losers." If one chooses wrongly in terms of the religious beliefs one embraces, one is then a loser. And one can assume that a person would

[402] *The Study Quran*, 5:50-60, pp. 302-309.

be hurt by choosing wrongly about religious beliefs. Having lost why are they then also said to incur God's wrath? Is this a double punishment?

And here is one of the problems with criminalizing apostasy or heresy–believing in the wrong religious tenets has already harmed the individual's soul. So, why should this person be subjected to criminal sanctions as well? Criminal sanctions as a form of retribution seem misplaced since the person is already a "loser" for having rejected Islam. Of course, perhaps criminalizing apostasy or heresy is meant to act as a deterrent–a possibility not mentioned in the relevant texts but something we will explore.

Criminal punishment can be justified in various ways, but it is rare to see deterrence mentioned in the Medieval period where retribution is so often associated with criminal punishment. In a later chapter we will explore in more detail the various forms of punishment and rationales for those punishments in religiously-inspired legal systems. Here we only note that deterrence can be accomplished with other-worldly punishments as well as with this-worldly punishments.

II. Canon Law and Heresy

Here is how James Brundage describes the early Canon law on the crime of heresy:

> Above all, the early canons defined the key elements of mainstream Christian doctrine and drew increasingly sharp lines between authentic Christians and others, whom they labeled heretics, apostates, and unbelievers. In addition, canon law in the early church sought to enumerate the powers and qualifications of bishops and other clerics, to define their obligations, and to provide for disciplinary measures to curb those who exceeded their authority or failed to measure up to the high standards of conduct expected of the clergy… In some situations, however, canonical judges felt obliged to penalize members of the church for heinous moral lapses or for serious deviations… the *audientia episcopalis* and other church tribunals, particularly councils and synods, asserted a penal jurisdiction over deviations from Christian faith to combat the threat of heresy.[403]

Heresy was considered a threat to the universal monotheism of the early church and church officials were instructed to confront heretics.

---

[403] James A. Brundage, *Medieval Canon Law*, London: Longman, 1995, pp. 11-12.

By around 1200, Canon lawyers began asserting full-scale criminal jurisdictions over Christians and non-Christians accused of heresy.

> It is not difficult to see how inquisitorial procedure soon emerged as the preferred method of dealing with suspected heretics. Even so, evidential problems continued to thwart heresy prosecutions and to deal with this problem church authorities sanctioned the use of questioning under torture when testimony was otherwise likely to be unavailable… They tried to justify its use in exceptional circumstances, however, on grounds that public welfare (*publica utilitas*) demanded that crimes should not go unpunished, and argued that even though torture sometimes forced people to confess to crimes they had not committed, its use would nevertheless deter others from committing real crimes.[404]

As Canon law moved more and more into the criminal domain to confront heresy, church officials were more and more drafted to be judges, and punishments became more severe. And significantly for us, such moves were sometimes justified in deterrence terms.

For various reasons, including the increasing literacy of the population of Europe, heretical views increased in the 12th century and the Church found itself struggling to overcome these competing views to its orthodoxy. As we will see in some of the chapters later in my book, inquisitions arose as a force that was organized and feared as the protector of the Christian orthodoxy.[405] The criminal prosecution of heretics became increasingly important for a church that saw itself confronted by many new religious views. But even before the 12th century, beginning with Constantine, the Church fought many battles against those they described as heretics.[406]

The crime of heresy was the most significant that the Canon lawyers had to confront because of its capacity to undermine the monopoly that the Church had on religious belief. It is significant that the Canon lawyers took a similar route to that of the Islamic lawyers in trying to use criminal prosecutions of heretics and apostates who threatened to undermine the dominant orthodox religious beliefs of religious regimes. In

---

404 Ibid., pp. 95-96.

405 See James B. Given, *Inquisition and Medieval Society*, Ithaca, NY: Cornell University Press, 1997.

406 See R. I. Moore, T*he Formation of a Persecuting Society*, Oxford: Blackwell Publishing, 1987, Chapter 1.

some respects, heresy and apostasy were more of a challenge to these religious regimes than open rebellion, and the criminal prosecutions were pursued with as much vigor as if there was an actual military battle being waged against the political enemies of these regimes. Yet, as we will see it is not clear why tolerance of other religious beliefs was indeed seen as such a significant threat to the society that the heretic must be killed.

III. Religious Orthodoxy and Deterrence

When a political regime's legitimacy is grounded in religious dogma, challenges to that dogma are often seen as challenges to the political regime itself. To punish heretics and apostates one would need to show that their beliefs somehow did harm to individuals or to the state. The justification of punishing heretics or apostates for retributive reasons would entail establishing their errant views and showing a connection between those views and harm. But this would be difficult to do, as we will see. Instead, these religious prosecutions and ensuing punishments for those who appear to be guilty were sometimes justified for deterrence reasons which had the advantage that the desired deterrent effect was somewhat independent of whether there was indeed actual harm caused by the heretics and apostates.

In the history of criminal law, justifications for punishment were normally based on retribution, as in the "eye for an eye" pronouncements of Hammurabi's code and the Hebrew Bible. It was also the case that some thinkers, like Plato, put forward a rehabilitation justification of punishment, especially in his last work, *The Laws*. Deterrence turns up at many stages along the way, but had rarely been a significant rationale for criminal punishment, until the Medieval period.

There is no advantage to the Christian or Islamic state to punish for retribution–God may wish to exact retribution but religious leaders here on earth did not need to do so as well, except for the ending of the blood-feud by substituting a system controlled by the state instead of one controlled by the old tribal or family leaders. What was needed was a method to curtail or at least diminish the spread of the heresy or apostasy. The fear of eternal damnation was often mentioned as a reason to stick with the orthodox religious beliefs. But something more earthly was also needed to solve what was in the end an earthly problem–how to prevent the deterioration of the state monopoly on the beliefs of the subjects of the state.

Here is a letter from Pope Urban II to Bishop Gebhard of Constance on how to deal with those who contradict the Canons of the Church:

> Having considered for a long time the question of excommunication, confirming the judgment of our holy predecessor we, with the Lord's inspiration, settled the matter thus. On the first level, indeed we decree that heresiarch of Ravenna, the invader of the Roman church, together with King Henry, the head of the same iniquity, is alien from all members of the Catholic Church... We wish that those who lapse either willingly or through negligence be received under this coercion of discipline so that fear is instilled in others.[407]

Notice that the penalty assessed for the heretic was supposed to instill fear not only in the heretic but in others who might follow him–and that such fear was meant to deter these others from being tempted to join the heretical schism.

Yet, excommunication is not itself as severe as some of the corporal and capital punishments employed in later centuries especially during the European inquisitions. Indeed, excommunication seems quite a fitting punishment for a "religious" crime. If a member of the society does not want to adhere to the orthodox beliefs, expelling him or her from the community seems a not-inhumane way to penalize the heretic. And insofar as community membership was thought to be a good, then threatening to take it away could also deter others from accepting unorthodox views. Excommunication would not require the religious officials to need the civil authorities to mete out the punishments for them.

In some societies, though, it may be that excommunication was to cut the heretic off from employment or welfare that was needed for the very survival of the heretic. In that case, the penalty of excommunication may be thought to be inhumane. In a totally intolerant society, excommunication may be very similar to killing the heretic outright. But short of that, this penalty seems to be consistent with a humane legal system. Excommunication is not necessarily like outlawry or exile since the person might still remain in the society and be the beneficiary of that society's bounty even as he or she is no longer a member of the religious community.

---

[407] *Pope Urban II: The Collectio Britannica and the Council of Melfi (1089)*, translated and edited by Robert Somerville, Oxford: Oxford University Press, 1996, pp. 141-142.

Excommunication is also something that potentially could be reversed if the heretic were to return to orthodox beliefs. Renouncing unorthodox beliefs is then like coming back into the fold. If the heretic is killed, of course, there is no such reconciliation with the religious community. What makes all of this more difficult is that in the religious community and the state, for both Islam and Christianity, being excommunicated can mean being exiled with no clear path back for the heretic. There was not only a state religion but also a determination that those who are not believers in the orthodoxy could be executed for something like treason.

IV. Was the Lack of Religious Tolerance a Problem?

It is clear that in both Islamic and Canon law, it was thought to be a virtue that there was no tolerance for heretical views. But were there also problems created by the lack of religious tolerance? In this section, I will sketch some of the problems encountered in our two legal systems with the lack of religious tolerance and then in the final section I will assess all of this in terms of the humaneness of these systems of law and their supporting legal thought.

One of the crucial problems with the lack of religious tolerance in the early Catholic Church was that in some sense it encouraged schisms and widened divides, especially between Rome and Constantinople that to this day has never been resolved. Since the Church leaders thought that any deviation from orthodoxy had to be eliminated those who thought that their ideas were only slight improvements on that orthodoxy had no where to go except out of the jurisdiction of Canon law altogether.

From a legal standpoint, the lack of religious tolerance for differing viewpoints meant that the Canon law was at risk of stultifying because of being frozen. In point of fact that is not what actually happened. A continuing series of councils and synods allowed some dissenting voices to be heard and some changes were mandated as a result. But this then created the problem that only certain changes were given any credence and it became difficult for the ordinary Christian believer to know what was law and what was heresy or apostasy.

Gratian's great contribution to Canon law was that he attempted to present many, often conflicting, views on a given subject, such as penitential confession, and then to suggest where the better arguments resided. Yet, when one reads through this text it is often hard to tell why one argument or position is indeed preferred by Gratian. Gratian modeled his great work on Justinian's digest–but like Justinian there remained many questions about how to resolve the differing positions presented since in the end it was not acceptable that these conflicts could occur together in a system of religious law that was largely intolerant of religious differences.

In Islam, one can see a similar dynamic in that various competing schools of jurisprudence arose and it took a well-informed scholar to be able to sort through the often competing ideas to discern what people should believe and what they should regard as apostasy. In fact the Medieval split between Sunni and Shiite versions of Islam has not been resolved to this day.

The lack of religious tolerance in these systems of law is especially problematical because the divisions internal to Christian and to Islamic doctrines if anything became more pronounced over time. Who was a heretic or apostate and who was a true believer in orthodoxy was thus very difficult to determine, and when it was determined it was difficult to justify harsh treatment of the heretical group and not the true believers.

Of course, if the societies in question had been more tolerant especially of close members the very idea of heresy or apostasy would have been confined to true outsiders. This would have created a different set of problems–the kind of us-versus-them mentality that has plagued countless societies over time. But at least the internal harmony of the society would not have been so persistently disrupted by claims and counter claims of heresy and apostasy.

And this points to one of the largest problems: what seems like heresy at one time may become accepted as orthodoxy at another time. If the society is not open to possible changes over time, what is orthodoxy will stultify and impede new ideas from being tested to see if they are better than the old ideas. Intolerance has the effect of diminishing the rise of new ideas, and it may turn out that those new ideas were crucial in the future for the survival of the society.

Another problem is that it may be difficult to tell which orthodox ideas were central to the religious system of legal thought. We can see this rather clearly with the debate about the celibacy of priests. Throughout the early Medieval period the Catholic Church debated whether it was an orthodox belief that priests should not marry when at the very beginning all priests either were or had been married. It is clear that what was considered orthodoxy changed over time and unclear why these changes were not considered heretical.

In Islam, there were changes that occurred within the Quran from early verses to later verses on such matters as alcohol consumption. Again, why was the later view against alcohol consumption considered orthodoxy and the earlier view, clearly found in the Quran as well, considered to be unorthodox, and even heretical? Intolerance to new or different ideas also makes it very hard indeed to interpret texts like the Quran, the Gospels, and the Hebrew Bible that contain contradictory religious beliefs. In Islam, later Quranic verses are said to override earlier verses–it is thought that in the early years for instance alcohol consumption could not be outlawed because it was too integral to the Arab societies from which Islam arose. Yet the Quran was supposedly revealed in only a relatively short period of time so the divergent texts are unlikely to be explained as emanating from different historical periods.

One last issue to consider in this section concerns the difference between heresy and apostasy. One difference is that the apostate once believed in the dominant orthodoxy and now does not, whereas the heretic is a more general category for those who simply hold different beliefs from the dominant orthodoxy. Why should it make any difference in terms of tolerance whether the unbeliever once believed or never believed in the dominant orthodoxy?

In practical terms, the apostate could be seen as the greater threat than the heretic because the apostate stands for an erosion of the adherents to the dominant orthodoxy which could be seen as a more pressing and immediate threat to that orthodoxy than the mere fact that there are people out there who do not have the orthodox beliefs. It is one thing to be tolerant of those who were born into a different religion than to be tolerant of people born into the orthodox religion who have rejected it. In both cases intolerance is a problem, as we have seen, but it is a greater practical problem concerning heresy since it does not necessarily threaten the status quo.

V. Heresy, Apostasy, and a Humane Legal System

It is easy today to think that criminalizing heresy or apostasy represent the epitome of an inhumane legal and political system. Such conclusions are easily supported in hindsight by looking at the horrors of the inquisitions that followed closely on the heals of the fixation with heresy and apostasy in earlier Medieval times. Yet, it is also easily imaginable that the excesses of the inquisitions did not need to follow on the criminalization of heresy and apostasy.

To take a step back, we can try to imagine the felt need for the crimes of apostasy and heresy. The early Christian emperors saw a need for a single religion to provide the social glue for the growth of the empire;

and this was also true of the early caliphs of Islam. And there was also a perceived need to have an extra-worldly basis for rallying fighters to defend and extend the realm of the Christian and Islamic empires. We can see this in more vivid detail in that there were horrible excesses of the Crusades and the jihads that were fought against the Crusades, but the idea of defending and extending an empire was facilitated by having a single religion.

Yet there is a significant difference between having a single religion in a territory as opposed to prosecuting any deviations, however insignificant, from that dominant religion. Having a single dominant religion in a territory is also consistent with having tolerance of other religions in that territory as can be seen most clearly in the way that the Roman empire came to accommodate many religions even as there was still a state religion of Rome. Having a dominant religion, even a state religion, is compatible with toleration for other religions. What is gained by having religious intolerance in such societies is that defense of the state can be coupled with defense of religion–but there is probably more that is problematic about that than what is to the good.

Intolerance to others and humane treatment of those others, while not formally opposed ideas are certainly practically opposed to each other, especially in a legal context. And using the criminal law to punish those who are heretics or apostates adds a whole new level of intolerance to merely shunning or morally condemning those who fail to subscribe to the orthodoxy.

We also find a problem in the mixing of religious and civil law with the prosecution of heresy and apostasy. In Canon law, the criminalization of heresy initially made the Canon law dependent on the civil authorities to perform the punishments and later to engage in the prosecutions, since Canon law tribunals were not initially set up to deal with much beyond family issues such as marriage, divorce, and inheritance. In dealing with these matters, Canon law judges acted primarily as mediators. But prosecuting heresy involved much more than mediation. And when especially severe punishments were handed down for heretics, Canon law lacked the police-power to coerce heretics or to administer the actual punishments that were this-worldly. In Islam there was from the beginning a merger of religious and civil law, but nonetheless there was a problem in having religious leaders mete out severe punishments in this world when it was God's other-worldly punishments that were the center piece of Islamic religion.

As we will see in examining the inquisitions in detail in later chapters, the Catholic Church became tainted for many centuries by the prosecutions of heretics that looked sometimes like persecutions. The punishments were so severe that civil authorities had to be enlisted to perform them, such as Joan of Arc being burned alive at the stake. The Church did not want to appear to be killing people–religious officials were in fact barred from doing so because it made them less pure, or at least appear so. When the Catholic Church got into the business of prosecuting heretics, the Church could not help but to be politicized and to its detriment in terms of humaneness. Islam was already in its early days a mixture of religious and civil law, but the pursuit of apostates also created problems for the basic humaneness of Islamic law. When religious leaders ordered severe punishment, or actually meted it out themselves, they did not appear to be merciful and caring.

We can at this point ask why criminal punishments needed to be handed down by religious courts in the first place. Why would Canon lawyers need actual fire for burning at the stake when eternal fire was available as a sanction for heretics and apostates? Similarly, why would stoning and other forms of capital punishment be needed in Islam when God's wrath was a clear form of punishment available? On deterrence grounds, eternal fire seems more fear-producing than being killed while on earth. And on retributive grounds, no matter how bad heresy or apostasy was portrayed, eternal damnation seems to be not a fitting punishment.

The crimes of heresy and apostasy, in keeping with religion's other-worldly features, could have been assigned only other-worldly punishments, but this did not happen in either Islamic or Canon law. Even so, this-worldly punishments could have been more like penance in that what was required of the offender was to pray more or to do more good works–housing the homeless, feeding the hungry, clothing the naked–well recognized goods in both of these traditions. Such penalties could have been part of a humane way to treat those whose unorthodox views were thought in some sense to be harmful to the society.

CHAPTER 18

DIVINE AND EARTHLY PUNISHMENT

Islamic and Canon law locates the authority of law in the divine commands of God. And discussions of punishments for violations of those commands is marked by having two tracks: one that is meted out here on earth especially by religious leaders, and one that is to be meted out after death. In the Canon law tradition, penance is the category that is most often discussed as the retribution for sin or crime. In the Islamic law tradition, making amends for one's sins is also discussed but not by reference explicitly to penance. We shall see though that Islamic law does have similar categories of retribution and punishment like penance as well. In the idea of holy war, one of the main motivations for fighting in a jihad or holy war is that by fighting one's sins are forgiven, and this includes sins that may be committed after that war has ended.

We begin in section one with a discussion of the idea of penance in Canon law, especially in the work of Gratian. We then, in section 2, look for an equivalent set of ideas to penance in Islamic law, especially in the debates about the meaning of certain categories found in the Quran and the Ahadith. In the third section I will argue that the two divine law traditions are closer than is often thought in how they understand divine punishment. Then in the fourth section we will see how these two legal traditions deal with earthly punishment, often in brutal fashion. And in the final section we will ask why there was a need for both kinds of punishment, and what having these two forms of punishment tells us about the motivation to obey the law.

I. Penance and Gratian's Work

The "father" of Canon law, Gratian, writing in the 12th century CE, devoted a major portion of his Decretal to penance, which is sometimes printed separately as *Tractatus de Penitentia*.[408] In the first

[408] Gratian, *Tractatus de Penitentia*, edited and translated by Atria A. Larson, Washington, DC: Catholic University of America Press, 2016.

distinction, the first question that Gratian considers is whether: "each person is able to make satisfaction to God by contrition of the heart alone and secret satisfaction without oral confession." And here is the first "position" Gratian considers on the way to answering the first question:

> There are those who say that anyone can merit mercy for an evil deed without confession to the church and to the judgment of a priest… [as] Augustine explains: "Great is the kindness of God that he has forgiven sins according to his promise alone. I do not yet announce with my mouth, and yet God already hears in my heart, for to say this very statement, ['I will pronounce'] is just like pronouncing the thing. For the will is taken to be the work."[409]

According to this position, to be forgiven of sin a person must pronounce in his heart that he or she is sorry, without having to speak these words or to be judged by a priest. The "work" or the penance is that the person has asked for forgiveness in his or her heart.

One important issue to be considered again in this section is the difference between sins and crimes. Crimes have "legal consequences" whereas sins can be merely internal. Civil law punishes crimes but divine law can punish, by providing penance, for thoughts that lack legal consequences.[410] Gratian argues that one can be guilty "in a multitude of ways" and then quotes Justinian's Digest that punishments should be meted out differently for each crime based on seven factors: "motive, person, place, time, quality, quantity, outcome."[411]

For Gratian, following Prosper of Aquitaine, a fifth century CE prelate, there are three forms of punishment here on earth: the punishment meted out by the civil law, the punishment based on the judgment of the priest who hears one's sins in confession, and the punishment that is self-inflicted by those who see that they have sinned and chastise themselves. These punishments are called "temporary penalties" and they are distinguished from punishment in the afterlife, the "eternal torture as God gives the retribution." One can "extinguish the flames of eternal fire" by accepting "a voluntary penalty of the most severe chastisement."[412] There is no benefit to avoiding human judgment here on earth given that one risks so much worse in the afterlife.

---

[409] Gratian, *Tractatus de Penitentia*, Distinction 1, question 1, First position, p. 3.
[410] See ibid., p. 11.
[411] Ibid., p. 9.
[412] Ibid., p. 17.

Gratian also presents arguments on the other side of this issue, especially concerning how the priest's judgment is crucial for providing the kind of penance that will preempt eternal damnation. In this respect, Gratian quotes Jerome, a Church father of the fourth century CE:

> Now the Canons indeed do not fix in a sufficiently clear manner the amount of time for doing penance for each evil deed so as to say concerning each individual deed how each one is to be emended, but rather they state that it is to be left to the judgment of an intelligent priest, because, for God, the amount of time does not have as much value as the amount of grief... For this reason, the Canons order that the lengths of penance ought to be shortened on account of the penitents' faith and way of life, and they judge that lengths of penance ought to be prolonged on account of negligence.[413]

Here the priest is necessary for setting the proper penance. Each sin and each sinner are to be judged differently and it is the intelligent priest whose job it is to judge and then to set the temporary temporal punishment that will save the sinner from eternal damnation.

We can end this section with just a few words from the 9th century CE bishop, Amalar of Metz, on the idea of penance and confession:

> Let each of us therefore flee to the lamentations of penance, since there is time to weep before we are struck down. Let us call before our mind's eye whatever we did in wandering astray, and let us endure punishment in our mourning for our vile actions... But let no one despair over the vastness of their sins. For he wiped away the faults of the indolent Ninevites with a penance of three days, and the converted thief earned the reward of life even upon the sentence of his death. Let us therefore change our hearts...[414]

In this view, there is no sin that is too grave that it cannot be forgiven–yet if it is not forgiven by a priest, after death there is nothing to be expected but eternal damnation. Amalar of Metz also gave us this pithy way to understand penance as the recovery after sin: "His resurrection was

---

413 Ibid., p. 67.

414 Amalar of Metz, *On the Liturgy*, Book 4.25.5-6, Cambridge: Harvard University Press, 2014, Vol. II, p. 481.

accomplished through an immortal body; ours is accomplished through penance.[415]

Penance is the sacrament that allows the Christian to regain full membership in the Church, but even more importantly it also in effect blocks the fate that awaits the unrepentant and forgiven sinner in the afterlife. So, while there are punishments in this life and the next, according to Canon lawyers and prelates it is much to be preferred to face even the worst punishments in this life since the punishments of the next life are not only very bad but also eternal.

II. Sin, Crime, and Punishment in Islam

In the Quran there is much discussion of sin and punishment, and for us the passages about grave sin (*kaba'ir*) are initially most interesting:

> Consume not each other's wealth falsely, but trade by mutual consent; and slay not yourselves. Truly God is Merciful unto you. And whosoever does that in enmity and injustice, We shall cause him to burn in a Fire; and that is easy for God. If you shun the grave sins (*kaba'ir*) that you are forbidden, We shall absolve you of your evil deeds and cause you to enter at a noble gate.[416]

It appears that there is a distinction here between grave sins, for which absolution will not come in this life, and evil deeds (lesser sins?) that can be forgiven in this life if one has avoided the grave sins. In any event some sins can be forgiven and then when this person dies he or she will be able to enter heaven through the noble gate.

The Quran also tells us that God "pardons much"[417] even as we also learn that some people will suffer "lasting punishment" for their grave sins.[418] The way to attain forgiveness for some (minor) sins seems to be not to commit grave sins. But it is also true that God is infinitely merciful and forgiving and so perhaps God may forgive those who commit grave sins, but we do not learn what the grave sinner is to do to obtain such forgiveness.

In another verse from the Quran it does seem that even grave sins can be forgiven in this world:

---

415 Ibid., 4.17.5, vol. II, p. 431.
416 *The Study Quran*, 4:29-31, pp. 204-205.
417 *The Study Quran*, 42:34, p. 1183.
418 *The Study Quran*, 42:45, p. 1185.

> Unto God belongs whatsoever is in the heavens and whatsoever is on the earth, that He may requite those who commit evil for that which they have done, and that He may requite those who are virtuous with that which is most beautiful, those who shun grave sins and indecencies, save what is slight; truly your Lord is of vast forgiveness.[419]

The infinite forgiveness for grave sins though, as some commentators have argued requires that first there be "repentance."[420]

The sins that are considered "grave" are listed in various Ahadith, as we see in this verse:

> Narrated by 'Abdullah bin 'Amar: The Prophet said, "Al-Kaba'ir (the biggest sins) are: To join others (as partners) in worship with Allah, to be undutiful to one's parents," or he said, "to take a false oath."[421]

These are the sins or crimes that deserve the strongest punishments, but the infinite mercy of God may forgive.

And yet we also find that the death penalty is assigned for grave sins or crimes, and we find that torture and mutilation are punishments as well that can be meted out for serious criminal acts. In fact, Muhammad is reported to have ordered the killing of people who had committed serious offenses, and even to have participated himself in the stoning to death of certain criminals. We see the use of the death penalty in the following Hadith:

> Narrated by Anas bin Malik: A Jew crushed the head of a girl between two stones, and the girl was asked, "Who has done this to you, so-and-so or so-and-so? (Some names were mentioned for her) till the name of that Jew was mentioned (whereupon she nodded in agreement). The Jew was brought to the Prophet and the Prophet kept on questioning him till he confessed, whereupon his head was crushed with stones.[422]

In part this reflects the use of the death penalty approved by Muhammad. In this Hadith there is also an account of the use of the death penalty for someone who confesses and in another Hadith we learn that "The Prophet

---

[419] *The Study Quran*, 53:31-32, pp. 1294-1295.
[420] *The Study Quran*, Commentary on p. 1295.
[421] Hadith 6870, Volume 9, p. 16.
[422] Hadith 6876, Vol. 9, p. 19.

killed a Jew for killing a girl in order to take her ornaments."[423] This shows that Muhammad not only ordered but also personally administered the death penalty.

In Islam, concerning divine retribution, God is portrayed as infinitely merciful and forgiving; but, in this life, punishments can often be quite harsh. Islamic law, to a certain extent, took over harsh punishments from the pre-Islamic Arabs. And it is clear that punishments were disproportionately administered based on who the person was–that is whether the sinner was a Muslim or not. Indeed, the case of the Jew who commits a sin or crime seems to show that one of the main factors that determines punishment is who the sinner or criminal is. And yet there is also a verse in the Quran that seemingly calls for what a Hadith calls "equal proportionality of punishment"–where the punishment scheme set out does not differentiate between different classes of sinners.[424] A Commentary on this verse is instructive:

> The understanding of *qisas* [retribution] in Islamic Law resembles *lex talionis* in Roman Law as well as other systems of compensation/retaliation in the ancient and premodern worlds… The majority of jurists make two points of equality a condition of *qisas*, or retribution: both the murder victim and the perpetrator must be free and be Muslims. They say that a Muslim would not be executed for killing a *kafir* (a disbeliever), nor a free man for killing a slave, though there would be some punishment in these cases if it were intentional murder. The Hanafi school, however, makes no distinction, since for it the operative part of the law is that a life is a life… and that it is the fact that a person has been slain, and nothing else is relevant.[425]

It is also worth noting that killing during war is treated differently, where the relevant question is whether the war had a just cause.

III. Islamic and Canon Law on Punishment and Penance

One of the first things to note as we compare the Islamic and Canon law on punishment is that both are deeply indebted to the Roman law. As just one example, punishment is determined by various factors, and one of these is the status of the person who is the victim and also the

[423] Hadith 6885, Vol. 9, p. 24.
[424] See *The Study Quran*, verse 2:178, pp. 77-78.
[425] *The Study Quran*, p. 77.

status of the perpetrator. Justinian's *Digest*, which was published just decades before the birth of Muhammad, collated most of the major laws of the Roman Empire. Many of the most significant documents of Roman law date from the first and second century, and were well known by the time of Muhammad and his early followers as they established the beginnings of Islamic law. And of course, Canon law also was very deeply indebted to Roman law–as can be plainly seen in the enormous number of references to Roman law in Gratian's codification of Canon law in the 12th century CE. Indeed, Gratian's code seems to parallel Justinian's code even in its structure.

A strong similarity between Islamic and Canon law is the idea that God is the ultimate source of rules and also the ultimate enforcer of those rules. And yet, God is also characterized in both traditions as a merciful forgiver. And those who most closely represent God on earth are also said to be merciful forgivers, although in both traditions there are well known excesses of punishment–such as the use of torture, extreme corporal punishment, and the death penalty. These excesses are best seen in Canon and Islamic law when dealing with heretics and apostates, as we have just seen in the previous chapter.

What is expected in order successfully to appeal for forgiveness varies: in Canon law it is a change of heart, and possibly also an oral confession to a priest; whereas in Islamic law it seems that forgiveness comes to those primarily who do not commit graves sins or crimes. Yet, in both traditions all of one's sins can be forgiven if one goes into battle for a just cause and at the direction of those who have proper authority, often religious leaders. In this respect, ideas of penance and punishment are also not fully distinguished either.

Penance becomes more than acknowledging to oneself that one has done wrong when a representative of the Church and hence of God must be appealed to as the judge of what will count as sufficient atonement. We also see something of this sort in the many cases where Muhammad is appealed to as judge of the correct punishment for those who have engaged in wrongdoing–and we find similar things said about those leaders of Islam who followed in Muhammad's footsteps. Islam lacks the formal "confessional" practices of Catholicism, but there are nonetheless many acknowledgements that Muhammad and his followers are to be the judges of what punishments should be inflicted–including cases where Muhammad is himself the executioner of those punishments.

There is also a similarity between these two systems of law in that there are different rules and different punishments depending on one's status. But there is more to this than is often acknowledged. Canon law's rules are mainly aimed at Christians, and Islamic law's rules are primarily aimed at Muslims. Roman Law was unusual in that it was universally binding but wide discretion was given to local parts of the Empire–so while Roman Law applied to all, there were many variances based on who one was–such as that Jews were allowed largely to govern themselves at least concerning matters of religious practice and family law.

IV. Assessing Earthly Punishment

In ancient times it is often claimed that virtually all punishments were brutal, especially since the death penalty was used so extensively. Yet, Medieval times are also characterized by brutality of punishment and this is especially curious since, as we noted, merciful forgiveness is so often also said in legal documents to be the hallmark of the systems of justice in Islamic and Canon law.

Some have traced the supposed brutality of Islamic law to the brutal methods of punishment of the non-Islamic Arabs from whom Islam arose. In the Middle Ages there was a breakdown in civil authority and a gap that religious leaders filled. But this alone would not completely explain the brutality of many of the punishments recorded at this time. Indeed, it is a puzzle, at least on first sight, that the ideas of merciful forgiveness would stand side-by-side with examples of brutal punishments. In part this can be explained by reference to the idea of God as an avenger of wrongdoing who is to be feared.

From the earliest of times, Islam has been known for and also criticized for such things as cutting off the hands of those who are caught in robberies. But as we have seen, in fact the Islamic law often talks of "equality of punishment"–which is comparable to the *lex talionis* of earlier times. It may appear brutal when a hand is cut off for having done an equivalent harm, but actually like *lex talionis* "equality of punishment" can be understood as attempting to stop the blood-feud and to stop much more severe punishments that had existed for the pre-Islamic Arabs and other peoples of ancient times.

It is curious that both Islamic and Canon law present two forms of punishment: earthly and divine–why is it not enough to have just one form of punishment? We can begin to formulate an answer to this question by turning to the idea expressed by Gratian that secret sins should be treated differently from sins that were public.

> For internal penance is one thing and external penance another. Internal penance is that which Augustine says, "Everyone who is made the arbiter of his own will is not able to begin a new

> life unless he repents his old life… But those things that are said about public satisfaction or oral confession should be understood in public and manifest offences… And public injury (as Augustine testifies) requires a public remedy. And so by the aforementioned authorities it is proven that manifest satisfaction and oral confession must be offered up for manifest sins. But it is not proven that hidden sins must necessarily be confessed to priest and expiated by his judgment.[426]

For hidden or secret sins, the sinner is the one who has to feel shame or guilt without the larger society's condemnation. And for this to occur, it seems that the sinner must fear the wrath of God if he or she does not engage in self-inflicted penance.

The idea seems to be that the control of behavior requires not only fear of state sanction but also fear of God's wrath. During the Middle Ages we find that there is still a serious problem of not having enough (or even any) police or jails to accommodate all of the wrongdoers. Realistically, people must have seen that the state could not punish all sins or crimes, and so the idea that those sins and crimes would nonetheless be punished in the afterlife by God's wrath made sense as a means of controlling the tendency to do wrong by the general populace.

Another idea that seems important to mention is that in the Middle Ages we find that the most minute behavior is scrutinized. The best example of this is in the monasteries and convents of the Catholic Church where when and whether to speak or eat or sleep is tightly regulated. It would be very difficult indeed for every person's behavior to be so scrutinized by a fellow human outside of monastery or convent so it is God who is said to always be watching and judging.

The regulation of thoughts and intentions is already discussed in Talmudic and Roman times, but it was the regulation of actions that was the main focus of the early criminal law. For hundreds of years intentional killing had been distinguished from unintentional killing–at least as early as Draco's code in ancient Greece. The idea that one could tell what a person's intentions are is thus quite ancient. But the idea that one could punish a person merely for one's thoughts or intentions seems to be peculiar to the Medieval period of legal thought. As we have seen, the kind of punishment for such thoughts is largely left to God's judgment in the afterlife.

---

[426] Gratian, *Tractatus de Penitentia*, Distinction 1, pp. 75-77.

One other idea that is worth pursuing here is that religion and politics, as well as religion and law, were not easily disconnected in Medieval times. Especially in divinely-inspired systems of law, one of the law's main objectives was to provide incentives for people to follow God's law. Civil punishments, religious sanctions, and fear of the fires in the afterlife blended together, all in the service of the same goal. Bishops found themselves passing judgment on what would otherwise seem to be strictly secular crimes; and princes found themselves similarly passing judgment on what would otherwise seem to be strictly religious sins. And, as we have seen, the Quran often does not distinguish between crime and sin. We will take up these issues in various ways in subsequent chapters, and in the final chapter we will consider the relation between religion and law in general in the Middle ages.

V. Sin and Penance, Crime and Punishment

There is a symmetry that is often today recognized but that did not characterize how punishment was understood in Medieval Islamic and Canon law. The symmetry would connect the idea of sin, understood as a violation of God's law, with penance, understood as how to appease or reconcile with God. And the symmetry would then connect crime, understood as the violation of the civil laws of a state or community, with punishment, understood as how the wrongdoer was to appease or reconcile with the community or state. In this final section we will speculate on why the modern symmetry seems not to have been accepted in Medieval times.

The most important reason why the symmetry did not hold in Medieval Islamic and Canon law systems was, as we saw in our Chapter 10, that civil law was ultimately supported by divine law. Those who violated civil law were offending against God, not merely one's community or state, since civil law was merely the divine law promulgated for a given community or state. Indeed, the ideas of sin and crime were often understood as interchangeable.

Yet, while sin and crime were often interchangeable, penance and punishment were not so understood. Indeed, the idea of penance does not play a prominent role in Islamic law, and in Christian writings penance was seen as an internal retribution whereas punishment was for external retribution. Nonetheless, bishops increasingly intervened in the civil affairs of their communities and states to impose or insist that punishment be imposed. And civil rulers also tried to dictate who should do penance and what form that penance should take.

In divine law systems, one could distinguish sin and crime, but to do so would not automatically restore symmetry. Civil authorities could be given the task of dealing with certain offenses against God's law, while other offences were left to those religious authorities who stood in a direct line to God. At some times it seems that this is indeed the way Medieval Christianity attempted some form of symmetry, but at other times there is no symmetry. In Islamic law, God's wrath and God's mercy are the backdrop for nearly all of the discussions of punishment. So, while Muhammad and his followers were the instruments of God's will, there was no clear distinction between punishing for sin and for crime.

It is also useful at this point to draw a distinction between retribution and reconciliation and to distinguish both from deterrence. Retribution is the idea that a person must make amends for his or her wrongful conduct. Retribution is premised on the idea of a balance being disrupted and that the person responsible needs to pay a price for the disruption. Reconciliation is a similar notion to that of retribution but it is less accusatory–a person has become estranged from his or her community and needs to do something to be welcomed back. Standing against both of these ideas is deterrence–punishment is to be meted out so that the wrongdoer, or another person tempted to be a wrongdoer, will have a disincentive to engage in wrongdoing.

Fear of God was a constant theme in Medieval times, and so was the hope for eternal reward. As we will see in the next chapter, fear of God's wrath and hope for eternal reward was what drove both crusaders and jihadists to risk their lives–they were promised that their sins would all be forgiven and that the "martyrs" would all go directly to heaven. Indeed, it sometimes seemed that there were only these options: eternal fire or eternal bliss. Fear of God can play a role in why people feel the need to do penance or accept punishment here in this world. Divine judgment can be affected by the showing in this world of remorse and piety that comes from penance or punishment.

While there is not much discussion of penance in Islamic law, there is discussion of some of what counts as the elements of penance as that term was used in Canon law. The leading idea of penance is that a person needs to make his or her heart, or soul, purified of evil thoughts and feelings. Here is where the idea of striving, that is the key component of jihad in its various forms, and of the fulfilling of the duty to go off to Just Wars. Striving is a matter of how one is disposed to behave, and it shares much with the early modern idea of endeavor. Indeed, as we have seen, Medieval legal thought is infused with the idea of intention–even more so than action–being the key idea in responsibility, especially criminal responsibility.

There is a related doctrine that we have not explored but is deserving of mention here, namely, some sinners and criminals preferred the harshest of this-worldly punishment so as not to face the eternal fires. There is much attention to avoiding the eternal fires by appealing to God's boundless mercy. Yet, even more attention is paid to the idea of doing good works in this life, or in having the best intentions to do good. This is presumably why Islamic and Christian texts talk so much about aiding the poor or those who were naked or starving. The attention to intention makes it possible for even poor people to serve the poor at least by having good intentions to do so.

SECTION VIII:

JUSTIFYING WAR

CHAPTER 19

MEDIEVAL JIHADS, CRUSADES, AND JUST CAUSES FOR WAR

Jihads in Islamic legal thought and crusades in Medieval Christian legal thought (especially Canon law) are often characterized as "holy wars"–wars fought for religious reasons, such as to conquer infidels or to convert heathens or polytheists. In this chapter I will set out some of the main similarities and differences between these two forms of "holy war." I shall mainly focus on the legal and political theory underlying jihads and crusades. I shall argue that these wars are at least as well characterized as wars for political ideology as for religion. And for this reason, even though very few theorists today would support a war for religious reasons, analyzing the legal and political thought behind the Medieval jihads and crusades can tell us something important.

I will begin by very briefly discussing two Just War concepts that are of importance to the assessment of jihads and crusades: the idea of just cause and the idea of proportionality. In the second section I set out some of the canonical texts from Islamic law and Canon law on "holy wars." In the third section I will suggest that there seem to be more similarities than differences in these views. In the fourth section I will argue that political ideology was often at the root of the defenses of jihad and crusade. Throughout, I will briefly explore the reasons given at the end of the Middle Ages against religious wars.

I. Just War, Just Cause, and Proportionality

The Just War tradition provides a way to assess the morality and legality of war. At the beginning of the Medieval period, Augustine of Hippo, provided the most influential statements of the criteria for a just war. And Thomas Aquinas, in the 13th Century, provided a more complete and also highly influential account of just war criteria. Several scholars have claimed that the ideas of a just war found in Islamic religious and legal texts were an important source for Aquinas. Today, Just War theory has made a strong comeback and is now a very robust area of scholarship.

The central claim of the Just War idea is that universal moral and legal criteria for assessing war can be defended, even as there is disagreement about the specific way the criteria are related to each other.[427]

Just cause is the idea that for a war to be justly initiated it must be motivated by a morally or legally good reason. The least contentious of just causes has, over the several millennia of these discussions, been self-defense. If one state is being attacked and has not provoked that attack, then the war waged against the attackers is considered to have a just cause. Another just cause, still somewhat contentious, is defense of innocent others. Self-defense, or defense of others, provide just causes, and have been recognized as such for nearly as long as there has been writing about war. This is not yet to say that the war that is so waged is a just war since there are other considerations than whether there is a just cause to wage war.[428] But establishing that there is a just cause is often thought to be the most significant hurdle to cross on the path to demonstrating that one is engaged in a just war. The party that wages a just war is considered to be acting defensively against the other party who is considered the aggressor. And in nearly all societies aggressive war has been considered immoral and illegal. In the Middle Ages, "illegal" means violating the (natural) laws of war.[429]

One reason why a war fought for a just cause is not yet considered a just war is that the anticipated destructiveness of a war may be disproportionate to the benefit of the cause for which the war is fought. The war may indeed be initiated for defending an outpost of a given state, but what it will take successfully to defend that outpost[430] may involve so much death and destruction as to make it unclear that the war will indeed be a just war.[431] As we will see, proportionality questions arise in the crusades and jihads that we will focus on in this chapter. Both jihads and crusades may have had a just cause but may have been nonetheless disproportionate and ultimately unjust.

---

[427] See *The Cambridge Handbook of the Just War*, co-edited by Larry May, Shannon Fyfe, and Eric Ritter, Cambridge: Cambridge University Press, 2017.

[428] Other jus ad bellum criteria include: legitimate authority, right intention, and necessity or last resort, as well as proportionality as we will see.

[429] See Larry May, *Aggression and Crimes Against Peace*, Cambridge: Cambridge University Press, 2008.

[430] Think of the case of the war waged between the UK and Argentina over the Falkland Islands.

[431] See Michael Newton and Larry May, *Proportionality in International Law*, Oxford: Oxford University Press, 2014.

In assessing just causes we should be aware that finding a reason to go to war that has a just cause may not be the end of the story even about just cause since there may be several reasons, several causes, for going to war in a given case where one of the causes is just but the other is not and in the balance of causes the war is deemed not to have a sufficient just cause to make us think that the war is just. This idea is linked to the idea that most wars are fought for mixed motives: to go to the aid of innocent others but also to gain access to oil reserves, for instance. In the case of the crusades and jihads of the 11th and 12th centuries CE, there may have been just causes-in defense of religion or co-religionists–but also causes of war that had to do with territorial gain or re-gain. When there are multiple causes for a war, as there often are, we cannot merely assess whether one of the causes is just in order to establish conclusively that the war overall has a just cause and is just.

II. Jihad, Crusade, and Holy Wars

The idea of a Medieval "crusade" is normally traced back to late November of 1095 with a sermon from Pope Urban II. Here is how Thomas Asbridge describes it:

> Urban declared that Christianity was in dire peril, threatened by invasion and appalling oppression. The Holy City of Jerusalem was now in the hands of Muslims–"a people… alien to God," bent upon ritual torture and unspeakable desecration. He called upon Latin Europe to rise up against this supposedly savage foe as "soldiers of Christ," reclaiming the Holy Land and releasing eastern Christians from "servitude." Enticed by the promise that this righteous struggle would purge their souls of sin, tens of thousands of men, women, and children marched out of the West to wage war against the Muslim world in the First Crusade.[432]

The term crusade was not actually used by Pope Urban II but was used a century or so later and was a transliteration of the French term, *croisade*, which meant the way or call of the cross.

On December 1, 1145, Pope Eugene III, called for all Catholics to go to the Mideast:

[432] Thomas Asbridge, *The Crusades*, NY: HarperCollins Publishers, 2010, p. 33.

> We exhort all of you in God, we ask and command, and for the remission of sins enjoin: that those who are of God, and above all, the greater men and the nobles, do manfully gird themselves; and that you *strive to oppose* the multitude of the infidels, who rejoice at the time in victory gained over us, and so to defend the oriental church… and to snatch many thousands of your captive brothers from their hands… [and to] war for the Lord.[433]

There are many things to comment on concerning the statement by this pope. First and foremost is that there is a call to go to war for God's sake to save imperiled Christians, a seemingly clear religious reason to go to war and to see such a war as involving a just cause. It is also interesting that the term "strive to oppose" is employed by this pope since that could easily be a translation not only of the Latin terms used, but as we will see also a translation of the idea of jihad.

Here are two verses from the Quran (c. 610 CE) that express the idea behind a holy war of jihad:

> He it is Who sent His Messenger with guidance and the Religion of Truth to make it prevail over all religion, though the idolaters be averse. O you who believe! Shall I direct you to a commerce that will save you from a painful punishment: that you believe in God and the Messenger and strive (jihad) in God's way with your wealth of souls? That is better for you, if you but knew. He will forgive your sins and cause you to enter Gardens with rivers running below, and goodly dwellings in Gardens of Eden–that is the great triumph–and something else that you love: help from God and a victory nigh… So We strengthened those who believed against their enemies and they came to prevail.[434]

Here it is very clear that the jihad is a war to overcome all religions other than Islam, and that those who engage in this striving for victory will triumph on many levels.

And we also learn from the Quran and other Islamic legal texts that "slaying infidels" is what Muslims are charged to do:

---

[433] Pope Eugene III, "The Papal Bull *Quantum Praedecessores*," in *A Reader of Medieval Laws, Edicts, and Orders*, translated by E. F. Henderson, Washington, DC: Madison and Monroe Press, 2013, p. 259.

[434] *The Study Quran*, 61:9-14, pp. 1367-1368.

> when the sacred months have passed, slay the idolaters wheresoever you find them, besiege them, and lie in wait for them at every place of ambush. But if they repent, and perform the prayer and give the alms, then let them go their way…[435]

Note though that if the infidels repent and either join Islam or stop opposing Islam and pay a tax, they can, and should, be saved.

In the Ahadith, we get clearer about the way that jihad is to be understood in Islamic law. The Book of Jihad (book 56) begins by quoting the Quran's verse 9:111:

> Truly God has purchased from the believers their souls and their wealth in exchange for the Garden being theirs. They fight in the way of God, slaying and being slain. [It is] a promise binding upon Him in the Torah, the Gospel, and the Quran. And who is truer to His pact than God? So rejoice in the bargain you have made. That indeed is the great triumph.[436]

This seems very clear indeed–the only way mentioned to achieve jihad is to slay the enemy of God or to be slain trying to do so. And this obligation is said also to be found in the Torah and the Gospel, so it is an obligation of all Abrahamic religions, not just Islam.

Those men who are called to fight for Islam will find a special reward waiting for them in heaven, as we see in several other Ahadith. Here is Hadith 2795:

> Narrated by Anas bin Malik: The Prophet said, "Nobody who dies and finds good from Allah (in the Hereafter) would wish to come back to this world, even if he were given the whole world and whatever is in it, except the martyr who, on seeing the superiority of martyrdom, would like to come back and get killed again (in Allah's Cause)."[437]

Being a martyr in God's cause is often mentioned in the Ahadith as the greatest thing to strive for–"I would love to be martyred in Allah's Cause and then come back to life again, and then get martyred, and then come back to life again and then get martyred and then come back to life again and get martyred."[438]

---

[435] *The Study Quran*, 9:5, pp. 506-507.

[436] *The Study Quran*, 9:111, p. 536.

[437] Hadith, 2795, Book IV, p. 51.

[438] Hadith 2707, Book IV, p. 52.

And yet Hadith 2782 only mentions the obligation to engage in jihad after the obligations of saying "prayers at fixed times" and being "dutiful to your parents."[439] Indeed Hadith 2783 then says:

> Narrated by Ibn 'Abbas: Allah's Messenger said, "There is no *Hijra* (i.e., emigration) (from Makkah to Madina) after the Conquest of (Makkah) but *Jihad* and good intention remain; and if you are called (by the Muslim ruler) for *Jihad*, go forth immediately."[440]

So having the intention to go to jihad is the key obligation and only after one has been commanded to go into battle is that the way that jihad must be satisfied.

Furthermore we learn in Hadith 2784 that women satisfy the obligation of jihad without fighting at all:

> Narrated 'Aishah (that she said), "O Allah's Messenger! We consider *Jihad* as the best deed. Should we not fight in Allah's Cause?" He said, "The best *Jihad* (for women) is *Hajj-Mabrur* (i.e., Hajj which is done according to the Prophet's *Sunna* and is accepted by Allah)."

Women satisfy the jihad by going on the Hajj, the pilgrimage to Mecca. It is thus clear that despite men being told that they should slay the enemies of Islam, there are other and perhaps better ways to satisfy the obligation of jihad. All of this is to say that while jihad can be said to be a call to slay or be slain, jihad also involves perhaps other greater obligations than fighting.

III. Comparing Jihads and Crusades

Jihads and crusades have much in common, seemingly more than the differences between them. Let us begin with some of the most commonly cited characteristics of jihad that are thought to be different from crusades. The call to the jihad of the sword must be answered unless a person has a disability like blindness that prevents participation in war. And another commonly cited characteristic of jihad is that martyrdom in the jihad of the sword will be rewarded with the highest place in heaven.

---

439 Hadith 2782, Book IV, p. 44.

440 Hadith, 2783, Book IV, p. 45.

Islam is often portrayed as a militant religion that makes serving in war the highest virtue, or so it is often claimed. But in fact the Quran lists praying five times a day and obeying one's parents as greater obligations than jihad, and in any event the most significant form of jihad is not waging war but having the right intentions in one's heart. And those Popes and bishops urging people to join the crusades did not single out going to war in service to God as the highest of all virtues either.

It is undeniable that being a martyr during a jihad is praised heavily in the Quran and the Ahadith. Indeed, here is Hadith 2818: "Allah's Messenger said, 'Know that paradise is under the shades of swords (Jihad in Allah's Cause).'"[441] This Hadith seems to say that paradise is only achieved or best achieved, by participating in the jihad of war. Yet, the call to the crusades also promises that all of a person's sins will be forgiven, even sins committed after returning from the crusades. So, the crusades were inspired by rhetoric, in some cases, that sounds surprisingly like the rhetoric that inspired people to join the jihad of the sword.

We can see the other similarities by realizing that inciting to violence is not the first or even the best way to understand jihad or crusade. In the case of jihads, many interpreters of the Quran point out that there are several types of jihad, all having to do with the root idea of striving to do one's duty before God. The "greater" jihad involves striving to overcome evil and the devil in one's own inner life. Jihad understood as striving to violently confront enemies of Islam is only considered to be the "lesser" jihad. As James Turner Johnson has put it:

> The concept of jihad, rooted in the earliest stages of Islamic history, fundamentally denotes striving or effort expended by the individual Muslim to walk in the path of God. The jihad of the sword, the "lesser" form of striving, according to one tradition associated with the Prophet Mohammed, is but one form alongside other, greater ones: the jihad of the heart (moral reformation), that of the tongue (proclaiming God's word abroad) and that of the hand (works in accord with the will of God)... Furthermore, not all wars of the Muslim community are properly jihad, since they may lack religiously defined purpose or authorization.[442]

---

[441] Hadith 2818, Book IV, p. 63.

[442] James Turner Johnson, *The Holy War Idea in Western and Islamic Traditions*, University Park, PA: Penn State University Press, 1997, p. 19.

It is obligatory that all Muslims strive to do what God commands, but God does not command that all Muslims take up the sword to satisfy the command of jihad as a form of striving to do what is right. Asma Afsaruddin has argued that in the Quran "there are more references to peaceful striving (against evil passions) than there are to armed conflict."[443]

There is a similar idea in Christian understandings of what is required of good Catholics concerning God's commands. Thomas Asbridge says:

> For centuries theologians had characterized the internal, spiritual battle that devoted Christians waged against sin as the 'warfare of Christ,' and monks were sometimes described as the "soldiers of Christ." [Pope Gregory VII] twisted this idea to suit his purposes, proclaiming that all lay society had one overriding obligation: to defend the Latin Church as "soldiers of Christ" through actual physical warfare.[444]

Indeed, as we saw, the term "striving" was applied to the obligations of Christians to lead a good life, much as was required in Islamic legal thought.

The main religious and legal texts that set out the obligations under God's law also provide similarities that are often quite striking. Of course, it is only surprising if one had ignored the fact that Mohammed proclaimed that Islam was an "Abrahamic" religion, and that he was merely the last in a list of Prophets that included Moses as well as Jesus. Mohammed also famously identified "the people of the book" as Jews, Christians and Muslims–setting the people of the book, those who were monotheists who followed the Bible, the Gospels, or the Quran as people who stood together against the idolaters and polytheistic pagans. And in Hadith 6861, we learn that those who believe in the one God should not be killed, "except for a just cause."[445]

IV. Political Ideology, the Crusades, and Jihads

Historians have debated whether the crusades and jihads were solely about religion or whether they were at least partially about

---

[443] Asma Afsaruddin, *Striving in the Path of God*, Oxford: Oxford University Press, 2013, cited in Malcolm Lambert, *God's Armies: Crusade and Jihad*, NY: Pegasus Books, 2016, p. 7.

[444] Thomas Asbridge, *The Crusades*, NY: HarperCollins Publishers, 2010, p. 16.

[445] Hadith 6861, Book IX, p. 13.

territorial gain or the promotion of a political ideology rather than a religion. In this section I will say a bit about the nature of religion in order to set the stage for discussing why wars fought for religious reasons are generally not acceptable today. The first task though is to try to explain how religion differs from political ideology

In the case of jihads, one should remember that Mohammed spent much of his adult life leading wars against his perceived foes, primarily other Arabs in what is now Saudi Arabia. And the first of the followers of Mohammed and the early caliphs worked greatly to expand the territory under Muslim rule. The focus on territory, that led to Islam conquering very large tracts of the known world, was said to be religiously inspired–the attempt to spread the universal religion of Islam to as much of the world as possible. But the spread of Islam was also a battle against other religiously based political institutions such as the Eastern Christian Church of the Byzantine Empire or the Zoroastrian religion of the Persian Empire. And the crusades pitted the Western Catholic Church's empire against the Islamic empire as well.

In the sense that the religions of the 11th and 12th centuries CE were territorial, the wars for religion were also highly political, even if not fought explicitly for a particular political ideology. We could speak of a "religious ideology" insofar as there were certainly clear social goals at stake such as the spread of the religiously-based dietary laws and family laws to increasingly large territories. Were there also political goals of the wars of Islam and the Western Catholic Church? It is certainly true that the crusades and the jihads that were in response to those crusades were aimed at determining which political institution should rule the Holy Land as well as large parts of the Mideast. But did it matter what kind of political institution ruled? It is hard to answer this question without speaking of the religion promulgated by various warring political entities. And this creates the problem of saying definitively that the crusades and jihads were about political ideology rather than religion. But it seems clear to me that political ideology not only "religious ideology" was one of the main motives of these war campaigns.

One reason to think that the crusades and responding jihads were driven by political ideology as well as "religious ideology" is that it really didn't seem to matter what was the religion of those who were attacked by the crusades or by jihads. In the case of jihads, the initial targets were polytheist Arabs, and a lot of the Quranic invocations of violent jihad are aimed against these polytheists. But when the jihads were turned against Christians, they were not any longer invoked to convert polytheists since the Christians are recognized in the Quran as fellow people of the Book–monotheists who like Muslims follow Abraham.

Another reason to think that political ideology was at least partially behind the crusades is that the first Popes to call for the crusades did so at least in part because of concerns about the territorial spread of Islam. The Holy Lands needed to be re-conquered from the Muslims because the Muslims were said to have limited access to the holy sites in Jerusalem and elsewhere in the nearby Middle East. Pope Eugene II, as we already saw, said that Christians should gird themselves in order "that you strive to oppose the multitude of the infidels, who rejoice at the time in victory gained over us."[446]

The crusades were portrayed as involving a war against infidels who had achieved victory over Christians in the Holy Land. And while the justification was often put in terms of relieving suffering it was apparently just as often put in terms of a territorial struggle. The liberation of the Holy Lands is a rallying cry that is only partially related to religious beliefs. And this assessment might be extended to the jihads, at least those waged in response to the crusades.

[446] Pope Eugene III, "The Papal Bull *Quantum Praedecessores*," in *A Reader of Medieval Laws, Edicts, and Orders*, translated by E. F. Henderson, Washington, DC: Madison and Monroe Press, 2113, p. 259.

PART C:

ENGLISH COMMON LAW AND EARLY ICELANDIC LAW

INTRODUCTION TO PART C

In the 12th century CE we find two systems of law that are remarkably unusual if not unique. In England and also in Iceland law was not a matter of a code or statutes instituted by kings or other members of the elite of the society. In England, what we have come to call the common law emerged–a system of law that begins in ancient custom and proceeds by one case after another decided by popular courts. While there had been popular assemblies in ancient Mesopotamia, classical Greece, and the Roman Republic, the law was made, or at least made authoritative, by kings and elite rulers. In England, law was made authoritative by appeal to the populace. In Iceland, even more striking was the idea that there were no kings or elite rulers, but it was assemblies that made law and it was the popular will that made law authoritative. In both cases, there is a very strong sense of the rule of law over the "rule of men."

We will confront the complexity and even the usefulness of the claim that law is nothing but what the sovereign says–a view made famous by the 19th century philosopher John Austin, a member of the English utilitarians. When kings do not make law, there is a question of who is the sovereign law maker. And while the execution of the law requires some kind of ruler with the power to deter law-breakers, the promulgation or production of law was to a certain extent separated from the executive branch of government. The underlying ideas in 12th century England and Iceland will seem very modern indeed, but we must remember that we are still only in the middle of the Medieval period, even as we also will come to recognize a 12th century renaissance.

SECTION IX:

SUBSTANTIVE AND PROCEDURAL LAW

CHAPTER 20

JUSTICE, CUSTOM, AND THE FORM OF LAW

In the early Medieval period, the model of law was that of the Roman Empire, where the emperor was a god or god-like figure whose word was law. But in the earlier Roman Republic, there were no emperors or kings for that matter–and this was by explicit founding document–the Twelve Tables. Law was made by the people's representatives–the members of the Roman Senate. In classical Greece, law was also made, and made authoritative, by the people sitting in the assemblies and courts. And as far back as ancient Mesopotamia, we find that assemblies at least made law authoritative if not actually made law themselves. Yet, for hundreds of years, the Medieval model was that of the Roman Empire–where the emperor was sovereign and handed down law from on high as it were. This is especially truc of Canon Law which was explicitly modeled on the law of the Roman Empire–with the pope taking the place of the earthly king as lawmaker.

In the early centuries of the new millennium in the middle of the Middle Ages, we find two societies that do not embrace king-made law but look to early judge-made law or to assemblies of the people to make law or to make law authoritative. The eleventh and twelfth centuries turn away from king-made law in two distinct ways, as seen in the early English Common Law and the Early Icelandic Law. There are very important differences between Icelandic and English Common law, but these two systems of law have in common that law was not handed down by elite rulers but was bottom up.

In this chapter we begin to explore the legal thought of two of the most significant Medieval legal theorists, Glanvill and Bracton, whose work established the English common law. We will also begin to examine the early Icelandic laws. In both cases it is interesting that the systems of law arose from new beginnings. In England the common law arose in spite of a turbulence of conquest in the case of the Normans led by William. And while William was a strong ruler, there is a sense that law had already arisen in spite of him. In Iceland, we have the apparent establishment of law by people arriving in an unoccupied land who did not recognize an overarching ruler.

In the first section we will contrast the ideas of law in England and Iceland in the 12th century CE. In the second section we look at the role of custom in the legal thought of these two countries–one of which did not seem to have an extant legal system at all until its colonization, and in the other despite the conquest by a foreign power customary law continued as it had before the conquest. In the third section we look to the concept of justice to see how the customary base of law affected the central idea of justice. And in the fourth section, we explore the importance of equity in these systems of law. Finally, we offer an assessment of how and why 12th century writs and pleas played an important role in the transformation of law into what is more recognizable today than had been true in the earlier Middle Ages and how to understand law once it is not rule by kings but rule by the people, at least in some sense.

I. Legal Pleas in 12th Century England and Iceland

We begin with a quotation from what is called "Glanvill," a treatise on law most likely written by King Henry II's Chancellor Rannulf Glanvill toward the end of the 12th century.

> Although the laws of England are not written, it does not seem absurd to call them laws–those, that is, which are known to have been promulgated about problems settled in council on the advice of the magnates and with the supporting authority of the prince–for this also is a law, that 'what pleases the prince has the force of law.' For if merely for lack of writing, they were not deemed to be laws, then surely writing would seem to supply written laws a force of greater authority than either the justice of him who decrees them or the reason of him who establishes them.[447]

We see here that Glanvill addresses one of the main theoretical issues concerning 12th century English law, namely, that it was not based on a code of law but on custom, which he tells us, seems to proceed from time immemorial.

Glanvill makes the argument that writing alone could not provide law with authority, or at least no greater authority than is provided by the justice or reason of the rules of law. It seems obvious that law derives its

---

[447] Glanvill, *The Treatise on the Laws and Customs of the Realm of England Commonly Called Glanvill*, edited and translated by G.D.G. Hall, Oxford: Oxford University Press, 1965, p. 2.

authority because of its consistency with the idea of justice or reasonableness, and writing does not provide either of those features. We also find here at the beginning of Glanvill's treatise a challenge to those who thought that law, to be properly law, had to be promulgated in writing. In what follows in his treatise we quickly see that there is a problem to be solved for unwritten law appears to be susceptible to arbitrariness or vagueness. For Glanvill, these problems are solved forthrightly by the system of writs, by a solid form for law that can have precise contours even though it is not written as a statute would be.

We will examine the English writs in more detail soon, but at the moment note that Glanville says he turns the customs into written form. So, while Glanvill starts off claiming that English law is customary and not a matter of written statutes, he soon turns to the procedures that apply at court. And he attempts to put into words the procedures he finds:

> But there are some general rules frequently observed in court which it does not seem to me presumptuous to commit to writing, but rather very useful for most people and highly necessary to aid the memory. I have decided to put into writing at least a small part of these general rules, adopting intentionally a commonplace style of and words used in court in order to provide knowledge of them for those who are not versed in this kind of inelegant language.[448]

We thus come to understand why Glanvill is said to have provided one of the first textbooks of the common law, a guide to students and others who wish to become versed in the unwritten customary law by reading a text that is admittedly quite surely not unwritten.

As an illustration we find the following writ or plea setting out how to initiate a suit:

> When anyone complains to the lord king or his justices concerning his fee or free tenement, and the case is such that it ought to be, or the lord king is willing that it should be, tried in the king's court, then the complainant shall have the following writ of summons:
> The king to the sheriff, greeting. Command N. to render to R., justly and without delay, one hide of land in such-and-such a vill, which the said R. complains that the aforesaid N. is withholding from him. If he does not do so, summon him by good summoners to be before me or my justices on the day

[448] Ibid. p. 3.

> after the octave of Easter, to show me why he has not done so. And have there the summoners and this writ. Witness Rannulf Glanvill, at Clarendon.[449]

These writs or pleas become the essential forms of pleading in 12th century England. Before suit can be initiated, the plaintiff must correctly determine the form of action that he wishes to pursue and then file the writ with the relevant court. As Glanvill then tells us, "on the appointed day the party summoned either comes or he does not," and then new forms follow.

It might be surprising that the writ system that is so closely identified with the origins of the English common law also appear in the Icelandic laws of roughly the same time period. In the Introduction to the Laws of Early Iceland, the translators say:

> It is generally agreed that the bulk of the material in our texts represent genuine laws approved by the Law Council, that by and large they reflect the state of Icelandic law in the twelfth century, and that their form is substantially the form they had in the Lawspeaker's recital. We are often reminded of the time and the place: we are told what we should do "here" at Dhingvollr "today" and "tomorrow" and what "I"–the Lawspeaker–have just said or am about to enumerate.[450]

And here is an example from these early Icelandic laws:

> Men may ask about the assembly attachment of people they wish to prosecute here at the Assembly, and ask today; or if they wish to challenge a court, ask tomorrow, though it is also lawful to the time courts go out to hear prosecutions. The man who wants to learn another man's assembly membership is to name witnesses–"I name witnesses to witness" he shall say, "that I ask all householders out loud at Logberg who has formally guaranteed N.N. legal domicile. What concerns me in that query is that I wish to know which neighbors I am to call in the case I have begun against him. I ask a legal asking."[451]

Here are the forms that must be used in the early Icelandic law. If one want to initiate a law suit one must first indicate who they are to sue, but just as importantly they must indicate who are the witnesses they will call

---

[449] Ibid., p. 5

[450]*Gragas I: Laws of Early Iceland*, translated by Andrew Dennis, Peter Foote, and Richard Perkins, Winnipeg, Manitoba: University of Manitoba Press, 1980, p. 13.

[451] Ibid., p. 55.

to substantiate their claims. In this respect the Icelandic law is very similar to English law in the 12th century CE.

The idea that seems to undergird these writs and forms is that a system of law can operate without an elaborate written code of law. In both cases, in England as well as in Iceland, it is procedure that leads the way and it is the substance of the law that will follow. Why it is that systems of law that are not grounded in elaborate codes is committed so obsessively to procedure is something we must understand from the outset if we are to make sense of the unusual Medieval laws and the underlying legal thought behind them.

Frederic Maitland tells us that the English common law begins in the 12th century with a few simple writs and then there is a proliferation of writs over the next few centuries.

> In these oldest forms–forms invented when as yet the parties had to appear in person and could only appoint attorneys by the king's special leave–the action may drag on for years, for the parties enjoy the power of sending essoins, that is, excuses for non-appearance… In the Middle Ages discretion is entirely excluded; all is to be fixed by iron rules… a 'form of action' has implied a particular original process, a particular mesne process, a particular final process, a particular mode of pleading, of trial, of judgment. But further to a very considerable degree the substantive law administered in a given form of action has grown up independently of the law administered in other forms… each has its own precedents.[452]

The collection of writs provided strict rules of law, but the writs did not fit into a single system of law, but each writ was a kind of law unto itself.

The collection of writs in effect substituted for the written code of law that various early English kings, such as Cnut, had promulgated. The writs were a kind of solidified custom, now quoting Henry Sumner Maine, and the substance of law is to be found in the "interstices" of the writs and other formal features of the law.[453] All of these writs and their substantive laws, made it possible for law to function in 12th century England and to be seen as authoritative and binding despite not being part of a larger written code of law that had been promulgated from on-high.

As we will see, it is also of interest that in Iceland there will be an impaneling of twelve people, mainly neighbors who have knowledge of

---

[452] F. W. Maitland, *The Forms of Action at Common Law: A Course of Lectures* (1909), Cambridge: Cambridge University Press, 1971, p. 3.

[453] Henry Sumner Maine, *Ancient Law*, London: John Murray, 1861.

what had occurred, and this is similar to the English juries that were not yet adjudicators of fact but a collection of witnesses who were asked to give their assessment of the suit. Maitland tells us that the Grand Assize was where the writ of right was presented and where "four knights of the neighborhood are summoned to choose twelve other knights who are sworn to say, to 'recognize' whether the demandant or the tenant has the greater right to the land."[454]

II. Custom in Medieval England and Iceland

In Medieval England, legal customs were said to have existed from time immemorial. In Medieval Iceland, legal customs were in effect established de novo when the first settlers arrived in Iceland from Norway. It is surely true that the Norse colonizers brought with them some of their old customs, but many aspects of the Icelandic law drew on unwritten rules that in effect were invented. And while the writs of England had some basis in immemorial custom, the actual form of the writs was also clearly invented as more and more writs were created for newly recognized wrongs that it was thought that the law should redress.

We can contrast what happened in the 12th century in Iceland and England with what happened 700 years earlier when the Germanic peoples invaded or were integrated into the Roman Empire. The Germanic tribes chose to go from customary unwritten law to written codes of law that in many respects resembled the Roman codes of law at the time. In Iceland at the time of settlement and England after the Norman Conquest a very different form of law was adopted than written codes. In this section I will attempt to begin to provide an answer to why Iceland and England took this different path.

And it is important to note that England and Iceland came to a similar system of non-top-down legal authority from very different starting points. In England, prior to the Norman Conquest, there were well established codes of law promulgated by various kings. Indeed, Thorpe has provided a large volume reproducing a set of these codes including the famous codes of King Alfred and of King Cnut. These codes had developed from customs that themselves were said to be from time immemorial.

Alfred, king of England at the end of the 10th century, describes his extensive code of laws in the following words: "These are the dooms

---

454 Maitland, ibid., p. 21.

which thou shalt set for them."[455] Here Alfred seems to suggest that his laws are in a sense codification of the age-old customs of England. And Cnut, king of the Danes and then also king of England in the beginning of the 12th century, also makes reference to ancient custom:

> This then is the secular ordinance which, by the counsel of my 'witan,' I will that it be observed all over England. That is then the first that I will; that just laws be established, and every unjust law carefully suppressed, and that every injustice be weeded out and rooted up, with all possible diligence, from this country. And let God's justice be exalted; and henceforth let every man, both poor and rich, be esteemed worthy of folk-right, and let just dooms be doomed to him.[456]

What we will need to investigate is how these codes relate both to ancient custom and also to the writs of the common law in the 12th century.

Maitland has this to say about how, if at all, the English codes are related to the common law and its writs in the 12th century:

> The writs of this period, so far as we can judge from the specimens that have been preserved, were penned to meet the particular circumstances of the particular cases without any studious respect for precedent.... the Writ of Right [is based on a] broad principle [espoused by Henry II]... we have little cause to believe that it was in force before Henry's day or that it ever was law in Normandy.[457]

Some of the writs were created by acts of Legislative Councils but some others seem to have been created by the judiciary to deal with specific wrongs that called out for adjudication. Here again is Maitland: at "the Council held at Northampton in 1176... the Mort d'Ancestor was created on that occasion... But the Novel Disseisin seems... [to have been] made at the Council of Clarendon in 1166."[458]

In the 13th century, Bracton provided us with a sense of how he saw the role of custom in English law:

---

[455] King Alfred, "The Laws of King Alfred," in *Ancient Laws and Institutes of England*, edited by Benjamin Thorpe, Cambridge: Cambridge University Press, 1860, p. 47.

[456] King Cnut, "The Laws of King Cnut," in *Ancient Laws and Institutes of England*, edited by Benjamin Thorpe, Cambridge: Cambridge University Press, 1860, p. 377.

[457] Frederic W. Maitland, *The Forms of Action at Common Law*, pp. 16-17.

[458] Ibid., p. 36.

> Though in almost all lands use is made of the *leges* and the *jus scriptum*, England alone uses unwritten law and custom. There law derives from nothing written [but] from what usage has approved. Nevertheless it will be absurd to call English laws *leges*, though they are unwritten, since whatever has been rightly decided and approved with the counsel and consent of the magnates and the general agreement of the *res publica*, the authority of the king or prince having first been added thereto, has the force of law.[459]

Here it seems that not all customs have the force of law in England but only those that have the authority of the king, the general agreement of the populace, and counsel and support of the "magnates" or the leading political officials.

In Iceland, people came from Norway in the 10th century with their customs and laws. Over the course of a few centuries, a complete system of law arose primarily from ancient customs. The early Icelandic laws are unusual for several reasons. First, the system of law seems to have been created and then approved in large part at the same time by a general assembly of the various tribes that had arrived in Iceland. Second, "the constitution on which the Icelandic legal system is based is much more the creation of theorists than an organic growth from immemorial custom–significantly there was no overarching "king or ultimate arbiter."[460]

A third and most surprisingly feature of the early Icelandic laws of the 12th century is that:

> the laws made no special provision for an executive arm. Acknowledgement of law, institution of proceedings, and execution of penalties were in the last resort matters of individual responsibility and choice: but a man would expect the support of his chieftain, and a chieftain would expect the aid of the assembly of men. Thus, for example, the chieftains were by law the superintendants of the confiscation courts which were held after men had been outlawed, but the prosecution of those outlaws had normally been undertaken by individuals acting in an entirely private capacity.[461]

---

[459] Bracton, *On the Laws and Customs of England*, translated by Samuel E. Thorne, Cambridge, MA: Harvard University Press, 1968, vol. II, p. 19.

[460] *Gragas I*: *Laws of Early Iceland* translated by Andrew Dennis, Peter Foote and Richard Perkins, "Introduction," p. 1.

[461] Ibid., "Introduction," pp. 3-4.

The Icelandic legal system operates on the basis of a code eventually adopted by the populace and written down from what had been agreed to orally. There is no sense that the law had been promulgated by a sovereign ruler, at least as we normally think of a sovereign in the Middle Ages.

Here is how the assembly procedures section of the Icelandic laws begins–notice that it is not about a king's act of promulgation:

> It is prescribed in our laws that we shall have four Quarter Courts. Each chieftain who has an ancient and full chieftaincy shall nominate a man to join a court. And those are full and ancient chieftaincies which existed when there were assemblies in each Quarter and three chieftains in each assembly. The assemblies are then not split up.[462]

Icelandic law does rely on chieftains to nominate members of the assembly and the courts, but it is then the members of such bodies that enact law in a way consistent with the ancient customs of the people who first populated Iceland.

III. Justice in 12th and 13th Century England and Iceland

Glanvill is a relatively short textbook for students of the law in England, where we do not find much in the way of legal theory. But a century later, Bracton supplies us with another legal textbook that begins, as did Justinian's *Institutes*, with attention to the idea of justice. Bracton's *De Legibus* (On the Laws and Customs of England) begins as follows:

> To rule well a king requires two things, arms and laws, that by them both times of war and peace may rightly be ordered. For each stands in need of the other, that the achievement of arms be conserved [by laws], the laws themselves preserved by the support of arms. If arms fail against hostile and unsubdued enemies, then will the realm be without defense; if laws fail, justice will be extirpated; nor will there be any man to render just judgment.[463]

Here justice is seen as following the laws, although it is also recognized that some laws can themselves be unjust.

Bracton provides us with several ways to understand justice, largely drawing on past understandings of this concept.

---

462 *Gragas I: Laws of Early Iceland*, p. 53.

463 Bracton, vol. II, p. 19

> Justice proceeds from God, assuming that justice lies in the Creator, [*jus* from man], and thus *jus* and *lex* are synonymous.... Since from justice, as from a fountain-head, all rights arise and what justice commands *jus* provides, let us see what justice is and whence it is so called. ... Justice is the constant and unfailing will to give to each his right. This definition may be understood in two ways, according as justice is taken to be in the Creator or in the created. If in the creator, that is, in God, the matter is clear, since justice is the disposition of God which in all things rightfully orders and justly disposes. God himself gives to each man in accordance with his deserts.... The definition may be understood in another way, that justice is in the created, that is, in the just man. The just man has the will to give to each his right, and thus that will is called justice. His will to give each his right refers to what is intended not to what is done.[464]

Bracton is here clearly influenced by Justinian but he provides important nuances about justice that differ from Justinian and other Roman conceptions of justice. It seems that what we are getting is a mixture of customary English law and Justinian's formulation of Roman law.

In Icelandic law, we do not find much in the way of theoretical commentary on the nature of justice, although what we would find from the theorists who essentially constructed the Icelandic legal code would be a combination of customary Norwegian and Icelandic legal ideas mixed with more contemporary ideas in 12th century Iceland. In early Icelandic law, justice is determined by the assemblies and courts, as would become true of English common law, as we will see.

Here is a selection from the Landnamabok from the 12th century CE concerning how law was characterized in early Iceland:

> Anyone transacting legal business before a court should first take an oath on the temple-ring, and, having called two or more witnesses, he should declaim the following words: "I call upon you to testify," he should say, "that I take an oath by the ring–a lawful oath...as I proceed to prosecute or to defend this case and to bear testimony, give verdicts or pronounce judgments, as truthfully and as much in accordance with the law as my knowledge permits me..." Three guardians of the

[464] Bracton, ibid., vol. II, 23.

> temples were selected according to their wisdom and sense of justice.[465]

The legal procedures established in early Iceland, as we can see, put a high premium on selecting judges who had "wisdom and sense of justice." It is especially important that judges have these virtues since there was no executive power.

And yet, one otherwise sympathetic commentator raises a worry about how justice was brought about in a governmental system without an executive branch.

> The Icelandic Commonwealth has attracted the interest of libertarians as the society of ultimate individual freedom, where even seats in parliament were a marketable commodity and the enforcement of law was privatized. Those who hold equality and social justice in high esteem may be less impressed. Still, it could be asked whether the Icelandic system offered the individual less opportunity to seek justice than a system of royal officials would have done in those times. At any rate, this was a society that gave many people good reason to think–and write–about problems of peace and justice…[466]

As the chapters in this part of the book proceed, we will have much opportunity to assess this claim and to see if justice without a system of strong government does have something to recommend it.

IV. Equity in 12th and 13th Century England and Iceland

Bracton provides an account of equity in the abstract, but we will also later see his use of equity practically. For the moment here is what he tells us of the abstract idea of equity:

> Equity is the bringing together of things, that which desires like right in like cases and puts all like things on an equality. Equity is, so to speak, uniformity, and it turns upon matters of fact, that is, the words and acts of men. Justice, [on the other hand], lies in the minds of the just. Hence it is that if we wish to speak properly we will call a judgment equitable, not just,

---

[465] Quoted in Jon Johannesson, *The History of the Old Icelandic Commonwealth*, Winnipeg, Manitoba: University of Manitoba Press, 1974, p. 56.

[466] Gunnar Karlsson, *The History of Iceland*, Minneapolis, MN: University of Minnesota Press, 2000, p. 27.

> and a man just, not equitable. But using these terms improperly, we call the man equitable and the judgment just.[467]

This conception of equity links equity to equality–like things are to be treated alike, and this gives us a kind of uniformity. Properly speaking, judgments are equitable insofar as they follow a pattern of like judgments. Justice is the virtue of people giving to each other person what is due to them. We can ascertain how to understand equity in the study of jurisprudence because equity is simply a discerning what is like and what is unlike in the facts of a situation. Justice, on the other hand, refers properly to the person who intends to give to each what they deserve, and is a matter of character.

Pollack and Maitland are quite clear in indicating the central role that equity played in nearly every aspect of early English Common Law.

> our king's court is according to very ancient tradition a court that can do whatever equity may require... It means that the royal tribunal is not so strictly bound by rules that it can not defeat the devices of those who would use legal forms for the purposes of chicane; it means also that the justices are in some degree free to consider all the circumstances of these cases that come before them and to adapt the means to the end... The need of a separate court of equity is not yet felt, for the king's court, which is not as yet hampered by many statutes or by accurately formulated 'case law,' can administer equity.[468]

The discretionary power of judges is in a sense at its height in such a system of law as we find in England in the 11th and 12th century, where rights can be referred to which "could not be asked for as a matter of strict right."[469] Indeed, Glanvill had said: "This legal constitution is based above all on equity."[470]

Icelandic law is also heavily dependant on a conception of equity. As with English judges, Icelandic judges were free to adapt the law so as to serve the specific interests of the people at a specific time. We can mark two different periods in this early history of Icelandic law–the first just after settlement, and the other just after a code of law was adopted. The existence of a code of law normally limits the discretion of judges and hence makes equity considerations less significant. Prior to the drafting of

---

[467] Bracton, vol. II, p. 25.

[468] Pollack and Maitland, *The History of English Law*, vol. I., pp. 189-190.

[469] Ibid., p. 190.

[470] Glanvill, p. 28.

the *Gragas*, the main compilation of laws, Icelandic law was marked by wide discretion. But, perhaps surprisingly, equity was also the hallmark of the system of law in Iceland even after the written statute law was formalized in the *Gragas*.

Systems of law such as those in Iceland and England, which are heavily dependent on the judgments of the common people, must be given discretion so that local facts and even local rules can be properly applied. Later in English law, we find formal courts of equity that became unique features of the English and American legal systems. But in the 11th and 12trh centuries, equity is the business of all of English courts and judges. In Iceland, equity is the business of the farmers and neighbors who make up the assemblies and courts. There are obvious problems when equity becomes run-away discretion, untethered from the written law. But in these early years of Icelandic and English law we are not yet at that point. The common people are seeking justice and equity for their neighbors just as they would expect it to be sought for themselves. We next say a bit more about how these systems of law saw the place of the common people in this process.

V. Rule by the People?

When we say that law was made by the people rather than by elite rulers, we must make several important caveats. Law was not made by women, elite or common. Law was also not made by slaves or those who failed to meet property requirements. And there were still elites involved–in Iceland it was the tribal leaders and in England it was the judges drawn often from the elites of English society. So, while it is true to say that law was a form of rule by the people this does not mean it was rule by all of the people or even a significant plurality of the people.

Yet, if we think of the other forms of law in the early Middle Ages we can see that the model that followed the law of the Roman Empire was significantly different than the law in Iceland and England in the 11th and 12th centuries. In this final section we will investigate in what sense it is true that Icelandic and English common law was indeed a form of "rule by the people" rather than "rule by elites." It is of course true that the elites are "people" too, so we will need to refine our ideas of "rule by the people" in this final section of the chapter.

Here is Pollack and Maitland talking about the age of Bracton and how it differed concerning status from Continental systems of law at the time.

> Closely connected with its uniformity is another distinctive trait: - in England the law for the great men has become the law for all men, because the law of the king's court has become the common law. For example, the primogenitary rules of inheritance are rapidly expanding downwards from their native home among the military fees through all the subsequent strata, and the one "formal contract" of English law can be made only by those who can write or hire others to write for them.[471]

Here we have the suggestion that the idea behind the "common law" was not merely that it was a law that was uniform, but that that law was also for the "common person" as much as for the elites.

In Iceland, it was even clearer than in England that the people were fully engaged with the law at every stage. The legislative power is wielded in England by the king operating through his judges, and yet it is ultimately the judges that decide when and whether a new writ is needed or that an old writ is to be given a new realm of jurisdiction. The legislative process in Iceland is in the hands of the assembly, and the assembly is composed of the farmers from the earliest of times in Iceland. It is true that the tribal chieftains can, and sometime do, exert outsize influence. But there are rules to which one can appeal in order to rein in those chieftains or even to replace them.

The translators of the *Gragas* point out a number of the features of the Icelandic system of law that were distinct and clearly favored the opinions of the common people:

> The part played by panels of neighbors is a much more distinctive Icelandic feature [than the idea of outlawry], and panel verdicts appear to take the place of various forms of compurgation common to the other Scandinavian laws... neighbors of standing... represented the best combination of local knowledge and impartiality that could be had, either because they lived closest to the place of action or to the man prosecuted. In the latter case, if there was room for doubt, it must have been assumed that general local satisfaction or dissatisfaction with the man in question would come out in the neighbors' verdicts. This innovation seems to have sprung from the conditions of settlement in Iceland where, to begin with, people did not have any large circle of kin or acquaintance of accepted standing to appeal to... Another

[471] Pollack and Maitland, *The History of English Law*, vol. I, pp. 224-225.

> distinctive feature of the Icelandic system is the detailed inclusion of everyone within the legal framework.[472]

Neighbors were called upon to be jurors and to function as the best source of common knowledge both about the character of the defendants and also of the rules that were most fairly to be applied to the cases at hand.

The fellow farming neighbors of Icelandic law and the common people of England were what the law was made for and most importantly who made the law. In the next chapter we will see how this worked in more detail as we look at the functioning of courts and assemblies, and especially the functioning of juries. But it should be clear by now how unusual were these two medieval systems of law–how different they were from the other medieval systems of law we have examined in previous chapters.

---

[472] *Gragas I: Laws of Early Iceland*, pp. 8-9.

CHAPTER 21

ASSEMBLIES, JURIES, AND JUDGES

In this chapter we will explore very important developments in the idea of juries and as in ancient times we will see that there is a close link between assemblies and juries–in both cases it is the people who take a leading role in the system of justice. In Iceland, assemblies played a very significant role in law-making and judging. Each of the parts of the code of law called the *Gragas* was probably submitted to the assembly for acceptance, and there was no ruler who was asked for authorization. In Iceland, the courts were an offshoot of the assemblies. In England, the courts played a role on their own in the making and applying of law in the Common Law system. And in both of these medieval societies we find juries taking on a greater and greater role in deciding how judgments were to be made. These developments were of the first importance and stand out from most of the other medieval legal systems of the time. In addition in this chapter we will say a bit along the way about some of the other contemporaneous law systems, especially in Wales.

In the first section we will examine some of the complex rules of the early Icelandic assembly. In the second section we examine the role of the jury in early Icelandic law. Then in the third section we encounter the English Common law jury and compare it to its Icelandic cousin–both may have developed from various Danish institutions. In the fourth section we will look to how judges were conceptualized in both Iceland and England in the 11th and 12th centuries CE. Then in the final section we will assess how unusual these systems of law were and why especially in Iceland but also in England these systems of law developed the way they did.

I. The Early Icelandic Assembly

We have a document written in the 12th century that is the first account of the assembly in early Icelandic history. Here is a selection from Ari's *Islendingabok* describing the system of assemblies:

> The Althing was established where it now is by the decision of Ulfljotr and everyone in the country, but before there was an assembly at Kjalarnes, which Þorsteinn, son of Ingolfr the settler, father of the Lawspeaker Þorkell Moon, held there together with those chieftains who attended it… Then the country was divided into Quarters, so that there were three assemblies in each Quarter; and in each place the members of the assembly had to conduct the prosecution of lawsuits together, except that there were four assemblies in the Northern Quarter… However, the same number of judges had to be nominated and there had to be the same number of members of the Law Council from that Quarter as from each of the others. And later the Quarter Assemblies were established.[473]

We find here references to the main institutions in the Icelandic legal system, each of which we will now attempt to explain in a bit more detail than was provided by Ari.

We have a good account of what was the Althing by the translator of Ari's *Islendingabok*:

> The Althing (or General Assembly) was a national assembly of free men held each year, the main seat of judicial and legislative activity for the whole of Iceland. It was probably based on regional assemblies held in Norway and elsewhere in Scandinavia, but differed from these in being countrywide and independent of any executive power.[474]

Here we find mention of one of the most unusual features of the early Icelandic legal system–there is no executive power, which raises the question of how the laws were enforced, a topic to which we will often return.

We should also explain the role of the Law Council and the Lawspeaker, especially the role played by these institutions in relation to the assemblies. Here is how the *Gragas* describes the Lawspeaker's role:

> It is also prescribed that there will always be some man in our country who is required to tell men the law, and he is called the Lawspeaker… When men have decided who it is to be, the Lawspeaker is to be appointed to the Law Council, and one man is to announce it and the others give their assent, and the

[473] Ari, *The Book of Icelanders* (*Islendingabok*), translated by Sian Gronlie, University College London: Viking Society for Northern Research, 2006, pp. 5-7.
[474] Ibid., p. 19.

> same man is to have it for three summers continuously unless men do not wish to change them… It is also prescribed that a Lawspeaker is required to recite all the sections of the law over three summers, and the assembly procedure every summer.[475]

The Lawspeaker took on an especially important role before the *Gragas* was written since he was the keeper of the oral version of the laws in the earliest of days in Iceland.

We also have an equally important institution called the Law Council, and again we can look to *Gragas* for an explanation of this institution.

> We shall also have a Law Council and hold it here at the General Assembly [the Althing] each summer, and it is always to sit in the place where it has been long since. There are to be three benches around the Law Council place, long enough for four dozen men to sit commodiously with each other. That is twelve men from each Quarter who have seats on the Law Council to decide there on laws and licenses and the Lawspeaker in addition. They are all to sit in the middle bench, and there our bishops rightly have places too… It is also prescribed that the Law Council shall go out on both the Sundays in the assembly and on the closing day of the assembly and at all other times that the Lawspeaker or the majority wish it and on every occasion when men want to clear the Law Council for a meeting. Men are to frame their laws there and make new laws if they will.[476]

The Law Council is the legislative branch of the Icelandic legal system and it is also, as we will see, the place where lawsuits are initiated. There is here a sense that the Lawspeaker performs some of the roles that a king performs in English Common Law, by calling the Law Council to order and indicating what should be on the agenda, as well as indicating what the existing law is that the Law Council and assembly should either affirm or change.

What is clear from all of this description of the institutions of the early Icelandic legal system is that it was based in almost every sense on the decisions of the people–primarily farmers and some tribal chieftains who were not treated much differently than the farmers. The members of

---

[475] *Gragas I*: *Laws of Early Iceland*, translated by Andrew Dennis, Peter Foote, and Richard Perkins, Winnipeg, Manitoba: University of Manitoba Press, 1980, p. 187.

[476] *Gragas I*, pp. 189-190.

the Law Council seem to be slightly more important than the regular assembly members, and the Lawspeaker is clearly the most important of all. But the Lawspeaker can really do very little without the support of the assembly and in any event the Lawspeaker has no independent executive power, and is limited in his legislative or judicial functions as well.

II. Juries in Early Icelandic Law

Here is a short passage from the *Gragas I* that will introduce us to some of the concepts we will need to explore in understanding the Icelandic jury.

> The chieftain to whose assembly group the man prosecuted belongs is to be called on to form [a panel] of twelve to give a verdict on whether that man has shared living quarters with the outlaw or not and thereby given him assistance. Testimony is to be given to match the number of times witnesses were named [in the original action].[477]

We find here that the chieftain is to pick a group of twelve to form a panel and that the panel is then to render a verdict about a factual matter that is being disputed in a trial. It is interesting that the panel or jury is to be of twelve men, just as is true of English Common Law juries at the same time.

We also learn how voting is to take place in the jury panels in another passage from *Gragas I*:

> The prosecutor is to name witnesses to witness that the other has finished challenging the panel or that he does not wish to challenge. Thereupon he shall ask the panel to deliver the verdict, It is prescribed that before the verdict is given they are first to swear oaths in the court… If they do not agree on what verdict they should give, those in the majority have the right to decide and they have to utter that verdict and all of them must give their assent, but the others are to say in the court that they would give a different verdict if they had the numbers to do so and state what verdict they would give.[478]

[477] *Gragas I*, p. 121.
[478] Ibid., p. 73.

Here we learn that the jury panel need not be unanimous in their verdict and that those in the minority are to give what their verdict would have been as well.

The jury panels do not issue verdicts about how a case is to be judged but only act as witnesses who give testimony about various factual matters such as where someone lives or what happened on a certain day. They are fact witnesses just as juries today are arbiters of fact, but they do not actually pass judgment on the disposition of the case. The role of the jury panels is more like what happens in a grand jury today in that they only give a preliminary verdict not the final determination of how to dispose of a given case. Here is how it is described in *Gragas I*:

> A man is to have called all the witnesses and panel members that are required for his conduct of the original suit, before the court goes out. It is lawful to call on a chieftain to form a panel of twelve before the court goes out and also at the court. The calling is rightly made if the chieftain hears it himself or if it is made at his place or if his booth-mates hear it. When a man wants to call for a panel of twelve, he is to name witnesses "to witness," he shall say, "that I ask you"–and name the chieftain–"whether you act in full chieftaincy which authorizes you to nominate complete courts and give panel-of-twelve verdicts. I ask a legal asking."[479]

The court is a subset of the assembly and this assembly will be asked eventually to decide the case not the jury panel. And in this respect we also find, as we will see, some commonalities with the early English Common Law jury which also did not reach ultimate verdicts but were more like witnesses.

There is an important feature of the Icelandic legal system that mirrors developments in the English system, namely that potential jurors can be struck off by the parties to the lawsuit–a major way that fairness of trial was secured.

> He is to swear an oath before he begins to challenge the panel. Afterwards he is to name witnesses "to witness that I give my word of honor that a man lives closer who has not been called" and name him and say which booth he belongs to. But if he challenges a panel on grounds of kinship, second cousins and men of closer kin are to withdraw, and three close kinsmen by marriage, where one man is married to another's mother or

[479] *Gragas I*, p. 63.

> daughter or sister. He is to challenge on grounds of kinship and of kinship by marriage with himself. He is to challenge on grounds of spiritual kinship those three for whom a man has stood sponsor at baptism or at prime-signing or at confirmation. A man is not to challenge on grounds of his own spiritual kinship with a panel member.[480]

These elaborate rules, and others as well, seem to be aimed at allowing the parties to a lawsuit to veto as witnesses and jurors those who would be biased against or in favor of one of the parties. As we will see, the early English Common law also allowed for such challenges so that witnesses and jurors were likely to be impartial–a key consideration in establishing the rule of law as having a fair system for adjudicating disputes.

One last point to consider is that juries in early Icelandic law were mainly fact witnesses, and their verdicts were only preliminary to the conclusions of the court which were issued by judges in the assembly. Here is a passage from *Gragas I*:

> If man has called for a panel of twelve, the chieftain is to nominate men of this assembly third to join him on this panel, and it is lawful for him to nominate either householders or household men. He is to nominate eleven men besides himself. The chieftain is to go to the court and invite the man who called on him to form a panel of twelve to challenge the panel, and name him and tell him where he has assembled the panel of twelve in the same way as a court.... Prosecution of every case shall come before defense unless it is one and the same and one man's defense is another man's prosecution. Where panels are called for the prosecution and the man who is to defend has witnesses, testimony is to come before panel verdicts, even though it goes with the defense.[481]

This discussion is a bit confusing but the use of jury panels was not taken directly from Norwegian law and seems to be unique.

Here is an interpretation of how best to understand the role of the jury panels in early Icelandic law by the translators of the *Gragas*:

> If the prosecutor proceeded by publishing at the assembly, he was expected to have called neighbors in the locality, those who actually lived closest to the place specified...In some cases it was necessary to have a panel of twelve members,

[480] *Gragas I*, p. 71.

[481] *Gragas I*, pp. 75-76.

> comprising a chieftain and eleven men selected by him. Courts probably had thirty-six judges… The prosecutor presented his case before them, with testimony of witnesses where appropriate and the verdicts of panels of neighbors he had assembled on whatever relevant matters he put to them to substantiate his suit… The judges could only find in accordance with the formal means of proof brought before them… The part played by panels of neighbors is a much more distinctive Icelandic feature… neighbors of standing… represented the best combination of local knowledge and impartiality that could be had…[482]

The witness panels in Icelandic law are in many respects very similar to the early juries in English Common Law, in that the verdicts they issue are on specific matters of local knowledge and are not, as juries are today, the determiners of guilt or innocence.

III. Juries in Early English Common Law

There are many references to juries in the early Common Law, especially in Bracton's *De Legibus*. We will see that there are significant differences between juries then and now, as well as perhaps surprising similarities between early Icelandic and English Common Law juries. Glanvill speaks of twelve lawful knights in the following passage:

> The tenant who has put himself upon the assize secures peace by such writs until the demandant comes to court and purchases another writ, which provides that four lawful knights of the county and of the neighborhood shall elect twelve lawful knights of the same neighborhood, who are to declare on oath which of the parties has the greater right to the landing question.[483]

As in early Icelandic law, twelve men from the neighborhood start the proceeding by swearing as to a matter of fact that is especially pertinent to a given lawsuit.

And we also find Glanvill describing these knights as constituting a jury in the following passage:

---

[482] *Gragas I*, Introduction, pp. 7-8.
[483] Glanvill, p. 30.

> When the assize reaches the stage where the recognition is made, then either the true legal position is well known to all jurors, or else some know and some do not, or else none of them knows. If none of them knows the truth of the matter, and they have stated this on their oath in court, recourse shall be made to others until such as know the truth of it are found. If, however, some know the truth of the matter and some do not, those who do not shall be rejected and others summoned to court until at least twelve can be found to agree on it.[484]

The jurors, the twelve knights, are those who know important facts that are at issue in the lawsuit. Only those who swear that they have such knowledge are allowed to be jurors.

But we also find in Glanvill the apparent reference to jurors being the body that convicts not merely the body that swears to important factual matters.

> To put it generally, whenever anything is done to the nuisance of a royal tenement or way or city, the resulting plea belongs to the crown of the lord king. Purprestures of this kind are investigated either in the chief Curia or before the justices of the lord king who have been sent into various parts of the realm to make such investigations by means of a jury of the countryside or neighborhood. When anyone is convicted by such a jury of having made such a purpresture, the whole of the fee which he holds of the lord king shall be at the king's mercy, and he shall restore his encroachment.

Here we have the closest thing to trial by jury in Glanvill but it is unclear that this is a major part of the procedures of trial, especially since this use of the jury is rarely mentioned in Glanvill.

When we turn to Bracton, a century or so later than Glanvill, things do not get clearer. But we can begin to see remaining difficulties in the following passage:

> The oath of the twelve knights chosen to speak the truth in a plea of the crown. 'Hear this ye justices that I will speak the truth as to that on which you shall question me on the lord king's behalf, and I will faithfully do that which you shall command me on the lord king's behalf, and for nothing will I

[484] Glanvill, p. 34.

> fail so to do to the utmost of my power, so help me God and these holy relics.'[485]

We see here that the jury is summoned to speak the truth about factual matters pertinent to the lawsuit, not to convict, although this is not ruled out.

In the early English Common Law, the idea of trial by jury was understood as a form of proof that was an option to trial by ordeal or trial by combat. We can turn to Pollack and Maitland for a sense of how to understand the early English jury:

> The essence of the jury–if for a while we use the term 'jury' in the widest sense that can be given to it–seems to be this: a body of neighbors is summoned by some public officer to give upon oath a true answer to some question... But what the jurors or recognitors of our twelfth century deliver is no judgment; they come to 'recognize,' to declare the truth.[486]

And Pollack and Maitland go on to say that the jury produces a "verdict of the neighbors instead of on battle or the ordeal"–it is a matter of proof not judgment of how the case is to be disposed of.[487]

We can learn one more thing from Pollack and Maitland that may be a difference in how juries were conceptualized in 12th century England as opposed to Iceland. They make three very important points about the early English jury:

> 1. Jurors are not arbitrators. We have seen, however, that the verdict of jurors becomes a common mode of proof...
> 2. The verdict of the jurors is not just the verdict of twelve men; it is the verdict of a *pays*, a "country," a neighborhood... The justices seem to feel that if they analyzed the verdict they would miss the very thing for which they were looking, the opinion of the country.
> 3. Lastly, we may already detect in the verdict of the jurors an element which we can not but call quasi-judicial. Whatever theory may have prevailed, the parties to an action are often submitting to "the country" questions which the twelve representatives of the country will certainly not be able to answer if they may speak only of what they have seen with their own eyes...

---

[485] Bracton, p. 329.

[486] Pollack and Maitland, vol. I, pp. 138-140.

[487] Ibid., p. 141.

> A little inquisitory zeal on the part of the king's commissioners might turn it into a mere examination of witnesses, whose divergent testimonies would be weighed by the court. Or again, their voice might be counted without being weighed and the verdict of the majority accepted.[488]

At the end here we see why Pollack and Maitland say that the verdict of the jury seems to contain something quasi-juridical. The verdict of the jurors may be that a certain person killed or raped, and this is not merely accepted as a statement of fact but also may be taken as a conclusion, as a judgment, and already a kind of conviction. It is unclear that the same can be said for the Icelandic jury, as we will see.

IV. Judges in Icelandic and English Common Law

In this section we will continue our comparison now focusing on the role of judges in Icelandic law and English Common Law. We begin by discussing several sections of *Gragas I* that are devoted to the role of judges.

> It is also prescribed that before they begin their judging they are to swear an oath, unless they have already sworn. They are to name witnesses. "I name them to witness that I swear an oath on the Cross, a lawful oath, and declare before God that I shall give such judgment as I think to be the law," It is also prescribed that they shall sum up men's cases, those first which have come first.[489]

Here we find that the judges must swear an oath that they will act on the basis of the law and then they are to examine the witnesses and hear from the two parties to a suit, providing summaries of what the parties say. These are the factors upon which they will make their judgments.

Later in *Gragas I*, we also learn more detail about how judges are to act in reaching their decisions. We learn for instance that a chieftain may "forbid the judges to judge" a case by vetoing a certain judge from hearing a case of someone who is from the judge's district.[490] We also learn that there may be attempts to intimidate judges or to coerce their verdicts–in such cases the remedy is to have the judges clearly separated

---

[488] Pollack and Maitland, vol. II, pp. 623-625.

[489] *Gragas I*, p. 79.

[490] *Gragas I*, p. 105.

from the rest of the assembly to keep the influencers at bay by providing "court-guarders."[491]

In Bracton's work we find some similar ideas about how to think of the role of judges in 13th century England.

> Some justices are major, general, permanent and of greater importance, who remain at the side of the king and whose duty is to correct the wrongs and errors of all others.... Their power is this: once a cause (one or several) is committed to them, though it is committed simply, their jurisdiction is extended to all matters necessary to determine the suit, so far as judgment and the execution of judgment are concerned, and so there is no incidental or emergent action preliminary to it. [But] they cannot extend their jurisdiction to other things or other persons, nor take cognizance of things other than those comprised in their commissions, since the limits of a mandate must be strictly observed.[492]

Here Bracton sets out the strict jurisdictional limits on judicial action and also indicates that some judges may be stationary and others must travel from county to county.

In describing the role of judges who travel, we get a good idea of the kind of characteristics that judges should have:

> The oath shall be this. Each will swear, one after the other, that in the counties into which they are to travel they will do right justice to the best of their ability to rich and to poor alike, and they will observe the assise according to the articles set, to be explained, and they will execute all that is right and just in matters pertaining to the crown of the lord king. And after his oath let each of them be instructed to promote, to the best of his ability, the advantage of the lord king.[493]

Later we are told that like the knights who become jurors the judges should be truthful and they should always obey the king's commands.

This last point lets us see how early English and Icelandic judges will differ, at least in theory. There are no kings in Iceland, so the obedience that the judge owes in Iceland is more directly to the people through the assemblies than it is in English Common Law. But in other respects the judges are to have similar characteristics, namely, to do right

[491] *Gragas I*, p. 80.
[492] Bracton, p. 308.
[493] Bracton, p. 309.

and justice as well as to be truthful and unbiased in not favoring the wealthy over the poor. In the final section of this chapter we will investigate how the lack of a monarch may have affected the way judges and juries were understood in early Iceland.

V. Being Responsive to Kings and Assemblies

It is true that English Common Law and early Icelandic law have many similarities, but the one major difference is that there were kings in England but not in Iceland in the 11th and 12th centuries. The kings did not make the law in the English Common Law system, but they played an important role nonetheless that was not filled by anyone comparable, except perhaps the assembly, in Iceland. We will explore this point in more detail in this final section of the chapter.

Let us begin by quoting from Robert Tombs's book *The English and Their History*, on how to understand the rise of parliament during the early Common Law period.

> Every post-Conquest monarch for 150 years suffered rebellions, mainly due to family rivalry. Moreover the unique power now claimed by the Crown led to attempts to bring the king under the rule of law as established by Magna Carta. Above all the troubled links with Normandy and with other parts of France placed a recurring strain on English politics. English kings were often away pursuing Continental interests. Their use of England as an endless source of money for wars caused rumbling discontent and was the greatest single reason why kings had to seek the consent of their subjects through parliaments.[494]

Even though England in the 11th and 12th centuries had kings, and Iceland did not, England also had parliaments that in some respects functioned like the assemblies in Iceland as a way for the people to have a major say in the way law was made and applied.

We should also note that the English Common Law was not at all like the legal codes of the Continent, and in this respect was more like the Icelandic *Gragas*. In both cases, the law texts did not "derive from a single code, as Roman law did." Instead, for the English the Common Law was based on a "compilation of precedents." [495] And the Icelandic laws

[494] Robert Tombs, *The English and Their History*, NY: Vintage Press, 2014, p. 62

[495] *The English and Their History*, p. 68.

embodied in the *Gragas* were similarly based on past precedents as well as custom from the Norwegian law of the period. The point is that the difference between England where there were kings and early Iceland where there were no kings was not as profound a difference in law as one might have expected.

We should note that changes in law could not be made by courts and the judiciary alone. In Iceland, the assembly had to assent to any changes in law. And in England, similar things could be said about the need for the assent by the king for a law to become authoritatively binding. There were other levels of government that also had to be consulted and from which disapproval could have negative effects on new law. In Iceland, the chieftains had to be considered, as was also true of the Law Council and most especially the Lawspeaker. These more informal requirements for a new law to be considered authoritative were often as important as the more formal requirements.

Yet the Lawspeaker, as powerful as he was in early Icelandic law, was not a king-like person. Most significantly, the Lawspeaker could not veto a new law. Nearly as significant is that the Lawspeaker did not have any executive powers, whereas the king in early English law was the chief enforcer and executioner of the laws. We will have occasion to consider this difference in greater detail in Chapter 26. At the moment we should merely note that without a king or king-like person the enforcement of law was tricky at best.

It is at least of symbolic significance that in England the king was associated with the law's authority, whereas in Iceland it was the assembly that was associated with the law's authority. This fact makes the Icelandic law look quite different from the English law. But, in both systems of law, it really was the people acting through the courts or the assembly that were the lawmakers and the authority bestowing body. And in this respect, there are more similarities than differences between these two Medieval systems of law.

We should also note that judges in both of these systems of law were very powerful indeed. It is well known that in English Common Law the judge could make new law by establishing a precedent that was then accepted by later judges. The system of writs was instituted so that no significant wrong would go unpunished or uncompensated. The writs were issued by the king's sheriff but this was only part of the story. It was the English judge who saw the need for a new writ and often initiated the move toward establishing that new writ. In Iceland, the judges who were also often chieftains had great power to create new law, even as it was ultimately the assembly that gave assent to the new law in the name of the people.

Another commonality between these systems of law is that at least some of the judges were to move in a circuit, from one geographical place to another over the course of a given year. This circuitry actually seems to have enhanced the role of the judges since in some respects a plaintiff had to go to great lengths and expense to follow the judges until his or her case was heard. The common people were also often not happy about such requirements that had to be met to achieve justice, and reformers in both systems called for an end to this practice. But it can also be said that the circuit riding judges were able to get a better sense of what the neighbors of the plaintiff or defendant felt about a particular lawsuit thereby advancing the work of justice rather than curtailing it.

In early Icelandic law, it is the assembly that is ultimately the institution to which judges, juries, prosecutors and other actors had to be responsive. In early English Common Law, it is the king that is ultimately the institution to which judges, juries, prosecutors, and other legal actors had to be responsive. Medieval Iceland lacked kings for three centuries; early English Common Law lacked assemblies for hundreds of years as well. These institutions–assemblies and kings–are obviously different institutions, and their presence or lack is an important difference in these systems of law. But it must be said that there was an emerging parliament in England, and there were elite leaders in Iceland such as the Lawspeaker as well as the various chieftains.

Yet, in both of these societies there is more commonality yet when we realize that law's authority was ultimately bestowed by the people–the king and the assembly owed their respective legitimacy to the consent or assent of the people, at least the free males of those societies. English Common Law is really the law of the common person, not the law of elites; and early Icelandic law is really the law of the citizen farmers who settled the country. In both cases, law was legitimated by processes that were bottom up not top down, in stark contrast with most other societies where law was imposed on the common people by secular or religious rulers.

CHAPTER 22

THE RULE OF LAW, MAGNA CARTA, AND THE OLD COVENANT

This chapter focuses on two ways that the rule of law was protected in the 12th and 13th century in England and Iceland. In both cases, the culminating and lasting contribution to future generations came in the Magna Carta, the Great Charter, signed between the English King John and the barons, and in the Old Covenant that was signed by the king of Norway with the people assembled in Iceland. Among other things, these documents sought to guarantee the rights of the citizenry against the possible, and indeed likely, oppression of the people by various kings.

The idea that the increasingly powerful Medieval kings needed to be reigned in was not controversial. What was controversial was that the people managed to force the king to recognize publically that he was not above, but below, the law and subject to sanctions if he abrogated the rights of the citizens. Magna Carta especially is now nearly synonymous with the rights of the people to due process and protection from abuse by the most powerful. But the actual story of Magna Carta is more nuanced than as it is normally portrayed. In addition, we will see a parallel story develop in Iceland where the citizenry found means to force the king of Norway to agree to protect the people's rights. In both cases the agreement is drawn in terms of the promised cooperation of the people with the king, now allowing the king to rule over and tax them but only under conditions of restraint.

In the first section of this chapter we look at the background to Magna Carta especially in the 12th century. And then in the second section we look at some of the most important provisions of Magna Carta and see how the rule of law was influenced by these provisions. In the third section we look at the idea of the traditional rights of freemen in Iceland. And then in the fourth section we look at specific legal provisions in Iceland, especially the Old Covenant, that were designed to preserve the rights of Icelanders. In the final section we assess the idea of the rule of law when the law and the assembly of the people confront each other, seeking a better understanding of how the rule of law and democratic governance fit together.

I. Magna Carta and its Twelfth Century Background

In order to set the stage for understanding how Magna Carta might be a model for the rule of law for many centuries afterwords, we need to understand what gave rise to Magna Carta. The first thing to note is that in twelfth century England, there was not a strongly centralized State. Indeed, if anything there was strong decentralized power. This decentralization took two significant forms. First, England was a feudal society, which meant that there were often quite strong feudal lords who reigned over large tracts of land in England and many did not feel that they were less powerful or authoritative than the king himself. Second, there were also many courts and systems of courts that had various levels of autonomy and subject matter jurisdiction.

England had had courts in existence for many years before Magna Carta in 1215. One type of older court was called "Courts of the Hundred." These courts were generally held as open-air meetings in the territorial districts called hundreds - larger than villages but not as large as counties or shires. Judges administered the Salic law of the Franks in these courts, and there was a kind of "manual of law and legal procedure for the use or guidance of free judges" of the hundred court.[496] Here there was a "deliberate attempt to furnish an alternative to violence and bloodshed."[497] These courts were autonomous of the king; the king "is merely represented in it by a class of officers who collect his share of the fines imposed."[498] Only much later does "the popular president of the Hundred Court, the Thingman disappear, and his place is taken by the Graf or Count, the deputy of the King."[499] From the earliest of times, England had autonomous local courts, and this was still true at the time of Magna Carta, in 1215.

Here is how the legal historian Frederick Maitland describes the Twelfth Century legal scene:

> At the beginning of the twelfth century, England was covered by an intricate network of local courts. In the first place these

---

[496] Henry Maine, *Dissertations on Early Law and Custom*, NY: Henry Holt and Company, 1886, p. 168.
[497] Ibid., p. 169.
[498] Ibid., p. 171.
[499] Ibid., p. 172.

> were the ancient courts of the shires and the hundreds, courts older than feudalism, some of them older than the English kingdom. Many of the hundred courts had fallen into private hands… Above all there rose the king's own court. It was destined to increase, while all the other courts were destined to decrease; but we must not think of it as a court of first instance for all litigants; rather it, like every other court, had its limited sphere of jurisdiction.[500]

And at the beginning of the thirteenth century, Bracton "is forced to make something like an apology for the activity of the king's court."[501]

In the twelfth and thirteenth centuries, there was great distrust for the king's court, as well as for the king's growing political and military power. Here is just one example of the difficulty faced by the growing strength of the crown:

> The problem of local government, then, was fast taking a new form, namely, how best to protect the weak from unjust fines and oppressions inflicted on them by local magistrates. The sheriff's local power was no longer a source of danger to the monarch, but had become an effective part of the machinery which enabled the Crown to levy with impunity its always increasing taxation.[502]

King John and the feudal barons had been warring about such matters for several years when things came to a crisis point. The barons refused to pay the king's taxes or to provide him with soldiers to fight for lands in Normandy that the king claimed as his by right. By the time of Magna Carta, the barons were in open rebellion and King "John found himself, for the moment, without power of effective resistance."[503] The barons "asked a plain acceptance of their plainly expressed demands" and King John was "constrained to surrender."[504]

Magna Carta was a charter, a kind of compact, drafted on June 15, 1215 and agreed to by the feudal lords on one side and King John on the other. The compact comes to take on mythical proportions by the

---

[500] Frederick W. Maitland, *The Forms of Action at Common Law*, Cambridge: Cambridge University Press, 1909, 1971, p. 10.
[501] Ibid., p. 12.
[502] William Sharp McKechnie, *Magna Carta: A Commentary on the Great Charter of King John*, Glasgow: John Maclehose and Sons, 1914, p. 16.
[503] Ibid., p. 35.
[504] Ibid., p. 38.

seventeenth century, especially due to the writings of the 17th Century English jurist Edward Coke. But it is not terribly controversial to say that Magna Carta was originally thought of as an agreement between parties that were roughly de facto equal in order to help dispel distrust and provide for harmonious relations within England. As one historian put it: "The barons on that day renewed their oaths of fealty and homage: this was the stipulated price of 'the liberties.'"[505] Magna Carta, the Great Charter between King John and the feudal barons, was primarily a bargain struck so that king could retain his crown and the barons could get assurances that the king would stop abusing his power. Both parties paid a high price to get what they desired from the compact.

Initially, Magna Carta did not appear to be anything other than an agreement struck between the leaders of England in the very early years of the thirteenth century. King John bristled under the terms of the charter and tried to extricate himself from its terms by enlisting the aid of the Vatican, which attempted to annul Magna Carta. But events intruded, making quite a difference. Here is William McKechnie's analysis:

> At a critical juncture, when fortune still trembled in the balance, John's death at Newark Castle, on the morning of 19th October 1216, altered the situation rendering possible, and indeed inevitable, a new arrangement of parties and forces in England. The heir to the throne was an infant, whose advisers found it prudent to reissue voluntarily, and to accept as their rule of government, the essential principles of the Charter that had been extorted from the unwilling John.[506]

So, in the very early years after its adoption the status of the charter changed.

Magna Carta was an agreement between semi-autonomous feudal lords and the king, and was in some respects like a multilateral treaty among sovereign States. Indeed I have previously written about the way that Magna Carta may help us in understanding such treaties. But Magna Carta as a historical document probably would not have had such an enormous impact if not for the fact that successive kings and parliaments continued to reaffirm it, each time allowing the Great Charter to live up to its name by both expanding its reach and confirming its permanency. The 17th century jurist, Edward Coke, claims that there were 29 reaffirmations

[505] Ibid., p. 40.
[506] Ibid., p. 47.

of Magna Carta from 1215 to the early seventeenth century.[507] By the early seventeenth century the charter was said to have established fundamental or constitutional law in England, despite its humble original meaning. Over time, the charter or "treaty" was expanded in scope and jurisdiction, and given a life of its own that would be the basis of many other founding documents such as the American Bill of Rights.

What is often cited as the most important provision of Magna Carta, and that which is closest to a provision of the American Constitution, is that of Chapter 39 (normally referred to as Chapter 29, from the 1225 revised version of King Henry III):

> No freeman shall be taken or imprisoned or desseised or exiled or outlawed or in any way destroyed, nor will we go upon him nor send upon him, except by the lawful judgment of his peers or by the law of the land.

These liberties are described at the beginning of Magna Carta, in Chapter 1, "to be had and held by them and their heirs, of us and our heirs forever."[508] This supposedly fundamental character of being final and immemorial probably did much to cement the importance of Magna Carta when the document was referred to over the centuries.

There are at least four distinct rights in Chapter 29 (39) of Magna Carta. First, is the right to trial by jury, which is so important that the other rights cannot be abridged unless a jury determines that such abridgement is justified. Second, is what came to be called the right of habeas corpus, the right not to be arbitrarily imprisoned. Third, is the right not to be desseised, which meant the right not to be arbitrarily dispossessed or deprived of citizenship rights, including the rights to certain "of any free tenements or of his liberties or free customs."[509] And fourth, is the right not to be outlawed or exiled arbitrarily, at least in part what is today called the right of non-refoulement, namely the right not to be arbitrarily sent out of a country where one resided to another country where one was likely to be harmed. These rights, including the vaguer right not to be destroyed in

---

[507] Faith Thompson, a contemporary historian, corrects this figure upward to a total of 44 including both parliamentary and royal decrees of affirmation of Magna Carta. See Faith Thompson, *Magna Carta – Its Role in the Making of the English Constitution 1300-1629*, Minneapolis, MN: University of Minnesota Press, 1948, p. 10.

[508] Note that this wording also conveys the idea that the Charter initially only applied to those who signed and their heirs, not to all of those living in England.

[509] This wording was added in the 1225 version of Magna Carta. See Faith Thompson, *Magna Carta*, p. 68.

any other way, are the core rights that were thought to be necessary to protect any substantive freedoms. For if one could be arbitrarily sent to prison, outlawed, or exiled, what good would substantive rights to property, or to receive compensation for military service, do.

The phrase, "by the law of the land," came to be understood as "due process of law" by the 14th Century. Indeed, Magna Carta is now so closely associated with due process rights that it is a bit of a shock to realize that the term "due process" does not appear in Magna Carta, except in this wide interpretation of the phrase "by the law of the land." The first explicit mention of due process of law as an interpretation of Magna Carta's Chapter 29 (39) seems to be in 1352 with the second of the six statutes during Edward III's rule:

> Whereas it is contained in the Great Charter of the Liberties of England, that none shall be imprisoned…unless it be by indictment of good and lawful people of the same neighborhood where such deeds be done, *in due* manner, or by *process* made by writ original at the common law.[510]

Thus, in just a few years, Magna Carta is cited to stand for the right of due process for all Englishmen, even though the phrase itself does not appear there.[511] It is not at all clear that this is what was foremost on the minds of the barons who sued to get the king to agree to this compact. Yet, even as the phrase habeas corpus also does not appear in Magna Carta either, surely the root idea, barring arbitrary imprisonment, is there in Chapter 29 (39).

II. Preconditions for the Rule of Law in England

The rights contained in Chapter 29 (39) of Magna Carta are what are sometimes referred to as fundamental law. A number of historians, including Holdsworth, date the idea of habeas corpus to an earlier time than Magna Carta. And interestingly, the earliest uses of habeas corpus also do not stand for such a broad right as due process, but only for the right to challenge one's imprisonment, a purely procedural right. Such rights do not specify any right to a particular form of treatment or liberty that the State must protect. Rather these rights are simply what minimally must be done so that arbitrariness does not creep into the way that people

---

[510] Faith Thompson, in her book, *Magna Carta*, p. 91, claims that this is the first mention of due process in the context of Magna Carta. My italics.
[511] Ibid., p. 92.

are deprived of their liberty by being incarcerated, outlawed or exiled. What is not initially clear is how pure procedural rights could come to be thought of as fundamental or constitutional law.

By the time of the 17th century, those who defended limitations on sovereignty found in Magna Carta a symbolic way to make their case that customary rights formed an immemorial law that restricted the prerogative of kings. As J.G.A. Pocock has said:

> In this way there grew up–or rather, there was intensified and renewed–a habit in many counties of appealing to "the ancient constitution," of seeking to prove that the rights it was desired to defend were immemorial and therefore beyond the king's power to alter or annul.[512]

These rights were imbued with a power stronger than reason, namely immemorial custom that no one could deny.

The great rights in Chapter 29 (39) of Magna Carta are best seen as procedural rights. They are not themselves what people sometimes mean by "due process rights" but they are some of the same as those listed in the canonical treatment of the rule of law by Lon Fuller.[513] Fuller does mention habeas corpus in passing, as part of the congruence between official action and declared rule. He lists this right along with the right to appeal, not as part of "procedural due process," but as rights "in part directed toward the same objective" as due process, in that lack of such rights can contribute to a broken or arbitrary system.[514] This seems right, if a bit more than can be easily defended as I will try to elaborate later in the chapter.

Perhaps, the provisions of Magna Carta's Chapter 29 (39) should be seen as "purely procedural," but in any event, they are not substantive in the normal sense of the term since they do not secure any particular liberty. Purely procedural rights would be those that are necessary for the efficacy of procedural rights, but do not have the normal features of being procedural themselves. Habeas corpus says only that there must be some ability of a prisoner to be made visible, to get his case reviewed, and this right can act in a way to deter the most egregious forms of arbitrariness–being disappeared. But it does not specify what that procedure should be.

---

[512] J.G.A. Pocock, *The Ancient Constitution and the Feudal Law*, Cambridge: Cambridge University Press, 1957, p. 16.

[513] See Lon Fuller, *The Morality of Law*, New Haven, CT: Yale University Press, 1964, 1969, Chapter 2.

[514] Ibid., p. 81.

Nonetheless, there is an important sense in which these rights are procedural, but one should note that there is a distinction between procedural rights that are a precondition even for other procedural rights, and procedural rights that are not a precondition for other rights. The provisions of Chapter 29 (39) were seen as crucial for "enforcing the law" especially for making sure that the legal rights were not denied by spiriting a potentially complaining party away, either into jail or out of the country altogether by outlawry. No rights would be secured without these rights of habeas corpus and other similar rights enforced.

Henry Sumner Maine well stated the most important point I am trying to establish in this section:

> So great is the ascendancy of the Law of Actions in the infancy of Courts of Justice, that substantive law has at first the look of being gradually secreted in the interstices of procedure; and the early lawyer can only see the law through the envelope of its technical forms.[515]

The substantive rights of liberty, especially the right to be free in one's bodily movements, are indeed first approached in a system of law that moved beyond the purely local, in this somewhat surprising way. Rather than focusing directly on substantive rights, perhaps it is procedural rights, such as habeas corpus that we should turn to, since the substantive rights developed much more slowly in medieval English legal debates.

It is also true that many other types of early law, including Irish and Indian legal systems, give "an extraordinary prominence" to procedure.[516] When early legal systems focus on procedure they display an awareness that what is most important is that "service to mankind was to furnish an alternative to savagery, not to suppress it wholly" by limiting but still partially allowing private remedies. As long as the appropriate procedures are followed, these private remedies were important since early tribunals often lacked the "power of directly enforcing their own decrees." [517] Procedures, like those that set limits on the arbitrary use of power, nonetheless allow a wide variety of enforcement mechanisms, something that is especially important when there is no centralized sovereign power.

Maitland tells us how the forms of action were absolutely crucial in determining whether there even was a wrong that had been committed.

---

[515] Henry Maine, *Dissertations on Early Law and Custom*, NY: Henry Holt and Company, 1886, p. 389.
[516] See, ibid., pp. 374 and 386.
[517] Ibid., p. 387.

As Maitland put it, one didn't see a wrong and then look for a form of action, but one first had to find a form of action before there was any wrong that was legally actionable. Maitland also explains how the growing importance and consolidation of forms of action contributed to the gradual increase in sovereign power within England. Here is how he characterized the incremental move toward centralized sovereignty:

> Had the worst come to the worst, the king might have claimed these things: jurisdiction over his own immediate tenants, jurisdiction when all lords have made default, a few specialty royal pleas known as pleas of the crown. To this he might have been reduced by feudalism... That his court should throw open its doors to all litigants...is a principle that only slowly gains ground.[518]

Magna Carta did not instantly transform English legal culture into a centralized system. Instead, procedural consolidation merely set the stage by restricting the form of law so that later a consolidation of substance could proceed. Parallels to Icelandic governmental structure will next be explored.

III. Iceland and the Traditional Rights of Freemen

While concern for their rights led the barons to force King John to protect rights by signing Magna Carta, concern for their rights probably led Icelandic farmers to forego rule by a king altogether. Here is how Jesse Byock puts it:

> the absence of an indigenous population freed the settlers from the need to cluster; giving the flexibility to settle wherever they wished without an initial competition for resources. A fundamental ingredient in the development of Icelandic governmental order and decision making is that Iceland was an immigrant society of freemen formed at a time when Scandinavian kings were enlarging their authority at the expense of the traditional rights of freemen.[519]

---

[518] Maitland, *Forms of Action at Common Law*, p. 11.

[519] Jesse L. Byock, *Medieval Iceland: Society, Sagas, and Power*, Berkeley, CA: University of California Press, 1988, p. 52.

Most of the settlers in Iceland were from Norway where there seems to have been an especially strong willed king who was not seen as respecting individual rights.

The settlers of Iceland seem to have come from Medieval Scandinavian societies where the settlers had struggled against their kings. Rather than attempting to sign agreements with their kings, as in the case of Englishmen in the 13th century, Icelanders left Scandinavian societies which were governed by kings and established a society in Iceland that had no kings and, at least initially, little in the way of government at all. Over time the need for laws became apparent, but Icelanders did not reach back to the laws of their Scandinavian homelands, or if they did it was only for some general guidance.

While the *Gragas* talks about how to treat slaves, most scholars believe that slavery had mainly disappeared in early Icelandic society–the society was primarily one of farmers and small shop keepers, such as alehouse owners. There were some members of the society who were recognized as chieftains, but these positions could be purchased and were not exclusively hereditary. It is true that over time some farmers became more wealthy than others and seem to have taken on more power in the society, but their power was not a legally recognized status that gave them more formal rights. Iceland was a society of freemen who were jealous of their freedoms in the way that people are who recognize what it is like not to have such freedoms.

It is perhaps only a coincidence that in the 13th century, Iceland came to accept the Norwegian king as their ruler–perhaps because of in-fighting among the chieftains. Yet, the Icelanders were concerned about their rights as freemen that had now been relatively secure for several centuries. Icelanders only accepted the Norwegian king due to an agreement struck between Icelanders and that king–the agreement was called "the Old Covenant," seemingly very similar to Magna Carta (the Great Charter) in England in the same century.

The Icelandic people gave up some of their independence by agreeing to be ruled by the Norwegian king. And the Icelandic people in return received a pledge that the king of Norway would protect Icelanders' rights and allow them some legislative autonomy. Specifically the Old Covenant stipulated these provisions:

> 1. That under oath they [the Icelandic farmers] agree to pay in perpetuity a tribute… to His Majesty King Hakon…
> 2. In consideration hereof the king will let us enjoy peace and the Icelandic laws...

> 6. In Norway Icelanders are to have rights as advantageous as they have ever enjoyed there…
> 7. We accept the earl as our overlord so long as he keeps faith with you and peace with us.
> 8. We and our descendants shall keep faith with you so long as you and your descendants keep this covenant, but be free of obligations if, in the opinion of the best men, it is broken.[520]

Here we see that Icelanders have their legal rights protected in exchange for recognizing obligations, primarily of paying taxes, to the Norwegian king.

Here is how Byock describes the most important provisions of the agreement between Icelanders and the King of Norway:

> Some kinsmen might be uncooperative and might even be inimical… The resulting confusion made Iceland in the mid-thirteenth century fertile ground for the expansionist policies of the Norwegian Crown. Aided by Norway's archbishop, the king offered Iceland's *baendr* a stable, if unpalatable, alternative to the turmoil caused by the quarrels of the *storgodar*, and the Icelanders at a series of local assemblies in 1262-1264 accepted the offer… The agreement, by which representatives from the northern and southern regions swore allegiance to the king, was called the Old Covenant (*Gamli Sattmali*). It guaranteed that the king would show deference to the Icelanders: "In return the king shall let us enjoy peace and the Icelandic laws"… it suggests that the Icelanders would have the right to accept or reject new legislation. Thus much of the traditional legislative power remained with the Icelanders[521]

Notice that the Old Covenant was between king and Icelanders, whereas Magna Carta was between the king and the barons.

The Old Covenant had several provisions that are of the highest significance for Medieval legal and political thought. Here is what Gunnar Karlsson says:

> The status of Iceland within [the kingdom of Norway] was set out in a treaty made at the Althing in 1262. This treaty was to enjoy long-lasting political significance…[as] the Old Covenant…. Three major things are clear. First, the Icelanders

---

[520] Translated by Jon Johannesson, in *A History of the Old Icelandic Commonwealth*, Winnipeg: University of Manitoba Press, 1974, pp. 282-283.
[521] Byock, pp. 75-76.

> were to become subjects of the Norwegian Crown, whereby the preservation of peace was to become the king's obligation. Second, Iceland was to remain a separate legal district, although no rules were set out about legislative power in the country. Third, the rule of taxation is clear.[522]

This agreement has obvious parallels with Magna Carta.

The 13th century is sometimes called the High Middle Ages because of the especially enlightened ideas that arose during that century. And here the idea is that the people, either through their assemblies or mediated through barons or other elites, should act to force the kings to guarantee the rights of the common people. This is clearly what was attempted by the Icelandic Old Covenant of 1262-4, as well as by Magna Carta in England in 1215.

IV. The Rule of Law in Iceland

One of the strengths of the Icelandic political system before 1262 was that there was a direct democracy where all of the people's assent was necessary for any change of law or for any new law–as was also true for the *Gragas* which attempted to somewhat codify the customary laws of Iceland, since even here the assent of the majority of the people was needed to ratify this code of law. The rule of law was associated with the fact that law was a matter of the popular will.

It is important to note here, as will become even more clear in later chapters, that the popular will of all citizens was nonetheless restricted to freemen–not slaves, not women, not even freedmen or serfs. Indeed, there is some concern that over time the wealthier farmers had an undue influence on the decisions of the Icelandic assembly. So, the political system in early Iceland was a direct democracy but only of one strata of the society.

Yet, the direct democracy intersected with the legal system in significant ways that affected the rule of law. Courts and panels of judges were effectively run out of the periodic assemblies, either the regional ones or the national assembly, the Althing. Iceland was governed by laws but the laws were a direct consequence of the decisions of the people. It is also important to point out that the populace was only asked for their assent. It was not expected that all of the citizens would participate in the writing of the laws–although apparently this was not ruled out. Rather the

---

[522] Gunnar Karlsson, *The History of Iceland*, Minneapolis, MN: The University of Minnesota Press, 2000, pp. 83-84.

practice seems to have developed in which certain chieftains or other people who were known to be especially wise were afforded the task of writing and changing the laws as was most beneficial to the people. The Icelanders saw themselves initially as not only being completely free to lay claim to whatever lands they wished but also to whatever laws they wished to institute. The question we will ask in the next chapter is whether such a seemingly unchecked system works out overall for the best of the society.

The Icelandic system did have two institutions that could have provided checks on an unfettered polity concerning the making or changing of laws. The first institution is that of the Lawspeaker and the second is the Law Council. The Lawspeaker is the closest thing to a fully recognized expert on the status of the law–but even as the Lawspeaker was supposed to have memorized all of the laws and to be able to recite any law when asked, the Lawspeaker was not necessarily considered an authority on what the law should be. The Law Council made important recommendations on legislation to affirm or change the laws of Iceland.

The various legal institutions in Iceland put a high premium on the law and set that law above any acts of Icelanders in the sense that these Icelanders could only change the law through procedures that themselves were recognized as having a kind of immemorial status. In these respects the Old Covenant and Magna Carta share much in common and have served as models of how the rights of citizens can be protected by law even against powerful kings.

V. The Rule of Law and Popular Governance

We will end this chapter by providing some brief reflections on how the rule of law might not only contrast with the rule of a single man, the king, but also with the rule of men, especially in assemblies and parliaments. In the case of such a conflict, it is not immediately evident that the rule of law should be placed above the rule of men. In this section we will also again look at the idea of customs, especially those that are said to have existed from time immemorial as we also ask whether such customs should have sway over the rule of men.

There is a sense in England that the judges and courts in the Common Law system of justice not only stood opposed to the king but to the emerging parliament as well. In Iceland the laws also stood against the king in the 13th century but also against the people insofar as laws restrict the arbitrary will of all. In both England and Iceland the emerging idea is that it is the procedures of the law that stand opposed to the will of the king and also to a certain extent the current will of the people.

Perhaps more interesting yet is that the rule of law also set limits on how the legislature and also the courts could operate. Here are just two of many examples in the *Gragas* of Icelandic law's restrictions on how courts operate:

> It is to be deemed as if a panel verdict is favorable to the other side if the man who called the panel delays until the sun comes onto Dingvollr.
> If in giving verdicts or testimonies men leave out any word that affects the case, then it is as if verdicts or testimonials are withheld…
> If a General Assembly court gives a wrong verdict, a summons is to be made for the judgment to be revoked and it is to be prosecuted before the Fifth Court that same summer. But if the principal in question is not there, it may be prosecuted the following summer.[523]

Indeed, the bulk of the *Gragas* is taken up with the procedures of the Assembly, and in many cases the procedures place limits on what the assembly can do or how it can do it even though it can be assumed that the Assembly's acts are the acts of the popular will.

In Icelandic law, the law stands over the executive branch, which is not very strong in any event since there is no king. The Icelandic law also stands over the legislative branch, the Law Council of the Assembly. And Icelandic law also stands over the judicial branch insofar as there are lots of legal restrictions on how courts operate. Similar things can be said of English Common law. The traditions and precedents of the common law stand over the king in many instances. The law stands over the emerging parliament and the other organs of government which make or change law. And the judiciary is limited in many ways by the law as well.

In both Icelandic and English law, the popular will is expressed in various ways, but that will is also restrained and restricted by the law. In this sense the rule of law not only restrains the king or other executive branch officials but the rule of law also restrains the will of the people. In other words, the rule of law is opposed not only to the rule of *man* but also to the rule of *men*. The rise of the importance of the rule of law was thus not necessarily a vehicle only for the people to use against the king. The rule of law was not necessarily a popular governmental institution.

[523] *Gragas I*, p. 121.

SECTION X:

STATUS

CHAPTER 23

WOMEN, WIVES, AND DAUGHTERS

In many respects early Icelandic and English Common Law offer unique perspectives in legal and political thought–but the status of women is not normally considered to be of this sort. Nonetheless in this chapter I will argue that there are indeed some unique, or at least highly interesting, ideas about the legal status of women in the 12th and 13th centuries in Iceland and England. We will find that in several respects the legal position of women in public affairs is somewhat better than many earlier societies. We will have occasion here to look at not only explicit legal texts but also sagas and tales in the literature of the peoples of Iceland and England.

In the first section we will explore the ideas of inheritance in Icelandic and English Common law, especially focusing on questions about the legal status of wives and daughters to their inheritances. In the second section we will follow with the related questions of how women and girls were regarded in marriage and the family in Iceland and England. We will here confront emerging ideas of communal property. We will also look at how these topics were dealt with in literature as well as explicit legal texts. In the third section we will begin to consider criminal law, to which we will give much more attention in later chapters, as to how women as defendants and plaintiffs were treated. In the fourth section we will look to how women were treated as witnesses and as potential jurors. And finally in section five we will attempt to draw out some comparative assessments as well as conclusions about women in early Iceland and English law.

I. Inheritance and Communal Property

In the very beginning of the Inheritance Section of the *Gragas*, we find the following law:

> A son free born and a lawful heir is to inherit on the death of his father and mother. If a son does not exist then a daughter is to inherit. If a daughter does not exist, then the father is to

> inherit, then a brother born of the same father, then the mother. If she does not exist, then a sister born of the same father is to inherit. If she does not exist, then a brother born of the same mother is to inherit. If he does not exist, then a sister born of the same mother is to inherit.[524]

From these provisions it appears that male heirs are given priority over female heirs when they are in the same relationship to the decedent, but female heirs are given priority over male heirs in many other circumstances. The general principle is made clear in the following:

> From then on the closest kinsman always stands to inherit. If there are several equally close who have the right to inherit, it shall be equally divided among all the branches, and a branch is counting from brothers and sisters. *If a man and a woman are equally close, then in that case the man is always to inherit.* If women are closest, then in that case there is also division of the inheritance among them."[525]

Male heirs have priority over female heirs, but only if males and females are of the same branch. Female heirs are recognized as having significant status as well.

We also find that inheritance is treated equally in case of desertion, as we see in this passage from the *Gragas II*:

> If a man separates from his wife and it is counted as desertion on his part and the bishop does not give him leave to marry, then his penalty is lesser outlawry if he makes a second marriage, and if he has children with that woman they do not become lawful heirs.
> If a woman separates from her husband with the result that it is counted as desertion on her part and she marries another man and the bishop does not give her leave, then her penalty is lesser outlawry, and the children she has with that man are not valid heirs.[526]

Earlier, men are clearly favored but here things look like they are roughly equal among the sexes.

Yet there are also some laws that seem to favor the woman over the man in certain inheritance situations.

---

[524] *Gragas II*, p. 3.
[525] *Gragas II*, p. 4, my italics.
[526] *Gragas II*, p. 7.

> A male is to inherit only if he is sixteen winters old. But a woman who is married, whether of sixteen winters or younger, she is to take an inheritance as soon as it comes her way and care of other people's property as well. If she is a widow younger than sixteen winters, then she is to take an inheritance and also care of other people's property if it comes her way as long as her legal administrator has authorized it.[527]

These cases are mixed in that females get to inherit at an earlier age than males, as long as the females are married, but the females also have to get authorization from a legal administrator–something that is not required of the male inheritor.

In the English legal textbook, Glanvill, from the late 12th century we find the following rule about inheritance:

> If anyone has a son and heir and also a daughter or daughters, the son succeeds to everything… the general rule is that a woman never shares in inheritance with a man unless there is a special rule in a particular city by ancient custom of that city. If, however, a man has several wives and by each of them has a daughter or daughters, all the daughters will come equally to the inheritance in the same way as if they were all of one and the same mother. When, however, anyone dies leaving no son or daughter as heir, if he has grandsons or grand-daughters born of a son or daughter, they will undoubtedly succeed in the same way as was laid down above for son and daughters; and subject to the same distinctions; for lineal descendants are always preferred to collaterals.[528]

So, while males are preferred over females in Medieval England, this is only true when they are equally placed, otherwise females can inherit even over males if the males are collateral rather than direct descendants.

According to Bracton, writing probably in the 13th century, males are preferred to females in the action titled "*mortdancestor*" (death of an ancestor), but Bracton is not as clear as the earlier text by Glanvill, or the later text by Britton, as we will see. Here is a statement of one of the writs concerning *mortdancestor* according to Bracton:

> The king to the sheriff, greeting. Summon by good summoners twelve free and lawful men of the neighborhood of such a vill to be before our justices at their first session when they come

---

[527] *Gragas II*, p. 8.

[528] Glanvill, p. 77.

> into those parts, ready to recognize on oath if such a one, the father (or "mother," "uncle" or "aunt," "brother" or "sister") of such a one was seised in his (or "her") demesne as of fee of so much land with the appurtenances in such a vill [etc.] and if he, such a one, is his (or "her") nearer heir…[529]

We see here that heirs can be females as well as males, but the relationship between them is best set out by Britton as we next see.

The English legal textbook called "Britton," probably dating from the end of the 13th or beginning of the 14th centuries, has a clear and concise treatment of inheritance rights of females.

> those who are found to be the nearest in the collateral degrees for ever are the right heirs… There are many things which constitute proximity and confer an inheritance and right of succession, to wit, sex, age, line, a particular inheritance, plurality of female heirs, form of gift, and blood. Sex, because the male is to be received and the female rejected, so long as there is a male heir apparent of the father by the same mother; but the daughter begotten on the first wife is to be preferred in the succession to the marriage granted with her mother to the male begotten by the same father on the second wife…. Line is material; because the daughter found in the direct line descending is to be preferred before the male found in the transverse line… Plurality of female heirs affects the succession, as in case of sisters perceners, who, whether they are begotten of one or of several mothers, all present themselves in the place of one heir, and no one of them is to be preferred before another… since they are all equally nearest.[530]

Here we see that males are preferred to females, but only when they are similarly placed. Females can be heirs in many situations in this summary of English Common Law, just as was true of Icelandic law from a bit earlier in time. Indeed, it is somewhat surprising to find that "Right of blood sometimes causes the female to exclude the male."[531]

---

529 Bracton, vol. III, p. 249.

530 Britton, *Britton: An English Translation and Notes*, translated by Francis Morgan Nichols and Simeon E. Baldwin, Washington, DC: John Byrne & Co., 1901, pp. 577-579.

531 Britton, p. 580.

II. Women in Marriage and Family Law

In their monumental book, *The History of the English Law Before the Time of Edward I*, Pollack and Maitland provide us with a concise statement of early English law concerning women:

> We have yet to speak of half the inhabitants of England. No text-writer, no statute, ever makes any general statement as to the position of women. This is treated as obvious, and we believe that it can be defined with some accuracy by one brief phrase: - private law with few exceptions puts women on a par with men; public law gives a woman no rights and exacts from her no duties, save that of paying taxes and performing such services as can be performed by deputy… But the woman can hold land, even by military tenure, can own chattels, make a will, make a contract, can sue and be sued. She sues and is sued in person without the interposition of a guardian; she can plead with her own voice if she pleases… The other half of our proposition, that which excludes women from all public functions, was subject to few if any real exceptions.[532]

In maters of marrying and raising a family, women in England in the 13th century were roughly equal to men, or so Pollack and Maitland claim. Yet, we also find that once a woman is married, her rights are greatly restricted by the overwhelming rights of her husband–"During the marriage, the wife can not contract on her own behalf. She can contract as her husband's agent."[533]

There is a kind of exception to marital property that some commentators find in England at this time, namely the idea of communal property, which we shall find in Icelandic law at roughly the same time. Here is a sense of the debate among some scholars:

> Sometimes the whole property of husband and wife, whether acquired before or after the marriage, falls into this community… But granted that there is this common stock, jurists have often found difficulty in deciding who… is really the owner of it. Some… have maintained that during the marriage the ownership of it is in truth with the husband, so large are his powers while the marriage lasts of doing what he pleases. Others will make the husband and wife co-owners, each of them entitled to an aliquot share of the undivided mass. Others,

---

[532] Pollack and Maitland, vol. I, pp. 482-483.
[533] Pollack and Maitland, vol. II. p. 405.

> again, will postulate a juristic person to bear the ownership, some kind of corporation of which the husband and wife are the two members.[534]

Pollack and Maitland are skeptical of communal property existing as a concept in English law, even as they admit that in Scotland, as well as in Iceland, there was such an important idea. Yet they also say that there is some evidence for communal property in early English law.

Perhaps of even more importance is the idea that the community of property can be unequally divided.

> A system of community need not be a system of equality. We do not mean merely that during the marriage the husband may and, at least in the Middle Ages, will have an almost unlimited power of dealing with the common fund; we mean also that there is no reason why the fund, when it has to be divided, should be divided in equal shares. Many schemes of division are found. In particular, it is common that the husband should take two-thirds, the wife one-third.[535]

While the wife cannot oppose her husband's will while the marriage lasts, upon its dissolution the wife may be able to take an equal share or some other distribution, which is not up to the husband to oppose.

In early Icelandic law, we find several instances of what could be called common property in marriage due to a partnership between the spouses. Here is one such example from the *Gragas II*:

> Man and wife have the right to make a partnership if they wish as long as it is a fair agreement between them and also fair towards their heirs. Betrothal agreements between man and wife must remain binding as long as betrothal witnesses are still alive and different agreements are not made. But if betrothal witnesses who remember the terms are not alive, then the law makes a partnership between them, given that he owned a mark or more when they joined the marriage and a bride-price was paid and they have been householding for three winters or longer. If man and wife make money from a state of poverty, then the law makes a partnership between them, and the law always makes a partnership between man

---

534 Pollack and Maitland, vol. II, pp. 400-401.

535 Pollack and Maitland, vol. II, p. 403.

> and wife in such a way that he owns two-thirds and she one third.[536]

As in early English Common law, when a community or partnership is established, the man gets two-thirds and the woman only one-third.

Such an arrangement also occurs in other arrangements in marriage as we see in this provision in the *Gragas II*:

> If they are both destitute, the children are to be divided between the families, two-thirds to the father's family and one-third to the mother's family. If one of them has more than enough for himself or herself, neighbors are to assess how much more that one can manage, and that some is to be contributed to the household where the children are. But responsibility for two-thirds of what they can manage is to pass to the father's family, for one-third to the mother's family.[537]

So, while there is a partnership or community created to deal with division of the marital estate, or the marital responsibilities, the partners are not treated equally.

In some respects, the greater amount of profit going to the man is offset by the greater responsibilities for caring for the children also going to the man. But we should not assume that that means that the husband and wife are somehow on an equal plain, for the husband clearly has the greater role and also the greater say in what occurs in the marriage. But we should also note that in some cases consent to join in the marriage is required from both parties. In Icelandic law this is clearest in some cases when a widow is betrothed.

> Where a widow is betrothed to someone, her consent is to be obtained unless her father gives her in betrothal, then he shall decide… Even without the consent of her legal administrator a widow has the right to give herself in betrothal to a man who previously had her to wife as long as there is no hindrance between them and they were not separated on account of dependents.[538]

---

[536] *Gragas II*, p. 67.
[537] *Gragas II*, p. 31.
[538] *Gragas II*, p. 53.

In the following sections we will explore in more detail some other circumstances where a woman has an equal status to a man in the 13th century CE in England and Iceland.

III. Women in Criminal Law

There is a very intriguing section of the *Gragas I* concerning women as victims of crime and when killing the perpetrator could be the appropriate response.

> There are six women a man has a right to kill for. One is a man's wife, two a man's daughter, three a man's mother, four is his sister, five is the foster-daughter a man has brought up, six is the foster-mother who brought a man up. It is prescribed that if a man arrives to find another man forcing a woman to lie with him there, a woman he has the right to kill for, and the man has forced her down and lowered himself down upon her, then he has the right to kill on her account there at that place, or likewise if he finds him in the same bed as the woman, so that they lie side by side, because it was his will to have wrongful intercourse with her, then a man has the right to kill on her account in both instances even if intercourse has not taken place.[539]

We learn here that men are appropriately the avengers of women who have been attacked, even if the woman has not actually been raped. In a later chapter we will see how such self-help was crucial for enforcement of the Icelandic laws given that there was no chief executive or police force. Indeed, we are told that this law is premised on the "intended" wrongful intercourse. And in effect this intended wrong is a capital crime.

In early Icelandic law, women can sometimes take charge of their own lawsuits but generally women must rely on their close male relatives for such lawsuits. Here is the law that is an exception:

> A widow or an unmarried girl of twenty or more is to have charge of her own lawsuits if they are assaulted or wounded with minor wounds, whether they wish to transfer or settle. They must not take more than the personal compensation fixed by law.[540]

---

[539] *Gragas I*, p. 154.

[540] *Gragas I*, p. 158.

So, for minor assaults a widow or unmarried girl of twenty may pursue legal action against her assailant, but only if minor injuries have been inflicted on her.

We also find another instance where a woman is given legal status on her own account in the following law concerning the wergeld owed as compensation for a killing or assault:

> There is also one woman who is both to pay and to take a wergeld ring, given that she is an only child, and that woman is called "ring-lady." She who takes is the daughter of the dead man if no proper receiver of the main ring otherwise exists but atonement payers are alive, and she takes the three-mark ring like a son, given that she has not accepted full settlement in compensation for the killing, and this until she is married, but thereafter kinsmen take it. She who pays is the daughter of the killer if no proper payer of the main ring otherwise exists but receivers do, and then she is to pay the three-mark ring like a son, and this until she enters a husband's bed and thereby tosses the outlay into her kinsmen's lap.[541]

When a woman is the daughter of a dead man who has no sons she can take the wergeld as if she were the son of the dead man; and if the woman is the daughter of a killer who has no sons she must pay the wergeld as if she were the son of the killer.

In early English Common law, here is how Glanvill characterizes the crime of rape and the plea that the woman must submit:

> In the crime of rape a woman charges a man with violating her by force in the peace of the lord king. A woman who suffers in this way must go, soon after the deed is done, to the nearest vill and there show to trustworthy men the injury done to her, and any effusion of blood there may be and any tearing of her clothes. She should then do the same for the reeve of the hundred. Afterwards she should proclaim it publicly in the next county court… it should be known that if anyone is convicted in this kind of plea the judgment against him shall be the same as in the crimes discussed earlier. Nor can the wrongdoer escape this by expressing his willingness, after judgment, to marry the woman he has defiled.[542]

---

541 *Gragas I*, p. 181.

542 Glanvill, pp. 175-176.

The crime of rape is one of the few exceptions[543] where a woman can accuse another on her own–a second case is where it is the woman's husband who was killed and she saw the event.[544] In this respect, early English Common law is similar to early Icelandic law. In both systems of law, women were only allowed to plead their own case in exceptional circumstances.

Bracton makes it very clear that women can only make an appeal to a court in their own behalf in two cases:

> We must see the cases in which a woman has an appeal. It is clear that there are no more than two by which one ought to be put to the duel or the grand assise, that is, only for a forcible harm done to her body, as for rape, as was said above, and for the death of her husband slain within her arms, and in no other way.[545]

We see nearly the same treatment of women in other early English Common law texts.

In Britton, we find several references to the crime of rape that help us see how women were able to sue for assaults on their own bodies:

> Rape is a felony by a man with violence on the body of a woman, whether she be a virgin or not. Of such felonies let inquiry be made; and whoever is attainted thereof, either at the suit of the woman by appeal of felony, or at our suit, shall have the same judgment as for the death of a man, whether the woman have consented after commission of the felony or not, as is contained in the Statutes of Westminster.[546]

Two things are significant: rape can occur even if the woman is not a virgin, and even if she has in some sense consented after commission of the act.

In another law from Britton we find special considerations that apply when there is a woman who is the victim of an alleged felony.

> As to women, our will is, that no woman shall bring an appeal of felony for the death of any man, except for the death of her husband killed within her arms, within the year and a day. For

---

543 Ibid., p. 173.
544 Ibid., p. 174.
545 Bracton, vol. II, p. 419.
546 Britton, p. 46.

> an infant killed within her womb, she may not bring any appeal, no one being bound to answer to an appeal of felony, where the plaintiff cannot set forth the name of the person against whom the felony was committed. With regard to an appeal of rape, our pleasure is, that every woman, whether virgin or not, shall have the right to sue for vengeance for the felony by appeal in the county court within forty days, but after that time she shall lose her suit; in which case, if the defendant confesses the fact, but says that the woman at the same time conceived by him, and can prove it, then our will is that it be adjudged no felony, because no woman can conceive if she does not consent.[547]

Here we find some added nuance to how women are treated as victims of crime. Being a virgin or not, she is able to make an appeal for vengeance on her own account. It is perhaps worth a comment that there is a false fact at the end of this law since there is now, and presumably there was then, no evidence that conception requires consent.

IV. Women as Witnesses and Potential Jurors

In early Icelandic laws, witnesses and juries are reserved for men, and women are excluded.

> It is prescribed by our laws that we shall have four Quarter Courts. Each chieftain who has an ancient and full chieftaincy shall nominate a man to join a court… Each chieftain is to nominate a man from his assembly third to join a court unless he has leave from the Law Council to do otherwise. A male of twelve winters or more, capable of taking responsibility for what he says or swears, free, and with a settled home, is to be nominated…. A man who has not learnt to speak the Norse language in his childhood is not nominated to join a court unless he has been in Iceland three winters or more.[548]

Women are excluded from nomination to join the court as jurors or even as witnesses in early Icelandic law.

There are very few exceptions which would allow women a role in public life–here is one of them:

---

[547] Britton, p. 96.

[548] *Gragas I*, p. 53.

> A man must baptize a child. But if he does not know the words or actions, it is lawful for a woman to teach him. The father of a child is to baptize if only no other men are at hand. But if a father baptizes his sick child himself, then he is to give up sharing a bed with his wife. If he does not give up sharing her bed, the penalty is lesser outlawry. His subsequent marriage is at the bishop's dispensation.[549]

Notice that women are not allowed to baptize, but only to instruct men in how to baptize, even though if the only male is the baby's father then the marriage can be dissolved.

In early English Common law there were also restrictions on women appearing in court as witnesses or jurors. Here is Glanvill:

> The tenant who has put himself upon the assize secures peace by such writs until the demandant comes to court and purchases another writ, which provides that four lawful knights of the county and of the neighborhood shall elect twelve lawful knights of the same neighborhood, who are to declare on oath which of the parties has the greater right to the land in question.[550]

Knights are always men, and never women, in these times. Witnesses must come from the male population. In addition, the jury of twelve which is formed is to include only men and never women, again from Glanvill:

> Each juror summoned for this purpose must swear that he will not declare falsely, nor knowingly suppress the truth. The knowledge required from the jurors is that they shall know about the matter from what they have personally seen and heard, or from statements which their fathers made to them in such circumstances that they are bound to believe them as if they had seen and heard for themselves.[551]

These jurors are always to be men not women.

Yet there was one type of case where women were jurors in English Common law. Pollack and Maitland summarize the general point in their characteristic pithy manner:

---

[549] *Gragas I*, p. 25.
[550] Glanvill, p. 30.
[551] Glanvill, pp. 34-35.

> we never find women as jurors, except, as not infrequently happened, some expectant heir alleged that there was a plot to supplant him by the production of a suppositious child, in which case a jury of matrons was employed… In the ecclesiastical courts the rule seems to have been that a woman's compurgators ought to be women, just as a man's compurgators ought to be men, but apparently in the king's court a woman had to find male oath-helpers.[552]

With these very few unusual exceptions aside, English Common law did not allow women to be jurors or witness. The classes of exceptions will be revisited in the final section of this chapter.

V. Women in 12th, 13th, and 14 Century Legal Thought

We can begin the final section of this chapter by returning to the summary provided by Pollack and Maitland:

> private law with few exceptions puts women on a par with men; public law gives a woman no rights and exacts from her no duties, save that of paying taxes and performing such services as can be performed by a deputy.[553]

We might ask why inheritance rules were so skewed toward men if the private sphere puts women on a par with men. Perhaps inheritance is at least a mixed mode rather than strictly a matter of the private sphere. But what of the idea that men were to be head of household and that meant head of the women in that household, especially the wife or wives?

Furthermore, we could ask how the unequal status of women in the public sphere, where all decisions governing the lives of both men and women, was controlled exclusively by men, could be reconciled with such a different status in the private sphere? The fact that women pay no taxes would be an obvious case where the public status of women would affect her private standing since paying taxes was the main obligation of citizens in both early English Common law and Icelandic law. And of course the fact that women were forbidden to enter into the places where the assemblies were held would signal to all that women were not to be trusted with their own affairs even in the private sphere. So, as we proceed briefly to summarize the status of women in these societies we should keep a

[552] Pollack and Maitland, vol. I, pp. 484-485.
[553] Pollack and Maitland, vol. I, p. 482.

close eye on what evidence there is for thinking that women were really seen as equal to their husbands in the private sphere. Indeed, we should also pay close attention to whether the spheres really are separated in law.

In early Icelandic law, as well as in early English Common law, we find that as a matter of separation of the marital unit, the man takes two-thirds and the woman only one-third. The man has more responsibilities–especially for the support of children–but the division is not equal even taking that into consideration. The idea of a married couple forming a unit–where certain goods are held in common is an idea that could lead to a more equitable marriage arrangement than in ancient times. Yet, as Pollack and Maitland tell us, it is not clear that early English Common law did recognize common property of the marriage. In early Icelandic law it is also not clear that the married couple formed a legal unit that could own property and from which equal shares could be withdrawn when the marriage was dissolved.

And the fact that England recognized that women could be rulers as queens and that Icelandic sagas often portrayed very strong female characters, could be cited as another basis for thinking of women as if not equal to men at least not the husband's servant. Here is how one scholar describes the Icelandic sagas' views of women:

> The poetry and mythology presents divine female figures and identifies four images of human women: the warrior, the prophetess/sorceress, the revenger, and the inciter. Although the divine figures disappeared with the acceptance of Christianity, the human images survived for a millennium, not only in poetry but also in the prose of the heroic sagas of Icelanders.[554]

Here is a basis for strong female role-models even if these women characters were somewhat downplayed in Christianized times.

Looking to the status of women as witnesses and parties to law suits we find a mixed record but generally women were excluded from being a witness, with only few exceptions. This is an important consideration since being excluded from the legal domain, except as represented by a male, certainly made women second-class members of the society in public affairs. And it is my contention that this status would inevitably also affect the private sphere since it is not just in terms of paying taxes

---

[554] Jenny Jochens, *Women in Old Norse Society*, Ithaca, NY: Cornell University Press, 1995, p. 3.

but in virtually all other legal matters women were afforded at best second-class status.

One last consideration to contemplate, which we have also considered in earlier chapters concerning other societies, is the effect of the Christianization of England and Iceland in the early part of the second millennium. Marriage was affected in that bigamy was outlawed, but this then left the legal question of how to deal with the offspring of non-monogamous sexual affairs. In England and Iceland, the pagan and Christian images of women continued to offer different ideas, but except for the role of the women of the cloister there were few clear paths for ambitious actual women in these societies.

Insofar as Pollack and Maitland were right to think of early English Common law as providing for the equality of treatment for women in the private sphere, we do have some unique legal ideas here. But insofar as we can only find mixed support for Pollack and Maitland's thesis, which turned on being able to completely separate private and public affairs, we must resist the conclusion that things were unique and better for women here than in other Medieval societies. And in any event, in Icelandic law, which in so many ways resembles that of early English Common law, what was truly unique about Iceland–its lack of an executive branch of the government–is not clearly related to a more inclusive or equitable position for women in Icelandic society. We are reminded of how ancient Roman and Greek societies had strong roles for women in literature but where women did not have a clear corresponding role in the actual legal practices of the time.

SECTION XI:

CRIMINAL LAW

CHAPTER 24

OUTLAWRY AND INLAWRY

In early Icelandic law, where there was no organized executive branch of government, punishment for violation of the law often took the form of outlawry, where a felon was exiled from Iceland and had to relinquish all of his or her property. This punishment is actually called "full outlawry." There was also "lesser outlawry," which involved banishment from Iceland for three years and other penalties. The advantage of these penalties is that they could be executed by the population at large, without the need for police or kings or troops, all of which was missing from early Icelandic society.

In early English Common law, the idea of outlawry also played a prominent role, but not for the same reasons as in Iceland. In England, there was a king with his sheriffs and troops. But like in Iceland, enforcement of the law was not easy to accomplish with meager resources to devote to law enforcement. So, outlawry was a form of punishment that was "enforced" by the whole population, as in Iceland. There were also laws in England about how outlaws could be reunited with their communities, called "inlawry." In this chapter I will argue that this ingenious institution of outlawry (along with inlawry) allows us to see how law can be "enforced" without an executive branch of government, without a police force or other such institution which is feared by the population.

We begin then, in the first section, with an account of how the institution of outlawry operated in early Icelandic law. And then in the second section we discuss outlawry in early English Common law. In the third section we discuss the institution of inlawry in England. And in the fourth section we discuss the corresponding idea to inlawry in Iceland. Finally, we take up the question of how law was indeed "enforced" by means of outlawry and why it matters for our understanding of the motivation to obey the law in Medieval times.

I. Outlawry in Iceland

Many of the crimes listed in the *Gragas* call for outlawry as the penalty for breaking the law, sometimes "full outlawry" and more commonly "lesser outlawry." Here is how full outlawry is described by the translators of the *Gragas*:

> Full outlawry cast a man out of society. The outlaw forfeited his property and all his rights, civil, family, and ecclesiastical. He could not lawfully be given any assistance–sustenance, passage, or any saving advice. He might be killed by anyone with impunity and had a price on his head: this applied forever even if he escaped abroad.[555]

There were various ways that the outlaw could redeem himself which we will discuss later. But in general the outlaw was in effect removed from society by losing all rights and being shunned by the members of his or her society, as well as being at risk of losing his or her life if he or she returned to Iceland.

While full outlawry was reserved for very severe offenses, lesser outlawry was a common penalty for many even seemingly minor offenses. Here is how the translators of the *Gragas* describe lesser outlawry:

> Lesser outlawry involved payment of a "life-ring" (a mark in legal tender, one-eighth of which, i.e., one ounce, was called the "sustenance pledge") to a chieftain (waived if the chieftain was able to take an ox or cow from the estate as he was entitled to do), forfeit of other property, and banishment from Iceland for three years (starting within three years of the sentence)… Failure to abide by the rules meant total forfeit of immunity. While abroad the "lesser outlaw" enjoyed normal immunity.[556]

These forms of outlawry in Icelandic law were forms of punishment that courts could order.

In Gisli Sursson's Saga, we have a tale of revenge and outlawry that sheds some light on our topic:

> Then the Summons Days came round and Bork travelled west with forty men to summon Gisli to the Thorsnes Assembly… He prepared a case against Gisli for the slaying of Thorgrim to

[555] *Gragas I,* Annotated Glossary, p. 246.
[556] *Gragas I*, Annotated Glossary, p. 250.

> be presented to the Thorsnes Assembly… The next thing that happened was that Gisli sent word to Vestein's uncles, Helgi, Sigurd and Vestgeir, the sons of Bjartmar, asking them to go to the assembly and offer a settlement for him so that he would not be outlawed. They went to the assembly, but they made no headway with the settlement. Indeed, it was said that they handled matters so badly that they were close to tears before it was over. They related the outcome to Thorkel the Wealthy, saying that they dared not face Gisli to tell him he had been outlawed. Aside from Gisli's sentence nothing much took place at the assembly.[557]

This saga dates from the time of the *Gragas* and is generally regarded as presenting a fictionalized but relatively accurate portrayal of life in Medieval Iceland. We can learn from this saga that outlawry was a sentence passed by an assembly and that full outlawry was a sentence for a serious felony such as murder. This sentence was feared and felons tried to find alternatives that would be accepted by the assembly instead of outlawry.

The *Gragas I* has several sections dealing with outlawry. Here is part of two sections relevant to the accounts in the saga:

> Testimony of the announcement of judgment is to be brought or testimony of the settlement [by which he was outlawed and of] what terms were laid down for his outlawry and of what he was outlawed for and of where he was outlawed. Men are then to draw lots to decide how cases are to be brought forward. If men bring back here a man who was made a full outlaw that same summer, the penalty for it is full outlawry. If they did not know he was outlawed, they are not under penalty, unless they keep him for three nights after they learn of it and then the penalty is full outlawry. If men are to bring back here a man who was made a full outlaw the previous summer, they are to do one thing or the other, either kill him or take him to the man who got him condemned within half a month of learning that he had been outlawed. If [they] will do neither, their penalty is full outlawry.[558]

We can see here that full outlawry was a sentence or judgment of an assembly and it is enforced by way of threatening to sentence others to

---

[557] *Gisli Sursson's Saga*, in *The Sagas of Icelanders*, translated by Katrina C. Atwood, et al, NY: Penguin Books, 2000, pp. 527-529.
[558] *Gragas I*, p. 119.

outlaw if they aid the outlaw or fail to kill or turn him over should he be brought back to Iceland.

In terms of lesser outlawry we can cite another passage from *Gragas I* for aid in understanding how the process worked:

> Where a man is judged a lesser outlaw for malicious damage, then at the confiscation court such compensation for damage is to be paid to the man who prosecuted him as five neighbors assess by oath on a book. If compensation for damage is not paid at the confiscation court as prescribed, then as soon as the confiscation court is finished, he falls under the same penalty as if he had been judged a full outlaw at a General Assembly court, one not to be sustained and not to be given passage.[559]

Full outlawry is the penalty for not doing what one had been sentenced to do when one was sentenced to lesser outlawry. Again, lesser outlawry was enforced by threats of full outlawry in Medieval Iceland.

II. Outlawry in England

Britton, the textbook probably written in the late 13th century in England, provides the following provision about outlawry:

> And for the maintaining of peace, we will that when felony is committed, every one be ready to pursue and arrest the felons…
> If one or more be appealed of the death, and others of the force and accessory facts, let the principals be first demanded at three county courts to come and answer concerning the felony, and if they do not come to the fourth court, and are not mainprised to appear at the fifth, they shall be outlawed at the fourth…
> As to the punishment of outlaws in their lifetime… they be forejudged from all law, and put out of our peace… and he that shall kill them shall be acquitted of their death…and if they are taken and found to be outlawed by record of the coroner, they shall be hanged, and their chattels shall be ours, and their heirs disinherited of every kind of inheritance.[560]

We have here outlawry sentenced in a somewhat different way in England than in Iceland.

---

[559] *Gragas I*, p. 116.
[560] Britton, pp. 42-44.

Consider an example from English literature about Robin Hood in order to make this a bit more clear and vivid:

> LYTHE and listin, gentilmen,
> That be of frebore bode;
> His nae was Robyn Hode.
> Robyn was a prude outlaw…
> Of my good he shall haue some,
> Yf he be a por man…
> loke ye do no husbonde harme
> That tilleth with his ploughe
> No more ye shall no gode yeoman
> That walketh by gren-wode shawe;
> Ne no knight ne no squyer
> That wol be a gode felawe…
> Cryst haue mercy on his soule,
> That dyed on the rode!
> For he was a good outlawe,
> And dyde pore men moch god.[561]

This is taken from "A Geste of Robyn Hode." Robin is portrayed as having made a large loan which he could not repay and is subsequently outlawed.

Let me elaborate on these provisions and indicate the differences between outlawry in England and in Iceland. One of the first things to note is that unlike in Iceland, outlawry in England is not a normal punishment but a default punishment when the accused felon has failed to appear for his trial and sentencing. And if the accused felon does appear later he is subject to immediate execution in England but his or her fate is much less clear in Iceland. This is at least in part because there is no formal executioner in Iceland just as there is no formal executive branch of government either.

A similarity is that ordinary people can kill the outlaw with impunity in both Iceland and England. It is a major provision in early Icelandic law that the ordinary people enforce the law and outlawry, especially lesser outlawry where the felon must absent himself from Iceland for three years. There is enforcement by those who know the felon and can enforce his temporary exile.

One other dissimilarity is that in England outlawry seems to be a substitute for the death penalty when the accused felon cannot be found.

561. *A Geste of Robyn Hode*, reprinted in J. C. Holt, *Robin Hood*, London: Thames & Hudson, 1982.

This is very different than in Iceland where outlawry was a regular sentence administered by a court in a trial where the accused felon is present. Indeed, as I have said, outlawry was a crucial punishment in Icelandic society that had no executioner or other executive branch officers who could administer a sentence.

It is still a bit mysterious how the outlawry punishment worked in practice in Iceland–for instance was it a successful substitute for executing punishments through officers of the executive branch? Or was its lack of success something that contributed to the popular receptivity of the king of Norway who eventually took over the executive branch of government in Iceland? We will explore these questions later in this chapter.

III. Inlawry in England

There was a formal procedure by which an outlawed felon could be reconciled with his community in England.

> Inlawry ought of right to be granted in these cases, namely, where a man has been outlawed before the fourth county court… or if the cause of outlawry be found null, as if the man who was supposed to be killed be still alive… or if the outlaw was then in our service in war or castle, or if it be found that the occasion of the outlawry was not a felony.
> In these and other like cases, if the outlaws return and surrender themselves to our prison, and acquit themselves of the principal fact, the Justices shall certify us thereof.. and that the outlaws be restored to their lands and inheritances, save for their chattels, if they have given occasion of suspicion by flight.[562]

Here we see that in England the outlaw could be reinstated in society by being inlawed. And the inlawry procedures were ones that were also the source of myths and legends in England.

Let us turn again to the various accounts of Robin Hood who was portrayed a young man who was the subject of an illegitimate outlawry and who was consigned to live in Sherwood Forrest where the king's law could not reach him. As every schoolchild in the English speaking world knows, Robin Hood used his outlaw status to rally men and women who were also experiencing oppression by the crown to "rob the rich and give to the poor" until finally a new king who was less corrupt inlawed Robin

[562] Britton, pp. 44-45.

Hood, not only reinstating him in society but also rewarding him for his many good deeds while he was forced to hide from the king's sheriff of Nottingham and his armed men. Outlaws were given a certain cache because of such stories, unlike the way that outlaws were seen in Iceland at the same time.

Yet it was also true that in England unless formal inlawry was established, the outlaw not only could be killed with impunity but people were obligated to kill him if they came across him or her, wherever that might be. This is probably different from Iceland where it seems to be true that the outlaw could only be killed with impunity if the outlaw was found in Iceland and had not been inlawed. In Icelandic law, if the outlaw remained outside of Iceland the outlaw seems not to have been seen as subject to be killed with impunity, although these laws were quite complex especially about inlawry as we next see.

IV. Inlawry in Iceland

In early Icelandic law there was a "Confiscation Court" that dealt with penalizing people with lesser or full outlawry and if it was not held this could possibly result in reinstating those outlawed.

> There is to be a confiscation court for every man who is outlawed when a fortnight has passed from the Assembly at which he was outlawed. That court is to be held at the place which was his home when the case was begun against him before he became outlawed. Now if the man who got him condemned does not know where that is, the court is to be held at the home of that chieftain to whose assembly group the man who has been condemned belongs.[563]

In both full and lesser outlawry, the outlaw's property was to be confiscated to pay his debts and for the upkeep of his wife and children while he was exiled. These confiscation courts were real courts where there were jurors and witnesses who presented evidence of the thing the outlaw had done that got him outlawed and about the outlaw's financial obligations at the time of the outlawry sentence. The confiscation court was a proceeding that was in addition to, and took place after, there had been a trial in the assembly at which the sentence of outlawry was passed.

It is interesting to note the role of the chieftains in the outlawry process. While there was no king or other chief executive officer of the

[563] *Gragas I*, p. 88.

Icelandic government, there were various local officials, such as chieftains, who played a role in making sure that punishments were in fact meted out properly. The chieftains did not have other officers, such as police or army members, but they could draw on fellow group members to help with the "policing" of the outlawry punishments.

Another aspect of the Icelandic outlawry institution was that if the confiscation court was not held, especially in cases of lesser outlawry, penalties to others were assigned.

> If men do not hold a confiscation court for the men they have got condemned or if they do not hold it in accordance with law, the penalty is lesser outlawry… If they will not prosecute, then the case lies with those who had money owed them by him when he was outlawed. And if they will not prosecute, then the case lies with anyone who will. If a chieftain does not nominate a confiscation court, having been asked in accordance with law, or whatever failure on the chieftain's part causes it that the confiscation court is not held in accordance with law, the penalty for the chieftain is lesser outlawry, and the case lies with the man who asked for the confiscation court.[564]

Here we see that those who do not hold these confiscation courts when by law they should are themselves subject to the sentence of lesser outlawry. We have thus another method by which a system without police or soldiers can nonetheless enforce the rules of courts.

In addition, and now we get specifically to inlawry, *Gragas I* mandates that outlawry can be revoked as follows:

> The penalty for lesser outlawry is revoked if a confiscation court is not held for him in accordance with law; and those who should have held the confiscation court are to be prosecuted and their guilt demonstrated; and that case may be prosecuted by anyone who wishes, but the penalty of the lesser outlaw is revoked no matter who prosecutes them.[565]

This provision seems only to apply to lesser outlawry–it seems that full outlawry cannot be revoked in the above manner.

We do find the following provision which is helpful to a certain extent in understanding possible revocation of full outlawry:

---

[564] *Gragas I*, p. 95.
[565] *Gragas I*, p. 95.

> If permission is asked in the Law Council for terms of mitigation for anyone, a full outlaw or lesser outlaw, it only counts if all the men of the Law Council permit it and no one outside the Law Council forbids it by veto in such a way that those sitting in the Law Council hear it. But besides members of the Law Council no one else's words are to count in opposition to it unless they forbid it by veto.[566]

We learn here that "mitigation" of full outlawry, as well as lesser outlawry, can be accomplished through an appeal to the Law Council. But mitigation is not revocation, so there is still the question of how precisely someone who is a full outlaw has recourse to revocation of his outlawry.

One other significant provision in the *Gragas* is that a full outlaw can gain a reprieve by killing other full outlaws.

> [It is lawful] to kill outlaws for the reprieve of other outlaws who would have had the right to settle in cases they were outlawed for, other than thieving cases. If a man not himself under legal penalty kills an outlaw for reprieve of another outlaw, the last becomes an outlaw who may be given passage as soon as one outlaw is killed for his reprieve. If he kills yet another outlaw for his reprieve, then he becomes a lesser outlaw. And if he kills a third, then his reprieve becomes complete. There are the same steps of reprieve for an outlaw who kills other outlaws for his own reprieve.[567]

So, here is a significant difference between inlawry in Iceland and that in England. In England inlawry results from showing that outlawry was somehow improper or illegal; whereas in Iceland "inlawry," at least for full outlaws, comes primarily from killing three other outlaws.

It is not really surprising that Iceland has this view of "inlawry." The institution of outlawry is meant to provide meaningful punishments in a society where the government could not be counted on to administer any punishments. There is a sense that outlawry in early Icelandic law is a kind of vigilante punishment. By this I mean that it is up to the general population to mete out punishment since there are no officials of the government who will do so, largely because there are no governmental police or even a king with his sheriffs, as there was in England at the same time. And strongly encouraging outlaws to kill each other can be seen as part of the vigilante system.

---

[566] *Gragas I*, p. 98.
[567] *Gragas I*, p. 170.

The drawback to having outlaws kill each other in order to become "inlaws" is that it is likely that the most bloodthirsty killers will be the one's who are allowed back into society. Surely this is not an optimal system if the safety of the community, and especially the security of the society from killers, is to be paramount. It makes more sense to give reprieves to those outlaws who can demonstrate that they have been wrongfully convicted. But perhaps this conclusion fails to take seriously the very severe problems that result in a society where there is no executive branch of government and where people are harming one another.

V. When Law is not Backed by Threat of Imprisonment

In this final section I will reflect on some of the differences between early Icelandic law and those systems of law in ancient times, especially in classical Athens and the Roman Republic, where there were democracies and also no strong executive branch to back up the laws. In ancient societies, exile was used as a means of punishing serious crimes. So, in a sense some ancient legal systems were similar to those in Medieval Iceland and England.

Today exile may not seem like such a severe penalty but in earlier times when people depended on their families and close associates for their very survival, exile was nearly a death sentence. And if one adds to this the idea that an exile was also outside the defenses of his or her legal system then those who would kill the exile or outlaw were seen to act with impunity. So, the threat of being exiled or outlawed was a serious threat indeed. The threat of exile or outlawry is in some ways worse than the threat of imprisonment.

In ancient societies such as those in Greece and Rome, there was really no choice but to employ institutions like exile because there simply were no public prisons or police. But in Medieval Iceland, there was a conscious choice not to have a king or other chief executive. And there was already in other Medieval societies the institution of the prison and certainly, as in England, of sheriffs and other enforcement officers like the police. Of course in all these times, capital punishment was a practical alternative for the most serious crimes. As in ancient Babylonia, capital punishment and corporal punishment were employed extensively but it was seen that something like exile was nonetheless also needed.

Yet, if there is no police force or other enforcement mechanism, the threat of exile or outlawry may not be so severe. And in addition we have the very serious problem that vigilante justice will take the place of normal justice since exile and outlawry rely so heavily on the member of a given community deciding to cooperate with enforcement. Here there is room for a fair amount of uneven enforcement, even unfair enforcement, based on prejudices or longstanding feuds within a given community. The evenhandedness of the law is jeopardized when enforcement of the law is left in the hands of the general population and not in the police. The inconsistent enforcement that comes from enforcement of law by the general populace is a major issue for the idea of equity, or fundamental fairness, in law.

There is also the problem that the legitimacy of law may be hampered as well since some theorists say that law is only legitimate if it is backed by the threats of the sovereign. Unless we conceive of the general populace as the sovereign, there is no threat of the sovereign in Medieval Icelandic law. And even if the people are seen as sovereign, there is no consistency in these threats because of the inconsistent enforcement by the general populace.

Outlawry and inlawry are about membership in a group, where the members of the group act in each other's behalf. In early Icelandic law, the state was constituted by the interrelations of the Icelandic people. Since there was no ruler or even much in the way of government, the state was constituted by its membership. Removing someone from these relations was removing the person from the community and also from the state. This meant that the person so removed was no longer obligated to obey the law, but it also meant that the person was no longer subject to the protection of the laws either. Membership had its privileges and also its liabilities, as it were. We have not here addressed the problem of those who were residing legally in Iceland and England but who were not citizens with the dual status of obligations and protections.

In states that are largely or exclusively constituted by membership, exclusion from membership is a crucial form of punishment. As we have seen in this chapter, Iceland had a pure form of outlawry, where withdrawal of membership was the key component. England had a form of outlawry that was really a substitute for capital punishment when a felon could not be found. England was not largely constituted by membership, but was also constituted by a ruler and a government. Despite these differences, outlawry took on an important aura in the contemporary public accounts as well as sagas and tales of this period of the Middle Ages. The legal standing of the outlaw in turn of the millennium England and Iceland that we have just examined and in this chapter is relatively unusual in the history of legal thought. And the idea of outlawry and inlawry gives us a very good sense of how law was understood, especially how law was enforced and why it was thought that law was binding.

CHAPTER 25

THE CRIME OF DISRUPTING THE PEACE

In Medieval Iceland and England, most legal matters involved private disputes and this included what normally count today as assault-type crimes–one person assaults another and the assaulted person or his or her family or clan proceed against the assaulter. But it was recognized that some wrongs were better seen as public rather than private matters because the assault disrupted the peace in a significant way. In this chapter I will argue that this idea brings us closer to the contemporary legal thought about crimes and also connects in a significant way with the idea of outlawry we explored in the previous chapter.

In this chapter we begin with a discussion of the idea of disrupting the peace as a crime in the English Common Law. Then in the second section we explore some similar ideas in the early Icelandic law, especially concerning assault. In the third section we look at both English and Icelandic laws concerning murder. In the fourth section we tackle the idea advanced in these Medieval legal systems that some matters simply could not be subject to private settlement. And finally we try to work out how the idea of disrupting the peace changed the legal thought about criminality in the Middle Ages, an idea at the heart of our own contemporary ideas of criminality today. Throughout we will approach criminality in such a way that it relates to our previous chapter on outlawry as a sentence for especially grievous assaults.

I. Disturbing the Peace in England

Here is an important commentary on the status of criminal law in Medieval England by the distinguished nineteenth century legal scholar Sir James Stephen:

> Offenses against the State constitute the first great division of complete substantive offenses. The first and most general object of all political associations whatever is to produce and to preserve a state of things in which the various pursuits of

> life can be carried on without interruption of violence, or according to the well-known expression of our law, to keep the peace. Every crime is to a greater or lesser extent a breach of the peace, but some tend merely to break it as against some particular person or small number of persons, whereas others interfere with it on a wider scale, either by acts which strike at the State itself, the established order of Government, or by acts which affect or tend to affect the tranquility of a considerable number of persons, or an extensive local area.[568]

In some sense all crimes disturb or disrupt the peace, but some acts such as high treason have as their aim the dissolution of the State or the Government, whereas other criminal acts "affect the tranquility of a considerable number of persons or an extensive local area."[569]

Stephen points out that if treason succeeds, the State ceases to exist and then it isn't "within the scope of the criminal law. They put an end to all existing law."[570] Stephen discusses regicide as the most common form of treason:

> It is obvious that to kill the king must be the readiest and most natural means of effecting a political revolution in any kingdom, and that the attempt to do so would be the first step in such a revolution. Probably the killing of the queen and of the eldest son and heir apparent might be treated as treason by way of a sort of compliment to the king.[571]

At various points in later sections we will discuss how this idea was to fare in early Icelandic law where there was no king and no royal family. But overall, we will not mainly concern ourselves with this extreme form of disturbance of the peace but will rather examine the forms of assault that although not utterly disruptive of law, nonetheless cause major harm to the population.

---

[568] James Stephen, *A History of the Criminal Law in England*, London: Macmillan and Co., 1883, vol. 2, p. 241.
[569] Ibid.
[570] Ibid., pp. 241-242.
[571] Ibid., p. 249.

II. Disturbing the Peace in Iceland

In Medieval Icelandic law, one of the most important results of an assault is that the felon is to agree to "a peace guarantee."[572] Here, as in English Common Law, we have the central idea that after crimes have been committed, the felon is to act in various required ways to reestablish the peace that has been disrupted by the criminal act. Indeed, reconciliation between the assaulter and the one assaulted, as well as the families of both parties, is crucial to achieving "a truce" upon which the peace of the community can be reestablished. Unlike in English Common law, though, early Icelandic law seems to have preferred private settlements of most assaults. But as we have also seen in the previous chapter, some offenders are seen as having so disrupted the peace that they should remove themselves, or be removed, from the community either temporarily or permanently.

We can wonder why Iceland allowed some criminals to work out private settlements. Is this a remnant of earlier times when the wergeld was prominent? In this sense it is clear that Iceland was drawing on such heritage of the Norse societies from which Icelanders arose, since there is a section of the *Gragas I* following the long chapter on homicide that deals with what is called "the Wergeld Ring List." I will speak more about this in a moment. But it is also worth asking if the retention of or reversion to private settlement structures was due to the fact that Iceland did not have a central enforcement institution that would have likely come with a ruler and his government. Probably because there was no strong government that could settle disputes in cases where the peace had been greatly disrupted, such cases as of killing are settled privately.

Iceland relied extensively on private settlement plans. The wergeld ring list is one such plan that we will now address in some detail. In the *Gragas I*, we are told that "There are four wergeld rings fixed by law." Each ring is worth a certain amount of money or its equivalent. The ring list assigns specific members of the victim's family as entitled to receive the wergeld and specific members of the assailant's family that is required to pay the wergeld. The wergeld payments are specifically called forms of "atonement."[573]

The wergeld list followed the descent lineage of a family even to various remote cousins so that there was certain to be someone who was to receive and someone else who was to give the wergeld. It is crucial for wergeld to operate as a mechanism of nonviolent atonement that these two

---

[572] *Gragas I*, p. 183.
[573] *Gragas I*, p. 175.

parties be clearly identified as a matter of law. Unlike in earlier times, the Icelandic wergeld list also allowed for outlawry to be an acceptable form of atonement in lieu of the monetary amounts specified in the various wergeld rings.

The punishment of outlawry operated at various points in the wergeld process. Perhaps most significantly, if the assailant made a truce with the family of the victim and then breached that atonement arrangement the punishment was full outlawry. And if the terms are paid but the aspects of the peace is broken then other penalties are assessed: "If a man breaks his peace guarantee after atonement is paid, the personal compensation of every one of the payers is doubled in relation to that man, and moreover no one is to settle in such suits without prior leave."[574] We also find this very strong law near the end of the first half of the *Gragas*:

> There were causes of dispute between A and B but now they are settled and atoned with money, as the valuers valued and the tellers told and the judges judged and receivers received and carried away, the cash in full and each ounce produced, handed to him who should have it… But the one of you who tramples on treaties made or smites sureties given, he shall be an outcast despised and driven off as far and wide as ever men drive outcasts off.[575]

These various provisions are said to be based on "ancient law in our country" by which is meant primarily Norway since Iceland at this time is a relatively new country. Yet, very similar things are said in England about ancient law. In an important sense, these legal provisions concerning how to treat grievous assault are portrayed in both England and Iceland as having been true for a long time even though the laws appear to be issued in the very recent past. In the next section we look more closely at the laws concerning various forms of homicide and corresponding punishments in both England and Iceland.

III. Homicide in Iceland and England

Murder is an act that poses various challenges to any legal system since the victim of the crime is no longer alive to press his case against his assailant. In this respect murder is especially disruptive of the peace of a society since the normal avenues for treating the criminal act as a matter

---

[574] *Gragas I*, p. 183.

[575] *Gragas I*, pp. 184-185.

between two parties is upended. While a crime like treason is a straightforward assault on the government and the laws of a society, murder is only slightly less a straightforward assault on the laws since the murderer in effect takes away the party who is most aggrieved as well as the witness to the crime who in most cases has the greatest knowledge.

Let us begin with the early Icelandic laws primarily found in the *Graga*s. If an assault of a certain type takes place the penalty is lesser outlawry.

> It is prescribed that if men meet as they travel and one man makes what the law deems an assault on another, the penalty is lesser outlawry. These are five assaults deemed such by the law: if a man cuts at a man, or thrusts at him, or shoots or throws at him, or strikes at him. And it counts as an assault if a man swings a weapon and a panel gives a verdict that he meant the stroke to land, and he was moreover at such close range that for that matter it could have landed if it had not been stopped on its way…[576]

So, for these relatively minor assaults the penalty was still fairly severe–lesser outlawry, which basically meant exile for three years and loss of significant amounts of one's property.

We learn that full outlawry (generally just called "outlawry") is reserved for more serious assaults, not all of which involve killing but all forms of assault seem to involve intent to harm and creation of actual harm, not merely attempted harm.

> The sixth assault deemed such by law occurs when a man fells another, and the penalty for that is outlawry. It is a fall if a man goes down on one knee or hand, and especially if he falls further than this. The seventh assault is when one man shakes another and the penalty is outlawry. The eighth is when a man wrests something from another's grasp; the penalty is outlawry. The ninth is if a man throttles someone; the penalty is outlawry… It is also prescribed that if a man wounds someone the penalty is outlawry... If a man kills someone, the penalty is outlawry.[577]

So, these assaults are deemed sufficiently serious to warrant the grave penalty of full outlawry, where the assailant is sentenced to permanent

---

[576] *Gragas I*, p. 139.
[577] *Gragas I*, pp. 139-140.

exile and loss of all of his or her property. And it appears that the form of assaulting that is most in need of severe punishment is that killing that is intentional and completed not merely attempted.

In the case of killing, there was an additional penalty, called the killing penalty, which was an additional amount of money that was owed to the victim's family and was not merely the money owed as a matter of previous debts incurred or inheritance owed to one's heirs. In this way there was an attempt to add a kind of private settlement in the case of killing that was in addition to outlawry and other confiscations of property. In part this additional penalty seems to have been meant to placate the relatives of the victim who in some respects had the right of revenge.

In early English Common law, crimes that threatened the peace were also subject to some of the most severe punishments. The treatment of murder in particular, as well as other forms of homicide, is given clear expression in Glanvill:

> There are two kinds of homicide. The first is called murder: this is done secretly, out of sight and knowledge of all but the killer and his accomplices, and so he cannot be immediately followed by the hue and cry which is required for the relevant assize. No-one is allowed to make an accusation of this kind unless he is a blood relative of the deceased, and within this limit proof of the accusation is awarded to him who is nearer the stock of the descent, to the exclusion of the remoter.
> There is another kind of homicide which in ordinary speech is called simple homicide. In this plea no-one is allowed to prove an accusation unless he is a blood relative of the deceased or bound to him by homage or lordship, and can speak about the death from what he has seen himself.[578]

Punishments are severe for homicide but there is not the same attention to differences in punishment for these offenses as for the status of the writs and the differences in types of homicide in this early law textbook.

In Bracton, this is how offenses against the crown are understood in the context of criminal conduct:

> We must first see how a general summons having been issued [to attend] before the justices in eyre at an appointed day and place, a summons which ought to allow at least a fortnight's interval, they ought to proceed and in what order. They ought first to proceed with the pleas of the crown, in which both

[578] Glanvill, p. 174.

> major and minor criminal actions are determined, unless the lord king has ordered them to proceed in another way in some particular place... First of all, of the king's peace and justice and the breaches thereof by murderers, robbers, and burglars... And that if they have heard the hue and cry raised against such men, that immediately on hearing it they and their household, the men of their land being assembled, will follow the trail through their own land... until the wrongdoers are apprehended...[579]

Here it is murder that is mentioned first in the short list of crimes that most affect the peace of the crown.

Bracton then addresses the punishments that follow when someone has been convicted of crimes against the crown.

> [Some of these crimes that are called] capital, which lead to corporal punishment, sometimes death, sometimes dismemberment, according as they are major or minor, some are public and some private, and of the public crimes some carry a heavier punishment because of the person against whom they are directed, as the crime of lese-majesty, as where something is done against the person of the king himself, a crime which surpasses all others with respect to the punishment inflicted...[580]

Crimes that most disrupt the king's peace, including killing of the king as well as other murders, are subject to the most severe punishment. Although we also learn that in the case of killing or plotting to kill the king there is more punishment yet than simply capital punishment:

> If he is convicted he shall suffer the extreme penalty with torture, the loss of all his goods, and the perpetual disherison of his heirs, who are admitted neither to their paternal nor their maternal inheritance. For this crime is so serious that his heirs are hardly permitted their lives... Security for prosecuting having been furnished, as aforesaid, let the accused be arrested at once and consigned to gaol, nor is he to be released by pledges or bail without special instructions from the lord king, any more than if he had committed homicide.[581]

---

[579] Bracton, vol. II, 327-328.
[580] Bracton, vol. II, p. 334.
[581] Bracton, vol. II, pp. 335-336.

Thus "the capital crime called homicide that partly concerns the king, whose peace is broken, and partly the private individual who is slain wickedly, and in breach of the king's peace," is assigned the most severe of punishments.[582]

We can also see the concerns about homicide in particular in the following provision in Britton:

> If the defendant cannot aid himself by any exception, let it be in his election to defend the felony by his body, if the defendant be able to fight, or by the country; and if he will not put himself on his defense, let him be put to penance until he prays to do it. And according to the event of the battle, or of the verdict of the country, judgment shall be given. The punishment of felons who have committed homicide shall be death, with disherison of their heirs, with further punishment if the occasion requires it.[583]

Once it is established that the felon killed without justification capital punishment plus disinheriting, plus additional monetary penalties, is the punishment–similar to that of Iceland at the same time.

IV. Problems in Settling Homicide Privately

Throughout the Middle Ages, the problem of personal revenge-taking is perhaps the most important problem to be overcome by emerging criminal law systems. As we saw in earlier chapters, the Germanic tribes settling in Europe employed the wergeld as one common device introduced to make compensation for serious crimes a matter of state sanctioned penalty not vigilante justice. In addition, with the Christianization of Europe and elsewhere before the turn of the millennium, the idea of penance, a punishment from God, was also introduced to stop this-worldly revenge-taking. In the period after the turn of the millennium, we have seen England and Iceland, two nations on islands, try other means, such as outlawry, but still relied on some forms of private settlement of criminal matters.

Perhaps paradoxically we have also seen that in Iceland the threat of the public punishment of outlawry was employed to coerce the parties to reach a private settlement agreement for crimes. There were elaborate fee-schedules adopted–the ring wergeld system–that preserved some of the

[582] Bracton, vol. II, p. 340.
[583] Britton, p. 95.

older wergeld model of the Germanic tribes and made the parties more likely to employ it because of the alternative outlawry penalty. In England, the king's court was a kind of court of last resort where parties instead preferred a more localized remedy for their grievances resulting from crimes. There were methods of payment here as well that could be privately enforced.

Iceland is an especially interesting case since there was not much truly public enforcement of law in terms of governmental action–public action relied on the collective actions of the people. Outlawry relied on people to guarantee that the outlaw did in fact remain outside of the boundaries of Iceland. But more importantly the compensation court and the settlement agreements were largely privately enforced–again with the added incentive that lesser outlawry would fall upon those who did not help enforce these measures.

While there was still revenge-taking, there was also the emerging idea that allowing private individuals to settle matters by taking revenge was in some still inchoate sense harmful to the community at large. When vigilante justice pervades the society there is a sense that the society is lawless–public laws are only enforced when there is sufficient private vengeance. But then it is not the equal enforcement of the laws but really such arbitrary enforcement that it is as if the laws did not exist at all. The intermediate step away from vigilante justice is to have the larger society control revenge-taking, before the society can step fully away from private enforcement altogether.

V. Criminality as Disturbing the Peace

In this chapter we have focused on how criminality came to be seen as something both public and something that required the private actions of the populace, especially where the governmental enforcement apparatus was weak or nonexistent. The linchpin in the public approach to crime was to conceive of criminality as disturbing the public peace. In this final section we will return to Bracton and other legal theorists of the early centuries of the new millennium to try to understand why disturbing the peace became such a strong vehicle for moving the idea of criminality out of the private domain.

We have already examined some of the passages in book II of Bracton concerning the Pleas of the Crown, and we will now look at some of these passages with a somewhat different purpose:

> let one of the senior and more distinguished among [the justices] publicly declare in the presence of all the reason for their coming, the purpose of the eyre and the advantage to be derived from keeping the peace... These remarks having been made, the justices ought to betake themselves to some private place and call before them four or six or more of the greater men of the county, who are called "buzones" of the county and on whose nod the views of others depend...[they] must swear that they will not harbor outlaws, robbers, burglars, nor join with them, nor with those who harbor them, and if they know of any such they will cause them to be attached and show they have done so to the sheriff and his bailiffs.[584]

There are several things of importance we can learn from these fascinating passages.

First, the justices of the king who arrive in a county should normally explain how disturbing the peace is harmful to the county and why legal proceedings before the justices is important in a return to keeping the peace after a crime has been committed. Second, it is important that the justices enlist the nobles of the county to "nod" to the others in the county thereby adding their authority to what the king's justices will ordain. Third, the justices then get the key members of the county to swear that they will help the king in prosecuting criminals and making sure that those who have been sentenced to outlawry, for instance, will not be harbored by the people of this county.

It is curious in the account just cited from Bracton that the justices are counseled to meet with the county nobles "in private." We see here the mixing of the private and public even in this provision of the law which is clearly aimed at providing a public process for dealing with crimes. Yet it is also clear that the process described here is meant to be one that is focused on the king and his sheriffs as the ultimate judges and enforcers of violations of the criminal law. The private interactions of the county's nobles with the wrongdoers are not sufficient for providing the peace of the community.

We see similar although also somewhat different considerations as Iceland coped with the keeping of the peace. As we have seen, early Icelandic law relied on a distinctive use of the idea of outlawry, indeed the translators of the *Gragas* say: "outlawry is the predominant feature of the penal system."[585] We raised questions in the previous chapter about how exactly this system worked. And here as we consider the criminal law we

---

[584] Bracton, vol. II, pp. 327-328.

[585] *Gragas I*, introduction, p. 8.

see that such questions are now of paramount importance since the system of fines established in Iceland did not adequately deal with the most serious of criminal conduct.

The translators of the *Gragas* also provide us with an insight that makes the matter of criminal punishment even more puzzling:

> The part played by panels of neighbors is a much more distinctive Icelandic feature [than outlawry] … it must have been assumed that general local satisfaction or dissatisfaction with the man in question would come out in his neighbors' verdicts. This innovation seems to have sprung from conditions of settlement in Iceland where, to begin with, people did not have any large circle of acquaintances of accepted standing to appeal to, so that a compurgation system could hardly be introduced. The cooperative communes of neighboring householders (*hreppar*) which functioned under national law but were largely self-regulatory, must have had their origins in the same conditions.[586]

The communities were arranged into self-regulating communes, and yet we still have to understand what the enforcement mechanism was, especially if the communities were not bound together by kin relationships.

If there were self-regulating communities in early Iceland it seems to me that the tight-knit communities were probably the most important. But these were artificial communities not ones formed on the basis of natural kinship. So, like the counties that were the main political units in England at the same time some kind of pressure was needed to keep the peace. In England the pressure was external–from the king and his sheriffs. In Iceland, it seems that the pressure was internal but not in a normal sense of natural.

This is the abiding puzzle concerning Icelandic law in the Medieval period: how was a legal system without a national enforcement system or even a national government able to enforce its laws. How was the peace maintained and how were disturbances of the peace deterred? The early Icelandic communities were formed by contiguous farms settled by outsiders, that is, by people who had never lived in Iceland before. Indeed, in some ways Iceland was truly *terra nullius* so there were no preexisting kinship groups or estates dating from time immemorial as were claimed in England. Apparently people settling in Iceland decided to form a self-enforcing system of law that was primarily broken down into small

---

[586] *Gragas I*, introduction, pp. 8-9.

communes with one or more chiefs in charge but with very little force behind them.

The enforcement system in Iceland worked at maintaining the peace and deterring disturbances of the peace by social pressure. And what this shows in general is that a top-down coercive enforcement structure is not necessary for the maintenance of the rule of law. This idea, that a top down enforcement structure was crucial for a legal system, is in need of much further exploration, both practically and theoretically–certainly more than it has occasioned so far given the paucity of critical inquiry into early Icelandic law and its similarity and difference with early English Common law in the same time period.

SECTION XII:

INTERNATIONAL LAW

CHPTER 26

PEACE SETTLEMENTS

Early Icelandic law and English Common law represent law of a people who had either just settled in a barren place or people who had intermixed with Conquerors and established peoples. Yet soon after the new systems of law were to be established, there were strong outside forces that threatened the existence of these societies. In both cases the source was the same: invading Viking and other Norse nations. Yet, there were many differences as well, since in Iceland the original settlers were also Norse so the invaders were of their own group as it were, whereas in England while the Danes had formed a significant part of early England, the Norse Vikings were truly outsiders trying to take over a foreign people. In this chapter, inspired by these developments, we discuss how peace settlements were achieved and specifically what the character of the treaties was.

We will begin by looking at Icelandic law's treatment of domestic peace settlements. In the second section we look at the peace treaty signed between Iceland and Norway in the 13th century. In the third section we return to the Great Charter (Magna Charta) which among many other things established terms of peace between barons and King John in England in 1215. In the fourth section we look at the charter struck between King John and Pope Innocent in which the king gave up certain rights of England in exchange for various remissions of sins and mercy from the pope. Finally, we look to the various documents considered in these sections for a sense of how peace settlement was understood in the 13th century in Iceland and England.

I. Domestic Peace Settlements in Iceland

An important part of a legal settlement in Iceland often involved a required "truce speech" where the parties pledge not to seek revenge or renege on a reconciliation agreement. Here is a selection from the *Gragas I* on this topic:

> All know the events of the discord between A and B but now their friends have intervened and seek to reconcile them. Now A, on behalf of his heir and all the people for whom he has the right to give truce, gives truce to B until the settlement meeting they have appointed, and B accepts truce from A for himself and his heirs and all the people for whom he needs to accept a truce. And first in this truce is God Himself, who is supreme, and all saints and every sacred relic, the pope in Rome and the patriarch our king and our bishops, and all Christian people. I nominate twelve men to join in this truce between A and B who now stand on opposite sides in these matters, and he is to name the twelve men. After that man who makes the truce speech is to name two or more witnesses "to witness that this truce which has just been set shall be full and firm between all men who come to this gathering and for as long as men remain at this meeting and until each man comes back to his home"... May God be gracious to him who keeps truce but harsh to him who breaks it... if a man is put under penalty for truce-breaking, then the twelve men who were nominated to join in the truce have the right to take his personal compensation from his goods, forty-eight ounce units.[587]

Here we see that the language of truces and settlements was used in domestic matters in order to convey, in part, the seriousness of the parties agreeing to stop revenge-taking and wait for the results of court proceedings.

We also find that when court cases are indeed settled the parties must deliver a speech, the "Peace Guarantee Speech," which commits the parties to accept the terms of the settlement and not to work to undermine these terms. There was also a very stiff penalty for those who then failed to keep to this peace guarantee.

> You are now to be men reconciled... You shall share knife and meat-bit and all things with each other like family and not like foes. If matters come up between you that are other than smooth, you shall redress with cash and not redden the spear. But the one of you who tramples on treaties made or smites at sureties given, he shall be an outcast, despised and driven off as far and wide as ever men drive outcasts off... He shall shun churches and Christian people, house of God and man, every home save hell.[588]

[587] *Gragas I*, pp. 183-184.
[588] *Gragas I*, pp. 184-185.

So, those who break these peace settlements will be sentenced to be outcasts, and this is true of the worst of outcasting since it means that no place will ever be their home again, except hell.

II. Peace Treaty between Iceland and Norway

Here is a translation of the agreement reached in 1262 of what might be called a vassal treaty between Iceland and Norway:

> 1. that under oath they agree to pay in perpetuity, a tribute amounting to twenty ells for each payer of the thing-tax to his Majesty King Hakon and to King Magnus, and at the same time they yield to them their country and agree to become their subjects. This tribute is to be collected by chief administrators of the local districts (*hreppstjorar*) and then brought by them aboard a ship and placed in the hands of the king's deputy, at which point they shall have no further responsibility with regard to these payments.
> 2. In consideration hereof the king will let us enjoy peace and the Icelandic laws.
> 3. Six ships are to sail from Norway to Iceland during each of the next two summers; from that time forth their number shall be decided according to what the king and the most judicious farmers in Iceland believe to be in the best interests of the country.
> 4. Any inheritance which falls to Icelanders in Norway is to be given to them, however long it may remain due, as soon as the rightful heirs, or their legal representatives, present themselves to claim it.
> 5. The land-dues are to be abolished.
> 6. In Norway, Icelanders are to have rights as advantageous as they have ever enjoyed there and which you (King Hakon) have yourself determined in your letters; you are to maintain peace for us in so far as God gives you the strength to do so.
> 7. We accept the earl as our overlord so long as he keeps faith with you and peace with us.
> 8. We and our descendants shall keep faith with you so long as you and your descendants keep this covenant, but be free of all the obligations if, in the opinion of the best of men, it is broken.[589]

---

[589] Jon Johannesson, *A History of the Old Icelandic Commonwealth*, translated by Haraldur Bessason, Winnipeg, Manitoba: The University of Manitoba Press, 1974, pp. 282-283.

This is best seen as a vassal treaty in that Iceland gives up the right to govern itself in exchange for protection from the state, Norway, which will now incorporate Iceland into its realm.

Yet, as Johannesson tells us, the terms of the agreement were set by Iceland making the agreement more complex than at first it may seem:

> Although the term "peace-treaty" (*sattargjord*) is employed in the context of the covenant, it is really, in its form, a unilateral agreement, as it was composed by the Icelanders alone. But although there is no mention of it, one must surmise that the approval of the king's representative was obtained. On the other hand, the covenant is bi-lateral in content in that it takes into account both *the responsibilities* undertaken by the Icelanders and *the rights* they stipulated in exchange for their commitments.[590]

In what follows in this section we will explore some of the significant points of this "peace settlement."

Gunnar Karlsson provides a clear summary of three of the most important points of the treaty between Iceland and Norway:

> It can hardly be said that this document gives a clear prescription of the intended constitutional status of Iceland. Three major things, however, are clear. First, the Icelanders were to become subjects of the Norwegian Crown, whereby the preservation of peace was to become the king's obligation. Second, Iceland was to remain a separate legal district, although no rules were set out about legislative powers in the country. Third, rule of taxation is clear; the stipulation refers to ells of homespun, which was originally a strip of marketable homespun (c. 50 cm. 91.6 ft.) long, two ells (c. 1 yard) broad… This would not be called heavy taxation nowadays, but by medieval standards it may have been quite severe.[591]

So, basically Iceland gave up the right to govern itself and agreed to pay a perhaps heavy tax in exchange for the Norwegian king's pledge to protect the Icelanders and respect their ancient rights. This is similar in important respects to other peace agreements in the thirteenth century, a subject we take up in greater detail in the final section of this chapter.

---

[590] Ibid., p. 283.

[591] Gunnar Karlsson, *The History of Iceland*, Minneapolis, MN: University of Minnesota Press, 2000, p. 84.

One question worth asking is why Iceland would agree to these terms, even to propose them in the first place, when the terms seem so strongly to favor Norway. One answer offered by commentators is that Iceland could no longer enforce its laws and maintain internal peace without some kind of coercive force. But the next question is why Iceland didn't develop its own internal police force and army rather than turning to a foreign power for this enforcement. It is very interesting to note, as Karlsson does, that during the internal debates about what to do about lawlessness, the envoy sent by Norway to Iceland, who was a cardinal, "called it improper that this country did not serve under some king, as all other countries of the world."[592] Of course, the cardinal could have been answered by the establishment of a king from among Icelanders rather than importing one from Norway.

III. Magna Carta and Domestic Agreements in England

The most famous of the internal agreements in Medieval England is Magna Carta, an agreement struck between King John and the chief barons of England where John was forced to recognize various rights of Englishmen in exchange for the barons agreeing to provide money for the various wars that King John wished to wage. Here is a bit of the wording of that Great Charter from the Preamble and Chapter One:

> John, by the grace of God, king of England, lord of Ireland, duke of Normandy and Aquitaine, and count of Anjou, to the archbishops, bishops, abbots, earls, barons, justiciars, foresters, sheriffs, stewards, servants, and to all his bailiffs and liege subjects, greeting. Know that, having regard to God and for the salvation of our souls… [we have granted as underwritten]…
> In the first place we have granted to God, and by this our present charter confirmed for us and our heirs for ever that the English church shall be free… We have also guaranteed to all freemen of our kingdom, for us and our heirs forever, all the underwritten liberties, to be had and held by them and their heirs, of us and our heirs forever.[593]

---

[592] Ibid., p. 86.

[593] *Magna Carta*, 1215, in *Magna Carta: A Commentary on the Great Charter of King John*, translated with an introduction by William Sharp McKechnie, Glasgow: James Maclehose and Sons, 1914, 2000, pp. 186 and 191.

In exchange for the king guaranteeing many "ancient" rights, the barons agreed to keep paying taxes to the king according to the schedules of payment of old.

As we saw earlier, it is of interest that King John was not happy to be forced to sign the Magna Carta at Runnymede in 1215. Indeed, he prevailed upon the pope at the time to condemn the agreement as null and void before any of the provisions had been enacted. Kings were considered to be heads of state just as popes were heads of the church, and apparently they each understood that their interests were best served by protecting each other at this time. Indeed we have seen in the case of Iceland that the cardinal sent by Norway to intervene in Icelandic affairs argued that they should have a king ruling them, a position that may seem strange since, on the face of it, the church did not appear to have any clear stake in the dispute about whether Iceland should affiliate under Norwegian rule. In the next section we see another aspect of the connection between kings and popes, where the king of England was forced to accept the supremacy of the pope in certain matters, signaling that the popes had at least as much power as kings. And peace treaties between kings and popes were proposed to spell out the domains of each of these powerful rulers.

IV. Charter between England and the Pope

For an example of a kind of external peace settlement in England, let us turn to the document called "John's Concession of England to the Pope" from 1213, which begins in a very similar way to that of Magna Carta.

> John, by the grace of God, king of England, lord of Ireland, duke of Normandy and Aquitaine, count of Anjou, to all the faithful of Christ who shall look upon the present charter, greeting. We wish it to be known to all of you, through this our charter, furnished with our seal, that inasmuch as we had offended in many ways God and our mother the holy church, and in consequence are known to have very much needed the divine mercy, and cannot offer anything worthy of making due satisfaction to God and to the church unless we humiliate ourselves and our kingdoms: - we wishing to humiliate ourselves for Him who humiliated Himself for us unto death, the grace of the Holy Spirit inspiring, not induced by force or compelled by fear, but of our own good and spontaneous will and by the common counsel of our barons, do offer and freely concede to God and His holy apostles Peter and Paul and to our mother the holy Roman church, and to our pope Innocent

> and to his catholic successors, the whole kingdom of England, and the whole kingdom of Ireland, with all their rights and appurtenances, for the remission of our own sins and that of our whole race, as well as for the living as for the dead; and now receiving and holding them as it were a vassal from God and the Roman church... As a sign moreover of this our perpetual obligation and concession ... the Roman church shall receive yearly a thousand marks, sterling... saving to us and to our heirs our rights and liberties and regalia... and we bind ourselves and our successors not to act counter to them. And if we or our successors shall presume to attempt this... he shall lose his right to the kingdom, and this charter of our obligation and concession shall always remain firm.[594]

Like the peace settlement struck between Iceland and Norway, this agreement struck between England's King John and Pope Innocent is a vassal treaty. At least at this time, the king of England had to recognize that the pope was more powerful than the king concerning these important matters.

V. Peace Settlements in the 13th Century

Peace settlements and treaties were employed extensively in Medieval law, both domestically and internationally, in England and Iceland in the thirteenth century. This is a kind of self-help in which people were held accountable by making them promise to accept punishments if those people violated the law. The act of agreement to maintain or reestablish the peace, accompanied by an oath, is a way to bind the wrongdoer to accept, and not interfere with, the punishment institutions of the society. This act of acceptance of the person's role in the peace is an enforcement mechanism that does not rely on the fear of the police or the army and is suited to the situation faced in the Middle Ages where the police or army were weak or nonexistent. And in the case of rulers binding themselves there was probably little other alternative.

Let us turn to some of the oaths that accompanied the agreements of the 13th century. Here is the oath that the people of Iceland took in their peace agreement with the Norwegian king:

---

594 King John, *John's Concession of England to the Pope*, in *Select Historical Documents of the Middle Ages*, translated by Ernest F. Henderson, London: George Bell & Sons, 1892, pp. 430-431.

> To this end I place my hand on the Holy Bible and call God to witness that under oath I do grant King Hakon and Magnus the land as well as the allegiance of a royal subject and tribute in perpetuity according to conditions named here and as our written agreement bears testimony. May God be as gracious to me as I am truthful; as wrathful if I lie.[595]

As we have seen, this was really a unilateral agreement and hence fits the model of the other peace agreements signed by Icelanders who have broken the law.

In the *Gragas*, we find the terms of the "peace guarantee speech" that Icelanders, both offenders and victims, must articulate as follows:

> Now the pair of you hold the same book–and on the book now lies the money which A pays in atonement for himself and his heir born and not born, conceived and not conceived, named and not named. B takes guarantees of peace and A gives everlasting guarantees of peace which shall be kept while mold and men survive.
> Now A and B agreed and of one mind wherever they meet on land or water, on ship or ski, at sea or on steed, sharing oars or bailer, thwart on deck plank if need be, each reconciled with the other as father with son or son with father in all their dealings. Now they put their hands together, A and B. Keep the peace well in accordance with the will of Christ and of all those men who now hear the guarantee speech. May he who keeps the peace have God's grace but let him who breaks true guarantees of peace have His wrath, but His grace him who keeps them. Be prosperous your reconciliation and let us be witnesses of it who are here present.[596]

Notice that the form of this agreement is much the same as the agreement of peace with the Norwegian king–an appeal to God to act wrathfully against the peace breaker and mercifully toward the peace keeper.

In English law of the thirteenth century we also find an oath that is employed to seal Magna Carta:

> Wherefore it is our will, and we firmly enjoin, that the English Church be free, and that the men in our kingdom have and hold all the aforesaid liberties, rights, and concessions, well

[595] Translated in Jon Johannesson, *A History of the Old Icelandic Commonwealth*, Winnipeg, Manitoba: University of Manitoba Press, 1974, p. 283.
[596] *Gragas I*, p. 185.

> and peaceably, free and quietly, fully and wholly, for themselves and their heirs, of us and our heirs, in all respects and in all places for ever, as is aforesaid. An oath, moreover, has been taken as well on our parts on the part of the barons, that all these conditions aforesaid shall be kept in good faith and without evil intent. Given under our hand–the above-named and many others being witnesses–in the meadow which is called Runnymede, between Windsor and Staines, on the fifteenth day of June, in the seventeenth year of our reign.[597]

King John makes the agreement here also seem as if it is a unilateral agreement, except that the barons also signed a parallel agreement as well, making the whole a bi-lateral agreement.

We can also see how King John handled treaties with foreign powers as well in the following oath connected to John's Concession to the Pope:

> I, John, by the grace of God, king of England and lord of Ireland, from this hour forth will be faithful to God and St. Peter and the Roman church and my lord pope Innocent and his successors, who are ordained in a catholic manner: I shall not bring it about by deed, word, consent or counsel, that they lose life or members or be taken captive. I will impede their being harmed, if I know of it, and will cause harm to be removed from them if I shall be able: otherwise as quickly as I can I will intimate it or tell of it to such person as I believe for certain will inform them. Any counsel which they entrust to me through themselves or through their envoys or through their letters, I will keep secret, nor will I knowingly disclose it to anyone to their harm. I will aid to the best of my ability in holding and defending against all men the patrimony of St. Peter, and especially the kingdom of England and the kingdom of Ireland. So may God and these holy Gospels aid me.
> I myself bearing witness in the house of the Knights Templars near Dover in the presence of… on the 15th day of May, in the fourteenth year of our reign.[598]

Here King John, representing England and Ireland, signs a peace settlement with Pope Innocent, representing the Catholic Church and the

---

[597] Magna Carta, Chapter Sixty-Three, in *Magna Carta: A Commentary on the Great Charter of King John*, p. 479.

[598] King John, "John's Concession of England to the Pope," in *Select Historical Documents of the Middle Ages*, translated and edited by Ernest F. Henderson, London: George Bell & Sons, 1892, pp. 431-432.

Vatican. As we have seen the terms are highly similar to the internal peace agreement King John signed with his own barons.

We have seen four different forms of peace settlement and we will now say a bit about each form before concluding this chapter. The first, and in many ways the most unusual form of peace settlement is drawn between two parties each of whom are human persons–a party who is the victim of a harm and a party who perpetrated the harm. This internal peace settlement comes to us from medieval Iceland. As we have seen, this peace settlement was very important for a society that had no ruler or police force that could enforce the law. It is also of importance that the agreement by the perpetrator is to make amends and the victim to accept the amends, and that both parties would not pursue revenge against the other. Here the parties are individual people, unlike the next peace agreement which conceives of the people as a collectivity that can be represented by those of noble birth.

In England we find another form of internal peace agreement: that reached between the king and the barons, where the barons represented the people of England as a collectivity. Magna Carta was the kind of internal peace agreement that guaranteed the rights of the people and granted to the king the right to demand payment of taxes and to have his laws followed. Magna Carta was thus important for maintaining peace within England in the Middle Ages. This is an internal peace agreement since no parties outside of England are involved. It is unusual since the barons stand in for the "people" and are one party which is opposed to the king representing the government.

We find a third kind of peace settlement in which the people of Iceland, as a collectivity, make an agreement with a foreign head of state, the king of Norway. This is an external peace agreement in that a foreigner is a party to the agreement. This would be a standard kind of agreement today if it were not for the fact that this treaty is not between two heads of state. Indeed, what makes this treaty unique, as with many other things in Iceland, is that it is the people not the head of state in Iceland that makes the agreement with the king of Norway. And of course this is because there was no head of state in Iceland at this time. The "head of state" was the people sitting as a collectivity in assembly.

The fourth kind of peace settlement is the most common, a pact between heads of state. But our example is somewhat unusual as well in that we have the king of England signing an agreement with the pope. The pope is not strictly speaking a head of state but a head of a religion. It is true that the pope had armies at his command and even reigned over a territory. But the treaty is really about the religious members of the church rather than about the political interests of the pope. Nonetheless, this treaty is an external peace agreement that most closely resembles those of today.

So, we have four models of peace agreements, two internal and two external, but like many things in the Middle Ages, each of these agreements is unusual in contemporary terms. And each of these forms of agreement were extant in the thirteenth century–in the middle of the Middle Ages as it were. In each form of agreement we have a different way to conceptualize the people and the interests of their country. Yet in all four, it is peace that is the object of the agreement.

Concerns about peace can involve worries about external threats and also worries about internal disruptions and harm. In some ways, the idea of outlawry that we have examined in previous chapters displays how being sent out of the country is one way to deal with those who are threats to the internal peace. But Magna Carta shows a different concern, a worry about the increasing power of the king and the harm he can do to the people of his own country. And we find that external forces can be both problematic and also helpful to maintaining the peace. In the case of Iceland, the peace treaty was drafted in order to gain help from the Norwegian king to deal with internal problems in Iceland that apparently could no longer be dealt with by Icelanders on their own.

The Church plays a role in some of the peace agreements in the thirteenth century. King John seemed to see the usefulness of the pope for maintaining peace in England. Indeed, King John also managed to get the pope to intervene in English affairs to nullify Magna Carta. We saw that the legate sent to Iceland to argue for the king of Norway made his case on the basis of the claim that it was ordained by God that all societies should be ruled by kings. In the early 14th century, Marsilius of Padua wrote a very important text that is called "The Defender of the Peace." This text was roundly condemned by church officials because it blamed them for being the greatest impediment to peace in these times. We have seen that the Church did indeed intervene in the internal affairs of countries like England and Iceland. Yet, we have not seen what Marsilius did, namely that the Church was the greatest impediment to peace. But we will have to reserve judgment on this issue until we examine the arguments of Marsilius in future chapters.

PART D:

NEO-ARISTOTELIAN JURISPRUDENCE

INTRODUCTION TO PART D

In these chapters we find ourselves toward the end of the Medieval period where there are philosophers from several very different backgrounds who made major contributions to legal and political thought. Because of this bounty of riches, we will spend our time with these theorists and only occasionally dip into the legal practice of this period. The philosophers all have one thing in common: they claim Aristotle as their inspiration and defend a version of natural law theory that Aristotle also seemed to have embraced. The philosophers we will consider are first, Averroes, the Arabic interpreter of Aristotle who tried to reconcile Aristotle with the Quran and related Islamic texts. Second, is Moses Maimonides, perhaps the greatest Jewish philosopher of all time, who worked to reconcile the Torah and Talmud with Aristotelian philosophy. Then, third, we have Thomas Aquinas, the monumental expositor of Catholic natural law theory, who was also a committed Aristotelian, calling Aristotle simply "The Philosopher" (he also called Averroes simply "The Interpreter"). And then our fourth thinker is the Italian secular theorist, Marsilius of Padua, who argued that a true Aristotelian should actually reject the claims of the Catholic Church to supremacy in jurisprudential matters. These four Medieval philosophers: Averroes, Maimonides, Aquinas, and Marsilius, are such important legal and political thinkers that we will spend all of the following chapters of Part D of this book on their writings.

Section XIII:

Natural Law, Equity, and Procedural Law

CHAPTER 27

DIVINE LAW

We begin these chapters by examining the role played by certain religious texts, especially the Quran, the Torah, and the Gospels, in the legal and political thought of the Neo- Aristotelians philosophers of the 12th through 14th centuries CE. The religious texts are said to transmit God's divine law for humans and also to be the guiding light for those legislators tasked with creating human law. For three of our thinkers, the divine law is higher than human law. Indeed, there is a reference to Antigone's adherence to a higher law in defying the king's declaration that no one should bury her brother. The eternal law is properly the higher law, with the divine law seen as the way the eternal law was transmitted to humans by the major religious texts of the religions of Islam, Judaism, and Catholic Christianity. Marsilius also supports the idea of a higher law, but is critical of the idea that the Pope or other Catholic Church officials have any special authority in the domain of human legislation–God's eternal law, as the divine law texts are interpreted to mean by various religious leaders, is appropriate for matters of religion but not of civil law.

In the first section of this chapter we will discuss the various approaches to the eternal law of God that undergirds both divinely inspired religious texts and also natural law, which is itself the subject of the next chapter. Then in the second section we examine how Averroes approaches divine law. And in the third section, we see how Maimonides understands divine law. This is followed by the fourth section on Aquinas and his elaborate treatment of the relationship between eternal law and divine law. In the final section we examine the criticisms that Marsilius makes of some of the arguments advanced by the religiously oriented Neo-Aristotelians who preceded him.

I. The Eternal Law as God's Higher Law

As I just indicated, a good place to start this discussion is with the ancient Greek drama *Antigone*, referred to by some of our thinkers to help us make initial sense of the idea of an eternal "everlasting" law. Here is Antigone speaking:

> Yes; for it was not Zeus that had published me the edict; not such are the laws set among men by the justice who dwells with the gods below; nor deemed I that thy decrees were of such force, that a mortal could override the unwritten and unfailing statutes of heaven. For their life is not of today or yesterday, but from all time, and no man knows when they were first put forth.[599]

Here is a text from Sophocles that Aristotle himself refers to in order to ask about whether there is a higher law than that law created by earthly lawmakers. It is interesting that Averroes also refers to Antigone in explaining the universal law, as we will see. We get a clear sense of how a higher law is understood and when that law can be appealed to in cases where a conflict of human law exists.

The eternal law is a law that has no known beginning or end and is connected to the dictates of God. Here is Aquinas:

> a law is nothing else but a dictate of practical reason emanating from a ruler who governs a perfect community. Now it is evident, granted that the world is ruled by Divine Providence, as was stated in I, 22, A1-2, that the whole universe is governed by Divine Reason. Wherefore the very Idea of the government of things in God the Ruler of the universe, has the nature of a law. And since the Divine Reason's conception of things is not subject to time but is eternal, according to *Prov.* 8:23, therefore it is that this kind of law must be called eternal.[600]

We see several things in this brief quotation. First, the argument is premised on two things being true without proof, that the world is ruled by God, and that a quotation from the Biblical book of Proverbs can establish the validity of a premise in the argument. Both of these ideas are also found in Averroes and Maimonides, for they assume the existence of God who has certain powers and also that religious texts can be treated as conveying truths.

---

[599] Quoted in J. Budziszewski, *Commentary on Thomas Aquinas's Treatise on Law*, Cambridge: Cambridge University Press, 2014, p. 60.

[600] Aquinas, *Treatise on Law*, Question 91, A1-4, translated by Budziszewski, p. 64.

Aquinas gives us a sense of what eternal laws are and which are the laws that other types of law, such as divine and natural law, participate in. We will talk of the "participates in" relation a bit later in this chapter and the next. For the moment I wish to highlight that eternal law for Aquinas, as well as for the other religiously oriented Neo-Aristotelians, is simply God's law, the higher law that Antigone and others have spoken of over the millennia.

Here is how Maimonides characterizes God's law in his multi-volume work, the *Mishneh Torah*:

> All the precepts which Moses received on Sinai, were given together with their interpretation, as it is said, "And I will give to you the tables of stone, and the law, and the commandment" (Ex. 24:12). "The law" refers to the Written Law; "the commandment," to its interpretation. God bade us fulfill the Law in accordance with "the commandment." This commandment refers to that which is called the Oral Law. The whole of the law was written by our teacher before his death, in his own hand.[601]

Here God's law is characterized as the law that was presented to Moses by God in both oral and written form. The written law was a scroll to be kept by each tribe of the Israelites in "the Ark for a testimony."[602] And the law of God was not to be added to or diminished from.

And here is how Averroes understands what are called universal laws that we find in his commentary on Aristotle's *Rhetoric*:

> The laws which define what is unjust and what is not unjust are those that are specific to a particular group of inhabitants in the city and those that are common to all inhabitants in the city. Of these two types, there are written laws and there are unwritten laws. By unwritten laws, I mean those that naturally exist in all people… These laws are also generally called universal laws in this respect. Nobody knows when these laws were laid down and who laid them down… This is like what Aristotle has said about a man famous among [the Greeks]. When it was reported that this man was not properly buried according to the law of his country, the excuse given about the manner of his burial was that he was buried according to the universal law, which is

[601] Maimonides, *Maimonides Introduction to Mishneh Torah*, in *A Maimonides Reader*, edited by Isadore Twersky, Springfield, NJ: Behrman House, Inc., 1972, p. 35.
[602] Ibid.

> the law of nature, and therefore the manner of his burial was just and not unjust.[603]

For Averroes, universal, or eternal laws, are laws that do not merely apply to specific groups or specific cities, but which are God's law for all people.

We finish this section with a passage from Marsilius on the different kinds of law in a polity:

> law can be considered in two ways: in one way, simply in itself, so that it does no more than give an indication of what is just or unjust, advantageous or harmful; and as such it is called the science or doctrine of right. In a second way it can be considered inasmuch as a command given in respect of its observation, which coerces by means of penalty or reward meted out in this world...[604]

Marsilius goes on to say that some acts cannot be coerced by means of earthly penalties and rewards and instead require coercion in terms of heavenly penalties and rewards. Marsilius does not regard the latter as higher or somehow better than the former. We will spend more time later on Marsilius's views.

So, all the Medieval Neo-Aristotelians recognize earthly laws as well as laws that are in some sense beyond the earthly domain. All but Marsilius talk of a law that is eternal or universal and everlasting, and call that law a higher law. As we have seen the speech by Antigone is a model of how the everlasting law is given priority over even valid earthly law. As we will see the higher law is identified as a moral or religious law that has been handed to humans in religious texts that are said to be God's word. In the following sections we will look at how the divine law, the received word of God, was understood in quite different religious traditions: Catholic Christianity, Judaism, and Islam, before returning to the critical comments of the secular Marsilius.

---

603 Averroes, *Averroes's Middle Commentary on the Book of Rhetoric*, Book I.13.2, in *Three Arabic Treatises on Aristotle's Rhetoric*, translated by Lahcen Elyazghi Ezzaher, Carbondale, IL: Southern Illinois University Press, 2015, p. 163.

604 Marsilius of Padua, *The Defender of the Peace*, translated by Annabel Brett, Cambridge: Cambridge University Press, 2005, p. 53.

II. Divine Law for Averroes

Averroes, like Maimonides who is roughly his contemporary, expresses the idea that divine law is law especially for followers of Islam but also for all humans. For Averroes, the Quran is the source of Islamic divine law, but Aristotle is also a source of the law that Averroes discusses. Aristotle did discuss universal or eternal law as did other ancient Greeks when addressing Antigone's conflict about whether to obey the law of her king or the law of gods. But Aristotle did not think that the Greek laws of his day were divine laws, indeed there are few specific references to eternal law of the gods in Aristotle's writings.

In trying to reconcile Aristotle's philosophy with the Quran and other sources of divine law, Averroes sought also to reconcile reason with faith. Here is how Averroes reconciles philosophical views on justice with religious views:

> With respect to God's justice and injustice, the Ash'arites held a very odd view from the standpoint of both reason and religion. They took a position on this issue which is not only one which was not proposed by Scripture, but also runs counter to it. They maintained that, regarding this matter, the visible world differs from the invisible world, claiming that in the visible world justice and injustice are attributed [to a person] by virtue of certain restrictions religion imposes on his actions. Thus, whenever a person performs what is considered just from the standpoint of religion, his action is just; but whoever performs an action, which religion regards as unjust, is unjust. They added that if one is not obliged or restrained by religion, there will be no actions performed by him that can be described as just or unjust, so that all his actions are just. Accordingly they committed themselves to the view that here on earth there is nothing that is just or unjust. This view is the utmost absurdity. It follows [on this view] that nothing [in the visible world] is good or bad in itself. Yet it is self-evident that justice is good and injustice bad...[605]

For Averroes, arguments from faith or religion and arguments from reason are reconciled in that religion does not make things just or unjust but merely provides education so that people can see for themselves what is

---

[605] Averroes, *Faith and Reason*, translated by Ibrahim Najjar, Oxford: One World, 2001, p. 115.

just or unjust. And yes, God has made unjust people but God is not unjust for doing so.[606]

Averroes argues throughout his most significant works, especially his so-called trilogy, that philosophical interpretation inspired by Aristotle has a strong role in the interpretation of divine works such as the Quran. Here is a comment from the translator of one of Averroes's works, *The Decisive Treatise*:

> the *Decisive Treatise* is characterized above all by the legal context in which Averroes couches his whole exposition as well by his repeated references to, and even attacks upon, the jurists and dialectical theologians. His abundant recourse to Quranic verses and to language highly evocative of the Muslim revelation amply indicates that he seeks to present this argument as something like a plea before a tribunal in which the divine Law of Islam is the sole authority… his goal is to determine the connection between this Law and wisdom, or philosophy. Even though he defends or explains the latter in terms set by the former, he does not thereby concede its subservience… Neither priority nor ascendance is at issue: the connection to be determined is close to one of parity–that is, agreement on all levels.[607]

Averroes indeed argues that the divine "Law makes it obligatory to reflect upon existing things by means of the intellect… by means of intellectual syllogistic reasoning."[608] And it is to Aristotle that Averroes turns for the kind of syllogistic reasoning that he believes to be needed by those who would interpret the divine law.

Averroes provides us with what he calls a scientific understanding of divine law and jurisprudence, as in the following passage:

> You ought to know that what is intended by the Law is only to teach true science and true practice. True science is cognizance of God (may He be blessed and exalted) and of all the existing things as they are, especially the venerable ones among them;

---

[606] See the Preface to the translation of Averroes's *Faith and Reason*, ibid., pp. 1x-xiv.

[607] Translators introduction to Averroes's *Decisive Treatise and Epistle Dedicatory*, translated by Charles E. Butterworth, Provo, Utah: Brigham Young University Press, 2008, pp. xix-xx.

[608] Averroes, "Decisive Treatise," in *Decisive Treatise and Epistle Dedicatory*, translated by Charles E. Butterworth, Provo, Utah: Brigham Young University Press, 2008, p. 2.

> and cognizance of happiness in the hereafter and of misery in the hereafter. True practice is to follow the actions that promote happiness and to avoid the actions that promote misery; and cognizance of these actions is what is called "practical science." These [actions] are divided into two divisions. One is the apparent, bodily actions. The science of these is called "jurisprudence." The second division is actions of the soul–like gratitude, patience, and other moral habits that the Law calls to or bans. And the science of these is what is called "asceticism" and "the sciences of the hereafter."[609]

Jurisprudence is the philosophical science that concerns the study of law here and now whereas asceticism is the study of law in the afterlife. In both cases, divine law guides human behavior and both philosophy and religion have a place in these studies.

In Averroes's "Epistle Dedicatory" we also find a few comments that are useful at this early stage in our examination of Neo-Aristotelian jurisprudence.

> How can it be conceived that the Peripatetics [Aristotelians] among the sages are of the opinion that eternal knowledge does not include particulars, when they are of the opinion that it is the reason for premonition with respect to dreams, revelation, and inspiration. This is what appeared to us as a way of resolving this doubt. It is a matter to be neither disputed nor doubted. God is one who conduces to what is correct and guides to the truth.[610]

Aristotelians are especially well-versed in the kind of method that is needed for religious texts like the Quran. And Averroes also claims that "the group [of philosophers] is the people who make the most of them [the divine Laws] and have the most faith in them."[611]

---

[609] Ibid., p. 23.

[610] Averroes, 'Epistle Dedicatory," in *Decisive Treatise and Epistle Dedicatory*, translated by Charles E. Butterworth, Provo, Utah: Brigham Young University Press, 2008, p. 42.

[611] Averroes, "Appendix," in *Decisive Treatise and Epistle Dedicatory*, translated by Charles E. Butterworth, Provo, Utah: Brigham Young University Press, 2008, p. 43.

III. Divine Law for Maimonides

Here are several passages from Maimonides's *Guide* where he spells out how he sees the divine law:

> the facility or difficulty of the Law should not be estimated with reference to the passions of the wicked, vile, morally corrupt men, but should be considered with reference to the man who is perfect among the people. For it is the aim of this Law that everyone should be such a man. Only that Law is called by us divine Law...
> Law that takes pains to inculcate correct opinions with regard to God, may he be exalted in the first place, and with regard to the angels, and that desires to make men wise, to give him understanding, and to awaken his attention, so that he should know the whole of that which exists in its true form–you must know that this guidance comes from Him, may He be exalted, and that this Law is divine.[612]

Here Maimonides tells us that *divine* law has as its aim to make humans perfect–and on the assumption that *human* law has as its aim only to stop us from harming one another. Divine law aims at wisdom and understanding–again a very different goal from that of human law that only aims to get people to minimally cooperate with each other.

In the *Guide* we also find a clear statement of the fact that the law handed down to Moses is a written law for all times.

> the prophesy of *Moses our Master* is different from that of the others, we shall say that the call to the Law followed necessarily from that apprehension alone. For nothing similar to the call addressed to us by *Moses our Master* has been made before him by any one of those we know who lived in the time between Adam and him. Correspondingly, it is a fundamental principle of our Law that there will never be another Law. Hence according to our opinion there never has been a Law and there never will be a Law except the one that is the Law of *Moses our Master*... As for Moses, you know what was said to him, what he said, and what all the people said to him: *This day we have seen that God doth speak, and so on.*[613]

---

612 Maimonides, *Guide of the Perplexed*, translated by Shlomo Pines, Chicago: University of Chicago Press, 1963, vol. I, pp. 381 and 384.
613 *Guide*, pp. 378-380.

The law that Moses was handed and which he then transmitted to the Jews was the divine law of God, in the account given by Maimonides.

It is of interest that Maimonides thought that the scriptures handed down to Moses had a special status, different from other supposed scriptures. The Quran, for instance, recognizes the Biblical scriptures of Moses as also sources of divine law. And this is also true of Aquinas although he takes the typical Christian stance that the "New" Testament is superior to the "Old" Testament, even as he allows that the Old Testament is a source of divine law. Maimonides does not here seem to recognize sources of divine law in the other great religions of his time.

In Maimonides great work, the *Mishneh Torah*, we also find that the law of Moses is the divine law.

> Every Israelite is under an obligation to study Torah… Among the great sages of Israel, some were hewers of wood, some drawers of water, while others were blind. Nevertheless, they devoted themselves by day and by night to the study of the Torah. They are included among the transmitters of the tradition in the direct line from Moses.[614]

Here we face the idea that the Torah, the first five books of the Hebrew Bible, is regarded as the direct word of God handed to Moses. And the prophets and other interpreters of the Torah (presumably including Maimonides himself) are also transmitting God's divine law.

In general, divine law for Jews, as for Medieval Muslims and Christians, is truly law but also truly God's word. In this respect, the Bible, Quran, and Gospels are religious texts but also legal texts–for divine law is both the expression of the word of the divine God and also the laws for those who believe in that God. Yet, there is also a sense that insofar as divine law is God's eternal law expressed in writing for humans that that law is not merely for the believers in a particular religion with a particular conception of who God is, but for all humans who have been created by the same God and owe obedience to that God's laws.

Yet, there remains the interesting problem that while divine law is critical for all three of these great religions and their Medieval interpreters, the sources of divine law, or the priority of them, that each discusses is different for each of them. If divine law is truly law, and law for all humans, then there is a problem when what counts as divine law for

---

614 *Mishneh Torah*, Book One: Knowledge, Chapter 1, 8-9, in *A Maimonides Reader*, edited and translated by Isadore Twersky, Springfield, NJ: Behrman House, Inc., 1972, pp. 64-65.

all humans varies from one religious tradition to another. The issue of the scope of the divine law is perhaps more difficult a problem than even the source of that divine law.

IV. Divine Law for Aquinas

Here is how Aquinas describes the divine law and indicates why it was needed in addition to other laws.

> Besides the natural and the human law it was necessary for the directing of human conduct to have a Divine law. And this for four reasons. First, because it is by law that man is directed how to perform his proper acts in view of his last end. And indeed if man were ordained to no other end than that which is proportionate to his natural faculty, there would be no need to have any further direction of the part of his reason, besides the natural law and human law, which is derived from it. But since man is ordained to an end of eternal happiness which is proportionate to man's natural faculty, as stated above, therefore it was necessary that, besides the natural and human law, man should be directed to this end by a law given by God.
>
> Secondly, because, on account of the uncertainty of human judgment, especially on contingent and particular matters, different people form different judgments on human acts; whence also different and contrary laws result. In order therefore that man may know without any doubt what he ought to do and what he ought to avoid, it was necessary for man to be directed in his proper acts by a law given by God, for it is certain that such a law cannot err.
>
> Thirdly, because man can make laws in those matters of which he is competent to judge. But man is not competent to judge of interior movements, that are hidden, but only of exterior acts which appear; and yet for the perfection of virtue it is necessary for man to conduct himself aright in both kinds of acts. Consequently, human law could not sufficiently curb and direct interior acts; and it was necessary for this purpose that a divine law should supervene.
>
> Fourthly, because as Augustine says, human law cannot punish or forbid all evil deeds: since while aiming at doing away with all evils, it would do away with many good things, and would hinder the advance of the common good, which is necessary for human intercourse. In order, therefore, that no evil might

> remain unforbidden and unpunished, it was necessary for the Divine law to supervene, whereby all sins are forbidden.[615]

This account of why divine law was needed is the most detailed of all of the Neo-Aristotelians, and we will examine it in what follows of this section of our chapter.

For Aquinas then, divine law was transmitted from God through Moses and Jesus's disciples so as:

> 1. to direct humans toward their eternal end;
> 2. to unerringly guide humans who have many conflicting human laws;
> 3. to guide and curb our interior states;
> 4. and to forbid all sins and evils.

Divine law has a clear role in directing our inner lives and moving us toward our heavenly end. But in addition, for Aquinas, divine law also can supplement or even take the place of human law in those cases where human law is likely to be unclear or to fail to take a comprehensive view of the wrongs humans need to be dissuaded from committing. As we will see, as long as divine law is kept in its own domain concerning primarily matters of sin understood religiously, there are fewer problems than when divine law becomes a competitor with human legislator-made law.

Sin and crime are distinguished for Aquinas, as we will see in much more detail in a later chapter. Suffice it here to point out that human law does not prohibit all sins, but only those human acts that cause harm or are some kind of wrong to another human that are typically regulated by criminal law. And yet, maintains Aquinas and nearly all Aristotelians, it is important that humans are encouraged toward positive acts rather than merely turned away from negative acts. One of the most important aspects of Aristotle's *Ethics* was his two chapters devoted to the virtues and what it would take to instill them in humans. The secular law was not the way to instill the virtues, or so argued Aquinas and his fellow Medieval Neo-Aristotelians. And this is one of the principal reasons for the divine law and its incentives of divine reward for those who act virtuously.

In addition, human law is not especially good at dealing with the internal acts of humans rather than their external acts. Mere thoughts are not generally criminalizable. But the divine law can deal with thoughts, especially intentions, as all of the Neo-Aristotelians held, despite their

[615] Aquinas, T*reatise on Law*, pp. 98-106.

differences in what they counted as the sources of divine law. Divine law is here a kind of supplement to human law.

An additional reason that Aquinas gives for the need for the divine law is that natural law is not knowable for some humans. As we will see in more detail in the next chapter, for humans to know the natural law they must have properly functioning consciences. Yet, some humans are either too young or too mentally infirm to understand the natural law that is imbedded in each of us. For these people there is a need that the written divine law of the scriptures be presented to them so that they can come to know what God expects of them. Again, this is most controversial when it concerns strictly secular matters, while it is less controversial when the things God is said to expect of us concern religious matters.

V. Marsilius's Critical Comments on Divine Law

Marsilius is our fourth Medieval Neo-Aristotelian to be considered but unlike the previous three (Averroes, Maimonides, and Aquinas) he is deeply skeptical of the ideas of divine law. We get an early sense of his position in the first book of his *The Defender of the Peace*, as follows:

> However apart from the grounds for positing religions which are believed without demonstration, philosophers… have–very aptly–paid attention to an entirely different reason for handing down divine religions… to induce in men a reverence and fear of God and a desire to avoid the vices and cultivate the virtues. For there are certain acts that a legislator cannot regulate by human law, as in those which cannot be proven to be present or absent in anyone but which cannot escape God–who according to their fiction, laid down these religions and commanded their obedience, on the threat or promise of eternal penalty or reward for doers of good or bad deeds…[616]

Here Marsilius indicates that divine laws can serve a useful purpose, one which human laws cannot, but he then shows his critical perspective when he calls these divine laws "fictions" which have been invented by religions. Divine laws are not laws properly so-called but fictions used to fool the people. Marsilius then goes on to show why exactly religions in general and divine laws in particular are actually pernicious.

---

[616] Marsilius of Padua, *The Defender of the Peace*, pp. 28-29.

Toward the end of the first book of *The Defender of the Peace*, Marsilius identifies an "unusual cause of the intranquility or discord of cities or realms."[617]

> some of the bishops who follow him [the pope] in the apostolic or Episcopal see of Rome, especially after the time of the Roman emperor Constantine–say and assert that they are superior to all the other bishops and priests of the world in respect of every kind of jurisdictional authority. Some indeed of the more recent of them say that they are superior not only to these, but also to the princes, communities, and individual persons of the world... The sense of this title among the Roman bishops is therefore this, that just as Christ had plentitude of power and jurisdiction over all kings, princes, communities, collective bodies and individual persons, so they too, who call themselves vicars of Christ, should have the plentitude of coercive power, defined by no human law.[618]

Marsilius calls this usurpation of human lawmaking authority by bishops and popes to be a "pernicious plague" and that such usurpation can be traced back to the idea that divine law gives religious rulers authority over secular law.[619]

Marsilius then identifies one of the most pernicious acts taken by religious leaders of the Catholic Church, the excommunication of anyone who challenges them and the ensuing "persecution from the violent hands of the Roman bishops and their accomplices."[620] As we will see in later chapters, the infamous inquisitions can be seen as a direct result of the kind of persecution of the perceived enemies of Rome that Marsilius has identified.

Marsilius argues that it is the interpretation of the texts supposedly presenting divine law that has caused the pernicious plague on peace that he seeks to expose and counter. He begins by showing that various terms are misused, such as the term spiritual.

> the term "spiritual" is predicated of the divine law and of the teaching and learning of commands and counsels in accordance with it and through it. Into this signification come all the sacraments of the church and their effects, all divine grace, all

[617] Ibid., p. 129.
[618] Ibid., pp. 132-133.
[619] Ibid., p. 136.
[620] Ibid., p. 139.

> the theological virtues... Further according to another signification this word is habitually taken for any voluntary human action or even passion, enacted upon oneself or another, for the sake of meriting the blessed life of the world... Most recently of all, however inappropriately, some people stretch this term to cover the voluntary actions and omissions on the part of priests or bishops, deacons, and other ministers of God's temple, which are transitive in respect of the convenience or inconvenience of someone other than the doer for the status of this worldly life. Again, they stretch this term–even more improperly–to the possessions and temporal goods of these men (both moveable and immoveable) and to certain proceeds from temporal goods which they call tithes, so that on the pretext of a word they can be exempted from the norm of civil laws and princes.[621]

So, part of Marsilius's critique of the abuse of the texts of divine law is that certain terms found in those texts are stretched so as to cover not only things of the Church but also to cover things of the state. And also that priests and bishops, etc., are said to be exempt from the criminal law even when they clearly act from "carnal" rather than "spiritual" motivations.[622]

In addition, Marsilius argues most cogently that the exemption from secular judgment and the cooptation of judgment by ecclesiastical authorities is utterly without foundation in the very divine texts the religious leaders claim as their source of authority. Here is a long section-heading that well represents Marsilius's argument in this respect.

> On the canonical scriptures, the commands or counsels and examples of Christ, and those of the saints and approved doctors of the evangelical law who expound them; by which it is plainly demonstrated that in virtue of the words of Scripture, neither the Roman nor any other bishop or priest or cleric can claim or ascribe to himself any coercive Principate or contentious jurisdiction, still less the supreme, over any cleric or layperson. And moreover that on the counsel and example of Christ, they should, especially within communities of the faithful, refuse such Principate if it is offered or granted to them by one who has authority to do so; and again, that all bishops without distinction should be subject to the coercive judgment or Principate of him who has dominion by the

[621] Ibid., pp. 148-149.

[622] Ibid., p. 150.

> authority of the human legislator, especially if the legislator is faithful.[623]

We can thus see that Marsilius believes that the interpretation of the texts of divine law cannot provide grounds for authority over secular matters and that Scripture, even if correctly transmitting the word of God's law can at most provide authority over religious members but not secular rulers. For Marsilius this is a matter of the proper domain of various types of law–and we ascertain the domain by examining the authority of these various laws.

---

[623] Ibid., p. 159.

CHAPTER 28

NATURAL LAW

In the 12th through the 14th century, the Neo-Aristotelians made some of their greatest contributions through how they came to understand the idea of the natural law, and this was especially true of Aquinas for whom the natural law was his signature theoretical idea. We also see how the idea of natural law was developed from Aristotle's writing in the century before Aquinas by the great Islamic scholar Averroes and the great Jewish philosopher Maimonides. And we will see how secular theorists writing after Aquinas began to question the idea of natural law - Marsilius said he was happier talking about the quasi-natural law.

In the first section of this chapter we recall some of Aristotle's remarks on the idea of a natural law and then turn to Averroes for his Medieval interpretation of Aristotle's views. In the second section we turn to Maimonides who made extensive use of the idea of natural law even as he did not always identify these ideas as ones of natural law. Then in the third section we sketch Aquinas's theory of natural law. In the fourth section we discuss how conscience and morality are linked to natural law, especially for Aquinas. In the final section we look to Marsilius for the beginnings of an attempt to deflate natural law as overriding all positive law in favor of a positive law common to all peoples. Indeed, throughout this chapter the idea of the relationship between natural and positive law will be the leitmotif.

I. Aristotle and Averroes on Natural Law

Here is a passage from Aristotle's *Nicomachean Ethics* on natural and positive law:

> Of political justice part is natural, part legal–natural, that which everywhere has the same force and does not exist by people's thinking this or that; legal, that which is originally indifferent, but when it has been laid down is not indifferent, e.g. that a prisoner's ransom shall be a mina, or that a goat and

> not two sheep shall be sacrificed, and again all the laws that are passed for particular cases, e.g. that sacrifice shall be made in honor of Brasidas, and the provision of decrees. Now some think that all justice is of this sort, because that which is by nature is unchangeable and has everywhere the same force (as fire burns both here and in Persia) while they see change in the things recognized as just... It is evident which sort of thing, among things capable of being otherwise, is by nature; and which is not but is legal and conventional, assuming that both are equally changeable.[624]

Here the natural part of justice is that "which everywhere has the same force and does not exist by people's thinking this or that." What is here called the legal part of justice is that which is "conventional" and "originally indifferent" until it has been laid down. We will see throughout this chapter that this idea had a profound impact on the Medieval theorists, who espouse what I am calling "Neo-Aristotelian Jurisprudence."

In Aristotle's *Rhetoric*, we likewise find important statements of what would become the natural law theory.

> If the written law tells against our case, clearly we must appeal to the universal law, and insist on its greater equity and justice. We must argue that the juror's oath "I will give my verdict according to my honest opinion" means that one will not simply follow the letter of the written law. We must urge that the principles of equity are permanent and changeless, and that the universal law does not change either, for it is the law of nature, whereas written laws often do change.[625]

Here again we see that Aristotle talks of a law of nature that is universal and distinguishes this universal law that is unchangeable with the written law that often does change.

Averroes was familiar with both Aristotle's *Nicomachean Ethics* and his *Rhetoric* and was highly influenced by both works. Here is a bit of his *Commentary on Aristotle's Rhetoric*:

> By unwritten laws, I mean those that naturally exist in all people. They are the ones in which everyone naturally sees

---

[624] Aristotle, *Nicomachean Ethics*, 1134b18-33, translated by W. D. Ross, in *Basic Works of Aristotle*, edited by Richard McKeon, NY: Random House, 1941, p. 1014.

[625] Aristotle, *Rhetoric*, 1375a25-34, translated by W. Rhys Roberts. in *Basic Works of Aristotle*, edited by Richard McKeon, NY: Random House, 1941, p p. 1374.

> what is just and what is unjust, even if there does not exist between one person and another any agreement or contract. These laws are also generally called universal laws in this respect. Nobody knows when these laws were laid down and who laid them down… [this] universal law is the law of nature.[626]

Like Aristotle, Averroes speaks of the law of nature as a universal law that exists in all people and is universally binding and knowable by all humans.

Averroes makes a very important distinction that is only sometimes recognized by the great social contract theorists of the 17th century. He distinguishes between written laws found in all societies and laws of nature:

> As to written laws proper to each particular people they are like the laws according to which some people consider that one should not kill animate beings –that is, animals–for that is unjust. In effect, this is not an obligation among all people, nor is it an obligation by nature.[627]

Here actually we have a tripartite distinction: laws specific to a certain society, laws common to all societies, and laws of nature. The latter two types of law are universally binding but for different reasons. It is a contingent matter that laws common to all societies are indeed commonly propounded; but it is a matter of necessity that laws emanating from God apply to all people.

For Aristotle as for his most prominent Medieval interpreter, Averroes, the law of nature exists independently of human will but is nonetheless within each human. As we will see, Maimonides and Aquinas will develop this idea, connecting it to a kind of sensibility or conscience.

II. Maimonides and Natural Law

Here is a passage from Maimonides great work, *The Guide of the Perplexed*, written about the same time as the work of Averroes we just examined.

---

[626] *Averroes's Middle Commentary on the Book of Rhetoric*, Book I.13.2, in *Three Arabic Treatises on Aristotle's Rhetoric*, translated by Lahcen Elyazghi Ezzaher, Carbondale, IL: Southern Illinois University Press, 2015, p. 163.

[627] *Averroes's Middle Commentary on the Book of Rhetoric*, Book I.13.2, in *Three Arabic Treatises on Aristotle's Rhetoric*, translated by Lahcen Elyazghi Ezzaher, Carbondale, IL: Southern Illinois University Press, 2015, p. 163.

> Now as the nature of the human species requires that there be those differences among the individuals belonging to it and as in addition society is a necessity for this nature, it is by no means possible that his society should be perfected except–and this is necessarily so–through a ruler who gauges the actions of the individuals, perfecting that which is deficient and reducing that which is excessive, and who prescribes actions and moral habits that all of them must practice in the same way, so that the natural diversity is hidden through the multiple points of conventional accord and so that the community becomes well ordered. Therefore I say that the Law, although it is not natural, enters into what is natural. It is a part of the wisdom of the deity with regard to the permanence of this species of which he has willed the existence, that he put it into its nature that individuals belonging to it should have the faculty of ruling.[628]

For Maimonides, "Law," by which he means God's law handed down from God to Moses, is not itself natural, but "enters into what is natural." But since Maimonides consistently debunks the idea that God has anything like human attributes, we cannot discern what God's law is by understanding God in terms of the Biblical stories told about him. We must reach beyond the allegorical meanings.

Instead, we need to understand nature and its laws as a way to understand God. As the translator of the *Guide* tells us:

> Maimonides speaks… of the attributes of action, i.e., of the application to God of such names as the "merciful," "revengeful," and so forth…. the use of these attributes is due to an anthropomorphic interpretation of natural or historical events regarded as beneficent or untoward. Quite evidently, the man who is granted knowledge of God, for instance Moses, must go beyond these anthropomorphic descriptions and grasp the workings of natural order. The chapter appears to indicate that the only positive knowledge of God possible to man consists in his understanding the natural phenomena.[629]

---

[628] Moses Maimonides, *The Guide of the Perplexed*, translated by Shlomo Pines, Chicago: University of Chicago Press, 1963, vol. II, p. 382.
[629] *Guide of the Perplexed*, p. cxv.

Indeed, Shlomo Pines goes on to say that "knowledge of the system of nature may represent the essence of God."[630] It appears that knowledge of the natural law is also knowledge of God's law for Maimonides.

Another commentator on Maimonides's often difficult texts tells us the following about how the laws of nature were understood by Maimonides: "Maimonides insists that just as there is gradation and purposiveness in the process of nature and biology, so there is in history and religion. The laws of nature, cosmic as well as human, remain immutable."[631] Knowledge of the laws of nature allows for knowledge of the "moral virtues" which are understood to be "moral qualities useful for life in society."[632]

Maimonides connects the law of nature to morality and to the nature of humans. Humans have a nature insofar as they are part of nature, and by studying human nature, in ourselves for instance, we can come to understand nature and what its laws are. The laws of nature for humans, which also are the laws of morality for humans, set the parameters of what is valid law. As we will see, the connection between human nature and the natural law is also an important connection for Aquinas, to whom we next turn.

III. Aquinas and Natural Law

For Aquinas, there are two ways to gain insight into God's eternal and universal law. As we saw in the previous chapter, one source of understanding of God's eternal law is divine law–the law that is revealed in the scriptures and other holy documents that God has transmitted to his representatives for promulgation. There is though another way to understand the eternal law and that involves natural law, the law that God has embedded in each human, as a matter of human nature. The question to ask is: how do we gain access to what is internal to ourselves? In order to answer this question we devote this and the next section.

The centerpiece of Aquinas's moral, political, and legal theory is the concept of natural law, which has pride of place in his *Treatise on Law*. We begin with this statement of the relation of human nature to the law of nature:

---

630 Ibid.

631 Isadore Twersky, *Introduction to the Code of Maimonides (Mishneh Torah)*, New Haven, CT: Yale University Press, 1980, p. 390.

632 Ibid., p. 388.

> the natural law is consequent to human nature. But human nature, as a whole, is one; though as to its parts it is manifold. Therefore, either there is but one precept of the law of nature, on account of the unity of nature as a whole; or there are many, by reason of the number of parts of human nature. The result would be that even things relating to the inclination of the concupiscible faculty belong to the natural law. [633]

So, for Aquinas, "natural law is consequent to human nature." One commentator says of this passage: "the natural law is what it is because human nature is what it is."[634] Human nature is part of nature in general, and nature in general has laws that govern it. These laws follow from one principle that is applicable to all natural beings.

Aquinas goes on, in Question 94 of his *Summa Theologica* from which his *Treatise on Law* is drawn, to argue that the precepts of the natural law are in effect propositions in a practical syllogism:

> the precepts of the natural law are to the practical reason, what the first principles of demonstrations are to the speculative reason; because both are self-evident principles. Now a thing is said to be self-evident in two ways: first, in itself; and secondly, in relation to us. Any proposition is said to be self-evident in itself, if its predicate is contained in the notion of the subject: although, to one who knows not the definition of the subject, it happens that such a proposition is not itself self-evident. For instance, this proposition, "Man is a rational being," is in its very nature, self-evident, since who says "man," says "a rational being": and yet to one who knows not what a man is, this proposition is not self-evident. Hence it is that, as Boethius says, certain axioms or propositions are universally self-evident to all; and such are those propositions whose terms are known to all, as, "Every whole is greater than its part," and "Things equal to one and the same are equal to one another." But some propositions are self-evident only to the wise, who understand the meaning of the terms of such propositions: thus to one who understands that an angel is not a body, it is self-evident that an angel is not circumscriptively in a place: but this is not evident to the unlearned, for they cannot grasp it.[635]

---

633 Aristotle, *Treatise on Law*, p. 238.
634 Ibid.
635 Ibid., pp. 241-242.

It is important to note here that when Aquinas talks of a practical syllogism he is referring directly to Aristotle's idea that while a demonstrative syllogism has two premises that support a conclusion as a piece of knowledge, the practical syllogism has two premises that support a conclusion that is an action–these premises move the person to act not merely to know something.

It is also very important to recognize that the natural law is grounded in self-evident propositions–propositions that do not need, and may not have, any further support. Those who are wise can then discern what actions they are required by God to perform. But those who are not wise, who do not understand the propositions or premises of the practical syllogisms of the natural law, will not be moved to act as they should. For these unwise people, Aquinas has argued that the divine law is needed–the unwise can read, or learn from, the scriptures and then be moved to do what he or she is obligated by God to do.

Here is another passage from the *Treatise on Law* concerning the way we learn of the natural law:

> Now a certain order is to be found in those things that are apprehended universally. For that which, before aught else, falls under apprehension, is "being," the notion of which is included in all things whatsoever a man apprehends. Wherefore the first indemonstrable principle is that "the same thing cannot be affirmed and denied at the same time," which is based on the notion of "being" and "not being": and on this principle all others are based, is stated in Metaphysics IV, 9. Now as "being" is the first thing that falls under the apprehension simply, so "good" is the first thing that falls under the apprehension of the practical reason, which is directed to action: since every agent acts for an end under the aspect of good. Consequently, the first principle of practical reason is one founded on the notion of good, viz. that "good is that which all things seek after." Hence this is the first precept of law, that "good is to be done and pursued, and evil is to be avoided." All other precepts of the natural law are based upon this: so that whatever the practical reason naturally apprehends as man's good (or evil) belongs to the precepts of the natural law, as something to be done or avoided.[636]

Earlier in his *Treatise on Law*, Aquinas had said that the function of the natural law is "the light of natural reason whereby we discern what

[636] Ibid., pp. 243-244.

is good and what is evil" and is "nothing else than an imprint on us of the Divine light... nothing else than the rational creature's participation of the eternal law."[637] Now we are also told that by practical reason we are able to apprehend what is good or evil and this is the way that the natural law works to get us to know what God has obligated us to do and to refrain from doing it.

Being is the first thing grasped in metaphysics by means of demonstrative reason; and good is the first thing grasped in practical matters of law and morality. Indeed, it is interesting that the "good" of the practical syllogism in Aquinas's account is the same for both law and morality. It is for this reason, as we will see in the next section, that when it can be demonstrated that a putative law is contrary to the good then that law ought not to be obeyed because it is not a proper law.

The natural law is instilled in humans to such an extent that each human has a natural inclination to do good.

> there is in man an inclination to good, according to the nature of his reason, which nature is proper to him: thus man has a natural inclination to know the truth about God, and to live in society: and in this respect, whatever pertains to this inclination belongs to the natural law; for instance to shun ignorance, to avoid offending those among whom he has to live, and other such things regarding the above inclination.[638]

There is something like an instinct, a special kind of inclination, that is impressed in humans, and that allows them to apprehend the good or evil in the world. In addition, this is the natural "law" in us, a rule or measure of our acts. Those who are wise can then discern what is good or evil and conform their actions either toward the good or away from the evil.

IV. Conscience and Morality

In Part I, Question 79, Article 12 of the *Summa Theologica*, from which the *Treatise on Law* is another part, Aristotle discusses the nature of conscience or *synderesis*. Here is what he says:

> *Synderesis* is not a power but a habit; though some held that it is a power higher than reason; while others said that it is reason itself, not as reason, but as a nature. In order to make this clear

---

[637] Ibid., p. 80.
[638] Ibid., p. 247.

> we must observe that, as we have said above (A. 8), man's act of reasoning, since it is a kind of movement, proceeds from the understanding of certain things–namely, those which are naturally known without any investigation on the part of reason, as from an immoveable principle,-and ends also at the understanding, inasmuch as by means of those principles naturally known, we judge of those things which we have discovered by reasoning. Now it is clear that as the speculative reason argues about speculative things, so that practical reason argues about practical things. Therefore we must have, bestowed on us by nature, not only speculative principles, but also practical principles. Now the first speculative principles bestowed on us by nature do not belong to a special power, but to a special habit, which is called *the understanding of principles*, as the Philosopher explains (*Ethics* VI, 6). Wherefore the first practical principles, bestowed on us by nature, do not belong to a special power, but to a special habit, which we call *synderesis*. Whence *synderesis* is said to incite to good, and to murmur at evil, inasmuch as through the first principles we proceed to discover, and judge of what we have discovered.[639]

Conscience or *synderesis* is the faculty or special habit that allows for humans to distinguish good from evil and right from wrong.

We also see conscience or *synderesis* turning up quite a lot in Aquinas's discussion of natural law. Aquinas distinguishes *synderesis* from *conscientia* as Budziszewski says in his Commentary on Aquinas's *Treatise on Law*:

> *Synderesis*, which St. Thomas had discussed much earlier in the Summa, is one of several different things contemporary people mean by "conscience," but which St. Thomas carefully distinguishes. It is the natural disposition or "habit" by which the mind understands the first principles of practical reason, the necessary starting points of all deliberation about what to do. *Conscientia* is the act of judgment that applies it.... *synderesis* [is] deep conscience.[640]

Deep conscience is the apprehension of what is good or right, where conscientia is the specific act of judgment where the deep insights of *synderesis* are applied to a particular case where a person must decide how

---

[639] Aquinas, *Summa Theologica*, translated by the Fathers of the Dominican Province, 1948, Vol. I, p. 407.

[640] Commentary on Aquinas's, *Treatise on Law*, p. 231.

he or she should act. Our concept of conscience tends to incorporate both of these.

In Article 96 of the *Treatise on Law*, Aquinas addresses the question of how conscience is related to human law, not merely to natural law. Here we will discuss several statements of Aquinas that will help us understand how conscience relates to human law.

> Laws framed by man are either just or unjust. If they be just, they have the power of binding in conscience, from the eternal law whence they are derived, according to Proverbs 8:15: "By Me kings reign, and lawgivers decree just things." Now laws are said to be just both from the end, when to wit, they are ordained to the common good, and from their author…that is to say when then the law that is made does not exceed the power of the lawgiver–and from their form, when, to wit, burdens are laid on subjects, according to an equality of proportion and with a view to the common good. For, since one man is a part of the community, each man in all that he is and has, belongs to the community; just as a part, in all that it is, belongs to the whole; so that on this account, such laws as these, which impose proportionate burdens, are just and binding in conscience, and are legal laws.[641]

Conscience then only binds people to obey human-made laws that are just and proportionate.

Aquinas summarizes his view by quoting from the *Acts of the Apostles*: "We ought to obey God, rather than man."[642] We are bound to obey human-made laws only if they do not conflict with natural law, and the way to figure this out, roughly, is to appeal to one's conscience to see whether or not obeying the human law in question would indeed promote the common good (or repel evil). Conscience then binds us to obey human law only when the human law conforms with the natural law and ultimately with God's eternal and universal law. Here we come to one of the main tenets of natural law theory, especially as it is understood today–a person is obligated as a matter of conscience only to obey just laws.

In the section of the *Summa Theologica* called *De Obedientia*, it is clear that unjust laws are not to be obeyed:

> It must be said that a man is so far obliged to obey secular princes, as the order of justice requires; hence if their authority

---

[641] Aquinas, *Treatise on Law,* p. 383.

[642] Ibid., p. 389.

> is not just but usurped, or if they command that which is unjust, a subject is not obliged to obey, except according to the circumstances, to avoid scandal or peril.[643]

As we will see in the final section, when a law is said to be invalid because it is immoral, this need not imply that it is God's order that comes into contact with human law–indeed such a view is consistent with the nonexistence of God. But here in the Middle Ages, it is an aberrant view to say the least to think that God's law is not the source for all other valid law, or at least that human law could oppose God's law and still be obligating.

Yet, we still have the problem that some people seem not to have a conscience, or not to be affected by conscience. Aquinas responds:

> sometimes a man is unable to make use of that which is in him habitually, on account of some impediment: thus on account of sleep, a man is unable to use the habit of science. In like manner, through the deficiency of his age, a child cannot use the habit of understanding of principles, or the natural law, which is in him habitually.[644]

Being too young may mean that conscience as *synderesis* will not allow for the discernment of principles of morality; and conscience as *conscientia* may be similarly hampered in applying principles of natural law or morality because of other deficiencies.

So, Aquinas is able to maintain that all humans have a conscience in that there is the habit of discernment and of judgment in all, but that not all can actualize these aspects of mind. In such cases, divine scripture will be needed as it were to operate in place of conscience to provide the deficient person with the moral guidance he or she is blocked from having on his or her own. Indeed, at some points Aquinas seems to say that only those humans who are wise can do without divine scripture to determine which human-made laws should be obeyed.

V. Marsilius and Quasi-Natural Law

Marsilius provides a unique take on the natural law idea and also provides a characteristically critical dimension to the debates. We can start

---

643 Translated by Alexander Passerin D'Entreves, in *The Medieval Contribution to Political Thought*, NY: The Humanities Press, 1959, p. 34.

644 Aquinas, *Treatise on Law*, p. 236.

by looking at what Marsilius says about quasi-natural law in his discussion of the origin of the civil community.

> Now as long as human beings were in a single household, all their actions, and especially those which we shall later call "civil," were regulated by the elder among them as by the more discerning: without, however, any law or custom, in that these could not as yet be discovered. But it was not only the men of the single household who were regulated in this way, but also, almost in the same way, those of the first community which is called the village–even if differently in some respects. For although it would have been licit for the head of the single household to pardon or punish domestic wrongdoings entirely at his wish and pleasure, this would not have been licit for him as the chief of the first community called the village. The reason is that in this community, it was necessary for the elder to dispense what was just and advantageous by some reasonable ordinance or quasi-natural law, because so it seemed appropriate to everyone by a kind of equity and without much examination, purely by the common dictate of reason and a certain duty of human society.[645]

The quasi-natural law is what people would all come up with as the most reasonable of laws governing communities.

The translator of Marsilius, Annabel Brett, makes the following comment on the above passage and others in *The Defender of the Peace*:

> Central to Marsilius's analysis of knowledge is that it is *cumulative*... the law is "an understanding forged from the understanding of many." Thus knowledge requires a community of people exercising their intelligence and it requires a continuity and a communication of that intelligence from one generation to the next. In other words, it has a *history*. Marsilius has no theory of natural knowledge, just as he has no theory of natural law as the natural illumination of the mind in moral matters. Following Aristotle, Marsilius argues that what people call natural law means simply those political standards that are the same everywhere; the village elder regulates the primitive community not by natural but by quasi-natural law. Knowledge is historical and *by the very same token* political: there is no wholly natural or immediate knowledge, no cognitive grasp that requires no community of understanding.[646]

---

[645] Marsilius, *The Defender of the Peace*, p. 16.
[646] Ibid., p. xviii.

In this account, Marsilius is actually the true Aristotelian on the topic of natural law, and it is indeed true that for the Greeks and the Romans it was not often true that the natural law (*jus naturale*) and the law common to all peoples (*jus gentium*) were carefully distinguished.

Yet it is also true that Marsilius follows in the footsteps of the Neo-Aristotelians in thinking that an immoral law is not a valid law.

> For men are gathered into a civil community in order to pursue their benefit and the sufficient life and to avoid their contraries. And therefore any convenience or inconvenience that can affect all ought to be known and heard by all, so that they can pursue their benefit and avoid its contrary. But of such nature are laws, as the minor proposition assumed. For the greater part of the entire common human sufficiency rests in their being rightly established, whereas under iniquitous laws there is only intolerable slavery, oppression and misery for the citizens, which ultimately results in the dissolution of the polity.[647]

Here Marsilius endorses an important tenet of natural law theory, namely, that for law to be valid it must not be iniquitous.

Marsilius seems to think of natural law as simply the common law of all peoples. In this way of thinking, natural law or quasi-natural law is disconnected to eternal law. It is true that there is a kind of universality to law if it is indeed common to "all" people but the commonality could be a contingent matter and not something that is ordained from God. And while Marsilius does not go so far as to disbelieve in God, his legal and political thought is so secular that there is little hope of the link being made between law common to all people and law derived from God.

Yet, there is a sense that Marsilius would support the idea that we saw espoused in Aquinas about the importance of conscience in determining which laws are indeed truly obligatory. Conscience can be a kind of inner voice or habit that moves people to do what is good or right without having conscience connected to God; indeed conscience can be independent of the existence of God altogether, and at times Marsilius comes close to endorsing a view like this. But then he seems to back away and instead of being critical of God Marsilius remains steadfastly focused on his criticisms of the Church and pope.

In the secular development of the idea of natural law, some endorsed the view that Marsilius was right to insist that the natural law

---

[647] Ibid., p. 71.

was not always to be placed above positive law. As Otto Gierke has shown:

> The deeper were the inroads that were made into the domain of ecclesiastical and temporal legislation by this idea of a Law of Nature which even legislators might not infringe, the more urgent was the need for a definition of the principle which set limits to a law-giver's power. As to the breadth and import of the principle there were abundant controversies. But the very elasticity of the limiting idea could in all circumstances save the principle. Men agreed that the rules of Natural Law could not be altogether abrogated by Positive Law but still those rules might be, and ought to be, modified and developed, amplified and restricted, regard being had to special cases. In this sense a distinction was often drawn between the immutable first principles and the mutable secondary rules…[648]

The idea here is to follow Marsilius in thinking that the natural law is only a quasi-natural law–and this for two reasons. First, it is only a natural law in a restricted sense of the term natural; and more importantly, second, it only supplies immutable general principles not secondary principles.

We can hearken back to a point made by Aquinas that the conscience which is *synderesis* only gives humans access to the normative principles by which they must generally live their lives. But perhaps the conscience that is *conscientia*, the specific application of the natural law, requires other principles, secondary principles, which are not immutable but highly variable throughout the human population. We all know that murder is wrong, as an immutable principle of the natural law, but we do not necessarily know whether to judge this particular case of killing, e.g. setting aged relatives to drift on icebergs, is to be judged a case of murder.

If we follow the secularists such as Marsilius and the early modern social contract theorists, we cannot tell that a law properly propounded is not valid on moral or natural law grounds until we cast our faculty of judgment upon the case and try to discern which first principles might be relevant and what secondary principles would apply the primary principles to the case at hand. This is a theory of natural law we will not see fully elaborated until the works of Grotius, Hobbes, and Locke, among other 17th century legal and political theorists. Yet, we see strong glimpses of such a view in the writings of the 14th century thinker, Marsilius of Padua. But it is fair to say that Marsilius was not at all representative of

---

648 Otto Gierke, *Political Theories of the Middle Ages*, translated by Frederic William Maitland, Boston: Beacon Press, 1958, p. 76.

Medieval natural law theory–for that view, we must stay with the works of Averroes, Maimonides, and Aquinas.

CHAPTER 29

EQUITY

For those legal theorists who supported a natural law theory, one of the pressing questions was what the institutions would look like that allowed for otherwise properly valid law to be overridden by moral considerations. In Aristotle's work, much was made of the concept of equity, or natural fairness, as an institution to ameliorate the harsh conditions of the application of strict justice. As we will see, Averroes again is the closest to Aristotle–indeed Averroes's commentary on Aristotle's *Rhetoric*, where equity is sketched, is where we find the most detailed discussion of the Neo-Aristotelian view of equity. Maimonides relied on Aristotle but also the very long tradition among Jewish scholars commenting on the Torah and Talmud who placed equity squarely at the forefront of Jewish jurisprudence. Aquinas connects natural law with ideas of natural fairness, as Aristotle did, but also moves the debate into more detailed treatment of this concept. And finally, we again find Marsilius providing the beginnings of a secular account of equity as a legal institution that was also deeply indebted to Aristotle but more to Aristotle's *Politics* and *Nicomachean Ethics* than to his *Rhetoric*. During this period we also find that England began to develop original institutions to deal with equity such as the Chancellor's court and ultimately the Court of Equity itself.

In this chapter we begin with a quick summary of Aristotle's account of equity in his three texts just mentioned. Then in section two we look at the nuances that Averroes added in his commentary on Aristotle's *Rhetoric*. In the third section, we turn to a summary of the ancient Jewish traditional account of equity and how it was adapted by Maimonides. In the fourth section, we look at the views of Aquinas in his *Treatise on Law* concerning equity. And we then conclude with the secular treatment of this topic by Marsilius relating it to the English Common Law tradition at this time.

I. Equity and Fairness for Aristotle

Aristotle's discussion of equity is brief in both his *Nicomachean Ethics* and in his *Rhetoric*, but it has had a very profound influence on the ideas of justice and equity in the history of legal and political thought. In the *Nicomachean Ethics*, Aristotle discusses political justice as divided in two parts: "part is natural, part legal,-natural, that which everywhere has the same force and does not exist by people thinking this or that; legal, that which is originally indifferent, but when it has been laid down is not."[649]

Equity is then discussed by Aristotle in the following way to distinguish it from one sort of justice.

> the same thing is just and equitable...the equitable is superior...the problem is that the equitable is just, but not the legally just but a correction of legal justice... all law is universal, but about some things it is not possible to make a universal statement which shall be correct...[650] To say what the legislator would have said had he been present.[651]

Equity is then defined to be "a correction of law where it is defective owing to its universality."[652]

For Aristotle, political justice, a form of particular justice, has two components. One part, natural justice, is universal ("which everywhere has the same force"[653]), and does not depend on what people think is politically just. The other, legal justice, was "originally indifferent" until it was "laid down." The idea of natural justice also had a powerful impact on the idea of natural law in the way Thomas Aquinas extended Aristotle's ideas in the Middle Ages.

Here is a long passage from Aristotle in his *Rhetoric* to give us a sense of how equity was understood in its most sophisticated form.

> There are two kinds of just and unjust conduct toward others... The second kind makes up for the defects of the written law. This is what we call equity; it is, in fact, the sort of justice which goes beyond the written law. Its existence partly is and partly is not intended by legislators; not intended, where they

---

649 Aristotle. *Nicomachen Ethics*, 1134b18, translated by W. D. Ross, in *Basic Works of Aristotle*, edited by Richard McKeon, NY: Random House, 1941, p.

650 Ibid., 1137b10.

651 Ibid., 1137b23.

652 Ibid., 1137b27.

653 Ibid., 1134b18.

> have noticed no defect in the law; intended, where they find themselves unable to define things exactly, and are obliged to legislate as if that held good always which in fact holds good usually; or where it is not easy to be complete owing to the endless possible cases presented, such as the kinds and sizes of weapons that may be used to inflict wounds–a lifetime would be too short to make out a complete list of these. If, then, a precise statement is impossible and yet legislation is necessary, the law must be expressed in wide terms; and so if a man has no more than a finger-ring on his hand when he lifts it to strike or actually strikes another man, he is guilty of a criminal act according to the written words of the law; but is innocent really, and it is equity that declares him so. From this definition of equity it is plain what sort of action, and what sort of persons, are equitable or the reverse. Equity must be applied to forgivable actions; and it must make us distinguish between criminal acts on the one hand and errors of judgment, or misfortune, on the other… Equity bids us to be merciful to the weakness of human nature; to think less about the laws than about the man who framed them, and less about what he said than about what he meant; not to consider the actions of the accused so much as his intentions, nor this or that detail so much as the whole story; to ask not what a man is now but what he has always or usually been. It bids us remember benefits rather than injuries, and benefits received rather than benefits conferred; to be patient when we are wronged; to settle a dispute by negotiation and not by force; to prefer arbitration to litigation–for an arbitrator goes by the equity of a case, a judge by the strict law, and arbitration was invented with the express purpose of securing full power of equity.[654]

There are several meanings, or at least several divergent strains, of equity described here. In the next section we will discuss how Averroes's commentary on Aristotle's *Rhetoric* came to interpret equity.

II. Averroes's Interpretation of Aristotelian Equity

Averroes, following Aristotle, distinguishes between written and unwritten law in relation to the idea of justice.

---

[654] Aristotle, *Rhetoric*, 1374a18-1374b22, translated by W. Rhys Roberts, in *Basic Works of Aristotle*, edited by Richard McKeon, NY: Random House, 1941, pp. 1371-1372. I have slightly altered the translation at the beginning of the quotation.

> [Aristotle] said: First, we must define the act of wrongdoing, and then speak of each of these three things.
> Then we say: An act of wrongdoing is injury inflicted voluntarily by way of transgression of the law. The law is of two kinds: it is either special or general. Special laws are written laws that one fears will be forgotten if they are not written, and they are proper to each particular community of people and each particular nation. As to general laws, they are unwritten laws recognized by all, like reverence toward parents and gratitude toward the benefactor.[655]

Averroes goes on to say that

> unwritten laws… are also generally called universal laws in this respect… They are often contrary to written laws, and they are used for persuasion to demonstrate that what one believes to be unjust according to the written laws is not unjust… according to universal law, which is the law of nature.[656]

Here, without using the term equity, Averroes sets out the main point of equity in an Aristotelian account of justice–equity is a law of nature, a universal law, which is unwritten and can be used as a matter of argumentation to show that what was believed to be unjust is not.

We also find Averroes talking about the kind of arguments that might lead us to disregard the strict interpretation of a law in favor of one that is more equitable.

> [Aristotle] said: These are the things by which we establish that something is more useful or more harmful. As to the things by which there is permission and interdiction, enough has been said about them earlier.
> However, the most important and greatest thing concerning these is the discourse on the things by which one is able to produce excellent persuasion in the subject matter of law and also by which one is able to give counsel regarding laws more useful than [that] which does not exist… for each political regime, there are laws that are useful to it, and they are the laws by which the city achieves its freedom and sustenance. Valuable and significant laws are just laws–that is laws instituted on the basis of justice–laid down by the head of the city-state or by the person authorized by the head. These

[655] Averroes's *Middle Commentary*, p. 142.
[656] Ibid., p. 163.

> valuable laws–that is, just laws–differ from one political regime to another depending on their ends.[657]

Sometimes people are obligated by their laws to act a certain way, but other people would not be so obligated. Only universal laws of nature obligate all people. And when written laws are in conflict with the law of nature (as equity) the latter should dictate the proper obligations of people.

Averroes seems to put greater weight than did Aristotle on the distinction between written and unwritten laws. But there is little doubt that Averroes and Aristotle both worry about the same issues concerning equity. Here is yet another example. Averroes tells us: "So they erred about the intention of the Lawgiver and were misguided and made others misguided."[658] Interpretation of laws so that one finds the intent of the lawgiver is of the essence of the pursuit of equity. Averroes, as with other proponents of Neo-Aristotelian jurisprudence recognizes that the strict interpretation of a law, according to literal methods often fails to uncover the intent of the lawgiver and leads the ruler and the people who rely on his interpretation into error. It is the correct method that brings out the equitable interpretation of the laws.

III. Maimonides and Equity in Jewish Law

Aaron Kirschenbaum provides a good summary of how equity was generally understood in Jewish law:

> In a sense, equity is a function of the administration of the law. This is especially true in Judaism. The basic tenet of historical Judaism is the unquestioned acceptance of the Torah, the Five Books of Moses, as the literal Word of God, His Law. To the prophets of Israel, to the sages of the Talmud, and to the rabbinic heirs of the "Tradition, the statement of law–with all its sanctity–is not the law; that is, it never exhausts God's Word. The Oral Torah, equally of divine origin, complements and supplements it, gives it body and substance. But even the Oral Law cannot exhaust God's Word. Its ultimate fulfillment is in the ongoing process of administering God's law: by textual exegesis, ritual guidance, judicial interpretation, rabbinic decision-making–all applying the halakhic rules to individual cases. Indeed, the Rabbis never arrogated to themselves a truly codificatory role of superseding the Law of Moses; even as

---

[657] Ibid., pp. 128-129.

[658] Averroes, *Decisive Treatise*, translated by Charles E. Butterworth, p. 30.

> legislators they regarded themselves as doing no more than administering God's law through "minor" external modification with the purpose of preserving it as He intended.[659]

The intent of the lawgiver in Aristotelian terms is here understood as the intent of God who is the divine lawgiver. Equity is a way for minor adjustments to be made in the way the law is administered so as to bring judicial decisions into greater conformity with God's intent.

Just as there is no Arabic term for equity, it is also true, as we learn from Kirschenbaum that

> Jewish law has no term for "equity." This becomes evident when the Rabbis compare Moses and Aaron. Moses, they say, is the embodiment of uncompromising justice, for his motto is *yikov hadin et hahar*, "Let the law cut through the mountain," which is the Hebrew approximation of *fiat iustitia ruat coelum*, "Let justice be done though the heavens collapse." In contrast stands Aaron, who loved peace, pursued peace, and made peace between a man and his fellow. Instead of equity, with its precise connotation, the Rabbis say *shalom*, "peace," a word with a rather broad and amorphous meaning… A study of the word *yosher* as it is found in the response literature of the Middle Ages reveals a connotation of uprightness, fairness, and propriety, essentially similar to the meaning of the word in Scripture. Halakhists often contrast it with the formal, rigorous rule of biblical law positively, as "the right way," the correct decision that is the product of intuitive justice and fairness. This connotation comes very close to–but is not identical with–the legal concept of equity.[660]

As we will see, Maimonides employs the category of equity, if not the term, in his writings in the Middle Ages of the sort that Kirschenbaum indicates.

In Maimonides multi-volume work, the *Mishneh Torah*, we find many discussions of how laws are to be interpreted and applied. Here are some passages from the *Book of Judges*:

> So far as traditional laws are concerned, there never was any controversy. If there was any, we may be sure that the tradition does not date back to Moses, our teacher. As for rules derived

---

[659] Aaron Kirschenbaum, *Equity in Jewish Law: Halakhic Perspectives on Law*, NY: Yeshiva University Press, 1991, pp. 4-5.
[660] Ibid., pp. 7-8.

> by means of hermeneutical principles, if they received the sanction of all the members of the Supreme Court, they were binding. If there was a difference of opinion among them, the Supreme Court followed the majority and decided the law in accordance with their opinion. This principle obtained also with respect to decrees, ordinances, and customs. If some felt that there was need for instituting a decree, for enacting an ordinance, or for discontinuing a practice, and others were of the opinion that there was no reason for the new decree or ordinance, or for the abandonment of the practice, they discussed the matter, followed the majority opinion and acted accordingly... If the Great Sanhedrin, by employing one of the hermeneutical principles, deduced a ruling which in its judgment was in consonance with the Law and rendered a decision to that effect, and a later Supreme Court finds a reason for setting aside the ruling, it may do so in accordance with its own opinion, as it is said: *and unto the judge that shall be in those days* (Deut. 17:9), that is, we are bound to follow the directions of the court of our own generation.[661]

Here Maimonides recognizes the importance of several concepts that play a prominent role in the idea of equity. Most importantly, judges are to be given discretion in interpreting laws so as to take account of the conditions at the time–so that what was thought to be a good interpretation of a law at one time might be revised so as to make the interpretation of the law consistent with what the lawgiver would have wanted to prescribe in today's times.

Another aspect of equity that Maimonides takes up is that the application of law is supposed to result in judgments that display fairness. Indeed, the attention to fairness is scrupulous in some types of case, especially capital cases as we see in these passages:

> He who is condemned to death is led forth from the court while one with a signaling flag is stationed at the door of the court and another, at some distance from him, is mounted on a horse. A herald precedes the culprit, announcing, "So-and-so is going forth to be executed by such-and-such a death, because he committed such-and-such an offense in such-and-such a place at such-and-such a time, and So-and-so and So-and-so are the witnesses against him. Whoever knows anything in his favor,

[661] Maimonides, *The Code of Maimonides, Book Fourteen: The Book of Judges*, translated by Abraham M. Hershman, New Haven, CT: Yale University Press, pp. 139-140.

> let him come forward and state it." If one says, "I have something to say in his behalf," the signalman waves his flag, and the horseman runs and brings the culprit back to court. If he is found not guilty, he is set free; otherwise, he is led forth to be executed. Should the accused himself say, "I have something to say in my favor," although there may be no substance in what he has to say, he is returned once, aye even a second time, because it is possible that overwhelmed by fear, he was unable to marshal his arguments and that on being brought back to court (once again), he might regain his composure and offer a plausible plea. If after he has been returned to court no substance is found in what he said, he is once more led to the place of execution. Should he assert a third time that he has a statement to make in his own behalf, if there is some cogency in his statement, he is brought back. This is done even many times. For this reason two scholars accompany him that they may listen to what he says.[662]

The procedure outlined here is breathtakingly fair to the accused–making things much like they are sometimes in the United States where a death penalty will only be administered after there is a complete exhaustion of appellate motions.

Kirschenbaum offers us a good summary of Maimonides view of equity when he examines Maimonides rejection that "An eye for an eye" is to be understood literally.

> equitable interpretations of statute are not regarded as intrusions or "reinterpretations" of the text based upon extrinsic considerations. On the contrary, many equitable interpretations are the products of the interpreter's search for the "true," original, authentic meaning of the passage. Maimonides regards a literal interpretation of the lex talionis as simply wrong: intrinsically wrong on the basis of word usage and wrong on the basis of the contexts and implications of related passages… More pronounced are the considerations of justice and fairness as the underlying reasons for the adoption of the nonliteral, equitable interpretation.[663]

Maimonides goes to great length to show that monetary compensation was both the intent of *lex talionis* and also the fairest way to understand this doctrine.

---

[662] Maimonides, *The Book of Judges*, ibid., pp. 36-37.

[663] Kirschenbaum, *Equity in Jewish Law*, p. 29.

IV. Aquinas, Natural Law, and Equity

Aquinas concerns himself late in the *Treatise on Law* with the question of when if ever a judge could favor or disfavor a particular plaintiff or defendant. The idea of discretion for judges is importantly considered here in Question 97:

> Dispensation, properly speaking, denotes a measuring out to individuals of some common goods: thus the head of a household is called a dispenser because to each member of the household he distributes work and necessaries of life in due weight and measure. Accordingly in every community a man is said to dispense, from the very fact that he directs how some general precept is to be fulfilled by each individual. Now it happens at times that a precept, which is conducive to the common weal as a general rule, is not good for a particular individual, or in some particular case, either because it would hinder some greater good, or because it would be the occasion of some evil, as explained above. But it would be dangerous to leave this to the discretion of each individual, except by reason of an evident and sudden emergency. Consequently he who is placed over a community is empowered to dispense in a human law that rests upon his authority, so that, when the law fails in its application to persons or circumstances, he may allow the precept of law not to be observed. If he grant such permission without any such reason, and of his mere will, he will be an unfaithful, or an imprudent dispenser: unfaithful if he has not the common good in view; imprudent, if he ignores the reasons for granting dispensations.[664]

Aquinas presents the idea of discretion, a key component of equity, as a mixed blessing. Discretion allows judges to decide in a way that deviates from the strict letter of the law; but when too much discretion is allowed, problems ensue. The partial answer to this predicament is to make sure that discretion is itself only employed in service of a principle that is aimed at the good of the particular person or community.

Aquinas's position is made especially clear in two more passages from Question 97 of his *Treatise on Law*:

> When a person is dispensed from observing the general law, this should not be done to the prejudice of, but with the intention of benefitting, the common good.

[664] Aquinas, *Treatise on Law*, pp. 452-453.

> It is not respect of persons if unequal measures are served out to those who are themselves unequal. Wherefore when the condition of any person requires that he should reasonably receive special treatment, it is not respect of persons if he be the object of special favor.[665]

The idea that is crucial here is that the intention of the judge or other person employing discretion and making exceptions should be the source of the justification of not following the law or rule.

And we also learn that Aquinas even allows for some discretion in how the natural law is understood to be binding.

> Natural law, so far as it contains general precepts, which never fail, does not allow of dispensation. In other precepts, however, which are as conclusions of the general precepts, man sometimes grants a dispensation: for instance, that a loan should not be paid back to the betrayer of his country, or something similar.[666]

In this respect it is especially interesting that the canonical 19th century case of equity concerned a grandson who, learning that he was about to be disinherited by his grandfather, killed him so as to benefit from the will. In this case, the majority of the judges argue that the grandson should not inherit because he would be profiting from his own wrongdoing. The grandson's killing of his grandfather is like the betrayer of his country–these are situations that call for dispensation or discretion from what would otherwise be required by strict justice in following the law.

J. Budziszewski provides a commentary on these passages that is especially helpful for us as we end this discussion of equity for Aquinas.

> As St. Thomas has argued… the general precepts of natural law are always binding, but the more detailed conclusions that follow from them are binding only in most cases; there are a few exceptions. May I ever steal? Never. May I ever refuse to return to someone an item of property he has entrusted to me? Usually, no, but in a few cases, yes; for example, if Joe asks me to return his rat poison because he wants it to commit suicide, I should refuse. Now consider two human laws: One that enforces the root precept of natural law "Never steal," another that enforces the branch precept of natural law "Always return property held in trust when the owner demands

---

[665] Ibid., pp. 455-456.

[666] Aquinas, *Treatise on Law*, p. 456.

> it." No dispensation is possible from the former human law, but dispensation is possible from the latter human law. When? In exactly those cases in which the natural law precept on which it is based has lost its binding force.[667]

And while the conclusion that Budziszewski draws still leaves much room for clarification, the idea seems to capture the relation between natural law precepts and the discretion or dispensation of equity for Aquinas's version of Neo-Aristotelian jurisprudence. As we move into more secular accounts of equity we will see that there are nonetheless remnants of the idea that equity maps onto natural law in significant ways for judges.

V. Marsilius and English Common Law on Equity

We begin this section of our chapter on equity with a quotation from Henry Sumner Maine, the great 19th century historian of legal thought:

> A time always comes at which the moral principles originally adopted have been carried out to all their legitimate consequences, and then the system founded on them becomes as rigid, as unexpansive, and as liable to fall behind moral progress as the sternest code of rules avowedly legal… It is easily seen by English lawyers that English Equity is a system founded on moral rules; but it is forgotten that these rules are the morality of past centuries–not of the present.[668]

We see here that equity can become as rigid as statutes. By the end of this section we will take up this problem identified by Maine. But first we will explore the secular ideas of equity for Marsilius.

We return to a passage from *The Defender of the Peace* that we have seen in another context:

> For although it would have been licit for the head of the single household to pardon or punish domestic wrongdoings entirely at his wish and pleasure, this would not have been licit for him as the chief of the first community called the village. The reason is that in this community, it was necessary for the elder to dispense what was just and advantageous by some reasonable ordinance or quasi-natural law, because so it

---

667 Ibid., p. 457.

668 Maine, *Ancient Law*, p. 69.

> seemed appropriate to everyone by a kind of equity and without much examination, purely by the common dictate of reason and a certain duty of human society.[669]

Equity is here discussed as a dictate of reason and as a reasonable ordinance.

Later in his work, *Defender of the Peace*, Marsilius explicitly addresses Aristotle's treatment of equity in his *Nicomachean Ethics*:

> It is further appropriate that in the future prince this virtue [of justice] should be accompanied by another, called "epiekeia," by which the judge is guided (especially as regards his inclinations) in those matters in which the law is deficient. Hence Aristotle says in *Ethics* IV, the treatise on justice: "And this is the nature of epiekeia, that it gives guidance to the law where it is deficient because of the particular." This, I think, is what the jurists want to call "equity." For it is a benign interpretation or tempering of law in a particular case, which the law includes within its universal rigor but in which the law is said to be deficient to the extent that it has not excepted it from its rule; and yet had it anticipated that it would come about, it would have made an exception from the universal rule, either through a certain modification or absolutely. Still further, on top of these virtues there is also required an unusual love or goodwill on the part of the future prince towards the polity and the citizens. For this means that the actions of the prince are directed towards both the common advantage and that of individuals, in concern and in goodness.[670]

Legal interpretation here is seen as a "tempering" of the harshness of the literal interpretation of a law. And for Marsilius the ultimate goal is to interpret and to apply the law so as to benefit the community. This way of understanding equity can give rise to quite a robust discretionary authority for the judge, something that the English Common lawyers at about the same time were working diligently to restrain even as they recognized that the "king's conscience" could be appealed to as a source of the tempering that Marsilius discusses.

Consider some passages from Frederic Maitland's lectures on equity from the beginning of the 20th century, discussing the 13th century origins of equity in England:

---

[669] Masilius of Padua, *Defender of the Peace*, p. 16.
[670] Ibid., pp. 84-85.

> In Edward I's day, at the end of the thirteenth century, three great courts have come into existence, the King's Bench, the Common Bench or Court of Common Pleas, and the Exchequer... One of the three courts, namely, the Exchequer, is more than a court of law. From our modern point of view it is not only a court of law but a "government office," and administrative or executive bureau...[and] there is the Chancery which is the secretarial department... At the head of the Chancery stands the Chancellor, usually a bishop... He is not yet a judge... But the Chancery has a certain limited power of inventing new writs to meet cases as they arise.[671]

The ability to issue new writs means the creation of remedies that in a sense go beyond the existing law of statutes. The Chancery Court is later called the Equity Court. This court was "not bound by precedent" but there were nonetheless procedures available for matters that the king felt should be heard, especially in fairness to the defendant.[672]

It is especially interesting that the Chancery Court dealt with the law from the standpoint of conscience. One legal scholar says that "the chancellor's court of conscience... began around 1370" and another legal scholar says that there was an explicit connection between chancery and the conscience of the king in 1391. By the 15th century there is a petition that "asks the chancellor to summon the defendants 'to come before you in the King's Chancery, which is the Court of Conscience, there to answer thereto as reason and conscience demand.'"[673]

In English case law at this time we also find attempts to specify what conscience was and why the Chancellor was to rule on this basis. Fortescue makes some general comments about conscience. The word, he says, "comes from *con* and *scioscis*. And so together they make "to know with God" to wit: to know the will of God as near as one reasonably can." This observation is significant for various reasons–notably that it makes judgment in conscience an effort to discern and do God's will. This fairly firmly places the measure of conscience in the law of God, and suggests that the judge in conscience is attempting, in some sense, to know as God knows... The conscience invoked appears not to have been particularly that of the litigant nor that of the Chancellor, but rather a somewhat disembodied or impersonal notion... So, the common complaint

---

[671] F.W. Maitland, *Equity: A Course of Lectures*, revised by John Brunyate, Cambridge: Cambridge University Press, 1909, 1936, pp. 2-3.

[672] See ibid., pp. 7-8.

[673] Quoted in Dennis R. Klinck, *Conscience, Equity, and the Court of Chancery in Early Modern England*, Burlington, VT: Ashgate Publishing Co., 2010, p. 13.

was that a person has acted "against conscience," not "against his conscience."[674] Like Aquinas, this links the law of nature or the law of God with conscience, and then also links to the legal notion of equity that is taken from Aristotle.

We can now begin to see the origins of the idea that equity is a matter of morality, the objective morality of right and wrong as it is understood in modern times. For Aristotle, equity is a kind of natural justice or fairness. In the Middle Ages, equity is the king's conscience, or what the king or his chancellor think God's law is, adapted to a particular case. And hence we come to the idea that is central to Henry Sumner Maine's 19th century account that equity is the correction of formal law by reference to the laws of nature and principles of morality.

The Anglo-American system of jurisprudence is the only one that established discrete courts of equity. And these courts can be traced back into the 13th and 14th centuries as we have just seen. Equity in the Middle Ages, in its institutionalization or in its abstract conceptualization, is associated with a kind of discretion or dispensation from formal law. But the problem was how to restrict the discretion so that judges could not merely overturn law in favor of their own interests or in some arbitrary manner. Equity was restricted by certain objective considerations. A judge was not to make conscience-based judgments on the basis of subjective interests but on objective moral norms. In this regard, equity was associated with natural law, just as had been true for the ancient Greeks, who largely invented the idea of equity.

Religion mixed with law in many ways in the Middle Ages, and we can see this clearly in the various ways that equity was conceived. Even in the seemingly secular English Common law, the earliest courts of equity administered by the chancellor normally had a bishop as the chancellor. And Marsilius, surely one of the most secular of the Medieval theorists, talked about equity serving the common good, and then saw the common good in terms of a quasi-natural law, as we saw in the previous chapter.

In all of these accounts of equity, morality plays a role in what counts as obligating law. But because the hallmark of the Middle Ages is the strong connection between religion, even highly organized religion, and law, the morality that is at the core of equity is a kind of religious morality–right and wrong as God would see it–a fully objective morality. But there was also a secular equity that was a natural principle or set of

---

[674] Quoted in ibid., p. 17.

principles, a principle of natural justice to which judges could appeal to disregard or dispense with the written law of the statutes.

SECTION XIV:

STATUS AND CRIMINALITY

CHAPTER 30

HERETICS

One of the characteristics of the history of Medieval legal and political thought is the way that religion and law are entwined in so many different ways. There are positive consequences such as in the way that equity came to have a central place in legal and political thought; but there are also negative consequences such as the ferocious focus on heretics in many aspects of law. In this chapter we will begin to take account of some of the ways that religious intolerance for heretics came to influence legal and political thought of the 12th to 14th centuries CE. In Chapter 31 we will look closely at two particular trials in this period, the trials of the Templars and of Joan of Arc. Then in Chapter 32 we will discuss more general issues in criminal law in this period. But for the current chapter we will see how heresy was regarded across our group of Neo-Aristotelian legal thinkers.

We begin in the first section with the Arabic Neo-Aristotelians, expanding our gaze slightly to include Averroes's discussions of what he calls "innovations." In the second section, we survey the extensive writings of Maimonides on heresy. And then in the third section we see even more extensive treatment of heretics in Aquinas's writings. In the fourth section we turn to Marsilius and others in Italian city-states at this time including Dante. And then in the fifth section we begin to see the institutional changes that occurred due to the writings of the legal and political theorists about how to treat heretics–almost always quite severely. This will then set the stage for a special look at two infamous trials, the trial of the Templars and the trial of Joan of Arc.

I. Innovations and Heresy in Averroes

We begin with Averroes's account of certain "innovations," a term he uses to stand for heretical ideas.

> Of the innovations that sprang up around this issue is the question regarding these attributes: "Are they identical with the essence or additional to it; that is, are they intrinsic or

> nominal?" By "intrinsic" I mean attributes that describe the entity as such, not because of an additional meaning of the entity itself, as when we say "one and eternal." By "nominal" I mean attributes that describe the self on the basis of some notion subsisting in it. The Ash'arites call these attributes nominal, meaning that these attributes are extraneous to the entity, meaning that [God] knows and that His knowledge is extraneous to Himself and that He is living, but life is additional to Himself, as is the case with visible [entities]. From this they are compelled to conclude that the Creator is a body, because then we would have an attribute and a substantive, a subject and a predicate, since that is the case with bodies. They must, then, concede that the entity is self-subsistent and the attributes subsist in it; or else that each one [of the attributes] is self-subsistent and thus the gods are many. This is the position of the Christians who believe in a Trinity of three Persons: Existence, Life, and Knowledge. Regarding this the Almighty says: "Unbelievers too are those who have said that Allah is the third of the three.[675]

So, while these differences with Islam are called "innovations" it is clear that Averroes regards those who hold to these innovations as unbelievers who are to be condemned for holding these views.

Averroes saw that the kinds of confusion that he had illustrated were such that they would lead not just to innovative heresy but ultimately to condemnation by God.

> When the lawgiver, God's blessing and peace be upon him, saw that something like this was bound to happen with respect to his religion, he said: "My community shall be split into seventy-two Sects, all but one shall be consigned to hell." He meant by that the one Sect that followed the literal meaning of Scripture and did not interpret it, divulging [its interpretation] to the public. Now if you ponder the state of this [our] religion at the present time and the widespread corruption it is exposed to due to interpretation, you would realize that this illustration is sound… As a result of this confusion and muddling, people split into two groups, one who took it upon itself to denounce philosophy and the philosophers and the other to interpret Scripture and assimilate it to philosophy. However, all this is an error; for Scripture should be accepted on its face value and the harmony between religion and philosophy should not be

[675] Averroes, *Faith and Reason*, translated by Ibrahim Najjar, Oxford: Oneworld Publications, 2001, p. 51.

> divulged to the ordinary people because such divulgence amounts to divulging philosophical conclusions without providing them with any proof thereof. To divulge philosophical conclusions to people who do not possess the demonstrations thereof is neither lawful nor permissible…[676]

As the translator of these passages says: "the statements of Scripture are either explicit and hence do not call for any interpretation, or ambiguous and hence should be interpreted exclusively by the learned… this interpretation should not be divulged to the general public, who are not able to fathom its meaning."[677]

Averroes elsewhere talks of a "ferocious form of punishment" for those who engage in willful wrongdoing.[678] But Averroes does not focus on what form that punishment will take, although there was certainly much in the Quran that he could have drawn on for explicit forms of punishment of heretics. But as primarily a philosopher it was not for Averroes to think of the kinds of acts that could count as ferocious forms of punishment of the unbelievers and those who maliciously sought to confuse the people. We cannot say the same of Maimonides and Aquinas who did talk about the forms of punishment due to the unbelievers and other heretics, as we will see.

In terms of the curious doctrine that the mass of people should not be told of the truths of religious faith, Averroes was not alone in this assessment since as we will next see Maimonides also held a similar view. Yet it is not at all clear that such a doctrine should be associated with any form of view that is said to follow from Aristotle's writings. It is well-known that Plato, as well as other ancient thinkers such as the Pythagoreans, held that the truths should be held closely by the philosophers and wise men, only teaching the masses by means of myths. But Aristotle stood against such doctrines–even though he was likewise no defender of democracy. We begin the next section of this chapter with a discussion of Maimonides's reasons for withholding from the masses the truths of religious faith as well as the penalties that should befall those who did what would lead the masses into heresy, in his *Guide of the Perplexed*.

---

676 Ibid., pp. 68-69.
677 Ibid., p. 4.
678 Averroes, *Middle Commentary on Aristotle's Rhetoric*, p. 145.

II. Maimonides and Heresy

Leo Strauss argues that *The Guide of the Perplexed* "contains a public teaching and a secret teaching. The public teaching is addressed to every Jew including the vulgar; the secret teaching is addressed to the elite."[679] As part of his argument, Strauss says:

> he makes a distinction between the view of the Law regarding providence and the true view (III 17, 25). He could well have said that the true view is the secret teaching of the Law. Instead he says that the true view is conveyed through the book of Job, a nonprophetic book whose characters are not Jews, and that is composed of an unknown author... marks a progress beyond the Torah and even beyond the prophets... Or to state the matter as succinctly as Maimonides does in the last chapter, the science of Law is something essentially different, not only from the post-biblical or at any rate extra-biblical legal interpretation of the Law, but from wisdom, i.e., the demonstration of the views transmitted by the Law, as well.[680]

Like Averroes, Maimonides does not think that the vulgar should be taught the word of God, but here he also seems to say that the Bible, as God's law given to Moses, is not to be the subject of demonstration for the elite either. And in this respect, Maimonides departs from Averroes to a certain extent.

Both Averroes and Maimonides argue for a kind of direct acquiring of wisdom from being exposed to the word of God. Both also reject the idea that study of the written word of God is something that the vulgar can or should engage in. They differ in that Averroes seems to place great stock in the ability of elites to work out the ambiguous parts of the written texts, and should be guided by faith instead, whereas Maimonides is skeptical that faith can get anyone to the wisdom of God's word. In the end, Averroes is a believer in the role of philosophical speculation and demonstration for the elite to achieve knowledge of God's Law, whereas Maimonides remains skeptical that either faith or philosophical demonstration can lead to wisdom, although a few philosophers (presumably like himself)

---

679 Leo Strauss, "How to Study the Guide of the Perplexed," in Maimonides, *The Guide of the Perplexed*, translated by Shlomo Pines, Chicago: University of Chicago Press, 1963, vol. I, p. xvii.

680 Ibid., p. xxxvi.

"were capable of grasping the philosophical doctrines" that would lead to wisdom.[681]

Maimonides is though as concerned as Averroes in the goal of stamping out aberrant interpretations of God's word or heresy, especially among philosophers. Heretics abounded not only among the common or vulgar people, but even more dangerously among the "philosophers and would-be philosophers."[682] As we will see in this section, Maimonides is more willing than Averroes to discuss what should be the fate of those who espoused heretical views.

Maimonides addresses the difficult issue of how to understand that "God sends down calamities upon an individual without their having been preceded by a sin…"[683] But we get a much more nuanced view in the *Mishneh Torah*, as in the following passages:

> He who repudiates the Oral Law is not to be identified with the rebellious elder spoken of in Scripture but is classed with the epicureans [whom any person has a right to put to death]. As soon as it is made public that he has repudiated the Oral Law [he is cast into the pit and is not rescued from it]. He is placed on a par with heretics, epicureans, those who deny the divine origin of Scripture, informers and apostates–all of whom are ruled out of the community of Israel. No witnesses or previous warning of judges are required. [Whoever puts any of them to death fulfills a great precept, for he removes a stumbling block.][684]

We see here that heretics are to be killed. More importantly, the killing of heretics does not turn on a court judgment that they have committed heresy. And indeed, it is an obligation of a person who knows a heretic to kill him directly. The harshness of these passages from Maimonides seems in keeping with Averroes's "ferocious forms of punishment" for the heretic as well.

III. Aquinas and Heresy

In Aristotle's discussion of heresy in his general discussion of unbelief, we find the following passages:

---

[681] See ibid., p. cxviii of the translators introduction to *The Guide of the Perplexed.*
[682] Ibid.
[683] *Guide*, vol. II, Ch. 24, p. 497.
[684] Maimonides, *The Book of Judges*, p. 143.

> he that holds the Christian faith aright, assents by his will, to Christ, in those things which truly belong to His doctrine. Accordingly, there are two ways in which a man may deviate from the rectitude of the Christian faith. First, because he is unwilling to assent to Christ; and such a man has an evil will, so to say, in respect of the very end. This belongs to the species of unbelief in pagans and Jews. Secondly, because, though he intends to assent to Christ, yet he fails in his choice of those things wherein he assents to Christ, because he chooses not what Christ really taught, but the suggestions of his own mind. Therefore heresy is a species of unbelief, belonging to those who profess the Christian faith, but corrupt its dogmas.[685]

Here we have a carefully drawn statement on the nature of heresy of Christians as a species of unbelief based on the acceptance of corrupt dogmas.

In Aquinas's view, heresy is properly a sin which is squarely within the authority of the Church to punish.

> We are speaking of heresy now as denoting a corruption of the Christian faith. Now it does not imply a corruption of the Christian faith , if a man has a false opinion in matters that are not of faith, for instance in matters of geometry and so forth, which cannot belong to the faith by any means; but only when a person has a false opinion about things belonging to the faith…certain doctors seem to have differed either in matters the holding of which in this or that way is of no consequence, so far as faith is concerned, or even in matters of faith; which were not as yet defined by the Church; although if anyone were obstinately to deny them after they had been defined by the authority of the universal Church, he would be deemed a heretic. This authority resides chiefly in the Sovereign Pontiff.[686]

The pope is considered the sovereign determiner of what heresy is and what it is not. And the Church thus has the authority to deal with the heretic as a matter of the Church's legal authority over matters of Christian belief.

Aquinas then addresses whether heretics should be tolerated and how their sins should be dealt with.

685 Aquinas, *Summa Theologica*, p. 1218.
686 Ibid., pp. 1219-1220.

> With regards to heretics two points must be observed: one on their side, the other on the side of the Church. On their own side there is the sin, whereby they deserve not only to be separated from the Church by excommunication, but also to be severed from the world by death. For it is a much graver matter to corrupt the faith which quickens the soul, than to forge money, which supports temporal life. Wherefore if forgers and other devil-doers are forthwith condemned to death by the secular authority, much more reason is there for heretics, as soon as they are convicted of heresy, to be not only excommunicated but even put to death. On the part of the Church, however, there is mercy which looks to the conversion of the wanderer; wherefore she condemns not once, but after the first and second admonition, as the Apostle directs: after that if he is yet stubborn, the Church no longer hoping for his conversion, looks to the salvation of others by excommunicating him and separating him from the Church, and furthermore delivers him to the secular tribunal to be exterminated thereby from the world.[687]

Here we have the separation of the penalty of excommunication, surely a Church matter, from execution which is said to be a matter for the civil authorities.

It was important that the Church not be the executioner but only the entity that removes the sinning heretic from the congregation. There is a kind of division of labor envisioned: the Church penalizes the soul of the heretic by excommunication whereas the civil authorities penalize the body of the heretic by execution. And we also find that the Church "should not protect them from the sentence of death."[688] But the Church should not be the one that does the executing. In the trials of heretics we find, as we see in the next chapter, the Church prosecutes the heretics and condemns the convicted heretic to excommunication but delivers the heretic to the civil authorities often to be burned at the stake, at least in part so that the Church officials do not have blood on their hands.

IV. Marsilius on Heretics

The secular perspective of Marsilius comes out especially clearly in his treatment of heretics. He argues that the civil authorities should be the ones that prosecute and punish the crime of heresy, and that the Church

---

687 Ibid., p. 1220.
688 Ibid., p. 1222.

officials should not play any role in these proceedings, contrary to the religiously-oriented thinkers we have just been examining. Here is the puzzle he presents us with at the beginning of his detailed chapter on heresy:

> But one might well raise a doubt about what we have said. For if (as shown earlier) jurisdiction over all those who must be constrained in this present life by coercive judgment, and the imposition and exaction of penalties in goods or in person, belongs to the prince alone by the authority of the human legislator, then the coercive judgment of heretics or those who are otherwise infidel or schismatic, as well as the imposition, exaction, and allocation of penalties in goods or in person, will belong to this prince. But this seemingly presents itself as a difficulty. For since it apparently belongs to the same authority to recognize, to judge, and to correct a misdeed, and it belongs to a priest (i.e. a priest or a bishop) to discern the crime of heresy, and no one else; it will certainly seem, then, that the coercive judgment or restraint of this crime and others like it belongs to a priest or bishop alone. Moreover, the judgment and exaction of penalty upon a delinquent belongs to him against whom, or against whose law, the delinquent has sinned. But this is a priest or bishop: for he is the minister and judge of divine law, against which any heretic, schismatic, or other infidel inherently sins, whether the sinner be a collective body or an individual person. It remains, therefore, that this judgment will belong to the priest and not to the prince.[689]

This is a characteristically clear and cogent statement of the puzzle about heresy. We will now take up how Marsilius proposes to solve this puzzle.

Marsilius begins his solution to the problem of who should judge and punish the heretic as follows:

> anyone who sins against divine law should be judged, corrected, and constrained according to that law. However, the judge in respect of it is twofold: one a judge… who has the coercive power to constrain aggressors of this law and to exact punishments from them, and this judge is one alone, sc. Christ… But Christ willed and ordained that all who transgress this law should be judged by coercive judgment in the world to come and be constrained by penalty or punishment in that world alone, and not in this… There is indeed another judge in respect of this law, viz. a priest or bishop. But he is not judge… in the sense

[689] Marsilius, *Defender of the Peace*, p. 232.

> that it would belong to him to constrain, in this world, anyone who transgresses this law… He is a judge in [that]… it belongs to him to teach, exhort, reveal in error, and reprove delinquents and transgressors, and to terrify them by his judgments of their future damnation…[690]

Yet, says Marsilius, neither Christ nor the priests and bishops can punish or coerce in this world and so we must look for another kind of judge in cases of heresy. We must seek a judge of matters in this world who has the authority to coerce in this world as well.

But now we have the problem that human judges generally have authority over matters of human law, not divine law. And then it is a question of whether heresy has indeed been made a crime of human law, for only when this is true can a heretic, in Marsilius's opinion, be coercively judged in this world. Here is the relevant discussion of what is needed for such a determination, first in general terms, and then in the particular case of heresy.

> we should notice that in any coercive judgment in this world, certain things need to be investigated, in an orderly fashion and so far as is relevant, before a sentence of acquittal or conviction is passed. One, whether the saying or action imputed to the accused is indeed of such a nature as it is said to be. And this is to know in advance what it is that is said to be committed. Two, whether doing something of this kind is forbidden by human law. Three, whether the accused did or did not commit it... The prince should be made certain of the first point by those who are expert in any particular discipline, to whom it belongs to consider the inherent what-it-is or nature of the saying or action that is imputed to the accused; for these experts are judges of such things… in which the prince has granted them the authority (… "a license")… The prince should be aware of the second point, sc. whether such a thing, if committed, is forbidden by law or not, from the law in its last and proper signification, in accordance with which the prince must exercise his function by the authority of the legislator. The third point that needs to be known is whether the person who is charged with the crime of heretical speech or activity did actually say or do that crime; and this judgment can be made by both the learned and the uneducated through their

[690] Ibid., p. 233.

> external and internal senses. The usual term for these people is "witnesses."[691]

According to this rather extensive analysis by Marsilius, there might be a role for clergy in a trial for heresy, but not the role that the other theorists we have examined have called for.

Basically the clergy could play the role of experts on what constitutes possible grounds for heresy–with the prince ultimately deciding how the contours of this crime are to be understood. The determination of guilt or innocence though would be treated as in other criminal proceedings–by an examination of witnesses and the application of the law to the facts of the case. The key though, according to Marsilius, is this:

> For a person is not punished by the prince just because he sins against divine law. For there are many mortal sins and sins against divine law, like fornication, which the human legislator permits even knowingly, and which a bishop or priest neither can nor should forbid by coercive power. But if a person, sc. a heretic, sins against divine law and that sin is also prohibited by human law, then he is punished in this world as a sinner against human law. For this is the precise or primary and inherent cause by someone constrained by penalty or punishment in this present world...[692]

As Marsilius then concludes, "judgment over heretics... belongs to the prince alone by the authority of the human legislator, and not to any priest or bishop whosoever as a result of the fact that they sin against divine law."[693] The priest or bishop can have a role in the proceedings, but not one as the authoritative judge of crimes of heresy committed, and punished, in this world.

V. Emerging Inquisitorial Tribunals for Heretics

In the 12th and 13th centuries various tribunals were established for the specific purpose of prosecuting heretics and stopping the spread of heresies. The best known were those tribunals organized by the Catholic Church, especially in Western Europe and England. What were called heresies often involved only minor divergences from Catholic orthodoxy either in terms of dogma or obedience to central governance by the

---

[691] Ibid., pp. 235-237.
[692] Ibid., p. 237.
[693] Ibid., p. 238.

Church. These heresies had begun to be identified in the 10th and 11th centuries but came under greatest scrutiny and prosecution in the centuries of the Middle Ages that followed.

It is initially of interest that the persecution of heretics was seen as a matter of judicial control. The law and legal authorities were enlisted to aid the Church in stopping the various heresies. And as we have already seen, there was a fierce battle over whether the use of trials and punishments of the state in connection to heresies should be governed by the Church through its bishops and priests or by the lay authorities who were normally recognized as governing trials and punishments. While the Church would use excommunication of early heretics, some lay leaders saw an opportunity to exert their authority by adding the penalty of execution which was not something Church leaders could administer on their own.[694]

The "inquisition" was the term used for the various trials that were launched by both religious and secular leaders to counter the heretical challenges to the Catholic Church. By the middle of the 12th century a trial was held for a particularly violent heretic in Brittany where there was first a Church tribunal that excommunicated the heretics and then they "were delivered to the lay power and burned."[695] This seems to have become a model for the later trials, especially the very high-profile trials of the Templars in the 14th century and of Joan of Arc in the 15th century, the subject of our next chapter, Chapter 31.

Here is how James Given describes the change in approach to heresy that occurred in the late 12th century.

> When popular heresy became a significant problem in the 12th century, the church experienced some embarrassment in dealing with it. Canon law was unclear on the proper procedure for handling heretics, and effective institutional means for identifying, prosecuting, and punishing them were lacking. Church authorities were long confused about what heretics believed and practiced, and the temptation to identify contemporary dissidents with those found in the pages of the church fathers was strong… In the course of the late twelfth and early thirteenth centuries, the church remedied these deficiencies in its treatment of its heretics. Decrees of councils and popes defined canon law concerning heretics. In 1184 Pope Lucius III issued the decretal *Ad Abolendam*. This

[694] See R. I. Moore, *The Formation of a Persecuting Society*, Oxford: Blackwell Publishing Co., Second edition, 2007, pp. 22-25.
[695] Ibid., p. 23.

> declared all heretics and their believers, defenders, and favorers to be excommunicate. Those found guilty of heresy were to be turned over to the law powers for appropriate punishment (the nature of which was left unspecified). Bishops were required twice a year to visit those parishes where heresy was reported and search out suspected heretics. In 1199 Innocent III in the decretal *Vergentis in senium* took the important step of assimilating heresy to treason as defined in Roman law. The property of heretics was to be confiscated by secular lords and their heirs disinherited. As the church clarified its laws concerning heretics, so did lay rulers. The emperor Frederick II incorporated the canon law strictures into imperial law and decreed that the punishment for unrepentant heretics was to be death at the stake. This became the penalty universally applied throughout Western Europe, including the kingdom of France… By the end of the thirteenth century, the church possessed an elaborate and well-developed body of law dealing with the problem of heresy.[696]

The stage was set for the trials of heretics that would last well into the modern era.

The institutions that were initially enlisted to prosecute and punish heresy were in many ways just the old institutions put into service for the crime of heresy. What was new was that the Church more freely used the punishment of excommunication than it had before, and that lay leaders worked with Church leaders so that a civil trial could follow closely on the heals of the ecclesiastical trial of the heretic. This new set of procedures reflected the growing concern about heresy especially in the Catholic Church. As we have seen, heresy was a problem for Islam and Judaism, but not nearly to the same extent as for Catholicism. Here is James Given:

> Central to the Medieval church's campaign against heresy was the creation of a specialized institution, charged specifically with the task of identifying, prosecuting, and punishing heretics and their sympathizers. When the local bishops had not succeeded in stamping out heresy, the papacy embarked on a policy of appointing special judges delegated to pursue heretics. In selecting men to carry out this task, the pope turned to the new mendicant orders that had come into existence in the early thirteenth century, the Dominicans and Franciscans.

[696] James B. Given, *Inquisition and Medieval Society*, Ithaca, NY: Cornell University Press, 1997, pp. 13-14.

> The Dominicans, in particular, had a special vocation for combating heresy.[697]

It is interesting that in the context of our current chapter, Thomas Aquinas was a member of the Dominican order and that he lived at the time of the first of the inquisitorial tribunals, the special courts set up to deal with heresy.

We can see the way that the Catholic Church had become entwined with the civil law of Europe in the way that heresy came to be one of the most significant crimes, on the same order as treason. And in part this was because heresy challenged not only the Church but the civil system of government and law that had been linked so inextricably to that church. The same could certainly have been said of Islam, and the penalties for heresy and apostasy were often equally severe in Islamic societies as in Christian ones. The Quran had dealt with such matters in detail–but Christian religious texts had not been so clear about the threat of heresy and how it was to be treated. Judaism did not have a connection to an empire at this time and so heresy was dealt with solely as a religious matter.

We should note in ending though that the inquisitorial tribunals were soon to be used not only for Christian heretics but also for prosecuting Jews and lepers–as well as others thought to be common enemies of the Church and its community. The idea that heresy was a kind of treason was also applied to the worries about Jews. And it is not much of a leap to think that people with incurable communicable diseases were also a threat to community in the way that treason could be. The inquisitors saw their job to be that of protecting their communities from all sorts of outside assaults, both spiritual and physical. This in part explains the zeal by which the inquisitors pursued their prey as we will see in much more detail in the next chapter.

---

[697] Ibid., p. 14.

CHAPTER 31

THE TRIALS OF THE TEMPLARS AND JOAN OF ARC

In the 14th and 15th centuries, the crime of heresy was of special interest to religious scholars and secular lawyers alike. There were several very high-profile trials for heretics that were prosecuted by the "inquisitions." In this chapter we will look at two of these trials: the first is a trial for heresy prosecuted against the Templars, a celibate lay order that aided Christendom in the Crusades; the second was a trial for heresy and other charges against the teenage Joan of Arc, who had rallied French troops against the English. In both cases, the inquisitors took on very popular groups and individuals in seeking among other things to show that disobedience to the Church was a kind of heresy that could lead to being burned at the stake.

In the first section we survey some of the facts concerning the trials of the Templars. In the second section we similarly survey the facts of the trial of Joan of Arc. In the third section of this chapter we discuss the trial procedures for prosecutions employed by inquisitors. In the fourth section we examine the use of torture, or the threat of torture, in prosecutions for heresy. In the final section we draw some general conclusions about the inquisitions and argue that the abuses of the inquisitions surely outweighed any possible gains, even for the Church in its battle against various forms of heresy. Throughout we are aided by remarkably detailed accounts of these trials that survived for us today.

I. The Charges Against the Templars

Malcolm Barber starts us off with a good description of the Templars and what they were accused of:

> The Templars were a military religious order, founded in the Holy Land in 1119. During the twelfth and thirteenth centuries they acquired extensive property both in the crusader states in Palestine and in Syria and in the West… Until the Templars

> were forced to leave 'Arlit they had functioned as defenders of the holy places and Latin settlements in Palestine and Syria for 172 years without a break. They had begun modestly when, in 1119, two French knights, Hugh of Payns and Godfrey of Saint-Omer together with a small number of companions, volunteered to protect pilgrims travelling from the port of Jaffa to Jerusalem and the surrounding holy places… and to serve the sick.[698]

The Templars were similar to the Hospitallers, and they had sewn "a distinctive red cross onto their mantles." The Templars grew in number and built castles throughout the Middle East. They also grew substantially in wealth, receiving land and money from many wealthy Christians at their deaths. The pope saw them as an especially important ally as they became known as bankers for Church leaders.

On October 13, 1307 the leading Templars living in France were arrested and "charged with serious heresies encompassing the denial of Christ, the spitting on the crucifix, indecent kissing and homosexuality" as well as idol worshipping.[699] The Templars in France had been arrested by agents of the king and turned over to prosecutors. But the pope was initially opposed to the prosecution and it took six months from the time of arrest until the trial could begin with the pope's reluctant blessing (perhaps granted under coercion by the king).

One of the first things the inquisitors did was to seize the Templars' land, which raises the initial question of whether there was a hidden reason for arresting the Templars unrelated to their supposed acts of heresy. Indeed, the trials of the Templars in the early 14th century enriched the religious and political leaders who orchestrated the trials. Some critics have said that it was probably as much a matter of jealousy and greed that drove these trials as was the concern about the crime of heresy, as we will see. One early accuser of the Templars said:

> For a long time they remained faithful to their noble vows, carrying out their duties fairly satisfactorily. Afterwards they forgot about humility… and abandoned the patriarch of Jerusalem, who had established their Order…They refused him obedience that their predecessors had shown him. They even

[698] Malcolm Barber, *The Trial of the Templars*, Cambridge: Cambridge University Press, 1978, 2003, p. 1, 7.

[699] See ibid., p. 1.

> caused many problems for the churches of God by removing their tithes and unjustly harassing their possessions.[700]

It is clear that their financial wealth and power was at the heart of the concerns about the Templars.

Yet when the first arrests were made in the early 14th century, various salacious charges were the public rationale for the objection to the Templars as we see here:

> To the king's great astonishment and horror, persons "worthy of faith" had recounted to [King Philip IV] the criminality of the brothers of the Temple who… when they were received into the Order, denied Christ three times and spat three times on his image. Then, stripped of their secular clothing, and brought naked before the senior Templar in charge of their reception, they are kissed by him on the lower spine, the navel, and finally on the mouth, "in shame of human dignity, according to the profane rite of the Order." Moreover, by a vow of their profession, they are then obliged to indulge in carnal relations with other members of the Order, "being required without the possibility of refusal." Finally, "this unclean people forsake the font of life-giving water" and make offerings to idols.[701]

Homosexuality and denouncing of Christ were among the chief charges against the Templars in their trial in France.

II. The Charges Against Joan of Arc

We are fortunate to have a detailed account of the trial of Joan of Arc that took place from January to May in 1431; indeed some of this account appears to be a verbatim transcript. Here is a letter that King Henry VI wrote concerning the charges against Joan of Arc:

> Henry, by the grace of God, king of France and England, to all who will see this present letter, greeting.
> It is sufficiently notorious and well known how for some time past, a woman calling herself Joan the Maid, abandoned women's clothes and dressed and armed herself like a man, a thing against divine law and abominable to God, and condemned and forbidden by every law. She committed cruel

---

[700] Translated in ibid., p. 16.
[701] Translated in ibid., p. 59.

> murders and, as reported, seduced and abused simple people by trying to convince them that she was sent by God and knew heavenly secrets, with other dangerous beliefs most scandalous and prejudicial to our holy catholic faith. While fostering these deceptions and engaging in hostilities against us and our people, she was captured fully armed before Compiegne by some of our loyal subjects, then brought to us as a prisoner. And because many have suspected and accused her of superstition, of spreading false dogmas and of crimes of treason against divine majesty, we have been urgently entreated by the reverend father... to surrender Joan to the reverend father for questioning and examination, so that gathering a proper assembly, he can proceed against her according to the rules and regulations of divine and canon law... We therefore command our men and officers guarding Joan to release and deliver her to the reverend father, without refusal or contradiction, whenever he asks them. We further command all our men of justice, officers or subjects, both French and English, neither to hinder nor in any way to disturb him or any others who are ordered to attend, take part in, and hear this trial...[702]

It is of interest that the first of the charges mentioned was that Joan of Arc wore men's clothing, supposedly contrary to divine law. But the trial was for heresy and treason as we will come to see, and as the letter mentions but does not single out as chief among the charges.

We can see better what the main legal charges against Joan of Arc were by seeing the summons issued by Pierre Cauchon who ordered Joan to appear before the inquisitor of France, Jean Graverent.

> A certain woman commonly called Joan the Maid was caught and taken in our diocese of Beauvais, and our most serene and Christian prince the king of France and England delivered and released her entirely to us, under grave suspicion of heresy, that we might initiate proceedings against her in matters of faith.... Therefore, peremptorily summon the said Joan, so gravely suspect of heresy, to appear before us in the castle of Rouen at eight o'clock in the morning of Wednesday, February

---

[702] Henry VI, "Letter regarding the Delivery of Joan to Pierre Cauchon," January 3, 1431, in *The Trial of Joan of Arc*, translated by Daniel Hobbins, Cambridge, MA: Harvard University Press, 2005, p. 40.

> 21, to answer the truth to the articles and questions and to other accusations, and to be dealt with according to law and reason.[703]

Here it is clear that heresy is the main charge and in this document the only charge for which Joan will be tried.

One historian has provided an analysis of the legal and also the political basis for the trial of Joan of Arc. Here are some passages that are revealing:

> Joan of Arc was tried as a heretic not because she was a woman, although that factor played an important part, nor because she heard voices, but because she heard voices telling her to attack the English. Joan believed that God favored the French: God was on her side. This problem surfaced several times during the interrogations… As long as she insisted on this point, that her voices were saints telling her to attack the English, she was doomed. Such a claim challenged the legal basis for the Anglo-Burgundian regime formed by the Treaty of Troyes in 1420… Her judges needed to show that her voices were false. The motivation for the trial was political because Joan's claims were political: if true, they would have invalidated the English claim to legitimate rule in France… On the other hand, the theological task of demonstrating Joan's claims to be false opened the door to all the other accusations designed to show that Joan was a heretic, such as her clothing, her fighting, and her refusal to submit to the Church. This dual nature of the trial is what makes it such a challenge to analyze.[704]

The trial was for heresy but heresy was both a theological and a political crime in the early 1400s.

Heresy was a theological crime in that it was a violation of theological orthodoxy or of various doctrines and creeds thought to be central to Catholic faith. And because of the close intertwining of the state and church, heresy was also a political crime in that it was a form of treason by violating the civil laws and failing to recognize the church's role in maintaining the authority of the king and Catholic leaders. Joan of Arc refused at various points to recognize the authority of the Church

---

[703] Pierre Cauchon, "Summons from Pierre Cauchon, Ordering Joan to Appear," February 20, 1431, in *The Trial of Joan of Arc*, translated by Daniel Hobbins, Cambridge, MA: Harvard University Press, 2005, pp. 47-48.

[704] *The Trial of Joan of Arc*, translated and introduced by Daniel Hobbins, ibid., pp. 20-21.

elders and ministers who put her on trial, and by denying their authority she showed herself to be a heretic by not submitting herself to the church's authority. But her heretical beliefs also led her to challenge the civil authorities, recognizing as king a person who was not ordained to be king at the time in France.

We can see the political aspect of the heresy trial in a few more passages from the trial account:

> Asked what instruction the voice gave her for her soul's salvation, she said it taught her to behave herself and go to church, and said to her, Joan, that she must come to France... The voice told her that she must raise the siege of the city of Orleans. She said the voice next told her that she, Joan, must go to Vaucouleurs to find Robert de Baudricourt, the captain there, and that he would supply her with men.[705]

So, part of her heresy was that she took up arms against the king that the pope had recognized as the legitimate king of France. And it certainly did not help Joan of Arc's case that we also find that Joan is insolent toward her accusers as when: "She told us the bishop 'You say that you are my judge. Take care what you do, for in truth I am sent from God, and you put yourself in great peril.'"[706]

III. Trial Procedures and the Inquisitions

Here is a recent summary of the of inquisitorial procedure drafted by Bernard Gui in his book of inquisitorial procedures from the early 14th century in Toulouse:

> When a suspect was brought to Bernard Gui's attention, a citation was sent out. If the person concerned did not appear, he was provisionally excommunicated, a sentence which became definitive after the lapse of a year... The secular authorities were empowered to arrest the suspect...The accused was interrogated by the inquisitor and his assistants, and a summary of the proceedings was recorded by a notary. The aim was to establish guilt, either by confession or by the use of testimonial evidence. He was not allowed a defending advocate, even if he could have found one, and witnesses were reluctant to testify in his behalf for fear of guilt by association. Hostile

[705] Ibid., p. 54.
[706] Ibid., p. 59.

> witnesses were allowed to remain anonymous on the grounds that they might otherwise be intimidated, and the accused could only read a précis of their depositions. In contrast to secular proceedings, all kinds of witnesses could be used, even perjurers, criminals, and the excommunicate. The accused could only list his enemies in the hope that some names would coincide with the witnesses.[707]

The inquisitions did not allow the defendant much in the way of procedural or substantive rights, especially concerning having counsel or challenging witnesses.

In the trial of Joan of Arc, approximately a century after the trial of the Templars, the procedures employed were similar. Here is a summary of the procedure employed in Joan of Arc's trial:

> Joan's trial was an ecclesiastical procedure covered under canon law, the law governing the medieval Church… a heresy investigation carried out under the legal procedure known in canon law as inquisition. At its core, inquisition was a trial procedure in which the judge himself… brought charges against the defendant…The essential feature of inquisition was that the accusation against the defendant came in the form of a public outcry or general belief that the accused had committed a crime… Once infamy had been established–that is, the existence of public outrage–the bishop or another ecclesiastical judge could summon the defendant and investigate the truth of the accusations. The judge was to present the defendant with a list of charges in the form of chapters or articles. The judge could then require the defendant to swear an oath to tell the truth. Especially in the fifteenth century, the judge was assisted by a "promoter" who prosecuted the case… The manuals encouraged the judge to ask for assistance from experts ("assessors") in law and theology, a recommendation that Pierre Cauchon took very seriously… Proof of guilt could be established through the testimony of witnesses or of the accused (the primary method in Joan's case), but the ultimate proof was confession.[708]

In the inquisitions of the 14th and 15th centuries, the main procedure was to extract a confession from the accused. To this end there was no counsel for the accused and all sorts of hearsay and prejudicial testimony was allowed.

[707] Summarized in Malcolm Barber, *The Trial of the Templars*, pp. 28-29.
[708] *The Trial of Joan of Arc*, pp. 14-16.

Clergy testified as experts in the law, not merely in canon law. This is surely why the "inquisitions" have had such a bad name down through the centuries. But there were other reasons as well, including the extensive use of torture that we will take up next.

IV. Torture and Psychological Intimidation in Inquisitions

If one of the points of an inquisition was to obtain a confession from the accused, then it is fairly easy to see why torture would have been a common practice either as employed to obtain a confession or as something threatened to secure a confession. Here is one account of the instructions to inquisitors in the Templars cases about the procedures to be employed to seek the desired confession.

> The instructions next explain the treatment which should be handed out to those who persisted in their denials even after questioning on this close pattern. They are to be put on "a restricted diet, namely bread and water and a few other refreshments, unless infirm, weak or for any other reason in need, in which case more may be administered to them." If they still have not told the truth, nor have been convicted in any other way, they should be shown the confessions made by the grand master and the other leaders, contained in the apostolic bull, and they should be told of the great many Templars who have freely confessed. If there is a Templar who has a good record of persevering in his confession he should be sent to talk to them in an effort to convince them. Finally, if this is not efficacious, torture should be threatened and the instruments shown to them. As a last resort torture should actually be applied, at first lightly, and always in accordance with proper procedures, that is in the presence of an appropriate cleric, and "without excess."[709]

The Templars were the subject of nearly systematic torture, and so the fact that the torturers followed proper procedure seems a bit beside the point, as we will discuss in the final section of the chapter.

We can also see how torture was threatened in Joan of Arc's trial, as we see from this summary of the 15th century inquisitorial trial manual:

> In strictly legal terms, the long interrogation of Joan was directed toward this one end. Here a role appeared for torture,

[709] Malcolm Barber, *The Trial of the Templar,* pp. 133-134.

> which might encourage the confession. Civil courts regularly used torture, which they had recovered from Roman law. In the early 14th century, however, Clement V regulated its use in ecclesiastical trials after abuses occurred. Although torture seems to have been used less often in the later Middle Ages (inquisition manuals and records rarely make mention of it) it certainly did not disappear. Joan of Arc herself was threatened with torture–primarily, it seems, as a strategy to encourage her confession, though three of thirteen assessors did recommend its use.[710]

While Joan of Arc was not tortured in the normal corporal ways she was definitely tortured psychologically as the trial summaries make abundantly clear.

As an example of a kind of psychological torture, Joan of Arc was repeatedly denied her request to attend mass and the sacrament of confession–all of this apparently aimed at intimidating her into making a confession to the inquisitors rather than to a confessor.

> Then after reading of these letters, the promoter urgently requested that the woman be ordered to appear before us in judgment, according to the summons, to be examined on specific articles of faith, and we granted this request. In the meantime, since the woman had asked to hear Mass first, we explained to the assembly that we had consulted the worthy lords and masters, and that, given the crimes of which she was accused and the shameful attire she insisted on wearing, they had decided we should postpone permission for her to hear Mass or attend divine office... Asked by us to say the Our Father, she said that if we would hear her confession, she would gladly say it for us. And after we asked her many times to say it, she replied that she would not say the Our Father unless we heard her confession...Then we the bishops forbade Joan to return from her prison cells in the castle of Rouen without our leave...[711]

The withholding of the sacraments, especially of confession, and even the hearing of mass, were designed to work psychologically on Joan as if she had been put on the rack. It pained her to be deprived of the solace of the rituals she had come to know since she was a child.

---

[710] *The Trial of Joan of Arc*, translated and edited by Daniel Hobbins, p. 16.
[711] *The Trial of Joan of Arc*, pp. 48-51.

In addition, I would point out that in the trials of the Templars and of Joan of Arc there was significant intimidation by having a large number of well-known clergy and professors as the team that accused and questioned during the inquisitions. The sheer number of these people–ranging into the dozens–and one after another questioning for hours was surely also designed to coerce. Here is a list of the people who were part of Joan of Arc's inquisition in her ordinary trial in addition to the main inquisitor:

> Brother Jean Le Maistre, vice inquisitor, presiding, assisted by reverend fathers, lords, and masters: Giles, abbot of Fecamp, Pierre, prior of Longueville, Jean Beaupere, Jacques de Touraine, Nicolas Midi, Pierre Maurice, Gerard Feuillet, Erard Emengart, Guillaume le Boucher, Maurice de Quesnay, Jean de Nibat, Jean le Fevre, Jacques Guesdon, Jean de Chatillon, doctors of theology; Raoul Roussel, doctor of canon and civil law; Jean Guerin, doctor of canon law; Robert Le Barbier, Denis Gastinel, Jean le Doux, licentiates of canon and civil law; Nicolas de Venderes, Jean Pinchon, Jean Basset, Jean le Fontaine, Jean Colombel, Aubert Morel, Jean Duchemin, licentiates of canon law; Andre Marguerie, archdeacon of Petit-Caux, Jean Alespee, Nicolas Caval, Geoffroi de Crotay, licentiates of civil law; Guillaume Desjardins and Jean Tiphaine, doctors of medicine; Guillaume Haiton, bachelor of theology; Guillaume de la Chambre, licentiate of medicine; Brother Jean Duval, Brother Ysambard de la Pierre of the Order of Friars Preachers; William Brolbster and John Hampton, priests.[712]

By my count there were 40 or more people who were theologians, doctors of medicine, canon lawyers, civil lawyers, and clergy of various descriptions from both France and England. This was an incredibly prestigious and also intimidating group, indeed it seems that the aim was probably to intimidate for why else would so many be required to attend?

V. Assessing the Use and Abuse of Inquisitions

To start at the most positive, heresy was considered an assault on the social order, as I said, the equivalent of treason against the state. When the state and the church are deeply intertwined, as they were in the Middle Ages in Europe, then it is very close to treason to attack or undermine the

[712] *The Trial of Joan of Arc*, p. 119.

church. So, one can see the heresy trials of the fourteenth and fifteenth centuries as the normal reaction to real threats to the existing order of the state and church. This is perhaps the strongest that can be said, if indeed the heresy claimed really did threaten the existing order and the authority of the church and state.

In addition, the crime of heresy was ill-defined as a crime since so much of it was due to the mental state of the accused–where the idea of willfully rejecting Church dogma required an examination of the accused's will. In trials where it is the state of mind of the accused that needs to be plumbed, rather than an examination of the facts, there is some plausibility in using coercive tactics to elicit confessions about the accused's state of mind. So, this is one of the strongest reasons for the use of torture in these heresy trials, if it were not for the fact that torture rarely works–people generally will say what they think their inquisitors want them to say to get the torture or coercion to stop. So, it is not a good tactic if what is wanted is the truth.

The charge of heresy is related to the failure to obey church authority in that the dogma denied by the heretic was that the church had the authority to dictate obedience. While this is a dubious claim, at least one can say that there is something to investigate that might warrant the conviction of the crime of heresy. And one can see that the disobedience of the church leadership is indeed related to the kind of thing that a traitor does concerning civil authority. But remember that the crime of heresy was punished, like the crime of treason, by death. So, the willful failure to obey church authority concerning matters of dogma does not seem to be the kind of thing that warrants the death penalty unless the act of disobedience in some significant sense threatened the very order of the church in the way that some acts of treason threaten the order of the civil authority. Nonetheless this is a kind of middle case, not nearly as bad as what we will take up next.

On the other side of the coin, consider some of the most outrageous charges, namely that heresy could be shown by demonstrating that a woman wore men's clothing, or that heresy could be shown by demonstrating that a man kissed another man on the lips. These charges, against Joan of Arc and the Templars respectively, are similar in that they concern the violation of a cultural norm recognized at the time. But in what sense is the violation of these norms an act of heresy? Or if it is an act of heresy, is it the kind of heretical act that warrants the death penalty? It seems that the death penalty would only be warranted if the heretical act really was like an act of treason. Yet, bending gender norms hardly seems of this sort.

Another obvious criticism of inquisitions that results from our analysis so far is that they seem to fail to distinguish among aberrant acts–such as acts of denying that women should not ever dress in men's clothing even when they are doing men's jobs versus acts of denial of the virgin birth or the resurrection of Christ. Or there is the failure to distinguish between offering a kiss as a sign of brotherhood and hence denying that men should never kiss other men, versus denying that people should tithe to support the legitimate activities of the Church.

Next we must consider the clear use of lies and fabrications in the charges against the alleged heretics in the two cases we have examined. The charge of rampant homosexual practices, including forced sex, among the Templars does not appear to have had any supporting evidence presented at the various trials. Similarly, the charge that the Templars were forced to spit on the cross also appears not to have any evidentiary support. When trumped up charges are added, it normally means that the other charges are considered too weak to sustain a guilty verdict.

In the case of Joan of Arc, the claims that she deceived various religious and civil leaders by lying to them also appears to have scant supporting evidence presented at her trial. It is true that she claimed to hear voices of various saints and angels. This could be evidence of lying if one thinks that there are no angels or saints whose voices Joan could have heard. But the problem for the inquisitors was that they did believe that angels and saints could speak to normal people so that Joan claiming to hear these voices is not proof that she was lying, or at least should not have been seen as proof by people who thought such voices were possible.

These heresy trials have been roundly condemned over the centuries since the time when they occurred. Those who have mounted partial defenses have stressed that we must look at things from the perspective of the people living at that time rather than from our own perspectives. And I agree with this last claim, but only up to a certain point. The abuses that took place can in some instances be justified by reasonable fear of the heretics disrupting the social order. But when the fears were unreasonable, for any person who is thinking clearly, then we should not dismiss the criticisms. In the last few paragraphs of this chapter I want to address the larger challenge to criticisms of legal practices that they must be only assessed from the perspective of the people at the time.

While many norms are culturally specific, there are nonetheless universal norms as well. Some of these norms are encapsulated in human rights terms. The use of torture and other coercive measures to extract false confessions during the inquisitions cannot easily be justified solely by appeal to cultural norms because there are other norms at stake as well.

It is initially worth noting that obtaining a false confession or one that was quite likely to be false cannot easily be justified even in terms of the cultural norms of the time. The only plausible justification for the use of torture and other forms of psychological intimidation is that this was the only way to get truthful confessions. To ferret out the true heretics and stop them from threatening the social order, it was surely important to find those who were heretics–coercing non-heretics can't serve any purpose that would justify torture and other forms of psychological intimidation.

But from the standpoint of human dignity and human rights, as universal values, torture and psychological intimidation could only very rarely if at all be justified because these tactics are themselves such a direct assault on human dignity. By design, torture is meant to stretch to the limits what humans can bear in terms of pain. The theory is that at the point where the pain is utterly unbearable, the person will admit to anything to get the pain to stop. At that point, the person has ceased to be in control of himself or herself and the torturer is now in control. This then denies the person's will and with it the dignity of the person.

The Neo-Aristotelian ethical position espoused by the great legal and political thinkers of this time, especially Maimonides and Aquinas, and also Averroes and Marsilius, would not have countenanced the denial of the free will of the person. Even as these Medieval thinkers did not necessarily condemn torture, from their philosophical premises they certainly should have condemned the torture used in the inquisitions. Of course, the Aristotelian views were mixed with religious views, and the religious views may have at least condoned torture as a means of countering evil. But the denial of the human spirit implicit in torture certainly runs contrary to Aristotle in *De Anima* and *Metaphysics* Book X.

CHAPTER 32

CRIMINAL JUSTICE AND CAPITAL PUNISHMENT

In this chapter we will explore the ideas of criminal justice and punishment with special emphasis on capital punishment. The Neo-Aristotelian legal theorists we have been examining held strong views about criminal justice and punishment, although they differed on whether to support capital punishment. Nonetheless, all of these theorists supported strong corporal punishment. It is not initially clear how these views were related to those of Aristotle, and so this will be our first task. I will argue that it seems that the religious views of these theorists are more responsible for their views on the death penalty than their Aristotelian sympathies.

In the first section we will take up the criminal justice views of Averroes, looking especially at how he supports his views from Aristotelian premises. In section two we look at Maimonides's theory of criminal justice and punishment. And in the third section we turn to Aquinas's views of criminal justice and punishment. Then in section four we examine the views of our theorists regarding two specific forms of punishment, first corporal and then capital punishment. And in the final section we attempt to draw some conclusions about the reasons why some Neo-Aristotelian theorists supported capital punishment and others did not. We will also look at the secular theorists at this time to see if the religious beliefs of the three Neo-Aristotelians were driving their views of punishment.

I. Averroes's Aristotelian View of Criminal Justice

In Averroes's commentary on Aristotle's *Rhetoric*, we find a lengthy discussion of criminality and appropriate punishments for those who commit crimes. Following Aristotle, Averroes first discusses the nature of wrongdoing:

> Aristotle said: First, we must define the act of wrongdoing, and then speak of each one of these three things [the doer of the wrongdoing, the person who suffers the wrongdoing, and act of wrongdoing itself].
> Then we say: An act of wrongdoing is injury inflicted voluntarily by way of transgression of the laws.[713]

We can see that Averroes is at pains to show that his view of the nature of wrongdoing is greatly indebted to Aristotle. Indeed, Averroes's reference to voluntariness is one of the most important components of wrongdoing for Aristotle.

Next we see the discussion turn to the causes of wrongdoing and how this affects the society's proper reaction to wrongdoing:

> Aristotle said: Since we established this matter, our discussion has come to the point where we must explain the motives behind the acts of wrongdoing…
> Thus the acts of wrongdoers are undoubtedly due to one or another of seven causes: one of them is chance; the second, nature; the third, compulsion; the fourth, habit and character; the fifth, reasoning; the sixth, anger; the seventh, appetite. All except the ones coming from reasoning, are the divisions of poor judgment that we have mentioned earlier.[714]

Averroes then proceeds to discuss each of these causes of wrongdoing until he comes to anger:

> The end of wrongdoing that is due to anger is revenge. Revenge is something other than punishment, for punishment is inflicted for the sake of the person punished, either for his own good or for the good of the city, or inflicted for the pleasure felt because of the punishment itself.[715]

And it is the connection between wrongdoing and the society's response in terms of punishment that interests Averroes just as much as it did Aristotle.

In discussing how people evade punishment for their wrongdoing, Averroes points to the way that some people make friends of their judges or corrupt the judges by paying them. And in a comment that is certainly as true today as it was then, Averroes says: "What motivates sly and

---

[713] Averroes, *Middle Commentary on Aristotle's Rhetoric*, p. 142.
[714] Ibid., pp.143-144.
[715] Ibid., p. 145.

cunning people to do wrong is that they present the act of wrongdoing in such a manner as to make other people believe it is not a wrongful act."[716] Here is the way that rhetoric can have clearly negative effects on the criminal justice system. It is also true, though, that sometimes this rhetorical move is acceptable such as when the person has engaged in wrongdoing out of necessity, as when a person is in need because he or she is poor.

Another significant excuse of wrongdoing is when the wrongdoing "is inflicted on those who have, intentionally or unintentionally, committed something bad and indecent in the eyes of people." But in this case "the doer of such an act is not considered a wrongdoer."[717] Punishment is a kind of wrongdoing, but such a kind that it is not really considered *wrong*doing because the doing is in reaction to someone else's wrongdoing, now understood as a punishment rather than a wrongdoing.

Averroes then tackles the difficult subject of when a person is due forgiveness rather than punishment. He sets out eleven premises that he says he has derived from Aristotle, each of which are relevant today as well. I will focus on several of these in the passages that follow:

> The first of the premises by means of which the offender asks for forgiveness for the offences that must be punished according to the written law–that is, those premises that Aristotle discussed in this book [the *Rhetoric*]–is that the offender says, "Oh punisher, you must not follow the model of this particular rule with regard to the punishment that accordingly must be imposed on me, but you must follow the model of the character of the legislator who laid it down for the purpose of forgiveness and mercy"...
> The third premise is that [the offender] says, "The punishment inflicted on me must not be based on the act that appears to have been done by me, but it must be based on intention and choice"...
> The sixth premise is that [the offender] reminds the judge who imposes the sentence of the good things rendered from the part of the wrongdoer to the person being wronged...[718]

These grounds for clemency tell us quite a lot about how Averroes views proper punishment and mercy. Here forgiveness is an important virtue

[716] Ibid., p. 158.
[717] Ibid., p. 161.
[718] Ibid., pp. 167-168.

when it is grounded in special considerations or especially considerations of context that would countenance not following a strict rule of justice.

But for Averroes, there are classes of wrongdoing that should not be forgiven or treated less harshly, even in these circumstances.

> For acts of injustice like these–that is, those that fall upon the houses of God and upon his friends–there is no forgiveness, no clemency, and no forbearance, since forgiveness and clemency for such acts are not required by any kind of interest; but in cases like these the judge must inevitably carry out the sentence, either for vengeance against the criminal only or for the sake of the general good.[719]

Notice here that wrongdoing that offends God is treated most severely. It is not clear that Averroes can find passages in Aristotle to back up this claim, and indeed it seems that Averroes is being more influenced here by his Islamic background than by his reading of Aristotle. We will have more to say about this issue in the final section of this chapter.

II. Maimonides and Criminal Justice

In Maimonides work, The *Mishneh Torah*, we find a discussion of crime and punishment that is influenced, to a certain extent, by Aristotle, but also by the tradition of the Torah and the Talmud. He begins his treatment of murder in his Book of Torts as follows:

> If one slays a human being, he transgresses a negative commandment, for Scripture says, *Thou shalt not murder* (Exod. 20:13). If one murders willfully in the presence of witnesses, he is put to death by the sword, for when Scripture says, *He shall surely be punished* (Exod. 21:20), we have learned from tradition that this means death by the sword. Whether one slays another with an iron weapon or burns him in a fire, he is put to death by the sword.[720]

We will say more about the death penalty later in this chapter, but at the moment notice that murder is to be severely punished and the rationale is largely drawn in terms of the Torah, the first five books of the Hebrew Bible.

---

[719] Averroes, *Middle Commentary*, p. 170.

[720] Maimonides, *The Code of Maimonides, Book VI: Book of Torts*, p. 195.

The general idea is that there must be an "avenger of the blood." Maimonides explains how in most cases the avenger should be the closest family member of the victim. But if there are no close family members, or if they do not want to avenge the blood of their kin, then "the court must put the murderer to death by the sword."[721] In some respects this is an extension of *lex talionis* ("an eye for an eye") also of the Torah, although first articulated much earlier in Hammurabi's code from ancient Mesopotamia of 1750 BCE.

Yet there are important exceptions to the idea that people are to be blood avengers.

> If a murderer kills willfully, he may not be put to death by the witnesses or the spectators before he is brought to court and condemned to death, for Scripture says, *That the manslayer die not until he stand before the congregation for judgment* (Num. 35:12). The same rule applies to anyone who is liable for death at the hands of the court because he has transgressed and committed a crime. He may not be put to death until he is sentenced by the court.[722]

When the court is the "avenger" then certain procedures must be followed giving to the alleged perpetrator certain rights and demanding that there be evidence and witnesses against him.

In understanding Maimonides's theory of criminal justice it is important to see that he subscribes to what he calls the "negative commandment, that we have no pity on the life of the pursuer."[723] In this view, when a continued pregnancy risks the pregnant woman's life, the fetus is treated as a pursuer and "the child inside her may be taken out, either by drugs or by surgery because it is regarded as one pursuing her and trying to kill her."[724]

In addition we should note that Maimonides distinguishes between the death penalty in this world and in the next.

> If however, one hires an assassin to kill another, or sends his slaves to kill him, or ties another up and leaves him in front of a lion or another animal and the animal kills him, and similarly if he commits suicide, the rule in each of these cases is that he is a shedder of blood, has committed the crime of murder, and

[721] Ibid., p. 195.
[722] Ibid., p. 196.
[723] Ibid., p. 196.
[724] Ibid., pp. 196-197.

> is liable for death at the hand of Heaven; but there is no capital punishment at the hands of the court.[725]

So, if one sheds blood "through an agent" or kills oneself then for these murders "the judgment is reserved for Heaven."[726]

Maimonides acknowledges that sometimes death is not sentenced to avenge but a slightly lesser punishment may be inflicted as deterrence.

> If the king does not kill them, and the needs of the time do not demand their death as a preventive measure, it is nevertheless the duty of the court to flog them almost to the point of death, to imprison them in a fortress or a prison for many years, and to inflict severe punishment on them in order to frighten and terrify other wicked persons, lest such a case become a pitfall and a snare, enticing them to say, "I will arrange to kill my enemy in a round-about way, as did So-and-So, then I will be acquitted."[727]

So, deterrence as well as retribution are valid bases for punishment according to Maimonides.

Finally, it is worth noting that Maimonides acknowledges that the reason for the death penalty being employed in certain cases, but not employed in other cases that seem worse, has to do with the harm to society.

> This, however, is not done to other persons guilty of crimes involving the death penalty at the hand of the court; rather, if one is condemned to death, he is put to death, and if he is not liable, he is allowed to go free. For although there are worse crimes than bloodshed, none causes such destruction to civilized society as bloodshed. Not even idolatry, nor immorality nor desecration of the Sabbath, is the equal of bloodshed. For these are crimes between man and God, while bloodshed is a crime between man and man. If one has committed this crime, he is deemed wholly wicked, and all the meritorious acts he has performed during his lifetime cannot outweigh this crime or save him from judgment…[728]

---

725 Ibid., p. 199.
726 Ibid.
727 Ibid., pp. 199-200.
728 Ibid., pp. 207-208.

As far as human affairs are concerned, where punishment is of this world not the next, killing a fellow human causes the most serious destruction of society and must be punished very severely.

III. Aquinas on Criminal Justice and Punishment

For Aquinas, law is the written expression of what is right. His argument is here indebted to Isidore of Seville as well as to Aristotle again.

> Just as there pre-exists in the mind of the craftsman an expression of the things to be made externally by his craft, which expression is called the rule of his craft, so too there pre-exists in the mind an expression of the particular just work which the reason determines, and which is a kind of prudence. If this rule be expressed in writing, it is called a *law*, which according to Isidore (*Etym*. v. 1) is a written decree: and so law is not the same as right, but an expression of it.[729]

Wrongdoers break the law and that in itself is a sign that they violate what is right and deserve to be punished in some form or other.

We get a good summary of Aquinas's position on criminality and punishment by Charles Nemeth in the following:

> Reason is the 'proximate rule of morality' in human affairs. Human reason is "itself a reflection of Divine reason or the Eternal Law, directing human action to the goal of life." The implications of this type of criminology are extraordinary. First, St. Thomas would be less inclined to listen to the usual panoply of excuses that rush forth in the criminal defense. From his mountaintop, the criminal agent knows the good. His intellect already has been sculpted with the essence of right and wrong. His *mens rea* has already been presumptively discovered because the criminal's mind can readily discover the "wrongness" of the criminal undertaking.[730]

Each human knows the good and what is right and wrong to do, in Aquinas's view, and thus when wrongdoing occurs it is easy to see the justification for punishment that results.

---

[729] Aquinas, *Summa Theologica*, pp. 1425-1426.

[730] Charles P. Nemeth, *Aquinas on Crime*, South Bend, IN: St. Augustine's Press, 2008, p. 35.

Aquinas believes that there is a kind of forfeiture of rights by those who engage in wrongdoing.

> By sinning man departs from the order of reason, and consequently falls away from the dignity of his manhood, insofar as he is naturally free, and exists for himself, and he falls into the slavish state of the beasts by being disposed of according as he is useful to others. This is expressed in Ps. xlviii. 21: *Man when he was in honor, did not understand; he hath been compared to senseless beasts, and made like to them*, and Prov. xi. 29: *The fool shall serve the wise*. Hence, although it be evil in itself to kill a man so long as he preserve his dignity, yet it may be good to kill a man who has sinned, even as it is to kill a beast. For a bad man is worse than a beast, and is more harmful, as the Philosopher states (*Polit*. i. 1 and *Ethic*. vii. 6).[731]

We find here references to the book of Psalms from the Bible and also to two of the works of Aristotle for support. Aquinas views the dignity of all men as the crucial moral consideration in how people are to be treated. But the respect owed to all people is sometimes overcome when these people engage in sin, that is, when they act against reason. In such situations, people become more like beasts and may also, like beasts, be killed in order to achieve something useful for the community.

Specifically with respect to murder, capital punishment is an appropriate punishment in many cases but interestingly Aquinas does not think that the death sentence should be carried out by clerics.

> God works in all things without exception whatever is right, yet in each one according to its mode. Wherefore everyone should imitate God in that which is specifically becoming to him. Hence, though God slays evildoers even corporally, it does not follow that all should imitate Him in this. As regards Peter, he did not put Ananias and Saphira to death by his own authority or by his own hand, but published their death sentence pronounced by God… The ministry of clerics is concerned with better things than corporal slayings, namely with things pertaining to spiritual welfare, and so it is not fitting for them to meddle with minor matters. Ecclesiastical prelates accept the office of earthly princes, not that they may

[731] Aquinas, *Summa Theologica*, vol. III, p. 1461.

> inflict capital punishment themselves, but that this may be carried into effect by others in virtue of their authority.[732]

According to this view, clerics may participate in trials that lead to capital punishment but they do this only as delegates of the secular authorities. The clerics should not participate either by ordering or administering the death sentence since they have more important things to do in God's name and it is also "not fitting for them to meddle with minor matters." It is of course curious that capital punishment is here seen as a minor matter, but we should realize that the comparison is to those things that God has specifically ordained to be the job of the clerics–and promoting the spiritual life of the community is seemingly of a different and higher order of importance than inflicting capital punishment.

IV. Capital Punishment

One of our Neo-Aristotelian thinkers, Averroes, stressed forgiveness and was a reluctant supporter of capital punishment at best, but the other two, Maimonides and Aquinas, were enthusiastic supporters of capital punishment. We will look at each of these views before, in the final section of this chapter, assessing why these Neo-Aristotelian thinkers took the views they did. Aristotle wrote much on the topics of our chapter and it is certainly possible to come away with conflicting messages about crime and punishment from Aristotle's texts. Indeed, as we will see, if one stresses the forgiveness and clemency aspects of Aristotle's account one will get a different view than if one stresses the need for a certain kind of vengeance, also to be found in Aristotle's texts.

So, let us start with Averroes who spends much attention on forgiveness, mercy, and clemency. In Aristotle's account of equity in Book 5 of the *Nicomachean Ethics*, as well as in his *Rhetoric*, he clearly recognizes that mercy is an important concept in law, seeing mercy and equity as a counter-force to a harsh justice that could demand revenge. Here is a relevant passage from the *Nicomachean Ethics*:

> It is plain then, what the equitable is, and that it is just and is better than one kind of justice. It is evident also from this who the equitable man is; the man who chooses and does such acts, and is no stickler for his rights in a bad sense, but tends to take less than his share, though he has the law on his side, is

[732] *Summa Theologica*, vol. III, p. 1462.

> equitable, and this state of character is equity, which is a sort of justice and not a different state of character.[733]

Even though it would be right to act a certain way, toward a wrongdoer for instance, equity dictates that one demand less than one has a right to demand.

Since Averroes comments on the *Rhetoric* as well as the *Nicomachean Ethics*, we could also cite a passage on equity, part of which we saw earlier, from the *Rhetoric*:

> if a man has no more than a finger-ring on his hand when he lifts it to strike or actually strikes another man, he is guilty of a criminal act according to the written words of the law; but is innocent really, and it is equity that declares him so. From this definition of equity it is plain what sort of action, and what sort of persons, are equitable or the reverse. Equity must be applied to forgivable actions; and it must make us distinguish between criminal acts on the one hand and errors of judgment, or misfortune, on the other… Equity bids us to be merciful to the weakness of human nature; to think less about the laws than about the man who framed them, and less about what he said than about what he meant; not to consider the actions of the accused so much as his intentions, nor this or that detail so much as the whole story; to ask not what a man is now but what he has always or usually been. It bids us remember benefits rather than injuries, and benefits received rather than benefits conferred; to be patient when we are wronged…[734]

Here we see most clearly the connection between mercy and equity, and in the specific context of criminal proceedings. It seems clear that this is the part of Aristotle's philosophy that most influenced Averroes.

Averroes did recognize, though, in some cases, especially in cases of blasphemy or heresy, that mercy is not called for and we must treat the wrongdoer harshly. Here again is a short quotation cited earlier:

> For acts of injustice like these–that is, those that fall upon the houses of God and upon his friends–there is no forgiveness, no clemency, and no forbearance, since forgiveness and clemency

---

[733] Aristotle, *Nicomachean Ethics*, translated by W.D. Ross, in *The Basic Works of Aristotle*, edited by Richard McKeon, NY: Random House, 1941, p. 1020.

[734] Aristotle, *Rhetoric*, 1374a18-1374b22, translated by W. Rhys Roberts, in *Basic Works of Aristotle*, edited by Richard McKeon, NY: Random House, 1941, pp. 1371-1372. I have slightly altered the translation at the beginning of the quotation.

> for such acts are not required by any kind of interest; but in cases like these the judge must inevitably carry out the sentence, either for vengeance against the criminal only or for the sake of the general good.[735]

So, in special kinds of cases, vengeance-based severe punishment, including capital punishment, can be appropriate.

Turning now to Maimonides, we see a very strong defense of capital punishment especially in cases of murder where the assault on the community welfare is most apparent. His arguments are largely couched in terms of his interpretation of various scriptural passages, especially from the book of Deuteronomy. As we have seen the idea espoused by Maimonides is that when blood is spilled there must be an "avenger of the blood." But as we have also seen in some cases capital punishment is not to be sought, and in some other cases capital punishment can only be administered after there has been a guilty verdict issued by a court of law.

Another important part of Maimonides doctrine is that if the killing of one person by another is inadvertent, at least in some case, the slayer "must go into exile from the district where he has slain to a city of refuge."[736] Maimonides again draws on the Bible as well as the ancient practices of the Israelites to support his views.

> The injunction to set aside cities of refuge is a positive commandment, for Scripture says, *Three cities shalt thou separate for thee* (Deut. 19:2). The rule concerning cities of refuge applies only to the land of Israel. There were six such cities, three set by Moses, our Teacher, in Transjordan and three by Joshua in the Land of Canaan. A city of refuge may not be situated either in a small town or a large city, but only in a town of medium size. It must be situated only where there are markets and where there is a water supply. If there is no water supply, one must be provided.[737]

So, while some killers are to be avenged, there are other killers who can go into exile in a city of refuge–and all of this follows closely the actual practices in ancient Israel.

Maimonides also has a discussion of how the killing of a killer can be seen as itself not a spilling of blood that would require either further killing or exile.

---

[735] Averroes, *Middle Commentary*, p. 170.
[736] Maimonides, *Book of Torts*, p. 209.
[737] Ibid., pp. 218-220.

> After measurements have been taken and the nearest city is determined, the slain person must be buried where he lies; the elders from Jerusalem then return home, and the court of that city must bring a heifer provided by its citizens and take it down to a valley with a swiftly flowing stream, this being the meaning of the scriptural expression *rough* (Deut. 21:4). There they must break its neck from behind with a chopper, and the court of that city, together with all its elders, even if there be a hundred of them, must wash their hands at the place where its neck is broken and there in the valley say in Hebrew the following words: Our hands have not shed this blood, neither have our eyes seen it (Deut. 21:7), meaning, "We did not let this slain person come to us and send him away without food, nor did we see him and let him go unaccompanied." Then the priests must say in Hebrew: *Forgive, O Lord, thy people Israel, whom thou hast redeemed, and suffer not innocent blood to remain in the midst of the people Israel* (Deut. 21:8), and they go away, and God forgives the blood…[738]

This ritual of the breaking the neck of the heifer is then mentioned often as a ritual that makes it clear that some spilling of blood, or interacting with those who have spilled blood, is not itself a forbidden spilling that would deserve punishment.

Finally, let us return to Aquinas and indicate the sources that influence his robust support for the death penalty. As we saw above, Aquinas quotes often from Scripture, as is true of Maimonides, but Aquinas also quotes from Aristotle on these issues of crime and punishment. Here are two short passages from texts of Aristotle that Aquinas quotes:

> *Nicomachean Ethics*, Book VII, Ch. 6: Now brutishness is a less evil than vice, though more alarming… for a bad man will do ten thousand times as much evil as a brute.[739]
> *Politics*, Book I, Chapter 2: A social instinct is implanted in all men by nature, and yet he who first founded the state was the greatest of benefactors. For man, when perfected, is the best of all animals, but when separated from law and justice is the worst of all … if he have not virtue, he is most unholy and the most savage of animals…[740]

---

[738] Ibid., p. 221.
[739] Aristotle, *Nicomachean Ethics*, *Basic Works of Aristotle*, p. 1047.
[740] Aristotle, *Politics*, translated by Benjamin Jowett, in *Basic Works of Aristotle*, NY: Random House, 1941, p. 1130.

Aquinas cites these passages from Aristotle to show that in certain cases humans behave worse than brute beasts and can be killed to protect the society just as is true of the killing of a brute beast that threatens people's lives.

But we have also seen that Aquinas thinks that some forms of killing should only be punished in the next life, and that clergy should not be the ones who engage in capital punishment. But Aquinas, unlike Averroes and Maimonides, seems equally influenced by Aristotle and by various religious texts. Indeed, Aquinas refers to Aristotle throughout his *Summa Theologica* as simply "the Philosopher" making it clear that Aristotle has pride of place in his own thinking. Yet, there are constant references also to scripture.

Let me just mention one of the many arguments that Aquinas advances to support the death penalty as not itself amounting to murder. In a very famous passage in his chapter on murder, Aquinas talks of self-defensive killing and implies that a state may kill a murderer in self-defense.

> Nothing hinders one act from having two effects, only one of which is intended, while the other is beside the intention. Now moral acts take their species according to what is intended, and not according to what is beside the intention, since this is accidental… Accordingly the act of self-defense may have two effects, one is the saving of one's life, the other is the slaying of the aggressor. Therefore this act, since one's intention is to save one's own life, is not unlawful.[741]

Here we see that Aquinas also engages in his own philosophical argumentation that is not necessarily indebted to either Aristotle or the scriptures.

V. Secular and Divine Punishment

All three of the Neo-Aristotelian thinkers we have discussed in this chapter, Averroes, Maimonides, and Aquinas, are influenced by their reading of Aristotle but also by their respective religious traditions. In this last section of the chapter, I wish to argue that the religious views seem to have much more to do with their views of punishment, especially capital punishment, than did their readings of Aristotle, with the possible

---

[741] *Summa Theologica*, vol. III, p. 1465,

exception of Aquinas. We shall also have occasion to ask again about the relation between religion and law in the Middle Ages.

The religions of Judaism, Christianity, and Islam all hold to some variation of *lex talionis* ("an eye for an eye"). The rabbis in the Talmud express the view that *lex talionis* should not be taken to be literally true, but only that proportionality of punishment to match the crime is the model. Christianity stressed that the revenge model of *lex talionis* was to be tempered by the New Testament emphasis on love, but by the time of the late Middle Ages the rise of the inquisitions marked a return to severe punishments to match the perceived severity of the crime. Islam also stresses the need for mercy, even as it incorporates older Arabic customs such as severing limbs and beheading for certain crimes. These religious views came to play a strong role in the writings respectively of Averroes, Maimonides, Aquinas.

Greek philosophical treatment of crime and punishment was not as overwhelmingly retributive as the religious traditions that dominated the Middle Ages. Indeed, Plato argued–in his last work, *The Laws*–for the idea that criminal offenders should be reeducated so they could be productive members of society again. And we saw that Aristotle often stresses the role of equity and mercy as overriding the harshness of strict justice. So, it is less likely that the Greek philosophical tradition would have supported the use of capital punishment on the scale that it took in the Middle Ages, whereas it is more likely that religious influences were more important in this respect than the Greek philosophy of Aristotle and others.

For the three Neo-Aristotelians we have focused on, religion had a large influence on their legal views. Indeed, the religious influence on these legal thinkers accounts for a lot of their similarities. Christianity and Islam drew heavily on the Hebrew Bible, and so we can see that there were obvious connections among the religious influences on the Neo-Aristotelian legal thinkers. And it was true of legal thinking in the Middle Ages that religious views intermingled with the legal. Indeed, many have rightly seen the influence of religion on law as one of the hallmarks of the Middle Ages in general.

Maimonides tells us that the way he structures his "Code" is by first articulating the commandments he finds in the Torah and then specifying the legal implications of those commandments. Averroes tells us that he is guided by the Quran in all aspects of his legal writings. And Aquinas creates an entire field of jurisprudence from the scriptural insights he finds in both the Old and New Testaments. Indeed, natural law jurisprudence has remained indebted to its religious inspiration to our own day. And Jewish law, practiced all over the world, has also remained indebted to Maimonides's articulation of the commandments and the laws he derived from them. The same can be said about Islamic law today; it is a mix of the Quran and the interpretations of the legal implications of the Quran by Medieval writers like Averroes. Even the secular legal writers quoted extensively from religious texts to support legal views as in Marsilius's *The Defender of the Peace*.

In this chapter we have seen the defense of capital punishment drawn in terms of the religious views of the time, as nearly overriding the strong Greek influence especially of the recently rediscovered Aristotelian political works. From the standpoint of mercy and equity, the resurgence of *lex talionis* is not a welcome development. Religious influences on the law are not always seen, especially from perspectives today, as positive. But as we will see in the next chapter, religious influences on the ideas of war and peace were, again from our perspective today but also from a universalist morality, much more positive.

SECTION XV:

INTERNATIONAL LAW

CHAPTER 33

THE JUST WAR

While religion had a negative impact on trials such as that of Joan of Arc, religion seems to have had a positive impact on the law of war, an idea deeply embedded in religious thought since at least the time of Cicero. In this chapter we will explore the way that the Neo-Aristotelian legal and political theorists of the 12th through the 14th centuries expanded and developed the idea of a just war in various ways. I will argue that most of these developments are highly positive, although there is also a worrying movement to allow most tactics if the war itself is judged to be good or holy. We will also see that the secular Neo-Aristotelians, especially Marsilius, made important contributions to the ideas of the Just War.

In the first section we will take up the views of Averroes about "jihad" or holy war and look specifically at the range of military tactics justified by reference to this Quranic concept. In the second section we will look at Maimonides's view of war from an admittedly Biblical perspective, and specifically the idea that some enemies, such as the followers of Amalek, could be slaughtered. In the third section we will look at the most significant thinker of this period to address the Just War, Aquinas, who linked the justification of initiating and waging war to the natural law. In the fourth section we will briefly encounter the secular Aristotelian views of Marsilius on the importance of and the tactics for achieving peace. And in the final section I will argue that these developments in the 12th through the 14th centuries were largely positive in terms of restraining the initiation of war but of only mixed value concerning the conduct or waging of war.

I. Averroes and Jihad

Averroes wrote a book, Al-Bidaya, which was a legal handbook for students and others studying the Quran and the laws that can be found in this religious text. Here is an important passage from Averroes's book:

> Scholars agree that the jihad is a collective not a personal obligation... According to the majority of scholars, the compulsory nature of the jihad is founded on [Quran 2:216]: "*Prescribed for you is fighting, though it be hateful to you*"... The obligation to participate in the jihad applies to adult free men who have the means at their disposal to go to war, and who are healthy, that is, not ill or suffering from chronic diseases.... Scholars agree that all polytheists should be fought...[742]

Here we find that when a holy war, a jihad, has been declared it is the collective obligation of adult free Muslim men of sufficient means to wage war against all polytheists. And the main source of such an obligation, Averroes tells us, is the Quran.

There are nonetheless various limitations on how even a holy war should be conducted.

> Damage inflicted upon the enemy may consist in damage to his personal property, his person, or violation of his personal liberty, i.e. that he is made a slave and is appropriated. This may be done, according to the Consensus (*ijma*) to all polytheists: men, women, young and old, important and unimportant. Only with regard to monks do opinions vary; for some take it that they must be left in peace and that they must not be captured, but allowed to be unscathed and that they may not be enslaved.[743]

Here it looks like there are not many restraints on tactical activities during war.

Yet just a few paragraphs later Averroes discusses a dispute that has arisen about whether captives should be slain or enslaved.

> Most scholars agree that, in his dealings with captives, various policies are open to the Imam. He may pardon them, enslave them, kill them, or release them... Some scholars, however, have taught that captives may never be slain... The controversy has arisen because, firstly, the Quran verses contradict each

---

[742] Averroes, Al-Bidaya, in *Jihad in Classical and Modern Times*, translated and edited by Rudolph Peters, Princeton, NJ: Marcus Wiener Publishers, 1996, , pp. 29-33; reprinted in *The Morality of War: Classical and Contemporary Readings*, edited by Larry May, Eric Rovie, and Steve Viner, Upper Saddle River, NJ: Prentice-Hall Inc., 2006, pp. 21-22.

[743] Ibid., *The Morality of War*, p. 22.

> other in this respect; secondly, practice [of the Prophet and the first caliphs] was inconsistent; and lastly, the obvious interpretation of the Quran is at variance with the Prophet's deeds.[744]

So, Averroes acknowledges that there is a major dispute about whether captives can be enslaved or killed.

And we then learn that there is also a major dispute about whether women can be slain or enslaved during war as well. We then come to an infamous passage that seems to spare women but provides a blanket license to kill all enemy males.

> As regards injury to the person, that is, the slaying of the enemy, the Muslims agree that in times of war, all adult, able-bodied, unbelieving males, may be slain… There is no disagreement about the rule that it is forbidden to slay women and children, provided that they are not fighting, for then women, in any case, may be slain. This rule is founded on the fact that according to authoritative Traditions, the Prophet prohibited the slaughter of women and children and once said that a woman who had been slain: "*She was not one who would have fought*."[745]

So, unlike others we will examine in this chapter, Averroes believes that all adult unbelieving males may be killed in war, he nonetheless supports the view that women and children are not to be targeted. The reason is the same for both groups: only those who are likely to fight should be subject to targeting, with the exception being those who actually are fighting. The implication here is that even if a person is not fighting or even threatening to fight he can be killed because he could have fought.

Averroes holds the view that wars can only be initiated according to rather strict, religious, reasons: "either conversion to Islam, or payment of a poll-tax."[746] But concerning the fighting of a war, the limits are less strict than those of other Neo-Aristotelians. Only women and children are to be spared, and not even captives can assuredly be spared. During a holy or just war the guiding norm seems to be: one is entitled to kill anyone who could be an enemy fighter. The Quran is the most important source of the laws of war for Averroes, although the practices of the Prophet Mohammed and the caliphs are also an important source for these laws of

[744] Ibid., p. 22.
[745] Ibid., p. 24.
[746] Ibid., p. 25.

war. In an earlier chapter, when we were contrasting the Crusades with the jihads, we came to note some of these points already, but now we can see the rationales more clearly. The two divisions of the Just War tradition are addressed by Averroes: jihad or holy war is only waged against religious unbelievers, and the tactics during war should not target women or children.

II. Maimonides, Amalek, and Killing During War

Maimonides begins his discussion in chapter 5 of Treatise V of his code, *Mishneh Torah* as follows:

> The primary war which the king wages is a war for a religious cause. Which may be denominated a war for a religious cause? It includes the war against the seven nations, that against Amalek, and a war to deliver Israel from the enemy attacking him. Thereafter he may engage in an optional war, that is, a war against neighboring nations to extend the borders of Israel and to enhance his greatness and prestige. For a war waged for a religious cause, the king need not obtain the sanction of the court. He may at any time go forth of his own accord and compel the people to go with him. But in case of an optional war, he may not lead forth the people save by a decision of the court of seventy-one.[747]

Maimonides distinguishes between religious wars that, like Averroes, he believes can be fought justly, and "optional" wars that can be fought for territorial gain, for instance, but only with the consent of a court.

Also like Averroes, Maimonides holds that a just religious war can be fought against all enemy males.

> No war is declared against any nation before peace offers are made to it. This obtains in an optional war and a war for a religious cause, as it is said: *When thou drawest nigh unto a city to fight against it, then proclaim peace unto it* (Deut. 20:10)… If they refuse to accept the offer of peace, or if they accept the offer of peace but not the seven commandments, war is made with them; all adult males are put to death; all their money and little ones are taken as plunder, but no woman or minor is slain… This applies only to an optional war, that is, a war against any other nation; but in a war waged against the

[747] Maimonides, *The Code of Maimonides Book 14 The Book of Judges*, p. 217.

> seven nations or against Amalek, if these refuse to accept the terms of peace, none of them is spared… it is said: *Thou shalt blot out the remembrance of Amalek* (Deut. 25:19).[748]

We will say more about Amalek in a minute. Note here that while there are some restraints, once a peace proposal has been rejected most wars can be just wars. And also note that during war while there are some restraints even little children can be taken as "plunder," although women and children should not be killed.

We find that certain acts are forbidden during war in several passages from Maimonides:

> It is forbidden to cut down fruit-bearing trees outside a (besieged) city, nor may a water channel be deflected from them that they wither, as it is said: *Thou shalt not destroy the trees thereof* *Deut. 20:19). Whoever cuts down a fruit-bearing tree is flogged… It may be cut down, however, if it cause damage to other trees…The Law forbids only wanton destruction.[749]

So, wanton damage to the sustenance of a community is forbidden during war, and "one who smashes household goods, tears clothes, demolishes a building, stops up a spring, or destroys articles of food" transgresses the law of war.[750]

A man who has joined the fighting forces in a just war is morally required not to be fearful or fainthearted.

> Once, however, he has joined the ranks, he should put his reliance upon Him who is the hope of Israel, their Savior in times of trouble. He should know that he is fighting for the oneness of God, risk his life, and neither fear nor be affrighted. Nor should he think of his wife and children, but, forgetting them and all else, concentrate on the war… he is accountable for the lives of all Israel.[751]

This statement makes the obligation to fight extremely strong indeed, somewhat undercutting some other things that are more ameliorative.

---

[748] Ibid., pp. 220-221.
[749] Ibid., p. 222.
[750] Ibid., p. 223.
[751] Ibid., p. 227.

One of the most puzzling and disturbing features of Maimonides's view is that Amalek and those who are associated with him should be slaughtered. This view is supposedly grounded in passages from Deuteronomy: "to destroy the seed of Amalek, as it is said: Thou shalt blot out the remembrance of Amalek (Deut. 25:19)."[752] Here is the passage from Deuteronomy to see the context:

> Remember what Amalek did to you on your journey, after you left Egypt–how undeterred by fear of God, he surprised you on the march, when you were famished and weary, and cut down all the stragglers in your rear. Therefore when the Lord your God grants you safety from all your enemies around you, in the land that the Lord your God is giving you as a hereditary portion, you shall blot out the memory of Amalek from under heaven. Do not forget![753]

Here we learn that Amalek and his followers did not spare the lives of the Jews who were fleeing Egyptian persecution. The story of the attempt of Amalek to wipe out the Jews is retold every year in the Jewish festival called Purim. And it is celebrated that the Jews took their revenge on Amalek by annihilating him and his followers. It is disturbing that Maimonides brings up this story with reference to the rules of war, seemingly countenancing massacre and even genocide. So even though there is much to admire in the restraint that Maimonides calls for during war there is a dark side to his doctrine as well.

III. Aquinas, Natural Law, and the Just War

For one of the most straightforward descriptions of the central Just War doctrine, we can turn to a section of Aquinas's *Summa Theologica*:

> In order for a war to be just, three things are necessary. First, the authority of the sovereign by whose command the war is waged. For, it is not the business of a private individual to declare war because he can seek for redress of his rights from the tribunal of his superior. Moreover it is not the business of a private individual to summon together the people, which has to be done in wartime… Second, a just cause is required, namely

---

[752] Ibid., p. 207.

[753] *Tanakh: The Holy Scriptures, The New JPS Translation*, Philadelphia: The Jewish Publication Society, 1985, p. 313.

> that those who are attacked, should be attacked because they deserve it on account of some fault… Thirdly, it is necessary that the belligerents should have a rightful intention, so that they intend the advancement of good, or the avoidance of evil…. For it may happen that the war is declared by the legitimate authority, and for a just cause, and yet be rendered unlawful through a wicked intention.[754]

For each of these conditions of a just war, Aquinas cites Augustine, who is justly regarded as the originator of the Just War tradition, as Aquinas is considered its most persuasive defender. These three conditions for a just war have formed the basis of the Just War tradition which extends into our own day. The number of conditions has increased, and there is a debate about whether Aquinas's third condition, rightful intent, is indeed one of those conditions, but the core as explained here by Aquinas has been hugely influential.

Today, there is a division of ideas into what is now called *jus ad bellum* and *jus in bello* (with some thinkers beginning to work on the idea of *jus post bellum*). Aquinas made major contributions to each of these areas of thought. Jus ad bellum concerns the rules and laws of initiating war. Here Aquinas said that the war must be initiated by a legitimate authority for the war to be justly initiated. Aquinas also argued, as we saw above, that the just war must be conducted for a just cause, specifically to confront an enemy that is at fault and deserves to be attacked. Today, the just cause most prominently discussed is self-defense, although there is also more and more support for the just cause of defense of innocent others ("humanitarian" war), something Aquinas would clearly also support. And Aquinas also talks about wars having a rightful intent. This idea is not as prominent today but it would take us too far afield to go into the technical debate about why that is so.

Aquinas also addressed the area of the Just War called *jus in bello*, the rules and laws for how a war should be conducted. As we saw, Aquinas discusses how to deal with prisoners as well as the property of the enemy, topics that are of the first importance for those who subscribe to the Just War today. There are hints given that make me think that Aquinas also thought that a Just War must be concluded justly as well, the *jus post bellum*, although we do not have many texts that address that topic directly.

In a provocative and important section of another part of the *Summa Theologica*, Aquinas raises the question of whether it is ever

---

[754] Aquinas, *Summa Theologica*, vol. III, pp. 1353-1354.

lawful to kill the innocent, a topic regularly addressed today under the *jus in bello*.

> An individual man may be considered in two ways: first, in himself; secondly in relation to something else. If we consider a man in himself, it is unlawful to kill any man, since in every man though he be sinful, we ought to love the nature which God has made, and which is destroyed by slaying him. Nevertheless, as stated above, the slaying of a sinner becomes lawful in relation to the common good, which he corrupted by sin. On the other hand the life of righteous men preserves and forwards the common good, since they are the chief part of the community. Therefore it is in no way lawful to slay the innocent.[755]

If we understand this doctrine in relation to killing during war, we can see why such killing requires that the one killed be in some sense at fault, or in other words not innocent. For, if the enemy soldier were innocent, it would not be lawful to kill him because it is an act of murder, in Aquinas's view.

What underpins the idea that each person has value as a creature God has made in his image, is the natural law as Aquinas understood it. According to the natural law doctrine subscribed to by Aquinas, each person has a soul which is valuable in itself to be maintained. This doctrine is indebted not only to the Church Fathers and the Bible but also to Aristotle's book *De Anima*, which articulates the idea that persons have a soul that is different from other animals. Aristotle says: "The case of mind is different; it seems to be an independent substance implanted in the soul and, to be incapable of being destroyed."[756] Following Aristotle, Aquinas recognizes the importance of the soul, especially the soul of a person with a mind, as being indestructible but also that the body of a man may be destroyed.

In his *Summa Theologica*, Aquinas addresses the question of whether it can be justified to lay ambushes and otherwise deceive the enemy in war, another topic addressed today under the *jus in bello*.

> The object of laying ambushes is in order to deceive the enemy. Now a man may be deceived by another's word or deed in two ways. First, through being told something false, or through the breaking of a promise, and this is always unlawful. No one ought to deceive the enemy in this way, for there are

---

[755] Aquinas, *Summa Theologica*, vol. III, p. 1464.

[756] Aristotle, *De Anima* (*On the Soul*), 408b18, translated by J. A. Smith, in *The Basic Works of Aristotle*, p. 548.

> certain rights of war and covenants which ought to be observed even among one's enemies (*De Offic.* i)...Wherefore much more ought the plan of campaign be hidden from the enemy. For the reason among other things that a soldier has to learn is the art of concealing his purpose lest it come to the enemy's knowledge, as stated in the Book on Strategy by Frontinus. Such like concealment is what is meant by an ambush which may be lawfully employed in a just war. Nor can these ambushes be properly called deceptions, nor are they contrary to justice or to a well-ordered will. For a man would have an inordinate will if he were unwilling that others should hide anything from him.[757]

In this view, there are rights of war that ought to be observed in all cases, such as not being lied to or otherwise deceived. But it seems not to be a right of war that one not have things concealed from him. It is natural to conceal some things and hence it is not a right of ours that nothing ever be concealed from us.

IV. Marsilius and Peace Conditions

In his work, *The Defender of the Peace*, Marsilius draws on Aristotle's *Politics* to set out the reasons for tranquility or intranquility in a city.

> Since, then, it is the due action of the prince which is the efficient and preservative cause of all the said benefits... that action will itself be the productive cause of tranquility.... And if there is anything that of itself impedes the action of this part, intranquility and discord will arise from their productive cause viewed in a generic sense; although it has various species and modes of which–insofar as they arise from the usual processes–Aristotle gave sufficient notice in book V of his civil science, which we have called the *Politics*. There is, however, a certain unusual cause of the intranquility or discord of cities or realms, which took its occasion from an effect produced by the divine cause outside all habitual activity in things, and which... neither Aristotle nor any other philosopher of his time or before was able to perceive.... some of the bishops who follow [the pope] in the apostolic or Episcopal see of Rome–especially after the time of the Roman emperor Constantine–say and assert that they are superior to all the

[757] Aquinas, *Summa Theologica*, vol. III, p. 1356.

> other bishops and priests of the world in respect of every kind of jurisdictional authority… not only to these but also to all princes, communities, and individual persons of the world…[758]

Marsilius warns that it is the Catholic Church that is the greatest impediment to peace and that the usurpation of even civil authority by the pope and bishops is the most important impediment to peace not necessarily the wars being fought between the nation-states at his time.

We can hearken back to our discussion in an earlier chapter (32) on the inquisitions to begin to understand what worried Marsilius. At one point he speaks of "the terror of the violent power of the priests" as one of the things that most worries him and is a cause of intranquility.[759] But it is the threat to the authority of civilian rulers that seems most to vex Marsilius and we can see that worry also expressed in the way the inquisitions' trials were being run at his own time. The Catholic Church leaders threatened and coerced the civilian leaders. Indeed, we can see the attack on the Templars as an attack on an organization that modeled itself on certain religious orders and could have been seen as usurping them–hence the need for the inquisitions that eventually brought down this very powerful civilian group, who after all had built and maintained some of the most famous of the castles of Europe and the Middle East at roughly the time of Marsilius.

As we see with Marsilius, there is a downside to the influence of religion on politics and law, and this is epitomized in the Middle Ages by the way religious leaders sought to undermine and even supplant civil authorities. The political or legal rule of the pope and his bishops is not necessarily a bad thing, but Marsilius makes a very good case for thinking that religious overreach is often a major source of intranquility.

V. Religion and the Just War

The very strong interlinking of religion and law in the Middle Ages was seen as problematic in our earlier discussion of the inquisitions, and earlier still of the crusades. What we have been exploring in the current chapter is a partially positive result in the laws and rules or war under the influence of the main religious traditions of the Middle Ages. Religion enters into discussions of the law of war in terms of largely moral constraints on initiating and conducting war.

---

[758] Marsilius of Padua, *The Defender of the Peace*, pp. 128-129, and 132.
[759] Ibid., p. 140.

War is often discussed in purely prudential terms–when to declare war and the strategy and tactics most conducive to winning a war. The religious influence on these topics can be seen in the terminology developed today in light of the Medieval religious influences: the justice or rightness of initiating war (*jus ad bellum*), the justice or rightness of conducting war (*jus in bello*), and the justice or rightness of ending war (*jus post bellum*). The discussion of the rightness or justice of a war is a largely moral discussion. This discussion is spurred on by the religious view that rulers should be led by divine or natural law in all that they do, even in war. That there is a just as well as an unjust way to initiate or conduct war is an advance on the solely prudential discussion of war centered only on how to win.

Religion plays a clearly positive role in political and legal discussion by stressing the difference between acting in accord with, instead of contrary to, God's law. God's law as it regulates affairs in this-world is typically drawn in terms of moral norms and rules, and these are sometimes even codified as laws. Here the influence of religion on war is highly positive, as a restraint on the use of violence on the scale that war epitomizes. Any ideas that can lead to less people being killed instead of more is a positive thing, and we have seen that that is precisely the aim of the rules and laws of war when the Just War is given prominence.

At least one way that religious influence can be negative is when religious leaders encourage the initiating of war. Averroes, Maimonides, and Aquinas all find that wars waged to overcome heathens and other non-believers in a certain religion, is ultimately justified and this can be seen, I believe, as a very bad influence of religion on the thinking about war. Indeed, Maimonides is especially strong in articulating the idea that war for religious reasons, by reference to the Torah, is justifiable. The just cause of spreading one's own religion and defeating other religions is also defended by Averroes with reference to the Quran. And we can again clearly see this dangerous idea in Aquinas's writings about how war can be initiated to convert those who are in error in terms of their religious ideas. The Spanish Conquistadors relied on such ideas to wage war against the Incas as well as to enslave them, as we will see in the Appendix.

Another way that religion can have a negative influence is when religious leaders encourage inhumane tactics. Here we can think again of the case of Amalek and the encouragement of massacres. The claim by Maimonides that God demands that all followers or descendants of Amalek should be slaughtered, even children, so that Amalek's seed is destroyed, is a case in point. This injunction is backed by passages from the Torah. Yet, the doctrine that Maimonides espouses is one that countenances genocide and other massacres. It does not make it better that this case of genocide is supported by the Bible.

It is perhaps surprising that the views of Averroes (supported by the Quran), Maimonides (supported by the Torah and Talmud), and Aquinas (supported by both New and Old Testaments of the Bible) would yield such similarities. Yet we know that the "New" Testament drew on the "Old" and that the Torah is the first five books of the "Old" Testament. We also know that the Quran is deeply, and expressly, indebted to the Bible. So, the fact that the way war is understood by the religiously-inspired writers of the 12th to 14th centuries is not really so surprising. In their various ways, each of these religious traditions is drawn on for the idea of a Just or Holy War.

It is the moral views supported by these religious texts that make for important advances in thinking humanely about war. But some of the abuses of war are also unfortunately supported by these same thinkers and the religious texts they draw on. As with the excesses of the inquisitions, so the religious wars of this period are conducted with a moral zeal that should give us pause.

But the idea of a Just War (and perhaps also, but less so, a Holy War) was an advance over the purely pragmatic ideas of war that were often espoused by political leaders. If nothing else the added moral and religious ideas made leaders stop and think before they rushed headlong into war or undertook an especially savage tactic of war. Savagery was certainly always in the background of war-thinking as long as winning over the demonized enemy is prized.

So, we are left with a mixed message at the end. Religious influence on war thinking is at its best when it inspires deeply moral restraint, but at its worst when religion inspires demonization of the heathen or disbeliever, especially when the demonization is engaged in with zeal. The Just War tradition is developed by religiously-inspired thinkers in the 12th to 14th centuries. And the idea of the Just War, as developed in those centuries continues to have strongly positive effects today. But we also find that religiously-inspired thinking about war also has led in the past as well as in the modern period to the kind of zealous devotion to overcoming the enemy that has unfortunately marked some of the worst atrocities of wars then and now.

APPENDIX

INDIGENOUS LAW IN THE AMERICAS AND AFRICA

CHAPTER 34

CUSTOMARY LAW, WRITTEN LAW, AND COLONIZATION

The most significant problem in addressing indigenous legal and political thought concerns the lack of written texts such as the code of law of Hammurabi in ancient Mesopotamia. In Africa and the Americas of the Middle Ages, there were very few if any such texts. And there were not legal theorists who wrote treatises either. Indeed, most of what we know about legal thought in these regions in the Middle Ages comes from accounts written by colonial rulers or those who accompanied them in their assaults on indigenous communities in, for instance, Nubia and the Sudan in Africa or in Mesoamerica, Peru or the Plains of the Southwest in what is now the US.

Most significantly, there was no written language in many of these regions at the end of the Middle Ages. This was true in Peru among the Incas and among the Nubians along the southern Nile where literacy was mostly confined to religious texts. The Aztecs in Mesoamerica had a written language, a hieroglyphic form of writing that has not yet been fully deciphered. The peoples of the Sudan and the US Plains were largely nomadic.

Once colonization began in Nubian Africa by Islamic Arabs and in the Americas by the Spanish and Portuguese Christians in the late Medieval period we have many reports about the state of the law and even how law was conceived in these regions. But the reports are often written by the colonizers who made assumptions about the practices of the conquered people that made them sometimes seem like other Europeans or like barely human savages.

We are lucky to have some reports by indigenous people who were educated by the colonists, such as the spectacularly detailed account of life among the Incas by Garcilaso de la Vega el Inca, whose father was a conquistador and his mother an Incan princess. There are also some narratives about the Aztecs and the Nubians, for instance, but what we lack are indigenous legal texts to study in the way we have in all of the other parts of this book. Most of the texts we have are written by colonizers, such as the very important work known as the Florentine Codex written by Fray Bernardino de Sahagun, a Spanish born Franciscan missionary, about Mesoamerica at the time of the conquest. We will also make reference to the accounts of Islamic Arabs who travelled with merchants and armies who attempted to conquer Nubia and the Sudan.

In the first of the two parts of this appendix, we will set the stage by discussing in more detail the way that knowledge of the customary law in indigenous societies can be studied even if there is no written law. I will argue that colonization has made the effort of understanding the legal thought of indigenous people especially hard, but not impossible. In the first section, we will examine some of the sources that will be employed. In the second section we will discuss how those sources reveal indigenous legal thought at the end of the Middle Ages. In the third section, we will discuss customary law in Peru and Mesoamerica. In the fourth section we will discuss customary law in Nubia and the Sudan. And in the final section we will attempt to explain how customary law differs from written, especially statutory, law for indigenous peoples. Throughout we will examine law in indigenous societies at the end of the Medieval period which in many ways resembles law in some of the most ancient of times, covered in my book "Ancient Legal Thought" but who are living thousands of years after those ancient people.

I. Colonization and Sources of Indigenous Law

When a group of people with a written language colonizes a people without a written language, the history of the colonized is often written by the colonizers. There are both positive and negative results of this set of events. On the negative side, the story will often be skewed politically in favor of the colonizing, portraying the colonized as backward and impoverished who are in need of aid from the colonizers. And the story is also often one that misrepresents the colonized. On the positive side, a people whose culture was not known outside of its society is to a certain extent made transparent, especially for scholars who can sift through the biases of the colonizers' accounts to understand that culture.

In some cases, the negative side can be ameliorated if the indigenous people can tell their own story, admittedly in the imperfect language of the colonizers, or settlers as they are often referred. In this set of chapters at the end of my book we will mainly have to rely on indigenous people educated by the colonizers or members of the colonizer group who interviewed and studied the indigenous people. In using these sources it will be important to keep in mind the limitations of the sources.

Yet, it is my firm belief that we must attempt to understand law for these indigenous peoples lest we leave out of our account of Medieval legal and political thought a very important set of ideas.

Another consideration to keep in mind is that the customary law of many indigenous people is not necessarily the same at the time of conquest as it had been for the thousands of years that preceded the event of conquest. Such a consideration is especially important in the context of Mesoamerica and Peru since the law and even the ruling peoples at the time of the Spanish conquest, the Aztecs and Incas especially, had only been the dominant people in these regions for a little more than a century before the Spanish conquest.

In addition, the idea of indigenous law and politics is itself a bit vague. The term indigenous means "originating or occurring naturally in a particular place; native." And yet the people who occupy Peru and Mesoamerica in the 15th and the beginning of the 16th centuries were not native to these lands, or not the only ones who were, and it is a mistake to think of them as the natives of these regions but rather as themselves the conquerors or even the colonist people in respect to the native populations that had occupied Peru and Mesoamerica for thousands of years. The law and politics of the Incas and Aztecs is not really indigenous in these senses, although the Incas and Aztecs were Indian peoples occupying and ruling Peru and Mesoamerica at the end of the Middle Ages. Yet, even to call them Indian, which typically means aboriginal inhabitants, is also not fully clear since it remains a matter of dispute which people were first in the Americas.

Returning to the idea of sources of indigenous law and politics, we face yet another problem in that since most of this law is customary and not written law, we must rely on the memories of the people who live in Peru and Mesoamerica and elsewhere who try to recount what their ancestors told them about the law and politics of their people. As we will see there are better and worse sources, and some of the best are indeed those who recount what their ancestors have told them. Those who lived for most of their lives among the indigenous people probably are more reliable guides to the legal and political thought of their people, but even this is not always true as we will see in the case of Garcilaso, for instance, who spent most of his life in Spain.

II. Indigenous Thought at the End of the Middle Ages

The first thing to say about indigenous legal and political thought at the end of the Middle Ages is that there is no single thing we can call indigenous thought. There are similarities among some of the Indians in the Americas but less so when compared with the indigenous peoples of Nubia or the Sudan in Africa. As we will see in the second chapter of this appendix, capital punishment was quite commonly used in indigenous societies, but that is also true of many Medieval societies that were not indigenous, as we have seen in previous chapters.

It is also clear that nearly all indigenous societies at the end of the Middle Ages link customary law to religious rites and rules of various sorts. And indigenous legal thought was no exception to this rule. For example, the priests of the Incas and Aztecs were also public officials who had secular roles to play in the society as well as their religious roles.

Indigenous legal thought of many societies placed mercy and equity on a par with justice, indeed equity is often placed as a higher goal than strict justice. For example, as we will see, the idea of the merciful ruler was ubiquitous and especially in Incan society praise was heaped on those rulers who refused to take revenge on their enemies. The idea of discretion was also discussed in relation to mercy as was true of other non-indigenous Medieval societies.

As we see in many instances of colonialism, in the case of indigenous law and politics at the end of the Middle Ages some of the colonizers were especially cruel in the destruction of the indigenous traditions and customs. And the rationale given is often that the *indigenous* practices were also cruel–when in fact the practices set up to replace the indigenous law were often crueler than what preceded the colonizers. Influenced by the inquisitions in Europe, the Spaniards employed torture and capital punishment on a very large scale against the indigenous peoples of Peru and Mesoamerica.

III. Customary Law in Medieval Peru and Mesoamerica

Despite having a highly sophisticated civilization, the Incas did not have a written language. The legal system of the Incan empire, which lasted for a century and a half before the Spanish conquest, was a system of customary law. The Aztecs as well as the Mayas had a written language, which has not been fully deciphered even today, but nonetheless also seemed to rely on a system of customary law, or at least we have not found evidence of a written code of law for these peoples. What has survived are largely oral accounts handed down from generation to generation. Luckily, we have some very good written accounts from the middle of the fifteenth century by people either with indigenous backgrounds or who made themselves very conversant with indigenous legal, political, and religious practices.

Here is how one historian describes the Aztec legal and political system from the accounts written by chroniclers:

> It was typical of the whole character of the Aztec state that the army and the administrative machinery concerning tribute developed the most rapidly. Legal administration was also developing… a complicated network of law courts developed. The tribunals sitting in the calpulli constituted the lowest court. All other more serious cases were addressed to a higher court, the Tlacxitlan. This court consisting of three judges was also competent to judge all cases concerning members of the ruling class. Cases which concerned the highest offices of state, or those concerning capital punishment, came before an even higher court under the direction of the "Snake Woman." Every twelve days the Chief Speaker personally took over the conduct of this court… Both the Chief Speaker and the Snake Woman were at the same time important priests… The most venerated of the priests … performed considerable executive functions.[760]

Aztec law and politics were segregated by class just as was true of the rest of the society. There were apparently different courts for these different classes.

Concerning the Incas, Katz tells us that they also had different legal treatment of different classes:

> The Inca nobility was on the other hand a much more privileged and closed group than that of the Aztecs. Both in Mexico and in Cuzco a noble who had committed an offense was taken before a special court. However judgments differed. In Cuzco punishments were not particularly harsh and frequently consisted of pillorying in public; in Mexico punishment was much more severe. While the ordinary man had to reckon with a reprimand, a noble could be executed for the same offense…[761]

---

[760] Friedrich Katz, *The Ancient American Civilizations*, Edison, NJ: Castle Books, 1969, 2008, pp. 200-202.
[761] Ibid., pp. 317-318.

While the Inca nobility was more privileged it was also more severely punished than commoners compared to how the nobility was treated by the Aztec law.

Garcilaso de la Vega El Inca provides a first-hand account of the Incan society and laws from the accounts of his relatives (although some scholars think he provides an idealized version of Incan affairs[762]). Garcilaso quotes Padre Blas Valera about the Inca legal and political system and also confirms his account with his own experiences:

> What they called the "common law" was that which enjoined on all Indians (except the aged, the children, and the sick) the duty of laboring collectively on all public works, such as building temples and houses for the kings and chiefs, cultivating the soil, constructing bridges, making roads, and similar operations. What they called the "law of brotherhood" was that which obliged all the inhabitants of every village to assist one another in ploughing, sowing, bringing in the harvest… The law and favor of the so-called poor required that the blind, dumb, lame, and paralyzed, the aged and infirm, chronic invalids, and others who were unable to till the soil and feed themselves by their own labors should be maintained from the public stores.[763]

The laws of the Incas were designed to regulate the distribution or redistribution of the societal benefits. Some 19th century socialists saw the redistributive laws of the Incas as a model of a socialist welfare state.

The Incan state tried to incorporate aspects of the legal systems of the Indians who had been conquered by the Incas. As Nathan Wachtel has said, "the imperial Inca mode of production was based on the ancient communal mode of production which it left in place, while exploiting the principle of reciprocity to legitimate its rule."[764] The Indians of Peru were a communal people and their Incan conquerors continued the state practices of redistribution of wealth, and employed the legal structure to aid in this process.

---

[762] See Katz, ibid., p. 289.

[763] Garcilaso de la Vega El Inca, *Royal Commentaries on the Incas and General History of Peru*, translated by Harold V. Livermore, Austin, TX: University of Texas Press, 1966, vol. I, pp. 262-263.

[764] Nathan Wachtel, "The Indian and the Spanish Conquest," in *The Cambridge History of Latin America*, vol. I, edited by Leslie Bethell, Cambridge: Cambridge University Press,1984, p. 216.

In Mesoamerican society just after the conquest there was also a well functioning and highly efficient legal and political system that regulated some economic as well as personal relations by reference to Aztec law as we see in this discussion by Susan Kellogg:

> As these cases suggest, a lawyer's success in property disputes, especially those heard in the 16th century, often depended on his ability to persuade the audiencia that a litigant had a legitimate "prior right" to the property, a right that may be rooted in pre-Hispanic custom, particularly inheritance or purchase. The court's procedures stressed the individuality of the disputes...[765]

The earliest Hispanic courts followed the customs of the Aztec courts that ruled on economic matters but only as they applied to individual claims for property and inheritance, not as a matter of redistribution of economic benefits as was the case in Incan courts.

A serious problem in understanding the pre-Aztec legal and political system is that the Aztecs as conquerors tried to wipe out the history of those times.

> One of the achievements of the Mexica [Aztec] at the height of the political and cultural development (roughly speaking the last 60 years before European contact) was the forging of images of their own origins, development and identity. Around 1430 their ruler Itzcoatl ordered the burning of the ancient books, both annals and those of religious content, on the grounds that: "It is not necessary for all the common people to know the writings: government will be defamed, and this will only spread sorcery in the lands: for they contained many falsehoods."[766]

Even in the case where there had been written legal records, the practice of the Aztecs greatly harmed the ability to know of these written texts. It was not until the time of the Spanish conquest that a written record was produced setting out the customary legal system of the Aztecs in Medieval Mesoamerica.

---

765 Susan Kellogg, *Law and the Transformation of Aztec Culture, 1500-1700*, Norman, OK: University of Oklahoma Press, 1995, p. 18.

766 Miguel Leon-Portilla, "Mesoamerica Before 1519: The Early Civilizations of Mesoamerica, The Mexicas (Aztecs)," in *The Cambridge History of Latin America*, vol. I., p. 14.

IV. Customary Law in Medieval Nubia and Sudan

In Nubia, which has existed as a separate state for most of its several millennia history immediately south of Egypt, it was the Islamic invaders and conquerors that brought attention to the Nubian's customary legal and political system. Here is how one recent historian puts it:

> In his earliest work on Nubia, Reisner opined that "...its history is hardly more than an account of its use or neglect by Egypt, its enrichment or impoverishment by changes of the Nile and the climate." While this view hardly does justice to the Nubians' own contribution to their history, it is nevertheless true that from the earliest of times until the end of the Middle Ages the story of their cultural development can be told largely in terms of the influence of their northern neighbors.... That situation ended forever in the late Middle Ages with the appearance of a "third party" who did not go away.... The coming of the Arabs ended forever the pre-eminence which the Nubians had enjoyed among their African neighbors... by a wave of Islamic expansion.[767]

We find that as Mesoamerica and Peru were invaded and conquered by the Spanish, so Nubia and Sudan were invaded and conquered by Islamic Arabs.

The consequence of the Islamic conquering of Nubia was that a society that had lacked a written legal code now had one in the Quran and the various other sacred books of Islam. But we also are able to get a picture of the customs and laws of the pre-Islamic Nubians by the writings of the Nubian's conquerors and colonialists. Nubians were literate and there are some written records that have been found,

> however [literacy's] functional role does not seem to have been correspondingly enlarged. The surviving texts, both formal and informal, are mostly of a religious character; they tell us little either of everyday life or of secular history. Throughout the Middle Ages it would appear that commerce and government functioned largely without the benefit of writing... To the foregoing generalization...Qasr Ibrim seems to represent an exception... Along with the usual number and variety of religious texts, the Qasr Ibrim material also seems to contain a large number of commercial and legal documents...

---

[767] William Y. Adams, *Nubia: Corridor to Africa*, Princeton: Princeton University Press, 1977, 1984, pp. 547-548.

> [which] are in Arabic… The Arab conquest of Egypt, following less than a century after the Christianization of Nubia, left…Nubia's only close relations with Moslem countries…. and our knowledge of personalities and events in the medieval period has therefore come chiefly from the reports of Arab historians and geographers.[768]

The account of religious and legal customs of Nubia in the Middle Ages comes then from those Arab conquerors and colonialists, much as was true in Mesoamerica and Peru concerning their Spanish conquerors and colonialists.

As far as we can tell, the legal system of Medieval Nubia seems to be relatively egalitarian in the application of the law to various classes of people with the exception of the ruling class. We should not overlook the idea sometimes expressed in Medieval Nubia that there was a "legal fiction that all the king's subjects were his slaves."[769] Of course, this is a kind of egalitarianism but not one that speaks well of Nubian legal thought. The more common idea would have been that the king must protect all of his subjects equally.

There are similar things to be said about Medieval Sudan concerning its colonization by Islamic Arabs. In the early 15th century the king of Borno in West Africa protested the colonialists' attempt to enslave his indigenous people, as we see in this document, quoting the Borno king, from c.1418.

> May God prolong your days in the land. Restrain the Arabs from their debauchery. God (who is exalted) said: "As for those who strive in us, we surely guide them to our paths, and lo! God is with the good." He [the Prophet] (peace be unto him) said: "Each of you is a shepherd, and each of you is responsible for his flock." It says in al-Hikma: "But for the sultan you would eat each other." And he (who is exalted) said to his Prophet David (peace be unto him): "O David! Lo! We have set thee as a viceroy upon the earth; therefore judge aright between mankind, and follow not the desire that it beguile thee from the way of the God. Lo! Those who wander from the way of God have an awful doom, forasmuch as they forgot the Day of Reckoning."[770]

---

[768] *Nubia: Corridor to Africa*, ibid., pp. 448-449.

[769] *Nubia: Corridor to Africa*, ibid., p. 437.

[770] Al-Qalqashandi, "A King of Borno Protests Enslavement of his People by Arabs," in *Medieval West Africa: Views from Arab Scholars and Merchants*, translated

We get a sense here of the practices of the Arab colonizers of Medieval Sudan but also a sense that the king was supposed to be as a shepherd of his flock, and also that judges are to act righteously and seemingly in an egalitarian manner among the people.

We learn from H. J. Fisher about the beginnings of the Arab conquest of Sudan in the following passage: "The first establishment of Islam in the central Sudan occurred at the beginning of our period [c. 12th century], with the conversion of the *mais* of Kanem. Thereafter the faith spread gradually."[771] And we also learn that by the 15th century most of Sudan was ruled by Arab colonialists:

> About the middle of the fifteenth century, the legitimate Tunjur ruler, Shau or Sau, was overthrown by his half-brother, Dali, founder of the Kayra dynasty, which continued in Darfur until the Mahdist conquest of the 19th century. Dali, the son of Ahmed al-Ma'qur, extended the range of organized government dividing the country into five principal provinces; and he established a system of criminal law, which in due time was written down as the Book of Dali, the Katib Dali. The basis of the law was not Islam, but rather the need for adequate revenue for the government. Instead of capital punishment and imprisonment, for all crimes both serious and trivial Dali prescribed fines, payable in cattle or cloth.[772]

While the laws of Dali in the Sudanese region of Darfur seem to be humane, since they eliminated capital punishment, we see here that there was a financial reason for the rewriting of the criminal law. It is nonetheless quite interesting that even though the Arab colonialists had converted Sudan to Islam from the 12th century onwards, by the 16th century at least some of Sudanese law was no longer based on the Quran.

V. Customary and Written Law for Indigenous Peoples

One question to ask is whether customary law in indigenous societies was likely to allow for more or less mercy and discretion than in

---

and edited by Nehemia Levtzion and Jay Spaulding, Princeton, NJ: Markus Wiener Publishers, 2003, p. 106.

771 H. J. Fisher, "The Eastern Maghrib and the Central Sudan," in *The Cambridge History of Africa*, Vol. 3, edited by Roland Olivier, Cambridge: Cambridge University Press, 1977, p. 312.

772 Ibid., p. 303.

written systems of law. Here is Garcilaso's understanding of Incan thought on this topic:

> The judge had no discretion about the penalties required by law, but was obliged to apply them in their integrity, under pain of death for infringement of the royal command. They held that if the judge had discretion the majesty of the law, established by the king with the opinion and consent of the gravest and most experienced men of the Council, would be diminished. Moreover such gravity and experience was wanting in single judges, and the use of discretion would make them venal and open the door to the purchase of justice by bribery or importunity, leading to utter confusion in the state, since each judge would do as he thought fit and it was not right that anyone constitute himself a legislator, when his duty was to execute what the law prescribed, however rigorous.[773]

Garcilaso points out that most penalties were death–"Thieves, murderers, adulterers, and incendiaries should be hanged without mercy."[774] Yet because this was seen as divine justice, the strict enforcement of the law led to a relatively crime free situation in Peru under the Incas.[775]

Yet, Garcilaso also tells us that compared to the Indian laws that were replaced by those of the Inca,

> The eldest and most prudent members of the tribe reminded them that they had long known that the Incas' laws were good and their government mild, since neighboring tribes had submitted years before: the Incas treated their subjects like their own children, and not like vassals at all; and all the lands they had taken were those that were not needed…[776]

Here we see that a certain amount of mercy was shown nonetheless by the Incas, at least by comparison with earlier Indian legal systems.

In addition, Garcilaso also discusses the two aspects of law and governance of the Incas that is most in line with seeing that they valued mercy.

> On account of the foresight of the Incas for the good of their subjects, Padre Blas Valera says that they should not be called

[773] Garcilaso de la Vega El Inca, vol. I, p. 96.
[774] Ibid., vol. I. p. 226.
[775] Ibid., vol. I, p. 97.
[776] Ibid., vol. I, p. 224.

> kings at all, but prudent and careful guardians or wards. The Indians, to express this in a word, called them "lovers of the poor" … [and] any judge, governor, or lower official who was found to have been guilty of injustice or to have committed any other fault in his office was punished more severely than any private person for a similar crime, and the more severely according to the degree of his office, for they said that it was intolerable that any who had been chosen to give justice should do wrong or that one set to punish crime should commit it, this being an offense to the Sun and to the Inca who had chosen him to be better than all his subjects.[777]

The Incan legal and political system was premised on the idea that the people, especially the worst off, should be treated fairly and that judges who failed in this respect were themselves some of the worst offenders.

The Aztecs are known for their brutality in dealing with their enemies. Yet, we also learn, in the Florentine Codex of Fray Bernardino de Sahagun, in addition to severe punishments at least one king ended the practice of creditors seizing goods and even children of the poor:

> Tlacxitlan [the highest criminal court]: there were the rulers, the princes, and the high judges. All the complaints of the lower classes and common folk they were heard and judged. And all death [sentences] they were meted out; either they would strangle one with a cord, or stone him to death, or slay him under wooden staves, beaten; or some nobleman or judge was to be shaven [as a disgrace], or driven [out of the land], or confined or made a commoner; or one would be seized and jailed in a wooden cage. And they delivered slave from [undeserved] bondage. [When] Moctezuma was lord, there was famine for two years and many noblemen sold their sons and maidens. When Moctezuma heard of this, he commanded that all [these] noble youths be brought together, and that their masters be told that their goods [which they had paid for them] were to be restored and returned to them. With large capes and mantles, and dried maize grains he paid the price for the noblemen. And a double forfeit he then paid in order to redeem and deliver the noblemen from bondage.[778]

---

[777] Ibid., pp. 100-101.

[778] Fray Bernardino de Sahagun, *Florentine Codex: General History of the Things of New Spain*, translated by Arthur J. O. Anderson and Charles E. Dibble, Salt Lake City, UT: University of Utah Press,1954, 1979, Book 8, p. 41.

Notice that in the Aztec legal and political system it is the nobles who are treated most mercifully, unlike in the Inca legal system. And it seems that while both legal systems have very severe penalties, the Aztecs have even more severe penalties for the commoners than for the nobles.

In Medieval Nubia and Sudan the penalties for criminal behavior were also severe but we find mercy valued especially among judges and rulers. In both cases the conquerors and colonizers were Islamic Arabs who brought the law of the Quran–Shari'a–to Nubia and Sudan. Here is Adams on Medieval Nubia:

> The ideological and legal basis of the Nubian monarchy seems to have been little different from that of other medieval states. The temporal power of the king was, in theory, absolute, and his subjects were regarded as his slaves. He was the sole landowner of the kingdom, conferring and revoking tenures at his pleasure. Whether the royal power was limited in practice by any sort of governing council is uncertain…[779]

When Nubia was conquered by the Arabs at the end of the Medieval period, the introduction of Islamic law did not seem to change things significantly, at least according to Adams and other historians of Nubia.

In the case of Sudan, the story is more complicated than that of Nubia. Yet as we will see the introduction of Islamic law, a form of written law, was not as major a development as one might think initially. And in part this is because while Islamic law was written law when it was introduced among largely illiterate peoples of the Sudan it was transmitted as oral or customary law. This is in many ways a return to the time of the origins of Islamic law when the probably illiterate Mohammed memorized the Quran and similarly transmitted it to those who committed it to memory.[780] Indeed, H. J. Fisher tells us that:

> *Mahrams*, or letters of privilege, show how highly the local rulers valued the service of prayer. One *mahram* exempts the descendants of the imam, Abdullah Dili, from military service and jihad, from the responsibility of entertaining the chiefs and from other customary tasks, and from fines–a useful list of

[779] Adams, *Nubia: Corridor to Africa, pp. 462-463.*

[780] See Part B of my book where Islamic legal thought is discussed in detail.

> some of the duties which an ordinary citizen might owe the state–having only the obligation to pray.[781]

Here we see that Islamic law was not enforced in all its aspects and similar things can lead us to see how law was conceptualized in those societies that were colonized by Islamic Arabs.

We end this chapter by reflecting on whether and how much it mattered for indigenous societies that their law was customary and largely unwritten compared to the law after conquest that was written. Perhaps counter-intuitively customary law in the indigenous societies we have examined was applied in many ways more strictly than the written law that came to replace it after conquest and colonization. But this was not true of the administration of mercy, which seemed to be greater in customary legal systems than in those that were based on written texts. What could be the reason for this disparity since in modern times anyway the use of discretion and mercy seem to go hand-in-hand?

In the case of the Incas, there simply was no written language in which the law could be expressed. Incan law was interpreted strictly perhaps because the law could not be easily changed–it was not a matter of a legislator making small or large changes and then publishing the new law. Also to give discretion to the judges meant, as we saw, that the law could not be known and the unjust manipulation of law would be very hard to ferret out. Yet, the judge or ruler could be merciful without raising such fears since, so it appears, the worry about bias was that justice could be bought by the wealthy or powerful not that the poor and weak would be treated more mercifully and less severely.

For the Aztecs, who clearly had a written language in which law could be expressed, they chose at one point to burn the law books so law became only customary again. It appears that the Aztec rulers did not want the people to know the law. But this does not yet give us reason why strict adherence to that law was prized. It is true that the Aztec law favored the nobility over the commoners in certain important ways, and it might have seemed to be better that the commoners could not as easily understand this. Having made law disproportionately severe for the commoners, there is then a sense, perhaps, that judges could now be merciful so as not to antagonize the commoners. Such a result is certainly possible but not as satisfying an explanation as that just provided for the Incan law. In both cases, though, things seem to have gotten worse with the advent of the

---

[781] H.J. Fisher, "The Eastern Maghrib and the Central Sudan," in *The Cambridge History of Africa*, Vol. 3, edited by Roland Olivier, Cambridge: Cambridge University Press, 1977, p. 319.

Spanish and their written law. In Medieval Africa, colonization seems to have helped make law more humane primarily because Islamic law seems to have been more merciful than the tribal indigenous law.

CHAPTER 35

PRISONERS OF WAR AND WAR-THINKING

One of the major differences between Incan and Aztec legal and political thought concerned the rules of war. The Aztecs were known for ritually killing all prisoners captured on the battlefield, whereas the Inca practiced extensive clemency and tried to incorporate defeated enemies into the larger Incan society. In this second chapter of the Appendix we will explore this difference and also discuss other thinking about war in indigenous societies of the Americas and Africa at the end of the Middle Ages. Despite being often characterized as barbarians or only developing a warrior class, indigenous peoples of the Americas and Africa often showed enormous restraint in dealing with the enemies after a war came to an end. The war-thinking of these indigenous peoples was certainly more complex than is generally acknowledged.

In the first section of this chapter we look at the Aztecs' and their infamous human sacrifices of their enemy soldiers and the thinking about war that seemed to undergird these practices. We also look at the rationale given by the Conquistadors for waging war on the Aztecs. In the second section we contrast the Aztec practices with those of the Incas, also looking at other ways that they conceptualized war. In the third section we look at the so-called warrior societies of the Plains Indians of what is now the United States, noting that there were characteristically peaceful means of settling disputes short of war. In the fourth section we look briefly at Nubia and the Sudan as a point of contrast with the indigenous peoples of the Americas. And in the final section we draw out some conclusions and argue that indigenous war-thinking was often quite subtle and nuanced in keeping with the rest of the jurisprudence of these peoples.

I. Aztec Sacrifices of Enemy Prisoners

When the Spanish conquistadors first reported back to their Spanish rulers about the Aztecs in Mesoamerica their accounts were full of stories of human sacrifice, especially of prisoners of war. On the basis of such accounts the conquistadors argued that the "heathen Indians" needed to be defeated so as to stop their inhumane practices. Here is what is believed to be a first-hand account by a conquistador, Bernal Diaz del Castillo of the sacrifices of Spanish soldiers captured in battle:

> There was sounded the dismal drum of Huichilobos and many other shells and horns and things like trumpets and the sound of them all was terrifying. We all looked to the lofty Pyramid where they were being sounded and saw that our comrades, whom they had captured when they defeated Cortes, were being carried by force up the steps and they were taking them to be sacrificed. When they got them up to a small square in front of the oratory where their accursed idols are kept, we saw them place plumes on the heads of many of them and with things like fans in their hands they forced them to dance before Huichilobos, and after they had danced they immediately placed them on their backs on some rather narrow stones which had been prepared for sacrifice and with stone knives they cut open their chests and drew out their palpitating hearts and offered them to the idols that were there. Then they kicked the bodies down the steps and Indian butchers who were waiting below cut off the arms and feet and flayed the skin off their faces and prepared it afterwards like glove leather with the beards on and kept those for the festivals… In the same way they sacrificed all the others and ate the legs and arms and offered the hearts and blood to their idols.

This gruesome and astonishing account is confirmed by some other sources and gives us a vivid account of the human sacrifice of prisoners of war by the Aztecs. And as Friedrich Katz comments: "The mass sacrifices were the most usual but not the only form of human sacrifice." [782]

We also hear accounts of mass murder and plunder by the Aztecs of the enemy villages they conquered. Here is an account drawing on Diego Duran's, another conquistador:

> Once the enemy line, which was generally near the defending capital, was broken, the attackers flocked into the city confines. While some fell upon the enemy who had retreated on to the steps of the temple pyramid, others began to plunder the houses and kill their inhabitants. The plundering and killing lasted until the leaders of the defeated army sued for peace and

[782] Bernal Diaz de Castillo, *The Conquest of New Spain*, translated by Alfred Percival Maudesley, London: Hakluyt Society, 1910, iv. p. 149, quoted in Friedrich Katz, *The Ancient American Civilizations*, pp. 164-165

> offered tribute.... it was by no means an easy matter to convince the troops to stop massacring and plundering. Often the officers and the members of the military orders had to round on the troops whose rejoinder was "that it was their reward and their pay, and that they had not come risking so much in order to die."[783]

Those who were not killed during the massacre were then taken back home by the Aztecs to be sacrificed to their gods.

II. Incan Thinking About War

Let us consider the Incas' thinking about war, as contrasted with that of the Aztec's, with a summary from Garcilaso:

> The system the Incas adopted in conquering new territories and their method of teaching the inhabitants to adopt a civilized and political way of life are certainly not things which should be omitted or despised. Since their earliest kings, who were imitated by their successors, they never waged war unless moved by causes that seemed to them sufficient, such as the need that the barbarians should be reduced to a human and civilized existence, or offenses and injuries inflicted on their subject peoples by untamed neighbors. Before they went to war, they used to warn their enemies one, two, or three times.[784]

We see here that the Incas thought of war as a matter to be conducted with restraint and according to a set of reasonable rules and guidelines.

We also learn that the Incas unlike the Aztecs normally did not kill those who they captured on the battlefield,

> The Incas stood by their ancient custom of not destroying their enemies in war, but conquering them with kindness, and waited until the Yuncas [one such conquered people] should tire and give in of their own accord... [the Incas] suffered the weariness of battle and the persistence of the Yuncas with great patience; they were determined not to destroy the enemy,

---

783 Diego Duran, *Historia de los Indios de nueva Espana*, Mexico City: 1867,vol. I, p. 332, translated and quoted in Katz, ibid., p. 153.

784 Garcilaso, vol. I, p. 264.

> but short of killing them, they pressed and harassed them as much as they could.[785]

And we also learn after the struggle was over, typically:

> The Incas received them with their usual clemency and advised them in the gentlest terms they knew to return to their villages and houses and seek to be good subjects of their lord the Inca so as to deserve his favors: all that had gone before would be forgiven and never more brought to mind.[786]

The Incas normally did not kill those defeated on the battlefield but forgave them and incorporated them into the Incan empire as true subjects.

We can also see a similar strategy employed by the Incas concerning those who would wage a rebellion or civil war.

> Inca Huaina Capac, desiring to display his natural clemency, and taking pride in his title of Huacchacuyac, "lover of the poor," would spare all the common people; and as to those who were present and who had been the authors and executors of the treacherous act, and therefore deserved death, they too would be pardoned, except that one in ten among them would be executed as a record and punishment of the crime. To this end they were to draw lots by tens, and the least fortunate should die, lest they should have occasion to say that the Incas had picked on those they most hated out of anger or rancor.[787]

We see again the emphasis on pardon and clemency by the Incas as strongly influencing the way that the Incas viewed their enemies.

In comparing the Aztec and Inca on ritual human sacrifice we can see a clear difference as Katz has written:

> How would mankind influence the gods? The first way lay in sacrifice. However Inca sacrifices were very different in Peru from those among the Aztecs. They were not meant to feed the gods and to protect the world from extinction, but only to win their goodwill. Human sacrifices existed among the Incas, but on a much smaller sale that in Mesoamerica. Such sacrifices were made only on special occasions… and perhaps a few prominent prisoners of war. As in Mesoamerica, their hearts

---

[785] Garcilaso, vol. I, pp. 352-353,

[786] Garcilaso, vol. I, p. 341.

[787] Garcilaso, vol. I, p. 548.

> were torn out of their breasts. Nevertheless these sacrifices only represented a fraction of the number carried out in Mexico.[788]

The Inca certainly had a more restrained and even legalistic way of approaching war and especially the treatment of prisoners of war than did the Aztecs.

III. Indians of the US and War-Thinking

One of the first things that comes to mind, even if one knows little of US Indians, is the idea that smoking a peace pipe is a crucial "institution" among many of these indigenous peoples. Here is a passage from *The Cheyenne Way*, a groundbreaking book by an anthropologist and a legal theorist.

> The same matter of multiple budding leads to further observation which the American official regime of precedent tends to obscure, and which the older emphasis of the social disciplines upon "patterns" and "institutions" also tend to hide. We refer to the phenomenon of the unsuccessful precedent, and of the tendency or urge which does *not* develop. An admirable instance from the Cheyenne will be recalled in the use of the pipe in settlement, with its magnificent possibilities both of working adjustment and of the relevant chief's influence upon what it would be proper to do.[789]

Smoking the peace pipe was a way to end a quarrel before it got out of hand, or to end a battle or war that needed to find an end.

John Ladd discussed the general ethical perspective of the contemporary Navajo and how their traditions are related to their modes of thinking.

> Any philosopher who visits the Navajos cannot fail to be impressed by the extent to which "talking it over" and "thinking hard" are prized and practiced by these people. Hasty and undeliberated actions are frowned upon. Every decision made must first be discussed by all who happen to be around and it is thought desirable to consult everyone, especially the

---

[788] Katz, *The Ancient American Civilizations*, p. 301.
[789] Karl N. Llewellyn and E. Adamson Hoebel, *The Cheyenne Way*, Norman, OK: University of Oklahoma Press,1941, pp. 60-61.

> older and wiser members of the family… Furthermore, it is evident that this emphasis on public discussion is a theme deeply rooted in Navajo culture, since their religious myths are full of accounts of family councils among the Holy People who "talked it over before doing anything about it."[790]

The Navajo even have a prohibition on quarreling as well as against killing. The general form of thinking manifested here is that talking things out is the proper way to behave not to employ violence. And according to Richard Brandt, the Hopi, who are the descendants of the Anasazi of Medieval and earlier times, says: "It is a reflection of Hopi individualism that there was no 'draft.' According to Tawaqwaptiwa, 'It was up to a man, if he wanted to go on the warpath. If he doesn't want to go, let him stay at home. He isn't necessarily a coward; he just doesn't want to go.'"[791]

While one popular conception of North American Indians is as a warlike people, in fact most Indians living in what is now the US at the end of the Middle Ages and the beginning of the Modern Era were not warlike people. Warriors were indeed prized, as they were among many indigenous societies (certainly including Incans and Aztecs), but the rules of war tried to restrain the impetus to violence and war. The idea that war should be avoided was the most prevalent.

IV. Treaties and Military Conquest in Medieval Africa

In the early Middle Ages, Arab forces tried to conquer Nubia. The most significant battle seems to have been the second Battle of Dongola which ended in 652 with a negotiated truce that guaranteed the sovereignty of a non-Muslim nation in this early history of Islam.[792] Here are some of the provisions of this "peace treaty":

> Covenant from the Amier Abd Allah ibn Sa'd ibn Abi Sarh to the king of the Nubians and to all the people of his kingdom: a covenant binding upon great and small among the Nubians from the frontier of the land of Aswan to the border of that land of Alwa. Abd Allah ibn Sa'd ibn Abi Sarh has established it for them as a guarantee and a truce to be effective among

[790] John Ladd, *The Structure of a Moral Code: Navajo Ethics*, Cambridge, MA: Harvard University Press, 1957, p. 203.

[791] Richard Brandt, *Hopi Ethics*, Chicago: University of Chicago Press, 1954, p. 357.

[792] See William Y. Adams, *Nubia: Corridor to Africa*, p. 452.

> them and the Moslems of Upper Egypt who live adjacent to them, as well as other Moslems and client peoples [*dhimmis*; i.e. Christians and Jews]. Verily, you are of Nubia enjoying the guarantee of Allah and that of his messenger Mohammed, the Prophet; with the condition that we will not wage war against you, nor declare war against you, nor raid you, as long as you abide by the stipulations which are in effect between us and you. [Namely] that you may enter our territories, passing through but not taking up residence in them, and we may enter yours through but not taking up residence in them. You are to look after the safety of any Moslem or ally [of the Moslems] who lodges in your territories, until he departs from you.... You are to look after the mosque which the Moslems have built in the courtyard of your capital, and you are not to prevent anyone from worshipping in it, or interfere with any Moslem who goes in it and remains in its sanctuary until he departs from it. And you are to sweep it, keep it lighted, and honor it.... It shall be incumbent upon any Moslem to defend [you] against any enemy who attacks you or to prevent him on your behalf from doing so, from the frontier of the land of Alwa to the land of Aswan.

This treaty was referred to as the *Baqt* treaty, and it "not only remained in force but largely determined the course of Moslem-Nubian relations for six hundred years." [793]

By the end of the Middle Ages, Nubia was again confronted by Islamic Arab invaders. As Adams tells us:

> Not only in Nubia but all across Africa adherents of the newly revitalized faith moved south over the Saharan caravan tracks and into the rich but culturally backward steppelands beyond...they brought with them a special kind of civilizing tradition; a civilization made by and for desert dwellers. It demanded neither learning nor literacy, but only a profession of faith and the performance of a few simple obligations... No longer an outpost of Mediterranean civilization in the darkness of inner Africa, the Nubians found themselves part of a new mosaic of Sudanic civilization which spread right across the continent.[794]

The colonization of Nubia seems to have succeeded by superiority of numbers of Arabs over Nubians, but more interestingly the Nubians were

[793] Translated and quoted in William Y. Adams, *Nubia: Corridor to Africa*, p. 451.
[794] Adams, ibid., pp. 548-549.

not warlike in ideology whereas the Arabs "possessed a martial spirit" and Nubians succumbed to the appeal of the new version of Islam that stressed the common heritage of exploited peoples across Africa.[795]

When the Europeans came as conquerors in the very end of the Middle Ages, they brought with them a warrior thirst that was quite different from that of the Nubians or Sudanese. Despite the long tradition of a just war tradition among European Christians, the Christian conquerors in Africa, like the conquistadors in the Americas, were not greatly restrained by the rules and laws of war that had so consumed the Neo-Aristotelians of the 12th and 13th centuries.

V. Peace-making and War-Thinking in Indigenous People

The Incas were largely pacific people even as they marshaled considerable war-power to overcome the peoples the Incas incorporated into their empire. Indeed, the Incas seem to have been less war-like than those they conquered or those, the Spanish, who ultimately conquered the Incas. The Aztecs were considerably more war-like than the Incas, and the Aztec practices in turning prisoners of war into human sacrifices to their gods showed a condoning of violence that was largely absent among the Incas. The Plains Indian tribes of what became the US, especially the Cheyenne, Hopi, and Navajo, were less war-like than the indigenous Indians in Mexico and Peru. Especially among the Cheyenne there seems to have been negotiators and peace-makers. And the Navajo had traditions that were to serve them well when they came to establish their own court system that rivaled that of the early United States government.[796] In what we have been surveying, there is tradition of war-thinking that is deeply infused with ethical ideas as well as ideas of restraint. In this last section we will explore these ideas in more detail.

The Incas and Aztecs achieved their empires through conquering many indigenous nations–and all in a relatively short time. But the way the conquered indigenous people saw those they conquered seem to have been quite different. The Incas assimilated the conquered nations into the Inca empire, allowing them to keep practicing their religions and to attain a modicum of self-governance. By contrast, the Aztecs subjugated the conquered peoples and kept them in line by various tactics that terrorized them.

---

[795] See Adams, ibid. p. 547-548.

[796] See Raymond Austin, *Navajo Courts and Navajo Common Law*, Minneapolis, MN: University of Minnesota Press, 2009.

One can surmise that the war-thinking of the Incas and Aztecs were also very different. It is certainly true that both Incas and Aztecs used military might to confront and conquer. The Incas sought to improve the lives of those they conquered, and hence created reasonably loyal subjects. The Aztecs seem to have exploited their new subjects and made it likely that these subjects would be willing to oppose the Aztec rulers when anyone challenged the Aztec empire, as happened with the arrival of the conquistadors. The Incas seemed to see war as a vehicle for extending their domain, but wanted a peaceful and content society. The Aztecs seemed to see war as simply a means of asserting power over others for the Aztecs' own gain.

Friedrich Katz has written about this comparison in illuminating ways a few passages of which I quote here:

> The differences between the two empires in respect to state integration were radical. While the Inca set up a rigid system of administration throughout their empire, carried out gigantic movements of population, encouraged public works, threw up a network of roads... among the Aztecs there was hardly a sign of any of this in their conquered territories. There was no state administration, but only collectors of revenue.... The fact that the Aztecs neither wanted to nor were able to carry out a large scale integration of their Imperium had lasting consequences. If the overthrown people could not be won over, naked terror had to be used.... Aztecs troops swept through all the villages and could plunder them at the discretion of the army. The Inca troops were kept at a distance from villages ... In theory at least the inhabitants of the Inca Empire could complain to the central authority about the Inca administration. Complaints about the many excesses of the Aztec tribute collectors were unknown in Mesoamerica. The prisoners of war captured by the Inca, with the exception of a few leaders who were executed, were liberated and returned to their villages. Prisoners of war taken by the Aztecs faced the inevitable sacrificial death.[797]

The Incas seem to have conquered so as to create an egalitarian empire whereas the Aztecs conquered merely to increase the power of the Aztec elite class.

[797] Friedrich Katz, *The Ancient American Civilizations*, Edison, NJ: Castle Books, 1969, 2004, pp. 314-316.

These differences also help explain why the warriors in the Inca armies were primarily drawn from the people the Inca had conquered, but not so for the Aztecs.

> Since the Aztecs had to fight their battles themselves, the need for elite warriors was substantially greater than among the Inca and they could put only a limited number of soldiers into the field. From a military standpoint, the individual warrior's experience in battle was presumably more significant than it was among the ordinary Inca soldiers, who were in the first place peasants.[798]

Even though the Aztecs had a more professional army there appears to be more restraint on the part of the peasant army of the Incas.

Turning northward, there seem to have been no indigenous societies in what is now the US that set out to conquer other indigenous peoples to form an empire. We have most indigenous societies valuing warriors, but we also have a strong respect for peace-making practices as well. And the warriors were neither professionals nor peasants, but probably best conceived as somewhere in between.

In this respect, it is worth mulling over again the idea of smoking the peace-pipe as well as other rituals to bring parties together rather than set them off to wage war against each other. Here again is how Llewellyn and Hoebel describe this practice:

> An admirable instance from the Cheyenne will be recalled in the use of the pipe in settlement, with its magnificent possibilities both of working adjustment and of the relevant chief's influence upon what it would be proper to do. Such a device has in it, in germ, everything up to and including deliberative consultation of all the chiefs before one of them would undertake a mission, and up to becoming the exclusively available device.[799]

Richard Brandt points out that one of the meanings of "Hopi" is peaceable: "And Hopi are probably right that their disapproval of aggressive behavior is developed to an unusually high degree."[800]

---

[798] Katz, ibid., pp. 316-317.

[799] Karl N. Llewellyn and E. Adamson Hoebel, *The Cheyenne Way*, Norman, OK: University of Oklahoma Press,1941, p. 61.

[800] Richard Brandt, *Hopi Ethics*, Chicago: University of Chicago Press, 1954, p. 177.

Finally, let us say a bit about peace-making and war-thinking in Nubia and Sudan at the end of the Middle Ages. Nubians had been known as fierce and loyal soldiers in the ancient Egyptian pharaohs' palaces and armies. In later times Nubians were captured as slaves and forced into service of Medieval Egyptian and Christian armies. Yet, we see that by the time of the Islamic Arab conquest of Nubia, the Nubians had become a peace-loving people who became easy targets of slave-traders. Indeed, the history of slavery in the Medieval Africa of Sudan and Nubia is an unpleasant reminder that in some cases taking on a peaceable disposition, rather than a war-like one, can be problematic if there are unscrupulous people ready to take advantage, as was true in Africa and among other indigenous people at the end of the Middle Ages.[801]

[801] See William Y. Adams, *Nubia: Corridor to Africa*, Princeton: Princeton University Press, 1977, pp. 452-453.

BIBLIOGRAPHY

Adams, William Y. 1977, 1984. *Nubia: Corridor to Africa*. Princeton: Princeton University Press.

Aelfric, Abbott. 1840. *Pastoral Epistle*, in *Ancient Laws and Institutes of England*. Vol. II. Edited by Benjamin Thorpe. Cambridge: Cambridge University Press.

Aethelbirht, King. 1840. *The Laws of King Aethelbirht* in *Ancient Laws and Institutes of England*. Vol. I. Edited by Benjamin Thorpe. Cambridge: Cambridge University Press.

Afsaruddin, Asma. 2013. *Striving in the Path of God*. Oxford: Oxford University Press, cited in Malcolm Lambert. 2016. *God's Armies: Crusade and Jihad*. NY: Pegasus Books.

Agobard. 1986, 2014. *Liber Adversus Legem Gundobadi*. Translated in Robert Bartlett, *Trial By Fire and Ordeal; The Medieval Judicial Ordeal*. Brattleboro: Echo Point Books.

Ahadith. 2015. *The Translation of the Meaning of Sahih Al-Bukhari*. 9 volumes. Translated by Muhammad Muhsin Khan. Riyadh. Saudi Arabia: Maktaba Dar us Salam.

Aistulf, King. 1973. *Laws of King Aistulf* in *The Lombard Laws*. Translated by Katherine Fischer Drew. Philadelphia: University of Pennsylvania Press.

The Alamannic Laws. 1977. *The Laws of the Alamans and Bavarians*. Translated by Theodore John Rivers. Philadelphia: University of Pennsylvania Press.

Alfred, King. 1840. "The Laws of King Alfred". In *Ancient Laws and Institutes of England*. Vol. I. Edited by Benjamin Thorpe. Cambridge: Cambridge University Press.

Amalar of Metz. 2014. *On the Liturgy*. 2 volumes. Cambridge, MA: Harvard University Press.

Alger of Liege. 2007. *De Misericordia*. Translated in Martin, Brett. "Finding the Law: The Sources of Canonical Authority Before Gratian". In *Law Before Gratian*. Edited by Per Andersen, Mia Munster-Swendsen, and Helle Vogt. Copenhagen: DJOF Publishing

The Anasazi. 2013. Edited by Charles River Editors. Boston: CreateSpace Independent Publishing Platform.

Angers. 2008. *The Formulary of Angers*, in *The Formularies of Angers and Marculf: Two Merovingian Legal Handbooks*. Translated by Alice Rio. Liverpool: Liverpool University Press.

Aquinas, Thomas. 1948. *Summa Theologica*. 5 volumes. Translated by the Fathers of the Dominican Province. NY: Benziger Brothers.

Aquinas, Thomas. 2014. *Treatise on Law* in *Commentary on Thomas Aquinas's Treatise on Law*. Translated by J. Budziszewski. Cambridge, Cambridge University Press.

Ari. 2006. *The Book of Icelanders* (*Islendingabok*). Translated by Sian Gronlie. University College London: Viking Society for Northern Research.

Aristotle. 1941. *De Anima* (*On the Soul*). Translated by J. A. Smith in *The Basic Works of Aristotle*. Edited by Richard McKeon. NY: Random House.

Aristotle. 1941. *Nicomachean Ethics*. Translated by W. D. Ross in *Basic Works of Aristotle*. Edited by Richard McKeon. NY: Random House.

Aristotle. 1941. *Politics*. Translated by Benjamin Jowett in *Basic Works of Aristotle*. Edited by Richard McKeon. NY: Random House.

Aristotle. 1941. *Rhetoric*. Translated by W. Rhys Roberts *in Basic Works of Aristotle*. Edited by Richard McKeon. NY: Random House.

Asbridge, Thomas. 2010. *The Crusades*. NY: HarperCollins Publishers.

Augustine. 2015. *On the Good of Marriage.* Translated by C. L. Cornish. NY: CreateSpace Independent Publishing Co.

Augustine. 1984. *The City of God.* Translated by Henry Bettenson. NY: Penguin Books.

Averroes. 2008. "Appendix". Translated by Charles Butterworth in *Decisive Treatise and Epistle Dedicatory*. Provo, Utah: Brigham Young University Press.

Averroes. 1996. Al-Bidaya, in *Jihad in Classical and Modern Times*. Translated and edited by Rudolph Peters. pp. 29-33. Princeton, NJ: Marcus Wiener Publishers; 2006. reprinted in *The Morality of War: Classical and Contemporary Readings*. pp. 21-26. Edited by Larry May, Eric Rovie, and Steve Viner. Upper Saddle River, NJ: Prentice-Hall Inc.

Averroes. 2008. "Decisive Treatise". Translated by Charles Butterworth in *Decisive Treatise and Epistle Dedicatory*. Provo, Utah: Brigham Young University Press.

Averroes. 2008. 'Epistle Dedicatory". Translated by Charles Butterworth in *Decisive Treatise and Epistle Dedicatory*. Provo, Utah: Brigham Young University Press.

Averroes. 2001. *Faith and Reason*. Translated by Ibrahim Najjar. Oxford: One World.

Averroes. 2015. *Averroes's Middle Commentary on the Book of Rhetoric*. Translated by Lahcen Elyazghi Ezzaher in *Three Arabic Treatises on Aristotle's Rhetoric*. Carbondale, IL: Southern Illinois University Press.

al-Barbahari. 2014. *Sharh as-Sunnah*. 2 volumes. Translated by Abdus-Sami' Abdus-Salam. Birmingham: Dar Makkah International.

Barber, Malcolm. 1978, 2003. *The Trial of the Templars*. Cambridge: Cambridge University Press.

Bartlett, Robert. 1986, 2014. *Trial By Fire and Ordeal; The Medieval Judicial Ordeal*. Brattleboro: Echo Point Books.

Bauer, Dominique. 2007. "From Ivo of Chartres to the *Decretum Gratiani*: The Legal Nature of a Political Theology Revolution" in *Law Before Gratian*. Edited by Per Andersen, Mia Munster-Swendsen, and Helle Vogt. Copenhagen: DJOF Publishing.

The Bavarian Laws. 1977. *Laws of the Alamans and Bavarians*. Translated by Theodore John Rivers. Philadelphia: University of Pennsylvania Press.

Benedict. 1982. *The Rule of St. Benedict in English*. Edited by Timothy Fry. Collegeville, MN: The Liturgical Press.

Bloch, Marc. 1973. *Feudal Society, vol. II: The Growth of Ties of Dependence*. Translated by L.A. Manyon. Philadelphia: University of Pennsylvania Press.

Boissonade, Prosper. 1927. *Life and Work in Medieval Europe*. Translated by Eileen Power. London: Routledge & Kegan Paul Ltd.

Bracton. 1968. *On the Laws and Customs of England*. 4 volumes. Translated by Samuel E. Thorne. Cambridge, MA: Harvard University Press.

Brandt, Richard. 1954. *Hopi Ethics*. Chicago, IL: University of Chicago Press.

Britton. 1901. *Britton: An English Translation and Notes*. Translated by Francis Morgan Nichols and Simeon E. Baldwin. Washington, DC: John Byrne & Co.

Brundage, James A. 1995. *Medieval Canon Law*. London: Longman.

Buckland, W. W. 1908. *The Roman Law of Slavery*. Cambridge: Cambridge University Press.

Budziszewski, J.2014. *Commentary on Thomas Aquinas's Treatise on Law*. Cambridge: Cambridge University Press.

Byock, Jesse L. 1988. *Medieval Iceland: Society, Sagas, and Power*. Berkeley, CA: University of California Press.

Calixtus II, Pope. 2013. *The Dictate of the Pope*. Reprinted in *A Reader of Medieval Laws, Edicts, and Orders*. pp. 315-316. Translated by E. F. Henderson. Washington, DC: Madison and Monroe Press.

Carlyle, A. J. and R. W. Carlyle. 1909, 1970. *A History of Political Theory in the West*. 6 volumes. London: William Blackwood & Sons.

Charlemagne, Emperor. 2013. "Capitulary of the Emperor Charlemagne," in *A Reader of Medieval Laws, Edicts, and Orders*. Translated by E. F. Henderson. Washington, DC: Madison and Monroe Press.

Charlemagne, Emperor. 1991. *Lex Salica Karolina* in *The Laws of the Salian Franks*. Translated by Katherine Fischer Drew. Philadelphia, PA: University of Pennsylvania Press.

Cauchon, Pierre. 2005. "Summons from Pierre Cauchon, Ordering Joan to Appear". February 20, 1431 in *The Trial of Joan of Arc*. Translated by Daniel Hobbins. Cambridge, MA: Harvard University Press.

Cicero. 1949. *De Inventione* in *Cicero II*. Translated by H. M. Hubbel. Cambridge, MA: Harvard University Press.

Clovis, King. 1991. *Pactus Legis Salicae* in *The Laws of the Salian Franks*. Translated by Katherine Fischer Drew. Philadelphia: University of Pennsylvania Press.

Cnut, King. 1860. *The Laws of King Cnut* in *Ancient Laws and Institutes of England*. Edited by Benjamin Thorpe. Cambridge: Cambridge University Press.

Constitutions of Clarendon, 1164. 1892. Translated by Ernest F. Henderson in *Select Historical Documents of the Middle Ages*. pp. 13-14. London: George Bell & Sons.

Crime, Law, and Society in the Later Middle Ages. 2009. Translated and edited by Anthony Musson. Manchester: Manchester University Press.

Cushing, Frank Hamilton. 1967. *My Adventures in Zuni*. Boulder, CO: Filter Press.

Al-Dawoody, Ahmed. 2011. *The Islamic Law of War*. NY: Palgrave Macmillan.

D'Entreves, Alexander Passerin. 1959. *The Medieval Contribution to Political Thought*. NY: Humanities Press.

Diamond, A. S. 1971. *Primitive Law Past and Present*. NY: Routledge.

Diaz de Castillo, Bernal. 1910. *The Conquest of New Spain*. Translated by Alfred Percival Maudesley. London: Hakluyt Society.

Drew, Katherine, translator. 1949, 1976. *The Burgundian Code*. Philadelphia, PA: University of Pennsylvania Press.

Drew, Katherine Fisher, translator. 1991. *The Laws of the Salian Franks*. Philadelphia: University of Pennsylvania Press.

Drew, Katherine Fisher, translator. 1973. *The Lombard Laws*. Philadelphia PA: University of Pennsylvania Press.

Driver, G. R. and John C. Miles. 1952. *The Babylonian Laws*. 2 volumes. Oxford: Oxford University Press.

Duran, Diego. 1867. *Historia de los Indios de nueva Espana*. Mexico City.

Ecclesiastical Institutes in *Ancient Laws and Institutes of England.* Vol. 2. 1840. Translated by Benjamin Thorpe. London: The Commissioners of the Public Records of the Kingdom.

The Ecloga in *The Laws of the Isaurian Era*. 2017. Translated by Mike Humphreys. Liverpool: Liverpool University Press.

Edgar, King. 1840. *Canons Enacted Under K. Edgar*, *De Confessione* in *Ancient Laws and Institutes of England.* Translated by Benjamin Thorpe. Vol. II. London: The Commissioners of the Public Records of the Kingdom.

Emon, Anver M. 2010. *Islamic Natural Law Theories*. Oxford: Oxford University Press.

Eugene III, Pope. 2013. *The Papal Bull: Quantum Praedecessores* in *A Reader of Medieval Laws, Edicts, and Orders*. Translated by E. F. Henderson. Washington, DC: Madison and Monroe Press.

El Fadl, Khaled Abou. 2001. *Speaking in God's Name: Islamic Law, Authority, and Women*. London: One World Publications.

Fisher, H. J. 1977. "The Eastern Maghrib and the Central Sudan" in *The Cambridge History of Africa*. Vol. 3. edited by Roland Olivier. Cambridge: Cambridge University Press.

Francis. 2013. *The Rule of St. Francis of Assisi* in *A Reader of Medieval Laws, Edicts, and Orders*. Translated by E. F. Henderson. Washington DC: Madison and Monroe Press.

Fuller, Lon. 1964, 1969. *The Morality of Law*. New Haven, CT: Yale University Press.

Gaius. 1946. *The Institutes of Gaius*. 2 volumes. Translated by Francis De Zulueta. Oxford: Oxford University Press.

Garcilaso de la Vega, El Inca. 1966. *Royal Commentaries on the Incas and General History of Peru.* 2 volumes. Translated by Harold V. Livermore. Austin, TX: University of Texas Press.

Geldart, W. M. 1911, 1933. *Elements of English Law*. London: Thornton Butterworth, Ltd.

Gierke, Otto. 1958. *Political Theories of the Middle Ages.* Translated by Frederic William Maitland. Boston: Beacon Press.

Given, James B. 1997. *Inquisition and Medieval Society*. Ithaca, NY: Cornell University Press.

Glanvill. 1965. *The Treatise on the Laws and Customs of the Realm of England Commonly Called Glanvill.* Edited and translated by G.D.G. Hall. Oxford: Oxford University Press.

Goetz, Hans-Werner. 1995. "Social and Military Institutions," in *The New Cambridge Medieval History II: c. 700-c.900*. Edited by Rosamond McKitterick. Cambridge: Cambridge University Press.

Gratian. 2016. *Tractatus de Penitentia*. Translated by Atria A. Larson. Washington, DC: The Catholic University of America Press.

Gratian. 1993. *The Treatise on Laws.* Translated by Augustine Thompson. Washington DC: The Catholic University of America Press.

Gragas: Laws of Early Iceland. 1980. 2 volumes. Translated by Andrew Dennis, Peter Foote, and Richard Perkins. Winnipeg, Manitoba: University of Manitoba Press.

Gregory of Tours. 1986, 2014. *De Gloria*. Translated by Robert Bartlett in *Trial By Fire and Ordeal; The Medieval Judicial Ordeal*. Brattleboro: Echo Point Books.

Gregory VII, Pope. 1892. "Decree of November 19, 1078," in *Select Historical Documents of the Middle Ages*. Translated by Ernest F. Henderson. London: George Bell & Sons.

Grimwald, King. 1973. *Laws of King Grimwald* in *The Lombard Laws*. Translated by Katherine Fischer Drew. Philadelphia: University of Pennsylvania Press.

"The Third Lay of Gudrun." 1969. In *Poems of the Vikings: The Elder Edda*. Translated by Patricia Terry. Quoted by Robert Bartlett in *Trial by Fire and Water* p. 204, p. 18. Indianapolis: Hackett Publishing.

Gundobad. 1949, 1976. *Book of Constitutions or Law of Gundobad* in *The Burgundian Code*. Translated by Katherine Fischer Drew. Philadelphia: University of Pennsylvania Press.

Halphen, Louis. 1977. "Germanic Society in the Early Sixth Century" in *The Barbarian Invasions: Catalyst of a New Order*. Edited by Katherine Fischer Drew. Huntington, NY: Robert E. Krieger Publishing Company.

Hallaq, Wael B. 1997. *A History of Islamic Legal Theories*. Cambridge: Cambridge University Press.

Henderson, Ernest F. translator. 1892. *Select Historical Documents of the Middle Ages*. London: George Bell & Sons.

Henry IV, King. 1892. "Answer to Gregory VII of January 24, 1076" in *Select Historical Documents of the Middle Ages*. Translated by Ernest F. Henderson. London: George Bell & Sons.

Henry VI, King. 2005. "Letter regarding the Delivery of Joan to Pierre Cauchon of January 3, 1431" in *The Trial of Joan of Arc*. Translated by Daniel Hobbins. Cambridge, MA: Harvard University Press.

Von Heyking, John. 2007. "Taming Warriors in Classical and Early Medieval Political Theory," in *Ethics, Nationalism, and Just War*. Edited by Henrik Syse and Gregory M. Reichberg. Washington, DC: Catholic University of America Press.

Hobbins, Daniel. translator. 2007. *The Trial of Joan of Arc*. Cambridge, MA: Harvard University Press.

Hoebel, E. Adamson. 1954. *The Law of Primitive Man*. Cambridge, MA: Harvard University Press.

"Robin Hood" *A Geste of Robyn Hode* reprinted in J. C. Holt. 1982. *Robin Hood*. London: Thames & Hudson.

Howard, A. E. Dick. 1964, 1998. *Magna Carta: Text and Commentary*. pp. 24-25. Charlottesville: University of Virginia Press.

Ine, King. 1840. *The Laws of King Ine* in *Ancient Laws and Institutes of England.* Vol. I. Edited by Benjamin Thorpe. Cambridge: Cambridge University Press.

The Institutes of Polity in *Ancient Laws and Institutes of England.* 1840. Translated by Benjamin Thorpe. Vol. II. London: The Commissioners of the Public Records of the Kingdom.

Irene, Emperor. 2017. *The Novels of Irene* in *The Laws of the Isaurian Era*. Translated by Mike Humphreys. Liverpool: Liverpool University Press.

Isidore of Seville. 2008. *De Ecclesiasticis Officiis*. Translated by Thomas Knoebel. NY: The Newman Press.

Isidore of Seville. 2006. *The Etymologies*. Translated by Stephen A. Barney, W. J. Lewis, J. A. Beach, and Oliver Berghof. Cambridge: Cambridge University Press.

Isidore of Seville. 2018. *The Sententiae*. Translated by Thomas Knoebel. NY: The Newman Press.

Ivo of Chartres. 2010. *Sermo VI* quoted in *Canon Law and the Letters of Ivo of Chartres*. Translated by Christof Rolker. Cambridge: Cambridge University Press.

Janin, Hunt, editor. 2004. *Medieval Justice*. London: McFarland and Company, Publishers.

Jochens, Jenny. 1995. *Women in Old Norse Society*. Ithaca, NY: Cornell University Press.

Johnson, James Turner. 1997. *The Holy War Idea in Western and Islamic Traditions.* University Park, PA: Penn State University Press.

John, King. 1892. *John's Concession of England to the Pope* in *Select Historical Documents of the Middle Ages*. Translated by Ernest F. Henderson. London: George Bell & Sons.

Johannesson, Jon. 1974. *The History of the Old Icelandic Commonwealth*. Winnipeg, Manitoba: University of Manitoba Press.

Justin. 2007. *Dialogue with Trypho*. Translated by A. Robinson and J. Donaldson. Quoted in Louis J. Swift, "Early Christian Views on Violence, War, and Peace in *War and Peace in the Ancient World*. Edited by Kurt A. Raaflaub. Oxford: Blackwell Publishing Ltd.

Justinian, Emperor. 1932. *Justinian's Code* in *The Civil Law*. Vol. 13. Translated by S.P. Scott. Cincinnati: The Central Trust Co.

Justinian, Emperor. 1932. *Constitutions of Justinian – Sixth Collection, Seventy-Eighth New Constitution* in *The Civil Law* vol. 16. Translated by S.P. Scott. Cincinnati: The Central Trust Co.

Kames, Lord Henry Home. 1765. *Principles of Equity*. London: Alex, Lawrie, and Co.

Karlsson, Gunnar. 2000. *The History of Iceland*. Minneapolis, MN: University of Minnesota Press.

Katz, Frederick. 1972. *The Ancient American Civilizations*. London: Orion Publications.

Kellogg, Susan. 1995. *Law and the Transformation of Aztec Culture*. 1500-1700. Norman, OK: University of Oklahoma Press.

Kern, Fritz. 1956. *Kingship and Law in the Middle Ages*. Translated by S. B. Chrimes. NY: Frederick A. Praeger Publishers.

King, P. D. 1972. *Law and Society in the Visgothic Kingdom*. Cambridge: Cambridge University Press.

Kirschenbaum, Aaron. 1991. *Equity in Jewish Law: Halakhic Perspectives on Law*. NY: Yeshiva University Press.

Klinck, Dennis R. 2010. *Conscience, Equity, and the Court of Chancery in Early Modern England*. Burlington, VT: Ashgate Publishing Co.

Ladd, John. 1957. *The Structure of a Moral Code: Navaho Ethics*. Cambridge, MA: Harvard University Press.

Lambert, Malcolm. 2016. *God's Armies: Crusade and Jihad*. NY: Pegasus Books.

Leon-Portilla, Miguel. 1984. "Mesoamerica Before 1519: The Early Civilizations of Mesoamerica, The Mexicas (Aztecs)" in *The Cambridge History of Latin America*, vol. I. Edited by Leslie Bethel. Cambridge: Cambridge University Press.

Levy, Leonard W. 1999. *The Palladium of Justice: Origins of Trial by Jury*. Chicago: Ivan R. Dee, Publishers.

Formulae Liturgicae in use at Ordeals (Ninth Century). 2013. Reprinted in *A Reader of Medieval Laws Edicts, and Orders*. Translated by E. F. Henderson. Washington, DC: Madison and Monroe Press.

Liutprand, King. 1973. *Laws of King Liutprand* in *The Lombard Laws*. Translated by Katherine Fischer Drew. Philadelphia: University of Pennsylvania Press.

Llewellyn, K. N. and E. Adamson Hoebel. 1941. *The Cheyenne Way: Conflict and Case Law in Primitive Jurisprudence*. Norman, OK: University of Oklahoma Press.

Levtzion, Nehemia .1977. "The Western Maghrib and Sudan in *The Cambridge History of Africa* vol 3. Edited by Roland Oliver. Cambridge: Cambridge University Press.

The Lombard Laws. 1973. Translated by Katherine Fischer Drew. Philadelphia, PA: University of Pennsylvania Press.

Magna Carta. 1215, 1914, 2000. In *Magna Carta: A Commentary on the Great Charter of King John*. Translated with an introduction by William Sharp McKechnie. Glasgow: James Maclehose and Sons.

Maimonides, Moses. 1972. *Maimonides's Introduction to Mishneh Torah* in *A Maimonides Reader*. Edited by Isadore Twersky. Springfield, NJ: Behrman House, Inc.

Maimonides, Moses. 1972. *Mishneh Torah*. Book One: Knowledge in *A Maimonides Reader*. Edited and translated by Isadore Twersky. Springfield, NJ: Behrman House, Inc.

Maimonides, Moses. 1949. *The Code of Maimonides, Book Fourteen: The Book of Judges*. Translated by Abraham M. Hershman. .New Haven, CT: Yale University Press.

Maimonides, Moses. 1954. *The Code of Maimonides, Book Eleven: The Book of Torts*. Translated by Hyman Klein. New Haven, CT: Yale University Press.

Maimonides, Moses. 1963. *The Guide of the Perplexed.* 2 volumes. Translated by Shlomo Pines. Chicago: University of Chicago Press.

Maine, Henry Sumner. 1861. *Ancient Law*. London: John Murray.

Maine, Henry Sumner. 1886. *Dissertations on Early Law and Custom*. NY: Henry Holt and Company.

Maitland, F. W. 1909, 1936. *Equity: A Course of Lectures*. Revised by John Brunyate, Cambridge: Cambridge University Press.

Maitland, F. W. 1971. *The Forms of Action at Common Law: A Course of Lectures* (1909). Cambridge: Cambridge University Press.

Marsilius of Padua. 2005. *The Defender of the Peace*. Translated by Annabel Brett. Cambridge: Cambridge University Press.

Marculf. 2008. *The Formulary of Marculf* in *The Formularies of the Angers and Marculf: Two Merovingian Legal Handbooks*. Translated by Alice Rio. Liverpool: Liverpool University Press.

May, Larry. 2008. *Aggression and Crimes Against Peace*. Cambridge: Cambridge University Press.

May, Larry. 2019. *Ancient Legal Thought*. Cambridge: Cambridge University Press.

May, Larry, Shannon Fyfe, and Eric Ritter, co-editors. 2017. *The Cambridge Handbook of the Just War.* Cambridge: Cambridge University Press.

May, Larry. 1987. *The Morality of Groups.* Notre Dame, IN: University of Notre Dame Press.

May, Larry. 1992. *Sharing Responsibility*. Chicago: University of Chicago Press.

McKechnie, William Sharp. 1914. *Magna Carta: A Commentary on the Great Charter of King John*. Glasgow: John Maclehose and Sons.

Moore, R. I. 1987. *The Formation of a Persecuting Society*. Oxford: Blackwell Publishing.

Nemeth, Charles P. 2008. *Aquinas on Crime*. South Bend, IN: St. Augustine's Press.

Newton, Michael and Larry May. 2014. *Proportionality in International Law*. Oxford: Oxford University Press.

Nicol, D. M. 1988. "Byzantine Political Thought," in *The Cambridge History of Political Thought: c. 350 – c. 1450*. Edited by J. H. Burns. Cambridge: Cambridge University Press.

Law of the Northumbrian Priests. in *Ancient Laws and Institutes of England* vol. II. 1840. Translated by Benjamin Thorpe. London: The Commissioners of the Public Records of the Kingdom.

Pocock, J. G. A. 1957. *The Ancient Constitution and the Feudal Law*. Cambridge: Cambridge University Press.

Pollack, Frederick and Frederic William Maitland. 1898. *The History of English Law Before the time of Edward I*. 2 volumes. Cambridge: Cambridge University Press.

Al-Qalqashandi. 2003. "A King of Borno Protests Enslavement of his People by Arabs" in *Medieval West Africa: Views from Arab Scholars and Merchants*. Translated and edited by Nehemia Levtzion and Jay Spaulding. Princeton, NJ: Markus Wiener Publishers.

The Study Quran, 2015. Translated and edited by Seyyed Hossein Nasr. NY: HarperCollins.

Rahim, Abdur. 1911. *The Principles of Muhammadan Jurisprudence*. London: Luzak & Co.

Ratchis, King. 1973. *Laws of King Ratchis* in *The Lombard Laws*. Translated by Katherine Fischer Drew. Philadelphia: University of Pennsylvania Press.

Reinhard, Wolfgang. 2011. *A Short History of Colonialism*. NY: Manchester University Press.

Rio, Alice. 2009. *Legal Practice and Written Word in the Early Middle Ages: Frankish Formulae, c. 500-1000*. Cambridge: Cambridge University Press.

Rio, Alice. 2017. *Slavery After Rome: 500-1100*. Oxford: Oxford University Press.

Rolker, Christof. 2010. *Canon Law and the Letters of Ivo of Chartres*. Cambridge: Cambridge University Press.

Rothair, King. 1973. *Rothair's Edict* in *The Lombard Laws*. Translated by Katherine Fischer Drew. Philadelphia: University of Pennsylvania Press, 1973.

as-Sadr, Muhammed Baqir. 2003. *Lessons in Islamic Jurisprudence*. Translated by Yoy Parviz Mottahedeh. Oxford: One World Publishers.

De Sahagun, Fray Bernardino. 1954, 1979. *Florentine Codex: General History of the Things of New Spain*. 13 volumes. Translated by Arthur J. O. Anderson and Charles E. Dibble. Salt Lake City, UT: University of Utah Press.

von Savigny, Carl. 1829. *The History of the Roman Law during the Middle Ages*. Translated by E. Cathcart. Edinburgh: Adam Black.

Schacht, Joseph. 1982. *An Introduction to Islamic Law*. Oxford: Oxford University Press.

Al-Shafi'i, Muhammad ibn Idris. 2013. *The Epistle on Legal Theory*. Edited and translated by Joseph Lowry. NY: New York University Press.

The Sirmondian Constitutions in *The Theodosian Code*. 1952. Translated by Clyde Pharr. Princeton, NJ: Princeton University Press.

Shoemaker, Karl. 2011. *Sanctuary and Crime in the Middle Ages, 400-1500*. NY: Fordham University Press, 2011,

Smalley, Beryl. 1973. *The Becket Conflict and the Schools*. Oxford: Basil Blackwell.

Stephen, James. 1883. *A History of the Criminal Law in England*. 3 volumes. London: Macmillan and Co.

Strauss, Leo. 1963. "How to Study the Guide of the Perplexed" in Maimonides *The Guide of the Perplexed*. Translated by Shlomo Pines. Chicago: University of Chicago Press.

Stuart, Gene. 1988. *America's Ancient Cities*, Washington DC: National Geographic Society.

Gisli Sursson's Saga in *The Sagas of Icelanders*. 2000. Translated by Katrina C. Atwood, et al. NY: Penguin Books.

Tacitus. 1952, 1979. *The Histories*. Translated by Alfred John Church and William Jackson Brodribb. Encyclopedia Britannica. Reprinted by Franklin Mint Corporation, Franklin Center, PA: The Franklin Library.

Thacker, Alan. 2005. "England in the Seventh Century" in *The New Cambridge Medieval History, Vol. I: c. 500-c.700.* Edited by Paul Fouracre. Cambridge: Cambridge University Press.

Theodosius II, Emperor. 1952. *The Theodosian Code*. Translated by Clyde Pharr. Princeton, NJ: Princeton University Press.

Thomas, Cyrus. 1890. *The Cherokees in Pre-Columbian Times*. NY: N. D. C. Hodges, publisher.

Thompson, Faith. 1948. *Magna Carta – Its Role in the Making of the English Constitution 1300-1629.* Minneapolis, MN: University of Minnesota Press.

Tombs, Robert. 2014. *The English and Their History*. NY: Vintage Press.

Twersky, Isidore. 1980. *Introduction to the Code of Maimonides (Mishneh Torah).* New Haven, CT: Yale University Press.

Ullmann, Walter. 1966. *The Individual and Society in the Middle Ages*. Baltimore, MD: The Johns Hopkins University Press.

Ullmann, Walter. 1961, 1966. *Principles of Government and Politics in the Middle Ages*. NY: Routledge.

Urban II, Pope. 1996. *The Canons of Melfi* in Robert Somerville, *Pope Urban II*. Oxford: Oxford University Press.

Urban II, Pope. 1996. *Pope Urban II: The Collectio Britannica and the Council of Melfi (1089).* Translated and edited by Robert Somerville. Oxford: Oxford University Press.

Vinogradoff, Paul. 1909. *Roman Law in Medieval Europe*. London: Harper and Brothers.

The Visigothic Code. 1910. Translated by S. P. Scott. Boston: The Boston Book Company.

Vitoria, Francisco. 1532, 1917. *De Indis* (*On the Indians*). Translated by John Pawley Bate. Washington DC: The Carnegie Institution of Washington.

Wachtel, Nathan. 1984. "The Indian and the Spanish Conquest," in *The Cambridge History of Latin America* Vol. I. Edited by Leslie Bethell. Cambridge: Cambridge University Press,1984.

Walker, Thomas A. 1899. *A History of the Law of Nations*. Vol. I, Cambridge: Cambridge University Press.

Wallace-Hadrill, J. M. 1977. "Roman Survivals in Frankish Gaul," excerpted in *The Barbarian Invasions: Catalyst of a New Order*. Edited by Katherine Fischer Drew. Huntington, NY: Robert E. Krieger Publishing Company.

Wemple, Susan Fonay. 1981. *Women in Frankish Society: Marriage and Cloister 500 to 900.* Philadelphia: University of Pennsylvania Press.

Van de Wiel, Constant. 1991. *History of Canon Law*. Louvain: Peeters Press.

INDEX